DEFENSE'S NUCLEAR AGENCY
1947 – 1997

DEFENSE THREAT REDUCTION AGENCY
U.S. DEPARTMENT OF DEFENSE
WASHINGTON, D.C.
2002

PREFACE

Defense's Nuclear Agency, 1947-1997, traces the development of the Armed Forces Special Weapons Project (AFSWP), and its descendant government organizations, from its original founding in 1947 to 1997. After the disestablishment of the Manhattan Engineering District (MED) in 1947, AFSWP was formed to provide military training in nuclear weapons' operations. Over the years, its sequential descendant organizations have been the Defense Atomic Support Agency (DASA) from 1959 to 1971, the Defense Nuclear Agency (DNA) from 1971 to 1996, and the Defense Special Weapons Agency (DSWA) from 1996 to 1998. In 1998, DSWA, the On-Site Inspection Agency, the Defense Technology Security Administration, and selected elements of the Office of Secretary of Defense were combined to form the Defense Threat Reduction Agency (DTRA).

This publication has been reviewed by concerned government agencies and its contents have been cleared for release to the public. Although the manuscript and its appendices have been cleared, some of the official sources cited in the notes and bibliography may remain classified. Finally, in democratic societies history is an iterative process, written and rewritten over many generations. Consequently, while this book is an official publication of the Defense Threat Reduction Agency History Series, the views and interpretations expressed are those of the authors and editors and do not necessarily represent those of the Department of Defense.

The Prologue sets the stage for the national and international events leading up to the founding of AFSWP in 1947. The history of AFSWP and its descendant organizations is presented in eight narrative chapters that cover logical periods of evolution and development. These chapters are followed by appendices that provide further background on organizational transitions, including charters, chronology, and an agency time line. Chapters are arranged in chronological order and cover the evolution of the agency, as portrayed against the larger backdrop of military and political currents. Each chapter addresses external influences, internal program response, ancillary programs, and transitions. Issues that overlap chapters are revisited. Although it is difficult at times to separate the agency's mission from the larger Department of Defense (DoD) or the Atomic Energy Commission (AEC), the text is centrally focused upon the department's nuclear agency over five decades, 1947–1997. Technical issues and terms, so much a part of a technical defense agency, have been held to a minimum; an abbreviation/acronym list is provided in the appendix for reference. Photographs and illustrative matter for this history were obtained from the Defense Threat Reduction Information Analysis Center (DTRIAC) Archives, Kirtland Air Force Base, New Mexico, and from other government sources.

Numerous individuals, organizations, and consultants contributed to this volume, all under the guidance of a history manuscript Review Committee. The production effort of *Defense's Nuclear Agency, 1947-1997* began in 1997 with agency research and oral history interviews conducted by History Associates, Inc., that set the historical foundation for the text. Those interviewed for this volume included: Colonel John A. Ord, Admiral John T. Hayward, Dr. Frank Shelton, Vice Admiral Robert Monroe, Vice Admiral John T. Parker, Dr. Harold Brode, Dr. Paul Carew, Dr. Fred Wikner, Dr. Marvin C. Atkins, and Dr. Robert Brittigan. Other individuals associated with the agency contributed technical commentary and advice during chapter development: Dr. John Northrop, Dr. Edward Conrad, Dr. Joseph Braddock, Dr. Donald Sachs, Dr. Eugene Sevin, Dr. Francis Wimenitz, Dr. Paul Caldwell, and Donald Moffett. The Review Committee consisted of: Dr. C. Stuart Kelley (DTRA), Dr. Joseph Harahan (DTRA), Adrian Polk (Logicon/RDA), Eugene Driscoll (DTRIAC), Don Alderson (DTRIAC), and Christian Brahmstedt (DTRIAC). The Agency is indebted to the editor of this history, Christian Brahmstedt, who has been associated with this effort, in a production capacity, since its inception. Adrian Polk's contribution to this book cannot be overstated. He was the guiding light for the organization of the early chapters and he reviewed carefully the technical content and presentation of the later chapters. His insight and remarkable memory for detail added substantial depth. Dr. Kelley's and Dr. Harahan's determination to see this effort through to completion are gratefully acknowledged. The detailed security review for this volume was accomplished by John Bilsky, DTRA, and Herb Hoppe, Logicon/RDA. DTRA extends its appreciation to both Mr. Bilsky and Mr. Hoppe for their thorough professional review. This review was complex, with many issues needing resolution. Throughout they made valuable contributions and their stimulating questions improved the final product substantially.

We hope you enjoy reading this history of our Agency as much as we enjoyed preparing it.

September 24, 2002

TABLE OF CONTENTS

PREFACE i

TABLE OF CONTENTS iii

PROLOGUE v

CHAPTER ONE 1
    THE POST-WAR TRANSITION, 1946 TO 1948

CHAPTER TWO 47
    THE ROLE OF THE MILITARY IN NUCLEAR MATTERS, 1949 TO 1952

CHAPTER THREE 95
    THE SPRINT FOR SUPREMACY, 1952 TO 1957

CHAPTER FOUR 131
    SOME SECOND THOUGHTS, 1957 TO 1963

CHAPTER FIVE 171
    A NEW PARADIGM, 1963 TO 1970

CHAPTER SIX 215
    ANOTHER WAY, 1970 TO 1980

CHAPTER SEVEN 257
    A REBIRTH OF CONFIDENCE, 1980 TO 1988

CHAPTER EIGHT 293
    POST-COLD WAR ERA: NEW MISSIONS, 1989 TO 1997

APPENDICES
    APPENDIX A: BIBLIOGRAPHY 327
    APPENDIX B: ACRONYM LIST 353
    APPENDIX C: CHRONOLOGY 357
    APPENDIX D: AGENCY CHARTERS 395
    APPENDIX E: AGENCY THROUGH THE DECADES CHART 445
    APPENDIX F: INDEX 449

PROLOGUE

A series of scientific discoveries heralded the birth of mankind's utilization of the atom. In 1911, British experimental physicist Ernest Rutherford proposed the nuclear model for the atom based on experimental data. Niels H. Bohr, a Danish physicist, contributed to the understanding of atomic particles, including the behavior of electrons in orbits around protons. In 1938, German chemists Otto Hahn and Fritz Strassman discovered fission products after irradiating uranium with neutrons. Lise Meitner, an Austrian physicist, interpreted this as being caused by the neutron-induced fission of uranium. Her interpretation led to over 100 papers being published in 1939, essentially defining the modern theory of atomic fission. Later, in a letter drafted by colleagues led by Hungarian theoretical physicist Leo Szilard, Albert Einstein wrote to President Franklin D. Roosevelt on August 2, 1939: "It may become possible to set up a nuclear chain reaction in a large mass of uranium, which would... lead to the construction of... extremely powerful bombs..." The National Defense Research Council, under Vannevar Bush, supported research in 1940 that indicated applications to weapons development were not as "remote" as earlier thought. In a Presidential review on October 9, 1941, President Franklin Roosevelt chartered a Top Policy Group and directed that the U.S. Army take the lead in a maximum effort to develop an atomic bomb.

On August 13, 1942, the U.S. Army Corps of Engineers, issuing General Order 33, established the Manhattan Engineer District (MED), the cover name for "Project Y," the atomic bomb development project. Brigadier General Leslie R. Groves was chosen to head the MED project; General Groves selected Dr. J. Robert Oppenheimer, a University of California physicist, to lead the scientific effort. Together, they chose an isolated ranch school in Los Alamos, New Mexico, as the site for the atomic laboratories. On December 2, 1942, Enrico Fermi's research group, in a converted squash court at Stagg Field, University of Chicago, operated the world's first self-sustaining nuclear fission reactor, establishing the technical feasibility for building a weapon.

Approximately three years of highly classified research and development by scientists at Los Alamos led to an experimental weapon. On July 16, 1945, Los Alamos scientists detonated an implosion-type plutonium device, named *Trinity*, near the remote town of Alamogordo, New Mexico; the world's first nuclear detonation. On August 6, 1945, the U.S. Army Air Corps' 509th Composite Group dropped *Little Boy*, a uranium gun-type nuclear bomb, over Hiroshima, and, on August 9, dropped *Fat Man*, a plutonium implosion nuclear bomb, over Nagasaki. Shortly thereafter the Japanese government agreed to surrender, ending World War II on September 2, 1945.

Post-war bomb damage and radiation assessments of both Hiroshima and Nagasaki were conducted by the Navy's Bureau of Yards & Docks and the U.S. Strategic Bombing Survey. The extraordinary power of these early atomic weapons encouraged initiatives for international controls. Planning began in earnest for nuclear control initiatives, including the Baruch-Lilienthal Plan that the U.S. presented to the United Nations, which was rejected by the Soviets in 1946. At the same time, the momentum of demobilization in the wake of World War II was being felt within the MED as the scientists, engineers and other workers sought to return to their normal peacetime pursuits as rapidly as possible. Something had to be done to ensure that the atomic weapon technology was not lost and that the U.S. military remained prepared to employ nuclear weapons when and if necessary.

CHAPTER ONE

THE POST-WAR TRANSITION, 1946 TO 1948

"Before us now lies a new era in which the power of atomic energy has been released. That age will either be one of complete devastation, or one in which new sources of power will lighten the labors of mankind and increase the standards of living all over the world."

President Harry S. Truman,
Public Address to Governing Board of the
Pan American Union, April 15, 1946

EXTERNAL INFLUENCES

The destruction caused by the atomic bomb dropped on Hiroshima, Japan, on August 6, 1945, ushered in the nuclear age and forced military strategists to rethink the nature of warfare. Out of a world war that confirmed for many the triumph of democratic society over fascism, there was great public pressure to bring the military applications of atomic energy under civilian control. Many hoped that nations would unite behind some form of international control and totally ban nuclear weapons. "It did not take atomic weapons to make man want peace," J. Robert Oppenheimer, the father of the atomic bomb, wrote in 1946, "But the atomic bomb was the turn of the screw. It has made the prospect of war unendurable."[1] Military planners, however, viewed those prospects in a different perspective than the nation's most prominent civilian scientist. They had to consider that these weapons would change how wars would be fought. They also had to design strategies that would enable the Armed Forces to deliver the bombs quickly, effectively, and, in a period of shrinking budgets, inexpensively. The level of destruction brought by such "absolute weapons," in the terminology of one of the country's leading nuclear warfare theorists, Bernard Brodie, made military control imperative to those who had led the country's nuclear effort during the war, particularly General Groves, the head of the Manhattan Project. The *beating of the drums* of war had ceased, but because of the strategic and policy changes dictated by atomic weapons, in the years immediately following the hostilities, civilian and military officials struggled *to play the pipes of peace*.[2]

AN OUTPOST ON A NEW MEXICAN MESA

Major General Leslie R. Groves was concerned. By July of 1946, having successfully completed the founding requirements of the Manhattan Engineer District

(MED) task, the civilian scientists he had fought so hard to acquire were abandoning Los Alamos. Groves knew he would need something tangible to hold this intellectual core team together. In haste, he summoned Colonel Gilbert M. Dorland to Washington to discuss a "special project." Dorland, a property disposal officer for the MED, who was just recently posted to the nuclear production complex at Oak Ridge, Tennessee, boarded the next train to Washington. The next day Groves explained to Dorland the loss of civilian scientists who "...put the bomb together. We are going to have to provide military personnel, regulars, who are not going to be discharged over the next week or whatever, those who are regular members of the Corps of Engineers to take on this project." Groves' intention was to form a new unit, the Los Alamos office of the Manhattan District, which was to be activated in Albuquerque, New Mexico. There the 2761st Engineer Battalion (Special) would take over the bomb assembly function that the scientists were abandoning. He wanted the 2761st located on a small air base east of Albuquerque. He asked Dorland to go west and "...take a look around and tell me what you think." Dorland returned to Oak Ridge, packed his bags and left for New Mexico.[3]

Dorland's inspection provided the information Groves sought. For the next week, the Colonel met with MED officers in Los Alamos and at Oxnard Field (Sandia) in Albuquerque. Located east of the Rio Grande River on a mesa about six miles from Albuquerque, Sandia Base lacked any permanent facilities. The base consisted of single-story wood-frame prefabricated houses that had been shipped down from Hanford in April, a mess hall, warehouses, and a bachelor officers quarters. Dorland was amazed by what he found. Oxnard, called Sandia (Spanish: *watermelon*) by the new inhabitants, was little more than a landing strip surrounded by row after row of surplus fighters, bombers, and cargo planes. Owned by the Reconstruction Finance Corporation, the old planes shimmered in the desert sun, waiting to be cut up for scrap. Some of the military personnel at Sandia, Dorland thought, did not measure up to regular Army standards. Two days later the Colonel was back in Groves' office, reporting his findings and offering solutions to what needed to be done. The General replied, "Well, go do it," with a proviso cautioning Dorland to "...remember you have got to get along with the Air Corps and the scientists from Los Alamos."[4]

With the extent of his non-specific orders to "...go do it," Dorland headed west again, this time to take command of the 2761st Engineer Battalion (Special). The 2761st would later become the field operations command unit for the Armed Forces Special Weapons Project (AFSWP) at Sandia Base.

THE ORIGINS OF AFSWP

General Groves was not an easy man to please. He had been in his third year of studies at the Massachusetts Institute of Technology in June 1916, when he received a coveted and highly competitive Presidential appointment to the U.S. Military Academy, graduated fourth in his class on November 1, 1918, ten days before the armistice that ended World War I. Dick Groves (only those who did not know him called him Leslie), according to his biographer, was "...an intensely businesslike and almost precociously serious young man whose exaggerated self-confidence and bristling sarcasm tended to keep potential friends at a distance." Over the years, Groves developed a hard-charging, straight-ahead style that would characterize his military career. The construction of the Pentagon and the forging of the nation's atomic weapons complex reflected his drive and singleness of purpose.[5]

In the fall of 1945, as commanding officer of the MED, Groves could be justifiably proud of the achievements of the scientists and soldiers under his command. From his Washington, D.C., office in the new War Department building at 21st Street and Virginia Avenue, NW, just four blocks from the White House, Groves assessed the vast secret industrial complex he had built to design, manufacture, and deliver the atomic bomb. After Hiroshima and Nagasaki and the ensuing Japanese surrender, most Americans learned for the first time about such places as Oak Ridge, Hanford, and Los Alamos. For Groves, secrecy and science were critical elements in the success of the Manhattan Project.

Groves' wartime accomplishments were widely acknowledged and praised. President Harry S. Truman and Secretary of War Henry L. Stimson had awarded him the Distinguished Service Medal, the country's highest non-combat honor, for his role in developing the atomic bomb. To many, Groves and the Manhattan Project had been crucial to winning the war. The General was on the cover of *Business Week* and featured prominently in daily newspapers and popular magazines such as *Time*, *The Saturday Evening Post*, and *Collier's*. Fiorello LaGuardia, the popular and irrepressible mayor of New York City, had praised him in a ceremony on the steps of City Hall as the man who had "…accomplish[ed] the impossible."[6] Wartime achievements, however, did not necessarily translate into peacetime success. In fact, in the months after V-J Day as 1945 drew to a close, Groves' atomic empire was already crumbling, a victim to both the rapid demobilization of the military and the failure of politicians and other government officials to reach agreement on a postwar nuclear policy.

General Groves was no stranger to seemingly intractable problems. The atomic bombs dropped on Hiroshima and Nagasaki had—most historians agreed—forced the Japanese to surrender and hastened the end of World War II. Atomic weapons exemplified the triumph of the "can do" spirit of the American military and American scientists and engineers. The Manhattan Project was proof positive of Groves' ability to grapple with huge challenges and create workable solutions. Yet herein lay Groves' dilemma.[7]

Groves knew that peacetime would bring to an end the Manhattan Project and its singular purpose to build an atomic weapon. He recognized that the military role in atomic energy would be reduced. Since the government failed to establish nuclear weapons policy between the summer of 1945 and July 1946, Groves did not know how much reduction of the military's role would occur. "Since our objective [in the Manhattan Project] was finite," he later wrote, "we did not design our organization to operate in perpetuity."

J. Robert Oppenheimer and Major General Leslie Groves at Ground Zero in Alamorgordo, New Mexico, about two months after *Trinity* test, 1945.

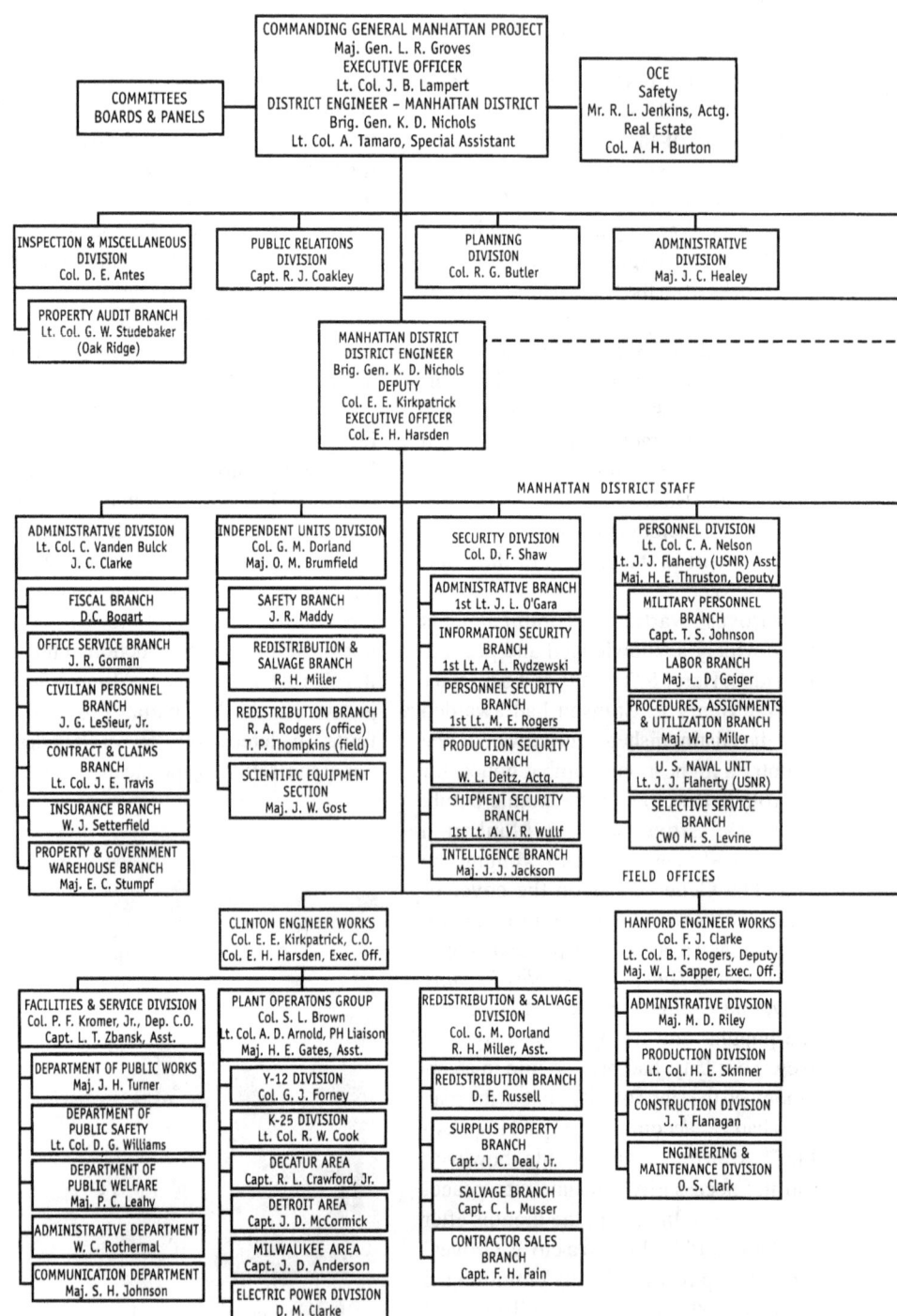

Manhattan Engineering District (MED) Organization Chart, 1946.

The Post-War Transition, 1946 to 1948

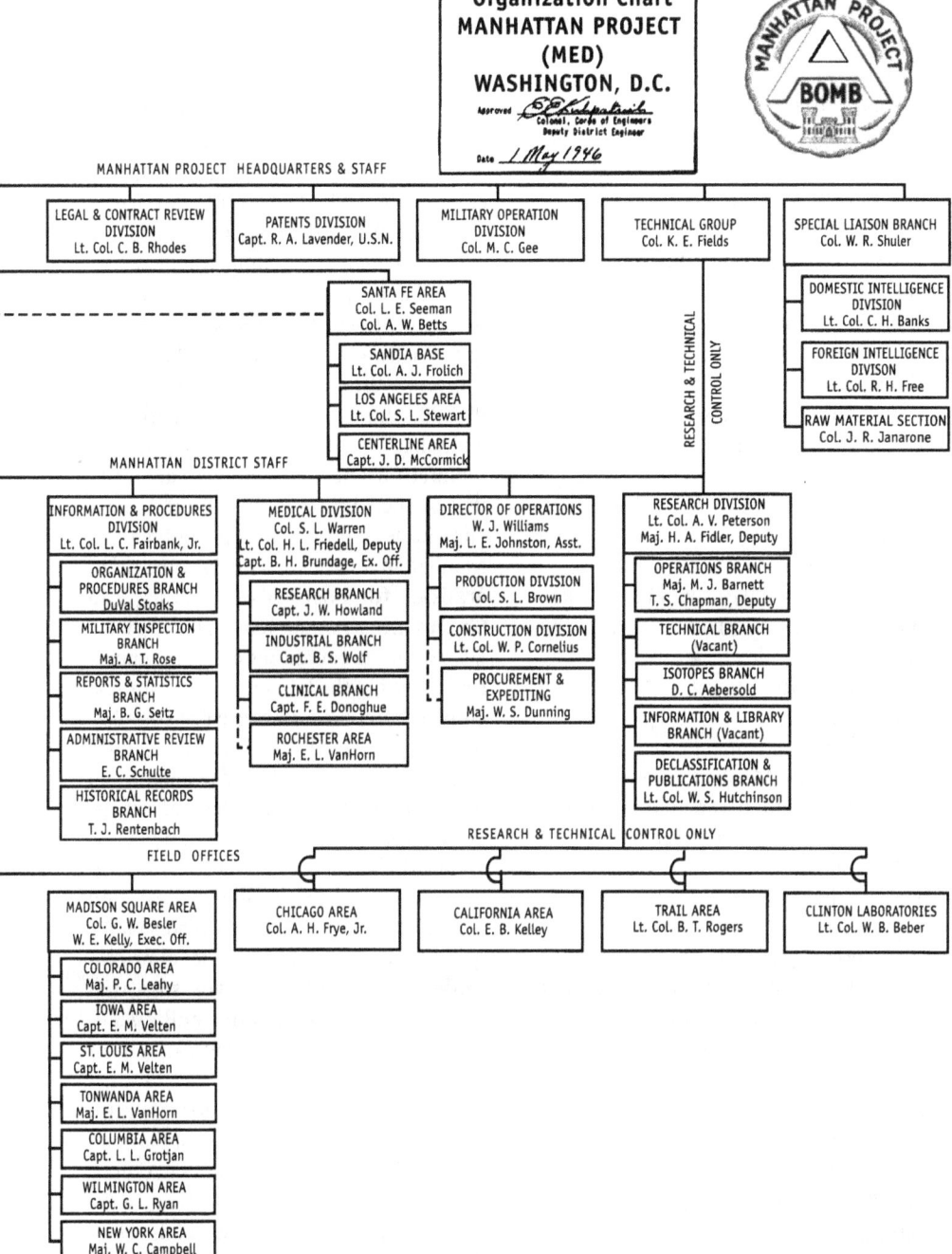

But the general fully expected that Congress would speedily act on a proposal to form a civilian commission to take over the Manhattan Project soon after the war.[8]

Since 1944, the Office of Scientific Research and Development, Groves, and lawyers in the War Department had drafted a number of versions of an atomic energy bill that would put the weapons complex under a largely civilian commission. The scientists and the military representatives, however, had not agreed on the details by the time the war had ended, dashing any hopes for a speedy resolution or transition to a domestic postwar atomic energy policy. Instead, Groves complained, there were a number of people "...pushing their pet schemes" and trying to "...advance their careers by displaying an interest in atomic energy matters." In the meantime, Groves sought to maintain operation of the Manhattan District's basic functions while carrying out the inevitable demobilization that came with peace.[9]

With no national policy in place, Groves ran the Manhattan Project as he saw best, even though he did not believe his assumption of such broad powers was justified after the war. Groves knew that many of the soldiers and scientists of the Manhattan Project longed to return to their more normal, prewar lives. To free up regular Army officers for the battlefield during the war, he had deliberately staffed the military side of the Manhattan District with noncareer reserve officers, who would quickly return to civilian life when they became eligible for discharge. "The great goal had been achieved," Groves said, "and there was nothing [for the scientists] to look forward to."[10]

Many of the scientists were already leaving to take up their former university research and teaching positions that they had left during the war. Moreover, the success of the atomic bomb had created a sharp demand for additional atomic physicists in academic institutions. Even junior men, Groves noted, were receiving offers "...far beyond anything they could have previously expected to get after even 20 years of experience." Military officers viewed the demobilization as a precursor to what had occurred after World War I, when boredom of garrison life was the major enemy and military careers advanced at a snail's pace.[11]

By the fall of 1945, Groves had to figure out how to reduce the Manhattan Project's wartime work force of more than 90,000, return facilities and materials to civilian use as rapidly as possible, and still maintain a nuclear weapons capability that meshed with whatever final American nuclear policy might evolve. The Manhattan District had made some preparations for postwar operations, and Groves moved to implement those plans. He set out to cut all but essential operations, closing the laboratory at Columbia University, considering its work completed. At Oak Ridge, he closed the liquid-thermal diffusion plant, S-50, and placed the older sections of Y-12, the electromagnetic separation plant, on standby. At Hanford, Groves terminated the operations of one of the chemical separation plants, closed the last heavy water facility, and sharply cut back the level of plutonium production. Groves said that "...we want to get rid of five million dollars worth of facility every week," one of his assistants later recalled.[12]

The fate of the Los Alamos laboratory in peacetime, however, demanded special attention. During the war, Los Alamos had combined two critical elements of the Manhattan Project, research and development and bomb production. That would now change. Groves wanted to keep a cadre of scientists in Los Alamos who would be available for future weapons improvement and development. Their leader, however, was leaving. Robert Oppenheimer, who had recommended the Los Alamos site and directed the scientific effort there since 1942, told Groves he was returning to his academic post at the University of California at Berkeley as soon as possible.[13]

In an attempt to keep the scientists together amid such uncertainty about their careers, Groves traveled to Los Alamos in August 1945 to reassure them. World War II was ending and Groves wanted to avoid a mass exodus of civilian and military staff from MED facilities. Loudspeakers were set up to allow the large crowd that gathered inside and outside the building to hear the general. Groves explained that President Truman was sponsoring an atomic energy bill that would establish a new federal agency to run the nuclear program and that he expected that the laboratory would continue as a research center for atomic weapons. There would still be the element of secrecy to their work, though their schedules would be far less strenuous.[14]

Groves' speech yielded mixed results. The civilians who disliked Groves during the war were not inclined to change their minds about him or the Army. "What we heard," one engineer recalled, "was a monologue of how great General Groves was; as a result the exodus from Los Alamos accelerated."[15] Though many of the wartime division leaders chose to leave Los Alamos, a number of younger men remained to head new divisions. Groves seized on the changes to move the bomb assembly function, an engineering rather than scientific operation, out of Los Alamos to Oxnard Field. More important, Oxnard was adjacent to Kirtland Field in New Mexico, which had served as a transit point for the climax of the Manhattan Project (*Trinity*) and was being developed after the war into a facility to load atom bombs into the specially modified B-29s, code-named *Silverplate*.[16]

General Groves addresses MED military and civilian workers at Los Alamos, August 29, 1945.

Groves still needed a new director to replace Oppenheimer. He wanted someone "...with sufficient prestige to secure the cooperation of his colleagues at Los Alamos, and the assistance of distinguished scientists throughout the country, particularly of those who were now leaving the project." In consultation with Oppenheimer, Groves named U.S. Navy Commander Norris E. Bradbury, a physicist and the number two man in the Explosives Division, as the interim director of the lab. In Bradbury, Groves finally found a blend of scientist and military officer who could maintain "...smooth relations between the civilian scientific staff and the military administrative officers." Such a combination, Groves hoped, might squelch the bickering between the two groups, which had plagued his own relationship with the scientific community during the war.[17]

As Groves struggled with reducing his operations while at the same time keeping them operable, he was frustrated by policymakers who continued to quarrel over how civilian control of atomic energy might be best accomplished. Groves believed he needed to act in the absence of any specific orders. With Bradbury in place to cover his scientific flank, Groves moved to strengthen his military contingent. He had concluded that, to ensure a smooth transition to whatever organization eventually would assume the responsibilities of the MED, he needed about 50 regular Army officers to run the weapons complex in the meantime. Drawing on the lessons of his wartime experiences, especially the running battles with civilian scientists who made no secret of their contempt for the military and its secrecy restrictions, Groves put out the word that he preferred West Pointers, officers who, as cadets, had been among the top 5-10 percent in their class scholastically. If forced to compromise, Groves allowed that he would also consider men who graduated in the top 10 percent. "A successful athletic career," he recalled, one that demonstrated "...a more than average determination and will to win, was a particular asset."[18]

Groves asserted that the new officers had to command the respect of those already in the Manhattan Project, particularly the scientists. Scientists, Groves had discovered, "...were most critical of anyone whose mental alertness did not equal or excel theirs." The general wanted men who "...were young enough to break into the atomic field, but who were senior enough in rank to have demonstrated their ability to accept heavy responsibilities." Younger men, those under 35, he believed, would be more acceptable to the scientists, nearly all of whom, Groves said, "...were extremely young."[19]

Normally, finding 50 replacement officers would not be difficult. But Groves' special requirements caused a barrage of protests from the War Department Gen-

Norris E. Bradbury and J. Robert Oppenheimer at MED-sponsored weekly scientific colloquia gathering in Los Alamos.

Robert P. Patterson, Secretary of War, 1945-1947.

eral Staff, which did not agree that the Manhattan Project should have the pick of the best officers. Groves' appeal to the new Army Chief of Staff, General Dwight D. Eisenhower, was unsuccessful. Groves argued that "...there was no place for anyone in the atomic field who was not a super-superior officer." Placing lesser men in the Manhattan Project, he insisted, "...would lead to adverse reactions among our scientific personnel, and through them, among the rest of the academic world and the press." Clearly, Groves did not wish to suffer from another round of headaches such as those he had experienced from the scientists at Los Alamos.[20]

In August 1946, the General carried his case for selection priority to Robert P. Patterson, the Secretary of War who succeeded Henry L. Stimson in late September 1945. Patterson called in General Eisenhower and General Thomas T. Handy, who had served as Acting Chief of Staff before Eisenhower's appointment. Both men opposed Groves on the personnel issue, believing that there were other important Army operations, especially overseas, requiring the best officers besides the Manhattan Project. After a heated discussion, Patterson settled the dispute. "I agree with Groves," he said. "I want him to have as many officers as he decides he needs and the quality he thinks he needs, and I want him to have complete freedom of choice." Groves had won a major victory. "Only the high quality of our regular officers enabled us to weather the difficult period of demobilization between V-J Day and the activation of the Atomic Energy Commission," he concluded in his memoirs.[21]

The ability to select specific personnel was a critical triumph for Groves. With Oppenheimer, Groves more than any other individual could claim parenthood for the American nuclear program. The inability of Congress to pass an atomic energy bill genuinely troubled him. Groves viewed the Manhattan Project as *his baby*, and he keenly recognized that it could not have a secure peacetime future without appropriate legislation. Thus, between the summer of 1945 and August 1946, the MED would exist in awkward adolescence, never quite making the transition between a temporary wartime project and a permanent part of the country's defense establishment.

Moreover, Groves was uncertain of his own role or, for that matter, the Army's role in the postwar nuclear program. No commander liked uncertainty, and Groves clearly disliked his caretaker position. Nonetheless, he would make the best of the situation. As MED employees were cut back by as much as half in some facilities, Groves was able to fill critical positions in 1945 and 1946 with his select officers. They proved to be excellent choices for the job. "A... surprising large percentage of these... officers in key positions," the Army historian of the Manhattan Project wrote, "stayed on until the latter part of 1946, and many of those who did resign continued with the atomic project in a civilian capacity." Groves' action ensured that the military would have a continuing presence in the nuclear program, regardless of the outcome of the debate over the atomic energy bill in Congress.[22]

Groves wanted the military to have more than a presence in the postwar period; it also required a mission. Since November 1945, Groves had worked with Oppenheimer and Bradbury to boost morale at Los Alamos. Deteriorating conditions at the laboratory, caused by the facility's uncertain future, the flight of the top scientists, and the lack of basic amenities in a city built during wartime, jeopardized the continued stockpiling of atomic weapons.

Operation CROSSROADS, the planned nuclear test series scheduled to begin at Bikini Atoll in June 1946, placed additional pressure on the scientists who were responsible for the development, fabrication, and assembly of the weapons. Groves turned to his long-time assistant, Brigadier General Kenneth D. Nichols, to find a solution.[23]

Nichols was the model of Groves' conception of an ideal officer. Slightly balding, thin, and ramrod straight, Nichols wore rimless glasses and looked every bit the intellectual who could deal easily with scientists. The looks were not deceiving. Nichols graduated fifth in the Class of 1929 from West Point, had earned two graduate degrees in engineering at Cornell, had taken graduate work in Germany, and completed a doctorate in hydraulic engineering at the University of Iowa before World War II. By 1937, Nichols had gained a coveted faculty appointment at West Point where he taught military and civil engineering and military history. In the summer of 1942, Nichols received orders to "...volunteer for a very important technical project, or be drafted." Soon he was working for the Manhattan Engineer District and General Groves.[24]

The two men complemented each other and worked well together, though they were a study in contrasts. With a full head of hair, heavy frame tending to paunch, and slightly rumpled appearance, Groves contrasted sharply with the lean, more soldierly Nichols. Nor did his education match that of his scholarly assistant. Groves had attended the University of Washington and the Massachusetts Institute of Technology before receiving a Presidential appointment to West Point.

Graduating in 1918 as World War I was ending, Groves began his Army career when promotions were few and far between. In the period between the wars, he graduated from the Army Engineer School, the Command and General Staff School, and the Army War College. At the time of Pearl Harbor, Groves was the Deputy Chief of Construction under the Chief of Engineers. Groves' academic background was typical for an Army officer of his generation, but it did not match up to the scientists with whom he dealt, a factor that nagged him, unfairly or not, during the Manhattan Project.[25]

WEAPONS DEVELOPMENT

At Groves' behest, Nichols examined the situation at Los Alamos and decided that to improve the rate of weapons development, the wide responsibilities of the scientists should be narrowed. In March of 1946, he wrote Groves proposing that outside contractors take over the fabrication of most bomb components. He also recommended that a new special military unit in the Manhattan District assume the final assembly of the weapons. Such changes, he argued, would free the scientists for the development of new types of bombs and thereby speed up the process.[26]

Nichols' concern about the snail's pace of bomb production was well founded. In 1945 and early 1946, all atomic weapons were laboratory weapons, handcrafted by the scientists at Los Alamos. As a result of peacetime personnel reductions throughout the nuclear weapons complex and the lack of a definitive postwar nuclear policy, advanced research and

Brigadier General Kenneth D. Nichols, first AFSWP Deputy Director.

design on a new generation of weapons was largely halted. Therefore, each bomb produced was based on the Mark III *Fat Man* implosion weapon dropped on Nagasaki. Improvements were made incrementally as each weapon was developed, fabricated, and assembled. The process was painfully slow. Scientists worked on every aspect of the weapon, and a group might take 30 days to complete the assembly of a bomb from the components. For example, the high explosive lenses, which would implode to achieve a critical mass in the plutonium core, were hand cast. Because of the complexity of the firing mechanism and the slow-drying adhesive that held the lenses in place, it took more than two days for a specially trained team of 39 scientists to assemble a Mark III bomb.[27]

In an effort to incorporate new weapons concepts that would increase a bomb's effective yield and increase the size of the stockpile, Groves and Oppenheimer had moved the weapons assembly division, Group Z-7 (Assembly), to Sandia Base at the end of 1945. The Z-Division was formed in July 1945 and named after its initial leader, Jerrold R. Zacharias. There was discussion at that time about having military personnel assemble the bombs for stockpiling, but up until that time all bombs exploded had been under civilian control.[28]

Nichols and Groves both realized the irony that there were very few weapons for anyone, civilian or military, to assemble. The head of the Manhattan District and his top aide belonged to a very select few who knew that, at the end of June 1946, the United States nuclear stockpile held sufficient components to assemble only nine weapons. General Eisenhower, the Army representative to the Joint

Housing units at Z-Division, (Zacharias), Sandia Base, February 1946.

Chiefs of Staff, and Secretary of War Patterson were the highest ranking government officials to be informed regularly of the stockpile numbers. No procedures existed for formally reporting on stockpile information to top military and civilian officials. Only the passage and implementation of the Atomic Energy Act would remedy that condition. In the meantime, President Truman, Secretary of State James F. Byrnes, Secretary of the Navy James V. Forrestal, and the rest of the Joint Chiefs were not briefed about the country's nuclear capability.[29]

OPERATION CROSSROADS

In fact, such a briefing might have horrified those officials. In 1946 the United States possessed very few nuclear weapons. Operation CROSSROADS, a planned series of three tests to investigate the effects of nuclear weapons on naval vessels during the summer of 1946, would require at least three nuclear components, called cores or pits, and perhaps a greater number of non-nuclear mechanical assemblies, which included the high explosives, electrical firing mechanisms, and outside casings. At that time, there were only nine bombs in the stockpile. The tests would use one-third of the country's nuclear arsenal. With plutonium production reduced from its wartime levels, the stockpile was not expanding. When Truman learned from Eisenhower of the small number of weapons in the stockpile in September 1946, he canceled the third CROSSROADS test at Bikini. The President probably did so realizing that only approximately six bombs remained in the stockpile, though he believed "...that was enough to win a war."[30]

Nevertheless, Operation CROSSROADS provided a unique opportunity to evaluate atmospheric nuclear weapon test data. Conducted in the Marshall Islands in the Central Pacific within the confines of Bikini Atoll, the 1946 test series consisted of Shot ABLE, air-dropped by a B-29 and detonated at an altitude of 520 feet on June 30, and Shot BAKER, detonated 90 feet underwater on July 24. The target naval vessels for both shots consisted of old U.S. capital ships, three captured German and Japanese ships, surplus U.S. cruisers, destroyers, and submarines, and a large number of auxiliary and amphibious vessels. The weapons used in ABLE and BAKER were of the same design as the one used in Japan on Nagasaki. Each had a yield of 21 kilotons (KT), the approximate equivalent of 21,000 tons of trinitrotoluene (TNT). The support fleet for Operation CROSSROADS consisted of more than 150 ships, which provided quarters, experimental stations, and workshops for most of the 42,000 men of Joint Task Force 1 (JTF 1), which administered the tests. Additional personnel during the tests were stationed on nearby atolls such as Enewetak and Kwajalein. Another senior group present through the CROSSROADS series was the JCS Evaluation Board, charged with advising the Commander of JTF 1 (Vice Admiral W.H. Blandy) in the planning of the tests and presenting to the JCS an evaluation of the results. This board included: Dr. K.T. Compton (President, MIT); Mr. Bradley Dewey (President, American Chemical Society); Major General Farrell (MED); General J.W. Stilwell (Commanding, Sixth Army Area); Brigadier General K.D. Nichols (AFSWP); Lieutenant General L.H. Brereton (Office of the Secretary of War); Vice Admiral Hoover (Navy General Board); and Rear Admiral R.A. Offsite (U.S. Strategic Bombing Survey).

Because of the very high level of secrecy surrounding stockpile information, few men realized the feeble sting of the country's nuclear weapons. Moreover, with the end of Operation CROSSROADS in September 1946, the scientists

Members of JCS Evaluation Board for Operation CROSSROADS, left to right, Major General Farrell, General Stilwell, Brigadier General Nichols, Lieutenant General Brereton and Vice Admiral Hoover.

who had assembled the weapons left the program. For the next six or eight months there was zero capability of assembling a weapon. Colonel Gilbert M. Dorland, officer in charge of the stockpile at Sandia, claimed, "We were plain bluffing. We couldn't have put the bomb together and used it."[31]

WHO WILL CONTROL THE BOMB?

Groves and Nichols moved quickly to remedy the problem. With the passage of the Atomic Energy Act in August 1946, they implemented the plan to place the responsibility for the assembly of nuclear weapons and the surveillance of the nuclear stockpile with the Army. Nichols still chafed at the fact that civilian scientists had continued to have "...a key part in the assembly and exploding of the bomb." That created for the military "...an intolerable situation," he emphasized in a September 1946 speech analyzing the military responsibilities under the Atomic Energy Act. Even as he spoke, Nichols knew that the Corps of Engineers was filling the vac-

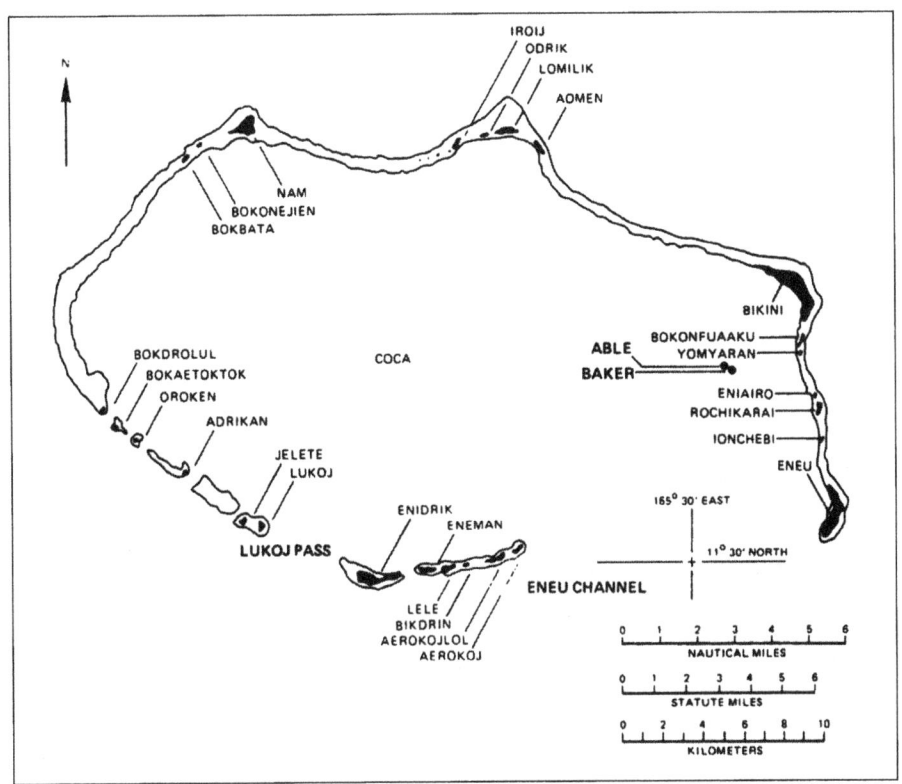

Bikini Atoll, 1946, showing ABLE and BAKER test sites for the CROSSROADS Test Series.

uum left by the departing scientists. In the summer of 1946, men began to gather in Albuquerque as the Pacific tests ended, military men selected by Groves and his assistants who would take over the responsibilities of assembly and surveillance.[32]

Lacking any precedent or historical guidelines, U.S. government officials and military officers at the highest level struggled throughout 1946 to find an appropriate policy governing both domestic and international control of nuclear weapons. All spring and summer, Congress argued over several possible versions of a civilian AEC that would assume the duties and responsibilities of the military's MED. The debate often focused on the relationship between the military's role and the extent of civilian authority over atomic weapons. It was not until August 1, when Truman signed the Atomic Energy Act, that a formal nuclear policy began to emerge.[33]

Laboring with the birth of nuclear policy, the Truman administration mired itself in the details. The search for the proper commissioners took several months. The same uncertainty applied to the international arena. Unsure of the actions of the Soviet Union and ambivalent over their own response, administration officials, scientists, and soldiers hammered out several versions of a plan for international control before agreement was reached. Then, abruptly, the administration shifted position and another proposal became the centerpiece of U.S.

CROSSROADS Series, Test BAKER, held on July 24, 1946, tested the effects of blast on surface ships.

policy at the United Nations. Touting international disarmament in one forum while testing nuclear weapons at the same time in another sent signals that many believed could be easily misinterpreted. Surrounded by high level indecision, Groves cautiously moved to keep his country's nuclear armor polished.[34]

SHAPING THE ATOMIC ENERGY COMMISSION

In August 1946, after months of behind-the-scenes deliberations and millions of words of public debate, Congress finally passed the McMahon Bill (Atomic Energy Act), named for its chief sponsor, Senator Brien McMahon, a Connecticut Democrat. The Atomic Energy Act was the result of a series of compromises, some of which were designed to limit the postwar role of the military.[35]

Although all sides in the debate had supported the transfer of the atomic energy program, including military applications, from the MED to a five-member civilian AEC appointed by the President, there was substantial disagreement about the shape of the Commission, the nature of the military's future mission under such an arrangement, and the level of military participation sufficient for the national defense. Groves supported a part-time commission with a military representative with extensive experience "...who is not going to forget for one minute that... defense must come first and other things will have to come afterward." McMahon, who had the strong support of scientists who had chafed under the strictures of the Manhattan District and now opposed any military control, wanted a full-time commission and sought to exclude the military altogether. McMahon received his full-time commission. But in the final bill, an amendment successfully pushed by Michigan Republican Senator Arthur H. Vandenberg, the uncle of the head of the Army Air Corps, General Hoyt Vandenberg, ensured that, although the commissioners would be civilians, the interests of the military would be fully represented to the Commission by a Military Liaison Committee (MLC).[36]

CONTROL AND CUSTODY

The issue of control and custody of nuclear weapons was equally crucial. Early versions of McMahon's atomic energy bill had given the Commission exclusive control over weapons research and development and the weapons stockpile. McMahon softened his position on research and development and changed the stockpile clause to read that the "...President from time to time may direct the Commission to deliver such quantities of weapons to the armed forces for such use as he deems necessary in the interests of national defense." The stockpile compromise continued to rankle with Groves and Nichols, but both knew in the summer of 1946 that the atomic arsenal was slim. With the Atomic Energy Act in place, however, the Army would now develop and articulate detailed weapons policy, before the Truman administration could select commissioners who would chart the course for the AEC and civilian control of atomic energy.[37]

Not surprisingly, Groves' closest aides, led by Nichols and his Chief of Staff, Colonel Sherman V. Hasbrouck, outlined the future relationships between the military and atomic energy in a two-day conference sponsored by the Manhattan District at Fort Belvoir, Virginia, on September 25-26, 1946. Although nuclear policy had yet to be defined by either the military or civilian parts of the government, Nichols' and Hasbrouck's papers provided a baseline for the defense establishment's views in the fall of 1946.

Nichols had lobbied long and hard for strong military control over atomic energy and was not at all pleased with the provisions of McMahon's bill. "The act as written," he told the officers on the first day of the conference, "may not be the best for getting the military end of the job done, but it is the way prescribed by law and the War and Navy Departments must find the way to work within its provisions to insure that the job is done properly." For Nichols, this meant that the military should control as much of the nuclear weapons program as possible.[38]

Nichols bluntly outlined the powers of the civilian commission but emphasized that the atomic bomb was "...a major part of our national defense and of primary interest to the military establishment." He noted the division of responsibility between the AEC and the MLC, whose members would be appointed by the Secretaries of War and Navy, emphasizing that the details for developing the military application of atomic energy or the production and custody of the weapons had yet to be settled. The logical division, he suggested, would be for the Commission "...to make all parts of the bomb, deliver these parts to the military, and the military would then have the responsibility for proper storage, assembly and delivery of the weapon," much the way "...our air forces acquire[d] airplanes."[39]

Nichols also stressed the importance of the military role within the AEC through the Director of Military Application, who, though under the Commission, had to be, by law, a member of the Armed Forces. That individual, Nichols argued, should control all aspects of weapons research, development, and production except that relating to nuclear material, which would be turned over to the military for conversion into weapons. He noted that all of the bombs exploded to that time had been assembled and fired by civilian scientists, "...a situation," he warned, "that from a military point of view should not be tolerated indefinitely."[40]

In calling for active military participation in the formulation of the country's foreign policy, Nichols anticipated the several policies that would come to shape the Cold War. He foresaw a country on constant alert, stocked with thousands of atomic bombs to be used in attacks of massive retaliation and assuring destruction of an aggressor. "The atomic bomb cannot be outlawed unless war is outlawed," he said. He maintained that atomic warfare "...lends itself best to a sustained aggressive surprise attack." Because a nation must deliver a "knockout blow" within the first few weeks, "...we can no longer prepare for an initial defensive war while our nation is mobilizing," as the United States had done before entering World War II. One part of the solution, Nichols said, was an extensive intelligence network to learn about the kinds of atomic energy research other nations were conducting. The second part of the solution was to discourage an attack by being prepared to retaliate "...with a similar attack multiplied a hundredfold." No nation, Nichols maintained, "...could stand up to a sustained atomic attack if they were not able to give equal or greater punishment in return."[41]

Preparedness would not come cheaply, Nichols warned. A potential enemy could easily support an atomic energy program costing "...tens of billions of dollars, particularly if they felt that by such an expenditure they could win a short aggressive war." But if the United States provided sufficient funding to develop and produce large numbers of weapons and devised ways other than the B-29 to deliver them, "...this nation [would be] undefeatable in war." He suggested that a funding level of $500 million per year would be adequate, though the country might need to increase the annual expenditures to $2 billion should the "...international situation become critical." He reminded his audience that regardless of cost, "...atomic warfare promises to be the cheapest form of death and destruction ever devised by man." It was up to the military, he told the officers, to educate the public and the nation's leaders to insure that such a defensive strategy received strong support.[42]

Nichols did not believe that a nuclear war was imminent; rather, he imagined that it was a possibility "...some fifteen to thirty years from now."[43] In any case, the United States must be prepared.

On September 26, 1946, at the AEC's Fort Belvoir Conference, General Groves, Rear Admiral William S. (Deke) Parsons, and other prominent officers from the Manhattan Project listened to Colonel Hasbrouck provide additional information on the bomb, most of it extrapolated from the military's experience in the war and at Operation CROSSROADS. Nuclear weapons, he explained, were not mass produced and could not "...be made like donuts rolling off a machine." Every bomb, therefore, was "...precious and must be conserved, safeguarded and expended wisely." He emphasized the strategic importance of nuclear weapons, contrasting the enormous cost of firebombing Tokyo in March 1945 with the results obtained by one B-29 and one atomic bomb six months later at Hiroshima and then at Nagasaki. After using hundreds of planes, thousands of air and ground crewmen, and thousands of tons of incendiary bombs, he noted, "...the Japs fought on." After dropping two atomic weapons, "...the Japs could take no more."[44]

Hasbrouck offered an additional example on the power and strategic value of atomic bombs. The Japanese had hammered away at Pearl Harbor with hundreds of planes for several hours, he pointed out, but at the CROSSROADS operation at Bikini earlier in the summer of 1946, "...a single bomb in a single moment [had] crippled a fleet." The nature of warfare had changed. He wondered if "...the day of the battleship and the big carrier [was] over." For example, what might have happened to the American fleet had the Japanese possessed such a weapon during the invasion of Leyte or to the Allied invasion force had Hitler been able to use one on the English Channel ports in June 1944, he asked rhetorically.[45]

The Colonel continued his discussion of the strategic value of atomic bombs by emphasizing the different ways the weapons might be used. Targeting was critical, Hasbrouck explained. He cited industrial cities, naval bases, embarkation ports, power dams, and reservoirs as the most appropriate and "remunerative" targets. Since the use of atomic bombs would be decided by the President with advice from the military, it was critical for the military to have the very best intelligence about potential targets so it could calculate the number of bombs necessary for destruction. It was also vital that the weapons be dropped with accuracy. A bomb dropped on "...Chevy Chase would not greatly hurt the federal installations in Washington," he noted dryly. To obtain the desired accuracy, he believed that the Air Force needed a "...comparatively small number of very highly trained bomber crews."[46]

Perhaps of equal importance, Hasbrouck continued, was the psychological impact of an atomic bomb. The war with Japan, he argued, had been brought to an end by a threat, the threat of continued bombing and the destruction of more cities. The Japanese "...did not *know* that we had even one more bomb. General Groves is probably the only one who knew." Hitler, he said, effectively used the threat of a "secret weapon" during the war. The United States had the same advantage with the atomic bomb. "There can be no doubt," Hasbrouck concluded, "that our present possession of this weapon is a stabilizing factor toward world peace."[47]

THE BARUCH PLAN AND INTERNATIONAL CONTROL OF ATOMIC ENERGY

The two-day conference was a crash course in nuclear policy from the veterans of the Manhattan Project for the postwar military planners. Experience with the uses and effects of atomic weapons was more apparent than either the shape of the government's postwar nuclear policy or the military's future relationship with the AEC, both of which were encountering major problems of definition. Even as Hasbrouck spoke, at the end of September 1946, of the atomic bomb as a stabilizing factor in world peace, he implied that nuclear weapons would continue to be a major part of postwar policy, reflecting a military position that had by then moved beyond the Truman administration's public posture of disarmament embodied in the Baruch Plan.

Establishment of the country's nuclear policy had been debated within the administration since early 1946 with mixed success. Secretary of State Byrnes appointed a panel headed by David E. Lilienthal, then the head of the Tennessee Valley Authority, and Undersecretary of State Dean G. Acheson to formulate such a policy. The group consisted of representatives from the business, scientific, and military communities, including General Groves. After nearly three months of discussion, the panel issued its findings. The Acheson-Lilienthal Report, as the proposal was called, did not seek to outlaw atomic weapons. "Any system based on outlawing the purely military development of atomic energy and relying solely on inspection for enforcement," the report stated, "would at the outset be surrounded by conditions that would destroy the system." Rather, the panel sought to control every stage of weapons production. Control, the report specified, would come from an international Atomic Development Authority that would keep track of potential violations as well as license acceptable activities such as research in nuclear medicine.[48] No sooner had the administration had its first view of the Acheson-Lilienthal recommendations when Truman, on Byrnes' advice, appointed noted Presidential advisor, millionaire financier, and major contributor to the Democratic party Bernard M. Baruch to present the U.S. position on atomic energy before the United Nations Atomic Energy Commission. Once more, American nuclear policy shifted. Baruch immediately rejected many of the provisions of the Acheson-Lilienthal Report on the basis that it [the Report] failed to deal with the central problem of enforcement. Baruch's plan called for "...sanctions against those who violated the rules" and required the United States to give up its nuclear monopoly only as other nations agreed to these terms. Finally, he stipulated that no nation could use the Security Council's veto power to block those sanctions. Baruch presented his proposal at the United Nations that summer.[49]

Not surprisingly, the Soviet Union rejected Baruch's ideas and immediately countered with its own proposal, which required immediate and total nuclear disarmament but lacked any provisions for inspection to see that signatories were following the rules. Further, the Soviets demanded to retain veto power in the Security Council. Throughout the summer, each side remained at the negotiation table, but, in fact, there was little chance that either side would agree to a compromise.[50]

The debate over the outcome of international control of nuclear energy became further muddied by Secretary of Commerce Henry A. Wallace. A former Secretary of Agriculture and Vice President under Franklin D. Roosevelt during most of the war, Wallace had acquired a reputation in Washington as a loose cannon. His brand of high idealism, attachment to

Bernard M. Baruch (center) presented to the United Nations the American Plan for International Control of Atomic Energy on June 14, 1946.

the controversial ideas of a Russian mystic of dubious character, and a willingness to publicly champion a foreign policy that was at odds with the administration's, insured that Truman would have to replace him. However, in the summer and fall of 1946, Truman had not felt comfortable enough in the office he had inherited to sack Wallace.[51]

As Groves, Nichols, and Hasbrouck were preparing for the military symposium on atomic weapons under a civilian authority, Wallace tried to torpedo his nation's policy for the international control of atomic energy. Wallace pointed to the Bikini tests and the production of the B-36 bomber that could carry a nuclear weapon from the continental United States to the Soviet Union, something the "silverplated" B-29s could not do, as evidence that the United States was not seeking accommodation with the Soviet Union. Wallace blasted Baruch's step-by-step disarmament plan and proposed instead to "…reach an agreement which will commit us to disclosing information and destroying our bombs at a specific time or in terms of specified actions by other countries, rather than at our unfettered discretion." Baruch was furious. He had never proposed that the United States unilaterally establish any timetable. But the major damage had been done. Although Truman fired Wallace soon thereafter, his administration had been thoroughly embarrassed. In addition, Baruch found himself occupied with patching over the damage at home. With so much vacillation within the administration and so much suspicion from the Soviets, an agreement on international control of atomic energy became impossible.[52]

Faced with an administration whose nuclear policy was conspicuous by its drifting and shifting on both an international and a national level, Groves and his officers in Washington had moved ahead in the fall of 1946 to define and articulate a formal military role in the new world of civilian-controlled atomic energy. Outlining their ideas to other officers at Fort Belvoir was only one aspect to their plan, however. Groves saw the basis for continued and vital military participation in nuclear weapons through upgrading the MED's presence in the field in Albuquerque, New Mexico. There, a new unit of superior, highly trained Army officers would control a critical point in the weapons production process: the assembly of atomic bombs and the training of officers to act as weaponeers for combat drops.

ESTABLISHING SANDIA BASE

Colonel Gilbert M. Dorland fit General Groves' profile for the men he wanted to run the Manhattan District's postwar operations. He had ranked twenty-first of 276 cadets at the U.S. Military Academy in the Class of 1936. While on duty in San Francisco, Dorland earned a graduate degree in civil engineering from the University of California at Berkeley in 1940. In August 1942 he shipped out with the 21st Engineers, serving as a battalion, then regimental, commander in North Africa and Italy. During the war, he earned the Bronze Star, the Legion of Merit, and the Order of the British Empire and won promotion to full Colonel in 1944.[53]

Dorland had returned from Europe and was finishing Command & General Staff School at Fort Leavenworth just as Groves was selecting regular officers for the postwar Manhattan District. The selection process, while sharply defined, was also extremely personal. It consisted largely of an intense canvass and discussion of West Pointers whose talents and qualifications were known to Groves and his assistants. Colonel James B. Lampert, General Groves' chief administrative aide in Washington, did much of the selecting, including suggesting Dorland. Lampert had been Dorland's classmate at West Point. In the summer, a number of these bright and highly motivated young officers received high priority orders to return from overseas. The posting carried a sense of stability; they were to report to New Mexico with their families.[54]

In late summer of 1946, while most of the scientists and military personnel from Los Alamos and Sandia were in the South Pacific rehearsing for the second test of Operation CROSSROADS, Colonel Dorland arrived in Albuquerque to take command of the 2761st Engineer Battalion (Special) as part of the MED. Within a month, a sufficient number of men had returned from Bikini or had been transferred from the Los Alamos Technical Services Unit to activate the battalion. He immediately formed a Headquarters and Services Company and Company A, which handled base security. Dorland would command two other companies once the men arrived for staffing. Company B, a technical company with the assignment of assembling atomic bombs, was to consist of 40 officers and 60 enlisted men, enough to form three assembly teams. In establishing Company B's mission, the Manhattan District provided that the military assembly personnel would perform only electrical and mechanical duties. In the summer of 1946, there was widespread belief that nuclear assembly was "...so complex that officers of the Armed Services did not possess sufficient knowledge to perform this work properly." Since many of the experienced assembly leaders had returned to civilian life, Company B would have to be largely self-trained from manuals and reports prepared at Los Alamos, supplemented by advice from the few knowledgeable scientists remaining in the project. Company C, when activated, would direct radiological monitoring.[55]

By September, the cream of the young officers selected by General Groves and his aides began arriving at Sandia Base. The men had orders to fly "immediate air" from Europe and the Pacific. Their families followed, usually by ship. One officer had travel orders to Sandia but had no idea where it was and wondered how he would get there. "Go to Albuquerque and ask," his intelligence officer whispered. The officers reported first to Washington, then toured the Oak Ridge operation before heading to New Mexico. The majority were graduates of the U.S. Military Academy from the classes of 1943, 1944, and 1945, primarily from the Corps of Engineers, with an additional sprinkling of honor graduates from Reserve Officer Training Corps (ROTC) programs. By the end of the month, approximately 25 officers had begun a series of orientation lectures conducted by Lieutenant Colonel A. (Al) J. Froehlich, the battalion executive officer, and Lieutenant Colonel John A. Ord.[56]

By October, the initial orientation lectures covering nuclear physics and the basic workings of the *Fat Man* atomic bomb needed to be replaced by more technical weapons assembly training. But, as Groves had feared, the scientists remained aloof, certain that "...none of those stupid Army people could understand the intricacies of an atomic weapon," Dorland recalled. The reason for this low regard of the military, he believed, was because the only soldiers they had dealt with during the war at Los Alamos were "...basically housekeeping types and security people." As a result, without much input from the scientists, for the first several months the military personnel serving as instructors were "...inadequately trained in the methods and techniques of bomb assembly," according to the unit's official history.[57]

One major difference between scientists and the military, aside from the long-

The Post-War Transition, 1946 to 1948

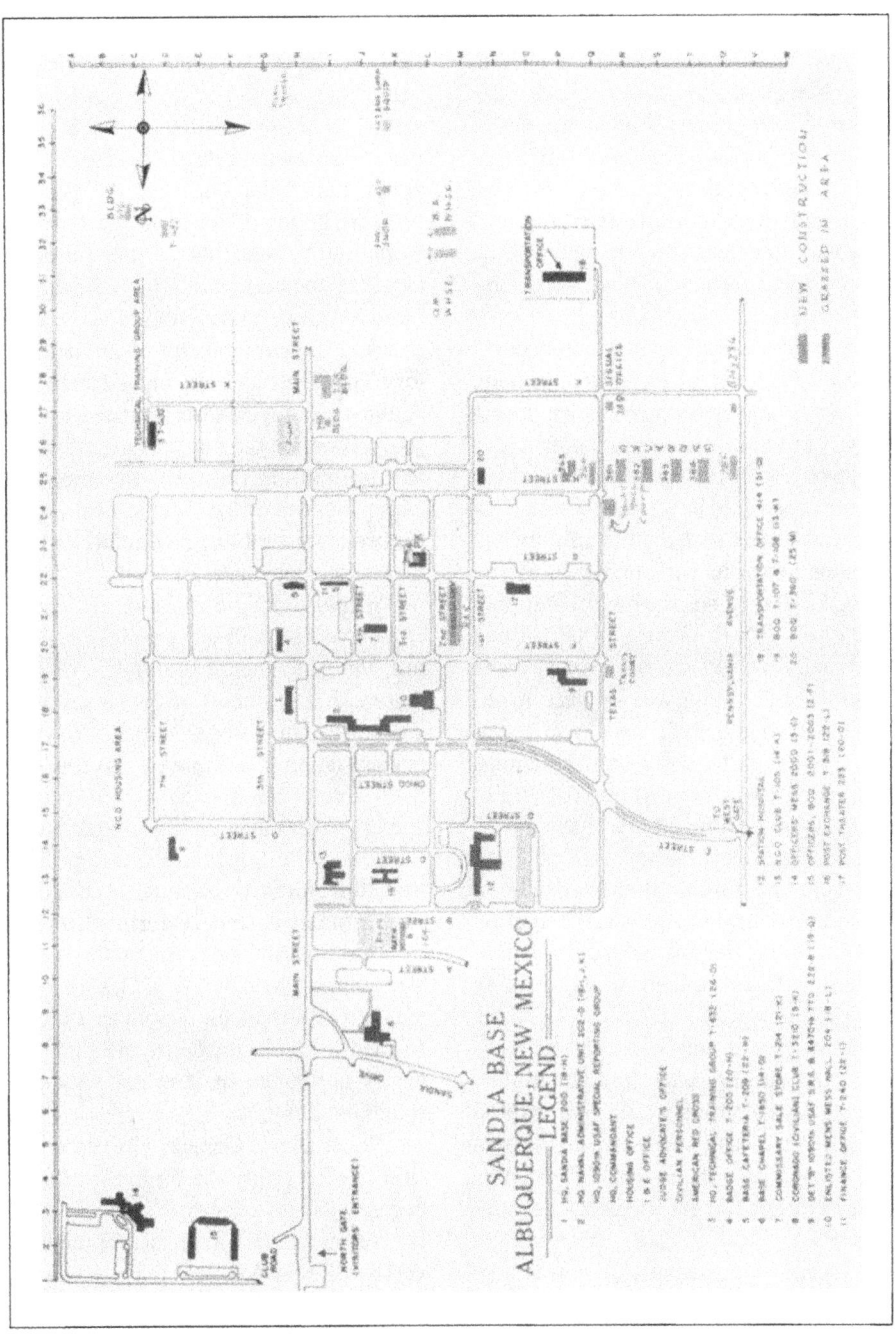

Layout of Sandia Base, Albuquerque, New Mexico, 1947.

standing disagreement about secrecy and security, was the approach each used in assembling a weapon. A team of scientists constructed the entire bomb in a series of steps, moving in a logical progression from one part to the second part, then the third, and so on until the assembly process was complete. Each member of the team worked at every stage in the assembly process. The military, on the other hand, used a variation of the procedures adopted from the Army arsenal system, which systematically broke down the assembly process into specific tasks, with a group of officers assigned to each. Later, the officers would be rotated to learn each of the separate tasks, but the military had no intention of its personnel performing all tasks during an assembly operation. Each group in the battalion performed different tasks. When the groups came together, everything was in place to assemble the bomb.[58]

To carry out the separate functions, Company B was divided into four training groups, Command, Mechanical Assembly, Electrical Assembly, and Nuclear. The Command Group, after its orientation on components, assembly, and operation of the bomb, began making logistical plans for the movement of an assembly team to a forward base. This involved the preparation of assembly kits, aircraft loading calculations, and time schedules. Eventually the group would also develop equipment to raise weapons with two sets of loading pits at the base and plan activities relating to test drops of dummy units.[59]

Training programs also evolved in the other groups. The Electrical and Nuclear Groups combined to create a self-instructed course on radio and fundamental electrical circuitry, using the manuals created by Los Alamos for Operation CROSSROADS. Ultimately, the Electrical Group focused on the Flight Test Box, a device that enabled the team to determine the readiness of the batteries and the electrical firing system. The firing system consisted of a series of circuits for the barometric switches and "Archies," converted radars that had been designed to protect fighter pilots from the rear but were used to detect the altitude for detonation as the bomb fell. They also developed a rotating-mirror camera that checked the simultaneity of the detonators. The Nuclear Group moved up to Los Alamos, where scientists provided on-the-job training on the nuclear assembly operation, putting the cores together and taking them apart. The Mechanical Group trained on assembling detonators and the high explosive lenses.[60]

While working with the spherical high explosive assemblies early in their training, the Mechanical Group discovered that several segments of the lenses were stuck together. After a couple of days of prying, tapping, and tugging to separate them, one of the men suggested using a solvent to dissolve the adhesive that held them together. Alcohol and gasoline proved fruitless, so they called in an expert from Los Alamos. He arrived, looked over the situation, and ordered the evacuation of the whole building. Gasoline and the high explosive, the neophytes learned, formed a highly unstable mix that was easily detonated by a minor shock or rough handling.[61]

Nonetheless, General Groves' decision to select only the brightest officers began to pay off. Many of the officers took courses in theoretical physics at the University of New Mexico. In the course of the training sessions at Los Alamos and with the Z-Division scientists posted at Sandia Base, the attitude of the scientists "…changed around completely," or at least enough to develop some respect for the soldiers, Dorland recalled. Over time, Los Alamos invited the military teams to occasional colloquiums for lectures by such luminaries as Edward Teller, Hans Bethe, Lise Meitner, and Enrico Fermi on the health hazards of atomic energy, the *Fat Man* implosion bomb, the *Little Boy* gun-type weapon, and the effects of atomic bombs.[62]

During the fall and early winter of 1946, only officers received bomb assembly training. By the end of the year, Dorland believed that his organization had some competence to assemble atomic bombs for combat, even though everyone connected with the project agreed that "a great deal of additional training was necessary" before the battalion could be said to have any reliable operational capability. With a cadre of trained officers in place by the end of the year, the 2761st began to recruit highly qualified enlisted men to fill jobs on the assembly teams. Three months later, when security clearances were obtained, noncommissioned officers began training in the Mechanical Group, specializing in high explosive assemblies and "canning" of bomb components for the stockpile.[63]

The training program was strained by an influx of novice Air Corps bomb commanders. In response, Dorland formed the Technical Training Group under the command of Lieutenant Colonel Ord. By the end of June 1947, every officer and most of the enlisted men had participated in three or more assembly operations and a number of special projects. But after nine months, following all the intense procedural and repetitive training, the special engineer battalion had yet to conduct an actual trial assembly or a joint training exercise with the Army Air Corps.[64]

Colonel Dorland was also concerned about his independent command at San-

Sandia Base guard tower and Building #452, viewed from the east.

dia. For four months, no one from Washington had even visited Sandia to find out how Dorland or the 2761st Engineer Battalion (Special) were doing. With the birth of the AEC and the growth of the training program, that *laissez faire* attitude was about to change.[65]

Dorland's first visitors were not military officers but the newly appointed commissioners from the AEC. In November 1946, the commissioners began touring most of the MED facilities that soon would belong to the Commission. After visiting Oak Ridge, the commissioners headed west. As their aircraft sped toward New Mexico, Robert F. Bacher, a Los Alamos physicist who had headed the group that designed the implosion weapon and the only scientist among the five commissioners, gave "...a vivid picture of the making of the bomb" and what to expect when they landed, according to Lilienthal. "We were so enthralled that for an hour or so we were hardly conscious of being anywhere at all."[66]

The commissioners had two scheduled stops in New Mexico. The first stop was Los Alamos where, on the morning of November 16, they spoke with the scientists, received a briefing on weapons research and production, and visited the bomb storage areas. During the briefing, they first heard the term "Alarm Clock," the code name for a thermonuclear device recently proposed by Edward Teller. But the commissioners sensed a lack of purpose among the scientists and a slow rate of weapons development and production. The country's nuclear arsenal, they learned for the first time, was not as sizeable as they had believed.[67]

That afternoon the group drove to Albuquerque to check out the operations at Sandia Base. Lilienthal described Dorland and his staff as "...alert and handsome young West Pointers, eager to learn the art of putting things together, a rather 'getting in on the ground floor' sort of thing." Lilienthal recorded in his journal that he asked numerous questions and learned "...quite a lot, particularly about what has *not* been done in the way of planning, coordination, and the like." Like Oppenheimer, Lilienthal found himself captivated by the beauty of the New Mexican mountains and concerned by the nuclear enterprises they sheltered. "There is something ironic," he confided to his journal, "about the contrast between these magnificent vistas of nature and the things I saw during the day."[68]

THE AEC AND AFSWP

In the afternoon of December 31, 1946, as much of Washington prepared to welcome the new year, President Truman and top officials from the military and the AEC met at the White House. The gathering was historic. By the stroke of Truman's pen, the Army's responsibility for the Manhattan District would be taken over by a civilian agency, the AEC. General Groves, who had commanded the MED since September 17, 1942, would be relieved by a General Manager, Carroll L. Wilson, a 36-year old engineer. The change came at the beginning of a new year. As 1946 became 1947, the Commission, according to new Chairman, David E. Lilienthal, would control "the most potent weapon of all time." But, he added, the Commission would also pursue "the peaceful and beneficial possibilities of this great discovery."[69]

The AEC, composed of a board of five full-time Presidential appointees, was to assume responsibility for most of the activities of the MED soon after passage of the legislation creating the Commission. But Truman took three months after the passage of the Atomic Energy Act in August to select the commissioners. In November, Chairman, Lilienthal, asked Groves and the military to run the operation until the end of the year. The transfer to civilian authority was set for December 31, 1946. The Chairman had no choice but to defer the transfer because the Commission had "...no offices, no funds, no secretaries, no staff, no budget, no files, and no property," as its historians have succinctly noted. Groves was not happy with the delay or the appointments. "Everyone knew that I was in a caretaker's position," he dryly recorded in his memoirs, and that there was "...no assurance that my views would be those of the Commission." Once the commissioners were appointed, Groves later complained, "...it was quite evident that my views would not be accepted without a long-drawn-out delay."[70]

A series of meetings at the end of November 1946 between the civilian commissioners and the military, represented by Groves and Nichols, emphasized how many devils lurked in the transfer details. The commissioners asked Groves for a detailed list of the facilities to be transferred from the MED. Lilienthal had interpreted the transfer section of the Atomic Energy Act to include all MED property to the AEC. Nichols was drafting such a list, Groves said, but it would not be ready by the end of the year. He added that he believed that nuclear weapons and weapons facilities, specifically Sandia and the Naval Ordnance Test Station at Inyokern, California, were excluded from the transfer. Groves, Nichols, and others believed it was essential to the strategic defense of the United States to have custody of all weapon stockpiles, affecting as it did, the "...potential efficiency and speed of action of the Armed Forces in the event that war is declared." The custody issue, always simmering, began to boil.[71]

The transfer was not easy for either the MED officers or the new commissioners. That General Groves viewed the Manhattan Project as his own creation was no secret. He confided to one of the commissioners during their talks that he "...was in the position of a mother hen watching strangers take away all her chicks." He thought the commissioners lacked much understanding about the technical issues of atomic energy and were in over their heads. Nichols agreed. He was annoyed that the commissioners seemed to ignore his advice on running the weapons complex and believed they were more interested in nuclear power than nuclear weapons. For their part, the commissioners thought that Groves and the military wanted to retain control over nuclear weapons despite legislation to the contrary. Consequently, they were suspicious of any departure from their interpretation that the AEC should receive all property and functions of the Manhattan District and viewed Groves' suggestions as attempts to get them to ratify military dominance before the Commission became fully operational. Officials within the Commission believed the Army was trying to undermine civilian control of atomic energy.[72]

Nichols did nothing to allay this concern. He continued his campaign for military control in the last weeks before the scheduled transfer and insisted that weapons, bomb parts, and fabricated materials ready for assembly be retained by the military. Nichols did not say so, but these were the very items under the custody of the 2761st Engineer Battalion (Special). Nichols intensified the Commission's distrust by submitting a draft of an Executive Order that would convey MED property to the AEC. In each paragraph Nichols had appended a clause excepting "...those functions, facilities, materials, and equipment of a military character which the Secretary of War or Navy and the Commission mutually agree" would remain with the military. The Commission

President Truman transfers control of the atom from the military representatives to the civilian Atomic Energy Commission, December 12, 1946. Seated, from left to right: Carroll L. Wilson (Commission General Manager), President Truman, David E. Lilienthal (Commission Chairman), Standing, from left to right: Sumner T. Pike (Commission member), Col. Kenneth D. Nichols (Deputy Chief of MED), Robert P. Patterson (War Department Secretary), Major General Leslie R. Groves (head of MED), Lewis L. Strauss (Commission member) and William W. Waymach (Commission member).

rejected Nichols' position. Secretary of War Patterson wrote Lilienthal at the end of January, stating that "I anticipate that when the matter has been reviewed by the President, he will direct that a certain number of bombs and bomb parts will be wholly within the custody of the Armed Services." Thereafter, both sides decided to let President Truman decide the custody issue.[73]

Nichols' last ditch attempts had failed. On Tuesday, December 31, Secretary of War Patterson, Groves, and Nichols, along with four of the five members of the AEC and its new General Manager, watched as President Truman signed Executive Order 9816 ending the Manhattan District. All MED property, including fissionable material, would go to the Commission, although some part – including Sandia Base, its physical properties, and Army and Navy personnel – would stay with the military. With the exception of his selected officers at Sandia, General Groves had little more than a paper command. Soon thereafter, he announced his retirement. Nichols' career in atomic energy also appeared to be stalled. By refusing to compromise on the custody issue, Nichols believed he had eliminated any chance of being appointed Director of Military Application, the highest military position at the AEC. In that regard, he was correct. Lilienthal spurned Nichols, the only candidate nominated by the military. After a two-month search, the Commission named Colonel James McCormack, Jr., of the Army Air Corps, a 1932 West Point graduate and Rhodes scholar, Director of Military Application. Nichols returned to a West Point teaching post.[74]

Unfortunately, none of these actions addressed the basic problems of defining operational responsibilities. The length of time taken to settle on the Atomic Energy Act had contributed to the drift in making decisions. As a result, the act gave birth to a set of Siamese triplets, three organizations – the Atomic Energy Commission, the Military Liaison Committee, and the Armed Forces Special Weapons Project – all figuratively joined at the hip and often heading in separate directions. The MLC was to "consult and advise" the Commission on "all atomic energy matters which the MLC deems to relate to military applications." As a matter of policy, the MLC would only advise; the AEC would develop, manufacture, and store nuclear weapons. Moreover, the Commission would have custody of all atomic weapons and fissionable material, as well as control access to classified atomic energy information.[75]

The clumsiness of such an arrangement was obvious to AFSWP officers at Sandia, who were caught in the middle between the Commission's drive to impose civilian control and the MLC's bid for greater military participation. Groves had compounded the confusion by having men from the special engineer battalion learn weapon assembly and testing, similar to the duties of Z-Division, the Los Alamos group stationed at Sandia under an AEC contract.

As a consequence, the custody issue continued to rankle all parties.[76]

THE ARMED FORCES SPECIAL WEAPONS PROJECT

When the AEC took control of the MED properties on January 1, 1947, Sandia Base remained under the control of the War Department, with General Groves still in command. Groves and Dorland expected Z-Division, the Ordnance Engineering Division and its laboratories, to remain as the center for research and development of the military aspects of atomic weapons under military control. A number of the officers from the 2761st battalion had been assigned to Z-Division, including Lieutenant Colonel Ellis E. Wilhoyt, who served as the alternate division leader. The Commission thought otherwise, however, wishing to retain control of Z-Division and its facilities on Sandia Base. The separation issue was complicated by the fact that both Groves and Nichols had left Washington in early January and the War Department had not yet hammered out a formal organizational structure for the battalion.[77]

By the end of January, the organizational issue was somewhat settled. A memorandum issued by Secretary of War Robert P. Patterson and Secretary of the Navy James V. Forrestal on January 29, 1947, generally referred to as the AFSWP Charter, established, "...effective midnight December 31, 1946, a joint Army-Navy atomic energy organization which will discharge all military Service functions relating to atomic energy and will be known as the Armed Forces Special Weapons Project." The head of the new organization was to be appointed by and report directly to the Chief of Staff of the Army and the Chief of Naval Operations. The two chiefs would also select a deputy from the opposite Service. Both the head of AFSWP and his deputy, the memo directed, would serve as members of the MLC to the AEC. The Chief of the AFSWP would assume responsibility for "...all military service functions of the Manhattan Project as are retained under the control of the Armed Forces." This included training of special personnel, coordination with the AEC in the development of atomic weapons of all types, technical training of bomb commanders and weaponeers, and participation with other agencies in developing joint radiological safety measures.[78]

The charter clearly anticipated the ultimate unification of the military Services. As if to emphasize the importance of AFSWP as the first interservice unit under the proposed National Military Establishment, Forrestal, in another memorandum to Patterson on the same day, underlined the word "joint."[79]

The military's failure to select an AFSWP director was surprising. Neither Army Chief of Staff General Dwight D. Eisenhower and Chief of Naval Operations Fleet Admiral Chester W. Nimitz had made a selection. Therefore, between the beginning of January and the end of February 1947, there was no officially appointed chief of AFSWP. During this period, Groves' aide, Colonel Hasbrouck, assumed Headquarters command in Washington as the senior officer of the organization. The offices of AFSWP were first headquartered in the new War Department Building, at 21st Street and Virginia Avenue, NW, where the Washington offices of the Manhattan District had been located. On April 15, 1947, the AFSWP offices were moved to the Pentagon; first on the fifth floor, and later, in October 1947, on the second floor in Corridor 2, due to security requirements. Little change could occur until the officials in Washington decided how the new joint organization would be constituted and its functions clearly defined.[80]

AFSWP OPERATIONS AT SANDIA BASE

All of the politics in Washington and the establishment of the AFSWP had little impact on the day-to-day operations at Sandia Base. Dorland continued to direct the activities of the 2761st Engineer Battalion (Special), and any changes he introduced were largely driven by local demands. By the beginning of 1947, training of officers had progressed to the point that the military was confident it had an organization capable of assembling an atomic bomb for combat. At the same time, Dorland and his staff saw the necessity for a great deal of additional training and that the development of procedures, organizations, and equipment left much to be desired.[81]

As Sandia Base expanded, more of the trained officers would be assigned to administrative duties. To relieve the pressure on training created by the reassignments, Dorland created a Technical Training Group, under the command of Lieutenant Colonel Ord. Ord was not an engineer. He was in the Signal Corps and been selected for duty with the Manhattan District at Sandia by Groves' Executive Officer, Colonel Herbert Gee, who, as district engineer in Jacksonville, Florida, had worked with Ord in constructing the Southern Signal Corps School, Camp Murphy, in 1942. Gee told Ord that his background in Army schools fit perfectly with what was needed at Sandia. Ord headed to Albuquerque in early September of 1946.[82]

Ord's first task was to recruit new instructors, especially those specializing in radio and radar electronics. In November 1946, he traveled to Fort Monmouth, New Jersey, to interview potential instructors from the ranks of both officers and enlisted personnel. After the usual complaints from the Army that the Manhattan District was stealing too many men, Ord successfully convinced Washington and Fort Monmouth to transfer his selections. By the time he set up the Technical Training Group in January 1947, Ord had assembled a team of instructors from both the Signal Corps and the Corps of Engineers. The group set up office and classroom space in old Civilian Conservation Corps buildings at the south end of the base. With only fans to battle the fierce New Mexican heat, Ord noted that "the generals had to sweat it out with the rest of us." Two of Ord's instructors, William R. Cherry and Ivan M. Moore, both second lieutenants from the Corps of Engineers, established a teaching laboratory in the "Farm," a building off Sandia Base near the loading pit at Kirtland Field. There they installed work benches and wired in the electrical outlets necessary to test a bomb's electrical components. The building was also used for assembling high explosive lenses.[83]

Ord's training methods were taken from the same book he had used at the Southern Signal Corps School—hands-on experience with actual equipment. This training method was particularly adapted to the maintenance and assembly of the bomb altimeter, an airborne radar unit that determined the altitude for firing the *Fat Man* implosion weapon. Ord put his students through their paces on actual equipment by altering the circuitry and challenging the men to find the problem. The one problem with Ord's alterations and hands-on training was that the radar units wore out after only a year of use. Replacements of specific components labeled for nuclear weapons were not easily obtained, but, fortunately, one of Ord's enlisted men, Master Sergeant James R. Corman, noticed that identical altimeters under a different name were stored in a warehouse on the base. Corman hauled the worn-out *Fat Man* altimeters to the warehouse, changed nameplates with their identical twins, and brought the new ones back to the weapons training center.[84]

For training men on the firing mechanism, Ord created a "reality check" process to ensure that the spark plugs (initiators) that fired the high explosive were properly wired and sequenced. The spark plugs were assembled in a rack and connected to the flight test box in the same manner as for an airborne bomb. With this equipment, students could test the firing order. Should the student make an error in testing, Ord recalled, "…the spark plugs would fire and announce to all the class that they had theoretically been blown up."[85]

Colonel Ord firmly believed that these training methods served to prevent such accidents under combat conditions. "We enforced a hard and fast rule," he said, "that there was but one way to handle every procedure—the right way." He tolerated no deviations from the checklists that covered every procedure; they were followed consistently, with no exceptions. Ord proudly pointed to the fact that there were no accidents while handling high explosives, changing initiators, or making insertions of active material.[86] In his recollections, he described the process:

> "…the initiators were assembled in a rack and connected to the flight test box for training on the latter, and if a mistake was made they would fire and embarrass a student. The same arrangement was used to fire the spark plugs and take a picture of the sparks using a high speed rotating mirror to test for simultaneity. This initial method of testing for simultaneity was time consuming and, I am told, was later improved. The adding of electrolyte to the batteries used in the bomb and their charging was also a critical operation."

As Ord's group had successfully employed enlisted men in the training pro-

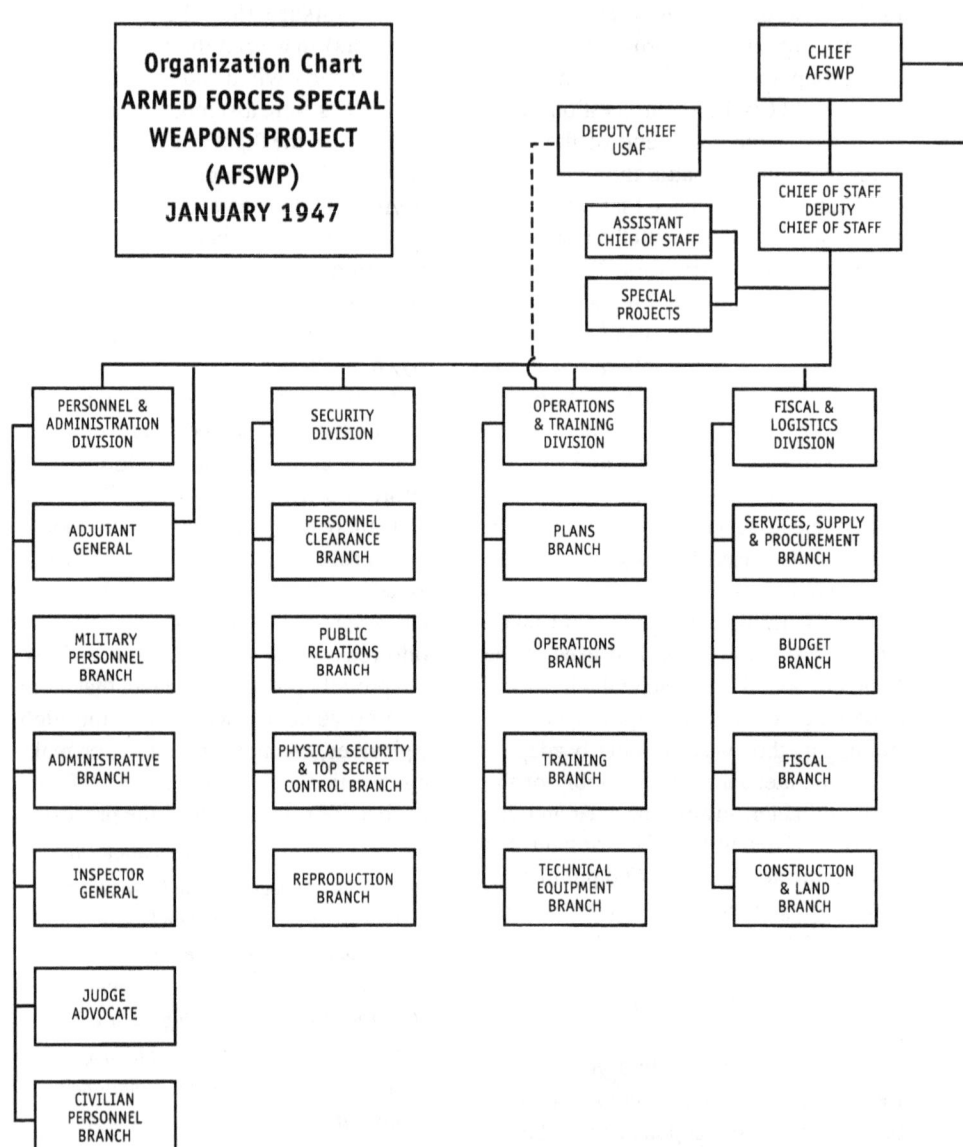

Armed Forces Special Weapons Project (AFSWP) Organization Chart, 1947.

The Post-War Transition, 1946 to 1948

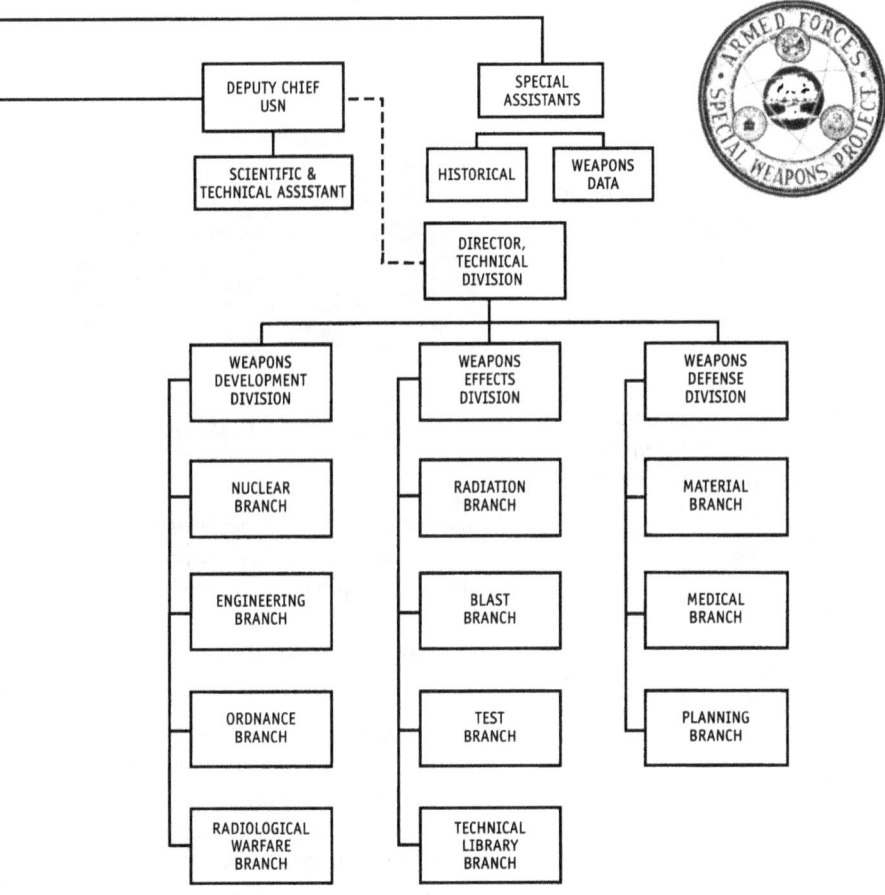

cess, it soon became obvious that the 2761st Engineer Battalion (Special) could not handle all the bomb assembly operations solely with officers. Enlisted men were also capable of doing the work, Dorland and his staff decided. Since certain elements of the Army had expressed some displeasure with sending the Service's best officer talent to Groves' special project, there was some urgency to the decision to recruit noncommissioned officers. Some enlisted men were already stationed at Sandia, carryovers from Los Alamos who were assigned to Z-Division after the end of the war, but they were not trained in weapons assembly techniques. In January, Dorland sent Major Oscar M. Brumfiel to Fort Belvoir to find highly qualified enlisted men from outside the Manhattan District. The enlisted men began arriving in February. After a month of processing all the necessary clearances, they began training as part of the mechanical assembly teams, working with high explosive assemblies, and "canning," or packaging, bomb components for the stockpile.[87] Ord remembered the quality of the enlisted men in his command in his recollections:

"I had no problem with training EM [enlisted men] to handle complicated radar equipment in the early forties, and the same proved true at Sandia Base. An interesting event took place one day that proved my point. The members of the AEC were visiting Sandia Base and we were putting on a 'country fair' type tour of our training facilities for them. A M/Sgt (who later was promoted to warrant officer) had proved very adept at learning the physics of the bomb and the monitoring of the pit during insertion, so I used him as the instructor at that station of the tour. [Colonel] Dorland was somewhat concerned that no officer was handling this task, but it was my neck that

Colonel John A. Ord, Commander, Technical Training Group, Sandia Base, 1947.

was out, and I let the sergeant do the job. When it appeared that the line of visitors had slowed up, I investigated and found that the AEC members were listening to the sergeant, asking questions, and were very complimentary of his performance."

In addition to the ongoing training programs, the men at Sandia Base began a number of special projects in the spring of 1947, several of which emphasized the interservice nature of AFSWP. For some time the Navy Department had wanted to modify *Midway*-class aircraft carriers to provide atomic bomb assembly sites aboard. Early in 1947, the Bureau of Ships and Sandia Base initiated discussions to determine the specifications for the shipboard assembly areas. The Army Air Corps also examined the possibility of having its own mobile assembly site. Not long after Operation CROSSROADS, the Air Corps suggested converting a C-97 cargo plane into an assembly facility. In late 1946, the design work commenced for adapting the interior of the C-97 for forward assembly operations, code-named CHICKENPOX. The Air Corps proposed another project, OPERATION 65, in the spring of 1947. Under this plan, the Sandia assembly teams and the Air Force would conduct a series of assembly tests in Alaska at Arctic temperatures, but the idea never went beyond the early planning stage.[88]

Another combined operation came from General Groves, who urged that officers of the special weapons battalion be trained as weaponeers for combat drops of atomic bombs. To implement this plan, Dorland's staff made arrangements with the 509th Bombardment Wing, the same unit that had dropped the atomic bombs on Hiroshima and Nagasaki and later at CROSSROADS, to take groups of five officers for a six-week tour at its base in Roswell, New Mexico, to orient them to the duties of air crew personnel.[89]

GROVES BACK IN COMMAND

At the end of February 1947, Eisenhower and Nimitz appointed Major General Groves Chief of AFSWP. His offices remained in the new War Department building on Virginia Avenue and 21st Street, NW, where the Washington offices of MED were located. Rear Admiral William S. Parsons was named Deputy Chief. By virtue of their positions, both men became members of the MLC. Groves assumed command of the remnants of his beloved MED, which consisted primarily of the operations at Sandia Base. From his new position, he could oversee limited operations in developing nuclear weapons. AFSWP acted for the Armed Forces in liaison with non-military agencies in the field of atomic energy, the exception being with the AEC, which by law dealt instead with the MLC.[90]

General Groves may have lost some power to the AEC, but he was not powerless. From his additional position on the MLC, he could influence policy, prodding the Commission to produce more nuclear materials and weapons and attacking the men who earlier had ignored his suggestions on running a nuclear program. He also retained a forum for his views on the custody issue. The Groves appointment kept the MLC and the AEC at battle stations.[91]

The nature of the atomic energy responsibilities of the military had been discussed among Groves and his staff for over a year, while Congress debated the atomic energy bill. As the senior military officer and perhaps the most highly respected in the field, at least by the military, Groves could shape the AFSWP organization to his own thinking. In a memorandum to Eisenhower, he quickly seized on some initial work begun by Hasbrouck to flesh out the organization of AFSWP to define more sharply its relationship within the nuclear weapons complex, and to establish a permanent charter for the organization. Groves reiterated AFSWP's basic responsibility for all military Service functions relating to atomic energy that were in the directive issued by Patterson and Forrestal. These included technical training of special personnel "...in all phases of the military use of atomic energy," providing military participation "...in research on development of atomic weapons of all types," and "...in developing and effecting joint radiological safety measures."[92]

Groves then expanded on these official responsibilities. He believed that AFSWP must have "centralized control" in atomic energy matters. In particular, Groves proposed that "...research contracts involving military application of atomic energy concluded by any agency of the Armed Forces will be concurred in by" AFSWP. The organization, he said, would take on the storage and surveillance of atomic weapons in custody of the armed forces, provide recommendations to assure a uniform policy concerning the security of atomic energy information, help prepare training courses for the military academies, assist in the preparation of staff studies and war plans related to atomic weapons, and prepare materials to educate the public on the military uses of atomic energy, "...particularly in connection with passive defense measures." Groves also offered to furnish AFSWP staff assistance to the MLC. But in reviewing AFSWP's relationship with the AEC, Groves carefully followed the guidelines outlined in the Atomic Energy Act of 1946 and no more.[93]

Nearly three months later, Eisenhower and Nimitz sent back their comments on Groves' draft organization plan. The two Service Chiefs were not inclined to give General Groves all the authority he sought. Where Groves had argued for "...centralized control of atomic energy activities," the high command limited AFSWP's role to "coordination." Where Groves had sought AFSWP concurrence in research contracts for military application of atomic energy, Eisenhower and Nimitz again restricted its authority to coordination. The revised memorandum contained a new provision that AFSWP "...will not enter directly into functions of operational command," assuming that special weapons project personnel would come under the command of a Task Force Commander.[94]

Critical to General Groves' and AFSWP's position in the military was its place in the chain of command. Groves wanted AFSWP to be considered in the same relationship as "...between the Director of any General Staff Division and other agency of the Army" or a "...Deputy Chief of Naval Operations and any other agency of the Navy." Eisenhower and Nimitz knocked that relationship down a peg or so by categorizing AFSWP as a Technical Service. Other changes in Groves' original memorandum also narrowed AFSWP's range of power within the Armed Services and in its dealings with the AEC.[95]

Groves could swallow most of the changes, but he found two simply unacceptable. AFSWP should be seen as a General Staff Division, he complained to an aide to Nimitz. Since his orders required him to report to the Army Chief of Staff and the Chief of Naval Operations, Groves asserted, "I should have direct personal access to these two officers such as enjoyed by Directors of General Staff Divisions in the Army." The AFSWP project, Groves confided, was of such importance as to merit personal attention. "It would be unfortunate if I had to deal through intermediaries." In addition, Groves took considerable umbrage at the idea that he lacked a command function. That was not true, he maintained, since he commanded the troops at Sandia. Moreover, requiring that AFSWP personnel be placed under Task Force command

MK V bomb being loaded on B-29 aircraft.

in the future, Groves thought, was "...unwise." The issue, he concluded, "...should be settled when the time comes."⁹⁶

There was good news and bad news for Groves. Eisenhower would concede that Groves should report to the Service Chiefs. But neither Eisenhower nor Nimitz would budge on the issue of command. Groves would be limited largely to staff functions except in special ordnance and technical training duties at Sandia. When the AFSWP Charter came up for modification in August, shortly after passage of the National Security Act of 1947 creating the Department of the Air Force, Groves found he had acquired a third boss, the Chief of Staff of the Air Force. The Air Force also assigned its own Deputy Chief to AFSWP, Brigadier General R.C. Wilson. Groves knew Wilson, who had worked with the Manhattan Project to modify B-29s to carry nuclear weapons and to train the crews.⁹⁷

For the rest of the year and through the end of February 1948, AFSWP's primary mission remained unchanged; that of training troops to assemble and store atomic weapons. The training would continue at Sandia and elsewhere, but the weapon storage function, according to an early AFSWP evaluation, did "...not reach the importance which was expected... because no atomic weapons have yet been turned over to the custody of AFSWP."⁹⁸

The custody issue continued to grate with Groves and the AFSWP command. In the transition period from military to civilian control of atomic energy, decisions regarding the ultimate custody of nuclear weapons were deliberately left vague. The contending parties had strong opinions which were diametrically opposed. Chairman Lilienthal of the AEC harbored no doubts that the civilian agency should have custody. Just as vigorously, Groves and Nichols believed it was imperative for the military to retain custody. With the AFSWP Charter more clearly defined, Groves turned his attention to the custody issue and began lobbying once more for nuclear weapons to be under military control.

General Groves raised the custody question in a series of meetings between the AEC and the MLC in the summer and fall of 1947. His timing, however, was not propitious. In July, several newspapers broke a story about the theft of secret documents from Los Alamos by two Army sergeants in 1946. Groves had persistently raised questions about the inability of civilians to properly care for nuclear secrets, and rumors circulated in Washington to the effect that Groves was behind the delayed leak to the papers as an attempt to discredit the Commission. But officials at the AEC were particularly amused by Groves' predicament since the theft had occurred under his command. Groves, of course, was not so amused. He sent one of his aides to question Commission staffers about the story, which served to annoy Lilienthal when he learned of the visit. Whatever the truth of the matter, the flare-up did nothing to promote Groves' custody campaign with the Commission.⁹⁹

A second, and more fatal, reason for Groves' failure was the fact that his effectiveness as the commander of AFSWP and as a member of the MLC had ended. He had overstayed his time. At the end of June 1947, Lilienthal had gone to the Pentagon to have lunch with General Eisenhower. Their conversation covered many topics, but the general often returned to Groves. "I know what a problem he is," Lilienthal remembered Eisenhower saying, "he was a czar during the war, and everything is a comedown for a man of his type." Eisenhower admitted that Groves had made many enemies "...because of the way he rode herd on everyone during the war." There were lots of ways to get things done, Eisenhower continued, that "...don't require humiliating people and making enemies of them." After all, he explained to Lilienthal, he had worked with both Field Marshall Bernard Montgomery and General George Patton, two of the most difficult personalities in the Allied armies.[100]

Eisenhower revealed that Groves had lost support from the senior military officers. Initially, the generals thought it wise to "...use him as long as he has anything to contribute" and "to pump him dry," Eisenhower explained. Now, perhaps, the well was dry. "If at any time he causes you trouble, let me know," he told the chairman, "and we will take him off." The flap over the lost documents certainly gave Lilienthal the provocation. He complained to his journal that he had had enough of Groves' "...sniping at us, sneering at us and running us down." The Commission, he concluded, had "...taken all the kicking around we intend to take."[101]

By September, Eisenhower told General Lewis H. Brereton, then Chairman of the MLC, that he had decided to relieve Groves of his AFSWP command. Brereton delivered the news to Lilienthal, with the caveat that Groves might stay on as a member of the MLC. Lilienthal said he would discuss the matter with the Commission but told Brereton that "...the minimum was the removal of Groves from the Special Weapons Command." For several weeks nothing changed.[102]

TRANSITION

Groves was a wily survivor and the beneficiary of a divided military. During a meeting with Secretary of the Army Kenneth C. Royall a month later, Lilienthal learned that the Secretary had strongly disagreed with Eisenhower's recommendation to relieve Groves, whom he described as "...the best-qualified man in the Armed Forces for the Special Weapons Project." Royall, who had worked with Groves in drafting the May-Johnson Bill and believed, as did Groves, that the McMahon Act was a mistake, wanted to keep Groves at AFSWP but replace him on the MLC. When asked for his opinion, Lilienthal pulled no punches. He pointed out that a civilian commission was responsible for atomic energy matters and that Groves had disagreed with the law, had no confidence in the men who administered it, and had "...conducted himself in a way that carried out his fundamental disagreement and opposition to the Commission." Lilienthal told Royall about a meeting of AFSWP officers at Sandia at which Groves had "crudely disparaged" the Commission and said "...it wouldn't be long until the Commission's mess of things would throw the whole business back in the Army's hands."[103]

That the military was waffling on Groves thoroughly aroused Lilienthal, and he fully vented his frustration on Royall. Groves, Lilienthal declared, thought that the Commission "...was no damned good." Groves believed that he, Groves, had all the answers, and "...he regarded it as a kind of sacred duty in his various capacities to prove his point." Lilienthal began to lecture the Secretary. The country was either entitled to civilian control under the McMahon Act with the full cooperation of the rest of the government or military control under Groves so everyone could cooperate with him. But the country could not have it both ways.[104]

When Lilienthal finished, Royall delivered the *coup de grace*. The three Chiefs of Staff, Royall said, had reached a unanimous conclusion that Groves would continue as head of AFSWP. Only the new Secretary of Defense, James V. Forrestal, could alter the decision. Lilienthal was astonished. In his view, "...the situation was heading for disaster." Groves would have to go. The Commission had done "...everything we knew how to do to make the situation [with Groves] workable," he explained. "But a time comes when no self-respecting men... can have any other course open to them, and still maintain their self respect." Nonetheless, as Lilienthal well knew, any final decision about Groves would be made by Forrestal.[105]

Economic and political instability in Europe and Soviet opposition to an agreement governing the international control of atomic energy set off alarm bells in Washington. To address Soviet expansionism in Central Europe, in early November 1947 the Air Force called for 70 combat groups consisting of 7,000 aircraft, including an expanded fleet of planes capable of delivering atomic weapons, to defend the United States and maintain world peace. The question of whether or not nuclear weapons would be available to the military in an emergency was back on the table. A week later, General Brereton, on behalf of the MLC, asked officials at the AEC to deliver to the Armed Forces "...all weapons now in stockpile and completed weapons and parts thereof ...at the earliest practicable date." For Lilienthal, the request was a policy issue to be settled by the President. His staff, following the lead of Commissioner Sumner Pike, wondered if it was even technically feasible to transfer nuclear weapons

Army Chief of Staff Dwight D. Eisenhower congratulates Leslie Groves on his promotion to Lieutenant General on January 26, 1948, a few days before Groves' retirement.

to the military on the grounds that the AFSWP lacked technical competence to handle or maintain them. In no rush to answer the MLC formally, the Commission asked Brereton for further clarification.[106]

In mid-December, the MLC reaffirmed its position on transferring custody of nuclear weapons to the military, for reasons of national security. It was a "...prerequisite for national security," the MLC argued, "...that all possible means of defense be available to the Armed Forces for instant use." The current arrangement between the AEC and the military was too complex and ponderous to permit a rapid response. The Armed Forces, the MLC asserted, "...must have the authority to place the forces and weapons at their disposal in strategically sound locations" for immediate use and delivery. The MLC admitted to some ambivalence about their request, however. The military was not sufficiently "...staffed and trained at the present time," the report conceded, to assume immediate custody. That must come gradually with additional training "...in the reasonable near future." The dilemma was a classic Catch-22 situation: as long as the AEC held custody of the weapons, the AFSWP unit at Sandia Base could not acquire the expertise necessary to assume custody.[107]

While the commission pondered Brereton's request, Forrestal asked his staff to examine the entire question of military organization for atomic energy. The report, submitted in January 1948 by Charles F. Brown, called for the abolition of AFSWP, whose functions, the report argued, could be absorbed by the three armed Services. The report also called for the elimination of the Division of Military Application within the AEC. That group's functions would be assigned to a more powerful MLC, appointed by the Secretary of Defense, with full authority to deal with the Commission for the military. Several weeks later, on February 2, General Groves announced that he was retiring at the end of the month from military Service to enter private business. No more, Lilienthal told his journal, would the Commission be troubled by "...having Napoleon sitting on Elba while his crew waited for *the Day*."[108]

General Groves' retirement was made the occasion for the enactment of an unusual bill by the Congress of the United States. This bill "authorized and requested" the President to appoint him, "without confirmation by the Senate," to the permanent grade of Major General in the Regular Army, effective as of the day prior to the effective date of his retirement; and, in addition, to place him on the retired list "with the rank and grade of Lieutenant General with honorary date of rank thereof as of July 16, 1945, which date commemorates the first explosion by man of an atomic bomb..." This bill, S.2223, was passed by the Senate on May 10, 1948 and by the House on June 16, 1948. It was signed by the President on June 24, 1948 and became Public Law 394A.[109]

Groves' retirement had removed but one voice in the custody debate. On March 1, 1948, the AEC released a report that restated the Commission's long-held view that the military did not have the technical expertise to assume custody of nuclear weapons. The report did, however, propose a joint AEC-AFSWP training program to prepare the military for surveillance and inspection duties. The Commission still held to its position that only the President could decide on the question of custody. The MLC, through Brereton, pushed Forrestal to take up the issue with President Truman. The Secretary turned to General Carl A. Spaatz for advice. Spaatz favored military custody but, in addition, wanted to place all responsibilities of AFSWP under Air Force control. The two men decided to delay any showdown with the President on the custody issue.[110]

After nearly two years of debate, the government officials, civilian and military, still could not agree on a unified nuclear policy. Indeed, both Groves and Nichols were painfully aware of the military's obligation in regard to nuclear weapons despite perceived civilian control; as Nichols would eloquently state: "The responsibility of the military is to see that if we must fight an atomic war, we win it. That still remains our responsibility..."[111] Consequently, AFSWP's centralized role in nuclear testing would go on, at *Camp Desert Rock*.

ENDNOTES

1. J. Robert Oppenheimer, *The Atomic Bomb and College Education*, quoted in *Bartlett's Familiar Quotations*, 16th Edition (Boston: 1992), p. 714.
2. Brodie, quoted in Steven L. Rearden, *History of the Office of the Secretary of Defense: The Formative Years, 1947-1950*, (Washington, D.C., 1984), p. 423.
3. Gil Dorland Oral History, p. 142.
4. *Ibid.*, pp. 142-43.
5. William Lawren, *The General and the Bomb*, (New York: 1988), pp. 43, 61.
6. *Ibid.*, p. 259.
7. Lawren, *The General and the Bomb*, pp. 259-60; Leslie R. Groves, *Now It Can Be Told: The Story of the Manhattan Project*, (Harper & Row, New York, 1962), p. 413.
8. Groves, *Now It Can Be Told*, pp. 389-90, 415.
9. Hewlett and Anderson, *The New World/ 1939-1946*, pp. 411-15, 624; Groves, *Now It Can Be Told*, pp. 389-90. Groves had integrated the scientists from the nuclear energy component of the Office of Scientific Research and Development into the Manhattan Project in mid-1943, though not without some friction. But in 1945, the transfer of an entire industrial complex for producing atomic weapons proved to be more difficult once the urgency of war and victory had dissipated. See Vincent C. Jones, *Manhattan: The Army and the Atomic Bomb*, (Washington, 1985), pp. 91-92.
10. Groves, *Now It Can Be Told*, pp. 390, 373, 376-77.
11. Hewlett and Anderson, *The New World 1939/1946*, p. 625. See also, Vincent C. Jones, *United States Army in World War II, Special Studies, Manhattan: The Army and the Atomic Bomb*, (Washington, D.C., 1985), pp. 583-85. On concerns about postwar careers, see Col. Gilbert M. Dorland Oral History, "Engineer Memoirs," April 1-3, 1987, Corps of Engineers Archives, p. 152.
12. Groves, *Now It Can Be Told*, pp. 377, 379; Hewlett and Anderson, *The New World, 1939/1946*, p. 624; Jones, *Manhattan: The Army and the Atomic Bomb*, pp. 580-85; David Alan Rosenberg, "U.S. Nuclear Stockpile, 1945 to 1950," *Bulletin of the Atomic Scientists* 38, no. 5 (May 1982): 27; Gilbert M. Dorland Oral History, "Engineer Memoirs," April 1-3, 1987, p. 141, Corps of Engineers Archives. There are varying estimates on the numbers employed by the Manhattan Project. The number of 90,000 is taken from Jones, *Manhattan: The Army and the Atomic Bomb*, pp. 584-85. The Army Air Corps also reduced its nuclear capability, cutting back the number of "Silverplated" B-29s (planes specially modified to carry an atomic bomb) from 46 during the war to 23 at the end of 1946. See Rosenberg, "U.S. Nuclear Stockpile, 1945 to 1950," p. 28.
13. Groves, *Now It Can Be Told*, p. 377; Hewlett and Anderson, *The New World/ 1939-1946*, p. 625; Jones, *Manhattan: The Army and the Atomic Bomb*, p. 581; Lillian Hoddeson, Paul W. Henriksen, Roger A. Meade, and Catherine Westfall, *Critical Assembly: A Technical History of Los Alamos during the Oppenheimer Years, 1943-1945*, (New York, 1993), pp. 399-400.
14. Groves, *Now It Can Be Told*, p. 377.
15. *Ibid.*, p. 377.
16. Groves, *Now It Can Be Told*, p. 377; Hewlett and Anderson, *The New World/ 1939-1946*, p. 625; Jones, *Manhattan: The Army and the Atomic Bomb*, p. 581; Hoddeson, *et al.*, *Critical Assembly*, pp. 399-400; Necah Furman, *Sandia National Laboratories: The Postwar Decade*, (Albuquerque, 1990), pp. 123-26.
17. *Ibid.*, p. 377.
18. Groves, *Now It Can Be Told*, pp. 373-74.
19. *Ibid.*, pp. 374-75.
20. Jones, *Manhattan: The Army and the Atomic Bomb*, pp. 583-85; Groves, *Now It Can Be Told*, pp.374-75. Eisenhower became Army Chief of Staff in November 1945. See Historical Office, Office of the Secretary of Defense, *Department of Defense, Key Officials, 1947-1995*, (Washington, D.C., 1995), p. 60.
21. Jones, *Manhattan: The Army and the Atomic Bomb*, pp. 541, 584; Groves, *Now*

It Can Be Told, p. 374; Patterson quoted in *Ibid.*, p. 376.
22. Jones, *Manhattan: The Army and the Atomic Bomb*, pp. 584-85. Jones also noted that the number of commissioned officers in the Manhattan Project dropped from more than 700 in September 1945 to a low of 250 in December 1946, just prior to transferring all the Manhattan Engineer District facilities to the Atomic Energy Commission. *Ibid.*, p. 584.
23. Jones, *Manhattan: The Army and the Atomic Bomb*, p.593; Kenneth D. Nichols, *The Road to Trinity*, (New York, 1987), p. 228.
24. Nichols, *The Road to Trinity*, 25-26, 29. As a fresh Second Lieutenant, Nichols had traveled to Nicaragua to survey a route for a proposed second inter-ocean canal where he encountered First Lieutenant Leslie R. Groves.
25. For Groves' background, see Groves, *Now It Can Be Told*, p. 465.
26. Jones, *Manhattan: The Army and the Atomic Bomb*, pp. 593-94.
27. Furman, *Sandia National Laboratories*, p. 132; Rosenberg, "U.S. Nuclear Stockpile, 1945 to 1950," p. 29.
28. Furman, *Sandia National Laboratories*, p. 132.
29. Rosenberg, "U.S. Nuclear Stockpile, 1945 to 1950," pp. 26-27.
30. *Ibid.*, p. 27; Truman quoted in Ibid., p. 27. Richard Rhodes in *Dark Sun* writes that there were but three cores in the stockpile and that CROSSROADS used two of them. Rhodes, *Dark Sun* (New York, 1995), p. 261. Stalin also realized that there were few weapons in the American stockpile based on information he received from Fuchs and perhaps other spies. See David Holloway, *Stalin and the Bomb*, (New Haven, 1994), p. 153.
31. Dorland, Oral History, April 1-3, 1987, Corps of Engineers Archives, pp. 153, 150.
32. Colonel K. D. Nichols, "Responsibilities of the Military Under the McMahon Bill: Atomic Weapons and Atomic Power," September 25, 1946, Record Group 374, Entry 19, Box 18, National Archives and Records Administration (NARA).
33. James T. Patterson, *Grand Expectations: The United States, 1945-1974*, (New York, 1996), pp. 115-17.
34. *Ibid.*
35. Jones, *Manhattan: The Army and the Atomic Bomb*, p. 596; Hewlett and Anderson, *The New World/1939-1946*, pp. 482-530.
36. Hewlett and Anderson, *The New World/1939-1946*, pp. 502-3; Groves quoted in *Ibid.*, 502. Hewlett and Anderson credit Eisenhower for being flexible on the role of the military as long as there was "reasonable liaison between the commission and the military Services." *Ibid.*, p. 511.
37. Hewlett and Anderson, *The New World/1939-1946*, pp. 511-12, 525. Quote on control of the stockpile from *Ibid.*, p. 512.
38. Nichols, "Responsibilities of the Military Under the McMahon Bill," pp. 98-101, 103.
39. *Ibid.*, pp. 99-102, 104.
40. *Ibid.*
41. *Ibid.*, pp. 116-17.
42. *Ibid.*, pp. 118, 117. At the same conference the next day, Nichols stated that "for a few billion you can build a few thousand [bombs] in a few years." See Hasbrouck, *Military Implications of the Atomic Bomb*, September 26, 1946, Ft. Belvoir, Virginia, 123, in RG 374, Entry 19, Box 18, "Notes on Atomic Energy," NARA II.
43. Nichols, "Responsibilities of the Military Under the McMahon Bill," p. 119.
44. S. V. Hasbrouck, *Military Implications of the Atomic Bomb*, pp. 123-24.
45. *Ibid.*, pp. 124-25, 128.
46. *Ibid.*, pp. 127-29.
47. *Ibid.*, p. 126.
48. Hewlett and Anderson, *The New World/1939-1946*, pp. 531-54; Rhodes, *Dark Sun*, pp. 231-33.
49. Rhodes, *Dark Sun*, pp. 239-40.
50. Hewlett and Anderson, *The New World/1939-1946*, pp. 590-97; Patterson, *Grand Expectations*, p. 117.
51. Patterson, *Grand Expectations*, p. 117.
52. Hewlett and Anderson, *The New World/*

1939-1946, pp. 598-619; Patterson, *Grand Expectations*, p. 117; Rhodes, *Dark Sun*, pp. 241-42.

53. Dorland, Oral History, 143-45; *Register of Graduates and Former Cadets, 1802-1990*, (West Point, NY, 1990), 436-37; Dorland to William C. Baldwin, March 12, 1987, attachment, "Military Service."
54. Ibid.
55. Dorland, Oral History, p. 144; Headquarters, 8460th Special Weapons Group, Sandia Base, "Early History of the Special Weapons Organization," September 1949, 1-3, in "First History of AFSWP, 1947-1954, Vol. 1, 1946-1948," Department of Energy, Coordination and Information Center, Accession Number NV0068990 (hereafter "First History of AFSWP," Vol. 1). See also, Gilbert M. Dorland to Lt. Gen. E. R. Heiberg III, May 3, 1985, in "History of an Engineer Special Weapons Battalion, 19 Aug. 1946 - 31 Dec. 1948," Research Program, U.S. Army Corps of Engineers.
56. William Taylor, ed., *Sandia Pioneer Reminiscences*, October 5, 1996, pp. 2, 4; "First History of AFSWP," Vol. 1", pp. 3-4.
57. "First History of AFSWP," Vol. 1, pp. 6-7.
58. "First History of AFSWP," Vol. 1," pp. 7-8. For a history of the Army arsenal system, see Merritt Roe Smith, *Military Enterprise and Technological Change*, (Cambridge, MA, 1985).
59. "First History of AFSWP," Vol. 1," pp. 7-8, 13.
60. "First History of AFSWP," Vol. 1," pp. 8-9.
61. "First History of AFSWP," Vol. 1," pp. 8-9; *Sandia Pioneer Reminiscences*, p. 3.
62. *Sandia Pioneer Reminiscences*, 3; "First History of AFSWP, Vol. 1," pp. 8-11; author's conversation with Ernest Graves, Sandia Pioneers' Conference, October 5, 1996.
63. "First History of AFSWP," Vol. 1, pp. 11-13.
64. *Ibid.*, pp. 11-13, 15.
65. Dorland, Oral History, pp. 143-44.
66. Hewlett and Anderson, *The New World/1939-1946*, pp. 641-42; David E. Lilienthal, (*The Journals of David E. Lilienthal: The Atomic Energy Years, 1945-1950*, New York, 1964), pp. 105-106, (hereinafter cited as *Lilienthal Journals*).
67. *Lilienthal Journals*, p. 106, emphasis in original; Hewlett and Anderson, *The New World/1939-1946*, p. 642.
68. *Lilienthal Journals*, p. 107.
69. *New York Times*, January 1, 1947, p. 28
70. Hewlett and Anderson, *The New World/1939-1946*, p. 638; Groves, *Now It Can Be Told*, p. 395.
71. Nichols, *The Road to Trinity*, p. 244; Hewlett and Anderson, *The New World/1939-1946*, pp. 643-44.
72. Hewlett and Anderson, *The New World/1939-1946*, p. 644; Nichols, *The Road to Trinity*, p. 245.
73. Hewlett and Anderson, *The New World/1939-1946*, pp. 651-52; "First History of AFSWP," Vol. 1, Chapter 4, 4.2.23.
74. Hewlett and Anderson, *The New World/1939-1946*, p. 655; Richard G. Hewlett and Francis Duncan, *Atomic Shield/1947-1952* (University Park, PA, 1969), p. 33; Nichols, *The Road to Trinity*, pp. 246-50. Nichols' rejection was short-lived. He assisted the transition to the AEC for another month, then continued to consult on atomic energy matters at the United Nations, in Congress, and with the intelligence community. In May 1947, Nichols reported to West Point where he had accepted an appointment in the department of mechanics.
75. Hewlett and Duncan, *Atomic Shield/1947-1952*, p. 136; "History of the Military Liaison Committee," MLC 085-46, p. 1.
76. Hewlett and Duncan, *Atomic Shield/1947-1952*, p. 136.
77. "First History of AFSWP, 1947-1954," Vol. 1, 1947-1948, Chapter 5, Sandia Base," 8-9, declassified version, DSWA Library; Nichols, *The Road to Trinity*, p. 247.
78. Forrestal to Patterson, January 29, 1947, RG 77, Entry 5, Box 58, Folder 322, "Or-

ganization-AFSWP."
79. Patterson and Forrestal to Chief of Staff, U.S. Army, and Chief of Naval Operations, January 29, 1947, General Counsel's Office, Forrestal to Patterson, January 29, 1947, RG 77, Entry 5, Box 58, Folder 322, "Organization-AFSWP"; "First History of AFSWP," Vol. 1," Chapter 5, pp. 8-9.
80. Patterson and Forrestal to Chief of Staff, U.S. Army, and Chief of Naval Operations, January 29, 1947, RG 77, Entry 5, Box 58, Folder 322, "Organization-AFSWP; "First History of AFSWP," Vol. 1," Chapter 4, Headquarters, 4.2.1. See also, Hasbrouck to Major M. N. Kadick, February 10, 1947, RG 77, Entry 5, Box 58, Folder 322, "Organization—AFSWP."
81. "First History of AFSWP," Vol. 1," p. 10; John A. Ord, "Evolution of the Technical Training Group, Sandia Base," n.d. (c. 1996), p. 1.
82. *Ibid.*
83. Ord, "Evolution of the Technical Training Group, Sandia Base," pp. 1-2.
84. *Ibid.*, p. 2.
85. *Ibid.*, p. 2. Ord adopted another Signal Corps idea to the classified world of Sandia Base. Rather than putting charts on poster board as was common Army practice, Ord wrote the information on white window shades which could then be rolled up and placed in a locked steel cabinet designed to hold classified materials.
86. Ord, "Evolution of the Technical Training Group, Sandia Base," p. 2.
87. "First History of AFSWP," Vol. 1," pp. 11, 13.
88. *Ibid.*, pp. 13-14.
89. *Ibid.*, pp. 14-16.
90. *Ibid.*, Chapter 4, Headquarters, 4.1.2, 4.2.1; Groves to the Chief of Staff, April 4, 1947, RG 77, Entry 5, Box 58, Folder 322, "Organization-AFSWP"; Hewlett and Duncan, *Atomic Shield/1947-1952*, pp. 131-32.
91. Hewlett and Duncan, *Atomic Shield/ 1947-1952*, pp. 131-32.
92. Groves to the Chief of Staff, April 4, 1947, RG 77, Entry 5, Box 58, Folder 322, "Organization-AFSWP."
93. *Ibid.*
94. Draft memorandum, Eisenhower and Nimitz to Groves, June 24, 1947, RG 77, Entry 5, Box 58, Folder 322, "Organization-AFSWP," passim, and "Memorandum for the Chief, Armed Forces Special Weapons Project," July 8, 1947, copy in General Counsel's Office, Defense Special Weapons Agency. This letter is the official document sent to Groves by Eisenhower and Nimitz.
95. *Ibid.*
96. Groves to Admiral DeWitt C. Ramsey, July 10, 1947, RG 77, Entry 5, Box, 58, Folder 322, "Organization-AFSWP."
97. Eisenhower, Memorandum No. 850-25-8, October 29, 1947, RG 77, Entry 5, Box 36, Folder "032.1 Legislation." See also, Forrestal to Eisenhower, Nimitz, and Spaatz, October 21, 1947, RG 77, Entry 5, Box 38, Folder "040 (OSD) Armed Forces Special Weapons Project"; "First History of AFSWP, Vol. 1," Chapter 4, Headquarters, 4.3.2; Hewlett and Duncan, *Atomic Shield / 1947-1952*, pp. 131-32. Spaatz was the first Chief of Staff of the Air Force, though Lieutenant General L. H. Brereton served as the Air Force representative and Chairman of the Military Liaison Committee.
98. "First History of AFSWP," Vol. 1, Chapter 4, Headquarters, 4.2.4-5.
99. *Lilienthal Journals*, pp. 221-24.
100. *Ibid.*, pp. 217-18.
101. *Ibid.*, pp. 218, 227-28.
102. *Ibid.*, p. 236.
103. *Ibid.*, pp. 249-50.
104. *Ibid.*, pp. 250-51.
105. *Ibid.*, pp. 251-52.
106. Hewlett and Duncan, *Atomic Shield/ 1947-1952*, pp. 149-50; Rearden, *The Formative Years*, p. 426.
107. Brereton quoted in Rearden, *The Formative Years*, p. 427; "First History of AFSWP, Vol. 1," Chapter 4, Headquarters, 4.2.24.
108. Hewlett and Duncan, *Atomic Shield/ 1947-1952*, pp. 151-52; Rearden, *The Formative Years*, p. 112; *Lilienthal Journals*, p. 287.

109. Congressional Record, June 16, 1948, pp. 8634, 8635, (Ref. 33).
110. Rearden, *The Formative Years*, pp. 427-28.
111. Colonel K.D. Nichols, Address, "Responsibilities of the Military Under the McMahon Bill," Fort Belvoir, VA, September 25, 1946.

CHAPTER TWO

THE MILITARY'S ROLE IN NUCLEAR MATTERS, 1949 TO 1952

"*A single demand of you, Comrades. Provide us with atomic weapons in the shortest possible time... provide the bomb–it will remove a great danger from us.*"

Josef Vissarionvitch Dshugashvili (Josef Stalin)
to the Peoples Commissar of Munitions,
August 1945

1948-1949: YEAR OF DECISION

The signals from Europe turned most ominous in the winter of 1948. In late February, while Congress in Washington debated the merits of the economic recovery offered by the Marshall Plan, the Communists, backed by the Red Army, took over the government of Czechoslovakia, thereby consolidating Soviet power in Central Europe. Truman compared the situation to the pre-war Central European crisis in 1938-39 after the Munich conference. For Truman, the Soviet takeover was history repeating itself. "Things look black," he wrote his daughter, Margaret. "A decision will have to be made. I am going to make it," he said. But the United States did nothing to change what had happened.[1]

A month later the Russians put the squeeze on Berlin. The city, controlled by all the victorious Allied powers – the United States, Great Britain, the Soviet Union, and France – was, in essence, an isolated island in the Soviet sector of divided Germany. The pressure, at first, was light but noticeable. Soviet representatives walked out of conferences, authorities stopped highway traffic on the pretense that the autobahns needed repairs, and soldiers held up rail traffic between Berlin and the western sectors of the country.[2]

At the end of March the Soviet military decreed that no rail traffic could leave Berlin without permission. General Lucius D. Clay, the commander of U.S. Forces in Europe and military governor of the American zone in occupied Germany, decided to test the Soviets by sending a test train with a few armed guards across the border into the Russian zone. He told his superiors in Washington that to permit Soviet control over military freight "...would be inconsistent with the free and unrestricted right of access in Berlin." Officials at the Pentagon agreed, and Clay sent a stern warning message to the Russians that their actions violated specific agreements among the Allies. Then he sent the test train west from Berlin. The Soviets dismissed Clay's protests; the train fared no better. The Russians shunted the train to a siding after it had traveled into the Soviet zone. There the cars sat for a few days before withdrawing "rather ignominiously," according to Clay. "It was clear," the general wrote in his memoirs, that "the Russians meant business."[3]

Clay also meant business. He rejected the possibility of an American withdrawal from Berlin, which he believed was psychologically the most important city in Europe for the West. "Evacuation," he told a group of reporters as he drew a symbolic line in the dirt with his shoe, "is unthinkable." As spring turned to summer, tensions grew. Then, on the morning of June 24, 1948, the Soviets closed all traffic from the western sectors into Berlin. Electricity from the Soviet zone was cut off. The blockade had begun.[4]

The Berlin crisis was the first ominous confrontation in the Cold War. Soviet Premier Josef Stalin hoped to block the establishment of a separate West German state and eliminate the Allied outpost in West Berlin. Khrushchev later recalled that Stalin's purpose in blockading Berlin was "...to exert pressure on the West to create a unified Berlin in a [German Democratic Republic] with closed borders." At the time, Truman saw through Stalin's ploy, concluding that the blockade was "...a major political and propaganda move... to force us out of Berlin." Knowing the Soviet's motivation, however, did not translate into how to respond to this Cold War skirmish.[5]

The underlying question, of course, was how much would each side shove and push before resorting to more than a clash of words. In retrospect, neither the Russians nor the Americans wanted war. Stalin, according to Andrei Gromyko, then Deputy Foreign Minister, believed that the Americans would not resort to nuclear war over Berlin. The Truman administration, in Stalin's opinion, was not run by "frivolous people" who would start a war.

Moreover, the Soviets controlled the blockade; if the West threatened hostilities, the blockade could be loosened and war averted.[6]

American policy makers did not believe the Soviets would go to war over Berlin either. Even as Soviet pressure increased in the spring and summer of 1948, General Clay, not one to underestimate the Russian threat, did not anticipate any shooting. He recognized that the situation was a political, not a military, operation. Moreover, Clay believed that the American monopoly of the atomic bomb and the threat of its use prevented a Russian invasion of the West. American intelligence also regarded a shooting war as unlikely. Although the Russians had a large army stationed in Germany, there were few means to keep it supplied should war erupt. The Russians had pulled up all the rail lines in East Germany except one and sent the rails and ties back to the Soviet Union as reparations for the damage the Nazis caused during the war. The remaining single track line running east from Berlin, which changed from a standard to a wider gauge in Poland, was entirely inadequate to supply fighting troops with supplies and material.[7]

The United States responded in two ways. The first response to the blockade came at the local level. Clay was determined to stay in Berlin, and his superiors in Washington fully supported that view. The morning the Russians closed the land corridors to the city, Clay called Air Force Lieutenant General Curtis E. LeMay, asking him to free up his cargo planes to assist Berlin through the air. The first C-47 transports arrived on the morning of June 25. The next day an organized airlift was under way, hauling thousands of tons of food and coal to the two airports under allied control; Templehof in the American sector and Gatow in the British. "Operation Vittles" had begun. Air Force pilots soon were passing out calling cards labeled "LeMay Coal & Food Co.," which guaranteed "round-the-clock service via the airlift." Later in the summer, Clay convinced the Air Force to provide 160 C-54s, a plane that carried ten tons of cargo as compared with the two-and-a-half ton capacity of the C-47s. Around the clock, flying by instruments in all weather, American and British pilots landed in West Berlin in the summer and fall of 1948 and into 1949. The steady drone of airplanes became part of the daily life for the beleaguered but indomitable Berliners. In mid-May 1949, after the Allies had flown more than 1,402,644 tons of food, coal, and other essential supplies into Berlin, the Soviets lifted the blockade.[8]

AFSWP PREPARES

Since 1946, the 2761st Engineer Battalion (Special), renamed the 38th Engineer Battalion (Special) in April 1947, had expanded its training operations at Sandia Base in a measured pace. Cutbacks in military funding, the transfer of nuclear control to a civilian agency, and the possibility of internationalizing atomic energy had drained any sense of urgency from AFSWP's activities at Sandia. Over its first year, the Special Weapons Group had acquired basic assembly skills but was hardly combat ready. With a stockpile of parts for fewer than 50 Mark III Nagasaki-type implosion bombs, classroom training and the development of standard operating procedures took precedence over operational exercises. Not until the fall of 1947 did AFSWP conduct its first joint field exercise, Operation AJAX, with B-29s from the 509th Bombardment Group of the Eighth Air Force and the First Air Transit Unit.[9] Operation AJAX was to practice and test the personnel and equipment in the rear/forward method of assembly, using a portable building at the forward assembly point at Wendover. An additional objective was to check the condition of the stockpile of bomb units.[10]

As the first joint operation, AJAX faced a number of coordination problems; some due to cuts in military funding which limited the equipment available for the exercise. Operational plans called for a two-stage assembly procedure, the initial assembly carried out on Sandia Base, from which the 509th would ferry the bomb and its components to a forward assembly base at Wendover Field, Utah, an air base some 100 miles west of Salt Lake City on the Nevada border. AFSWP personnel provided an orientation course for bomber crews on the handling and assembly of the weapons during the fall of 1947. Colonel Dorland, who commanded the 38th and was in charge of the operation, realized that more than bomb assembly teams were necessary, and he organized the first Special Weapons Unit consisting of a team of 109 technical, security, overhead and support personnel to handle the activities at the forward base. As preliminary planning shaped the operation, its major objectives became better defined.

The most ticklish problem faced by the joint group was determining the best place to assemble weapons at a forward base. Hangers and tents were leading candidates, but Dorland and his assembly teams determined that the only sure method of having a suitable facility available was to create a transportable unit. The group procured a 20' x 100' portable building of aluminum sheets over wood forms, equipped it with power plants, distribution lines, and all utilities, and loaded it on a transport plane headed for Wendover.[11]

On November 15, the B-29s began loading their cargo at Kirtland Air Force Base, New Mexico, then left for Wendover. For the next 10 days, Operation AJAX unfolded. At the forward assembly area at Wendover, the 38th inaugurated radiological safety procedures to prepare for an unexpected atomic explosion. A radiation safety team developed a disaster plan to keep damage to a minimum and allow the task force to continue its mission as far as possible. The maneuvers consisted of the complete assembly and "theoretical bombardment missions" of three strikes of two Mark III bombs. One of the six high-explosive bombs was used in a live drop at the Naval Ordnance Testing Station at Inyokern, California. Significantly, the AJAX operation did not involve fissile material. Nonetheless, the weapon was so bulky and heavy, Dorland later remembered, that "the plane jumped a hundred feet" as the bomb was released. More important to Dorland, his men had accomplished their mission of assembling and dropping an atomic bomb right on schedule. They took great pride in being able to take what they still viewed as a scientific device and turn it into a military weapon.[12]

Regardless of its successes, Operation AJAX was more important for its failures. Dorland and the 38th learned that communications between the forward and rear bases were inadequate, that the power supply of the portable assembly building was largely unreliable, and, perhaps most important, that "...under the existing law, with the AEC charged with procurement and custody of all atomic weapons, there was no adequate logistic support for the weapon." That experience, according to one officer, "...gave strong support to the contentions of the AFSWP and, indeed, the whole of the Armed Services, with respect to atomic bombs." As a consequence, General Robert F. Montague, the AFSWP commander at Sandia, recommended to Groves that the military be given a larger role in the surveillance of the stockpile. That was beyond Groves' ability to make happen.

Within a couple of months after the conclusion of AJAX, most of the 38th Battalion would be headed to a sun-drenched atoll in the Pacific named Enewetak, where they would have their opportunity to practice with nuclear cores by participating in Operation SANDSTONE.[13] For more than a year AFSWP had been planning for Operation SANDSTONE, a critical test of the first new weapon design since *Trinity*, but the troubles in Central Europe and in Berlin in the spring of 1948 gave the operation a sense of immediacy. In accordance with his objective to place the Army at the core of the country's nuclear program, Groves directed Dorland to provide for the maximum possible participation by the personnel of the 38th Engineer Battalion (Special) in this operation.

Following Groves' orders, Dorland filled every possible job with contingents of the 38th. Some men were to assemble the bombs, some were designated to take measurements of detonation phenomena and conduct and analyze effects tests, others were to participate in radiological safety drills, and a fourth group was assigned to security details with the main purpose of providing them with the opportunity to see the detonation and results. In December 1947, the first contingent went to Enewetak; others followed in the ensuing months. The 38th became part of the technical task group of Joint Task Force 7, and practically every officer and technical enlisted man in the unit traveled to the Pacific for at least one of the tests. When Nichols took command of AFSWP in March, only one skeleton bomb assembly group remained at Sandia.[14]

NICHOLS TAKES COMMAND

Major General Kenneth D. Nichols took command of a unit that seemingly stood at the very center of American military policy but one that was, nonetheless, emasculated by the politics, both civilian and military, that swirled about it. Nichols' frustration, even fury, with the AEC's attitude on maintaining custody of atomic weapons was clear in regard to AFSWP's preparation and training. He heartily endorsed the conclusions about custody that his men carried from AJAX. The AEC had presented Nichols with a classic Catch-22 situation: AFSWP could not achieve the level of technological familiarity necessary to be fully competent in nuclear weapons assembly without more nuclear experience, the very thing civilian authorities prohibited, in Nichols' mind, by retaining custody of the bomb. Full involvement of AFSWP at SANDSTONE would help break that dilemma.

Even as Nichols pushed for greater nuclear responsibilities for AFSWP, events in Berlin conspired to limit its participation. Nichols' alarm at Soviet actions in Berlin in March contributed to the dilemma. Nichols had asserted, at a special meeting of the MLC, that the situation in Berlin might well lead to war. He wanted to move the nuclear stockpile to new storage sites where they would be less vulnerable to sabotage or potential enemy air attack. He also suggested recalling civilians who had assembled atomic weapons during the war. Cueing on Nichols' remarks, Admiral Lewis L. Strauss, an AEC commissioner, warned Forrestal about the large number of weapons assembly teams already at Enewetak for the SANDSTONE tests. Strauss feared that a sneak attack on Task Force 7 at Enewetak might cripple or destroy the nation's ability to assemble nuclear weapons. The two men also discussed the possibility of postponing SANDSTONE altogether to preserve the stockpile and bringing back the assembly teams should they be needed for an emergency in Europe. SANDSTONE was not postponed, but the discussion did reflect the inadequacies of American nuclear preparedness.[15]

Military politics and interservice rivalries also served to constrain AFSWP's role. At the very time that the military sought control over the custody of nuclear weapons, the Air Force sought to be the dominant Service in handling atomic weapons, much to the concern of the Navy. In the spring of 1948, the Air Force pressed the Joint Chiefs of Staff to designate it as the exclusive agent of AFSWP "for operational command." The dispute clouded the future of AFSWP, particularly as possible reorganization of the special weapons project was then under review. Forrestal was inclined to favor the Air Force position, limiting the Navy to strategic bombing under the direction of the Air Force and to sorties on purely Naval targets. The Air Force, however, rejected even a secondary role for the Navy. Air Force Secretary W. Stuart Symington demanded that all Naval air operations involving nuclear weapons should be under Air Force control.[16]

Forrestal deflected the Air Force's grab for power. When the Secretary of

Major General Kenneth D. Nichols, Chief AFSWP, 1948-1951.

Defense received a report on the reorganization of the department's nuclear organization, he adopted some of its recommendations in an effort to settle the military's internal disputes. Rather than tuck AFSWP under an Air Force wing, Forrestal, at the insistence of the Navy, decided to retain AFSWP, which the Navy viewed as a positive force toward promoting interservice collaboration. In addition, he hoped the appointment of Donald F. Carpenter, Vice President of the Remington Arms Company, as chairman of the MLC might soothe the troubled waters separating the military and the AEC. Nichols, too, hoped to avoid the internal controversies and saw SANDSTONE as a reprieve from the debate and an opportunity for AFSWP to field assemble actual atomic weapons.[17]

Nonetheless, the dispute continued over the summer. A decision regarding the organization and responsibilities of AFSWP was intertwined with more general policy on the use of nuclear weapons. Forrestal called a meeting of the Joint Chiefs of Staff at the Naval War College in Newport, Rhode Island, in August 1948. Following this meeting, Nichols reported to the Air Force Chief of Staff in carrying out emergency war plans but, in exchange, each Service, including the Navy, would have access to atomic weapons. The compromise worked, at least to a point. Nichols made certain that AFSWP would work with both the Air Force and the Navy in developing a nuclear response capability, though he noted that Truman's strict budget limitations made it impossible to provide "...for the desires of both the Air Force and the Navy."[18]

Fears over events in Berlin and the exposure of the paucity of weapons assembly teams did give new urgency to another crucial facet of AFSWP, the transfer of nuclear weapons to the military in an emergency. While Groves, Nichols, and other military leaders had argued in vain for permanent custody of nuclear weapons, the generals, the AEC commissioners, and the President all agreed that the military needed to get the weapons quickly and efficiently in a national emergency. In early April, Carroll L. Wilson, the AEC General Manager, and General James McCormack, head of the Division of Military Application, met with the AFSWP commander at Sandia, to develop plans for the delivery of atomic weapons to the military in the event of an emergency. Within a week, the three men had coordinated transfer details to the degree that Wilson said there would be "...absolutely no delay."[19]

THE NUCLEAR CARD

The Berlin Airlift was the most direct Allied response to the Soviet blockade. Even so, it was limited in its goal to keep a western presence in Berlin. The Truman administration readily accepted Clay's domino theory regarding the Russian squeeze on Berlin. Czechoslovakia had been "...lost," Clay believed, and other European nations were menaced by Soviet actions. "When Berlin falls," he told Secretary of the Army Kenneth C. Royall in April 1948, "Western Germany will be next... We must not budge. If we withdraw, our position in Europe is threatened. If America does not understand this now, does not know that the issue is cast, then it never will and communism will run rampant." The airlift saved the moment, but its success could not have been anticipated in the dark spring of 1948. The airlift was but a *temporary bandage* remedy to maintain a symbolic presence in Berlin. It did not address the larger strategic issue facing the Allies with the Soviet Union, in the form of the Red Army, overrunning the badly outnumbered Allied forces in Western Europe. That policy aspect was left to the United States' seemingly invincible ultimate weapon, the atomic bomb.[20]

In the spring of 1948, even as the Russians began to apply the first pressure on Berlin, the Truman administration struggled to find an acceptable and realistic role for atomic weapons in formulating foreign policy against the background of shrinking military expenditures and growing antagonisms with the Russians in Europe. The United States and its allies clearly recognized the numerical superiority of the Red Army and the limited options available should war break out over Berlin and the Red Army move west. In a meeting with Truman and Secretary of State George C. Marshall, Forrestal emphasized the Allies' weakness should the Russians resort to military aggression. The country's total reserves amounted to just more than two divisions, only one of which could be deployed in Europe with any speed, he explained. At the end of the discussion, Truman said he sought diplomatic solutions "…in order to come to some kind of an accommodation to avoid war."[21]

Part of Truman's diplomatic response was the atomic bomb. Not that Truman had plans to use the weapon in Europe; he did not. In fact, plans for military use of atomic weapons were ill-formed at best. Although AFSWP, through Groves, Nichols, and their staffs, had suggested as early as 1946 how nuclear weapons might be employed in a war scenario, American planners were focusing on diplomatic, rather than military, applications in the spring and summer of 1948. The Berlin crisis served to prod policy makers to review the long-standing issue of civilian versus military custody and control of nuclear weapons. With so few nuclear weapons and nuclear weapon assembly teams available, the only diplomatic card that Americans could play was the threat of their country's nuclear monopoly.

Since Soviet leaders also knew these limitations, as historian David Holloway noted in *Stalin and the Bomb*, the nuclear card made little difference. But the Berlin blockade took on the characteristics of a major international crisis and therefore required a very public response. As the airlift was the practical response, so wagging a nuclear finger became the diplomatic response. It was a pretense. In reality, the United States was offering up a strategy of nuclear deception.[22]

In a period of demobilization, the atomic bomb was the ideal weapon, the solution to a shortchanged military planner's most pressing problem: how to achieve military superiority at the least cost. Nuclear bombs, as Nichols had explained in 1946, required fewer planes, fewer servicemen, and fewer weapons to achieve comparable levels of destruction. The Air Force promoted this view because of the importance it placed on a large air arm and, not incidentally, the lack of importance it gave to a Navy role. Most military and civilian authorities accepted that position, especially after rejecting the more costly non-nuclear alternative of universal military training in late winter of 1948. Public support remained high for Secretary of the Air Force Stuart Symington, air power, and the atomic bomb.[23]

The Berlin Airlift was an economic and political response to the Soviet blockade. The Allies also responded with another military airlift. Nuclear weapons carried no threat without the ability to deliver them. To give the atomic deterrent some public muscle, in mid-July the United States, with great fanfare, announced that 60 "atomic-capable" B-29 Superfortresses, part of the newly-formed Strategic Air Command (SAC), were being transferred to bases in Great Britain, within striking distance of the Soviet Union. Press reports noted that the planes carried no bombs on their trip across the Atlantic but that their machine guns were manned and loaded. Bomber crews, often accompanied by AFSWP personnel, would be on full alert throughout the Berlin blockade. After the blockade began, bomber units went on alert, adding that when relations over Berlin became further strained the bombers would head toward Europe. The Soviets, the Americans knew, could not fail to notice these heavy-handed public hints of nuclear deterrence.[24] As elements of the SAC prepared to fly to Britain, AFSWP officers in Albuquerque accelerated training of nuclear assembly teams to meet anticipated needs.

While the B-29 was indeed atomic-capable, the B-29s in England were not. In the summer of 1948, the atomic stockpile consisted of the same model of bombs dropped in World War II. Only the Silverplate B-29s of the 509th Bombardment Group, those that had been specifically reconfigured to accommodate the bulky weapons, were truly atomic-capable. Further, while the 509th was placed on a 24-hour alert, the group remained in the United States. The technological advances achieved in the SANDSTONE tests at Enewetak in the spring of 1948, which proved the feasibility of mass producing a smaller, more powerful bomb using less nuclear material, would eliminate the need for specially altered bombers, but those changes lay in the future. By the summer of 1948, American military commanders seriously considered establishing policy for the use of atomic weapons in the event of war, but the Truman Administration refused to make any substantive moves since diplomacy was still an option. In any case, Truman insisted that only he would decide to use the bomb. The President told Forrestal that he did not want "...some dashing lieutenant colonel [to] decide when would be the proper time to drop one."[25]

At the center of Truman's decision was the continuing dispute over who should control the atom. The rivalry between civilian and military control was as old as the atomic age, first pitting scientists against Groves and the Army, then

Strategic Air Command B-29 Silverplate Superfortress.

the AEC against the military. The controversy of custody and control was further exacerbated by a feud between the three branches of the Armed Services, something that the creation in the fall of 1947 of the National Military Establishment and a purportedly unified Department of Defense had failed to reconcile.

The crisis in Berlin served to sharpen the military's insistence on having custody of atomic weapons. Groves' replacement at AFSWP, General Nichols, was as adamant about the necessity for military custody as Groves had been, perhaps even more so. General Omar Bradley, Chief of Staff of the Army, asked Nichols to take over AFSWP the first week of March 1948, pending official orders and a promotion to the position. Nichols moved into AFSWP's Pentagon offices just as tensions over Czechoslovakia and Berlin increased. On March 5, Secretary of the Army Royall invited Nichols, Forrestal, John L. Sullivan, Secretary of the Navy, Stuart Symington, Secretary of the Air Force, Donald F. Carpenter, the new Chairman of the MLC, and AEC Chairman Lilienthal to dinner at his Pentagon office overlooking the Potomac. Royall hoped to promote better cooperation between the Armed Services and the AEC over nuclear weapons. The strategic application of atomic weapons became particularly urgent, given Soviet actions in Central Europe and a telegram that arrived that day from General Clay in Berlin. That evening General Clay's analysis from Berlin that Soviet attitudes toward the West were becoming increasingly hostile became the main topic of conversation.[26]

As the discussion evolved, military and civilian officials alike connected atomic weapons to a possible American response to Soviet actions. War in Europe seemed like a possibility, and atomic warfare would be part of the scenario. "How long would it take to get a number of 'eggs' to, say, the Mediterranean?" Royall wondered, using the slang term for atomic bombs. Symington noted that most Americans were "...misinformed about how quickly we could go into action and what we could do," meaning that the public did not sense the weakness of the atomic option. From the civilian perspective of the Commission, Lilienthal told the group that the most important need was to improve Sandia Base, "where the AEC and the military must fit closely." Royall had recently visited Sandia and agreed. "I saw it was a mess, just as Dave [Lilienthal] said, and something had to be done." He added that the Army was not doing it as fast as the AEC would like, but "we're moving that way." Nichols, who had just assumed command of Sandia on an interim basis, remained distrustful of Lilienthal and the AEC, which he believed had held up his promotion. He made no mention of the Sandia part of the discussion in his memoirs.[27]

The March 5 meeting did not accomplish Royall's goal of bringing the military and the civilian aspects of atomic energy closer together. President Truman made no bones about where he stood when he summoned Lilienthal, Nichols, and Royall to the White House six days later on March 11. He wanted the problem solved. Truman wanted everyone present to clearly understand that he wanted cooperation between the civilian and military agencies in matters of atomic weapons. "I know you two hate each other's guts," Nichols reported Truman saying to Lilienthal and him, but "I expect you two to cooperate." Both men agreed.[28]

Immediately, Nichols began to push for detailed plans for the use of atomic weapons, including their transfer to the military in case of an emergency. He met with General Albert M. Gruenther, the Director of the Joint Staff, to discuss AF-

SWP's activities. Nichols told Gruenther that AFSWP should be doing more planning and holding joint exercises with the AEC and the Air Force. Gruenther's response was a bombshell. He told Nichols that his aims violated a Presidential order not to plan on the use of atomic weapons. Nichols was flabbergasted and asked if he should stop working on such plans. "I'm not telling you to stop," Gruenther said, "I just wanted you to know that you are not in accord with present Presidential policy."[29]

At the end of March, Nichols went to Forrestal's office for a working lunch with Symington, Royall, the three Joint Chiefs, Under Secretary of State Robert A. Lovett, and Dwight Eisenhower, then president of Columbia University, to discuss the intensifying crisis in Berlin. Nichols, who was there to report on the country's atomic readiness, noted "...how easily Eisenhower assumed leadership of the entire group." Asked if the United States was able to deliver any atomic weapons, Nichols replied that the country could not. He explained that the only assembly teams, military and civilian, were at Enewetak for the SANDSTONE tests and "...that the military teams were not yet qualified to assemble atomic weapons." Eisenhower, Nichols recorded, told him "...in very definite terms to accelerate training and improve the situation at once." By the next morning, Nichols had briefed a joint meeting of the MLC and the AEC about the situation.[30]

Berlin provided the catalyst for Nichols to proceed with arranging for a more active military role in atomic weapons. Both at a policy level in the Pentagon and an operational level at Sandia, Nichols initiated action "...to perfect plans for transfer of atomic weapons to the military in case of emergency and to expedite training and equipping the military assembly teams." The Presidential directive, at least as far as Nichols was governed by it, was not placed on a back burner; it was taken off the stove.[31]

While he beefed up assembly training at Sandia, especially as the teams returned from the successful SANDSTONE tests in the spring and summer of 1948, Nichols once more attacked the custody issue head on. He found a willing and powerful ally in the Secretary of Defense. As Secretary of the Navy, Forrestal had viewed some level of military control of atomic weapons as essential to the national security. As Secretary of Defense, he had asked Truman in March 1948 to transfer custody of nuclear weapons from the AEC to the military. In June, Forrestal asked Nichols to prepare a memorandum for the President which recommended the military be given authority to withdraw weapons from the stockpile for training purposes or in a national emergency. Meetings between Forrestal and Lilienthal during the month failed to reconcile the military and civilian positions on custody. Nichols noted that the issue for the Commission was not the lack of technical competency of AFSWP, a reason usually given for keeping the bomb in civilian hands, but, as Lilienthal confessed in one of the June meetings, the real issue was civilian control of atomic weapons. "Emotion rather than reason," Nichols said of Lilienthal, "was the basis of his position." Both sides agreed to present their divergent views to Truman for resolution.[32]

Lilienthal's emotions stemmed from his conviction that the military was treating atomic bombs "...like any other kind of weapon." In Lilienthal's mind, they were anything but the same. Civilians, Lilienthal believed, served as a check on military assumptions, which he believed included the use of atomic weapons. Therefore, he drew a careful distinction between technical custody and underlying policy because the Berlin crisis had led the military to plan for the use of the bomb and the selection of appropriate targets. Thus, the custody issue took on increased importance in times of crisis.[33]

Lilienthal's views were also shaped by an earlier meeting, which AEC representatives held with Dr. Walter F. Colby, an intelligence expert from the University of Michigan. The Commission had asked Colby to explore with the Central Intelligence Agency (CIA) and other intelligence agencies how long it might be before the Soviet Union developed an atomic weapon. "The thing that rather chills one's blood," the chairman noted in his diary, "is to observe what is nothing less than lack of integrity in the way intelligence agencies deal with the meager stuff they have." He feared that in the future some President might order "a terrible atomic attack" in "anticipatory retaliation" based on the thinnest of intelligence reports. "No one will ever know what terrible things could ensue that might have been prevented," he concluded, "that may have been utterly needless."[34]

The custody showdown came at the White House on July 21. Lilienthal had learned from Clark Clifford, the President's legal and political advisor, that Truman favored keeping atomic weapons under civilian control. He passed Clifford's comment on to Forrestal, who carefully mulled it over. In the end, Clifford's warning was ignored. The Secretary of Defense was firmly committed to the notion that the end user of the bomb, the National Military Establishment, should have custody of it, partly because it would bring a concentration of authority and a unified command structure. With the military Services and AFSWP pushing for custody and the threat of Berlin giving urgency to the issue, Forrestal would not back away from an official Presidential decision. On the way to the White House meeting, Forrestal asked General Nichols if the custody issue was important enough to resign over should the President say no. "It certainly is important enough," Nichols replied, adding, nonetheless, "I hope you will not resign over the issue."[35]

On July 21, 1948, Forrestal, two of the Service Secretaries, Carpenter, his deputy from the MLC, William Webster, and the five AEC commissioners packed into Truman's office. Lilienthal believed it was the largest group he had seen in a Presidential conference since the summer of 1936. From the outset, the tone of the meeting was somber and serious. There were no light preliminaries. Truman, looking "worn and grim" according to Lilienthal, got right down to business. Sitting to the President's left, Forrestal began by asking Carpenter to read the military's single-spaced, two-and-a-half-page position paper on transferring the custody of nuclear weapons. In Lilienthal's view, reading the document word for word was "...mistake number 1." When Carpenter added that he also had additional supporting materials from the Secretaries of the Army, Navy, and Air Force and from the Joint Chiefs, Truman's patience was exhausted. "I can read," the President snapped, "curtly and not pleasantly," according to Lilienthal.[36]

Lilienthal then took up the objections of the AEC to any change in the existing civilian/military arrangements regarding nuclear weapons. He said that atomic weapons carried the widest kind of international and diplomatic implications. He emphasized policy issues, asking if the civilian control over atomic weapons as established in the Atomic Energy Act could be preserved by transferring custodial issues to the military. In short, Lilienthal argued that the present arrangement was working smoothly and that there was no need to change it, though he was careful to add that the decision was entirely the President's own. With Carpenter's reading gaffe in mind, Lilienthal stopped.[37]

The military men tried to salvage their position. Symington told the President that he had visited Sandia and "...our fellas [there] think they ought to have the bomb. They feel they might get them when they need them and they might not work." Truman, according to Lilienthal, was not impressed with this line of argument. Royall asserted that economics required military control. "We have been spending 98 percent of all the money for atomic energy for weapons. Now if we aren't going to use them, that doesn't make any sense." Lilienthal observed in his diary that if Truman was concerned about trusting "...these terrible forces in the hands of the military establishment, the performance these men gave certainly could not have been reassuring on that score."[38]

The AEC Chairman had correctly read the President. Truman told the group that he needed to consider atomic weapons in the light of international relations. He emphasized that the responsibility for using the bomb was his and a responsibility he intended to keep. With the politics of the 1948 campaign and the Berlin crisis as a background, Truman cautioned that "...this is no time to be juggling an atom bomb around." Three days later, on July 24, Truman announced that all aspects of the atomic energy program would remain with civilian authorities.[39]

The President's decision rankled the Pentagon. In dealing with Forrestal, Truman tried to ease his Defense Secretary's disappointment by explaining that political considerations were key to the decision. After the November election, he told Forrestal, "...it would be possible to take another look at the picture." But Forrestal openly fretted that the President's ruling had made it "difficult for me to carry out my responsibilities." Again, he raised the possibility of resigning, but his aides talked him out of such a course.[40]

The military did not see Truman's decision as irrevocable. One might evade the custody impasse. If AEC officials visited the AFSWP operation at Sandia, some generals believed, the members might be convinced that the military unit was "...fully qualified and could be ready for this responsibility in a comparatively short time." Nichols, consistently a hardliner on the custody issue, also disagreed with the President's decision. The outcome of the custody battle, he later wrote, taught him that "...patience, persistence, and the real threat of war would be required to obtain the right decision." In the meantime, he would bolster AFSWP's operational ability to transfer weapons to the military in an emergency.[41]

Donald Carpenter, the civilian brought in to head the MLC, had a different perspective. Caught between both warring parties, Carpenter did not believe that the President's decision had changed anyone's views. Relations between civilians and soldiers dealing in atomic energy had improved little. Part of the reason, Carpenter later said, were the strong views "...that members of the AEC thought all military officers were damn fools and officers thought all AEC people were damn crooks."[42]

THE SANDSTONE TESTS

The same week that Montague, McCormack, and Wilson settled the details for transferring nuclear weapons, engineers from the 38th Battalion (Special) completed laying several miles of submarine cable connecting a 200-foot steel tower rising above Entebbe, a small island on the north rim of the Enewetak Atoll in the Marshall Islands. The tower contained electronic test instruments to measure blast, thermal, and radiation effects. The assembly team, including AFSWP personnel, practiced arming a dummy weapon and testing the firing circuits. Other components of AFSWP served as guards, provided technical assistance, or worked in a radiation safety unit. Satisfied with the checks, the scientific director, Darol K. Froman, gave the order to fire the actual device. While the firing party proceeded to point zero, most of the task force relocated to the command center on Parry Island, 10 miles away.[43]

Operation SANDSTONE was to be the second test series held in the Marshall Islands, yet it differed from the first series (CROSSROADS) in that it was primarily an AEC scientific test series with the Armed Services serving in a supporting role. SANDSTONE's stated purpose was to proof test improved design atomic weapons. The weapons were tested at Enewetak by JTF 7 during April/May 1948. Three weapons were detonated in the test series, to include X-RAY (April 15), YOKE (May 1), and ZEBRA (May 15).

At 6:17 in the morning of April 15 the fireball of Shot X-RAY, the first test in the SANDSTONE series, rose from Enjebi. The brilliant light of the blast was visible in Kwajalein, some 300 miles to the southeast. Almost immediately scientists raced toward ground zero to collect critical samples and data on the shot. Drone planes filled the air collecting fallout samples, and a remote controlled tank began scooping earth off the island's surface. Using airplane relays, the Air Force quickly ferried test samples back to Los Alamos for full analysis. Within hours, the scientists in New Mexico confirmed what those in the Pacific strongly suspected, that the new design principles were a stunning success. The air sampling at SAND-

Scientists leaving shot island (Enjebi) just prior to X-RAY event, April 15, 1948.

STONE, conducted by the then top secret Air Force Office of Atomic Testing (AFOAT-1), demonstrated for the first time the feasibility of airborne radiological detection of nuclear explosions. Thereafter, such "sniffer" flights became part of an American long-range detection system that would keep a nose into the Soviet atomic energy program.[44]

X-RAY and the two tests that followed at Enewetak over the next month, YOKE and ZEBRA, demonstrated two new technological advances in bomb design.[45]

The implications of the data from the SANDSTONE tests, according to two historians of nuclear strategy, "...were enormous. Not only would weapons become more plentiful, but they could also be of increasingly diverse design," from lightweight tactical weapons to larger strategic bombs. The old 10,000-pound Nagasaki implosion bomb, requiring delivery in a single specially outfitted B-29, was immediately obsolete. The new core design also allowed the weapon to be prefabricated, thus marking the change from a laboratory device to a production weapon. Days of slowly adding a handful of atomic bombs to a tiny stockpile would soon be over. Suddenly, American scientists had created *more bang for fewer bucks*. A public announcement from the AEC following the tests allowed only that "...the position of the United States in the field of atomic weapons has been substantially improved." The military view was more optimistic. After SANDSTONE, Nichols said "we should be thinking in terms of thousands of weapons rather than hundreds."[46]

NEW PRESSURES AT SANDIA

Increased friction with the Soviet Union and the prospective boom in the production of nuclear weapons greatly boosted AFSWP activities at Sandia. To meet this increase, the 38th Engineer Battalion (Special) was reorganized into three Special Weapons Units soon after most of the men had returned from SANDSTONE. With a nucleus of trained officers from SANDSTONE and new officers who had finished the technical training course, the new units were to direct operational and field training. The war scare over Berlin created a crash program to train bomb assembly crews and, under the new schedule, the number of students, according to the unit historian, "...mushroomed by leaps and bounds" in the early summer of 1948.[47]

The growth proved to be too fast. Training programs expanded so rapidly that they were badly crippled by Los Alamos' inability to provide the necessary classified equipment, including test calibrators, flight test boxes, and other electrical meters. The equipment problem was another manifestation of the military/civilian dichotomy in nuclear weapons. The AFSWP training program experienced great difficulty in obtaining replacement parts from the AEC and in getting repairs completed on equipment. The soldiers complained about the Commission's policy of requiring all repairs of AEC equipment to be made by AEC employees, and, groused one Army engineer, "...this took time, sometimes causing classes to be held up." In the meantime, the new Special Weapons Groups remodeled a warehouse and office building to handle the expected materials and maintained a training program "...consistent with available equipment." One building, dubbed the "museum," held mock-ups of various models of atomic bombs. A nearby building contained two large bomb assembly areas complete with an elaborate monorail system on which the bomb components moved. When the needed equipment arrived in November, it arrived all at once in a "landslide," severely taxing the available storage space. Toward the end of

Operation SANDSTONE, Event X-RAY detonation, April 15, 1948.

1948, after much pressure from Nichols, production equipment, instead of prototype test equipment, began to appear in the training classes.[48]

Nichols viewed Soviet actions in Berlin with a wary eye. He would not have his unit be less than fully prepared for all contingencies. In March 1948, 250 paratroopers from Fort Hood, Texas, landed on the edge of Tijeras Canyon, southeast of Sandia Base. Base defenders repulsed the simulated attack, which tested base defenses of the technical area but did not involve atomic weapons or nuclear equipment. The next month, General Montague brought in 18 tanks and stationed them around the Ordnance, Igloo, and Technical areas. Security experiments were also conducted with the Air Force, trying out various aircraft and equipment configurations. AFSWP sought alternatives to hydraulic lifts to conduct bomb loading. Most air bases lacked special loading pits with hydraulic lifts to place nuclear weapons into the bombers. In May, a joint AFSWP-Air Force team successfully loaded a Mark III bomb into a B-29 using a standard aircraft hoist over a deep pit. Because of a need for a reserve of transport aircraft for bomb components, AFSWP experimented with both Air Force and Navy cargo planes to carry these units.[49]

FIELD OPERATIONS

As the training programs for bomb assembly teams increased, so did the number of field operations. In July, one company of the 38th held a joint exercise with the 509th Bombardment Group at Walker Air Force Base in Roswell, New Mexico. Operation BANJO involved the first operational employment of assembly units since AJAX in November 1947. It called for air transport of the entire unit with equipment and a transportable assembly building to a forward base and the assembly of five bombs at a forward base. Four of the weapons were to be used in a mock strike mission, the fifth was held as a spare. By completely assembling a weapon at a forward area, rather than the rear-forward area approach used at AJAX, AFSWP found that the rate of assembly considerably increased. AFSWP pronounced the operation a success, even though it was necessary to raid other AFSWP units to bring the complement of personnel up to strength for the maneuvers. Thereafter, field operations were held on a monthly basis.[50]

Field exercises grew in complexity. As units graduated from the training course, they practiced on continuous assemblies, aircraft loading operations, and finally in a field exercise in conjunction with an Air Force unit. In August, two Army companies and a Navy unit from AFSWP conducted a joint exercise with two Air Force units at Davis-Monthan Air Force Base in Tucson, Arizona. Code-named "COWBOY," the operation was an expansion of the rear-forward assembly method initiated in AJAX. COWBOY's goal was to assemble five weapons using a modified C-97 aircraft, code named "Chickenpox" as the B-29 was "Silverplate," to determine if the plane could be used as a forward assembly site. One of the C-97s contained an airborne assembly laboratory built into the aircraft. Other C-97s would carry a portable assembly building, called a "Palmer House," which was redesigned to eliminate the deficiencies experienced at AJAX. Two teams, one from the Army and one from the Navy, handled the rear assembly, the first operation to include a Naval assembly unit. The third AFSWP team conducted the forward check and final assembly. Results were mixed. By the time the fifth bomb had been assembled, the teams were exhausted. The time schedule for the delivery of an assembled weapon, 16 hours as suggested from an earlier exercise, proved impossible to meet. Rather, assembly time averaged about 24 hours for each bomb. However, this COWBOY exercise indicated that the Chickenpox C-97 assembly laboratory could be used operationally.[51]

Close coordination between the Air Force and AFSWP became increasingly critical, which COWBOY had demonstrated. Nichols arranged for monthly meetings between the staffs of the two organizations to brief him: General Lauris Norstad, and other top Air Force officers on the capabilities of the Air Force and AFSWP to deliver atomic weapons. The meetings, which began in September, gave each group a top level forum to analyze the continuing field operations and readiness plans.[52]

The AFSWP units had scarcely returned to Sandia from COWBOY when one company was sent to check out the assembly facilities at one of the recently built nuclear weapons storage bases in Texas. The permanent assembly facilities for the site had not been completed; however, two storage igloos had been recently modified into assembly facilities as a result of the Berlin crisis. Operation NUTMEG was designed to see if, indeed, the storage areas would suffice. Shortly after Labor Day 1948, an AFSWP detachment flew to Texas, toured the retrofitted storage bunkers, evaluated the equipment, and pronounced the igloos acceptable for weapons assembly.[53]

PREPARING FOR WAR

Just as NUTMEG was ending in September, Forrestal asked Nichols to come to his office for a meeting on the Berlin issue. There, the head of AFSWP was

Nose view of USAF C-97 aircraft used by AFSWP as forward assembly site.

joined by the Joint Chiefs, the three Service Secretaries, Secretary of State George C. Marshall, Generals Gruenther and Norstad, and Carpenter, head of the MLC. They discussed deteriorating relations with the Soviet Union and the growing prospects of a war. All agreed that "...a greater state of readiness to deliver atomic weapons was necessary." Nichols immediately accelerated AFSWP's activities. He expedited the training of assembly teams at Sandia and put additional pressure on Los Alamos to provide badly needed assembly equipment for the teams. He also sent a delegation to visit the United Kingdom with an eye toward installing nuclear weapons assembly equipment in key air bases. Nichols was extremely pleased with the direction that events had taken AFSWP and confirmed the central strategic role he and Groves had always envisioned for it. "It is amazing," Nichols later wrote in his memoirs, "how cooperation can be improved by a careful selection of personnel, clear-cut objectives, and a sense of urgency."[54]

Events in Berlin in the fall of 1948 also caused Truman to change his position on planning for the use of atomic energy, something he had rejected previously. "I have a terrible feeling that we are very close to war," Truman noted in his diary after a September briefing from his generals on the situation in Europe, "but I hope not." Caught between international tensions and his own proclivity not to use atomic weapons, Truman ordered the military to draw up operational plans that would rely on a nuclear response. AFSWP continued its monthly schedule of field exercises with a renewed sense of urgency.[55]

Operation WHIPPOORWILL, held over a two-week period in October 1948, combined the storage site experience of NUTMEG with the assembly operations conducted at BANJO and COWBOY. Again, elements from the 38th Engineer Battalion (Special) of AFSWP and the 509th Bomb Group of the Eighth Air Force joined to conduct the field operation. WHIPPOORWILL was the most extensive field exercise planned to that time. It consisted of assembling 11 bombs, 10 to be used in simulated bombing attacks with a single spare. Similar to AJAX, a plane would fly west, to Inyokern, California, and drop one of the bombs that had been assembled, less its fissile material. The purpose of the operation was to test forward base assembly conditions and the capabilities of an assembly team during extended maneuvers.[56]

Before a sizable number of high-ranking visitors anxious to see this new business of field assembly of atomic bombs, the assembly crew from Sandia established a new, and faster, standard time for assembling the Mark III weapons: 16 hours. Once again, however, fatigue proved to be a critical factor. The results suggested that outside labor, rather than assembly team personnel, be brought in to erect the portable assembly building so that the team's primary purpose would not be impaired. For the first three days it was possible to deliver three bombs a day; thereafter, the officers found, two bombs were a more realistic expectation. The bulky weapons still required numerous planes in the delivery/assembly process. Each bomb capsule required a separate aircraft, as did the balance of the bomb components. At its conclusion, officials believed WHIPPOORWILL had been the most realistic joint operation the Armed Services had ever conducted and proved the military's competency in assembling and delivering atomic weapons.[57]

Other exercises combined AFSWP units' Naval operations. The initial joint AFSWP-Navy operation had taken place in 1947, when Sandia developed shipboard assembly site specifications for the

Bureau of Ships. The Navy, seeking to protect its nuclear role against opposition from the Air Force, believed that it could develop an atomic capability by modifying certain large *Midway*-class carriers by strengthening their flight decks to accommodate larger aircraft capable of carrying atomic weapons. In late November of 1948, AFSWP's Navy Special Weapons Unit No. 471 flew to Norfolk, Virginia, to conduct Operation EASTWIND, an exercise to test bomb assemblies on one of the modified carriers. The Naval unit was to check the assemblies of both bomb types then in the stockpile, the *Little Boy*, the gun-type uranium bomb that had been dropped on Hiroshima, and the Mark III Nagasaki-type implosion weapon. The operation also included a third model, a prototype mock-up of the newly designed Mark IV bomb, the product of the results of SANDSTONE. The aim was to thoroughly review the technical work and investigate handling and weapons stowage problems.[58]

Including the Mark IV in EASTWIND was critical. The new weapon held the potential for being a smaller weapon in size and weight than the Mark III, crucial differences for sea-based aircraft. Because Naval aircraft could more readily carry a smaller weapon, the Mark IV revitalized the Navy's push to maintain an atomic carrier-based capability. Detailed results of Operation EASTWIND remain classified to this day. The AFSWP report simply noted that "…work was begun at once to correct the deficiencies noted." By the end of 1948, a Navy XAJ-1 aircraft, which would carry atomic weapons, had arrived at Kirtland for wiring and test loading of the three types of atomic bombs.[59]

The final exercise of 1948, held in the week before Christmas, drew on the experience of AFSWP's other operations during the course of the year. Operation UNLIMITED was a joint AEC-AFSWP exercise at Sandia designed to test the emergency transfer plans which dealt with the turnover of nuclear capsules to the military by the Commission. The exercise began with the simultaneous transmission of special code words from Washington to the field. Using dummy bombs, the complicated transfer procedure worked out between the military and the AEC began its first test. Nichols was uneasy. He had just enough confidence in the level of cooperation at the operational level to think the procedures could "…work under many but not all emergency situations." Nichols thought there were "…too many possibilities for a snafu."[60]

Nichols would not have full confidence in any transfer procedure until it was entirely under military control. Nonetheless, Operation UNLIMITED demonstrated that AFSWP and the AEC could satisfactorily transfer nuclear weapons in a timely fashion. The teams did recommend that Air Force rather than AFSWP personnel move weapons capsules to a forward base and that the capsules be transferred in a secluded area rather than at the more conspicuous gate of the ordnance area. All agreed that officials in Washington should initiate additional drills once every four to six months.[61]

At the end of 1948, Nichols looked back on the 10 months he had commanded AFSWP. He took heart that considerable progress had been made in the weapons program. Mark IV weapons were nearing production stage, the scarcity of fissionable material was easing, new smaller and lighter weapons were being developed, and a spirit of closer cooperation between civilian and military authorities had developed. Operation UNLIMITED had proved that atomic bombs could be transferred successfully without military custody. Nichols believed he could live with this arrangement, but, he added, "I hope for not too long."

But on the whole, 1948, the AFSWP head concluded, had been an exciting and demanding year. "I was glad to be back in a position of responsibility," Nichols later wrote. "I enjoyed it." He realized the changes taking place in 1948 were shaping a timetable that would eventually permit the military to assume full custody and surveillance of atomic weapons. Nichols' long-time goal seemed to be drawing closer.[62]

SEARCH FOR A CONTINENTAL TEST SITE

In early 1947, Admiral William S. Parsons, the Navy deputy to AFSWP, recommended that the United States establish a site within the continental United States for testing nuclear weapons. Lilienthal and the AEC rejected the idea, which surfaced again prior to SANDSTONE only to be driven into hibernation once more because of opposition from Los Alamos, which preferred a Pacific site. Issues of safety, security, logistics, weather, and costs that stemmed from the SANDSTONE operation, however, rekindled interest in a continental site. Most of the interest came from the Joint Chiefs of Staff and mainly flowed from budgetary worries. The AEC persisted in its opposition but did agree to a survey of possible sites within the United States, but only if the work was to be done in the utmost secrecy. Because of AFSWP's expertise in conducting radiological monitoring, especially the recent work at SANDSTONE, Parsons suggested that the radiological division could conduct the survey for the Joint Chiefs. In the late summer of 1948, the AFSWP assigned Project Nutmeg - not to be confused with Operation NUTMEG that occurred about the same time - to Navy Captain Howard B. Hutchinson.[63]

During the fall of 1948, Captain Hutchinson collected data from the Pacif-

Rear Admiral William S. Parsons, Navy Deputy to AFSWP and Deputy Commander of JTF-1 during CROSSROADS.

ic tests and Japan, especially looking at fallout patterns of radionuclides. With this information, Hutchinson believed he could identify those areas of the country where wind and weather would be most favorable to safeguard population centers. By 1949 he had finished the AFSWP survey. In his report to the AEC and the MLC, Hutchinson identified two primary regions: a stretch along the eastern seaboard between Cape Fear and Cape Hatteras and a large area in the desert southwest. Hutchinson preferred the Carolinas because of prevailing winds and ocean currents.[64]

That was as far as Hutchinson progressed. His report did not consider rather critical problems such as "...real estate, public relations, soil composition, safety, physical security, and logistics," the AEC noted. Nor did the Nutmeg report identify a specific area as a continental test site. The Carolina coast, in the opinion of the AEC staff, "...would obviously pose difficult domestic and possibly international relations problems." In the Commission's view, short of a national emergency, a continental test site was "...not desirable," and the report was shelved.[65]

PROGRESS ON BOMB ASSEMBLY

The results of SANDSTONE and the military's unsuccessful attempt to gain custody of nuclear weapons largely determined AFSWP's direction in 1949. The development of a simplified Mark IV production weapon permitted AFSWP to assemble bombs in far greater numbers than previously. Moreover, although Nichols had lost the custody battle at the Presidential level in July 1948, he quickly saw that the subsequent agreement that the AEC made with AFSWP to facilitate the transfer of atomic bombs in an emergency would prove to be an avenue by which the military could obtain a yet greater participation in handling nuclear weapons. Finally, revisions of the Atomic Energy Act of 1946 and a reorganization of the AEC's Division of Military Application in 1949 led to closer working relationships between the Commission and AFSWP.

Since the summer of 1948 when Truman decided to stay with civilian control of atomic weapons, Nichols had focused AFSWP's energies on strengthening the process by which the AEC would promptly deliver the needed number of weapons to the military. In late January 1949, Nichols recommended to the Commission that a formal agreement be worked out fitting the transfer of weapons to the actual war plans. Nichols emphasized that it was essential that weapons be delivered to field commanders not only at the proper time and in proper numbers but, with the development of the Mark IV weapon, also by proper model. He asked that the AEC maintain a transfer capacity for each weapon type equal to AFSWP's capacity to assemble that type. AFSWP, Nichols added, would notify the AEC of any changes in its assembly capabilities.[66]

The AFSWP general also requested his command's stake in stockpile matters be increased. AFSWP, he wrote Lilienthal, should make the necessary arrangements with war planners and field commanders to ensure stockpile utilization in accordance with the weapons' relative efficiency, subject to military requirements for particular types of weapons. Such an agreement, he concluded, would allow the AFSWP commander at Sandia Base to develop specific transfer schedules, by number and type, and maintain a current delivery plan with "...as many alternates as necessary." The AEC agreed to Nichols' suggestions five weeks later.[67]

Critical to Nichols' plan was AFSWP's assembly capability. At the time he sent Lilienthal the recommendations, AFSWP was able to assemble 10 Mark III bombs per day. By July 1, Nichols estimated, AFSWP's teams could assemble 20 old Mark IIIs and 30 new Mark IV weapons per day. By the end of the year, he predicted that daily assembly production levels would increase to 30 Mark IIIs and 50 Mark IVs. Nichols' estimates proved to be too low. By July, AFSWP, "...by the most efficient utilization of available personnel and equipment..." (meaning dispatching additional personnel from Sandia Base to weapons storage sites) was able to assemble 21 Mark IIIs and 24 Mark IVs, or 45 bombs per day, he told Lilienthal. By September, AFSWP could handle 63 bombs a day. Nichols now believed that his men could assemble approximately 100 per day by the end of the year. The assembly and transfer process had evolved so smoothly and efficiently in the course of the year that the AEC agreed to permit AFSWP personnel to "...handle nuclear weapons incident to their emergency transfer."[68]

TECHNICAL SURVEILLANCE

Nichols pushed for AFSWP to acquire greater nuclear responsibilities in areas outside the emergency transfer of weapons. For months he had argued that technical surveillance of the weapons stockpile should be a joint responsibility of the military and the AEC. If the AEC was responsible for weapons development and production, Nichols wanted AFSWP involved in laboratory and destructive tests, the analysis of tests and inspection data, and the determination of defects and preventive measures relating to atomic weapons. The three stockpile storage areas - Sites Able, Baker, and Charlie - became the focus of Nichols' campaign to extend AFSWP activities, if not control, in lieu of outright custody of atomic weapons.[69]

By the spring of 1949, General Montague, Sandia Base Commander, had cut an agreement with the AEC's manager of the Santa Fe Operations Office, Carroll L. Tyler. The arrangement, attempted to sort out some of the confusion inherent in the dual military/AEC responsibilities established in the Atomic Energy Act. It provided that the AEC and AFSWP would jointly occupy the storage sites. The military would support operations in the event of a national emergency and conduct training exercises and maneuvers at the sites. In addition, AFSWP would also participate in nuclear and non-nuclear inspection, surveillance, and assembly of weapons under AEC supervision. AFSWP soon took over the re-inspection of the non-nuclear electrical and mechanical components at Baker and Charlie sites and much of the nuclear surveillance as well.[70]

Increased weapons production, however, soon made the Tyler-Montague Agreement obsolete. Montague estimated that it would take the AFSWP inventory officer 10 to 14 days each month to complete the inventories at Los Alamos and the storage sites. Montague suggested revising the system to permit two AFSWP representatives at each storage site to conduct the inventory, one to survey the electrical and mechanical components and the other to inventory the nuclear material. Each of the individuals had to serve a full year on the assignment and could not be transferred between the storage sites, thereby eliminating the possibility that any one of them could obtain complete stockpile figures. The stockpile figures, with the approval of the AEC's representative at Sandia Base, were then forwarded to Nichols in Washington. Tyler agreed to Montague's changes. By the end of the year, AFSWP was participating in the inspections of AEC contractors in their final acceptance of major non-nuclear subassemblies to assure that the products would be acceptable for military use. Thus, the agreement provided a means for increased AFSWP responsibilities in the weapon production process and at the stockpile storage sites. Groves' goal of building a highly trained cadre of military personnel to handle nuclear weapons had been largely realized. By the end of 1949, the AEC had recognized the advanced technical training and weapons capabilities of military personnel far more than it had acknowledged previously.[71]

MEASURING NUCLEAR WEAPON EFFECTS

Perhaps the best example of the technical competencies acquired by AFSWP related to weapons effects testing and measurement. At SANDSTONE, the AFSWP contingent had performed some technical monitoring but generally believed that it had been underutilized. In the spring of 1949, Dr. Alvin C. Graves, the director of J Division at Los Alamos, asked that AFSWP assume the responsibility for measuring free air pressures at the planned 1951 atomic tests. Nichols readily agreed. The work, done in conjunction with the Naval Ordnance Laboratory at White Oak, Maryland, was to measure the blast effect of a bomb to determine the overpressure of the shock wave in free air. J Division hoped that AFSWP could assemble a group that would bring together balloon, blast, and instrument experts to manage a Free Air Pressure Group.[72]

By the end of the year, AFSWP, led by Lieutenant Colonel Alexander J. Frolich, had convened a team of experts located in the Washington, D.C. area to find methods for measuring blast effects. One proposed method involved taking measurements with impulse transmitters suspended at a height of 2,000 feet from barrage balloons.

In addition to the Naval Ordnance staff at the White Oak facility, the blast effects team soon included the Johns Hopkins Applied Physics Laboratory, based in Silver Spring, Maryland, which supplied an electronic instrument research and radio transmitter expertise, and the Army's Engineer Research and Development Laboratory (ERDL) at Fort Belvoir, Virginia, which undertook balloon research, design, and procurement. Under Frolich, the AFSWP Free Air Pressure Group, or Test Group as it became known, would firmly establish AFSWP's future administrative and technical credentials in nuclear effects, and became the basis for the main focus of the agency for the next 40 years.[73]

If new scientific and technical initiatives were being shaped under Frolich in Washington, activities at Sandia Base took on a new face as well. In December 1948, the designation of the 38th Engineer Battalion (Special) was changed to the 8460th Special Weapons Group. The change, which came at a time of rapid expansion, new weapons, and changing operational concepts, was part of a general reorganization of AFSWP that more closely reflected the Joint-Service nature of the weapons program. The 8460th became an administrative and operational command consisting of special units from all three Services, fully integrated into AFSWP. Experienced officers from the 38th, including Colonel Dorland, continued to lead the new Special Weapons Group.[74]

TOWARD A MARK IV STOCKPILE

Changes in nuclear weapons design made a significant impact on the activities of the Special Weapons Group. The first development was the modification of the Mark III Nagasaki-type bomb in 1947. For some time, the military had clamored for a weapon that could be field assembled in a short period of time and be reliable enough for the most stringent military applications. In the spring of 1949, the AEC delivered to the stockpile a modified Mark III, called a 31.* It was not a radically new weapon from the 30 but incorporated a more rugged and reliable firing system and permitted a considerable saving of time in field assembly. Concurrent with the development of the 31 bomb, the AEC delivered the Mark IV, or 40, bomb to the military for training in the late spring of 1949. The Mark IV was a production bomb designed "...to provide maximum speed in field assembly consistent with reliability of performance." Within weeks of working with the new weapon, AFSWP had realized that smaller, 46-man assembly teams could achieve the same rate of assembly under field conditions.[75]

---

* The first digit of the number 30 translated from the initial design number of the weapon, or Mark III. The second digit indicated the modification, or Mod, to the basic weapon. Thus the first modification to the original Mark III would be labeled a 31 bomb.

As they became part of the stockpile, the 31 and 40 type bombs significantly improved the performance of the special weapons units. By April 1949, a joint Navy/Air Force exercise in New Mexico used the *Fat Man* weapon for the last time. Whereas the assembly team worked eleven hours to assemble the now obsolete weapon, a team took only seven hours to assemble a modified *Fat Man*, the Mark III Mod 1 (31) bomb, the following month. By June, the 31 and 40 weapons were the only bombs for which SAC and AFSWP developed standard operating procedures, and AFSWP intensified its program at Sandia to train 10 SAC assembly teams, which would then be assigned to the SAC operating bases. At the same time, the Air Force began staffing permanent storage and assembly facilities at the three stockpile sites, using them as rear assembly bases in nuclear field exercises.[76]

SUPPORTING THE AIR FORCE

Since the early stages of development of assembly organizations, AFSWP and the Air Force had planned to conduct a field exercise under arctic conditions. The idea was to assemble and deliver an atomic weapon at a forward base in extremely cold weather. The Air Force, however, cancelled the drill scheduled for the winter of 1948 in the northern part of Alaska. The next fall, AFSWP and the Air Force tried again. In September 1949, a Special Weapons Unit left Sandia for Eielson Air Force Base in Alaska, to run a limited assembly exercise and generally prepare for a second outing later in the winter. The September exercise went off without a hitch except for the weather, which proved to be frustratingly mild. Afterward, cold tests on equipment and personnel were conducted in the cold chamber at Eglin Air Force Base in Florida.[77]

As American nuclear policy came to be centered more and more on the Air Force in 1949, the Technical Training Group at Sandia found itself inundated with SAC assembly organizations, which arrived at the base at the rate of one a month. General LeMay and SAC were eager to deploy these teams to air bases as quickly as possible, allowing only 12 weeks for team training and operational instruction. AFSWP complained of the "high pressure training schedule," which was hampered additionally by a shortage of equipment and training facilities. To ease the space problem, AFSWP erected a number of classrooms. The limited training time also raised doubts with the staff of the 8460th about the level of expertise and qualifications of SAC's *12-week wonders* when they left Sandia. To insure the highest standards of performance, technical knowledge, and operational readiness, Dorland established a proficiency board made up of experts from experienced assembly teams to pass on the functional skills of each unit prior to deployment. By mid-year, the length of Sandia's bomb assembly training course was cut to two months, with a fundamental course in electronics moved to Keesler Air Force Base, Mississippi, for Air Force personnel and to Treasure Island for the Navy personnel.[78]

One technical development, a result of switching to the production of the smaller Mark IV weapon, changed the training program for weaponeers.[79] With the bulky Mark III bomb, a weaponeer was needed on all flights to monitor the Flight Test Box, an instrument that tested the circuitry of bomb components during flight. General Montague recognized the possibilities of replacing the complicated and cumbersome Flight Test Box with a simple "go/no go" indicator. By the fall of 1949, research and development teams from AFSWP, the newly-established Sandia Laboratory, and the AEC had developed a simplified device known as an In-Flight Monitor. The new instrument permitted the bomb commander to assume the duties of the in-flight weaponeer, and the weaponeer training course was dropped from the AFSWP curriculum in the spring of 1950.[80]

The impact of the Air Force's elevated position in nuclear weapons was demonstrated by the growth in assembly teams in 1949. The year before, the Air Force had two Special Weapons Units; at the end of 1949, there were 12 operational units and three more in training. By comparison, the Army remained static at four, and the Navy added one unit in 1949, bringing its total to three. In addition, the preponderance of nuclear bomb commanders and weaponeers trained in 1949 were from the Air Force.[81]

A NEW AFSWP HEADQUARTERS

As AFSWP increased its field activities at Sandia Base, headquarters operations also expanded. AFSWP's offices on the second floor of the B Ring at the Pentagon had filled up early in 1949. The film library and photographic branch of the Radiological Defense Division had spilled into rooms on D Ring on the first floor. Security for the spread-out offices was, as AFSWP staff agreed, unsatisfactory. Therefore room for expansion was sought.

On August 29, 1949, AFSWP moved into new offices in the Pentagon. The space for the agency on Corridor Six of the first floor of B Ring combined AFSWP's headquarters staff and the photographic collection. The new space required considerable reconstruction, especially from the standpoint of security. The location lacked outside walls and windows and was illuminated only by artificial light. The outer walls were masonry construction from floor to ceiling, pierced only by a guarded single doorway for entrance and exit. A vault housing records from CROSSROADS was constructed of 8-inch brick; other vaults, which stored both film and records, were of 6-inch tile covered on the outside with an inch of plaster. A darkroom was added for photographic work. AFSWP designed a heavily soundproofed conference room, which was located next to the reception area, constructed with double soundproof walls and a double door. Steel burglar stops were installed in all the ceiling ducts. In all, AFSWP's new offices occupied more than 18,000 square feet; sufficient, it was decided, for current headquarters needs.[82]

A GREENHOUSE FOR NUCLEAR WEAPONS EFFECTS

On July 11, 1949, Admiral Tom B. Hill, Parson's replacement as Deputy Chief of AFSWP and Navy member of the MLC, asked that AFSWP assume responsibility for a program to study military effects of atomic weapons. Hill's request was an ideal task for the Joint Service unit to take on, and Nichols readily accepted. Hill had compiled a distinguished record under Nimitz in the Pacific during World War II. He sufficiently impressed Nimitz that the admiral invited him aboard the *USS Missouri* to be part of the Japanese surrender in Tokyo Bay on September 2, 1945. Eight months later, Hill took command of the *Missouri*, where he remained until becoming the Director of Atomic Defense in the Office of the Chief of Naval Operations in April 1947 and the Assistant to the Deputy Chief of AFSWP a month later. Two years later he became a Deputy Chief when Admiral Parsons retired.[83]

Hill believed that it was critical for the Armed Services to assemble as much information as possible regarding the effects of nuclear weapons from underwater, underground, and atmospheric tests. Other types of effects demanding study, he said, were blast, thermal radiation on structures and individuals, and ionizing radiation. He hoped that the studies would help refine the criteria used by the Armed Services in determining the effectiveness of atomic weapons against all types of targets. The Army and Navy immediately initiated programs under AFSWP's Development Division to carry through on Hill's request. The Air Force declined to join the program, citing the need for additional authorization. Nevertheless, by the end of 1949, the Development Division had gathered materials on underwater effects, including a study of base surge phenomena, and had contracted with the Naval Ordnance Laboratory to conduct a series of underwater explosions to gather additional data. AFSWP instituted a similar program with the Corps of Engineers on the effects of underground explosions, which also included a study of the possibility of a base surge emanating from that type of blast, and another with the U.S. Weather Bureau to evaluate the effects of weather on atomic explosions.[84]

Another result of Hill's order to gather more data on weapons effects was a handbook drafted in 1949 to explain unclassified areas of weapons effects information and to contribute to military training and civil defense planning. Written under the auspices of the Weapons Effects Classification Board, under Chairman Norris E. Bradbury, the director of the Los Alamos Scientific Laboratory, the volume was prepared jointly by the AEC and the DoD. This draft manuscript on the nature of weapons effects, published in 1950 as *The Effects of Atomic Weapons*, was the first in a series of important public documents explaining the technical and scientific phenomena of atomic weapons to the public, written by Dr. Samuel Glasstone and retitled *The Effects of Nuclear Weapons* (1957). Glasstone's pioneering works, partly based on an earlier effects manual entitled the "Smythe Report," described the same airblast, ground and water shock, thermal radiation, and nuclear radiation phenomena that Hill had initially outlined in his 1949 letter.[85]

RADIOLOGICAL WARFARE

Another effect of nuclear weapons that became part of AFSWP's mission was the potentiality of radiological warfare, which, like the weapons effects handbook, was an outgrowth of the investigations of AFSWP's Technical Branch of the Radiological Defense Division. The National Military Establishment and the AEC had established the Joint Panel on Radiological Warfare in late 1948, but the group did not begin work until the next year. The joint panel asked that the military develop an "...intensive study [of] the possible operational uses and military worth..." of radiological warfare, including a program of field testing. The panel asked that particular attention be given to Pa-233 (Protactinium 233) "...since this material is the most promising radiological warfare (RW) agent in the light of information presently available." Representatives from the Air Force, Army Chemical Corps, AEC, and AFSWP selected a site in the Dugway-Wendover, Utah, area where chemical, biological, and radiological agents and weapons might be field tested. The first contamination experiments were held in the late fall of 1949, using a 2,000-pound bomb to scatter radioactive Ta-182 (Tantalum). Satisfied with the first experiments, the JCS requested that the Technical Division continue its investigations so that an evaluation of radiological warfare could be completed by 1954.[86]

A MONOPOLY OF NONE

In July 1949, President Truman told a group of Congressional leaders that he no longer believed international control of atomic energy was possible. "Since we can't obtain international control," he announced, "we must be strongest in atomic weapons." Later events would prove his belief. The President soon authorized an increased weapon production program. To avoid the impression that the Soviet detonation had an impact on American decisions, Truman couched the expansion decision simply as part of the country's previous plans and capabilities. Within the year, atomic weapons came to occupy the focal point of U.S. military planning. The limited number of atomic bombs of World War II vintage became - as a result of the technological advances learned at SANDSTONE and expanded nuclear processing and production capabilities - the basic source of America's power. "The atomic strategy had, de facto, been further endorsed," according to two historians of nuclear strategy. Atomic weapons were "...economical, efficient, intimidating, and, above all, more available than ever."[87]

On September 20, 1949, the CIA completed a top-secret evaluation on the "Status of Atomic Warfare in the USSR." The Soviet Union's atomic energy program, the memorandum noted, was "...being vigorously pursued under a top priority." Nonetheless, the Joint Atomic Energy Intelligence Committee, comprised of technical experts from the AEC, CIA, State Department, and representatives from the military Services, estimated "...that the earliest possible date by which the USSR might be expected to produce an atomic bomb is mid-1950 and the most probable date is mid-1953." Three days later, on September 23, President Truman announced that "...within recent weeks an atomic explosion occurred in the USSR."[88]

Not only was the September estimate put forward by the CIA badly mistaken, it was obsolete even as it was being written. In fact, the September memo was a rehash of a series of annual estimates on Soviet nuclear weapons capability. CIA Director, Admiral Roscoe H. Hillenkoeter, had sent a similar memo to President Truman in July 1948 and again a year later, less than two months before the Soviet test.[89]

The intelligence estimates were based more on a consensus of official Washington thinking than on actual knowledge. Groves had estimated the Soviets would take 20 years; the consensus in the scientific community had been five years, or sometime in 1950; some had thought that the Russians would never solve the technical and industrial problems. So firmly did top military and civilian officials believe that the Russians were years behind the United States that, when the AFOAT-1 planes picked up radioactivity in their air filters, the President questioned the possibility of a Russian atomic bomb. If it was a bomb, he told Lilienthal, it was the product of German scientists. The new Secretary of Defense, Louis A. Johnson, believed that a Soviet reactor had exploded. Before Truman made the public announcement, he asked Lilienthal and others analyzing the fallout data to sign a statement that they indeed believed the Soviets had fired a bomb.[90] The U.S. nuclear monopoly had lasted just four years!

RUSSIAN PROGRESS

As the sun rose over the steppes of Kazakhstan, in the Soviet Union, on the morning of August 29, 1949, the country detonated its first atomic weapon.[91] Preparations for the detonation at this site, locally known as Semipalatinsk-21, had begun two years previously; a 30-meter tower had been erected and a workshop had been constructed. Aided by nuclear data – details of the plutonium implosion bomb – provided by Klaus Fuchs, the

Russian nuclear program was accelerated by American progress. Much of the Soviet research, headed by Igor Kurchatov and later, Andrei Sakharov, was initially conducted at secret facilities on the outskirts of Moscow; i.e., Laboratory No. 2, and later at Arzamas-16, approximately 450 miles northeast of Moscow. Arzamas-16 was known as the "archipelago" or center of atomic institutes in Russia and was soon dubbed "Los Arzamas" by American military and civilian nuclear researchers. The tower detonation on August 29, 1949 in Kazakhstan, about 165 kilometers west/southwest of the city of Semipalatinsk, proved that the Soviet Union possessed the capability to produce, assemble, and detonate a nuclear device.

JOE 1: The first Soviet nuclear test, detonated on August 29, 1949.

THE THERMONUCLEAR OPTION

Truman's downplaying of the effect of Joe 1 on the weapons expansion program hid another undercurrent pushing the technology of nuclear weapons: a thermonuclear bomb called the "Super." In 1946, a group of scientists at Los Alamos had discussed the theoretical feasibility of a hydrogen bomb. An H-bomb might be built in one or two years, they predicted. The scientists studied a detailed design of such a weapon, which they said was, "...on the whole, workable." By the following year, however, scientific advice was far less optimistic. In December 1947, Los Alamos reported to General McCormick, the Commission's Director of Military Application, that "...our progress to date in this field has been so limited that it will be many years before we develop the thermonuclear reaction for weapons purposes." The scientists also warned McCormack that any nation that could develop a "...bigger and better fission bomb than we have yet developed... will also be able to do at least as well as we have done on the thermonuclear project." The scientists, backed by Senator Brien McMahon, chairman of the Joint Committee on Atomic Energy, envisioned a return to a Manhattan Project drive to produce the new weapon. If the government wanted the Super, "...we had better get more brains to work."[92]

Many scientists soon turned cool to the prospects of a thermonuclear bomb. On August 18, 1948, from his position as Director of the Institute for Advanced Studies in Princeton, New Jersey, Dr. Oppenheimer submitted a draft report on long-range military objectives in atomic energy to Lilienthal, in which he counseled against developing the Super, "...in view of the magnitude and complexity of the problem, the special personnel requirements, and the uncertainties as to the characteristics of a feasible weapon." He also cited the "...extraordinarily difficult problems" of delivery, cryogeny, and tritium production as reasons to rely on "boosting" a fission weapon in the short term.[93]

The JCS, however, pressed for the development of a thermonuclear weapon. In early 1949, they stressed the importance of military uses of a hydrogen bomb, especially if costs were reasonable and its further development did not impair the production of other atomic weapons. With the success of Joe 1, the military stepped up its interest in the Super. In testifying before the Joint Committee on Atomic Energy in October, General Omar Bradley urged Congress to support a major effort to develop thermonuclear weapons. At the same time, two prominent scientists, Enrico Fermi and Isidor I. Rabi, strongly recommended that the United States not develop the Super on ethical grounds if the Soviets promised not to work on it either. The AEC's General Advisory Committee was even more definite. It opposed the Super even if the Russians proceeded with its development.[94]

Still the administration was undecided. Truman appointed a special committee consisting of Lilienthal from the AEC, Johnson from DoD, and Secretary of State Dean Acheson to review the issue. The pressure to build a hydrogen bomb focused the debate between those who developed weapons and those who would use them. On one side stood Edward Teller and other scientists at Los Alamos, who relished the scientific elegance of creating a new weapon and their military allies in the Pentagon who viewed the Super as the ultimate, and inexpensive, weapon in the race to stay ahead of the Soviet Union. The other side also favored nuclear weapons but preferred improving atomic bombs to developing thermonuclear weapons. Led by Oppenheimer, this group thought that the military wanted larger weapons to compensate for having such poor aim in bombing targets. The second group supported smaller atomic weapons that used less fissionable material so that the stockpile might be expanded even before the new nuclear production facilities began operating. Lilienthal also opposed the Super; appalled by the weapon's potentially awesome power and the arms race it would breed. This second group also had doubts as to the Super's military usefulness. Where might such a weapon be used, they wondered? They were horrified with its possible use on cities and large civilian populations. Atomic bombs were more practical, they argued, as they could be used against strictly military targets.[95]

By the end of 1949, the National Security Council and the military, led by Secretary of Defense Louis Johnson, had recommended that Truman direct the development of a super bomb. On January 31, 1950, Truman took the first step, directing the AEC to determine the feasibility of a thermonuclear reaction. Los Alamos took the lead, estimating that it could test the concept within two years if enough tritium was available. The laboratory asked that one of the production reactors at Hanford be converted to tritium production to meet this schedule. On June 8, the President approved the tritium production program. While problems regarding the production rate of Tritium and Lithium-6 continued to surface and more time was needed to develop a fusion weapon, the nation was firmly set on the thermonuclear path. The invasion of South Korea by Communist armies from North Korea two weeks later served to confirm Truman's decision.[96]

THE KOREAN INVASION

Two events in the first half of 1950 had an impact on the country's thermonuclear program: Korea and the Loper Memorandum. Of the two, Korea is far better known. North Korea's invasion of the southern half of the peninsula in June caused officials at the AEC and the MLC to review plans for GREENHOUSE, a weapon test series in the Pacific planned for the spring of 1951. There were rumblings from Washington that the test should be cancelled. The day after Truman named Gordon Dean chairman of the AEC, Robert LeBaron, head of the MLC, phoned to tell the new chairman that the military, including members of the MLC, wanted to withdraw from or cancel GREENHOUSE outright. The JCS wanted to free the Navy vessels committed to those tests for a blockade of North Korea.[97]

Dean, however, unlike his predecessor Lilienthal, was an outspoken proponent of nuclear weapons, including the Super, and not inclined to delay. His first decision as chairman after war broke out had been to transfer non-nuclear weapons components to the United Kingdom. His views on GREENHOUSE were equally firm. Pushing aside LeBaron's concerns of military opposition, Dean wrote in his diary that "the test *must go now*." For the next several months he fought to ensure that Joint Task Force 3, headed by Air Force General Elwood R. Quesada, would not be raided. Dean also lobbied for the establishment of a continental test site and was able to win Deputy Secretary of Defense Stephen T. Early over to both positions. By September, the Joint Chiefs had retreated, deciding that the military could indeed spare the resources for GREENHOUSE the following spring.[98]

THE LOPER MEMORANDUM

Before the Korean conflict erupted, the military drew on other public fears to increase the pace of nuclear weapons testing. Revelations of the extent of information passed to the Russians by accused spy Klaus Fuchs gave rise to the belief that the Soviets could not have achieved their nuclear success without Fuchs' perfidy. In truth, no one really knew how important Fuchs was to the Soviet weapons program. Early in 1950, LeBaron had asked AFSWP chief General Nichols and Brigadier General Herbert B. Loper, another member of the MLC, to estimate the damage done by Fuchs' disclosures. Their rather alarming and sensational conclusion was that the Soviets might be much further advanced in nuclear weaponry than Americans believed. "The USSR stockpile and current production capacity," the report stated, might be "equal or actually superior to our own, both as to yields and numbers." Moreover, they concluded gloomily, the Russians might even have a thermonuclear weapon in production. The Nichols/Loper report moved up the command chain to the desk of Secretary of Defense Johnson, the Joint Chiefs, and the President. After digesting the report, the military wanted a crash program to develop a super bomb, even if it meant cutting back on the existing atomic bomb program.[99]

Revelations of Fuchs' spying activities reverberated at AFSWP. There was a distinct possibility that Fuchs had betrayed the nature of the radar fuzing systems used in atomic weapons, thereby allowing the Soviets to jam and compromise radar systems. In view of this possible threat, AFSWP immediately began developing a more accurate barometric fuze than those used for the Mark I and III bombs. By the spring of 1952, the new fuze was ready to be included in the stockpile.[100]

Through the winter of 1950 the administration debated the fate of the Super. Finally, in late February, with a push from the Pentagon, the special committee of Acheson, Johnson, and Henry Smyth, who replaced Lilienthal as the AEC representative, advised Truman to prepare for production of hydrogen bombs. Truman, accepting recommendations of his advisors, approved the thermonuclear program on March 10 "…as a matter of the highest urgency." GREENHOUSE, scheduled for the following year, would test the thermonuclear theories being developed at Los Alamos by Teller and Stanislaw M. Ulam.[101]

OPERATION GREENHOUSE

Even as the SANDSTONE operation was being completed in the summer of 1948, planning had begun at Los Alamos for another nuclear test series scheduled for the Pacific Proving Ground in 1951. Los Alamos had formed J Division in July 1948 to design and conduct a test of a new concept growing out of SANDSTONE, to "boost" the efficiency of the nuclear explosion with a heavy isotope of hydrogen, deuterium. Deuterium, the scientists believed, would allow the explosion to achieve higher temperatures than previously obtained and, if successful, would provide the "trigger" for a thermonuclear reaction. Construction for the test series, code-named Operation GREENHOUSE, had begun on Enewetak in 1949, before Joe 1. An Army Engineer Construction Battalion and a civilian contractor had cleared sites on several test islands and had begun building a large plant for liquefying deuterium and buildings to test nuclear blast effects. Although Joe 1 hastened the movement of Mark IVs into the stockpile, it had little effect on the schedule for GREENHOUSE.[102]

The focus on the GREENHOUSE operation was weapons development, not weapons effects, and, as a result, AFSWP assumed a secondary role to Los Alamos scientists, especially those like Edward Teller who were eager to prove the theoretical feasibility of a fusion weapon. By mid-1950, Teller and his colleagues had looked at a system combining a deuterium-tritium booster with the core developed at SANDSTONE. But no one knew if the fission reaction would produce a fusion reaction. Teller's idea was to see if the fission reaction would ignite a small amount of deuterium and tritium in an adjoining chamber. As one scientist commented, "using a huge atomic bomb to ignite the little vial of deuterium and tritium was like using a blast furnace to light a match."[103]

Operation GREENHOUSE, similar to the SANDSTONE tests, was held at Enewetak. AFSWP's responsibility was limited to the blast effects on a number of military and civilian buildings. In all, AFSWP had six men at the tests, two to run the structures program and four handling radiation safety duties. Weapon development and science took front stage. Two shots, GEORGE and ITEM, would verify the thermonuclear concepts. GEORGE, fired on May 9, 1951, proved that the blast furnace worked. A fission bomb ignited the deuterium and tritium, which, in turn, contributed to the size of the blast. Two weeks later, ITEM proved that a small amount of tritium could dramatically boost the yield of fission weapons. While neither of the devices were weapons, the tests did establish the feasibility of fusion weapons but complicated planning for the country's expansion of its nuclear production capacity. Increased tritium production could be achieved only at the expense of plutonium production at the existing plants. Solving the hydrogen bomb mystery served only to heighten the dilemma of how to increase the stockpile before the new production facilities came on stream. By the first of January, 1951, there were approximately 300 atomic weapons in the stockpile.[104]

AFSWP AND CONTINENTAL TESTING

The threat to American security posed by the North Korean invasion renewed interest in establishing a continental test site and revived AFSWP's 1949 Project

Aerial view of storage area, aircraft ramp, and runway on Enewetak Island, Enewetak Atoll, during Operation GREENHOUSE, 1951.

Nutmeg report. The AEC and military looked at six possible sites before choosing an area called Frenchman Flat in the Nevada desert on the Las Vegas Bombing and Gunnery Range. By the end of 1950, the Air Force had turned over a large area to the AEC for testing atomic weapons. Originally called Site Mercury, the area would later be called the Nevada Proving Grounds and finally the Nevada Test Site (NTS). The name Mercury has been retained as the housing area, just outside the test range. Before the end of January 1951, Operation RANGER, the first series of atomic tests within the continental United States, was under way.[105]

RANGER constituted an ideal opportunity for increased AFSWP participation in a weapon test. But that did not happen. Los Alamos designed the RANGER series of tests to gather additional data for improving on the weapon design tested at GREENHOUSE in the spring of 1951. Since no weapon effects tests occurred, there was no AFSWP test group at RANGER, and only six men comprised the AFSWP contingent that did attend. Those men were placed in the Scientific Tests Section under the supervision of Los Alamos scientists and other AEC officials. Since RANGER tested new weapon designs, Los Alamos scientists, not AFSWP personnel, assembled the nuclear devices. Nonetheless, the test devices were dropped from Air Force planes and the military had a significant presence at RANGER. Over 350 servicemen participated, mostly in Air Force weapons delivery, weather, and cloud sampling programs.[106]

FIELD COMMAND

The contingent of officers, enlisted men, and scientists at *Camp Desert Rock,* located approximately 65 miles from Las Vegas, just outside the southern boundary of the Nevada Proving Grounds, formed the precursor of AFSWP's Field Command presence at Sandia Base. Field Command, AFSWP was officially designated by General Order No. 4, April 28, 1951, and its first Commander, General Robert F. Montague, was assigned responsibility for exercising command jurisdiction over and supervision of activities at Sandia Base and tenant organizations of AFSWP.

REVIEWING AFSWP'S MISSION

AFSWP's role in the planning for RANGER and for the upcoming test series in 1951 and 1952 emphasized a need for the agency to re-examine its function in the development of nuclear weapons. Early in 1951, General Herbert B. Loper, who had served as the Army representative to the MLC since November 1949, replaced Nichols as chief of AFSWP. Loper, according to Nichols, was "...a very capable engineer, easygoing but firm, and well liked by his associates." While Loper had worked with Nichols in drafting the memorandum about Fuchs and Soviet progress on nuclear weapons development, he had not been associated with Groves or part of the early development of AFSWP. Loper had been a deputy to General Omar N. Bradley when Bradley was chairman of the Joint Chiefs of Staff. In 1950 Loper had helped persuade policy makers not to use atomic weapons in Korea, opposing the views of General Douglas McArthur. There were too few weapons in the stockpile to be decisive, he had argued. Less than a year later, as the new chief of AFSWP, he decided that it was time to review and clarify the mission of the agency he now headed.[107]

Shot GEORGE, part of Operation GREENHOUSE at Enewetak Atoll, May 1951.

Since the establishment of AFSWP in 1947, Loper wrote to the Chiefs of the three Armed Services, a number of events had prompted him to re-examine AFSWP's mission. He explained that the responsibilities of the Department of Defense with respect to the operation of the stockpile had greatly expanded. So, too, had the level of military participation in test planning and evaluation of weapons effects. As a result, he believed that AFSWP had assumed new responsibilities while altering the scope of others. Therefore, Loper wrote, he had drafted a new mission statement and outline of AFSWP's responsibilities for the Joint Chiefs' review.[108]

Within six weeks, the Joint Chiefs had approved Loper's draft with only a few changes. Boiled down to the salient

Major General Herbert B. Loper, Chief AFSWP, 1951-1953.

points, AFSWP's major responsibilities, according to Loper and the Joint Chiefs, were providing specialized training and technical services, coordinating storage and surveillance of the nuclear stockpile with the AEC, planning continental and overseas weapons tests with other agencies, and determining and evaluating weapon effects from those tests. Under Loper's plan, AFSWP would continue its role in weapon development, procurement, and assembly. Loper recognized the increasing activities in the field of atomic energy assumed by staff divisions and subordinate agencies in the Departments of the Army, Navy, and Air Force. AFSWP would play a coordinating role under Loper's plan, an interdepartmental, rather than joint, agency, "...utilizing established agencies of the Armed Forces to carry out programs. Existing organizational structures will not be duplicated, nor will additional activities be established." The new directive accurately reflected AFSWP's central role in the country's expanding nuclear program.[109]

A TIME OF TESTING

Reveille blared over the loudspeakers at 2:00 am on November 1, 1951, as several sleepy-eyed officers from AFSWP dragged themselves from their tents at *Camp Desert Rock*. These AFSWP test participants were part of Operation BUSTER-JANGLE, the first nuclear combat training exercise conducted by the Armed Services. For several days the officers had conducted a series of orientation training activities for nearly 2,800 troops, the largest group of servicemen ever assembled to witness a nuclear test in the continental United States. AFSWP instructors used films and lectures developed at Sandia Base in Albuquerque to explain the characteristics of a nuclear detonation and the procedures to follow during the test, including a rehearsal of shot day activities. In the cold morning air, the men ate breakfast and trudged over to a long line of waiting trucks which would convey them from *Desert Rock* to an observation point overlooking Yucca Flat.[110]

Before dawn, the troops arrived at the observation point, some seven miles from ground zero. The AFSWP officers conducted a final pre-shot orientation. A minute before the blast, the order came over a loudspeaker for the observers to sit on the ground and face south, with their backs toward ground zero. The countdown continued, then came the announcement, "Bomb Away." Just after dawn, at 7:30, the men saw the sharp silhouettes of their huddled forms and helmets neatly outlined by the initial flash of white light from the blast. About 30 seconds later, when the light had dimmed, the AFSWP instructors directed the soldiers to turn and view the atomic fireball and billowing cloud from Shot DOG. The roar and the shock waves produced by the explosion swept over the troops. One battle-hardened veteran paratrooper, known mostly for his exquisite profanity, simply said, "It's extraordinary!"[111]

The participation of large numbers of troops at a nuclear test demonstrated the changing missions and responsibilities of the U.S. military as its leaders wrestled with the questions raised by the specter of atomic warfare. AFSWP was at the heart of these changes. Shifts in international politics, the growth of the atomic weapon stockpile, the marked increase in numbers of atomic weapon assembly organizations, and increased activity by all the Armed Services in the atomic weapons field forced AFSWP to review and clarify its own mission between 1948 and 1952. AFSWP's primary mission of bomb assembly training grew less important than inspecting the nuclear stockpile, preparing plans and budgets for military activities at atomic tests, providing technical and logistical services, and coordinating the study of military effects of atomic weapons. The increased military participation in test planning and quantification of weapons effects - culminating with the large joint military exercise at Shot DOG on November 1, 1951 - sharply illustrated the impact of events on AFSWP's operations in the early years of the Cold War.[112]

OPERATION BUSTER-JANGLE

Although its participation at RANGER had been limited, AFSWP's site studies had been critical to the decision to place the continental proving ground in Nevada. In addition, AFSWP's work became central to the planning of a second

Aerial photo of *Camp Desert Rock* showing rows of tents and Quonset huts, April 21, 1952.

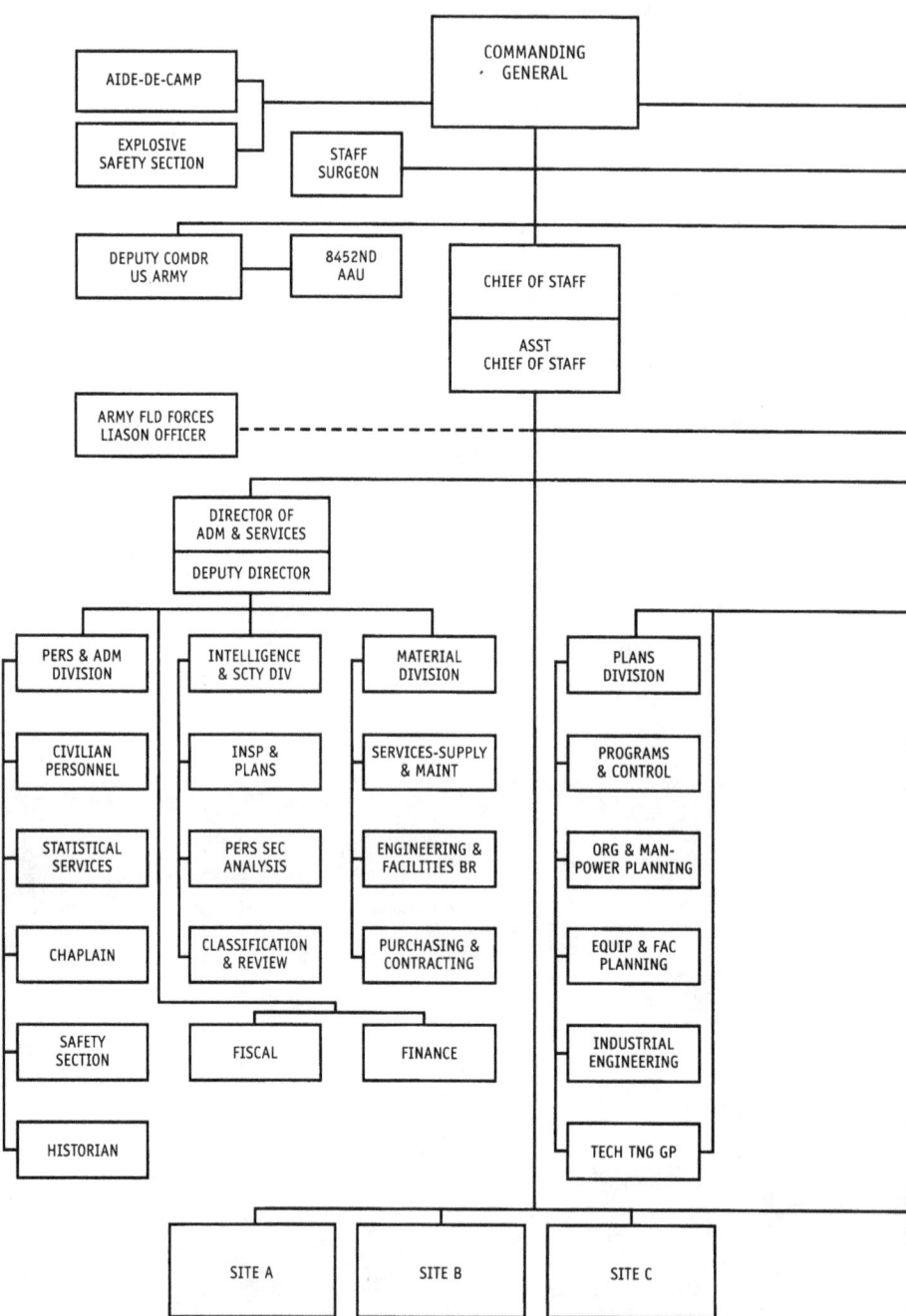

Field Command Organization Chart, 1952.

The Military's Role in Nuclear Matters, 1949 to 1952

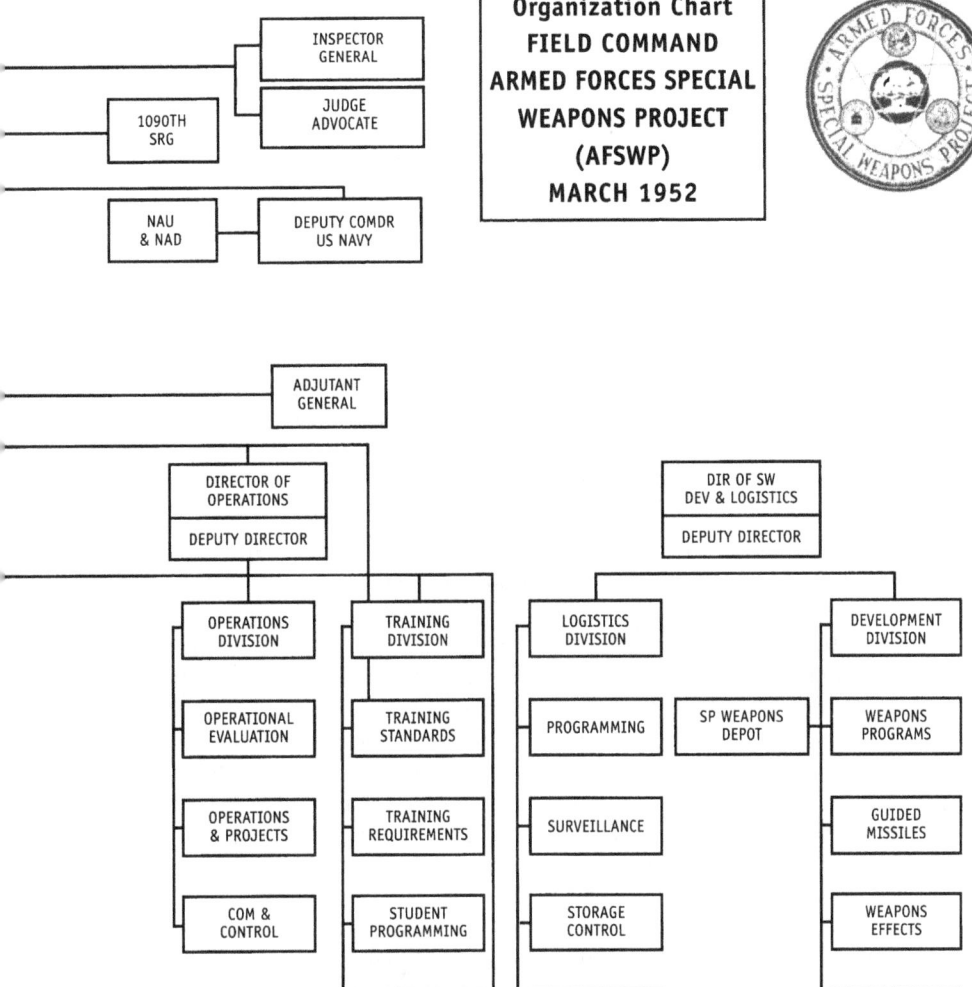

series of tests scheduled in the fall of 1951. In 1950, AFSWP and the AEC had selected a site on Amchitka Island in the Aleutian chain west of Alaska for a planned series of tests code named Operation WINDSTORM. For the test, AFSWP planned to fire two 20-kiloton devices, one at ground level, the second beneath the surface. At the end of November 1950, President Truman had endorsed those plans. At that point AFSWP asked the Army, Navy, and Air Force to submit proposals for the projects they wished to conduct at WINDSTORM. High on the Armed Services' list of programs was an examination of the effects and possible military value of an underground detonation. Another objective of the proposed series was to determine the effects of surface detonation. The AFSWP Research and Development Board weighed these proposals along with those submitted for another test series, Operation BUSTER, also planned for the fall of 1951. After re-reviewing the geology at Amchitka, AFSWP realized that prospects for obtaining useful data were not as good as once believed. Therefore, AFSWP recommended that the WINDSTORM test be held in Nevada rather than Amchitka and be made part of the BUSTER operation. The AEC agreed to AFSWP's recommendation. Subsequently, WINDSTORM was renamed Operation JANGLE and the two test series were to be conducted as consecutive phases in one series renamed BUSTER-JANGLE. The weapons effects test in the series would consist of one 20-kiloton airdrop and two 1-kiloton surface shots.[113]

Operation BUSTER-JANGLE demonstrated how complex nuclear weapons testing had become. In February of 1951, AFSWP had gone to the Joint Chiefs with an Army plan for the participation of troops in a combat training exercise at BUSTER. More than 150 different military units and armored battalions, paratroopers, transportation companies, engineers, and a veterinary detachment among others based from Washington, DC, to Chunchon, Korea, would participate. AFSWP did the planning and budgeting to pull the intricate operation together. BUSTER-JANGLE consisted of a number of weapon effects experiments, studying the physical results of blast and thermal radiation as related to the particular interests of the Armed Services, the Federal Civil Defense Administration, and the U.S. Public Health Service. For AFSWP, the test series provided a splendid opportunity to train new radiation monitors to augment its pool of experienced men.[114]

Operation BUSTER-JANGLE was an outgrowth of the increasing importance of atomic weapons in shaping U.S. defense policy. Military planners realized that atomic bombs would radically alter battlefield conditions. They wondered how troops would react to such powerful explosions. One historical reference they had was the behavior of Union troops in 1864, at the siege of Petersburg, Virginia during the Civil War. At Petersburg, Union sappers (Pennsylvania coal miners) mined a tunnel to the Confederate breastworks and planted tens of thousands of pounds of explosives. The following detonation opened a huge gap in the rebel fortifications. Rather than rush into the gap and seize the city, however, Union soldiers stood in wonder and awe of the explosion and found themselves completely defenseless as they attempted to scramble up the loose soil on the far side of the crater; the opportunity for advancement was lost. Perhaps, the commanders at NTS thought, atomic blasts would produce the same immobility.

The Army developed a war game scenario for BUSTER-JANGLE to evaluate troops on a nuclear battlefield. In this exercise, two mythical enemy armies had invaded the northwest coast of the United States, sending the U.S. forces retreating to the southeast. The enemy had driven the U.S. Sixth Army back to a line anchored by Los Angeles on one end and the Nevada desert on the other. In Nevada, the enemy had established strong defensive positions, supposedly impervious to a counterattack with conventional weapons. To gain the offensive, the American forces would use an atomic bomb dropped from a B-29, labeled Shot DOG, then advance to capture the enemy's positions.[115]

To conduct the war game, the military sent nearly 3,000 troops, mainly drawn from the Sixth U.S. Army based at the Presidio in San Francisco, to a hastily constructed encampment called *Camp Desert Rock*. The purpose of bringing troops to the test was to train soldiers in the tactical use of atomic weapons and to observe the reactions of soldiers to a nuclear detonation. At the same time, the men would be instructed in radiation protection. The Armed Services also wished to gather additional information on the effects of a blast on animals, field fortifications, and military equipment.[116]

While AFSWP had occupied a central role in the planning and coordinating stages of BUSTER-JANGLE, its role at the test was relatively small and largely advisory. The most prominent was a group of three officers who were assigned to *Camp Desert Rock* and provided technical assistance and radiological safety advice to the Army troops participating in Shot DOG. Before the shot, the group briefed observers and troops on nuclear weapons and their effects. Within an hour after the detonation, at least one AFSWP officer with a radiation monitor led the combat teams toward ground zero to inspect damage to animals, equipment, and fortifications. The group later assisted other military evaluation teams in assessing data and preparing weapon effects reports. In all, a total of eight AFSWP personnel participated in BUSTER-JANGLE, five of whom received radiation doses between one and three roentgens during their participation at the tests. The Army was pleased with the fact that none of the film badges worn by Desert Rock combat or support troops read above 0.225 roentgen, "...well beneath the militarily accepted limits," and far below the 3.9 roentgen limit established by the AEC.[117]

Although most of the *Desert Rock* troops departed after DOG, the Army requested that other units be allowed to witness two of the JANGLE shots: SUGAR, a surface blast, and UNCLE, an underground detonation. The AEC reluctantly agreed. The two JANGLE shots took place during the last two weeks of No-

SSgt. T.B. Davis and Cpl. J.E. Bell check B-29 aircraft for radioactivity after its return from "hot" area during CHARLIE event during Operation BUSTER-JANGLE, October 31, 1951.

vember 1951. Both had a yield of 1.2 kilotons, relatively small detonations when compared to the 21-kiloton DOG shot, but radiation levels from the ground shots proved to be much higher that those from an air-dropped weapon. The troops participating in the remaining JANGLE series observed the shots from a distance and toured the forward areas in buses. They received even less radiation than the shot DOG participants.[118]

The military's satisfaction with the results of BUSTER-JANGLE led the Joint Chiefs to push for continued weapons effects tests in Operation SNAPPER planned for the spring of 1952. The AEC and Los Alamos scientists viewed effects testing as a hindrance to weapons development, but the MLC strongly argued that nuclear tactics depended on a clear understanding of blast pressure data and the proper heights for air bursts. On January 2, 1952, the AEC and Joint Chiefs agreed on the urgent need for an air blast effects test. Loper and the AEC test organization worked out the details a week later in Los Alamos. To include the military participation, the series was renamed Operation TUMBLER-SNAPPER.[119]

The tests in the spring of 1952 marked an increased role in radiation monitoring at NTS. Los Alamos wanted to surrender its responsibility for radiation safety at the test site and the Department of Defense quickly offered to assume that role. The AFSWP headed that effort, under James B. Hartgering, a Medical Corps officer on the AFSWP staff. Hartgering planned the radiation safety monitoring programs for TUMBLER-SNAPPER and remained as an advisor after an Air Force officer was chosen to head the radiological safety group.[120]

Radiation safety took on increased importance with the reopening of *Camp Desert Rock* and the development of AFSWP's plans to place combat troops some 7,000 yards from ground zero. Once more military and scientific views clashed. The AEC, which thought seven miles was close enough, emphasized that something might go amiss with an air drop, such as an error in flight path or bomb release. Air Force Brigadier General Alvin R. Luedecke, a Deputy Chief of AFSWP, wrote the Commission that "...in the interest of indoctrination of ground troops to an extent which would be of value in readying them for the actual use of atomic weapons," the rules had to be revised. Troops should also be allowed to "...maneuver in the vicinity of ground zero as soon as practicable after the explosion." To Luedecke, "a safe but tactically sound distance" was 7,000 yards. In the end, the AEC gave in. If the Department of Defense, "...after review of the hazards involved, still feel that a military requirement justifies the maneuver, the Commission would enter no objection to stationing troops at not less that 7,000 yards from ground zero."[121]

The TUMBLER-SNAPPER tests were similar to BUSTER-JANGLE. Test CHARLIE, involving an air-dropped device of 31 kilotons fired on April 22, 1952, troops observed from trenches some 7,000 yards south of ground zero. They were asked a battery of questions relating to the psychological reactions to the blast, then advanced toward ground zero, moving within 200 yards of the area. Army paratroopers landed in an area north of ground zero. Radiation readings were relatively low, with readings more than .01 roentgen per hour confined within the immediate area of ground zero.[122]

The second test during TUMBLER-SNAPPER was conducted by the Navy and Marine Corps. DOG, which yielded 19 kilotons, was dropped just over a week later on the morning of May 1. Participants watched from the same trenches overlooking Yucca Flat. A Marine Corps

Front gate of Camp Mercury, later renamed Nevada Test Site.

Provisional Atomic Exercise Unit from Camp Pendleton and Camp Lejeune, the first to participate in a nuclear test, marched toward ground zero until stopped by unexpectedly high levels of radiation. Observers from the Navy took the same psychological survey and accompanied AFSWP monitoring teams during the initial survey of the ground zero area to learn radiological monitoring techniques. But there had been contamination and "...much recovery work was unavoidably delayed." Nonetheless, the military was satisfied with the care it had taken with the *Desert Rock* troops at TUMBLER-SNAPPER and would continue to push for troop participation at nuclear tests.[123]

By the end of 1951, AFSWP's role in atomic testing had evolved to be more active in the planning stages than in actual participation during the tests, an evolution closer to the role anticipated in the Atomic Energy Act than desired by General Groves in 1946.

TRANSITION

Between 1948 and 1952, atomic weapons had become a vital component of America's defense. The advent of the atomic age had a profound impact upon AFSWP, the first military unit established solely to deal with atomic weapons. The Berlin Crisis, the Soviet development of an atomic bomb, the Communist invasion of South Korea, the development and production of the Mark IV bomb, and additional technical advances in nuclear weapons design achieved by the scientists at Los Alamos intensified the basic AFSWP mission as defined in 1946. The Technical Training Group had significantly increased the numbers of classes coming through the program at Sandia Base, both in the training of weapons assembly teams and in courses for bomb commanders. Interservice training exercises between AFSWP and the other Services increased in frequency as AFSWP sought to refine and speed up both forward and rear assembly operations.

The administration's softening on the custody issue, particularly after the retirement of Lilienthal and the invasion of Korea, prompted Truman to increase AFSWP's responsibilities at the weapons storage sites in the United States and to transfer non-nuclear bomb components to the military at bases within the country and abroad and aboard aircraft carriers. Old grumblings by scientists and others at the AEC about military incompetence to handle complex nuclear weapons became muted as the weapons became less complicated, AFSWP technical training and experience expanded, and storage and surveillance costs borne by the AEC grew. The Commission readily recognized that its budget, already stretched to meet the demands for greater production, could be eased somewhat by allowing AFSWP to assume more of the duties relating to the stockpile.

AFSWP's original mission placed it on a Pentagon hot seat from the start. A stepchild of the three Services, AFSWP operated in an unexplored territory organized by the creation of the national military establishment. As interservice rivalries intensified over which Service would gobble up the largest slice of the

Soldiers from *Desert Rock* exercise sitting down, facing air-dropped DOG shot, part of Operation BUSTER-JANGLE, November 1, 1951.

nuclear pie, AFSWP was caught in the middle. Each Service branch wished to have its own capability. Held under the lamp of scrutiny and possible reorganization by the Pentagon, AFSWP was rescued by Forrestal at the Newport Conference in August 1948. Thereafter, the Services passed on more responsibilities, and less and less was heard about AFSWP's dissolution.

By 1952, AFSWP, because of its close relationship to the three Services, the MLC, the AEC, and other Washington agencies, had proved its value and the usefulness of an interservice organization. AFSWP would go forward, as its technical staff prepared for a whole new series of weapon tests during Operation IVY, including the first thermonuclear test.

ENDNOTES

1. William Manchester, *The Glory and the Dream*, (Boston, 1974), p. 441; James T. Patterson, *Grand Expectations*, (New York, 1996), p. 134.
2. Patterson, *Grand Expectations*, p. 134; Manchester, *The Glory and the Dream*, p. 441.
3. Lucius D. Clay, *Decision in Germany*, (New York, 1950), pp. 357-59, 365.
4. *Life*, vol. 24 (April 19, 1948): p. 47.
5. Khrushchev quoted in David Holloway, *Stalin and the Bomb*, (New Haven, 1994), p. 259; Truman quoted in Rhodes, *Dark Sun*, p. 325.
6. Holloway, *Stalin and the Bomb*, p. 260.
7. Clay, *Decision in Germany*, p. 359, 366; Rhodes, *Dark Sun*, pp. 326, 329-30.
8. Clay, *Decision in Germany*, pp. 366-68, 390-91; "The Squeeze on the Corridors," *Newsweek*, vol. 32 (July 26, 1948): pp. 30, 32. See also Robert H. Ferrell, *American Diplomacy*, (New York, 1969), p. 700.
9. "First History of AFSWP, vol. 1," p. 20.
10. "First History of AFSWP, vol. 1," pp. 18-20; *Ibid.*, Chap. 5, Sandia Base, 5.52a.
11. "First History of AFSWP, vol. 1," p. 20.
12. "First History of AFSWP, vol. 1," Chap. 5, Sandia Base, 5.52a-5.52b; "First History of AFSWP, vol. 1," pp. 20-21; author's conversation with Dorland, October 5, 1996, Alexandria, Virginia.
13. "First History of AFSWP, vol. 1," Chap. 5, Sandia Base, 5.52a-5.52b.
14. "First History of AFSWP, vol. 1," pp. 23-24.
15. See Hewlett and Duncan, *Atomic Shield/1947-1952*, pp. 159-60.
16. *Ibid.*, pp. 170-71; Rearden, *The Formative Years*, p. 428.
17. *Ibid.*; "First History of AFSWP, vol. 1," p. 24.
18. Hewlett and Duncan, *Atomic Shield/1947-1952*, p. 171; Rearden, *The Formative Years*, pp. 401-2; Nichols, *The Road to Trinity*, p. 265.
19. Hewlett and Duncan, *Atomic Shield/1947-1952*, p. 160.
20. Clay, *Decision in Germany*, p. 361.
21. Walter Millis, ed., *The Forrestal Diaries*, (New York, 1951), p. 459.
22. Gregg Herken, *The Winning Weapon: The Atomic Bomb and the Cold War, 1945-1950* (New York, 1980), pp. 246-48; Holloway, *Stalin and the Bomb*, pp. 271-72; Millis, *The Forrestal Diaries*, pp. 459-60.
23. Millis, *The Forrestal Diaries*, pp. 462-63.
24. Clay told Joseph Alsop that the bomb prevented the Soviets from invading western Europe. See Noel Francis Parrish, *Behind the Sheltering Bomb* (New York, 1979), p. 250. *New York Times*, July 16, 1948, 1; *Ibid.*, July 17, 1948, 3; *Newsweek*, Vol. 32 (July 26, 1948): 32; Herken, *The Winning Weapon*, p. 259; William R. Harris, *Functions of the Defense Nuclear Agency and its Predecessor Organizations, 1947-1994*, DDR-997-OSD, February 1995, p. 11.
25. Gregg Herken, *Counsels of War*, (New York, 1987), p. 33; Samuel R. Williamson and Steven L. Rearden, *The Origins of U.S. Nuclear Strategy, 1945-1953*, (New York, 1993), p. 88; Truman quoted in Rhodes, *Dark Sun*, p. 326.
26. Nichols, *The Road to Trinity*, p. 259; *Lilienthal Journals*, pp. 302-3.
27. *Lilienthal Journals*, p. 303; Nichols, *The Road to Trinity*, pp. 258, 259.
28. Nichols, *The Road to Trinity*, p. 259; *Lilienthal Journals*, p. 303.
29. Nichols, *The Road to Trinity*, p. 260.
30. *Ibid.*, pp. 260-61.
31. *Ibid.*
32. Rearden, *The Formative Years*, pp. 424, 282, 428-29; Nichols, *The Road to Trinity*, p. 263. Forrestal believed that the American people placed too much value on atomic weapons. He believed atomic bombs were powerful but not decisive. Royall, the Secretary of the Army, argued that nuclear weapons *might* be decisive. Both men agreed, according to Lilienthal, that nuclear weapons "were best and almost the only thing we had that could be used quickly." See the *Lilienthal Journals*, p. 377.

33. *Lilienthal Journals*, p. 374.
34. *Ibid.*, p. 376.
35. Millis, *The Forrestal Diaries*, pp. 460-61; *Lilienthal Journals*, p. 388-89; Rearden, *The Formative Years*, p. 430; Nichols, *The Road to Trinity*, pp. 263-64. Nichols did not attend the meeting.
36. *Lilienthal Journals*, pp. 388-89.
37. *Ibid.*, p. 390; Millis, *The Forrestal Diaries*, p. 461; Rearden, *The Formative Years*, p. 430.
38. *Lilienthal Journals*, pp. 390-91.
39. *Ibid.*, p. 391; Millis, *The Forrestal Diaries*, p. 461.
40. Rearden, *The Formative Years*, pp. 112-13; Millis, *The Forrestal Diaries*, p. 461.
41. Rearden, *The Formative Years*, pp. 112-13; "First History of AFSWP, vol. 1," Chap. 4-Headquarters, 4.2.25; Nichols, *The Road to Trinity*, p. 265.
42. Carpenter quoted in Rearden, *The Formative Years*, p. 113.
43. *Ibid.*, p. 163; "First History of AFSWP, vol. 1," Chap. 5, Sandia Base, 5.54.
44. Neal O. Hines, *Proving Ground*, (Seattle, 1962), pp. 83-87; Hewlett and Duncan, *Atomic Shield/1947-1952*, pp. 163-64; Rhodes, *Dark Sun*, pp. 369-70. As early as November 1946, the Army Air Corps, under a contract with New York University, instituted a program using "constant level" balloons which carried a Sonobuoy and FM transmitter launched from Alamagordo Army Air Field (now Holloman Air Force Base) to detect shock waves from nuclear explosions. The program, code-named *Project Mogul*, used balloons made from neoprene, which degraded in sunlight and fell back to earth. It was one of these balloons, a GAO report stated, that crashed near Roswell, New Mexico, in July 1947 and gave rise to the mysterious "flying saucer" and captured alien stories which persist to the present. See Philip Greenstein, "Radio Transmitting, Receiving and Recording System for Constant Level Balloon," Project Report No. 4, March 31, 1947; *New York Times*, June 14, 1997, 1, 6, and Ibid., June 15, 1997, Arts and Leisure, 38.
45. Williamson and Rearden, *The Origins of U.S. Nuclear Strategy*, p. 108; Rhodes, *Dark Sun*, pp. 320-21.
46. *Ibid.*; "First History of AFSWP, vol. 1," Chap. 5, Sandia Base, 5.54-5.55; Nichols, *The Road to Trinity*, p. 269.
47. "First History of AFSWP, vol. 1," p. 27.
48. *Ibid.*, Chap. 5, Sandia Base, 5.135-5.141.
49. *Ibid.*, 5.62-5.66.
50. *Ibid.*, p. 27; Chap. 5, Sandia Base, 5.55.
51. "First History of AFSWP," Vol. 1, Chap. 5, Sandia Base, 5.56, 5.63-6.64; "First History of AFSWP," Vol. 1," p. 27.
52. Nichols, *The Road to Trinity*, p. 266.
53. "First History of AFSWP," Vol. 1, Chap. 5, Sandia Base, 5.57; "First History of AFSWP," Vol. 1, p. 28.
54. Nichols, *The Road to Trinity*, pp. 266-67.
55. *Ibid.*, pp. 267-68.
56. "First History of AFSWP," Vol. 1, Chap. 5, Sandia Base, 5.58; "First History of AFSWP," Vol. 1, p. 28.
57. "First History of AFSWP," Vol. 1, Chap. 5, Sandia Base, 5.59.
58. *Ibid.*, 5.59-5.60.
59. Rearden, *The Formative Years*, pp. 397-98; Frank Camm, "Chronology of Early Days at Sandia Base," 1996, DSWA History Project Files. The Air Force opposed Navy participation in the atomic weapons program because of the limited stockpile and its desire to assume all responsibility for delivering atomic weapons. The results of SANDSTONE, which eased stockpile pressures and led to the development of smaller weapons, enabled the Navy to renew its demand to have carrier-based nuclear weapons. See Nichols, *The Road to Trinity*, p. 265.
60. Rearden, *The Formative Years*, p. 431; Nichols, *The Road to Trinity*, p. 268; "First History of AFSWP," Vol. 1, Chap. 5, Sandia Base, 5.61-5.62.
61. Rearden, *The Formative Years*, p. 431; "First History of AFSWP," Vol. 1, Chap. 5, Sandia Base, 5.61-5.62.
62. Nichols, *The Road to Trinity*, p. 268.
63. Text relies heavily on materials from Barton C. Hacker, *Elements of Controversy*, (Berkeley, 1994), pp. 40-42, in the passage on Project NUTMEG.

64. Hacker, *Elements of Controversy*, p. 40.
65. *Ibid.*
66. "First History of AFSWP," Vol. 2, Chap. 3, Headquarters, 3.2.39-3.2.40. In nuclear weapons terminology, a significantly new design receives a new Mark number. Subsequent improvements to the same basic design are designated with modification (or mod) numbers by changing the second digit.
67. *Ibid.*, Headquarters, 3.2.40, referencing Nichols to Lilienthal, January 26, 1949, and Carroll L. Wilson to Nichols, March 7, 1949.
68. *Ibid.*, Headquarters, 3.2.41, referencing Nichols to Lilienthal, July 19, 1949, and James McCormack to Nichols, October 27, 1949.
69. "First History of AFSWP," Vol. 2, Chap. 3, Headquarters, 3.2.34-3.2.35.
70. *Ibid.*, Headquarters, 3.2.35-3.2.37.
71. *Ibid.*, Headquarters, 1949, 3.2.30-3.2.32.
72. *Ibid.*, Headquarters, 3.2.43-3.2.49.
73. *Ibid.*
74. Beside Dorland, other Sandia "Pioneers" continued with the 8460th, including Captain John H. Cushman, Major Lowell L. Wilkes, and Captain D. A. Kellog. See "First History of AFSWP," General, pp. 29-30.
75. "First History of AFSWP," General, pp. 31, 33, 36.
76. *Ibid.*, 32.
77. *Ibid.*, 36.
78. "First History of AFSWP," General, p. 37; *Ibid.*, vol. 2, Chap. 3, "Headquarters, 1949," 3.3.10a-3.3.11.
79. Weaponeers: all inclusive term for assembly and deployment personnel associated with nuclear weapons.
80. "First History of AFSWP," Vol. 2, Chap. 3, "Headquarters, 1949," 3.3.12-3.3.13; *Ibid.*, 3.7.12-3.7.13.
81. "First History of AFSWP," General, pp. 36-37; *Ibid.*, Vol. 2, Chap. 3, "Headquarters, 1949," 3.3.4-3.3.10.
82. *Ibid.*, "Headquarters, 1949," 3.9.4-3.9.7 and 3.1.2-3.1.3.
83. "First History of AFSWP," Vol. 2, Chap. 3, "Headquarters, 1949," 3.2.1-3.2.3, 3.2.27.
84. *Ibid.*, 3.2.27-3.2.28; *Ibid.*, 3.6.11-3.6.12.
85. *Ibid.*, 3.2.24-3.2.25 and 3.7.10-3.7.11; Glasstone's first edition appeared in 1957. He wrote revised editions in 1962 and 1977.
86. "First History of AFSWP," Vol. 2, Chap. 3, "Headquarters, 1949," 3.5.53-3.5.57.
87. Williamson and Rearden, *The Origins of U.S. Nuclear Strategy*, pp. 109-11.
88. Michael Warner, ed., *The CIA under Harry Truman*, (Washington, 1994), p. 319; see also Rearden, *The Formative Years*, pp. 613, fn. 79. At the time of the Joe-1 explosion, the Applied Physics Branch of the Evans Signal Laboratory in Belmar, New Jersey, had developed an ultra-low frequency sound detection system for locating such explosions. Colonel Ord, who was assigned to Evans Laboratory, recalled that the system "...had obtained readings indicating a possible Soviet test..." but he was never told if President Truman factored this information in his announcement of the Soviet test. (Col. Ord to Chris Brahmstedt, April 3, 1998).
89. Holloway, *Stalin and the Bomb*, pp. 213-17, 220.
90. Nichols, *The Road to Trinity*, p. 272; Rhodes, *Dark Sun*, pp. 372-73.
91. Holloway, *Stalin and the Bomb*, pp. 215-17.
92. "MLC Comments Concerning H-Bomb Developments," June 16, 1954, Secretary's Files, AEC 493/37, Record Group 326, National Archives.
93. *Ibid.*
94. *Ibid.*, pp. 6-7.
95. Barton Berstein, "Truman, Acheson, and the H-Bomb," *Foreign Affairs* 60, no. 6 (June 1983): p. 21.
96. *Ibid.*, pp. 9-15.
97. Roger M. Anders, ed., *Forging the Atomic Shield: Excerpts from the Office Diary of Gordon E. Dean*, (Chapel Hill, 1987), pp. 65, 70-71.
98. *Ibid.*, pp. 70-71.

99. Hewlett and Duncan, *Atomic Shield/1947-1952*, pp. 415-16; Rhodes, *Dark Sun*, pp. 420-21. Report quoted in Rhodes. No one at Los Alamos, where scientists might have made a keener analysis of the impact of Fuchs' information, reviewed the report. *Ibid.*, p. 420. Even today, the impact of Fuchs' spying and its potential on Soviet nuclear weapons production is in debate. In the early 1950s, it was natural to credit Soviet success to stolen American secrets. Fuchs' confession fueled this attitude. Recent studies on the Soviet program, however, offer alternate interpretations of Fuchs and credit intelligence from other Soviet spies or sources as being more important, especially in the development of a thermonuclear weapon. Fuchs had left Los Alamos before the scientists had discovered a way to build a workable thermonuclear device. See David Halloway, *Stalin and the Bomb*, New Haven: 1994, and Frank H. Shelton, "A Perspective: Reflections on the Big Red Bombs," *Science & Technology Digest*, August 1996, p. 9.

100. Rhodes, *Dark Sun*, p. 450.

101. Hewlett and Duncan, *Atomic Shield/1947-1952*, pp. 415-17; Berstein, "Truman, Acheson, and the H-Bomb," 34; Rhodes, *Dark Sun*, pp. 419-21.

102. Rhodes, *Dark Sun*, p. 379; Hewlett and Duncan, *Atomic Shield/1947-1952*, p. 371; Defense Nuclear Agency, *Operation GREENHOUSE, 1951*, DNA Report 6034F, pp. 21, 226.

103. Rhodes, *Dark Sun*, p. 457.

104. DNA, *Operation GREENHOUSE, 1951*, pp. 157-58, 226; Richard G. Hewlett to author, June 27, 1997, DSWA History Project Archives; Rosenberg, "U.S. Nuclear Stockpile, 1945-1950," p. 26.

105. "Operation RANGER," DNA Report 6022F, Nuclear Test Personnel Review, February 1982, pp. 19-25.

106. *Ibid.*, pp. 42, 37-40, 50-64.

107. John Newhouse, *War and Peace in the Nuclear Age*, (New York, 1989) p. 83; Nichols, *Road to Trinity*, p. 282; Loper to Chief of Staff, U. S. Army, May 29, 1951, RG 374, Box 3, Folder 322, Field Command, Sandia, 1951-1971, NARA II.

108. *Ibid.*

109. Joint Chiefs to Loper, "Mission and Responsibilities of the Armed Forces Special Weapons Project," July 12, 1951.

110. Defense Nuclear Agency, "Shots ABLE to EASY: The First Five Tests of the BUSTER-JANGLE Series, 22 October-5 November 1951," DNA 6024F, 1982, pp. 67-68.

111. *Ibid.*, 68; Howard L. Rosenberg, *Atomic Soldiers*, (Boston, 1980), pp. 43-44.

112. See Herbert B. Loper to Chief of Staff, U.S. Army, May 28, 1951, RG 374, Box 3, Folder 322, Field Command, Sandia, 1951-1971, NARA II.

113. "Operation BUSTER-JANGLE, 1951," Defense Nuclear Agency, DNA 6023F, NTPR, 1982, pp. 20-22.

114. Hewlett and Duncan, *Atomic Shield/1947-1952*, p. 563; Defense Nuclear Agency, "Operation BUSTER-JANGLE, 1951, DNA 6023F, 1982, 135-152; Hacker, *Elements of Controversy*, p. 67.

115. Defense Nuclear Agency, "Shots ABLE to EASY," DNA 6024F, pp. 69-70; Rosenberg, *Atomic Soldiers*, p. 43.

116. "Operation BUSTER-JANGLE, 1951," DNA 6023F, 1982, pp. 46-48.

117. Defense Nuclear Agency, "Shots ABLE to EASY: The First Five Tests of the BUSTER-JANGLE Series, 22 October-5 November 1951," DNA 6024F, 1982, 65, 68; *Ibid.*, "Operation BUSTER-JANGLE, 1951," DNA 6023F, 1982, p. 144; Barton C. Hacker, *Elements of Controversy*, pp. 70-71. The NTPR study of Operation BUSTER-JANGLE, published in 1982, lists eight Navy participants from AFSWP, three Army representatives, and 12 Air Force participants. The highest radiation exposure to the AFSWP contingent was to one individual who received a total dose of 3.8 roentgen. See *Ibid.*, pp. 135-152.

118. Hacker, *Elements of Controversy*, p. 71.

119. *Ibid.*, 72-73.

120. *Ibid.*, 73.

121. Quoted in *Ibid.*, pp. 75-76.

122. Defense Nuclear Agency, "Operation Tumbler-Snapper, 1952," DNA 6019F, NTPR, 1982, pp. 3-4;
123. *Ibid.*, 4-5; Hacker, *Elements of Controversy*, pp. 78-81.

CHAPTER THREE

THE SPRINT FOR SUPREMACY, 1952 TO 1957

"*We are in the era of the thermonuclear bomb that can obliterate cities and can be delivered across continents. With such weapons, war has become, not just tragic, but preposterous.*"

President Dwight D. Eisenhower,
Republican National Convention,
August 23, 1956

ADVENT OF THE THERMONUCLEAR AGE

On the morning of June 30, 1952, AEC Chairman Gordon Dean and members of his staff entered the Oval Office for a meeting with President Truman. Accompanying them were General Kenneth E. Fields, the director of the AEC's Division of Military Application, and Norris E. Bradbury, director of the Los Alamos Scientific Laboratory. Fields opened a wooden case he was carrying and displayed for the President a scale model of MIKE, which was scheduled for testing at Enewetak in the autumn. As Bradbury and Fields explained, MIKE could not be considered a weapon prototype; it was too big, too heavy, and too much like a *Rube Goldberg* contraption to earn that designation, but the nation's hopes for beating the Soviet Union to the hydrogen bomb rested on MIKE.[1]

Drawing on the success in igniting a small amount of tritium in the GEORGE shot at GREENHOUSE a year before, the MIKE device would test the feasibility of igniting a substantial amount of deuterium in what, in essence, would be an immovable but powerful thermonuclear device. Los Alamos estimated that if it worked, MIKE would produce a blast equal to 5-10 megatons of TNT. The devastation wrought by such a weapon would be almost incomprehensible. So awesome was the possibility that the National Security Council asked the Psychological Strategy Board to consider how the American public might first be informed about the arrival of the thermonuclear age.[2]

Until MIKE could be fired, it was imperative to maintain the highest possible secrecy around that event, not just to keep information from the Soviet Union but also to avoid wild speculation that might terrify the American people. The words "thermonuclear" and "hydrogen bomb" were not to be spoken even within the security confines of the AEC, AFSWP, or the JCS.

The timing of the shot, scheduled for November 1, 1952 (Pacific Time), was also a concern of the administration. The

President was about to hit the campaign trail in an attempt to prevent the Republicans from putting General Eisenhower in the White House. Firing MIKE just four days before the Presidential election raised the danger of entangling the test in a political battle. Truman hoped that the test could be postponed at least until November 5, the day after the election, but when that proved impossible for technical reasons, he agreed to the scheduled date.

By late October the 2,000 military and civilian personnel in Joint Task Force 132, under the command of Major General Percy W. Clarkson*, were completing the installation on Elugelab Island on the northern rim of the Enewetak Atoll, 23 miles from Clarkson's base at Enewetak and Parry Islands on the south rim. The test device, weighing more than 80 tons, sat in a large building which housed the cryogenic plant needed to keep the deuterium fuel in liquid form. Stretching away from the black building was a low wooden helium-filled tube.[3]

As with GREENHOUSE, the overriding purpose of the IVY series was weapon development, so AFSWP had virtually no direct participation on the atoll. The agency, however, had a crucial role in planning and coordinating weapon effects tests to be performed by all three military Services. This planning effort spanned more than a year as AFSWP, headquartered at the Pentagon, determined what tests were needed and how they should be conducted. By the summer of 1952, AFSWP had negotiated an approved list of 21 projects. The Air Force was responsible for long-range detection of seismic waves and recording the fireball at a distance. Navy scientists conducted an extensive geophysical and marine survey of the atoll before the tests to establish a benchmark for measuring the effects of the blast. Navy teams also installed instrumentation to record underwater pressures, thermal radiation, and sea waves produced by the detonation while ships in the Navy Task Force were responsible for gathering fallout to measure intensity and distribution. The Army Signal Corps set up instruments to measure electromagnetic phenomena while the Chemical Corps was prepared to analyze fallout and cloud particles. Similar projects, but on a smaller scale, were set up for Shot KING, to be detonated after MIKE.[4]

OPERATION IVY

Concerns about weather conditions threatened to delay the firing of MIKE, but General Clarkson gave the order to fire as scheduled on the morning of October 31, 1952 (local time). By that time base operations at Enewetak and Parry Islands had been evacuated to Task Force ships, which retreated to positions east and south of the Enewetak Atoll to avoid possible fallout and blast effects. Most of the instrumentation installed by Scientific Task Group 132.1 performed as expected, and the yield of the shot was soon determined to be 10.4 megatons, at the upper end of the expected range. For observers on the ships, the experience of witnessing a shot in the megaton range was awesome. As one observer recorded after detonation of MIKE:

> "Accompanied by a brilliant light, the heat wave was felt immediately at distances of thirty to thirty-five miles. The tremendous fireball, appearing on the horizon like the sun when half-risen, quickly expanded after a momentary hover time and appeared to be approximately a mile in

---

* A June 30, 1951 JCS Letter of Instruction, with AEC concurrence, designated authority to General Clarkson, Commander of Joint Task Force 132, to activate Scientific Task Group 132.1, to oversee Operation IVY (Shots MIKE and KING) in 1952.

Firing party standing in front of MIKE device prior to detonation; left to right, H.E. Grier, S.W. Burriss, R.T. Lunger, and M.D. Sprinkel.

diameter before the cloud-chamber effect and scud clouds obscured it from view. A very large cloud-chamber effect was visible shortly after the detonation and a tremendous conventional mushroom-shaped cloud soon appeared, seemingly balanced on a wide, dirty stem. Apparently, the dirty stem was due to the coral particles, debris, and water which was sucked up high into the air. Around the base of the stem, there appeared to be a curtain of water which soon dropped back around the area where the island of Elugelab had been. The shock wave and sound arrived at the various ships approximately two and one-half minutes after the detonation, accompanied by a sharp report, followed by an extended rumbling sound. The pressure pulse and the reduced pressure period as received by the ear were exceptionally long. Although the upper cloud first appeared unusually white, a reddish-brown color could be seen within the shadows of its boiling mass as it ascended to greater height and spread out over the atoll area. At approximately H+30 minutes, the upper cloud was roughly sixty miles in diameter with a stem, or lower cloud, approximately twenty miles in diameter. The juncture of the stem with the upper cloud was at an altitude of about 45,000 feet." [5]

Within six hours the cloud had risen to 118,000 feet and appeared to have penetrated the tropical tropopause. Although the cloud moved to the northwest as expected, efforts to track it by ship and by aircraft from Kwajalein proved difficult as the cloud eventually split into four segments. With no land-based collection points north and west of Enewetak, a comprehensive map of MIKE fallout could not be drawn. MIKE had been a stunning success and its implications for the future were staggering.

THE EISENHOWER IMPRINT

Less than a week after the MIKE shot and the Presidential election, Roy B. Snapp, the secretary of the AEC, hurried to the Augusta National Golf Club in Georgia to brief the President-elect, Dwight D. Eisenhower, on what had occurred at Enewetak. Eisenhower initially seemed more interested in developing atomic energy for peaceful purposes, but he quickly sensed the significance of MIKE. He was troubled by the growing power of nuclear weapons and understood the scientific interest in developing more powerful and efficient weapons, but he thought there was no need "...for us to build enough destructive power to destroy everything." "Complete destruction," he said, "was the negation of peace." The United States needed enough force to meet the Soviet threat, but he neither feared the Russians nor thought that kind of fear should influence American foreign policy. Secrecy, however, was all important. The President-elect saw no need to release any information at all about the tests at Enewetak.[6]

Eisenhower reinforced these opinions in a secret two-hour meeting with officials at AEC headquarters on November 19, 1952. While he supported the Commission's efforts to build a growing arsenal of nuclear weapons, he was still uneasy about the possession of so much physical power. He seemed to understand the possibilities of human failure, misdirected ambition and treachery in the nuclear era. Eisenhower made clear a key principle of his administration: a dedication to economy in government, in terms of both funding and federal authority.

Eisenhower's decisive victory in the 1952 election–"I Like Ike" movement–swept Republicans into control of Congress for the first time in 20 years and brought about massive changes in the leadership of federal departments and agencies. Within DoD, as elsewhere, American industry with its conservative economic principles would have a strong voice. Eisenhower appointed General Motors President, Charles E. Wilson, to be Secretary of Defense and a few days later selected four industrialists to fill the positions of Deputy Secretary and the three Service secretaries. The nomination of John Foster Dulles to be Secretary of State in December of 1953 revealed Eisenhower's determination to take new and decisive initiatives in international affairs. That same month, before his inauguration, the President-elect made a trip to Korea. Shortly after his inauguration, to make certain that the war did not break out again, Eisenhower let it be known through diplomatic channels that "...we intend to move decisively without inhibition in our use of weapons." Thus, the threat of nuclear warfare was to be a significant element in American foreign policy in the new administration.[7]

During the hectic weeks that preceded his inauguration, the new President could not dispel the image of MIKE. Eisenhower did not refer directly to the thermonuclear development in his inaugural address on January 20, 1953, but there were overtones in his speech:

"Are we nearing the light—a day of freedom and of peace for all mankind? Or are the shadows of another night closing in upon us ... This trial comes at a moment when man's power to achieve good or to inflict evil surpasses the brightest hopes and sharpest fears of all ages... Science seems ready to confer upon us, as its final gift, the power to erase human life from this planet."[8]

THE CHALLENGE FOR AFSWP

Just a week before the President's inaugural address, Major General Herbert B. Loper, who had served for two years as AFSWP Chief, suffered a heart attack and was forced to retire from the Army. Fortunately, the agency had a highly qualified and experienced officer in Air Force Brigadier General Alvin R. Luedecke to assume leadership in the difficult months that lay ahead.

At the age of 53, Luedecke already had 21 years of military Service, beginning with a reserve commission in the Army when he graduated from Texas A&M in 1932. The following year he transferred to the Army Air Force, completed flight training, and served in air operations in the Canal Zone and as Assistant Military Attaché for Air in Central America. During World War II, he was Deputy Chief of Air Staff for the Army Air Force in the India-Burma theater and then Assistant Chief of Staff in the China theater. After the war he was an Air Force member of the Joint Strategic Plans Group of the JCS and Executive Secretary of the MLC before joining AFSWP in 1951.

In his new position General Luedecke would be the connecting link between the MLC, Field Command in Albuquerque, and the three Armed Services. With General Nichols' departure as Chief of AFSWP, his successors were not appointed to the MLC but served that body only as observers. For Luedecke, this arrangement proved no hindrance; rather, it gave him more flexibility. He continued to meet

Major General Alvin R. Luedecke, AFSWP Director, 1953-1957.

with the advisory committee regularly and had direct access to its members in all three Services, and particularly to Robert LeBaron, who served not only as Advisory Committee Chairman but also as Assistant to the Secretary of Defense (Atomic Energy). Luedecke, like his predecessors, reported directly to the JCS and to each of the chiefs individually. He had no direct line to Secretary of Defense Wilson or to the White House, but through LeBaron and the Joint Chiefs he could command attention at the highest levels.

Luedecke's headquarters command in the Pentagon was small, but it was staffed with experienced officers and civilian scientists.[9] Most prominent among the civilians was Herbert Scoville, Jr., who served as technical director and technical advisor to Luedecke. It was Scoville who had noted the lack of adequate data on height of burst curves taken in the BUSTER-JANGLE test series and who had initiated action to incorporate additional projects on this subject in the forthcoming UPSHOT-KNOTHOLE series, to be held in the spring of 1953.

While Scoville worked with Sandia and Los Alamos on weapon development for UPSHOT, the Weapons Effects Division had, since 1951, been developing plans with the Armed Services for weapon effects tests during UPSHOT-KNOTHOLE. By the time Luedecke took command in 1953, the division was working on preliminary plans for effects experiments to be conducted in 11 more test series tentatively scheduled for the next five years.[10] Planning was based on extended discussions with the Armed Services to determine what kinds of effects data were most critical for their operations and then to consider the experimental programs and instrumentation that would produce the data. Headquarters staff awarded contracts to defense and university laboratories for studies of the possible environmental effects of radiation from nuclear weapons during UPSHOT. The activities of the Weapons Test Division paralleled those of the Weapons Effects Division in terms of long-range planning and technical support of each test series.[11]

During AFSWP's first three years, the agency relied on such other government organizations as the AEC's national laboratories, the National Bureau of Standards, and the Army Chemical Corps, for research and development. In the 1950s, as typified by the effects testing during UPSHOT, AFSWP began to seek support from universities, industrial contractors, and service laboratories; a practice that became a permanent feature of the agency.

If AFSWP Headquarters was becoming a research and development agency, it was even more a training organization, as it always had been. The Operations and Training Division at Headquarters, in combination with the school facilities at Field Command, was responsible for a broad range of activities, beginning with training of military personnel assigned to AFSWP to assemble, handle, and store weapons and extending to individual training courses for air crews, staff officers, and atomic defense teams. The division also prepared films and orientation material for members of Congress and other government officials who would be observers at Operation UPSHOT-KNOTHOLE, as well as military units involved in exercises and maneuvers during some of the shots. During 1953 more than 7,000 military personnel would be involved in AFSWP training courses. In support of operations, the division coordinated training programs in atomic defense within DoD, conducted scores of technical training courses for air crews and DoD personnel involved in assembly and maintenance of nuclear weapons, and prepared dozens of training films. AFSWP carried out these training activities within the complex and often changing working relationships among the three Armed Services, the laboratories, and the AEC.[12]

Additionally, on October 16, 1953, the Secretary of Defense directed AFSWP to maintain "a centralized system of reporting and accounting to ensure that the current status and location" of each nuclear weapon "will be known at all times." This critical function resulted in the establishment of AFSWP's Atomic Warfare Status Center, which continued throughout the history of the agency.

NEW DIRECTIONS IN WEAPON DEVELOPMENT

In at least two ways, the Operation IVY Series, which included MIKE, KING, and other tests, marked a turning point in weapon development. The KING shot on November 15, 1952, with a yield of 550 kilotons, was the most powerful fission stockpile weapon ever detonated.

However, the tests were used not to produce larger fission weapons, but to develop a growing variety of small weapons, including new missile and rocket warheads and such tactical weapons as artillery shells and demolition munitions.

The first way that MIKE affected AFSWP involved the rapid proliferation of nuclear warhead designs, many of which could be adapted for use with a variety of weapon systems. This greatly increased the planning and coordination responsibilities for AFSWP in training courses, weapon test planning, warhead assembly, and weapon storage maintenance, both at Headquarters and Field Command.

The second way that MIKE affected AFSWP was that it launched the joint organization into the thermonuclear age, with all its risks and responsibilities. The enormous power of MIKE seemed to validate Lewis Strauss' prediction that the hydrogen bomb would represent a giant leap in nuclear weapon capability and hence would keep the United States ahead of the Soviet Union in the Cold War. The pressures on thermonuclear development brought by the JCS, the Joint Committee on Atomic Energy, and scientists like Ernest O. Lawrence and Edward Teller had a powerful impact, not just on the AEC and Los Alamos, but on AFSWP as well. MIKE demonstrated what was possible, but it did not lead directly to a deliverable thermonuclear weapon. Eisenhower saw that point at his very first briefing in Augusta, Georgia. He was concerned that it would take a year or more after MIKE to produce a deliverable weapon.

Dr. Edward Teller had become so impatient with the lack of progress at Los Alamos that he had resigned from the laboratory and, with support from the Joint Committee on Atomic Energy, had forced the AEC to build a second weapons laboratory operated by Lawrence Livermore's Radiation Laboratory at Livermore, California. The UPSHOT series in 1953 would be the first to include test devices from both laboratories.[13]

The painful fact was that a prototype of a deliverable thermonuclear weapon would not be ready for testing until Operation CASTLE in the fall of 1953 or the spring of 1954. In the meantime, Los Alamos and Sandia hastened to develop and produce "emergency" weapons, that is, models that could go into the stockpile without the assurances of full-scale testing.[14] Although these "emergency" weapons were not deployed, their development characterize the pressures of the Cold War in early 1953.

With weapon development moving toward smaller devices with smaller yields in parallel with the high-yield thermonuclear designs, the continental test site would be flooded with requirements for dozens of shots, while the Pacific test areas at Enewetak and Bikini Atolls would be reserved for the thermonuclear shots in the megaton range that were too large for detonation in Nevada. As the number of thermonuclear tests increased, operations in the Pacific would become almost continuous, as plans for new test series followed on the heels of those already completed.

Reflecting this change in the frequency of Pacific tests, the JCS abandoned the practice of creating a special Joint Task Force for each Pacific series and created Joint Task Force 7 as a permanent organization for those tests. In the short term, this change lightened the burden on AFSWP when the new Task Force took over responsibility for technical reports from IVY, but in April 1953, the JCS gave AFSWP responsibility for exercising "...within any Task Force organization, technical direction of weapons effects tests of primary concern to the Armed

Forces and the weapons effects phases of development or other tests of atomic weapons."[15]

EXPANSION OF FIELD COMMAND

AFSWP's operational arm at Field Command inherited greater responsibility as Pacific test and training roles increased. Field Command Director, Brigadier General Leland S. Stranathan and his deputy, Rear Admiral Frederick M. Trapnell, held jurisdiction over the base and all tenant organizations, including the buildings used by the Sandia Corporation, a subsidiary of Western Electric and a prime contractor of the AEC. Sandia Corporation had the task of taking designs created by Los Alamos and, beginning in 1953 by Lawrence Livermore Laboratories, transforming them into fully engineered and operational weapons. In this process, Field Command staff worked closely with the Sandia Corporation and the laboratories at Los Alamos and Livermore. Stranathan and members of his staff could make regular trips to Los Alamos for meetings with scientists on weapon design, while a small resident staff provided the same function at Livermore.

On-site training was a major responsibility of Field Command, both for weapon assembly teams and for those assigned to test and storage operations. Field Command continued to supervise the training and performance of military personnel assigned to weapon assembly, monitored AEC activities, revised production schedules as required, and maintained master schedules to establish priorities for personnel and facilities. In addition to operating assembly and storage facilities, Field Command coordinated testing of all kinds of electronic and other components of each weapon type, including drop tests, barometric pressure sensing, fuzing, and ballistic performance. With the Air Force, Field Command directed the modification of aircraft and ground-handling equipment to accommodate the variety of airborne weapons entering the stockpile. To speed the development of emergency weapons that would enter the stockpile without testing, the AEC, with AFSWP's assistance helped to define assembly procedures and proof-test an assembly kit, all in accordance with ground rules established by Los Alamos.[16]

With broad responsibilities for construction, supply, and logistics at Sandia Base, the weapon storage sites, and other Armed Forces installations throughout the nation, Field Command, in 1953, was a large organization that boasted 10,250 staff, consisting of 1,550 officers, 7,100 enlisted personnel, and 1,600 civilians.[17] As the tempo of continental testing increased, whole units of engineering and operations personnel moved from Sandia Base to the Nevada Proving Grounds to begin construction and installation of equipment months before a forthcoming test series. At the same time, Field Command had to adjust to direct participation in Pacific tests, a requirement that led to Agency coordination throughout 1953 with Joint Task Force 7.[18]

LUEDECKE INITIATIVES

In 1953, as new weapon designs emerged from Los Alamos and Livermore and additional storage sites were constructed for the increasing number of assembled weapons entering the stockpile, General Luedecke, like his predecessors, put the question of custody high on his agenda. A week after Eisenhower's inauguration Luedecke wrote a memorandum for the JCS proposing that DoD seek custody of just enough weapons "…to meet deployment and delivery requirements for initial strike operations of all strategic and tactical forces." Such an arrangement, in Luedecke's opinion, would suffice until

Brigadier General Leland S. Stranathan (center), Commander of AFSWP Field Command, along with Dr. Frank Shelton, (left) and Colonel Jack James (right) after Operation TEAPOT, Shot MET, in 1955.

the new administration had time to reexamine the thorny question of custody. Partial custody of the stockpile would not be an acceptable long-term solution, but in the short run it might improve security, operational flexibility, and military readiness. Certainly it would avoid another nasty fight with the AEC if complete transfer were not proposed. When asked in a session with the Joint Chiefs on February 10 to list the disadvantages of such a move, Luedecke admitted that partial custody would be inefficient, expensive, and not very practical for a number of reasons. The following week, however, he learned from Robert LeBaron that Secretary of State Dulles, in a meeting of the National Security Council, had maintained that nuclear weapons should be an integral part of the military weapon system and that all nuclear weapons should be transferred to DoD. Dulles further argued that DoD should be responsible for its own non-nuclear hardware, which LeBaron interpreted to include research, development, production, and storage of all non-nuclear components.[19]

Although Roger M. Keyes, the new Deputy Secretary of Defense, agreed with Dulles' position on custody, he asked the Joint Chiefs to reexamine the whole question. This request brought Luedecke center stage once again as he briefed the JCS on the opinions of Dulles and Keyes and then directed an AFSWP staff study, which he sent informally to the Joint Chiefs' Strategic Plans Committee. The result was a memorandum from the JCS to Secretary of Defense Wilson recommending transfer of the entire stockpile to DoD. Part of the package was a draft directive giving AFSWP responsibility for centralized control of, and accountability for, the stockpile. The Chief of AFSWP would report directly to the Secretary of Defense on the operational and technical status of the stockpile and would maintain a centralized system of reporting and accounting for the status and location of all weapons and components in DoD custody.[20]

Luedecke was also present at a meeting of the Special Committee of the National Security Council on April 15, 1953, to discuss the custody issue. Keyes and Air Force Chief of Staff General Hoyt S. Vandenberg spoke for the Defense Department. Walter Bedell Smith, Under Secretary, represented the State Department while Gordon Dean and two of his fellow commissioners opposed transfer of custody to DoD. Despite Keyes' strong arguments for transfer, Dean convinced the special committee that there was nothing wrong with Commission custody of the stockpile. The Commission understood the need for flexibility and readiness and assured the committee that the Commission could transfer weapons to the military within the time limits specified for an emergency situation.[21]

Keyes and Luedecke had one consolation. Just three weeks earlier Secretary Wilson had signed an agreement with Chairman Dean setting forth in detail a cooperative plan defining the functions and responsibilities of the two agencies in the development, production, and standardization of nuclear weapons. The agreement did not touch on the custody issue, but it did specify the roles of the AEC and the DoD in weapon conception, determination of feasibility, development, first production, quantity assurance, and stockpile maintenance. No longer would the Commission have sole authority in these areas; in each area both the AEC and the DoD would have complementary responsibilities. The AFSWP Weapons Development Division had spent months drafting each section of the agreement and had cleared its provisions with the three Armed Services. It was an agreement both the AEC and DoD could live with, and it gave the military Services, for the first time, a significant role in nuclear weapon development.

The new agreement, in fact, reflected cooperative procedures that were already being used. Early in 1953 AFSWP and the Commission's Division of Military Application had agreed to replace radar fuzes with barometric devices on some weapons after determining that radar fuzes gave no advantage in weapon effects but greatly increased operational and logistics problems in maintaining weapon reliability. At the same time Field Command and Sandia Corporation had worked out a plan to standardize fuzes for all weapons.[22] This agreement, with two amendments, remained in effect as of 1997 as the baseline document for clarifying nuclear weapon life cycle roles between the two departments.

Useful as the new agreement was, it did not resolve the custody issue, and Luedecke was not about to give up the fight. On April 17, he briefed Lewis L. Strauss, the former AEC Commissioner and now special assistant to President Eisenhower. In explaining the operation and maintenance of the stockpile, Luedecke was careful not to criticize the Commission in light of rumors that Strauss would soon replace Dean as chairman. Rather, he described the confusion and duplication of effort inherent in the existing arrangement under which the AEC maintained custody of the weapons while AFSWP was responsible for building and operating the storage sites. The following week Luedecke received a staff study by Headquarters and Field Command that concluded that transfer of "...the complete stockpile of atomic weapons and weapons components to DoD was necessary to ensure the military readiness and operational flexibility required by the Armed Forces to conduct atomic warfare."[23]

Before Luedecke could present his study to the JCS, he learned that the President was prepared to transfer custody to DoD. Acting on this rumor, Luedecke ordered the Plans Division to draft memorandums, directives, and agreements needed to implement the President's order. Field Command prepared similar orders, and all was ready for Presidential action by the end of May. Luedecke was impatient but optimistic. From what he could learn, the President intended to transfer 95 percent of the stockpile to DoD, and this was to be accomplished without public announcement in order to avoid any "...public reaction or international political implications."[24]

Although this rumor did not prove entirely accurate, in June the President did authorize deployment of some nuclear components to military installations outside the continental United States. A month later the AEC was directed to transfer the components to the Chief of AFSWP. It would be the first such component transfer to AFSWP and a chink in the custody armor of AEC.[25]

OPERATION UPSHOT-KNOTHOLE

More than a year of planning by Los Alamos, Livermore, and Field Command culminated in UPSHOT-KNOTHOLE, an 11-shot series at the Nevada Proving Grounds conducted in 1953. Now, for the first time, Field Command had full responsibility for all the military exercises in a Nevada test series. As with TUMBLER-SNAPPER series in 1952, Field Command faced the difficulties of melding the military projects with the ever-changing plans of the Los Alamos and Livermore scientists in scheduling and setting the yields for the diagnostic tests of new weapon designs. Ultimately, Los Alamos conducted six diagnostic shots during the UPSHOT program, five of which were tied to military and/or civilian effects tests in KNOTHOLE. Livermore had two diagnostic tests on novel weapon designs. Los Alamos devoted only three shots for weapon effects: two air drops to simulate combat conditions for troop maneuvers and one, GRABLE, a test of a nuclear warhead in an artillery shell fired from a 280-millimeter cannon, the first test ever of such a weapon. The effects tests conducted by Field Command included blast, thermal, and radiation measurements similar to those at SNAPPER, as well as survivability/vulnerability studies of trucks, railroad stock, communications equipment, and aircraft.[26]

Following troop exercises during the 1952 TUMBLER-SNAPPER tests, AFSWP began planning for DESERT ROCK V, part of UPSHOT-KNOTHOLE, in the spring of 1953. For weeks AFSWP negotiated with the AEC to obtain full responsibility for the safety of all troops and to set the safety criteria for radiation exposure. The Commission delayed approval for fear of public criticism if some troops were injured or exposed to excessive radiation doses. There was also concern that DoD would set exposure limits higher than the Commission had permitted in the past. Not until January 1953 was a compromise reached. The Test Manager (an AEC official) would set the overall radiological and safety criteria for the Nevada Proving Grounds but would oversee implementation only for those "...other than troops and troop observers." In fact, radiological safety tests for DESERT

280-mm "Atomic Cannon" in foreground just after detonation of Shot GRABLE, at Frenchman's Flat, Nevada Test Site, on May 25, 1953.

ROCK V and the UPSHOT-KNOTHOLE tests were conducted independently.[27]

More than 13,000 troops, along with officers and official observers, participated in the maneuvers following six of the 11 shots. At shot BADGER on April 18, 1953, two Marine battalions, entrenched 4,000 yards from ground zero, moved forward until one of the battalions encountered significant radiation levels and quickly withdrew. Twelve Army and Marine volunteer officers, entrenched at 2,000 yards, were shaken by the blast, sound waves, and falling debris, and had to be evacuated quickly to avoid undue radiation exposure. At another test a week later, two Army battalions at 4,000 yards and volunteer officers at 2,000 yards encountered much more severe conditions when the shot yield turned out to be 43 kilotons, or almost twice the yield of BADGER.[28]

More highly publicized at UPSHOT-KNOTHOLE than the military operations were the civil effects tests conducted in close cooperation with the Federal Civil Defense Administration. AFSWP provided scores of reports to civil defense officials after earlier tests, but here, for the first time, the general public witnessed the effects of nuclear explosions on such familiar objects as residential homes and automobiles, through both the eyes of hundreds of observers and the graphic photographs released to the press. The civil effects tests, in addition to the measurable offsite fallout from several of the shots, prompted inquiries–from the public and federal officials–about the safety of tests at the Nevada site.[29]

THE THERMONUCLEAR SPECTRE

Even before UPSHOT-KNOTHOLE, AFSWP officers at Headquarters and Field Command were making plans to participate in the test of a prototype thermonuclear weapon during the Operation

CASTLE Series in 1954. Working under great pressure to have the test ready on schedule, AFSWP personnel felt even greater tension when, on August 8, 1953, Soviet Premier Georgi M. Malenkov announced that the United States no longer had a monopoly on the hydrogen bomb. Until the Air Force could collect and analyze samples of fallout from the Soviet test, it was impossible to verify Malenkov's claim. In order not to reveal the United States' detection capabilities, the Eisenhower administration delayed any comment on the test, which became known as Joe 4. The President, as usual, was reluctant to make any statement other than a general announcement that a test had taken place in the Soviet Union. On August 19, the Air Force unit concluded firmly that "...a fission and thermonuclear reaction had taken place within Soviet territory." When Moscow radio announced later that day that the Soviet Union had conducted a thermonuclear test, Chairman Strauss released a statement confirming the event.

Congressman W. Sterling Cole, chairman of the Joint Committee on Atomic Energy, mirrored public reaction when he pointed out in a speech to the American Legion in October that the Russians had detonated a hydrogen weapon "...only nine months after our own hydrogen test." Even though President Eisenhower in a press conference referred to the Soviet achievement as the creation of a hydrogen bomb, there was no incontrovertible evidence that the Soviets had such a weapon. It would be several years before most scientists could agree that the Soviet device had "burned" some thermonuclear fuel, but it was in no sense a hydrogen bomb. The misconception about the nature of the Soviet test, whether sincerely accepted or deliberately promoted, had the effect of ratcheting up American efforts to perfect the hydrogen bomb as a response to what seemed a frightening escalation of the Soviet threat.[30]

As the AEC's absolute control of the stockpile began to erode in the fall of 1953, Deputy Secretary of Defense Keyes issued a directive updating the responsibilities of AFSWP. The Chief, AFSWP, was to report directly to the Secretary of Defense on the technical status of the stockpile and to advise him of any deficiencies that needed to be corrected. The Chief was to maintain a centralized system of reporting and accounting to ensure that the current status and location of atomic weapons and components in DoD custody were known at all times. He was to arrange for the transfer of weapons and components to storage sites in accordance with JCS war plans.

In addition, the Chief of AFSWP was to keep the three Service secretaries informed of: "...scheduling and performance

Protective lead-glass cloth schroud being placed on an Air Force pilot during sampling operations.

of nuclear and non-nuclear maintenance and minor modernization programs at both the national stockpile and operational storage sites." He coordinated major modernization schedules with the AEC. The Chief was also responsible for transportation and security of weapons and components between storage sites, internal security at the national stockpile sites, and for construction of facilities at these sites."[31]

THE EISENHOWER RESPONSE

In response to the growing Soviet threat in the autumn of 1953, President Eisenhower was moving in what seemed two parallel directions. The first course would lead the nation and the world to open nuclear technology for peaceful uses. The second would exploit the nation's arsenal of nuclear weapons as a deterrent to Communist aggression around the world.

In his very first discussions of nuclear energy as President-elect, Eisenhower had been engrossed with the prospects of developing a nuclear power industry. If the AEC could induce leaders of American industry to invest in the design and construction of nuclear power plants, it would be possible to demonstrate that nuclear energy could be more than an instrument of war, that it could be a beneficial force in the world. Further, by involving private industry, the President saw the possibility of avoiding heavy expenditures of federal funds. Building national security at home and abroad while balancing the federal budget was a key strategy for the new administration.

It was immediately obvious, however, that industrial participation would require amending the Atomic Energy Act, to allow private ownership of nuclear materials and ease the severe restrictions on access to technical information. As industry leaders responded enthusiastically to the President's overture, amending the

President-elect Dwight D. Eisenhower, 1953.

Atomic Energy Act became a popular subject in the halls of Congress and in industrial lobbies. In April 1954, a member of the Joint Committee on Atomic Energy introduced in the House of Representatives a bill that would give private industry access to nuclear materials.[32] It was probably this widespread interest in amending the act that induced General Luedecke to lay aside a proposal the AFSWP staff had drafted to solve the custody issue by amending the act so as to transfer all of the functions and authorities of the AEC to DoD.[33]

Efforts to revise the Atomic Energy Act by "simple" piecemeal amendments failed during the summer and fall of 1953 as the public debate became snarled in the complexities of patent law and the old battle between public and private power interests. By December, the Joint Committee on Atomic Energy had embarked on drafting an entirely new law, which would take another six months to work its way through Congress. It became apparent to all, including Keyes and Luedecke, that the new legislation would solve the custody issue, even if the DoD and the AEC had not reached agreement on the matter by that time.[34]

While the public debate over amending the act continued in 1953, the Eisenhower administration was engaged in its own internal discussions of how to introduce the American public to the frightening realities created by the growth of the nuclear weapon stockpile, and particularly the threat posed by thermonuclear weapons. Actually created in the final days of the Truman administration, Project *Candor* was an attempt to draft, in simple terms the public could understand, a description of the nuclear dilemma that the nation and the world faced: how could potential benefits of nuclear energy be realized without throwing the world into the horrors of nuclear war? One early proposal, soon abandoned, was to give the public some idea of the size and capability of the nuclear weapon stockpile. This proposal for *Candor*, like many others to follow, foundered on troublesome questions. Could the administration be candid without jeopardizing national security? Could the facts be stated in simple terms without misleading the public or in terms that would not create widespread anxiety? These and many other reservations blocked the acceptance of draft after draft of the *Candor* statement. By November 1953, the President's advisors had given up on *Candor* and were transforming the statement into one in a completely new context. The result was Eisenhower's dramatic presentation of his "Atoms-for-Peace" plan before the United Nations General Assembly on December 8, 1953. The President proposed not only to open access to nuclear science and technology to American industry and research institutions but also to launch a broad program of international cooperation in developing the peaceful uses of nuclear energy. Neither the DoD nor the AEC knew what was in the speech before it was delivered or knew at the time what it really meant. The "Atoms-for-Peace" plan would be a landmark of the Eisenhower administration, setting the context for much that the AEC and the DoD would accomplish in the next eight years.[35]

In contrast to the benign course the administration was pursuing toward peaceful uses of atomic weapons, the second course seemed more belligerent. Eisenhower was determined to move American foreign policy in the Cold War away from what he considered a defensive stance that merely reacted to Soviet challenges to a "New Look" in which the United States would take the initiative. The principles of the "New Look" appeared in a report presented to the National Security Council in October 1953.[36] The report concluded that military planning should focus on long term objectives rather than on specific Soviet threats. American forces worldwide were to be reduced in order to preserve the economic stability of the United States and its fundamental values and institutions. To replace the military forces withdrawn from abroad, the United States would be prepared, if necessary, to threaten to use, or actually use, its nuclear arsenal to deter, or failing this, to counter Communist aggression. The administration's "New Look" policy was to be a selective approach to the Soviet threat, an effort to keep the Communists off guard. As one scholar observed, the "New Look" policy was "...an attempt to combine a defensive nuclear military policy with an offensive strategy in the non-military field."[37]

Like Project *Candor* and the "Atoms-for-Peace" plan, the "New Look" emerged out of months of heated debate within the administration. Only by the end of 1953 had the President clearly defined these proposals in his own mind. A month after his "Atoms-for-Peace" speech, Eisenhower set forth the elements of the "New Look" in his State of the Union address. As a general principle of foreign affairs, he stressed the importance of maintaining good relations with America's allies, but the key to national defense was to deter aggression by maintaining "a massive capability to strike back." The President pledged to "take into full account our great and growing number of nuclear weapons," and he mentioned explicitly weapons designed "for tactical use." Nuclear weapons, he noted, would permit reductions in military force levels, an assumption reflected in the administration's fiscal year 1955 budget. It reduced military spending authority from $41.5 billion, proposed by President Truman in 1953, to $31 billion just two years later.[38]

In his State of the Union address, Eisenhower had revealed elements of the "New Look" without defining it as a whole. Such a definition came a week later, on January 12, 1954, when Secretary of State Dulles spoke before the Council on Foreign Relations in New York City. He declared that local defenses against Communism the world over would be reinforced by "...the further deterrent of massive retaliatory power." The United States would seek to deter the Soviets with "...a great capacity to retaliate, instantly, by means and at places of our own choosing." The speech implied that the United States might respond with strategic nuclear air power against the Soviet Union itself, or perhaps against Communist China, in the event of Communist aggression anywhere in the world.[39] The aggressive tone of Dulles' speech aroused a storm of criticism both at home and abroad. Those who did not read his speech carefully saw it as a commitment to respond to every incident with a massive attack with nuclear weapons; others considered it such a gigantic bluff so transparent that it would fail to deter aggression. Although Dulles responded to such criticisms by qualifying or elaborating on his initial statements, the President, Secretary of Defense, the JCS, and Congressional committees endorsed the concept of "massive retaliation." The concept in turn would shape the mission of DoD and AFSWP in the years ahead.

Indeed, the threat to use nuclear weapons by the United States was viewed by many as one of the chief bargaining chips used to secure the Korean armistice in July 1953. Eisenhower's belief that the tactical use of nuclear weapons against the North Korean honeycombed enemy dugouts would halt the Korean conflict, and send a strong message of retaliation to the Chinese. Passing this message of "potential use" to the Koreans was the President's intent. "...We dropped the word, discretely, of our intention...We felt quite sure it would reach Soviet and Chinese ears."[40]

The primary ammunition for massive retaliation was to be the thermonuclear weapon. As new AEC Chairman Lewis Strauss and Secretary Wilson pointed out to the President in early February, the JCS believed that thermonuclear weapons would "...insure that the United States maintain[ed] its superiority over the U.S.S.R." The Joint Chiefs were also convinced that "...the production of thermonuclear weapons is the cheapest method to obtain high yield weapons and improved destructive capability."

Following JCS advice, Wilson discussed with Strauss new military requirements for thermonuclear weapons. Strauss agreed that the Commission could meet the new requirements by July 1956 at a cost of $360 million for plant and equipment and $75 million in operating costs in the next fiscal year. The following day Eisenhower approved the proposed expansion.[41]

CASTLE SERIES: THERMONUCLEAR REALITY

For more than a year prior to the MIKE shot in 1952, the AEC's weapon laboratories and a score of military organizations coordinated by AFSWP had been preparing for the crucial test of a device that could be considered the prototype of a thermonuclear weapon. Until such a weapon was actually available, the United States would have no counter to the Soviet challenge embodied in Joe 4.

The American response came in Operation CASTLE, a series of six tests of thermonuclear devices at the Pacific Proving Ground (PPG) in the spring of 1954. Table 3-1 summarizes the tests during the CASTLE series and Table 3-2 details the types of weapon effects experiments approved by AFSWP.

With more than 10,000 personnel participating from the military Services, CASTLE was the first Pacific series in which AFSWP had direct field responsibility for DoD projects. Scientific advisors and military officers from AFSWP Headquarters and Field Command had consulted with scientists at the weapon laboratories on some aspects of experiments and tests, but the main burden on AFSWP came in the weapon effects tests at Bikini. Of the 1,300 persons working on the atoll in setting up the tests and instrumentation, the majority–uniformed personnel and civilians–participated in DoD programs. As in the past, AFSWP had solicited Service requirements for weapon effects information, assisted DoD laboratories in designing experiments, and dovetailed these experiments with the weapon designers[42] of Los Alamos and Livermore. AFSWP ultimately approved weapon effects experiments in the categories shown in Table 3-2.

All six tests were successful, but the most dramatic CASTLE test was Shot BRAVO, fired on March 1, 1954. The largest device ever fired during atmospheric nuclear testing by the United States, BRAVO, yielded 15 megatons. This high-yield test was made possible by the first use, by the United States, of Lithium-6 Deuteride, a dry thermonuclear fuel that eliminated the need for cryogenic equipment. Because the neutron cross-sections of certain isotopes were not well known at the time, the actual yield of BRAVO was nearly three times the predicted yield. Other and more ominous in-

Table 3-1. Summary of Events, CASTLE Series (March-May 1954).

Date	Test	Location	Yield (MT)
March 1	BRAVO	Bikini (Sandspit off Nam Island)	15
March 27	ROMEO	Bikini (Barge in BRAVO Crater)	11
April 7	KOON	Bikini (Surface off Eneman Island)	110 (KT)
April 26	UNION	Bikini (Barge off Iroij Island)	6.9
May 5	YANKEE	Bikini (Barge in UNION Crater)	13.5
May 14	NECTAR	Enewetak (Barge in MIKE Crater)	1.69

Table 3-2. Experiment Categories During CASTLE Test Series.[43]

Type of Experiment	Number
Blast wave propagation through air, ground, and water.	10
Initial neutron and gamma radiation, documentation of fallout, especially downwind deposition of weapon debris.	9
Blast effects on structures, tree stands, and sea mine fields.	5
Test of Service equipment and techniques.	6
Burst detection studies in electromagnetic pulse generation, airborne low-frequency sound, and collection of nuclear weapon debris.	3
Cloud photography.	1
Total	34

dications of the higher than expected yield were the high levels of radiation that made it impossible to return immediately to any part of Bikini, forcing Naval ships carrying test personnel to retreat to more than 50 miles south of the atoll. Unable to enter the Bikini lagoon, the principal vessels of the Task Group returned to the main base at Enewetak, 190 miles west of Bikini.

Before the end of the day, Air Force cloud tracking teams reported that winds aloft were carrying the radioactive cloud from BRAVO slightly northeast, toward a group of Marshall Islands that were beyond the danger zone established by Joint Task Force 7 for the CASTLE series. Early on March 2, 1954, the Air Force sent amphibious aircraft to Rongerik, 133 nautical miles from ground zero, to evacuate 28 military personnel who were part of the Joint Task Force. Later in the day the Navy dispatched destroyers from the Bikini area to evacuate native populations from other atolls. Almost 200 islanders were transported to Kwajalein, where they were treated for radiation exposure.[44]

The most unfortunate radiation incident from BRAVO was not discovered until March 14, when Japanese fishermen aboard the *Daigo Fukurya Maru* (Fortunate Dragon No. 5) returned to Japan with all 23 members of the crew suffering from radiation exposure. The ship's log indicated that the vessel had been about 82 nautical miles from Bikini at the time of the shot, just beyond the eastern boundary of the exclusion area. Within a week the incident created a sensation in the Japanese press as reporters wrote frightening stories about "ashes of death," while one newspaper reported that the Japanese people were "terror-stricken by the outrageous power of atomic weapons which they had witnessed for the third time."[45]

Even before ROMEO, the second shot in the CASTLE series, could be fired on March 27, Washington was seeking more information on the impact of BRAVO. General Kenneth E. Fields, the Director of the Commission's Division of Military Application, cabled General Clarkson, the Joint Task Force commander, for "...broad information on present opera-

Brigadier General Estes, PPG Operations Commander (in shorts) greeting Lieutenant General Curtis LeMay, SAC Commander (far right) and his party upon their arrival at Enewetak airstrip on April 12, 1954 during Operation CASTLE.

tional conditions" prevailing at the proving grounds, particularly "the fallout situation." AFSWP scientists joined those from the weapons laboratories in producing an analysis, "Radioactive Fallout Hazards from Surface Bursts of Very-High-Yield Nuclear Weapons."[46]

Before solid information on fallout was available, President Eisenhower had set in motion the establishment of a special Technological Capabilities Panel to study the danger of surprise attack on the United States by the Soviet Union. James R. Killian, Jr., president of Massachusetts Institute of Technology, submitted the panel's report to the National Security Council in February 1955. The report concluded that both sides would be vulnerable to surprise attack by thermonuclear weapons. The United States would hold the upper hand until 1960, but thereafter the panel predicted that an attack by either side with thermonuclear weapons would undoubtedly destroy more than cities or devastate regions; it would result in mutual destruction of the combatants.[47]

Faced with the staggering implications of thermonuclear weapons, the Office of Defense Mobilization joined a special interagency task force to revise minimum standards for dispersal of new industrial facilities from the ground zero of potential targets. Prior to BRAVO the standard had been 10 miles, but now with the enormous fallout pattern from that test, even tripling that standard would not offer protection from a cloud 40 miles wide and 200 miles long.⁴⁸

By early April 1954, the BRAVO test had raised international fears. Indian Prime Minister Jawaharlal Nehru called for a test moratorium, soon to be followed by statements from Pope Pius XII and Albert Schweitzer raising moral concerns about continued testing. Within a week both Dulles and Henry Cabot Lodge, the United States Ambassador to the United Nations, raised the question of a partial test ban. At a National Security Council meeting on May 6, the President spoke warmly in favor of a test moratorium. He believed that United States' sponsorship of a moratorium would gain a propaganda advantage over the Soviet Union. But even more important, Eisenhower thought it was wrong to treat "this terrible problem" negatively. He could not envision a long-term solution to the danger of nuclear warfare without first establishing a test ban. Only when he was convinced that a test ban was unenforceable at that time did the President, at least temporarily, abandon the idea.⁴⁹

In the absence of a nuclear test ban, the United States had no choice but to rush the development of an arsenal of thermonuclear weapons, despite, or even because of, the potential horrors of thermonuclear warfare. After viewing films of the IVY-MIKE shot, Prime Minister Winston Churchill had ordered all work on air raid shelters abandoned as useless, and he informed Eisenhower that the British would proceed with development of their own thermonuclear weapon.* ⁵⁰

---

* The first British atomic bomb was detonated within the hold of a supply ship, the *HMS Plym*, on October 3, 1952 during Operation HURRICANE, conducted off Australia's Monte Bello islands. The later British thermonuclear weapon development tests were conducted during Operation GRAPPLE in 1957, in the vicinity of Christmas Island in the South Pacific.

BUILDING THE NUCLEAR ARSENAL

Throughout the construction of the nuclear arsenal, AFSWP continued to have a central role within DoD. As General Luedecke explained to the House Committee on Appropriations 10 days after the BRAVO shot:

"In pursuing our three-way mission of technical, logistic, and training services, our basic principle has been to provide only those things which the Services cannot do themselves or which can be done more economically by one organization. In implementation of this principle, we have trained all the atomic weapons assembly organizations of the three Services. We secure from the Atomic Energy Commission all the training weapons and testing and handling equipment which must be manufactured by it. We are the focal point for the three Services in the military phases of research and development and testing of atomic weapons. We are thus able to prevent duplication and become the source of basic information leading to the military requirements for weapons development, weapons effects, and weapons defense."

In his presentation, Luedecke provided the figures shown in Table 3-3 to support AFSWP's 1955 budget. He reported that between 8,500 and 9,000 military personnel and about 1,700 civilian employees were assigned to AFSWP, stationed at either Headquarters, Field Command, or at AFSWP test sites.⁵¹

As the budget figures suggests, a large share of the resources (and personnel) of AFSWP were devoted in one way or another to supporting the continuing series of weapon tests in Nevada and the Pacific. In direct response to the fallout crisis created by BRAVO, AFSWP Headquarters set up a fallout study group to provide the JCS with a series of reports showing analysis and evaluation of radi-

Table 3-3. AFSWP 1955 Budget.

Category	Amount	1955 Budget
Maintenance and Operation		
Support of Testing Beyond Budgets of the Three Services	$11,786,000	
Training	$800,200	
Operation of National Storage Sites	$4,802,980	
Operation of AFSWP Headquarters	$774,275	
Operation of Field Command	$2,000,000	
Maintenance and Operation, Sandia Base	$6,417,805	
Total, Operation and Maintenance		$26,581,000
Research and Development		
For Full-scale Weapon Tests	$9,900,000	
For Laboratory Research	$2,350,000	
Total, Research and Development		$12,250,000
Procurement and Production*		$279,190
Total, AFSWP		$66,750,000

* With funds carried over from the previous year, the total amount available in this category was $28 million.

ation hazards resulting from weapon tests. The technical divisions at Headquarters, however, continued to fund scores of contracts at university and government laboratories to study the biological and biomedical effects of radiation, quite apart from the direct analysis of data from weapon tests.[52]

After the completion of the CASTLE series in May of 1954, Field Command personnel assigned to Task Unit 13 at the PPG returned to Sandia Base, and the Weapons Effects Division at Field Command began preparations for the next test series, Operation TEAPOT, to be conducted in the spring of 1955. Staff members of the Development Division were busy serving on 14 committees set up to study missile warhead designs while another committee continued work on the nuclear artillery projectile. During 1954, the Plans Division felt new pressures on staff with an added maintenance workload as a result of the increase in the numbers and types of weapons entering the stockpile. As design improvements came from Los Alamos and Livermore, retrofitting stockpile weapons became a significant agency effort.[53]

TEST OPERATIONS: WIGWAM, TEAPOT, AND REDWING

Since the underwater shot had been canceled at the CROSSROADS series in 1946, the Navy had been hoping to conduct such a test to observe the effects of a nuclear detonation on ships and submarines. Not until December 1952 did the JCS recognize the need for an underwater test and direct the Chief of AFSWP to begin planning. A month later AFSWP created the Special Field Project Division to give the planning group a place in the Headquarters organization.

WIGWAM was to be designed to determine the optimum yield of nuclear depth bombs and their lethal range against submarines and surface ships, particularly in terms of hull splitting and internal shock damage. The test would also help to judge the effectiveness of an underwater nuclear burst against convoy or task force formations as compared to a surface or air burst. It would also be necessary to study effects on marine biology, oceanographic phenomena associated with the explosion, problems of long-range detection, and shockwave phenomena.

Early 1953 was not a propitious time to launch a new project as the Eisenhower administration began looking for ways to reduce the defense budget. As a result, some ancillary atomic studies and research was canceled. Only one test was to be conducted on just two full-scale targets, both at the same depth but at different distances from the detonation. Not until late in 1953 was most of the funding restored and a third target added.

After considering dozens of possible targets, the Special Field Project Division settled on a simplified, conservative design, 120 feet in length, a prototype of the 563 class submarine. For the detonation, the Navy would use a nuclear weapon that could be easily adapted for suspension under sea and for remote control of the safe handling and firing sequence. The test would be conducted in the eastern Pacific, at least 50 miles from the coast and 200-600 miles south and southwest of San Diego.[54]

The most challenging feature of the test was designing the vast array of precisely spaced floats and barges on the surface that were tethered to the nuclear device and three targets 2,000 feet below the surface. Each of the barges above the targets had to be equipped with electronic cables and air hoses to blow the ballast tanks on the targets so that they could be lowered or raised to the surface. Once the preliminary design had been completed, the David Taylor Model Basin ran a series of tests of the array on a 1-to-13 scale early in 1954. Trials of a one-third scale model, off the Virginia coast in heavy seas later in the year with one target, resulted in some damage to air hoses and prevented surface handling and towing of the target at slightly negative buoyancy. The model performed sufficiently well, however, that confidence in a full-scale array surviving extreme sea conditions rose. At the same time, the Long Beach Naval Shipyard had begun constructing the three target vessels and modifying the barges that would carry the instrumentation for the targets.[55]

Trials of the full-scale array off San Diego in January 1955 went smoothly, but severe weather on the third day of the tests pulled the air hose and instrumentation cable out of one target and damaged another. The Naval group struggled through heavy seas back to Long Beach, where the target vessels were repaired and cables were modified.

Although WIGWAM was not to be conducted at the Pacific Proving Grounds, the designated test site was outside the continental United States. For that reason control of the test was assigned to Joint Task Force 7, and the Navy group in charge of the array was designated as CTG 7.3. On May 2, 1955, ships in the Task Group began moving to the test area from west coast ports. High seas on the way damaged the target vessels as they

Overhead view of Frenchman Flats; part of Nevada Test Site.

were being towed on the surface. Once repairs were made, the Task Force began assembling the five-mile array on May 12. Despite the severe weather, the array remained intact, and the test was fired midday on May 14. Although one target vessel was destroyed by the detonation and another damaged, the test produced solid data for determining the distances for lethal damage to submarines and surface ships by a deeply submerged nuclear weapon.[56]

Following normal procedures, the AEC provided the nuclear device for the test and WIGWAM was almost entirely a Navy operation. AFSWP, however, had played a vital role, first in providing the administrative structure and then participating in the planning, working out administrative channels with the Navy and other Services, and obtaining the necessary funding. Without AFSWP, the WIGWAM test never would have occurred.

In January of 1955, six weeks before the first shot in the Operation TEAPOT Series, Eisenhower summed up his views "...on our general needs in military strength" in a letter to Secretary of Defense Wilson. The letter contained nothing that had not been stated a year earlier in the President's presentation of the "New Look," but the short two-page document highlighted his principal convictions. The threat to the nation's security, the President wrote, was a continuing and many-sided threat that required a broad and sustained response that had to be "...founded on a strong and expanding economy, readily convertible to the tasks of war." In the face of rapid scientific and technical change, the President held that "...we should base our security upon military formations which make maximum use of science and technology in order to minimize numbers in men." Furthermore, the increasing destructiveness of modern weapons and the increasing efficiency of long-range bombers made the nation, "...for the first time in its history," vulnerable to a sudden enemy attack. The nation, Eisenhower concluded, had to maintain the capability to deter or blunt an enemy attack "by a combination of effective retaliatory power and a continental defense system of steadily increasing effectiveness."[57]

The Department of Defense could have had no better rationale for Operation TEAPOT, a 15-shot series (one nonnuclear test) scheduled for the Nevada Proving Grounds now renamed the Nevada Test Site (NTS), in the winter and spring of 1955. Four of the shots were related to what the President referred to as strategic bombing capability: Shots WASP and WASP PRIME were used to test air-drop delivery techniques; HADR was a non-nuclear high-explosive device detonated at 38,000 feet to calibrate delivery and technical equipment for Shot HA, a nuclear shot detonated on April 6. Shot ESS, a prototype nuclear demolition device, was detonated in a shaft 67 feet deep, and eight low-yield shots were detonated on towers on Yucca Flat. One shot, MET, fired on Frenchman Flat, was designed only for weapon effects tests.[58] Table 3-4 provides a summary of Operation TEAPOT events.

As in the earlier Nevada test series, TEAPOT combined the diagnostic measurements designed by Los Alamos and Livermore with the DoD projects, which included weapon effects projects and troop participation. In fact, the activities of the laboratories and DoD units were so closely scheduled through the Joint Test Organization that it was no longer necessary to assign a double name, such as UPSHOT-KNOTHOLE, to the series. It was named simply TEAPOT.

On the Defense side, Field Command's responsibilities were widespread and diverse. DoD assigned 11,000 military and civilian personnel to the test site, 8,000 of whom participated in DESERT ROCK VI. This test contingent was composed of support and administrative staff and military personnel from all Services participating as observers or as troops in exercises and maneuvers under a variety of post-shot conditions.[59]

The Joint Test Organization coordinated all scientific and technical operations, which included weapon diagnostics, weapon effects tests, effects on civilian populations, and an operational training program for DoD personnel and support services. Although relatively few individuals participated in these activities compared to the DESERT ROCK VI exercises, their personal responsibilities were critical to the gathering of test data and the success of the shots during the series.[60]

AFSWP Field Command, Los Alamos, Livermore, and the Civil Effects Test Group, staffed by the Federal Civil Defense Administration, comprised the four test groups at TEAPOT. Composed of scientists and technicians from military and civilian laboratories, support contractors, and the Armed Services, the test groups developed and conducted field experiments before, during, and after the detonations.

Field Command consulted with the laboratories in planning the shot series and coordinating the placement of diagnostic instrumentation, but its heaviest work came at the test site. For almost all the shots in the series, Field Command worked with each sponsoring organization in designing the experiment and deciding how to place the instrumentation for the experiment around the test site.

Table 3-4. Summary of Events, TEAPOT Series (1955).

SHOT	Sponsor	Planned Date	Actual Date	Local Time	NTS Location	Type of Detonation	Height of Burst (Feet)	Actual Yield (KT)
WASP	LASL	18 Feb	18 Feb	1200	Area 7	Airdrop	762	1
MOTH	LASL	22 Feb	22 Feb	0545	Area 3	Tower	300	2
TESLA	UCRL	25 Feb	1 March	0530	Area 9	Tower	300	7
TURK	UCRL	15 Feb	7 March	0520	Area 2	Tower	500	43
HORNET	LASL	6 March	12 March	0520	Area 3	Tower	300	3
BEE	LASL	10 March	22 March	0505	Area 7	Tower	500	8
ESS	DOD	15 March	23 March	1230	Area 10	Crater	-67	1
HADR	DOD	1 March	25 March	0900	Above Area 1	Airdrop	38,000*	(non-nuclear)
APPLE1	LASL	18 March	29 March	0456	Area 4	Tower	500	14
WASP PRIME	LASL	20 March	29 March	1000	Area 7	Airdrop	737	3
HA	DOD	4 March	6 April	1000	Above Area 1	Airdrop	36,520*	3
POST	UCRL	1 March	9 April	0430	Area 9	Tower	300	2
MET	LASL/ DOD	1 March	15 April	1115	Area 5	Tower	400	22
APPLE2	LASL	26 April	5 May	0510	Area 1	Tower	500	29
ZUCCHINI	LASL	1 April	15 May	0500	Area 7	Tower	500	28

* Mean sea level

Each experiment was organized as a project, ranging from seven to more than 20 projects for each of the shots. Many of the projects followed the patterns established at UPSHOT-KNOTHOLE for basic measurements of blast, thermal, and radiation effects, tests of equipment and operational techniques, and measurements in support of other projects, such as technical photography. Examples of the diversity and complexity of these projects are shown in Table 3-5, which lists the projects scheduled for Shot BEE on March 22.[61]

The Joint Task Organization, working with scientists from the AEC, took additional precautions at TEAPOT to avoid radiation exposures above the limits established by the Commission, and especially incidents of off-site fallout such as occurred at UPSHOT-KNOTHOLE. Nine of the fourteen shots at TEAPOT were less than 10 kilotons, to reduce the probability of offsite fallout. To further reduce the hazard of radiation, the Test Director delayed many of the shots until favorable weather conditions prevailed. The cumulative effect of these delays was that ZUCCHINI, the last shot in the series scheduled for April 1, was not fired until May 15.

Operation REDWING, similar to its

Table 3-5. Field Command Military Effects Group Projects, Shot BEE, March 22, 1955.

Project	Title	Participants	Estimated Personnel
1.2	Shock Wave Photography	Naval Ordnance Laboratory	2
1.10	Overpressure and Dynamic Pressure versus Time and Distance	Stanford Research Institute	15
1.14b	Measurements of Airblast Phenomena with Self-Recording Gauges	Ballistic Research Laboratories	6
2.1	Gamma Exposure versus Distance	Army Signal Corps Engineering Laboratories	4
2.2	Neutron Flux Measurements	Naval Research Laboratory	5
2.5.1	Fallout Studies	Chemical Research Laboratory; Chemical Warfare Laboratory	*
2.8a	Contact Radiation Hazard Associated with Contaminated Aircraft	Air Force Special Weapons Center	5
2.8b	Manned Penetrations of Atomic Clouds	Air Force Special Weapons Center	2
3.1	Response of Drag-Type Equipment Targets in the Precursor Zone	Ballistic Research Laboratories	5
5.1	Destructive Loads on Aircraft in Flight	Wright Air Development Center	*
5.2	Effects on Fighter Aircraft in Flight	Wright Air Development Center	2
6.1.1a	Evaluation of Military Radiological Equipment	Army Signal Corps Engineering Laboratories	3
6.1.1b	Evaluation of a Radiological Defense Warning System	Army Signal Corps Engineering Laboratories	3
6.3	Missile Detonation Locator	Army Signal Corps Engineering Laboratories	*
6.4	Test of IBDA Equipment	Wright Air Development Center	14
6.5	Test of Airborne Naval Radars for IBDA	Bureau of Aeronautics	3
8.1	Measurement of Direct and Ground-Reflected Thermal Radiation at Altitude	Bureau of Aeronautics	4
8.4b	Thermal Measurements from Fixed Ground Installations	Naval Radiological Defense Laboratory	3
8.4d	Spectrometer Measurements	Naval Radiological Defense Laboratory	*
8.4f	Bolometer Measurements	Naval Radiological Defense Laboratory	*
9.1	Technical Photography	Lookout Mountain Laboratory; AFSWC; Air Force Missile Test Center; EG&G	7
9.4	Atomic Cloud Growth Study	Air Force Cambridge Research Center; U.S. Weather Bureau; EG&G	*

* Unknown

thermonuclear predecessors, reflected the determination of President Eisenhower and his advisors to make thermonuclear weapons the keystone of national defense against Soviet attack. REDWING consisted of 17 shots, at the Pacific Proving Grounds, from May through July of 1956. Ten shots (11th at Bikini Atoll), each with a yield of less than one megaton, were fired at Enewetak, where weapon effects were unlikely to damage structures or endanger personnel working at the headquarters and main base of the operation. The other five tests (6th at Enewetak), all in the megaton range, were either surface shots or air drops at Bikini, 190 miles east of Enewetak. Table 3-6 summarizes the Operation REDWING tests.

REDWING was the first test of megaton weapons in the Pacific since the CASTLE series two years earlier, when fallout from BRAVO spread far beyond the exclusion area, caused radiation burns on islanders and Japanese fishermen, and aroused a worldwide storm of protest. In an attempt to allay the anxieties raised by another series of thermonuclear tests, the DoD and the AEC issued a joint press release a week before the first shot on May 9 to outline the precautions to be taken during REDWING. The press release described the improved fallout prediction

Table 3-6. Summary of Events, REDWING Series (May-July 1956).[62]

Date	Name	Location	Yield
May 4	LACROSSE	Enewetak (Surface)	40 KT
May 20	CHEROKEE	Bikini (Air Drop)	3.8 MT
May 27	ZUNI	Bikini (Surface)	3.5 MT
May 27	YUMA	Enewetak (Tower)	190 Tons
May 30	ERIE	Enewetak (Tower)	14.9 KT
June 6	SEMINOLE	Enewetak (Surface)	13.7 KT
June 11	FLATHEAD	Bikini (Barge)	365 KT
June 11	BLACKFOOT	Enewetak (Tower)	8 KT
June 13	KICKAPOO	Enewetak (Tower)	1.49 KT
June 16	OSAGE	Enewetak (Air Drop)	1.7 KT
June 21	INCA	Enewetak (Tower)	15.2 KT
June 25	DAKOTA	Bikini (Barge)	1.1 MT
July 2	MOHAWK	Enewetak (Tower)	360 KT
July 8	APACHE	Enewetak (Barge)	1.85 MT
July 10	NAVAJO	Bikini (Barge)	4.5 MT
July 20	TEWA	Bikini (Barge)	5 MT
July 21	HURON	Enewetak (Barge)	250 KT

capability available and the extensive monitoring network at the test site and beyond. Plans for surveying marine life in the Pacific and the expectation that yields expected at REDWING would be lower than those in 1954 were also described.

For the first time since the CROSSROADS test in 1946, uncleared observers were permitted during a test. Approximately 15 media observers and 17 officials from the Federal Civil Defense Administration were permitted to witness the LACROSSE and CHEROKEE shots, the first two in the series. CHEROKEE was a 3.8 megaton device dropped from a B-52 bomber, the first such event conducted by the United States. The shot did host some unique measurements, but it was primarily a demonstration of the ability to deliver large-yield thermonuclear weapons. Such a demonstration seemed essential after the Soviet Union announced the air drop of a thermonuclear weapon six months earlier, in November of 1955.[63]

Although weapon diagnostics and tests were the primary purpose of REDWING, AFSWP had a major role in conducting the series. Once again Headquarters staff evaluated, selected, and organized weapon effects projects while Field Command assisted the many military and civilian research groups in setting up experiments at the test site. Members of Task Group 7.1.3 began moving to the Pacific in January of 1956 with each project having one Field Command representative on hand.[64]

Field Command organized eight programs for REDWING, as shown in Table 3-7.

SEARCH FOR A TEST BAN

Even before the REDWING tests ended, the CHEROKEE shot became the source of a heavy attack on the test program. A few days after the air drop, General James M. Gavin, Army Chief of Research and Development, used the shot to illustrate the power and significance of the hydrogen bomb. He told a Senate committee that a bomb like CHEROKEE dropped on the east coast of the United States would "kill or maim seven million persons and render hundreds of square miles uninhabitable for perhaps a generation." Even worse, Gavin predicted that a similar attack on the Soviet Union would spread death from radiation across Asia to Japan and the Philippines. If the winds blew the other way, an attack on eastern Russia would eventually kill hundreds of millions of Europeans, including, some commentators added, half the population of the British Isles.[65]

Under pressure from the White House to release some information about the success at REDWING, AEC Commissioner Strauss told the public that the tests had "...achieved a maximum effect in the immediate area of a target with minimum widespread fallout hazard." He concluded that REDWING had proven "...much of importance not only from a military point of view but from a humanitarian aspect."[66] The Administration's attempt to use the "clean weapon" issue to counter the growing demand for an end to nuclear testing backfired when critics jumped on the implications in Strauss' statement that a weapon that could kill millions of people could somehow be called "humanitarian."

In the fall of 1956 nuclear weapons, for the first time, became an issue in a Presidential election when Adlai Stevenson, the Democratic candidate, told an American Legion convention that the United States should end the testing of megaton thermonuclear weapons. Although Eisenhower, with his access to classified information, could convincingly refute Stevenson's arguments, Steven-

Table 3-7. Operation REDWING Programs (May-July 1956).

Program	Type	Detail
1	Blast Effects	Experiment established basic blast and shock phenomenology of specific shots in various environments (10 projects).
2	Nuclear Radiation	Planned to obtain comprehensive fallout data for a model that would permit extrapolation to different devices, burst heights, and surface conditions; research on decontamination and nuclear radiation countermeasures; and studies of initial gamma and neutron radiation (17 projects, most at Bikini).
3	Effects on Structures	One experiment on the blast effect of multi-megaton detonations on industrial buildings (one project).
4	Chorioretinal Burns	Experiments on the eyes of animals at six shots (several projects).
5	Effects on Aircraft Structures	Experiments to test the reliability and delivery capability of aircraft subjected to weapon effects (9 projects).
6	Studies of Electromagnetic Effects	Experiments for long-range detection of nuclear explosions (6 projects).
7	Thermal Radiation and Effects at Cherokee	(7 projects).
8	Supporting Photography	For all projects in the military effects program.

son did succeed in making disarmament and nuclear testing major campaign issues and thus kept the debate before the American public.[67]

Once the election was over, the Administration returned again to the test ban issue. Since its first proposal in 1956, the Administration had taken the position that it would consider a test ban only when a foolproof system of international inspection had first been established. Now, in January 1957, United Nations (UN) Ambassador Henry Cabot Lodge presented a five-point disarmament proposal to the UN General Assembly. The key to the plan was a call for the end to the production of nuclear weapons under strict international supervision. There was even an offer to consider a future test ban if an international inspections system could be established. However, the preconditions demanded by the Russians (complete nuclear disarmament) ensured the American proposal would fail.

Facing this stalemate, the United States, the Soviet Union, and the United Kingdom pressed forward with nuclear testing in 1957. The Russians conducted a long series of secret tests from August of 1956 through April of 1957; the five April tests spreading heavy fallout levels, although this was not known in the West at the time. The British, ignoring impassioned opposition at home, fired their first thermonuclear test at Christmas Island in the Pacific on May 15. Two weeks later Joint Task Force 7 began another series of tests, Operation PLUMBBOB, in Nevada.

RB-57D sampling aircraft during test operations.

As the tempo of nuclear testing increased in 1957, so did public opposition. Albert Schweitzer captured world attention in his Nobel Peace Prize address on April 24, when he focused on the danger that radioactive fallout posed for human life. A month later Linus Pauling, in an address at Washington University in St. Louis, declared that "...no human being should be sacrificed to the project of perfecting weapons that could kill hundreds of millions of human beings." The response to Pauling's remarks was so favorable that he launched a petition, signed by 2,000 scientists, calling for an international agreement to halt testing. At the same time the Joint Committee on Atomic Energy launched eight days of hearings on fallout and radiation effects. The hundreds of pages of technical material printed in the hearings served as a convenient reference document for further public debates on the fallout issue.[68]

The international debate over fallout, beginning with Schweitzer's letter and continuing through the Joint Committee hearings, brought about an abrupt change in public attitudes. In the fall of 1956, 44 percent of respondents to a Gallup poll supported a test ban; while 63 percent of Americans thought the United States should end testing if all other nations so agreed. This shift in public opinion reinforced Eisenhower's strong interest in a nuclear test ban, as he spurred his Administration toward that goal.[69]

A CHANGE IN AFSWP COMMAND

During the first phase of the PLUMBBOB series in June of 1957, General Luedecke completed his tour as Chief, AFSWP, and retired from the Air Force to replace Kenneth Nichols as General Manager of the AEC. In his four years as head of AFSWP, Luedecke had reached most of the goals he had set for the agency early in 1953.

Luedecke had played a leading part in negotiating the transfer of most of the nuclear weapon stockpile from the AEC to AFSWP and then to each of the Armed Services. By 1954, AFSWP had become the control point for the allocation, distribution, and control of non-nuclear components. Field Command now had the funding it needed to build and maintain additional weapon storage sites in the continental United States and to assist the Armed Services in handling weapons at overseas bases and on Navy ships at sea. In 1955, Eisenhower had directed that weapons with yields of over 600 kilotons would remain in AEC custody, even if dispersed to military units, but in 1956 the Commission had agreed that military personnel could perform this task on its behalf. The Commission still maintained custody of some high-yield thermonuclear weapons, but most of the stockpile was in military custody where it was readily accessible in case of a surprise attack.[70]

In October of 1952, a few months before Luedecke took command of AFSWP, the Headquarters staff was just coming to realize that AFSWP was not to be only a bridge organization until the military Services could take over all aspects of developing, testing, acquiring, and handling of nuclear weapons. Rather, AFSWP would continue to have a research and coordination function for years to come.[71] AFSWP, under Luedecke's leadership, had assumed a central role within DoD and in its relationships with the AEC and its weapon laboratories. As a result, AFSWP had made a major contribution to the growth of the nuclear stockpile, now largely in the hands of the military Services. At the end of 1952, the nation had stockpiled 841 weapons with a total yield of almost 50 megatons. By the time Luedecke left AFSWP in 1957, the stockpile had grown to 5,543 weapons with a total yield of 17,546 megatons.[72]

Luedecke's drafts of legislation to amend the Atomic Energy Act of 1946 had not gone beyond AFSWP Headquarters, but he supported efforts at higher levels in DoD to amend Section 6 of the Act that gave primary custody to the Commission. In the end, the new Atomic Energy Act of 1954 not only clarified the language of Section 6 but also permitted the Commission to remove information primarily related to military applications from the Restricted Data category.[73] In the future, Restricted Data was to be reserved for weapon design only and limited to the AEC, while a lesser classification became available for weapon effects. These revisions gave the military Services much easier access to data they needed to plan for the effects of nuclear weapons.

Replacing General Luedecke at AFSWP in June 1957 was Rear Admiral Edward N. Parker. A native of Pennsylvania, Parker had graduated from the U.S. Naval Academy in 1925 and served mainly at sea prior to World War II. He took command of the *USS Parrott* in January of 1940 and immediately found himself at the hottest part of the sea war in Asia. He earned a Navy Cross for his capable leadership under heavy fire from a Japanese task force off Borneo in the Dutch East Indies in January 1942, shortly after hostilities began in the Pacific. Three weeks later, Parker won a second Navy Cross for bravery and seamanship in the Badoeng Straits, and a Silver Star a week later. By the end of 1942, Parker had won a third Navy Cross, which, with the exception of the Congressional Medal of Honor, was the Service's highest award for valor. In command of the *USS Cushing*, Parker "...engaged at close quarters and defeated a superior enemy force" near Guadalcanal, although the *Cushing* sank in the battle. In 1946 he received a commendation from the Secretary of the Navy for his activities at CROSSROADS. After a series of commands stateside and in the Mediterranean, Parker returned to

Rear Admiral Edward N. Parker, AFSWP Chief, 1957–1960.

Washington. For more than two years, from September of 1952 to the end of 1954, Parker served as Deputy Chief of AFSWP under Nichols. After two more years at sea, he came back to Washington as a Special Assistant to the Deputy Chief of Naval Operations (Plans and Policy) before reporting to his AFSWP assignment.[74]

Parker immediately confronted a number of issues that threatened the direction of nuclear testing. The most immediate was fallout from weapons testing. Anxiety about the danger of radioactive fallout was rapidly becoming a major public concern in the United States and abroad. Since the Japanese fishing boat incident during the CASTLE BRAVO test in 1954, President Eisenhower and other administration officials, Congressmen, scientists, and the public expressed increasing concern about radioactivity and atmospheric testing. The CASTLE BRAVO incident led the government to heighten its fallout precautions and intensify radiation monitoring in the field. The TEAPOT tests at NTS in 1955 incorporated these new policies.[75]

TRANSITION

General Luedecke's tenure as AFSWP Chief had been years of accomplishment and growth for the agency. The United States' growing arsenal of tactical and strategic nuclear weapons provided what the Eisenhower administration saw as a credible deterrent to Soviet aggression. Within a few months, however, under the helm of Admiral Parker, the agency would, once again, have to meet new challenges in creative ways, while the nation met the Soviet's newest challenge... in space.

ENDNOTES

1. Richard G. Hewlett and Francis Duncan, *Atomic Shield/1947-1952*, University Park, PA: Pennsylvania State University Press, 1962. p. 590.
2. Roger M. Anders, ed., *Forging the Atomic Shield: Excerpts from the Diary of Gordon E. Dean*, Chapel Hill: University of North Carolina Press, 1987, p. 218.
3. Defense Nuclear Agency, *Operation IVY*, 1952, DNA Report 6036F, December 1982, pp. 29-38.
4. "First History of AFSWP," Vol. 5, 3.10.13 - 3.10.16; Defense Nuclear Agency, *Operation IVY*, 1952, DNA Report 6036F, December 1982, pp. 118-176, 199-200.
5. Defense Nuclear Agency, *Operation IVY*, 1952, DNA Report 6036F, December 1982, pp. 187-188.
6. Richard G. Hewlett and Jack M. Holl, *Atoms for Peace and War, 1953-1961: Eisenhower and the Atomic Energy Commission*, Berkeley: University of California Press, 1989, pp. 1-5.
7. *Ibid.*, pp. 17-18; quoted in Ronald E. Powaski, *March to Armageddon: The United States and the Nuclear Arms Race, 1939 to the Present*, New York: Oxford University Press, 1987, p. 62.
8. *Public Papers of the Presidents of the United States, 1953: Dwight D. Eisenhower*, Washington, D.C.: Government Printing Office, 1960, p. 2.
9. In early 1953, the AFSWP Headquarters staff totaled 249, comprised of 154 military officers and enlisted personnel and 95 civilians. "First History of AFSWP," Vol. 6, 3.1.1 - 3.1.2.
10. "First History of AFSWP," Vol. 5, 3.8.6 - 3.8.7.
11. "First History of AFSWP," Vol. 6, 3.8.1 - 3.8.27, 3.10.1 - 3.10.24.
12. "First History of AFSWP," Vol. 6, 3.6.1 - 3.6.71.
13. Hewlett and Duncan, *Atomic Shield*, pp. 581-584; Hewlett and Holl, *Atoms for Peace and War*, p. 146.
14. "First History of AFSWP," Vol. 6, 3.7.59 - 3.7.60.
15. "First History of AFSWP," Vol. 6, 3.3.4 - 3.3.5; Chap. 4, Field Command, 4.3.16.
16. "First History of AFSWP," Vol. 4, 4.1.2 - 4.1.3, 4.4.3, 4.5.53 - 4.5.70; Vol. 5, 4.3.16; Vol. 6, 4.4.1 - 4.4.10, 4.4.20.
17. "First History of AFSWP," Vol. 6, 3.1.4.
18. "First History of AFSWP," Vol. 6, 4.6.1 - 4.6.6.
19. "First History of AFSWP," Vol. 6, 3.5.5 - 3.5.9.
20. "First History of AFSWP," Vol. 6, 3.5.10 - 3.5.12.
21. "First History of AFSWP," Vol. 6, 3.5.13.
22. "First History of AFSWP," Vol. 6, 3.7.1 - 3.7.5; Atomic Energy Commission, "An Agreement Between the AEC and the DoD for the Development, Production, and Standardization of Atomic Weapons," March 31, 1953, DSWA General Counsel's Files. The basic agreement, with some modifications, was still in effect in 1984 between the Departments of Defense and Energy.
23. "First History of AFSWP," Vol. 6, 3.5.14 - 3.5.15.
24. "First History of AFSWP," Vol. 6, 3.5.16.
25. "History of the Armed Forces Special Weapons Project," Latter Period, 1955-1958, Part I [henceforth cited as "AFSWP History, 1955-1958"], pp. 30-31.
26. "AFSWP History, 1955-1958," pp. 30-31; "First History of AFSWP," Vol. 6, Chap. 4, Field Command, 4.4.41 - 4.4.42'; Hewlett and Holl, *Atoms for Peace and War*, pp. 145-147.
27. Barton C. Hacker, *Elements of Controversy: The Atomic Energy Commission and Radiation Safety in Nuclear Weapons Testing, 1947-1974*, Berkeley: University of California Press, 1994, pp. 93-95.
28. *Ibid.*, pp. 96-99.
29. *Ibid.*, pp. 99-113; Hewlett and Holl, *Atoms for Peace and War*, pp. 150-159.
30. Hewlett and Holl, *Atoms for Peace and War*, pp. 57-59.
31. "AFSWP History, 1955-1958," Part I, pp. 31-34.
32. Hewlett and Holl, *Atoms for Peace and War*, pp. 27-32; *Congressional Record*, 83 Cong., 1 Sess., 3414, A2010.

33. "First History of AFSWP," Vol. 6, 3.5.72 - 3.5.73.
34. Hewlett and Holl, *Atoms for Peace and War*, pp. 119-122.
35. *Ibid.*, pp. 42-44, 50-57, 59-62, 65-67, 71-72; *Public Papers*, 1953, Eisenhower, pp. 813-822; Dwight D. Eisenhower, *Mandate for Change*, Garden City, NY, 1963, pp. 251-255.
36. NSC 162/2, October 30, 1953, *Foreign Relations of the United States, 1952-1954*, Vol. 2, *National Security Affairs*, Washington, D.C.: Government Printing Office, 1984, pp. 577-597.
37. Saki Dockrill, *Eisenhower's New-Look National Security Policy, 1953-61*, London: MacMillan, 1996, p. 4; Michael Mandelbaum, *The Nuclear Question: The United States and Nuclear Weapons, 1946-1976*, London: Cambridge University Press, 1979, pp. 50-52.
38. Samuel F. Wells, Jr., "The Origins of Massive Retaliation," *Political Science Quarterly*, 96. Spring 1981, pp. 31-33.
39. Glenn H. Snyder, "The 'New Look' of 1953," in W.R. Schilling, P.Y. Hammond, and G.H. Snyder, eds., *Strategy, Politics, and Defense Budgets*, New York: Columbia University Press, 1962, pp. 463-465.
40. Dwight D. Eisenhower, *The White House Years: Mandate for Change, 1953-1956*, Garden City, NY: Doubleday, 1963, pp. 180, 181.
41. Strauss and Wilson to the President, February 5, 1954; Eisenhower to Chairman, Atomic Energy Commission, February 6, 1954; Eisenhower Library.
42. Weapon design plans were then at the heart of a jurisdictional argument between DoD and AEC-DOE concerning where the interface should be drawn between weapon design and effects studies. The interface finally agreed on was that the AEC would calculate warhead outputs in as much technical detail as required to predict effects. This was significant additional work for the labs since it required them to continue calculations further out in time and radius than was required for their own purposes of burn and yield. The interface was between the warhead and weapon, which precluded DoD participation in weapon "design." However, DoD did assume responsibility for calculation of (i.e., x ray, gamma ray, neutron) penetration through the missile skin, the whole missile, and the atmosphere. Thus DoD never became a party to warhead design.
43. Defense Nuclear Agency, *Castle Series, 1954*, DNA Report 6035F, 1982, pp. 167-200.
44. Hewlett and Holl, *Atoms for Peace and War*, pp. 172-177.
45. American Embassy, Tokyo, *Daily Summaries of the Japanese Press*, Periodicals Division (microfilm), Library of Congress.
46. Fields to Clarkson, March 12, 1953, Department of Energy Historian's Office; Hewlett and Holl, *Atoms for Peace and War*, pp. 272-273.
47. James R. Killian, Jr., *Sputnik, Scientists, and Eisenhower: A Memoir of the First Special Assistant to the President for Science and Technology*, Cambridge: MIT Press, pp. 67-71.
48. "ODM Planning for Dispersal of Facilities," AEC Staff Paper 540/15, June 4, 1954, Record Group 326, National Archives.
49. Hewlett and Holl, *Atoms for Peace and War*, pp. 274-276.
50. *Ibid.*, p. 276.
51. House Committee on Appropriations, *Department of the Army Appropriations for 1955*, March 10, 1954, Washington, 1954, pp. 587-593.
52. "History of AFSWP," Part I, Chap. 7-4, pp. 7-38.
53. "First History of AFSWP," Vol. 6, 1953, Chap. 4, Headquarters, Field Command, 4.4.9 - 4.7.4.
54. "First History of AFSWP," Vol. 6, 1953, Chap. 3, Special Field Projects Division, 3.11.1 - 3.1.20.
55. Deputy Chief of Staff, Technical Services, to Historian, AFSWP, July 30, 1954, *History of the Special Field Projects*, January 1 - June 30, 1954.

56. Deputy Chief of Staff, Technical Services, to Historian, AFSWP, July 30, 1955, *History of the Special Field Projects*, January 1 - June 30, 1955.
57. Eisenhower to Wilson, January 5, 1955, National Security Archive.
58. Defense Nuclear Agency, *Operation Teapot 1955*, DNA Report 6009F, pp. 34-35.
59. *Ibid.*, pp. 25-26.
60. *Ibid.*, pp. 29-35.
61. *Ibid.*, pp. 81-130; Defense Nuclear Agency, *Shot Bee, A Test in the Teapot Series*, March 22, 1955, DNA Report 6011F, pp. 10-30.
62. U.S. Department of Energy, Nevada Operations Office, *United States Nuclear Tests*, July 1945 through September 1992, DOE/NV-209 (Rev. 14), Washington, D.C., GPO, 1995.
63. Defense Nuclear Agency, *Operation Redwing 1956*, DNA Report 6037F, pp. 21-23.
64. AFSWP, "Semiannual Report," Headquarters, Field Command, Vol. 1, January 1, 1956 - June 30, 1956, pp. 243-266.
65. Robert A. Devine, *Blowing on the Wind: The Nuclear Test Ban Debate, 1954-1960*, New York: Oxford University Press, 1978, pp. 80-81; Hewlett and Holl, *Atoms for Peace and War*, pp. 345-346.
66. Hewlett and Holl, *Atoms for Peace and War*, p. 347.
67. *Ibid.*, pp. 364-370.
68. *Ibid.*, pp. 389-391; Devine, *Blowing on the Wind*, pp. 120-129; Hacker, *Elements of Controversy*, pp. 190-191; Joint Committee on Atomic Energy, *Hearings on the Nature of Radioactive Fallout and Its Effect on Man*, May-June 1957, Government Printing Office: Washington, D.C., 1957.
69. Devine, *Blowing on the Wind*, pp. 139-142.
70. L.A. Ninnich, Jr. and Lewis L. Strauss, "Memorandum of Conference with the President," August 6, 1956; Eisenhower to Strauss, August 8, 1956, National Security Archives.
71. RADM W.K. Mendenhall, Jr., to General Loper, AFSWP, October 29, 1952, Record Group 374, National Archives.
72. U.S. Department of Energy, *Restricted Data Declassification Decisions, 1946 to the Present*, RDD-3, January 1, 1996, Appendix D.
73. Section 6, Atomic Energy Act of 1946, P.L. 585, 79 Cong., 60 Stat., pp. 755-775; Atomic Energy Act of 1954, P.L. 703, 83 Cong., 69 Stat., p. 919. Section 91 of the 1954 Act clarified the language of the old Section 6 by authorizing the Department of Defense "to manufacture, produce, or acquire any atomic weapon or utilization facility for military purposes." Section 142 of the new act removed weapon data from the Restricted Data category.
74. Biography, Vice Admiral Edward N. Parker, Navy Office of Information, Internal Relations Division, December 6, 1963; *Washington Post*, October 17, 1989.
75. Hewlett and Holl, *Atoms for Peace and War*, 451-52; Herbert F. York, *Making Weapons, Talking Peace* (New York: 1987), p. 117.

CHAPTER FOUR

SOME SECOND THOUGHTS, 1957 TO 1963

"So let us begin anew—remembering on both sides that civility is not a sign of weakness, and sincerity is always subject to proof. Let us never negotiate out of fear. But let us never fear to negotiate."

John F. Kennedy
Inaugural Address, January 20, 1961

THE SOVIET'S TURN: SPUTNIK

In the last half of 1957, there were changes in the strategic landscape that permanently altered the nation's perceptions of the balance of world power and that had a lasting impact on the Department of Defense and AFSWP.

On August 21, 1957, the Soviet Union tested an Intercontinental Ballistic Missile (ICBM) over a 4,000-mile trajectory extending the length of Siberia. The ICBM, (SS-6), carried a 10,000-pound payload (equivalent to a three-megaton warhead). The launch was carried out secretly and was initially known to only a few in the U.S. intelligence community. The Soviets subsequently announced that they had successfully tested a strategic missile with intercontinental range and claimed an imminent operational capability. Disbelief of the claim was the predominant reaction in national defense circles and, indeed, among the general public. The Soviet *Sapwood* ICBM was deployed in 1958, with an announced range of 8,500 kilometers (5,270 miles). It was, at the time, significantly more capable than any operational U.S. strategic missile system. The apparent Soviet advantage in intercontinental-range missiles helped fuel the "missile-gap" issue of the 1960 Presidential campaign and the U.S. determination to catch and surpass the Soviet Union in scientific/engineering expertise and achievements.

Any lingering U.S. disbelief in the Soviet's ICBM claim was dispelled less than two months after their ICBM test when, around dinnertime on October 4, 1957, technicians in New York City picked up Radio Moscow's announcement earlier that day: a Russian rocket had successfully launched an artificial satellite into orbit at the outer edges of the earth's atmosphere. Radio operators at the Radio Corporation of America facility in Riverhead, Long Island, soon confirmed the story, picking up the steady "beep...beep... beep" of the satellite's radio as it streaked over the eastern United States. Life magazine characterized the first man-made noise from space as an "...an eerie intermittent croak of a cricket with a cold." To American scientists, the radio transmission shattered notions of their country's scientific superiority. To the American military, the satellite served as a Cold War alarm: the Soviets now had the capability to deliver an intercontinental missile with a nuclear warhead. The world in the atomic age had just grown much, much smaller and Americans were expressing some second thoughts about Soviet technological development.[1]

The satellite was a stunning success. *Sputnik*, short for *Iskustvennyi Sputnik Zemli* or "Artificial Traveler Around the Earth," was a shiny 184-pound, man-made sphere, 22 inches in diameter, about the size of a large beach ball. Launched from the Baiknonur Cosmodrome in the Soviet Union and orbiting the earth at 18,000 miles per hour—at altitudes ranging from 300 to 560 miles—the satellite completed one revolution every 96 minutes. *Sputnik* contained rows of batteries to power two radio transmitters. Outside the satellite antennas sent the signals earthward. By the next morning, the Naval Research Laboratory (NRL) in Washington confirmed that the satellite had passed over the United States four times.[2]

The Russians were ecstatic. *Sputnik* was a technological and propaganda triumph, even though the satellite's orbit around the earth would only last six months. "The present generation," Radio Moscow boasted, "will witness how the free and conscious labor of the people of the new socialist society turns even the most daring of man's dreams into reality." In Washington, three visiting Soviet scientists told reporters that their country was ahead in engineering and science. "In America," one explained, "you have trouble recruiting young men to study science. In the Soviet Union, everyone wants to be a scientist." When told that their *Sput-*

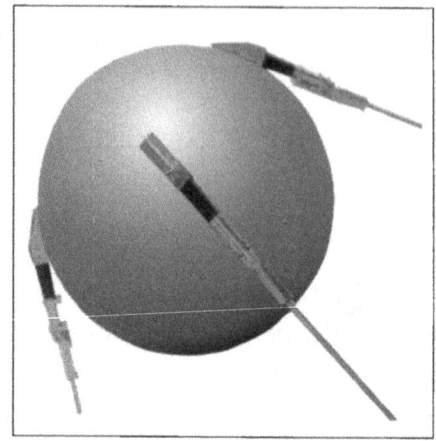

Model of Soviet Satellite: *Sputnik*.

nik was stealing the limelight from the World Series, another replied, "In Russia, scientists are not compared with football players." More painful and revealing, however, was the Russian assertion that "Americans design better automobile tail fins but we design the best intercontinental ballistic missiles and earth satellites."[3] Most Americans recognized the Radio Moscow statement as Cold War propaganda. Nevertheless, *Sputnik's* impact on Main Street USA was profound. On the whole, *Newsweek* magazine reported, Americans were concerned, not panicked. Rather, they "...seemed to have suffered a severe blow to their pride," conducting what one scholar has called "...a veritable orgy of national self-examination and self-criticism." Whatever position one took on *Sputnik's* immediate impact, few would argue with the NBC announcer who described the satellite's beeps as "...the sound which forever separates the new from the old."[4]

The beeps from space resonated most keenly in discussions regarding the military applications that *Sputnik's* launch implied. *Newsweek* noted that the difference in sending a 184-pound satellite into orbit and firing an ICBM "...with H-bombs instead of radio transmitters and batteries" was not great. "...very few technical changes," the magazine stated, needed to be made for these weapons to "...spew their lethal fallout over most of the U.S. or Europe." A scientist working on the Air Force Titan ICBM program put the military implications more succinctly. Unless the United States caught up to the Russians fast, he warned, "...we're dead."[5]

SPUTNIK, THE MILITARY, AND NUCLEAR WEAPONS

Sputnik's beeps sounded a sharp reveille for U.S. military planners. Three years before, in 1954, Dr. John von Neumann indicated that hydrogen bombs could be reduced in size to fit into a missile, prompting the military to raise von Neumann's concept to a top priority. Even so, the development of the Vanguard rocket, which was to launch the first U.S. satellite, had been largely divorced from the military's programs, and funding levels for all the rocket programs had been held under tight leash by the fiscally conservative Eisenhower administration. Rocket development had been further hampered by inter-service rivalries, primarily between the Army's Redstone missile program, developed by a team under the direction of German rocket scientist Dr. Wernher von Braun and the Air Force's triad missile program, represented by the Atlas, Titan, and Thor missiles. Then, on October 7, two days after *Sputnik* first orbited over the United States, the Soviets announced that they had successfully tested a hydrogen bomb warhead, presumably designed for an ICBM. Von Neumann's prediction of the marriage of thermonuclear weapons to missiles had become a reality but, to the country's chagrin, the United States had not led the way.[6]

Since the beginning of the Nuclear Age, DoD had conducted numerous weapons effects tests piggy-backed on AEC-sponsored shots as well as a number of specific DoD detonations designed solely for the purpose of effects measurements. In the late 1940s and early 1950s, military planners sought to understand the effects of nuclear weapons, including atmospheric, underwater, cratering, and surface explosions. How vulnerable were men and material, they wanted to know, to a nuclear explosion's blast, heat, shock, radiation and radioactivity? How would troops react? How well would tanks, airplanes, ships, docks, housing, underground shelters, and the like hold up? By the late 1950s, "...the effects of low-level or surface nuclear bursts were in general adequately understood," according to William E. Ogle, a Los Alamos scientist and Science Deputy to the military's Joint Task Forces at that time. However, with the advent of missile delivery systems and the threat posed by satellites, the planners changed focus completely, now concentrating their attention on the effects of high altitude and deep space bursts, especially on radio and radar. "The effects of high-altitude detonations were still very uncertain," Ogle noted. "On some subjects, the knowledge was still too dim to ask even the right questions." In fact, Ogle admitted, the level of knowledge of these blasts "...was still very primitive."[7]

While there was a great public outcry bewailing a possible "missile gap" and America's loss of scientific and technological leadership after *Sputnik*, the military's efforts to unite nuclear weapons and missiles had not lagged as much as the administration's critics argued. Work had begun soon after von Neumann had suggested that small thermonuclear weapons could be designed to be placed in a rocket. Von Neumann convened a meeting of the AFSWP Blast Panel at the agency's

Pentagon headquarters in February 1954. The discussions from that panel led to AFSWP's development of the DoD nuclear effects tests at TEAPOT and later test series.[8]

For its planning of the TEAPOT weapon effects program, which was to include the development and testing of a Nike-Hercules warhead, AFSWP acquired from Sandia the services of Dr. Frank H. Shelton, an expert on the phenomenology of high-altitude detonations. As Technical Advisor to AFSWP, Shelton provided detailed calculations for the effects from a small yield explosion at 40,000 feet, a standard air defense altitude for the high-altitude shot and extrapolated his figures for a 100,000 foot burst. Working with Shelton were Dr. Edward B. Doll, the AFSWP technical director at Field Command in Albuquerque and a fellow Cal Tech graduate, and Jack Kelso from the Headquarters blast group, who oversaw work on drone aircraft, shock wave, and surface-blast programs, among other DoD effects tests.[9]

As a result of their mutual interests, Doll and Shelton became good friends. In June 1955, Doll confided to Shelton that he had become increasingly worried that Soviet development of ICBMs with thermonuclear warheads put the United States at great risk. Doll believed he could respond more effectively by getting out of AFSWP. He told Shelton he was leaving the agency to join a private company in California to work on an Air Force missile program. In turn, Shelton had a surprise of his own for Doll: he would be leaving Sandia to take Pete Scoville's place as AFSWP's Technical Director.

NUCLEAR WEAPON EFFECTS

Public interest remained high in the biological effects of radiation on human health through the 1950s, but many of the studies done by the AEC remained classified. Instead, the public's imagination about the effects of nuclear warfare was captured by *On the Beach*, a best-selling apocalyptic novel by the Australian writer Nevil Shute. Appearing in the summer of 1957, Shute's book described a world slowly poisoned by radioactivity from the devastating explosions of thousands of "cobalt" bombs.[12]

AFSWP had its own version of nuclear war in 1957. With the expectation that better information would aid civil defense workers, the DoD and the AEC issued Samuel Glasstone's *The Effects of Nuclear Weapons*. The unclassified work, an update of a 1950 Glasstone study on the effects of atomic weapons, described the grim destruction caused by a nuclear blast. Glasstone also saw the dangers of worldwide fallout and long-term residual radiation, arguing that thermonuclear bombs could be used in radiological warfare as "...an automatic extension of the offensive use of nuclear weapons of high

Dr. Frank H. Shelton, Technical Director, AFSWP (1955-1959).

yield." Glasstone's analysis may not have been as dramatic as *On the Beach*, but its scientific accuracy lent credibility to Shute's vision of a nuclear apocalypse.[13]

The publication of Henry Kissinger's *Nuclear Weapons and Foreign Policy* and a series of Congressional hearings on fallout kept the cauldron of public concern with radioactivity bubbling in the summer of 1957. Kissinger made clear to a wide audience what most policy makers in Washington already understood: the U.S. policy of "massive retaliation" was no deterrent to a potential enemy who also possessed thermonuclear weapons. There would be no limited nuclear war, Kissinger argued. As Americans read Kissinger and Shute that summer, they also learned from hearings conducted by the Joint Committee on Atomic Energy about increasing levels of radioactive Strontium-90 appearing in soil and milk, radioactivity that would linger long after a cessation in weapons testing. Accordingly, scientists asked the AEC to "...hold testing to a minimum consistent with scientific and military requirements."[14]

Eisenhower was already considering a suspension of nuclear weapons testing. He had planned to introduce the notion of a limited test ban as early as 1956, but Adlai Stevenson grabbed the initiative in that year's Presidential campaign and the idea remained confined to policy discussions at the White House. Determined to end the arms race, Eisenhower hoped to end or limit nuclear tests and restrict the production of fissionable material to peaceful purposes. Nuclear testing had become a moral issue to some of Eisenhower's closest advisors, including Secretary of State John Foster Dulles. Neither the military nor the AEC supported a cessation of testing, arguing that some check against the deterioration of the stockpile and the development of new safety technologies were critical to national defense. Moreover, an effective detection system had to be in place before testing stopped so that knowledge about Soviet intentions and activities might better guarantee American security. The administration proposed the end of 1957 as a possible date to limit the country's nuclear testing program.[15]

Not surprisingly, some of the most strident opposition to a test ban came from nuclear scientists who argued that low yield, small, 'clean' fusion weapons could be developed and tested without creating a significant fallout hazard.

The military argued for continued testing. During the 1956 planning for the PLUMBBOB series, AFSWP's technical director thought it "...prudent to approach the 1957 DoD effects test series as though it might be the last atmospheric effects program."

JOHN was a DoD shot during the PLUMBBOB Series, which AFSWP Field Command held in Nevada between March and October 1957. JOHN tested the performance of an air-to-air "Genie" rocket with a nuclear warhead detonated at some 20,000 feet to assess radiation and blast effects on an aircraft as it banked away from the detonation. Three Air Force officers stood on the ground directly below the burst to "...demonstrate that air defense could occur above a population without danger to the population."[17]

While Field Command supervised DoD work at NTS during PLUMBBOB, AFSWP Headquarters continued to shape plans for high-altitude tests, codenamed HARDTACK, in 1958 to take place in the Pacific. Bruised by public outrage over radioactive fallout, AFSWP played down the dangers of fallout from testing to a Congressional committee. Dr. Frank Shelton claimed that atomic testing might be continued "...at the present rate for forty to fifty years and not create any danger from radioactive fallout." He told the Congressmen that it would take the equivalent of 1,500,000 Nagasaki bombs to bring the concentration of Strontium-90, a carcinogen that collected in human bones and caused bone cancer and leukemia, to the maximum permissible concentration. Other military and scientific representatives held opposing viewpoints on the concentration levels. At the same hearing, however, Shelton admitted that had the Marshall Islanders lived on the other side of the Bikini Atoll during the CASTLE-BRAVO test in 1954, "...all would have died."[18]

For all the public comments in support of a continued nuclear testing program, AFSWP moved cautiously in planning HARDTACK. The fallout precautions proposed in July 1957 by Dr. Alvin C. Graves of the Los Alamos Laboratory were, in Shelton's estimation, "...insufficient from a scientific point to warrant Department of Defense support." A series of meetings between AFSWP, the AEC, and Los Alamos scientists led Graves to revise his initial plans. Thereafter, AFSWP initiated a series of briefings to DoD officials, including the Joint Chiefs of Staff, and the former Presidential candidate and Democratic party leader Adlai Stevenson, on the status of fallout and testing.[19]

As talk of a testing moratorium grew louder throughout 1957, both the AEC weapons laboratories, Los Alamos and Livermore, and the military argued for more tests at HARDTACK. Although Admiral Lewis L. Strauss, Chairman of the AEC, told the President that he had cut the number of laboratory and military tests by half, Eisenhower expressed great concern to his advisors about the large number of HARDTACK tests and the excessive length of the series, which now stretched over four months into the summer of 1958. Eisenhower was frustrated by the plan to conduct numerous tests while arguing in the international arena for a policy to suspend testing altogether. He believed the rest of the world would lose faith in the United States as it followed this seemingly paradoxical policy.[20]

As a result of AFSWP's concerns, throughout 1957, on radioactivity altering the conduct of HARDTACK's fallout program, DoD staff urged the President to permit testing to gain information on specific weapon effects deemed critical to military applications. DoD planned two series of effects tests. One series consisted of underwater shots that would continue the investigations of nuclear explosions on Naval vessels begun at CROSSROADS and WIGWAM. The second series sponsored by DoD was to examine the effects of high-altitude nuclear blasts. Combined with the weapons design tests conducted by Los Alamos and Livermore, the HARDTACK series would fire as many nuclear devices as had been exploded in all prior Pacific tests. Throughout 1957, AFSWP pushed to conduct full-scale test programs examining large yield nuclear explosions at high altitudes, taking its case directly to Donald A. Quarles, the Deputy Secretary of Defense. Quarles supported the high-altitude weapon effects tests, and Eisenhower agreed. The decision came none too soon. Three days before the end of the PLUMB-BOB series, the Soviets had launched the world's first satellite into space.[21]

HIGH-ALTITUDE TESTING

Dr. Shelton welcomed fresh ideas and quickly recognized that one of the places in the Pentagon to get them was the newly formed Advanced Research Projects Agency (ARPA). On one foray, Major General Cyrus Betts, the head of ARPA, gave Shelton a paper by Nicholas C. Christofilos, a self-educated Greek immigrant who worked at the University of

Donald A. Quarles, Deputy Secretary of Defense, 1957 to 1959.

California's Lawrence Radiation Laboratory in Berkeley. Christofilos' paper suggested that electrons could be trapped in the magnetic field of the earth's upper atmosphere by a high-altitude nuclear explosion and would interrupt radio, radar, and other communications systems, perhaps damaging or destroying the fuzing mechanisms of ICBMs. Shelton and his predecessor, Scoville, who had become the Deputy Director for Science and Technology of the CIA, worried that the Soviets might also be thinking along the lines of Christofilos' paper and use a nuclear weapon to form a long-lasting trapped radiation belt and interfere with U.S. satellites. The Russians had detonated a large, high-yield weapon in 1956 and *Sputnik* intensified American concerns. The Soviet launching, in November 1957, of *Sputnik II*, a half-ton satellite capable of carrying a nuclear weapon into space, heightened concern at the Pentagon and at Langley.[22]

Christofilos' study was an extension of the DoD's interest in the effects of nuclear explosions in the outer atmosphere. In the early years of the missile age, military planners feared that electrons emitted by such large high-altitude nuclear blasts could become trapped in the earth's atmosphere and might possibly block the operation of ballistic missiles and defensive radar systems. In particular, AFSWP intensified its investigations into the nature of nuclear explosions at high altitudes and their generation of an electromagnetic pulse (EMP). Drawing on TEAPOT, AFSWP began planning, in mid-1956, a series of tests on the effects of EMP and high-altitude phenomenology which were, at that time, little understood testing addressed series of missile-launched ultra-high-altitude nuclear tests for the 1958 HARDTACK test series in the Pacific. There were numerous questions about the effects of missile-launched weapons and detonations in space, especially the effects of EMP on radio communications and equipment. This concept was discussed with AFSWP's Thermal Radiation Panel in late November 1956, and would be honed, over the next two years, and become an integral part of the HARDTACK Pacific test as part of the military's plan to carry out von Neumann's suggestion of designing a smaller nuclear weapon to fit into the warhead of a missile.[23]

Planned against a background of growing concern with worldwide radioactive fallout and President Eisenhower's inclination to call a moratorium on the U.S. nuclear testing program, HARDTACK would not be an easy series to conduct. The dangers of radioactive fallout, particularly of Strontium-90, were placed in perspective at a Congressional hearing in the spring of 1957. Nevertheless, many were not convinced that the danger from fallout was as insignificant as the agency suggested. Nuclear testing, according to much of world opinion, was the kind of saber rattling that enhanced international tensions and might lead to war. The Soviet Union, which had completed its test series in the spring of 1958, gained some propaganda victories by renouncing nuclear testing. Many in the United States, however, believed that continued testing was vital to American security and that the resulting fallout was an inconsequential price to pay. In any case, weapons designers hoped to avoid the fallout problem by developing radiologically 'clean' weapons to make testing more acceptable in world opinion.[24]

Against this international background, HARDTACK planners, including AFSWP, which was responsible for weapon effects data collection for DoD, were squeezed between those who believed the peace was enhanced through demonstrated deterrence and those who believed that peace would be the product of negotiations. The difficulties were further exacerbated by the difference in aims between the scientists and administrators created by the structure of the Joint Task Force, which would manage the series in the Pacific. There was the usual urgency to start and end a test series on time and to conduct the tests as economically as possible. "This urgency," William Ogle recalled, "could be produced by programmatic aims, economics, or political consideration, or simply the desire to get the operation over with and go home." For administrators, delays were cost prohibitive, on average approaching a million dollars for each day of delay. For scientists, however, each shot had an experimental purpose, and the need to take appropriate effects measurements often clashed with the "shoot it now" attitude of administrators. Disputes were often solved at the highest staff levels, but only after considerable discussion through the permanent AEC Laboratory and AFSWP structure rather than through the temporary Joint Task Force.[25]

The inter-service rivalry over missiles complicated AFSWP's job of preparing for the two high-altitude shots planned for HARDTACK. In May 1956, AFSWP recommended to the JCS that the Army's Redstone missile, the product of Wernher von Braun's German V-2 rocket scientists in Huntsville, Alabama, be used in ORANGE and TEAK, both planned to be conducted at Bikini Atoll or at Enewetak at the Pacific Proving Grounds.[26]

The Redstone missile possessed a number of critical advantages. The missile was produced at the Chrysler plant in volume; the Reynolds Metal Company fabricated some of the airframe components. Built to Wernher von Braun's specifications by the North American Rocketdyne Division, the Redstone developed 75,000 pounds of thrust using liquid oxygen propellant. The missile had an excellent record of successful launches at Cape Canaveral, Florida. Further, the missile was exceptionally mobile. Along with its launching, fueling, and auxiliary support equipment, the Redstone could be transported by cargo plane or by truck. The logistics of moving missiles and ground support equipment to the Pacific were relatively simple when compared with the Navy's Polaris missile, which would not be successfully launched until October 1957, and the Air Force's Atlas rocket, which would not have its first successful firing until late November of 1957. Nevertheless, over a year before possessing a proven workable rocket, the NRL and the Air Force Special Weapons Center recommended that AFSWP use missiles developed by their respective Services for the 1958 HARDTACK high-altitude weapons effects tests.[27]

As a face-saving compromise for the Joint Chiefs, AFSWP took its Redstone recommendation to two senior civilian officials at the Department of Defense, C. C. Furnas, the Assistant Secretary for Research and Development, and E. V. Murphee, Special Assistant to the Secretary of Defense (Guided Missiles). Both agreed with AFSWP's advice and forwarded their decision to Donald Quarles, the Deputy Secretary of Defense. Quarles, however, in consultation with AEC Chairman Lewis Strauss, canceled the two tests. At once, AFSWP and the Army worked to get the effects tests reinstated. Shelton convinced the Weapons System Evaluation Group of the JCS to keep the high-altitude shots. General Maxwell Taylor, the Army representative to the JCS, urged Quarles to change his opposition. By the end of August of 1957, Quarles agreed to proceed with ORANGE and TEAK as planned.[28]

The AEC, however, continued to block the tests. Strauss opposed the high-altitude shots because the flash might blind islanders on nearby atolls. After the fiasco with CASTLE-BRAVO fallout on the *Fortunate Dragon* and the Marshallese, he would not gamble with the health and safety of the islanders. The DoD, which had initially argued that eye burn from the flash would not be a problem, also began to have second thoughts. General Luedecke, the commander of

The Army's Redstone Missile.

Joint Task Force 7, did not believe that it was practical to control the 4,000 or so Marshallese that might be exposed to the flash hazard. Moving the launch site, however, would mean a five-month delay and would spoil critical measurements from an Army satellite put up in March 1958 to gather information from TEAK during its scheduled April test.[29]

Sputnik gave urgency to the tests. AFSWP proposed moving the tests to Wake, Midway, Christmas, or Johnston Island. Strauss agreed. He would approve the high-altitude tests on one condition: move the launch site from Bikini to Johnston Island, some 800 hundred miles to the southwest of Hawaii and approximately 1,500 miles northeast of Enewetak. At a meeting with Strauss and other senior government officials in April of 1958, Quarles agreed to the move. Redstone missiles would carry TEAK and ORANGE aloft from Johnston Island.[30]

Just as an agreement was reached on the Johnston Island location for the tests, the DoD and ARPA proposed three additional high-altitude tests in a new top secret series named ARGUS. The main purpose of ARGUS was to examine the "Christofilos effect." A conference of scientists held at Lawrence Livermore Laboratory in February 1958 concluded that

TEAK would not produce serious effects on military radio and radar systems but that a properly optimized shot might "...cause difficulties" for several months. Because of the uncertainty of the calculations, the group recommended firing a small shot to test the facts. It was too late in the planning to include the verification of Christofilos' concept during the HARDTACK series, but the idea was placed on a fast track test schedule for the ARGUS series to be conducted in August and September of 1958. On May 1, Eisenhower approved the additional series, which would be conducted operationally by AFSWP.[31]

TEAK AND ORANGE

For more than three minutes, the fiery bright flames that shot from the engine of the Redstone rocket were plainly visible in the night sky as the missile lifted off its launch pad at Johnston Island, at 11:50 pm on July 31, 1958. As the rocket reached an altitude of nearly 50 miles, the megaton-range warhead detonated. A huge, spectacular fireball erupted, reaching a diameter of more than 18 miles in three and a half seconds and rising at a rate of up to one mile per second. A brilliant aurora, produced by electrons from the TEAK explosion, developed at the bottom of the fireball and filled the sky with vivid colors.[32]

Throughout the Pacific, observers marveled at the blast. One observer, an Air Force lieutenant watching the sky around midnight that evening from his porch, recalled TEAK: "...it seemed to be a semi-circular fireball on the horizon... I just thought it was Honolulu or Pearl Harbor and I was dead."[33] The Apia Observatory in Western Samoa approximately 2,000 miles to the south described the "...violent magnetic disturbance," which heralded "...the most brilliant manifestation of the Aurora Australis [Southern Lights] ever seen in Samoa." The resulting persistent ionization of the low-density atmosphere cut high frequency radio communications with New Zealand for six hours. In Hawaii, where there had been no announcement of the test, the TEAK fireball turned from light yellow to dark yellow to orange to red. "The red spread in a semi-circular manner until it seemed to engulf a large part of the horizon," one resident told the Honolulu *Star-Bulletin*. The red glow remained clearly visible in the southwestern sky for half an hour. In Honolulu, military and civilian air traffic communications were interrupted for several hours. At the AFSWP's offices in the Pentagon, Admiral Parker grew concerned for the personnel on Johnston Island as hour after hour passed with no word regarding the test. Finally, some eight hours after TEAK had occurred, the word that all was well came from Luedecke, the commander of Joint Task Force 7 and soon to be General Manager of the AEC. The communications blackout worried others as well. Later AFSWP learned that one of the first radio messages received at Johnston Island once communications was restored was: "Are you still there?" By any measure, TEAK was a most impressive test.[33]

Spectacular as it was, TEAK was one of three HARDTACK weapon effects tests to study blast, thermal, and nuclear radiation effects at high altitudes, particularly as they might affect ballistic missiles. The first shot of Operation HARDTACK was YUCCA, a low-yield weapon of 1.7 kilotons launched from the aircraft carrier *USS Boxer* and carried aloft by a helium-filled balloon and detonated at 86,000 feet. Preparations for the YUCCA test brought old inter-service rivalries to the surface. The Air Force had designed and developed the balloon system for the high-altitude test, but the persistent surface winds on Enewetak made launches from the airfield uncontrollable

Johnston (Atoll) Island,* South Pacific, looking to the West (photo circa 1965).

and unreliable. With great reluctance, the Air Force accepted the suggestion of launching the balloon from the carrier, which could sail downwind to create zero velocity wind conditions. Just before midday on April 28, 1958, the *Boxer* turned downwind, and the balloon rose from the flight deck with the YUCCA device hanging from a cable below. At 2:40 in the afternoon, a radio command signal fired the weapon, much to the relief of several observers whose worst case scenarios included a free flying balloon being driven toward Japan by the upper level Krakatoan winds.[34]

The final test of a high-altitude detonation began just after TEAK. The Army Redstone crew returned to Johnston Island to make final preparations at the launch pad for ORANGE. During the evening of August 11, the missile was launched. When it reached 125,000 feet, the fire signal was sent to the missile with no apparent response. Someone had failed to throw a safety switch once the missile had cleared the island's safety zone. Technicians quickly discovered and corrected the

---

* Johnston Atoll (JA) or Johnston Island, located 717 nautical miles southwest of Honolulu, Hawaii, is operated and maintained by Field Command. The atoll consists of four coral islands: Johnston Island, Sand Island, North Island, and East Island. At just over 625 acres, Johnston is the largest island and base for all operations and management activities, including all personnel and community support functions. Although Johnston served as a staging area and test site during the atmospheric nuclear test series, its current mission (by Albuquerque Operations) is to support the U.S. Army chemical weapon storage and destruction program.

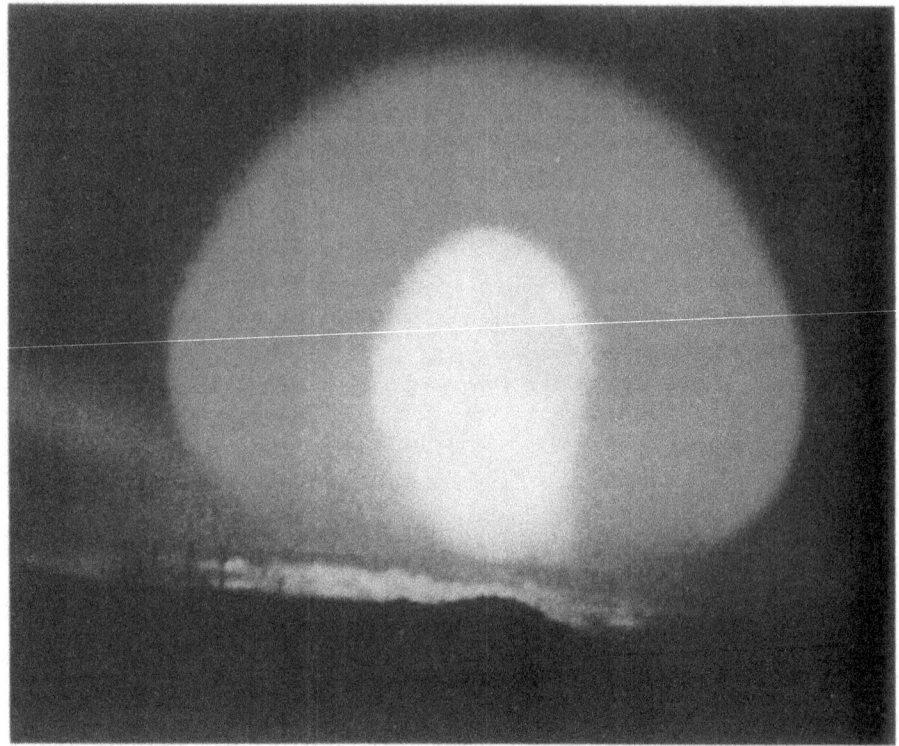

TEAK high-altitude shot; taken from Maui, 794 nautical miles from the explosion.

error, though the Redstone reached 141,000 feet before detonating. OR-ANGE's yield was equal to the TEAK shot, but less spectacular. The dramatic display of southern lights which TEAK generated raised considerable anxiety in Hawaii, but most observers in the islands were disappointed in ORANGE. One observer on the top of Mount Haleakala on Maui described the display as "...a dark brownish red mushroom [that] rose in the sky and then died down and turned to white with a dark red rainbow." While ORANGE was visible for about 10 minutes in Hawaii, it had little effect on radio communications.[35] The ORANGE event was a critical effects test for AFSWP. The nuclear weapon was salted with tracer elements so that the residence time for nuclear debris in the stratosphere could be determined.

AFSWP's U-2 high-altitude sampling program (HASP) had begun in 1956 but was kept secret within the agency. AFSWP was reluctant to share its HASP activities with even the AEC in order to protect its security. Additionally, information acquired through HASP flights shaped AFSWP's position on worldwide fallout patterns. This information was promulgated in Glasstone's *The Effects of Nuclear Weapons*, which was being written under AFSWP's and AEC's auspices in 1956-57.[36]

While some valuable information had been gathered from TEAK and OR-ANGE, many scientists in the nuclear weapons community considered the tests

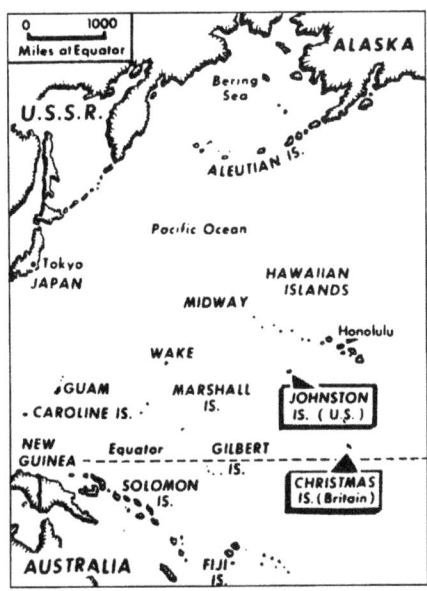

Location of Johnston and Christmas Islands.

to be only partially successful. Neither detonation had occurred where it had been planned and, due to cloud cover, detailed photographic coverage was incomplete. One Los Alamos scientist requested that AFSWP repeat the TEAK event, but the DoD maintained that it was satisfied with the results of the test and rejected the request on August 14, 1958. A week later President Eisenhower announced a one-year moratorium on nuclear testing, effective October 31, 1958.[37]

ARGUS

The rejection of a second TEAK test may have been in part due to another series of high-altitude tests scheduled for the South Atlantic at the end of August. The DoD and the AEC sought to detonate nuclear devices at far higher altitudes than both ORANGE and TEAK to obtain effects data on communications systems and long-range missiles. The central idea was to test Christofilos' idea that a defensive shield of high-energy electrons might destroy any missile attacking the country. At the direction of ARPA's Order No. 4, AFSWP designed ARGUS to determine if an Anti-Ballistic Missile (ABM) system might use radiation effects from nuclear detonations to create an umbrella of electrons to prematurely detonate missile warheads or jam the electronics of incoming missiles. A large number of scientists had advocated the development of a nuclear weapon ABM system, but the initial analyses from TEAK and ORANGE were inconclusive. In addition, scientist sought information about the feasibility of a high-altitude detection system that might complement seismic data gathered from a network of worldwide ground monitoring stations.[38]

Time, however, was running out for the scientists. Rockets capable of reaching heights far above the HARDTACK shots would not be ready for at least a year or more. With the prospect of a test ban going into effect before the end of 1958, the DoD proposed conducting a series of tests immediately, using available rockets that could reach an altitude of some 400 miles, where the experiment would be conducted at a point in the earth's magnetic field where an electron umbrella shield could be established. Since no existing test site proved acceptable, officials planned to conduct the series from Naval vessels in the South Atlantic, where, at roughly 45 degrees south latitude, the earth's magnetic field at a height reached by existing missiles was appropriate for trapping electrons in stable orbits. In selecting the South Atlantic, the military appreciated the fact that the area was remote and sparsely populated. Moreover, if asked, the AFSWP technical director for ARGUS later said there was an excellent "... likelihood that we could indefinitely maintain that [the tests] had never occurred."

Although the South Atlantic provided a good test site technically, there were international concerns. If the United States conducted a nuclear test in international waters, there was no good argument to prevent the Soviet Union from doing the same. Only when Eisenhower had received the concurrence of the Department of State and his scientific advisor did he approve the ARGUS series. At the end of April 1958, AFSWP, with the assistance of ARPA, began planning the South Atlantic operations to test, in late August 1958, the "Christofilos effect." This test would determine if an artificial electron belt trapped in space, similar to the naturally occurring Van Allen radiation belts, could act as a defensive shield.[39]

On April 28, 1958, a couple of days before Eisenhower formally approved the ARGUS series, Admiral Parker notified the skipper of the *USS Norton Sound*, Captain Gralla, that his ship had been selected to launch the missiles. AFSWP and Sandia began training sessions aboard the *Norton Sound* off the southern California coast to ensure adequate coordination among those responsible for the missile, nuclear device, and fuzing and to maintain tight security away from the rest of the flotilla in the Atlantic. After refitting the *Norton Sound* at the Navy's San Francisco Shipyard, the vessel headed south to conduct a series of test firings off Point Mugu, California. Technicians from Lockheed's Missile Systems Division led the exercise. Two launch failures, including one in which the third stage of the missile and the dummy nuclear warhead landed within 300 feet of the ship, led Lockheed to change their missile design. Back east, Rear Admiral Lloyd M. Mustin, the Task Force commander, moved into AFSWP offices in Washington to receive a steady stream of briefings on the technical aspects of the tests. Uncertain of the probability of a clean launching success even after the test firings, Mustin requested a third test shot, which was quickly approved. High winds and rough seas were of special concern to AFSWP, even though the *Norton Sound* could launch its missiles in spite of pitch and roll, high-sea conditions. AFSWP anticipated heavy cloud cover at shot time,

Starboard view of Admiral Mustin's (subsequent DASA Director) flagship–the *USS Tarawa*–underway in the Atlantic.

which would cloak the explosions from the ship crews and would necessitate aircraft photography and another instrumentation ship off the Azores.[40]

The ARGUS tests were to be held in complete secrecy. Although conducted on Navy ships, ARGUS used an older version of an Air Force solid fuel rocket. At the same time, ARGUS would study the feasibility of the Army's Nike-Zeus antiballistic missile, then in development. The nine ships of Task Force 88, under the command of Rear Admiral Mustin, quietly put to sea some three months after receiving Presidential approval for ARGUS. The key vessels for the series were the guided missile ship *Norton Sound*, a converted World War II seaplane tender from which the rockets carrying low yield atomic devices would be fired, and the *USS Tarawa*, an aircraft carrier outfitted with radar tracking equipment and anti-submarine reconnaissance planes. The *Tarawa* was to track the flight of the missiles and search the test area for prying Soviet submarines.[41]

On August 1, 1958, the *Norton Sound* departed from Port Hueneme California, and, under radio silence, skirted the west coast of South America, avoiding the Panama Canal, and rounded Cape Horn into the South Atlantic. The *Tarawa* and the remaining six support ships left Quonset Point, Rhode Island, on August 7. The flotilla headed south, losing a couple of Soviet trawlers in a hurricane in the Caribbean. On August 23, the radioman on the *Tarawa* received a cryptic radio message: "Doctor Livingston, I presume?" It came from the *Norton Sound*. The missile ship had arrived and rendezvoused with the rest of Task Force 88 by August 25, during the heart of winter in the southern hemisphere.[42]

Once Task Force 88 was in place in the lee of Gough Island, an uninhabited British possession in the South Atlantic,

Launch of Argus missile from *USS Norton Sound*, August 1958.

the ARGUS tests began. On August 27, 1958, five days after Eisenhower announced that a test moratorium would go into effect in the beginning of November, a 43-foot, specially modified X-17, a three-stage rocket fitted with a small nuclear warhead, roared off the deck of the *Norton Sound*. The second shot went off on August 30, and the third a week later on September 6. Each of the devices exploded some 300 miles into space. Mustin and an AFSWP staff member, Navy

Captain William Wallace, observed each of the shots from planes flying above the clouds.[43]

Shortly thereafter, *Explorer IV*, an American satellite launched a month before the first ARGUS test, passed through the artificially induced radiation belts several times a day for the next week or so, measuring effects data from the detonations. At the same time, in a related weapons effects investigation at Kirtland Air Force Base in Albuquerque, the Air Force fired 16 five-stage Jason rockets outfitted with radiation instrumentation some 450 miles into space. The three ARGUS firings were successful in that neither radioactive fallout nor nosy Russian submarines were detected in the test area. The ARGUS experiments were less successful in confirming the Christofilos effect. Dr. Herbert F. York, the chief research scientist at ARPA, admitted that while the radiation belts Christofilos anticipated had indeed occurred, the concentration of electrons was too small, too unstable, and too weak to prevent missiles from reentering the earth's atmosphere (serving as a protective shield). Nonetheless, ARGUS proved that a test series could be taken from concept to conclusion in an extraordinarily short period of time if interest and inter-service cooperation were present. "Ten months from the germ of an idea to its actual execution in outer space was just short of fantastic," York later wrote, still in awe of what AFSWP, the DoD, and Task Force 88 had accomplished.[44]

ARGUS was unique among U.S. nuclear testing operations. It was the most expeditiously planned and conducted series, the first launch of a ballistic missile with a nuclear warhead from a ship, and the only nuclear operation in the Atlantic Ocean. In addition, it was the only clandestine test series conducted by the United States. ARGUS involved neither diagnostic testing of a weapon design nor, strictly speaking, the effects of an explosion on military systems as did other test series. Rather, ARGUS was largely a scientific examination of the feasibility of Christofilos' theory that a very high-altitude nuclear detonation would create an electron belt that might interfere with communications and weapon performance.[45]

The epilogue to the top secret ARGUS series came some six months later when Hanson Baldwin, a *New York Times* military reporter, broke the story in March 1959 after determining to his satisfaction that the Soviets had gleaned much information from the tests. Baldwin, who specialized in reporting on the Navy, had the story as early as January 1959. The Pentagon was furious and, with White House support, tried unsuccessfully to block publication. After some internal debate at the newspaper, however, the editors decided to delay the story until March 19. To deflect Baldwin's scoop, Deputy Secretary of Defense Quarles called his own press conference the same day. With Roy W. Johnson and Herbert York from ARPA, William J. Thaler of the Office of Naval Research, and Frank Shelton from AFSWP sitting alongside, Quarles downplayed the military applications of the tests, emphasizing that the experimentation was focused on the scientific investigation of electrons in the upper atmosphere. York was a bit more candid. After describing Christofilos' theory, he told reporters that "...it became clear that if we could fire an atomic bomb above the earth's atmosphere and inside of the earth's magnetic field that some of the electrons would be spewed out with a sufficient energy and in such directions that they would be trapped." By examining what occurred after the explosion, York continued, "...we would be able to learn a great deal more about the lifetime, about the stability of these electron shells, etc., and that's essentially what has been accomplished."[46]

THE MORATORIUM AND TESTING READINESS

Even as Eisenhower announced that the United States would cease testing nuclear weapons in August 1958, he asked the DoD and AEC to maintain their capability to test. He had clearly recognized the heightened dangers that the marriage of missiles and nuclear weapons brought to international affairs, a risk made all too apparent by *Sputnik*. Ballistic missiles with nuclear warheads drastically reduced decision times for government leaders. With this in mind, in 1957 Eisenhower gave senior military commanders the authority to retaliate with nuclear weapons if the President could not be reached or was unable to respond to a nuclear attack against the United States. At the same time, Eisenhower hoped to avoid a nuclear armageddon. While strongly backing an end to the arms race and an end to radioactive fallout, Eisenhower did not want to be caught unprepared. Therefore, even as talks about a moratorium and a nuclear test ban treaty grew more productive, he asked his scientists to keep the nation's testing program at the ready.[47]

The suspension of nuclear weapons testing moved AFSWP responsibility from direct field nuclear testing to a focus on laboratory experimentation, theoretical studies, and field tests that would not involve nuclear explosions. On September 19, 1958, Neil McElroy, the Secretary of Defense, outlined AFSWP's new role. During the moratorium, McElroy wrote, AFSWP should "...continue the necessary research, laboratory, planning and budgetary activities within [its] present responsibilities" on the assumption that limited testing might resume by February 1960 and "...extensive test operations may be initiated by, but not earlier than, mid-1960." In the meantime, AFSWP would continue to coordinate with the AEC to gather essential nuclear information from all sources except actual nuclear testing.[48]

To facilitate discussions between the military and the AEC, Quarles, who had become the acting Secretary of Defense, established in October the Joint Atomic Information Exchange Group (JAIEG) within AFSWP under the policy guidance of the Secretary of Defense and the Chairman of the AEC. Under the agreement, AFSWP provided necessary administrative support and daily technical advice and assistance to the Group. Brigadier General R. H. Harrison, Deputy Chief of AFSWP, became the first head of the Joint Group. Harrison's group, which consisted of staff assigned by each military Service and the AEC, was also responsible for disseminating atomic information to foreign governments and regional defense organizations. The formation of JAIEG was more than a response to the moratorium. The new organization represented the increased responsibility of the military, sanctioned and implemented by Eisenhower a year earlier, to deal with nuclear issues outside the United States.[49]

AFSWP and the AEC adopted a cooperative approach to meet another growing concern, accidents involving nuclear weapons. After several months of discussions and negotiations, AFSWP and the Commission signed a joint agreement in February 1958 defining the areas of responsibility and operational procedures applicable to achieving a "...prompt, effective, and coordinated response" to nuclear accidents. Under this arrangement, the two agencies established the Joint Coordinating Center in Albuquerque using the resources of Field Command, AFSWP, and the AEC's Albuquerque Operations Office to provide assistance and information as required. The agreement stipulated that for accidents occurring within the United States, the Army would have primary responsibility and command; for accidents elsewhere, the primary duty went to the agency having physical control of the weapon at the time of the incident. Events would soon overtake the fine points of this agreement.[50]

On March 11, 1958, two weeks after the nuclear accident response agreement, a B-47 bomber headed for North Africa accidentally dropped an atomic bomb over Mars Bluff, near Florence, South Carolina. According to the bomber crew, the safety device failed on a shackle which held the bomb in place. As a crewman tried to refasten the bomb, it broke loose and dropped through the bomb bay doors, nearly taking the crew member with it. The bomb dug a 20-foot crater near a farmhouse, setting off a high explosive arming plug, damaging several other buildings, and injuring six people, none seriously. Air Force police, unmindful of the new joint agreement and the Army's primary responsibility, quickly sealed off the area, swept it for any scattered bits of plutonium, and soon announced that "...there was not enough radioactivity present to make a Geiger counter click." Secretary of Defense McElroy explained that "...these are perilous times and that, as part of our security measures, strategic bombers are on 24-hour training," adding that "...this accident is one of the dangers." But, he assured the country, there had been no nuclear explosion and no radiation danger. Most people, according to one news magazine, feared an "atomic Pearl Harbor" and understood the need to keep bombers with nuclear weapons in the air at all times. Bill Gregg, a World War II paratrooper who owned the damaged farmhouse, agreed that the security was worth the danger. Assured that the Air Force would take care of all damage, he quipped, "I've always wanted a swimming pool, and now I've got a hole for one at no cost."[51]

DEFENSE REORGANIZATION ACT OF 1958

On April 3, 1958, President Eisenhower proposed to Congress a general reorganization of the Department of Defense. The nature of war and the requirements of national defense, he said, had changed fundamentally, and that "...separate ground, sea, and air warfare is gone forever. If ever again we should be involved in war, we will fight it in all elements, with all Services, as one single concentrated effort. Peacetime preparatory and organizational activity must conform to this fact."[52]

The President's plan called for a dramatic expansion in the authority of the Secretary of Defense, who henceforth would allocate funds among the Services, assign each Service combat roles in accordance with overall national strategy, select officers for promotion to the most senior rank, centralize all public relations, and, presumably, put an end to inter-service squabbling. The JCS was to be transformed into a senior staff responsible for assisting the Secretary in exercising unified direction. The act also authorized the Secretary to establish without further Congressional legislation such defense agencies as were necessary "...to provide more effective, efficient, and economical administration and operation" within the Defense Department.[53]

Despite scattered complaints from lawmakers about "Prussian-like centralization" and disgruntlement in some military quarters over the loss of autonomy the Services would suffer, by August the Defense Reorganization Act of 1958 had won Congressional approval and was ready for Eisenhower's signature.

Although the President spoke like a

visionary in introducing defense reorganization, his primary motivation was political. He was responding in large part to the anxieties engendered by recent setbacks in the Cold War. In the media and in Congress, Soviet breakthroughs in space and in the development of ICBMs were generally attributed not to Soviet technical superiority but to American bungling and mismanagement, chiefly among turf-minded Pentagon bureaucrats. "The Russians are catching up to us," charged retired Air Force Chief of Staff General Carl Spaatz, "not because we lack scientific and technical genius...[but] because our present defense organization is defective. With the best will in the world, it cannot make the best use of the brainpower and materials at its disposal."[55] Certainly there were well-publicized examples of duplication and waste in the weapons development arena. The latest round of Army-Air Force missile competition, between the Army's intermediate-range Thor and the Air Force's Jupiter, was estimated to have cost taxpayers an additional $500 million.

The nation's nuclear weapons program had also been disrupted by inter-service conflict. In public, there was no more avid defender of the program than AEC Chief Strauss, but privately he was a harsh critic. In a 1957 conversation with Deputy Defense Secretary Quarles, he "...compared it to the faltering missile program—too many designs, too much inter-service rivalry, too much time spent on engineering refinements, and too little time spent on developing radically new approaches."[56] The unprecedented scope and scale of HARDTACK exemplified his concerns. Not only did HARDTACK stretch AFSWP's field capabilities almost to the breaking point, it also heightened public sensitivity to the whole testing program at a time when it was already under critical scrutiny and thus hastened what the military and the AEC wished to avoid: a moratorium on testing.

BIRTH OF DASA

On August 22, 1958, two weeks after passage of the Defense Reorganization Act, AFSWP was ordered to conduct a full evaluation of its mission and responsibilities under the new defense structure. The review was completed in a fortnight, and, after evaluation and coordination, approved by the JCS by the end of December. On May 1, 1959, with the endorsement of Deputy Defense Secretary Quarles, AFSWP aquired a new name: the Defense Atomic Support Agency (DASA) and a new charter, and the AFSWP of old was retired. Within this new agency charter, the Joint Chiefs noted the growing dependence of the Armed Forces on atomic weapons and their continuing responsibility for logistical and administrative support of the nuclear stockpile. DASA became the first defense field agency established under the 1958 legislation.[57]

On paper, the creation of DASA was in accordance with the spirit of the Defense Reorganization Act. Nothing appeared to have changed aside from the nuclear organization's name and its reporting relationships. The DASA chief, whose position was to be rotated among the Services, would now report through the JCS to the Secretary of Defense. Requests for DASA's advice and assistance would now have to be approved either by the Office of the Secretary or one of the unified commands. The new charter gave DASA responsibility for supervising all DoD weapon effects tests, which had formerly been conducted by the individual Services. But in most other respects, DASA's new charter looked identical to the one under which AFSWP had operated since July 1951, and so did the organization itself. DASA's official history conceded that "...there were no apparent differences within the headquarters" between the old organization and the new.[58] Nor was there to be a change in leadership; Admiral Parker had agreed to stay on as director.

MORATORIUM IN ACTION

When it came to the reorganization of the defense establishment in general and the nuclear testing establishment particular, appearances were deceiving. In Eisenhower's mind, the Defense Reorganization Act was as much about forging the new institutional arrangements that would permit the Cold War to be gradually wound down as it did with the public purpose of confronting the Soviet threat more "efficiently." Increasingly uncertain about the validity of America's strategic assumptions, distressed by the prospect of a continuing arms race, and convinced that the new Soviet leader, Nikita Khrushchev, was more amenable than his predecessors to negotiations, Eisenhower, late in his second term, was determined to burnish his legacy as a peacemaker. For the President, the moratorium on nuclear testing was the harbinger of a relaxation of tensions that would hopefully lead to a nuclear test ban treaty, nuclear disarmament, and overall detente with Moscow.[59]

The transition from AFSWP to DASA reflected the change in the agency's fundamental purpose associated with the moratorium. For DASA, vast quantities of data from previous tests, especially HARDTACK and ARGUS, remained to be analyzed; the stockpile still required intensive maintenance; training had to be conducted; and war planners would still turn to DASA for advise as they pondered the role nuclear weapons would play on the battlefield of the future.

Some testing still went on in the laboratories. AFSWP-DASA had developed exploding wire experiments, where huge amounts of electricity, released instantaneously through an extremely fine wire, which literally *atomized* the wire. Dynamic loading machines, which used specifically designed conventional explosives or gases under pressure released through quick opening valves, simulated the rise time, peak pressure, and duration of a nuclear weapon's shock pulse.[60]

Based on the results of such laboratory experiments along with continuing theoretical calculations, DASA continued to expand its understanding of nuclear weapon effects. Through similar techniques, Los Alamos and Livermore were able to continue developing and stockpiling new weapons during the moratorium. "Testing" now consisted largely of extrapolating data from previous tests on similar warheads. Inevitably, some of the new weapons developed problems that had gone undetected in the laboratories. Original thinking on new designs, those for which no test precedents could be extrapolated, went largely by the board.[61]

PROJECT *Plowshare*

Another moratorium-stimulated stratagem was Project *Plowshare*, the aptly named effort to investigate civilian uses of nuclear explosions. As early as 1956, Dr. Herbert York, Director of Lawrence Livermore Laboratory, had raised the possibility of using the energy released by nuclear or thermonuclear reactions to produce electrical power, dig excavations for mines and canals, dredge harbors, and other practical uses. Livermore received approval to begin investigations, with the proviso that the *Plowshare* research not interfere with the weapons program. Funding averaged approximately $100,000 a year between 1956 and 1959.

The moratorium threw *Plowshare* into a new light. Some scientists, notably Edward Teller and AEC officials, started thinking about it as a way to compensate

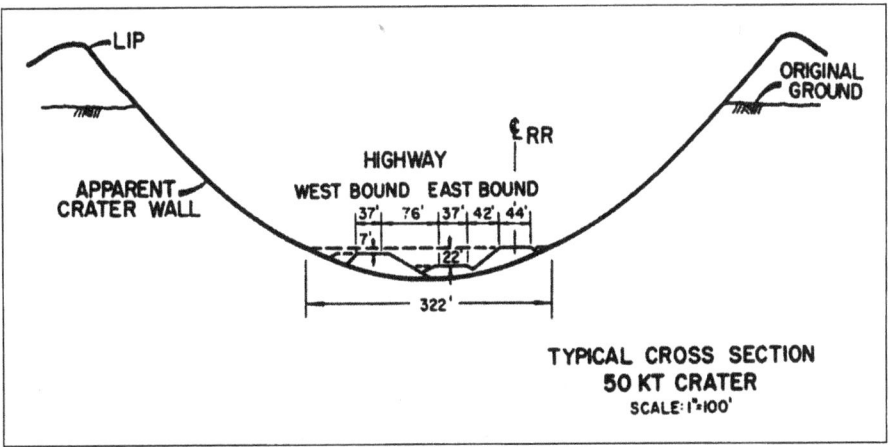

Example Project Plowshare Proposal: Use of nuclear explosive for excavation of mountain roadway from *Project Carryall*; Congressional Hearing, "Peaceful Applications of Nuclear Explosives-Plowshare," January 5, 1965.

for the absence of direct weapons tests during the moratorium, not as a subterfuge, but as a means of acquiring new information about nuclear behavior relevant to weapons testing. Fiscal year 1960 funding for Project *Plowshare*, primarily managed by the AEC Livermore labs, shot up to $6 million. DASA, however, was ambivalent, believing that any involvement by a Defense Department agency would be construed *ipso facto* as a violation of the moratorium. This ambivalence was increasingly shared by the administration, which saw *Plowshare* as a transparent evasion of the spirit, if not the letter, of the moratorium. When the Soviets, with their own voluntary moratorium, pointedly suggested that two could play the *Plowshare* game, the project quietly returned to the back burner.[62]

Later hearings on Project *Plowshare* before the Joint Committee on Atomic Energy in January 1965 expanded a wealth of creative uses for the "peaceful applications of nuclear explosives." Among these nuclear applications, espoused by Dr. Glenn Seaborg and Dr. John Kelly of the AEC in Congressional testimony, were proposals on underground engineering of all types, recovery of oil from shale and tar sands, recovery of underground gas, canal dredging and excavation, and harbor expansion.[63]

Despite these efforts to develop alternative approaches to nuclear testing, the heart of AFSWP's old mission was gone. In this area, the agency's future hinged on the outcome of U.S.-Soviet negotiations to achieve a test ban treaty, negotiations for which opened at 3:00 p.m. on October 31, 1959, at the Palace of Nations in Geneva.

The new global realities posed administrative as well as functional challenges for DASA. Among these challenges, funding was the thorniest. Considerations of economy were hardly absent from Eisenhower's calculations in promoting defense reorganization, and, with no nuclear tests to conduct, the best that DASA could hope for was funding to maintain a low level of readiness in case nuclear test-

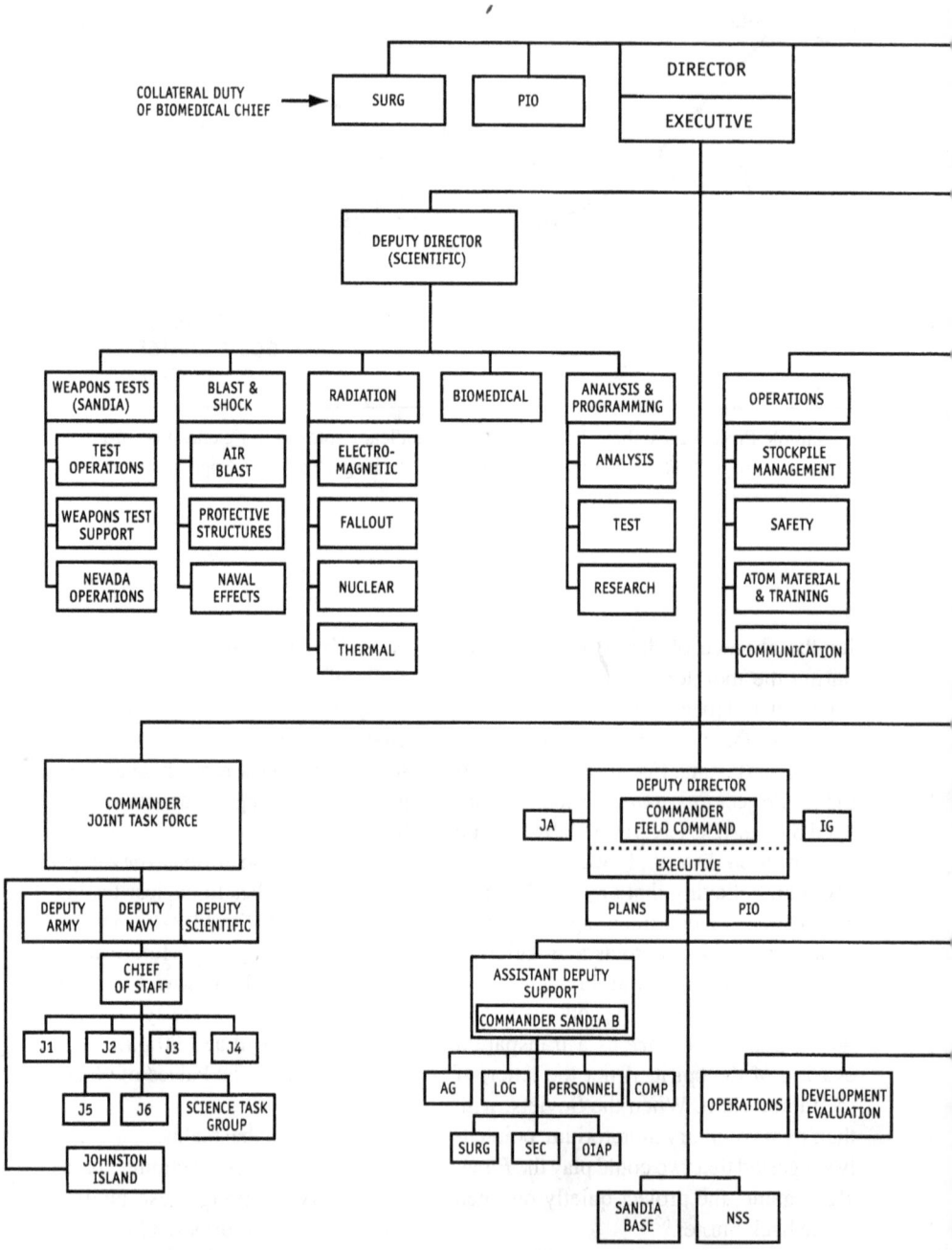

DASA Organizational Chart, May 1959.

Some Second Thoughts, 1957 to 1963

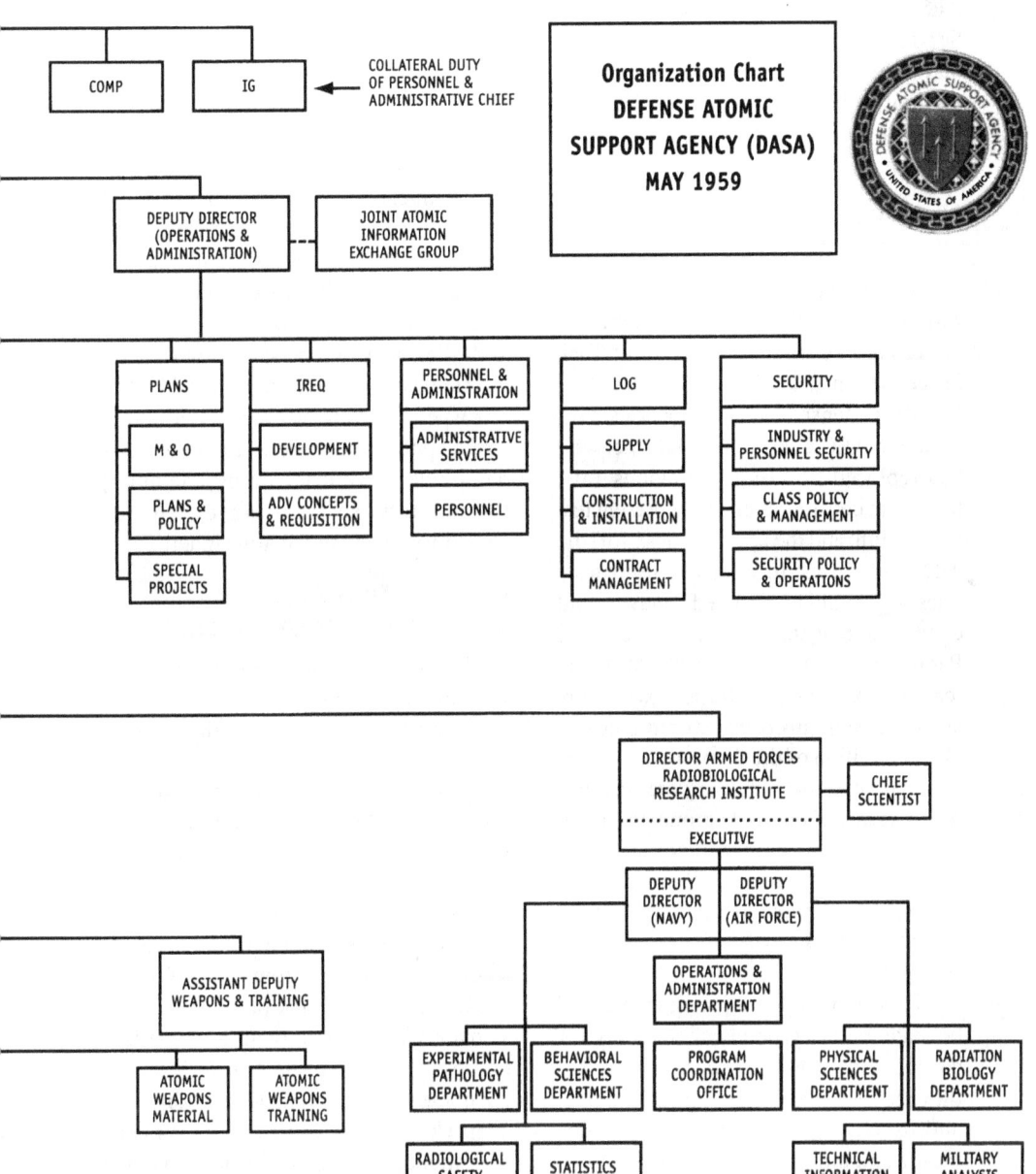

ing should resume. The transition from AFSWP to DASA provided that all the Services' nuclear testing budgets would be lumped together into a single appropriation under DASA's control. The adequacy of that appropriation was another question.

THE DISMANTLING OF JOINT TASK FORCE SEVEN

Among the first subordinate organizations to feel the effects of moratorium-related stringencies was Joint Task Force Seven (JTF-7). In March 1959, Deputy Defense Secretary Quarles suggested to AEC Chief John McCone, who had replaced Strauss the previous July, that "...in consideration of the present test moratorium and the uncertainties...[of] the nature, scope and locations of future tests if testing should be resumed," they should conduct a joint study on the future of the Pacific test infrastructure.[64] McCone readily agreed, both to the proposed study and the assumptions that would guide it. "In recognition of the domestic and international situation regarding the resumption of testing," the study group observed, "it may be too readily concluded that plans and preparations for overseas operations, in particular, could be safely relegated to the back burner, if not abandoned completely."[65]

They agreed that a strong case could be made on the grounds of economy for closing out the test facilities entirely. But they also warned of "...serious political and psychological consequences," domestic and diplomatic, if that were done. Unilateral dismantling of the test facilities, the study group concluded, would convey the message that the military regarded the atmospheric testing in the Pacific as unnecessary and, worse, eliminate any incentive for the Soviets to make comparable concessions of their own.

Despite the "relatively low probability" that the PPG would ever be used again for atmospheric testing, the study recommended the retention of the facilities on a much-reduced basis. Some base camp facilities and depots would be consolidated and others mothballed. All new construction came to an end. Communications equipment was turned over to contractors for conservation. As for JTF-7, its total authorized manpower was slashed from 945 to 206. Task Group 7.1, the group of scientists that had served as the liaison between the laboratories and the field, was entirely eliminated.[66] "In retrospect," wrote William Ogle, "this move appears as possibly the most serious single move made during the moratorium toward winding down our capability to test in the atmosphere."[67]

HIGH-ALTITUDE TESTING POSSIBILITIES

Implicit in the decisions about JTF-7 was another assumption: that, whatever became of the moratorium, the days of atmospheric testing for the United States were numbered. Given the emotions surrounding the fallout issue, military planners concluded that, if and when testing resumed, their focus would necessarily turn underground and to space.

Even underground and high-altitude testing was not free from political complications, however. The public controversy over ARGUS six months after the fact had less to do with testing *per se* than with the nuclear agencies' deliberate failure to keep Congress informed of their plans. The implication, disquieting in light of the ongoing test ban negotiations, was that tests conducted in outer space could go entirely undetected. Nevertheless, it was the fallout question that absorbed public attention immediately after the ARGUS revelations. To what extent was high-altitude testing safer than atmospheric tests? How high was high enough to prevent radioactivity from returning to earth? Congressional hearings in May of 1959 produced warnings from AEC, DASA, and public health experts that even a shot 30 miles up offered only a 50 percent margin of protection. However, at much higher altitudes—ARGUS had taken place approximately 300 miles above the earth—fallout dropped off dramatically. For DASA planners, this turned deep space into the next frontier for nuclear testing once the moratorium was lifted.

In particular, it revived interest in Project *Willow*, a Defense Department initiative designed as an ARGUS follow-on project, to test effects of nuclear explosions on communications, radar operations, and so forth. After the spring 1959 hearings, discussions began between DASA and the AEC to expand the scope of *Willow* to include AEC requirements for high-altitude testing, detection, and evasion.

The process soon bogged down, largely for budgetary reasons. One could hardly make a persuasive case for a project which, if nothing changed, would never be productive. It was especially difficult to make such a case for a project as costly as *Willow*. Operational and safety complexities led planners to switch the site of the proposed launch from Cape Canaveral to Johnston Island, adding $50 million to the projected cost. The agency requested $6 million for one phase of 1960 planning; it received $2 million. By early 1960, Project *Willow* was no further along than it had been a year earlier.[68]

HARDTACK II
AND THE DILEMMA OF UNDERGROUND TESTING

A week after the President's announcement of the moratorium, AEC Chief McCone had persuaded a reluctant Eisenhower to authorize "…one more test series" before the formal cessation of testing actually went into effect. The official name for the series, which consisted of 19 small shots, four of them underground, was HARDTACK II, although the press dubbed it "Operation Deadline." The test series took place at Yucca Flats, 90 miles northwest of Las Vegas, over a period of six weeks. The last blast occurred on October 30, 1958, just hours before the moratorium was to begin the following day.[69]

Meanwhile, negotiators in Geneva, James Wadsworth for the United States and Semyon Tsarapkin for the Soviets, had turned to the business at hand, fleshing out the agreements reached between U.S. and Soviet technical experts in Geneva over the previous summer. The central issue was verification and inspection. On the basis of the 1957 RAINIER blast, the Americans had concluded that it was seismically possible to detect underground blasts in excess of five megatons and to differentiate between a naturally occurring earth tremor and one caused by a nuclear detonation. This position was agreeable to the secretive Soviets, who opposed stringent verification. According to the experts' agreement signed on August 21, monitoring would be carried out from a network of 180 land- and sea-based stations around the globe.[70] But the shortcomings of the scientists' agreement was revealed soon after the Wadsworth-Tsarapkin negotiations got under way. Talks quickly bogged down over political questions, such as the composition of the seven-member control commission that would supervise the inspection arrangements and the nationalities of the commission's technicians.

Then a crucial substantive obstacle arose. In January of 1959, analysis of the data from HARDTACK II cast considerable doubt on the RAINIER-based assumptions embodied in the bilateral experts' agreement. HARDTACK II showed that the seismic signals produced by underground blasts were much weaker than RAINIER had indicated: detecting blasts down to five megatons would require as many as 1,000 on-site inspections or three times as many monitoring stations as the experts' agreement contemplated. To the Soviets, this represented an unthinkable intrusiveness. They cried foul, accusing the Americans of manipulating the data to justify reneging on the experts' agreement. Eisenhower was embarrassed and angry, for he had accepted the judgment of his scientists; judgment based on RAINIER alone, as a basis for a negotiating position that subsequent evidence proved untenable.[71]

Nevertheless, with the Geneva talks apparently headed for a breakdown, Eisenhower again turned to his scientists. The chairman of his Science Advisory Commission, James R. Killian, Jr., recommended the appointment of an investigative panel to review the HARDTACK II findings and to investigate ways in which existing monitoring technology might be improved, perhaps making it possible to retain the original Geneva monitoring framework. The panel, headed by university president Lloyd V. Berkner, reported its findings in March, and, for test ban treaty proponents, the news was not good. It reaffirmed the HARDTACK II conclusion and then raised a new issue that reinforced it: the so-called "big hole" phenomenon. Scientific evidence now showed that if an underground explosion took place in a large cave, as opposed to being drilled directly into the bedrock, it would be much more difficult to detect seismically.[72]

The Berkner Panel's concluding call for a crash program of seismic research provided further motivation for the VELA UNIFORM project, which produced major advances in underground test detection technology.[73] In the meantime, however, there was no method the United States and the Soviet Union could agree to for monitoring underground testing that was both effective and unobtrusive. Additionally, no method was known to effectively monitor nuclear testing in outer space. By the spring of 1959, even as the Geneva negotiators struggled on, it was clear that a comprehensive test ban treaty was beyond reach; a ban on atmospheric testing was all that could realistically be achieved.

Pressure began to build in the United States for a resumption of testing, if not in the atmosphere, then underground. Strauss and McCone had always had difficulty keeping their moratorium misgivings to themselves. Other defense officials were similarly candid in expressing their concerns about the United States falling behind in the arms race; they and their colleagues at the AEC took for granted that the Soviets were conducting underground tests even as they were pledging to adhere to the moratorium. By December, even Secretary of Defense Thomas Gates was calling for the resumption of underground testing. On the defensive, test ban treaty proponents agreed on a compromise proposal to the Soviets that would bar atmospheric testing and underground testing above a specified kiloton level, the latter to be determined based on a number of on-site inspections to be determined by Moscow. On December 29, 1960, Eisenhower announced the end of the moratorium, with the caveat that the United States would give notice before resuming testing. Six weeks later, he formally presented the compromise proposal to the Soviets.

Before the Soviets had a chance to react, France became the fourth member of the nuclear fraternity when it detonated a 60-kiloton bomb at Reggan, a remote Sahara oasis approximately 750 miles southwest of Algiers. It was the first atmospheric nuclear test in 16 months. French President Charles de Gaulle insisted that by developing an independent nuclear capability not responsive to Moscow or Washington, France was "...rendering a service to the balance of the world." Others saw it differently. In Africa, French embassies were the scene of violent protests. The hostility of eastern bloc nations was predictable, but even in Washington and London, the reaction was noticeably cool to what amounted to an ally's triumph. For the French, the blast highlighted the dangers of nuclear proliferation—and the fact that the window of opportunity to prevent nuclear weaponry from spreading to other, perhaps less responsible, governments would not stay open indefinitely.[74]

That sobering realization lent new urgency to the test ban negotiations. Two days after the French test, Soviet treaty negotiator Tsarapkin indicated that Moscow was studying the U.S. compromise proposal eliminating atmospheric tests and large underground tests. On March 19, 1961, he brought a counterproposal: in addition to the prohibitions proposed by the Americans, the Soviets proposed an end to smaller underground tests, but without provision for verification. The plan would be based on good faith, a scarce commodity in the Cold War. In the United States, ardent Cold Warriors quickly denounced the Soviet plan as a ploy that would permit Moscow to conduct smaller tests in massive numbers behind closed doors while U.S. compliance would be subject to the world's scrutiny. But Eisenhower was determined to have an agreement. As he told his advisors, unless the U.S. accepted the Soviet proposal as a basis for new negotiations, which he hoped to begin with Khrushchev during their upcoming summit in Paris, "...all hope of relaxing the Cold War would be gone."[75]

MORATORIUM ENDS

In October, 1961, the Soviets ended the moratorium by detonating a 50 megaton,* parachute-retarded weapon from a Tu-95 *Bear* strategic bomber over Novaya Zemlya test range. The weapon, named *Tsar Bomba*, was in response in Kruschev's specific command to Sakharaov and other bomb designers to pursue the quick development of a 100-megaton range weapon. Although this weapon was actually fielded and added to Soviet stockpile, it was deemed "militarily useless" due to its weight of 27 tons. The fabrication of the massive parachute used with this weapon actually disrupted the Soviet hosiery industry. In response to the threat imposed by Soviet nuclear tests, DASA was tasked with several program support initiatives in 1961; many in direct response to White House requests.

The DoD Damage Assessment Center (DODDAC) began operations in the Pentagon and at the underground Alternate National Military Command Center (ANMCC) at Fort Ritchie, Maryland in 1961. DASA contributed staff to DODDAC and to the Assessment Center's research programs.

In late 1961, at White House request, DASA staff analyzed the effects of a 100-megaton weapon detonated on the ANMCC at Fort Ritchie, and on proposed new underground facilities in Washington, D.C. DASA also supported the Joint Strategic Target Planning Staff (JSTPS), established at SAC, beginning in 1960. DASA and its contractors developed computer models of nuclear effects, notably airblast, based on data collected at NTS and Pacific test series.

---

* *Tsar Bomba*, the largest nuclear weapon ever constructed or detonated, was actually a 100-megaton bomb design, however, the yield on detonation was 50 megatons.

The U-2 Affair

Just before sunrise on May 1, 1960, a 31-year-old Air Force lieutenant rolled out of his bunk in the U.S. barracks at Peshawar, Pakistan. After breakfast, he squeezed into his flight suit and then into the cockpit of the plane that, if all went according to plan, would carry him over the Soviet Union and land in Norway 18 hours later. His name was Francis Gary Powers.[76]

First Lieutenant Powers, an Air Force pilot flying F-84 fighter aircraft, had been solicited by the CIA in 1956 to support a unique mission the agency was developing. With the imminent test flight of a new secret surveillance aircraft, the Lockheed U-2, the CIA began a crash program to train top-flight pilots in high-altitude surveillance. Powers entered U-2 training at Watertown Strip in Nevada and after several months began service at U.S. military bases in Turkey and Pakistan. Originally flying the U-2 along the Soviet borders for reconnaissance, the May 1, 1960 flight was to be the first direct traversing flight across the USSR from Pakistan to Norway. A little more than halfway though his flight, Power's U-2 was disabled by a Soviet surface-to-air missile near the city of Sverdlovsk. After bailout, Lieutenant Powers was taken into custody by local military and turned over to the KGB in Moscow.

The downing of his U-2 reconnaissance plane over Sverdlovsk set in motion a train of events that abruptly ended the Paris summit, all hopes for rapid progress toward a nuclear test ban treaty, and Eisenhower's dream of achieving detente between the United States and the Soviet Union. Eisenhower's disappointment was acute, but he would have undoubtedly had real difficulty selling to the Senate a treaty resembling the one that the Soviets had proposed; a treaty that would have frozen U.S. testing both above and below ground, and trusted the Soviets' pledge to do likewise.

Soon after the Paris summit failure, Wadsworth and Tsarapkin resumed negotiations in Geneva. But these were negotiations that were going nowhere, at least not until a new administration took office in Washington. With the Pentagon and the AEC clamoring for a reopening of test-

Becoming operational in 1955, the B-52 bomber served as a USAF mainstay front-line bomber.

ing, new President John F. Kennedy's expressed commitment to continuing the moratorium became increasingly difficult to sustain. After August 31, 1961, when the Soviets unilaterally resumed large-scale atmospheric testing, it became impossible. Kennedy's first reaction to the news of the Soviet decision, according to Theodore Sorensen, was "unprintable."[77] His second reaction was to order "the resumption of nuclear tests, in the laboratory and underground, with no fallout."

Meanwhile, the fledgling Soviet space program, still reveling in the success of the earlier launch of the *Sputnik* satellite, enjoyed another first; the launch of Vostok 1 from Baikonur in the Soviet Union, and the earth orbit of Yuri Gagarin on April 12, 1961. Gagarin's spacecraft circled the Earth once in an elliptical orbit with successful re-entry, making the Soviet Union's first cosmonaut a worldwide celebrity. Once again, American notions of superiority were shattered by the Soviet space triumph, yet it was this achievement that prompted the United States to launch its own program to "get a man on the moon" by the end of the 1960s.

OPERATION NOUGAT

Coupled with the fact that larger weapons and anti-missile weapons could not be tested underground under any circumstances and that each day seemed to bring reports of new and bigger Soviet atmospheric blasts, it is no wonder that Kennedy's inclination was increasingly to embrace a resumption of atmospheric testing. He announced that decision several months later, on November 30, 1961.[78] Kennedy's call for the resumption of nuclear tests with "no fallout" led to a hastily prepared program of underground testing at NTS, called Operation NOUGAT; a series of underground nuclear tests. The initial test, Shot ANTLER, got off to a rocky start on September 15, 1961. About an hour after the initial detonation, involving a 2.6 kiloton device, radioactivity vented from the tunnel complex into the atmosphere, destroying most of the data and rendering some of the test tunnels unusable for a month, despite around-the-clock clean-up efforts. Operation NOUGAT tests continued at NTS through 1961 and on into 1962, with more than 45 individual weapon-related tests; the

Lockheed U-2 Surveillance aircraft of the type used by Lieutenant Powers in 1960.

majority of which were tunnel or shaft-type tests.

Prompted by Soviet testing, the U.S. accelerated deployments of nuclear weapons to Europe late in 1961. The NATO nuclear stockpile virtually doubled between January 1961 and May 1965. The tension and pressure of the Cold War began to boil over.

DASA AFTER THE MORATORIUM

The change from AFSWP to DASA on May 1, 1959 was soon accompanied by a change in agency leadership. Admiral Parker resigned as DASA Director in August of 1960; taking his place on an interim basis was Major General Harold C. (Sam) Donnelly, commanding general of Field Command. In January of 1961, Major General Robert H. Booth took over the reins at DASA, where he would serve until health problems forced his retirement in 1964.[79] Born in Washington, D.C., in 1905, General Booth graduated from West Point in 1930. He attended the Air Corps flying school and then, with limited opportunity to put his flying skills to use in the peacetime Army, switched back to field artillery. He then began a long series of teaching and staff assignments: three years as an instructor of field artillery at Fort Sill, Oklahoma; four years in the mathematics department at West Point; and, after a year in combat against Japan, as an operations officer with a specialty in new weapons applications. Booth's postwar field commands took him to Germany, first in divisional and then in corps artillery. Before coming to DASA, he commanded the Second Army Air Defense Region at Fort Meade, Maryland. He had just completed his 31st year of active duty.[80]

Booth's wealth of administrative experience would be put to the test in rehabilitating a nuclear testing capability that, as Frank Shelton put it succinctly, "...had gone to pot" during the moratorium years.[81] NOUGAT's start-up difficulties, in which the first 11 underground tests all vented radioactivity to a significant extent, even though they were all AEC tests, still underscored the challenge DASA faced in meeting President Kennedy's stricture of "no fallout." But the agency now had the budgetary wherewithal to get the job done: the appropriation for fiscal year 1962 was nearly double that for fiscal year 1959, during the depths of the moratorium.[82] As DASA personnel continued their work in the Nevada desert into the early months of 1962, mishaps of the sort that vexed NOUGAT at the outset and that had prodded Kennedy to resume atmospheric testing, became less frequent. Underground testing was relatively new, and experience paid big dividends. Testers learned the relative advantages of tunnels for some applications and vertical holes for others. A search got under way for a

Major General Robert H. Booth, DASA Director, 1961-1964.

second site to augment the NTS; the Mississippi salt domes seemed especially promising. Veteran test engineers from AFSWP days, who had scattered to other assignments during the moratorium, returned to DASA. Booth ordered the recruitment of experienced radiochemists, who brought with them advanced techniques of data collection and evaluation. DASA logisticians unraveled bottlenecks in the delivery of materials—coaxial cable was for a time in particularly short supply—and heavy equipment. Labor unrest, particularly among the unionized pipe fitters and operating engineers, was ironed out when the workweek was reduced from 54 hours to 40. By January, a schedule of 24 NTS shots had been submitted to and approved by the President, a schedule consistent with the demands of national security and the capabilities of the test site.[83]

OPERATION DOMINIC

For all the progress stateside, the Pacific would be the main theater of nuclear test operations should atmospheric testing be approved. In preparation for resumption, Joint Task Force Eight (JTF-8), the successor to JTF-7, was activated. On October 21, 1961, the JCS assigned DASA the task of planning for the tests to be carried out under control of JTF-8.

JTF-8 was organized much like prior test organizations, incorporating elements of the military Services and their contractors, of the AEC and its contractors, and of other government agencies in its structure. Command went to Major General Alfred D. Starbird, who had served as the AEC's senior military officer since 1955. General Starbird was responsible to both the JCS and the AEC Chairman. He had three deputy commanders: one from the Navy, who also commanded the Navy Task Group (JTG 8.3); another was from the Air Force who commanded the Air Force Task Group (JTG 8.4); the third deputy was an AEC civilian, who directed all the scientific activities. Base support would be carried out by the same civilian contractor that had supplied these services in all the Pacific tests during the 1950s. Starbird had at his disposal 95 ships, 233 aircraft, and more than 19,000 military, civilian, and contractor personnel.[84]

General Starbird and his staff had a full plate with Operation DOMINIC, a series of 36 tests that began April 25, 1962. The principal location for the weapon development phase of the project was British-owned Christmas Island, a largely uninhabited atoll lying about 1,200 miles south of Hawaii. Christmas Island offered two principal benefits. First, it was *not* Enewetak, the obvious and best choice from a technical standpoint but problematic politically. Even U.S. allies, the State Department argued, might reasonably question whether Washington was doing right by the Marshallese under United Nations trusteeship in once again turning their tropical island into a nuclear firing range. Second, Christmas Island, 30 miles long, was considerably larger than Johnston Island, another frequent test site, but too small to accommodate any except the high-altitude shots planned for DOMINIC. The one drawback, of course, was that Christmas Island was British, but high level negotiations, culminating in a Bermuda summit meeting between Kennedy and Prime Minister Harold Macmillan, and a *quid pro quo* agreement allowing the British to use NTS for some test blasts of their own, settled that matter.[85]

DOMINIC was to be a comprehensive test series. It involved two key Navy tests (FRIGATE BIRD and SWORDFISH), a Defense Department rocket-launched high-altitude series, code-named FISHBOWL, plus a variety of nuclear weapons development tests designed by AEC

Operation DOMINIC, Shot TRUCKEE, June 9, 1962; 210 KT weapons-related airdrop at Christmas Island, South Pacific.

nuclear weapons laboratories. In approving DOMINIC, Kennedy imposed an approximate 90-day time limit; all tests were to be completed by July of 1962.

The Navy series (FRIGATE BIRD and SWORDFISH) and FISHBOWL were the most consequential for national security. FRIGATE BIRD, on May 6, marked the first firing of a Polaris submarine-launched ballistic missile (SLBM) system with a nuclear warhead, delivered by the submarine USS Ethan Allen. The missile traveled over 1,000 nautical miles before reentering the atmosphere and exploding as an air burst over the Pacific. It was the capstone of the development of the Polaris, which subsequently joined the long-range bomber and the land-based ICBM to form the three legs of the U.S. deterrent triad. SWORDFISH was both a weapon system test and a weapon effects test of the Navy's ASROC program, the development of a rocket-launched, antisubmarine nuclear depth charge. It, too, was a near-complete success.[86]

FISHBOWL, however, knew both success and failure, and the failures were spectacular. A high-altitude rocket was to be launched from Johnston Island, where a massive crash rebuilding program was under way, involving a new launch complex for Thor missiles and improvements to the island airfield. FISHBOWL's component shots, code-named BLUEGILL and STARFISH, were effects tests designed to answer two questions: whether neutrons and gamma rays from a nuclear blast were capable of neutralizing enemy reentry vehicles, and whether varying intensities of nuclear radiation would interrupt enemy radar and communications. Announcement of FISHBOWL brought protests from prominent scientists, who charged that they would disturb the Van Allen radiation belt, a vast field of protons and electrons recently discovered by Professor James Van Allen of Iowa State University and thought to be critical to the earth's radio communications. Van Allen himself gave BLUEGILL and STARFISH a clean bill of health, and President Kennedy added his own reassurances at his May 9 press conference.[87]

With the eyes of the scientific community focused on these two tests, it was naturally a great embarrassment when the BLUEGILL rocket had to be destroyed 10 minutes into the June 5 launch due to the failure of radar tracking. Two weeks later, on June 19, the STARFISH rocket barely got off the ground when the missile propulsion system exploded and the warhead had to be destroyed. In the second iteration of STARFISH, called STARFISH PRIME, the rocket left the launch pad on time and in one piece. But its detonation discharged billions of electrons into the Van Allen belt, belying AEC assurances that nothing of the sort would occur. BLUEGILL was also rescheduled, but this time the Thor rocket erupted in flames after lift-off and had to be destroyed, strewing considerable nuclear debris.[88]

Other tests in the FISHBOWL series had better results. CHECKMATE (October 20), KINGFISH (November 1), and, finally, on November 4, TIGHTROPE all went off much as planned. That was a good thing, for, as Air Force Chief of Staff General Curtis LeMay pointed out, there were no Thor missiles left in case any failed.

After observing the success of TIGHTROPE, Frank Shelton returned to his living quarters in a melancholy mood. "That was the 65th atmospheric nuclear weapon burst that I have observed in the past 10 years," he recalled saying to himself, "and I think it is probably the last one that I will ever see conducted in the atmosphere."[89]

Shelton was correct. From the perspective of DASA and the AEC, DOMINIC *had* been a major success. The test series had yielded data that proved indispensable for improving safety and reliability. It also increased the yield-to-weight ratio and the shelf life of the warheads. From these data eventually came a new generation of more advanced nuclear weapons.[90]

DOMINIC pointed up all of the liabilities inherent in nuclear testing— scientific, political, economic, and diplomatic. It had cost U.S. taxpayers more than $250 million. Kennedy's three month time limit had turned into six, and that for a significantly abbreviated series of tests. On at least one occasion, Kennedy's exasperation led him to consider calling off the whole exercise, only to learn that Soviet tests of devices far larger than anything contemplated for DOMINIC were proceeding apace.

THE CUBAN MISSILE CRISIS AND A NEW TREATY

Agency staff on Johnston Island, like tens of millions of other Americans, were glued to their radios and televisions on October 22, 1962, as Kennedy announced the discovery of nuclear-capable Soviet surface-to-surface, nuclear-capable missiles in Cuba and demanded that the Soviets remove them forthwith. The world held its breath as U.S. warships moved into position to enforce a blockade around Cuba. For DASA personnel assigned to Hickam Air Force Base in Hawaii, the long stretches of empty asphalt on parking ramps which customarily held as many as 50 military aircraft bespoke the gravity of the crisis; all had been recalled to the mainland to participate in the buildup of forces against Cuba.[91]

The Kennedy and Khrushchev brush with nuclear catastrophe had a sobering effect upon both leaders, who emerged from the experience determined not to repeat it. Kennedy, who had earlier dismissed Khrushchev's suggestion that a telephone "hot line" be installed between the Kremlin and the White House, now accepted the idea with alacrity. Both evinced a sense of urgency about coming to an agreement on curtailing nuclear testing and the arms race. In the exchange of notes that brought the missile crisis to a close, they expressed their mutual commitment to that cause. While the ensuing months saw enough posturing and haggling to raise questions about whether an agreement would ever be reached, the will was clearly there to achieve the breakthrough that had eluded the superpowers for five years.

President Kennedy hinted at the sort of peace he sought in a June 1963 Commencement Address at American University in Washington. In his speech, Kennedy announced the early agreement with Soviets to begin discussions "...on a comprehensive test ban treaty..." to "ban nuclear tests in the atmosphere." Kennedy continued his thoughts, explaining, "While we proceed to safeguard our national interests let us also safeguard human interest. And the elimination of war and arms is clearly in the interests of both."

The agreement was, however, a limited breakthrough, for the two sides were never able to bridge the American insistence on on-site inspections and the Soviets' refusal to consider them. "NATO spies," said Khrushchev, and that was that. With the exception of that point, the negotiations moved rapidly. Averill Harriman and the U.S. delegation arrived in Moscow on July 15, 1963; 10 days later, Harriman, Soviet Foreign Minister Andrei Gromyko, and the British representative, Lord Hailsham, signed the Limited Test Ban Treaty (LTBT). It consisted of a mere 800 words, a preamble and five articles prohibiting nuclear detonations in space, at high altitude, in the atmosphere, or under water. It permitted underground testing, but only to the extent that discharge of radioactivity was confined to the borders of the country doing the testing. On July 26, Kennedy again took to the airwaves, but this time it was to announce an agreement with the Soviets rather than an ultimatum. On October 7, after Senate hearings, he signed it into law. "No other accomplishment," wrote Theodore Sorensen, "ever gave Kennedy more satisfaction."[93]

Transition

DASA faced enormous change dealing with the world of the new treaty, which would be different from the world of the moratorium into which it had been born. In response to Senate (and Joint Chiefs of Staff) concerns that ratification would again play havoc with the country's nuclear capabilities, Kennedy pledged to the Senate that he would implement four specific safeguards to assure that nuclear readiness would be maintained. Safeguard A continued the underground nuclear test program. Safeguard B committed the United States to maintaining modern nu-

President John F. Kennedy signs the Limited Test Ban Treaty, 1963.

clear laboratory facilities and programs. Safeguard C established a National Nuclear Test Readiness Program. Safeguard D provided for improved verification of the Treaty, including continued work on VELA detection and seismic monitoring.[94] This ambitious mandate became DASA's mission during the mid-1960s under the aegis of the Limited Test Ban Treaty.

ENDNOTES

1. "Into Space," *Newsweek*, October 14, 1957, p. 38; "Soviet Satellite Sends U.S. into a Tizzy," *Life*, October 14, 1957.
2. "Red Moon Over the U.S.," *Time* 70, no. 16 (October 14, 1957): p. 27; "Into Space," *Newsweek*, October 14, 1957, p. 38; Robert J. Watson, *Into the Missile Age, 1956-1960: History of the Office of the Secretary of Defense, Volume IV* (Washington, D.C.: 1997) pp. 123-24.
3. "Soviet Satellite Sends U.S. into a Tizzy," *Life*, October 14, 1957, p. 35. As if in response to the Soviet comment, tail fins on American automobiles reached their apogee in 1957 and shrank in each year thereafter.
4. "Did Russia Steal Satellite Secret from U.S.?" *U.S. News & World Report* 43 (October 18, 1957): p. 44; "The U.S., Ike, and Sputnik," *Newsweek* 50 (October 28, 1957): pp. 31, 32, 35; Watson, *Into the Missile Age*, p. 124; *Time* 70, no. 16 (October 14, 1957): p. 27.
5. "Man's Awesome Adventure," *Newsweek* 50 (October 14, 1957): pp. 39-40.
6. "Man's Awesome Adventure," *Newsweek* 50 (October 14, 1957): pp. 40-41; Watson, *Into the Missile Age*, pp. 124-26.
7. William E. Ogle, *An Account of the Return to Nuclear Weapons Testing by the United States after the Test Moratorium, 1958-1961*, (Las Vegas: 1985), pp. 85-87, 89 (hereinafter cited as Ogle, "Return to Testing").
8. Shelton, *Reflections of a Nuclear Weaponeer*, pp. 7.5-7.11.
9. *Ibid*, pp. 7.18-7.22.
10. *Ibid*, pp. 7.5-7.25. Scoville went to the Central Intelligence Agency.
11. *Ibid*, pp. 7.22, 7.25.
12. Hewlett and Holl, *Atoms for Peace and War*, p. 452.
13. *Ibid*, p. 453. When the moratorium was announced in 1958, AFSWP decided that another revision of *The Effects of Nuclear Weapons* should be prepared. The version published in 1962 incorporated new information gleaned from the HARDTACK and ARGUS series, especially the effect on radio communications and radar and detection of distant explosions. See Glasstone, ed., *The Effects of Nuclear Weapons* (Washington: 1962), pp. vii-viii.
14. Hewlett and Holl, *Atoms for Peace and War*, pp. 455-56.
15. *Ibid*, pp. 361-70.
16. *Ibid*, p. 399.
17. Shelton, *Reflections of a Nuclear Weaponeer*, pp. 8.17-8.22.
18. *New York Times*, May 10, 1957; *Washington News*, May 10, 1957, reprinted in Shelton, *Reflections of a Nuclear Weaponeer*, pp. 8.9-8.11.
19. Shelton, *Reflections of a Nuclear Weaponeer*, pp. 8.49-8.51.
20. Hewlett and Holl, *Atoms for Peace and War*, pp. 456-57.
21. Defense Nuclear Agency, "Operation HARDTACK I, 1958," DNA 6038F, December 1, 1982, pp. 1-3; Shelton, *Reflections of a Nuclear Weaponeer*, pp. 8.51-8.52.
22. Shelton, *Reflections of a Nuclear Weaponeer*, pp. 8.40-8.42, 9.12; Defense Nuclear Agency, *Operation Argus 1958*, DNA 6039F, April 30, 1982, p. 1.
23. Ogle, *Return to Testing*, p. 101; Shelton, *Reflections of a Nuclear Weaponeer*, p. 8.46.
24. U.S. House, 85th Cong., 1st sess., Subcommittee of the Committee on Appropriations, *Hearings, Part 2, March 11, 1957, 1533-1551; Ibid., March 21, 1957, 1551-57;* DNA, "Operation HARDTACK I," DNA 6038F, p. 25.
25. Ogle, *Return to Testing*, pp. 90-91.
26. Shelton, *Reflections of a Nuclear Weaponeer*, pp. 8.34-8.35; Hewlett and Holl, *Atoms for Peace and War*, p. 482.
27. Shelton, *Reflections of a Nuclear Weaponeer*, pp. 8.34-8.35, 8.33.
28. *Ibid*, pp. 8.35-8.36.
29. Hewlett and Holl, *Atoms for Peace and War*, p. 483; Edward N. Parker, memorandum, "Joint Task Force-7 Relations with DASA Under the Proposed Reorganization," November 9, 1959, pp. 15-17.
30. Ogle, *Return to Testing*, pp. 101-2; Hewlett and Holl, *Atoms for Peace and War*, p. 483.

31. Hewlett and Holl, *Atoms for Peace and War*, p. 483; Ogle, *Return to Testing*, p. 101; Shelton, *Reflections of a Nuclear Weaponeer*, pp. 8.40, 10.6-10.21.
32. Shelton, *Reflections of a Nuclear Weaponeer*, pp. 9.35-9.36; Joint AEC-DoD Statement of Results of the TEAK and ORANGE shots in the 1958 HARDTACK Series, June 15, 1959, DSWA Technical Library, pp. 070-046.
33. Adrian Polk recollection of TEAK detonation, discussion with author, Alexandria, VA, September 29, 1999.
34. Shelton, *Reflections of a Nuclear Weaponeer*, pp. 9.35-9.36; quotes from Ibid., p. 9.39.
35. Ogle, *Return to Testing*, p. 100; Shelton, *Reflections of a Nuclear Weaponeer*, pp. 9.18-9.24; U.S. DOE, *United States Nuclear Tests, 1945-1992* (Las Vegas: 1993), p. 6.
36. Shelton, *Reflections of a Nuclear Weaponeer*, pp. 9.40-9.41.
37. *Ibid*, pp. 9.41, 8.4-8.5.
38. Ogle, *Return to Testing*, p. 106.
39. DNA, *Operation ARGUS*, DNA 6039F, pp. 20-21; Watson, *Into the Missile Age*, p. 461; York, *Making Weapons, Talking Peace*, pp. 180-81; *New York Times*, March 20, 1959, pp. 1-2; Shelton, *Reflections of a Nuclear Weaponeer*, pp. 10.17, 9.1. The Soviets and Americans discussed the issue of detecting very high-altitude nuclear detonations using a system of satellites. See p. 9.9.
40. Watson, *Into the Missile Age*, p. 461; Shelton, *Reflections of a Nuclear Weaponeer*, pp. 10.17, 10.15; Ogle, "Return to Testing," 103; DNA, *Operation ARGUS, 1958*, DNA 6039F, pp. 17-20; Hewlett and Holl, *Atoms for Peace and War*, p. 483. The other area in the world where the Christofilos effect could be easily measured because of the imperfect symmetry of the Earth's magnetic field was Iceland. See York, *Making Weapons, Talking Peace*, p. 149.
41. DNA, *Operation ARGUS 1958*, DNA 6039F, pp. 31-32, 53, 83-84; Shelton, *Reflections of a Nuclear Weaponeer*, p. 10.21.
42. *New York Times*, March 20, 1959, pp. 1-2; Shelton, *Reflections of a Nuclear Weaponeer*, pp. 10.5-10.15. Mustin would later become the head of DASA.
43. DNA, *Operation ARGUS 1958*, DNA 6039F, pp. 32-34; Shelton, *Reflections of a Nuclear Weaponeer*, pp. 10.20-10.21.
44. York, *Making Weapons, Talking Peace*, p. 149; Shelton, *Reflections of a Nuclear Weaponeer*, p. 10.21.
45. *New York Times*, March 20, 1959, pp. 1-2; Shelton, *Reflections of a Nuclear Weaponeer*, p. 10.15; York, *Making Weapons, Talking Peace*, p. 149. The secrecy of the ARGUS tests was blown when Hanson Baldwin, a military writer for the *New York Times*, got hold of the whole story in January 1959. After three months of discussions with the Pentagon, Baldwin ran the ARGUS story, much to the distress of Deputy Secretary of Defense Donald Quarles and other administration officials. See York, *Making Weapons, Talking Peace*, pp. 149-50.
46. DNA, *Operation ARGUS, 1958*, April 30, 1982, pp. 11-12, 1.
47. *New York Times*, March 20, 1959.
48. *Washington Post*, March 21, 1998.
49. "History of the Armed Forces Special Weapons Project: Latter Period, 1955-1958," Part 1, p. 39.
50. "History of the Armed Forces Special Weapons Project: Latter Period, 1955-1958," pp. 40-41.
51. Philip L. Cantelon and Robert C. Williams, *Crisis Contained: The Department of Energy at Three Mile Island* (Carbondale, Ill.: 1982), pp. 20-21; "History of the Armed Forces Special Weapons Project: Latter Period, 1955-1958," pp. 33-34. The agreement was extended to permit the Joint Center to include mutual assistance in radiation monitoring and medical safety for military or civilian radiation accidents. The Albuquerque Center later became known as the Joint Nuclear Accident Coordination Center. Cantelon and Williams, *Crisis Contained*, pp. 21, 78.
52. *U.S. News & World Report* 44 (March 21, 1958): pp. 55, 57; *Time* 71 (March 24,

1958): pp. 23-24; *Newsweek* 51 (March 24, 1958): p. 60; *Life* 44 (March 24, 1958): p. 48.
53. Eisenhower quoted in Watson, *Into the Missile Age*, p. 257.
54. William R. Harris, *Defense Nuclear Responsibilities: From the Armed Forces Special Weapons Project to the Defense Nuclear Agency, 1947-1971* (Washington, D.C., 1996), pp. 76-77.
55. *U.S. News & World Report* 44 (April 18, 1958); *New Republic* 138 (April 14, 1958): pp. 12-13.
56. Spaatz, "Where We *Went* Wrong—Plan for the Future," *Newsweek* 50 (December 30, 1957): p. 19.
57. Strauss quoted in Hewlett and Holl, *Atoms for Peace and War*, p. 457.
58. Harris, *Defense Nuclear Responsibilities*, pp. 77-78; Memorandum for the Chief, Armed Forces Special Weapons Project, 6 May 1959, Subject: Organization and Functions of the Defense Atomic Support Agency.
59. "History of the Defense Atomic Support Agency," Part I: Mission, Organization, Liaison, Strength, ch. 1, pp. 5-6.
60. The extent to which Eisenhower sought to perpetuate or terminate the Cold War has been widely debated. On this subject, see Stephen G. Rabe, "Eisenhower Revisionism," *Diplomatic History* 17, no. 1 (Winter 1993), esp. p. 111.
61. "Red Test Fallout Will Double 59's" [interview with Major General Robert H. Booth], *Army, Navy, Air Force Register* p. 83 (December 16, 1961): pp. 13-14; John S. Foster, Jr. to Starbird, June 2, 1959, DMA Collection, Box 3788, Department of Energy Archives.
62. Shelton, *Reflections of a Nuclear Weaponeer*, p. 11.1.
63. Hewlett and Holl, *Atoms for Peace and War*, pp. 528-30; Ogle, *Return to Testing*, pp. 135-36.
64. *Peaceful Applications of Nuclear Explosives-Plowshare*, Hearing before the Joint Committee on Atomic Energy, 89th Congress, First Session, January 5, 1965, US GPO: Washington, D.C.
65. Quarles to McCone, March 7, 1959, in *Report of the Study Group on Organization for Future Test Operations*, August 20, 1959, p. 8.
66. "Factors Bearing on the Organization and Planning for Future Weapons Testing," March 17, 1959, in Ibid., p. 10.
67. "Discussion," *Ibid.*, pp. 30-35. See also Joint Task Force 7, "Relations with DASA Under the Proposed Reorganization," November 1959.
68. Ogle, *Return to Testing*, pp. 128-29.
69. *Ibid*, pp. 131-32, 140-49.
70. Shelton, *Reflections of a Nuclear Weaponeer*, p. 10.2; Robert A. Divine, *Blowing On the Wind: The Nuclear Test Ban Debate* (New York, 1978), pp. 231-34.
71. Shelton, *Reflections of a Nuclear Weaponeer*, pp. 10.3-10.5; Divine, *Blowing on the Wind*, pp. 241-61.
72. Divine, *Blowing on the Wind*, pp. 231-40.
73. James R. Killian, Jr., *Sputnik, Scientists, and Eisenhower: A Memoir of the First Special Assistant to the President for Science and Technology* (Cambridge, Mass., 1977), pp. 165-68.
74. On VELA, see Ogle, *Return to Testing*, pp. 170-84.
75. *Time* 75 (February 22, 1960): p. 22; *U.S. News & World Report* p. 48 (February 29, 1960): p. 75.
76. Eisenhower quoted in Divine, *Blowing on the Wind*, p. 301.
77. Michael R. Beschloss, *May-Day: Eisenhower, Khrushchev and the U-2 Affair* (New York, 1986), pp. 13-17, 231-33, 379-80.
78. Sorensen quoted in Glenn T. Seaborg, *Kennedy, Khrushchev and the Test Ban* (Berkeley, Calif., 1981), p. 81.
79. *Ibid*, 89-90; Shelton, *Reflections of a Nuclear Weaponeer*, pp. 11.9-11.11.
80. "History of the Defense Atomic Support Agency, 1959-1969," p. 5.1.
81. "Joint Task Force Eight Moves Ahead," *Army, Navy, Air Force Journal and Register* 94 (March 17, 1962): p. 20; "Major General Robert Highman Booth, USA," in U.S. Army Center of Military History Archives.

82. Shelton, *Reflections of a Nuclear Weaponeer*, p. 12.21.
83. Harris, *Defense Nuclear Responsibilities*, p. 81.
84. Ogle, *Return to Testing*, pp. 242-302.
85. "Joint Task Force Eight Moves Ahead," p. 20; Joint Task Force Eight (Activation and Charter Development), in "History of the Defense Atomic Support Agency, 1959-69"; DNA, *DOMINIC I*, DNA 6040F, pp. 43-44.
86. Seaborg, *Kennedy, Khrushchev and the Test Ban*, pp. 108-10, 117-19, 126-31.
87. DNA, *DOMINIC I*, pp. 184-85, 196-99.
88. Seaborg, *Kennedy, Khrushchev and the Test Ban*, pp. 152-57.
89. Shelton, *Reflections of a Nuclear Weaponeer*, pp. 11.35-39; DNA, *DOMINIC I*, pp. 218-32; Ogle, *Return to Testing*, pp. 416-31.
90. Shelton, *Reflections of a Nuclear Weaponeer*, p. 11.63.
91. Hansen, *U.S. Nuclear Weapons*, pp. 88-89.
92. Shelton, *Reflections of a Nuclear Weaponeer*, pp. 11.60-11.63.
93. A useful evaluation of recent literature on the subject is Robert A. Divine, "The Cuban Missile Controversy," *Diplomatic History* 18 (Fall 1994): pp. 551-60.
94. Seaborg, *Kennedy, Khrushchev and the Test Ban*, pp. 263-82; Richard Reeves, *President Kennedy* (New York, 1993), pp. 545-51, 593-94; Arthur H. Dean, *Test Ban and Disarmament: The Path of Negotiation* (New York, 1966), pp. 86-92.

CHAPTER FIVE

A NEW PARADIGM, 1963 TO 1970

"*Yesterday, a shaft of light cut into the darkness. Negotiations were concluded in Moscow on a treaty to ban all nuclear tests in the atmosphere, in outer space, and underwater... to bring the forces of nuclear destruction under international control.*"

President John F. Kennedy,
Radio Address on Nuclear Test Plan Treaty,
July 26, 1963

NEW FRONTIER

It took several years for the full impact of Kennedy's *New Frontier* spirit to be felt within DASA. Through a series of steps in the 1960s, DASA was reshaped and reinvigorated by policies implemented by Secretary of Defense Robert S. McNamara. Based on the specifics of McNamara's nuclear policies, DASA's role in the American defense establishment moved to center stage. The "dreadful note of preparation" at the core of the Cold War rang loudly at DASA as the agency constantly tested the new nuclear weapon delivery systems that McNamara's policies demanded.

Kennedy's new generation of leaders faced the nuclear arms race with fresh approaches in strategy, in management, and in personnel. The President selected McNamara to head the DoD in 1961, bringing him to the cabinet only five weeks after he had accepted a position as Chief Executive Officer of Ford Motor Company. At the DoD, McNamara surrounded himself with a group of young advisors, disparagingly referred to by an older generation of military leaders as the "Whiz Kids." Fred Wikner, who served in DASA during the era, characterized the Whiz Kid leadership of McNamara as divided between budget specialists like Allen Enthoven and the "West Coast Nuclear Mafia" including Harold Brown, William McMillan, and the nuclear policy group at RAND Corporation. The Whiz Kids' philosophy affected strategic thinking about nuclear weapons development and testing policies, and even the internal structure of DASA itself.[1]

Like Kennedy, McNamara believed that an elite team of experts could invigorate organizations, including government. Throughout the business world in the 1950s, progressive companies had sought ways to tap into the technical intelligence of specialists through participatory management, matrix and project management, and other means that attracted what Charles McCormick called "the power of people." Such innovations bypassed older structures in which generalists at the top of the organization simply made decisions and issued orders.²

After the assassination of Kennedy in November 1963, President Lyndon B. Johnson kept McNamara as Secretary of Defense, and he was retained when Johnson was elected President in 1964.

The spirit of the *New Frontier* was embodied throughout the decade in federal and civilian service. At DASA, the *New Frontier* meant an influx of new talent and the promotion of staff with fresh ideas to positions of power and responsibility at the heart of the nuclear arms race. DASA, although a defense organization run by military officers and technical experts, had to adjust to this new style of management that gave a louder voice to brilliant, lower-ranking officers and scholarly civilians.

Lyndon B. Johnson, President, 1963 to 1969.

NEW GENERATION OF MISSILES

The first multiple-warhead weapon that the military developed was the submarine-launched Polaris A-3. This multiple reentry vehicle (MRV) weapon, deployed first in 1964, carried three warheads. All three reentry vehicles (RVs) went to the same target, enveloping the area with the combined nuclear effects of the three weapons.³ As McNamara endorsed the perfection of the concept, later models of both SLBMs and ground-launched ICBMs mounted "independently targetable" reentry vehicles that could attack separate targets. Minuteman III, the submarine-launched Poseidon C-3, Trident C-4, Trident D-5, and Peacekeeper were all sophisticated multiple independently targetable reentry vehicles (MIRVs).

The United States deployed its first Minuteman II missiles in 1965 and the first Minuteman IIIs in 1970. Minuteman III was the first U.S. missile equipped with MIRV capability, each with its own nuclear warhead. The missile deployed its RVs early in the trajectory and the nuclear-tipped RVs proceeded on their own course to different specific targets.⁴

Multiple warheads, although having a total yield considerably less than that of the single warhead they replaced, if optimally separated over a large target, would cause much greater damage than the single high-yield warhead. The ensuing requirements for new families of low-yield, light, and physically small warhead designs resulted in a considerable challenge for the design laboratories. The MIRV technology—allowing each RV to be sent to a totally separate target—provided a larger number of targets to be covered by a single missile launch. The separation of the RVs as they approach their targets dictates the hardness required to avoid fratricide (disablement of a *friendly* weapon system resulting from a nuclear environment generated by *friendly* weapons). It was also required that, in any defensive ABM environment, a single ABM burst not destroy more than one attacking RV. Designing such RVs and their carrier missiles to withstand the effects of defensive nuclear weapons became the central technology thrust of DASA for the following decade.

With steadily increasing Soviet deployment of nuclear warheads, and with the U.S. policy of rotating older missiles into retirement while moving to newer models, the total ICBM armaments of the two superpowers reached parity in 1969, with a growing Soviet lead in subsequent years (see Table 5-1). "Throw weight" issues escalated numbers of warheads in a single missile, which favored the USSR and exacerbated the disparity shown in this table.

As a requirement of the Single Integrated Operability Plan established by SAC in 1964, a sufficient number of American nuclear weapons had to survive a first strike to be capable of subsequently inflicting unacceptable damage on the Soviets, thus deterring the original attack. To achieve sufficiency, the U.S. nuclear arsenal had to increase vastly. The 1960s saw the greatest growth in number and variety of nuclear warheads and delivery systems of the whole Cold War period. The proliferation of new missiles and weapons created a crowded agenda for DASA, to include testing the survivability of those weapons under simulated nuclear battle conditions.[6]

Secretary McNamara detailed the logic of building such a vast arsenal when he appeared before the House Armed Services Committee in January 1964 to present his defense program and budget. He spelled out the extremes of policy positions, ranging from "overkill" to "full first strike" capability. The overkill advocates pushed for the capability to destroy Soviet cities in retaliation for a first strike by the Soviets. The "full first strike" advocates focused on the ability to attack Soviet arms capacity first. McNamara explained to Congress that a strategy allowing the United States to survive a first strike and to respond by destroying remaining or residual nuclear forces in the enemy arsenal required a vast number of weapons. The total needed was even more than necessary to destroy cities in the "overkill" strategy.[7]

Through all of his presentations before Congress, McNamara's concept of weapons as instruments of negotiation and communication continued to shape policy. McNamara's weapons policy, announced publicly through Congress, would serve to communicate to the Soviet Union a believable and credible willingness to retaliate against any use of nuclear weapons. McNamara took a di-

Table 5-1. Total U.S. and USSR ICBM Deployed from 1962 through 1970.[5]

Year	USA	USSR
1962	294	75
1964	834	200
1966	904	300
1968	1,054	800
1970	1,054	1,300

rect interest in the precise details of which delivery system was most effective, which weapons were to be included in the stockpile, and how well those weapons could be expected to perform against Soviet defenses. He demanded that the Office of the Secretary of Defense be more involved with the individuals who developed and tested the reliability of the weapons. Given the high level of concern about the reliability of nuclear weapons, DASA's testing work took on extreme importance through these years.

By 1965, McNamara's shift away from a manned-bomber delivery system to reliance on ground-launched and sea-launched missiles was well under way, much to the dismay of Air Force leaders like General Curtis LeMay. McNamara announced that the nation's strategic missile forces, which had almost tripled in fiscal year 1963-64 and had more than doubled again in fiscal year 1964-65, would continue to increase, but more slowly, over the next several years. McNamara had included in the 1964-1965 budget support for some 800 Minuteman I missiles, augmented by 150 Minuteman IIs. The Minuteman II missiles were expected to provide increased payload, longer range, a smaller circular error probable (CEP),* and greater flexibility in choice of pre-assigned targets. In addition, the Minuteman II missiles could be launched by commands from an airborne command post.[8]

Due to their high cost of operation and maintenance, McNamara phased out earlier generations of missiles, including the Atlas D and E models as well as the Titan I. The yearly cost of maintaining the new Minuteman missiles was about $100,000 per missile, he claimed, while the earlier missiles cost approximately 10 times as much.[9] For such practical budgetary reasons, the American arsenal of ICBMs leveled off in 1970, while the less cost-conscious Soviets added new missiles to their collection of aging older models. The perceived growing lead of the Soviet nuclear arsenal dismayed U.S. strategists who believed that sheer numbers of missiles, no matter how outmoded or costly to maintain, would be important during disarmament talks and in impressing other nations, even if their obsolete characteristics might prove unreliable in an actual war. Edward Luttwak, in particular, believed that McNamara's concern with budget matters blinded him to the diplomatic and political aspects of total missile numbers.[10]

The Air Force side of the debate over nuclear weapons surfaced early in 1965, when Senator Barry Goldwater expressed concern over the reliability of silo-based American missiles. Goldwater, a reserve Air Force general and a staunch defender of SAC's manned bomber approach to strategic defense, argued that McNamara had ignored the advice of generals and listened too intently to civilian planners. McNamara responded with a public and very detailed argument, emphasizing that Minuteman missiles were dispersed in sites "hardened" to protect them from nearby nuclear bursts, with one missile per silo. The Minuteman missiles, he noted, were much less vulnerable than manned bomber delivery systems since the detonation of a thermonuclear weapon over a SAC base would destroy all its bombers on the ground. Citing calculations of probable penetration of Soviet defenses, McNamara demonstrated that missiles had higher rates of dependability and reliability than did aircraft.[11] Through such calculations, McNamara

---

* Circular Error Probable: A measure of the delivery accuracy of a weapon system; specifically it is the radius of a circle around a target of such size that a weapon aimed at the center has a 50-percent probability of falling within the circle.

aimed at getting the highest destructive capability possible for each dollar expended. He viewed that capability as part of the effort to mount the most credible retaliatory force, to communicate "the dreadful note of preparation" as loudly and convincingly as possible.

In 1963, McNamara supported developing an American ABM, the Nike-X. He explained to Congress that this missile represented an improvement over the Nike-Zeus, which he had reduced to a study program that focused on reentry phenomena and defense techniques. The Nike-X system included the Sprint missile, which boasted high acceleration capability. This ABM was also able to discriminate between reentry objects, such as the missile booster, chaff, decoys, and the actual warhead. The Nike-X system included a Multi-Function Array Radar; its ability to track a large number of incoming items simultaneously would avoid the problem caused by decoys overloading the missile's radar system. The Nike-X system, with several sites around each city, could be hardened against attack, thus improving reliability of the total defensive system. A prototype of the radar system was planned for installation at White Sands, New Mexico, in the summer of 1964.[12]

Even though McNamara spoke highly of the promise of Nike-X in his 1963 presentation to Congress, over the next two years he became convinced that mounting an ABM system would further provoke the arms race. Based on this reasoning, he turned against the Nike-X system. He concluded that almost any defense would simply stimulate a responding offense and that once some form of credible capability to destroy the other side in a second strike existed, the arms race might be stabilized. However, both to American supporters of a defensive ABM system and to his Soviet opponents, the logic of defense rather than simple reliance on the fear of retaliation seemed more compelling than the concept of deployed offensive weapons as signals of intent. The disparity between McNamara's concept of weaponry and that of the Soviet leadership soon surfaced.

In June of 1967, Soviet Premier Alexis Kosygin visited the United Nations in New York City. After arguing over whether President Johnson would visit New York to meet Kosygin or whether Kosygin would go to Johnson in Washington, the two settled on a halfway point, Hollybush Hall at Glassboro State College in southern New Jersey. At their June 23 meeting, President Johnson tried to explain the U.S. opposition to fielding an ABM system. Johnson called on McNamara to relate the position of the Unit-

U.S. Army Nike-Hercules missile.

ed States to the Soviet representatives. McNamara stated that a proper U.S. response to a Soviet ABM force would be expansion of American offensive forces. "If we had the right number of offensive weapons to maintain a deterrent before you put your defenses in," said McNamara, "then to maintain the same degree of deterrence, in the face of your defense, we must strengthen our offense." Therefore, an ABM would accelerate the arms race, McNamara claimed. "That's not good for either one of us." It all seemed perfectly logical to McNamara, who expected Kosygin to immediately understand the concept. Kosygin, however, could not believe his ears. Rather, he saw weapons in much more traditional military terms. Kosygin's face flushed in anger. "Defense is moral," said Kosygin. "Offense is immoral."[13]

Following the meeting, McNamara returned to Washington, discussed policy with the Joint Chiefs, and decided to proceed with the MIRV program. The United States did not plan to deploy MIRVed weapons unless attempts to negotiate a treaty prohibiting deployment of defensive systems failed to outlaw ABMs.[14] As it turned out, ABMs were eventually limited, but only after both the United States and the Soviet Union had adopted MIRV technology.

McNamara said that the construction of MIRV systems was "an insurance program to counter what we feared would be a widespread deployment of the Soviet ABM system."[15] Later, McNamara regarded the decision to begin MIRV technology and initiate a new round in the arms race as a tragic move. He came to see that the MIRV systems themselves, rather than preventing weapons escalation, only took it to a higher and even more potentially destructive level.[16]

In 1966, members of Congress leaked reports that the Soviets were building an ABM system around Leningrad, the so-called Tallinn Line. Despite the opposition of McNamara and many advisors, the pressures increased on Johnson to build an ABM system in response to the Tallinn Line. The Army claimed that their planned Nike-X system would work well as a U.S. ABM system and that it could be deployed at a cost of $8.5 to $10 billion. This investment, the Army claimed, would protect 25 American cities.

American intelligence agencies debated whether the Tallinn Line was actually an anti-missile system. Analysts within the CIA believed the Soviets had built an anti-bomber defense system, while the Defense Intelligence Agency (DIA) reported that the Tallinn Line would strike at incoming missiles as an ABM system.[17] Both agencies correctly understood that the Galosh system deployed around Moscow consisted of a Nike-type anti-missile system, and if the DIA view of the Tallinn Line were correct, it would mean the Soviets already had two ABM systems (Galosh System and Tallinn Line System).[18]

In mid-1967, McNamara quietly shelved the Nike-X program. Instead of balancing the Soviet ABMs with U.S. ABMs, the United States would seek a credible ability to overwhelm ABM defenses with MIRVed weapons, just as he had warned at Glassboro. Once they had decided not to support the Nike-X ABM program, due to its limited defensive capacity, Johnson and McNamara successfully resisted the Army's pressure to restore it to the budget and the arsenal.

Transition to the "New" DASA

All these decisions taken by McNamara and Johnson with regard to weapons, both defensive and offensive, required that DASA shape the nuclear weapons effects testing and stockpile management program accordingly. Each high-level policy created specific new challenges and agenda issues for the agency. The decision to ensure an American second-strike capability, with deployment of Polaris SLBMs, required testing many new weapons systems. The Soviet deployment of their ABM system, despite McNamara's warning that it would accelerate the arms race, made ever more urgent the requirement that American weapon systems be protected against the effect of defensive, nuclear-weapon-tipped ABMs. DASA would need to be able to test the new U.S. systems to ensure their capability in a nuclear environment.

The signing of the LTBT early in 1963 and the resulting cessation of atmospheric tests required that DASA develop new methods to test the effects of nuclear weapons on military weapon systems. At the same time, it is essential to recognize that several other fundamental changes in the Cold War had further effects on DASA's mission, its agenda, and its internal structure. Those changes included managing the sheer size of the new stockpile that emerged as a consequence of the national policy of assured destruction. During the Johnson years, DASA's stockpile management responsibilities, both numerically and geographically, vastly increased. Changing military priorities caused the nuclear stockpile to escalate from approximately 12,000 weapons in 1959 to over 22,000 two years later. The significant increase of weapons in the system required more staff at the stockpile sites maintained by DASA. The Soviet Union also increased its stockpile, but at a more gradual rate. The total Soviet stockpile did not exceed 22,000 until 1988, when the Cold War was about to end and the Strategic Arms Reduction Talks (START) soon put both arsenals into decline.

The changing arms race, with its focus on missile delivery systems and new

Secretary of Defense Robert McNamara and Secretary of State Dean Rusk, 1964.

defensive systems, imposed other pressures on DASA. ICBMs and other missiles would travel at thousands of miles per hour, resulting in less than 30 minutes warning time from the moment the incoming weapons were detected until they detonated. To have a viable assured response in such a short time required a constant state of readiness to launch. If the United States had to be prepared to respond almost instantly to a surprise attack, its nuclear weapons had to be in the hands of the Services that would employ them. Thus, the older concept of stockpile management by DASA and AEC, with only "operational" weapons in the hands of the Services, no longer made sense.

Even the AEC believed that the custody issue was moot, a far cry from the heated days of civilian-military control arguments in the late 1940s. On July 11, 1966, Glenn T. Seaborg, AEC Chairman, formally recommended the transfer to military control, seeing "no practical purpose" in continued AEC control.[19]

Through 1966, DASA and the AEC worked out changes to the stockpile agreement giving more authority to DASA. In January of 1967, the draft of the new stockpile agreement was sent to the President. Johnson ordered the AEC to deliver all completed nuclear weapons to the DoD on February 10, 1967, bringing to an end the era of civilian custody of the nuclear arsenal. The AEC signed the new agreement on March 10, and the DoD signed it on March 20. Under the new agreement, the AEC continued to be responsible for safety, quality assurance, and retrofit programs, and would have access to weapons in the stockpile for these purposes. The Services and DASA exercised all other day-to-day responsibilities.[20]

Compared with the heated discussions in 1946 about custody, the quiet ending of the policy of civilian control reflected not a major debate but simply recognizing reality. With the deployment of ready-to-launch nuclear weapons in missile silos, aboard submarines, at SAC bases, and at NATO bases in Europe, physical custody and possession was already in military hands. Given the readiness posture, AEC control of the arsenal was maintained through the President's role as Commander-in-Chief.[21]

Part of the policy of readiness required keeping some weapons airborne *at all times*. Such readiness required safety measures to prevent accidental detonation as well as to prevent lower-ranking officers from making unauthorized decisions to launch or drop. The SAC policy of flying in proximity to the Soviet borders with operational hydrogen bombs aboard meant that the chances of an accident or incident in which nuclear weapons fell to the ground and broke or their non-nuclear high explosive components detonated on foreign territory greatly increased. While such Broken Arrow[*] incidents had occurred before over the United States and over international waters, taking airborne weapons close to the Soviet borders increased the chances of such an incident over the territory of a friendly country. Thus, on the one hand, instant readiness meant that the responsibility for the stockpile shifted away from DASA to the respective Services. On the other hand, readiness only increased the likelihood of accidents involving weapons in aircraft, aboard ships, and in transit that might require DASA's expertise in handling nuclear weapons.

McNamara's endorsement of multiple warheads also affected DASA's responsibilities and requirements. Both the MRV and MIRV, like the ABM, raised specific new technological considerations that DASA had to investigate. MRV or MIRV weapons, if employed, would descend on targets, exploding within a few minutes or possibly within a few seconds of each other over targets, some only hundreds of yards apart. ABM systems, when armed with nuclear devices, would intercept incoming missiles outside the earth's atmosphere. Each of these considerations required that DASA explore new mechanisms to cause damage and invent new means of testing to determine the effects of nuclear weapons detonated in outer space upon delivery systems and the incoming RVs.

In July 1969, Melvin Laird, Richard Nixon's Secretary of Defense, made the final decision to introduce true MIRVs into the force, with the first such deployment of Minuteman III under way in 1970. For DASA, the introduction of MIRV planning and then deployment through the late 1960s and early 1970s meant a burgeoning of new agenda items in these years.[22]

---

[*] *Broken Arrow:* a DoD term to identify and report on an accident involving a nuclear weapon/warhead or nuclear component.

During a full-scale war, both Soviet ABMs and U.S. MIRVs would create a "nuclear environment" in which U.S. missiles would be exposed to radiation from other explosions when in space, or to radiation, heat, and blast when in the atmosphere. In the 1940s and 1950s, when planners had expected all or most nuclear weapons to be delivered by aircraft over targets, none of these factors had been envisioned. A single weapon might present a threat to the delivering aircraft as it hastened from the area, but no one had considered what the effect of a nuclear weapon would be upon a second nuclear weapon. ABMs and MIRVs changed all that.

In order for a missile to survive to deliver its warhead in a MRV, MIRV, or ABM environment, the delivery system and warhead components required thorough testing, to assure their hardness to these environments. Designers had to undertake a host of improvements to harden nuclear weapons and their delivery and launching systems against the effects of other nuclear weapons. The nature of those effects at the high altitudes of incoming missiles had to be determined, and new specifications had to be developed to guard weapon systems against those effects.

The quickly escalating arms race of the years following 1963 involved delivery systems and defensive systems that catapulted DASA into a central role. The agency rather quickly found a new agenda of crucial interest to the Secretary of Defense and to nuclear planners. A larger stockpile, a higher risk of accidents, many new weapons and weapon systems that had to be tested against nuclear weapon damage under ABM and MIRV environments, and difficult new limitations imposed by the LTBT required a very high order of scientific and administrative capability by DASA. The Director, Defense Research and Engineering (DDR&E) Harold Brown, took the lead in ensuring that the organization was restructured to handle the rising tide of issues.

POLICY CONSEQUENCES FOR DASA MANAGEMENT

The various developments in international weapons policy and Defense Department management principles during the 1960s created pressures to change the way DASA did its work. Internal management was affected and changed with the recognition, by McNamara and throughout the DoD, that high-level policy had to be shaped by current advice from scientists and engineers, not just politicians and policy specialists. The "Whiz kid" philosophy meant that the status, recognition, and reporting channels for the scientists and engineers at DASA had to be modernized and modified. The variety of management reforms and administrative changes that took place inside the agency did not come in isolation, but were internal consequences of powerful external factors. The reforms DASA would undertake during the mid-1960s came because the agency's mission, as redefined under McNamara, required a much greater level of scientific and technical expertise than had been envisioned in its original 1959 charter. The general concept of upgrading the status and improving the voice of scientific and technical staff made its way from Kennedy and McNamara into DASA through a series of specific directives, reports, committee studies, and finally, through a set of revisions to the DASA charter.

Shortly after taking office, McNamara and his staff developed 120 broad questions, many of which led to book-length reports. For DASA, question number 97 was crucial: "What must be done in order to enhance the capability of our in-house research and development laboratories?"

McNamara assembled Task Group 97 to develop an answer. Eugene Fubini, a deputy to Brown, served as Task Force Chairman. Fubini also served on a number of science advisory boards through the decade before retiring from government, later becoming a director of Texas Instruments Company and long-term member of the Defense Science Board.

Fubini's Task Group 97 conducted field visits and interviews with laboratory personnel and reported in 1961 with five basic recommendations for the Services. Fubini urged that each laboratory have a well-defined mission, adequate supplies of competent manpower, improved personnel policies to raise morale, simpler procedures for programming and budgeting, and better facilities. Partly in response to the Fubini report, McNamara asked the Services to provide extended tours of duty to military officers assigned to laboratories and to raise salaries for technical personnel. DASA, like the Service laboratories, began to benefit from the respect for scientific training that permeated DoD under McNamara and Brown.[23]

A separate study, headed by David Bell, director of the Bureau of the Budget, also focused on research and development. The Bell report, similar to Fubini's Task Group 97 report, urged strengthening of all government in-house research capacities and particularly stressed the lack of clarity in the relationship between military officers and civilian technical staff in the military Service labs. Both the Fubini and Bell reports served as part of the justification used by Brown in reorganizing all DoD scientific enterprises, and DASA in particular, during the mid-1960s.[24]

In June of 1961, Brown established the Ad Hoc Committee on Nuclear Weapons Effects and appointed RAND physicist William McMillan as chairman. The so-called McMillan Committee played an influential role in establishing priorities for DASA's nuclear test program in the early 1960s. Like the Fubini and Bell reports on a broader scale, the McMillan Committee urged greater participation by scientists in decision making at DASA. From the perspective of those working within DASA, the McMillan Committee reports, not the broader Bell and Fubini studies, were the more immediate documents stimulating reform.[25]

A step in the direction of clarifying the role of DASA was a clearer delineation of the separate duties of AEC and DASA, made by agreement between the two agencies in mid-November of 1962. AEC Chairman Glenn Seaborg and Deputy Secretary of Defense Roswell Gilpatric set out the specific division of labor between the AEC and DASA on November 14, 1962. They agreed that the AEC would be responsible for weapons development, testing, stockpile confidence testing, effects tests on warhead components, and management of NTS. DASA, in turn, would be responsible for providing test facilities and some of the associated hardware necessary for environmental diagnostics and data recording, field support, and test-related funding. DASA was to integrate test results into useful documentation, disseminate evaluations, and perform survivability and operability testing for DoD weapon systems. Yet this clarification did not address the more profound issue of ensuring a good flow of technical information from the agency to the policy makers.[26]

In order to develop specific organizational reforms to restructure DASA, the Deputy Secretary of Defense directed, on November 30, 1962, that the DoD's Director of Organizational and Management Planning, Solis Horwitz, conduct an analysis of the functions, responsibilities, and charter of DASA. Horwitz served as chairman of a study group with representatives from the military Services, from the JCS, from DDR&E, and from DASA itself. The Horwitz report noted that Brown, as DDR&E, believed the technical continuity in DASA required strengthening, especially in regard to weapon effects testing. The study reviewed the origins of DASA, showing that AFSWP actually preceded the formation of the Department of Defense, and that DASA's charter did not reflect the new organization of DoD or the role of the Secretary of Defense.

In short, the Horwitz group recognized what Brown and the McMillan group had come to realize: that DASA, as the agency dealing with nuclear weapons within the DoD, should be able to affect DoD policy in these areas at the highest level. The Horwitz group made 12 recommendations, including the elevation of the rank of the chief of DASA to a three-star officer and creating explicit channels of communication between DASA and the Office of the Secretary of Defense.[27]

The DASA charter originally drafted by Donald Quarles in 1959 had given the agency the responsibility to supervise the conduct of full-scale DoD weapons effects tests. But supervising and conducting tests did not necessarily suggest that the specialists of the agency could affect policy at a higher level, nor did it assure even within the agency that the views of scientific personnel would carry weight against those of Service personnel.[28] Another aspect of the 1959 mission was a limited role of assisting the JCS in providing advice to the Secretary of Defense. Technical assistance envisaged in the 1959 charter was subordinate to policy making. DASA advice would have to filter through the JCS before getting to the Secretary of Defense in Quarles' original scheme.[29]

Following the McMillan Committee recommendations, McNamara considerably modified the 1959 charter by issuing DoD Directive 5105.31 on July 22, 1964, signed by Deputy Secretary of Defense Cyrus Vance. The changes outlined in this 1964 Directive converted the organization from one headed by a "chief" supported by two deputies as well as a chief scientist, a chief of staff, and three deputy chiefs of staff to a much simpler one headed by a "director."[30] In the new organization, the director would be supported by two major deputy directors: one for Science and one for Operations and Administration. This change was central to the concerns of McMillan.

The 1964 directive also indicated that when the deputy directors of DASA were military officers, they would normally be from Services different from the director. In practice, the director would be a three-star officer, while the Deputy Director for Operations and Administration was usually a two-star officer, as was the Commander of the Field Command, while the Deputy Director for Science (later Science and Technology) was a civilian scientist.[31] In terms of budgetary responsibility, the Research, Development Test & Evaluation (RDT&E) budget and some of the Operation & Maintenance were under the complete control of the Deputy Director, Science and Technology (DDST). This post of DDST would be crucial. By the simple stroke of creating two deputy directors, the role of scientific personnel within the organization was suddenly made parallel and equal in importance to operations and administration. This organizational change was intended to allow feedback and advice from the technical side, as well as from the administrative side, directly to the agency's head.[32]

As part of the elevation of the role of scientists, Brown ordered the McMillan Committee to report directly to the direc-

Early gathering of the Scientific Advisory Group on Effects (SAGE).

tor of DASA as a Scientific Advisory Group on Effects (SAGE).[33] By this measure, the outside consulting group became incorporated as a highly-respected and high-powered brain trust, well populated in its early days by experienced nuclear specialists from Lawrence Livermore, RAND, Sandia, and west coast private sector firms in the nuclear and defense businesses.[34] Through SAGE and direct communication between the Assistant to the Secretary of Defense (Atomic Energy), ATSD(AE), and sometimes through informal networking channels, control of DASA shifted dramatically in 1964 from the military Joint Chiefs to the civilian Secretary of Defense.

Table 5-2 presents an overview of DASA manpower authorizations for the period ending June 30, 1965. It includes DASA Headquarters, Field Command, Joint Task Force-8, and other support divisions within the agency. An agency organizational chart detailing the agency structure as of April of 1966 follows this table.

The transformation went beyond simply raising the visibility or the reporting level for technical advice. DASA transitioned from being a support agency to taking the lead within DoD in identifying, structuring, funding, implementing and overseeing the application of critical new programs. Specifically, the hardness and survivability programs of the nation's strategic systems, which the Services were most reluctant to address, became the primary focus of DASA's RDT&E program.

The changes in internal organization continued through the late 1960s. In 1965, the Weapons Test Division became the Test Command (at Field Command in Albuquerque, NM), which reported directly to headquarters DASA (now located in Alexandria, VA).[35] This change was an indication that the Office of the Secretary of Defense wanted more direct control over the research side of nuclear weaponry. Additionally, stockpile accountability, and all its related responsibilities, was turned over completely to

Table 5-2. DASA Manpower Authorizations, June 30, 1965.

	Off/WO	ENL	CIV	Total
Headquarters, DASA	(207)	(219)	(157)	(583)
Director	3		2	5
PIO	2	2	1	5
Comptroller	4	3	10	17
Subtotal	*(9)*	*(5)*	*(13)*	*(27)*
Deputy Director Operations & Administration	2		1	3
JAIEG	7		27	34
Operations Division	36	37	3	76
Plans Division	11	2	3	16
Requirements Division	12	1	4	17
Personnel & Administrative Division	8	34	32	74
Security Division	5	3	14	22
Logistics Division	2	3	19	24
Subtotal	*(83)*	*(80)*	*(103)*	*(266)*
Deputy Director Science & Technology	2	2	4	8
Radiation Division	18	7	10	35
Analysis & Programs Division	20	4	4	28
Blast & Shock Division	11	2	9	22
Bio-Medical Division	8	1	2	11
Weapons Tests Division (Sandia)	56	118	12	186
Subtotal	*(115)*	*(134)*	*(41)*	*(290)*
Field Command, DASA	(725)	(3154)	(1802)	(5681)
HQ Field Command, DASA	476	1232	1307	3015
Killeen Base	52	368	113	533
Bossier Base	39	321	88	448
Manzano Base	48	403	84	535
Clarksville Base	53	404	111	568
Lake Mead Base	57	424	99	580
JTF-8	57	102		159
Bio-Medical Division	36	21	169	226
TOE (901st ICD & 46th MP)	24	41		65
Grand Total	*1139*	*3592*	*2116*	*6847*

DASA Field Command. These reorganization efforts raised the administrative and leadership position of those engaged in scientific research, while turning over the more procedural and policing authority of stockpile management to the more strictly military and operational, administrative side of the organization. By transferring to Field Command the "caretaking" or "warehousing" side of the agency, Headquarters staff could concentrate on the more intellectually challenging technical work involving new weapon effects testing.

The 1964 Directive issued by Deputy Secretary Vance clarified the reporting channels to the Secretary of Defense, giving the Director, DDR&E, responsibility for approving or modifying the DASA research programs and giving the ATSD(AE) responsibility for exercising staff supervision over stockpile management. The underlying McNamara-Brown philosophy of tapping into technical talent through the chain of command received very practical and specific implementation in these reforms. In addition to the testing program and the question of stockpile management, the 1964 Directive clearly spelled out DASA's responsibilities in conducting courses for the military departments to train technically qualified personnel.

Under the reorganization of DASA in Directive 5105.31, issued July 22, 1964, the agency gained control over and operated the Joint Nuclear Accident Coordinating Center (JNACC). On July 28, 1964, as per DoD Instruction 5100.45, DDR&E Harold Brown assigned the DoD Data Center, then located in Santa Barbara, California, to DASA as the agency's primary information analysis center (IAC). Renamed as the DASA Data Center, and later the DoD Atomic Support IAC, this agency technical resource formed the impetus behind the current Information Analysis Center (DASIAC), which continues to serve the agency with analysis of scientific and technical data. Once DASA had become established as the premier DoD nuclear agency, these collateral activities logically came under the organization's aegis.[36]

Unlike the early days of the Manhattan Project, during which scientists were often drawn from academia, a new generation of civilian and military scientists emerged. Colonels and civilians with graduate degrees filled DASA's scientific and administrative positions alike. General Groves' early efforts to recruit the most talented officers continued to be part of the organizational culture. Therefore, rather than reflecting an internal division between civilian and military staff, the emerging cultural division within DASA tended to cut along other lines. On the one side was a group of scientists and engineers, both civilian and military, under the DDST, who were deeply involved in the technical questions of exactly how to most effectively and safely conduct weapon tests. On the other side was a group of administrators and managers who served under the Deputy Director for Operations, which also contained both civilian civil servants and career military officers. One observer of the cultural divide commented that it struck him as similar to the divisions within academia between faculty on the one hand and staff on the other.[37]

The first civilian DDST under the new system, Theodore Taylor, served from October 13, 1964, to August 31, 1966. The appointment of Taylor, who was never known as a steady administrator, reflected the effort to bring a representative of the new generation of brilliant young nuclear physicists into the agency.[38] Taylor's successor, Fred Wikner, served from September 1, 1966, through December 27, 1968. Wikner had worked for several West Coast nuclear firms, including Aerojet General Nuclear, qualifying him as a member of the "West Coast Nuclear Mafia." Like the appointment of Taylor, Wikner's appointment infused the agency with talent drawn from the country's growing nuclear physics community. Wikner initially joined DASA as Scientific Assistant to the Director, serving in that post for a year under Taylor, before becoming Deputy Director.[39]

A NEW DIRECTOR

Lieutenant General Harold C. Donnelly assumed the helm of DASA in 1964, having served as Acting Director from 1960 through 1961. General Donnelly, who had served as Commander of Field Command, was well connected within the Services and well positioned to be an advocate for testing new weapon systems nuclear survivability. A West Point graduate, Donnelly had served in World War II as Deputy and then Chief of Staff of the China-India-Burma Theater. He transferred to the Air Force in September 1947 when it was created and served at Air Force Headquarters until 1948.[40]

Lieutenant General Harold G. Donnelly, DASA Director 1964 to 1968.

DASA INNOVATIONS: UNDERGROUND TESTING

In the fall of 1966, the staff of the Deputy Director (Science & Technology) began developing programs responsive to problems of national significance, bringing more scientific rigor to nuclear weapon effects tests on equipment and on weapon systems. The DDST program meshed a thorough understanding of physical phenomena with larger policy issues, ensuring focus on the minute details of testing and experimentation.[41] These issues were addressed as the agency confronted a series of specific policy and practical problems that grew out of the new conditions of the 1960s arms race.[42]

Above all, the new national policy prohibiting atmospheric testing demanded innovative testing methods. After the LTBT went into effect in 1963, the nuclear weapons testing program faced fundamental difficulties. First of all, the last tests in the DOMINIC series of atmospheric tests in 1962 had demonstrated that when nuclear weapons detonated at extremely high altitudes, the released energy took the form of an intense radiation burst. In addition to the burst of x rays, gamma rays, and neutrons, which at these altitudes traveled over very great distances, high-altitude detonations produced an electromagnetic pulse (EMP), containing a flood of energy ranging across the spectrum. EMP was capable of damaging electronic devices over thousands of square miles. The STARFISH PRIME detonation in the DOMINIC series, exploded more than 800 miles from Hawaii, affected the streetlight system in Honolulu. Without the opportunity to conduct further high-altitude tests because of the test ban, the nuclear weapon testing program was faced with the challenge of how to measure the full dimensions of EMP effects and other radiation effects.

Another issue was the limited experi-

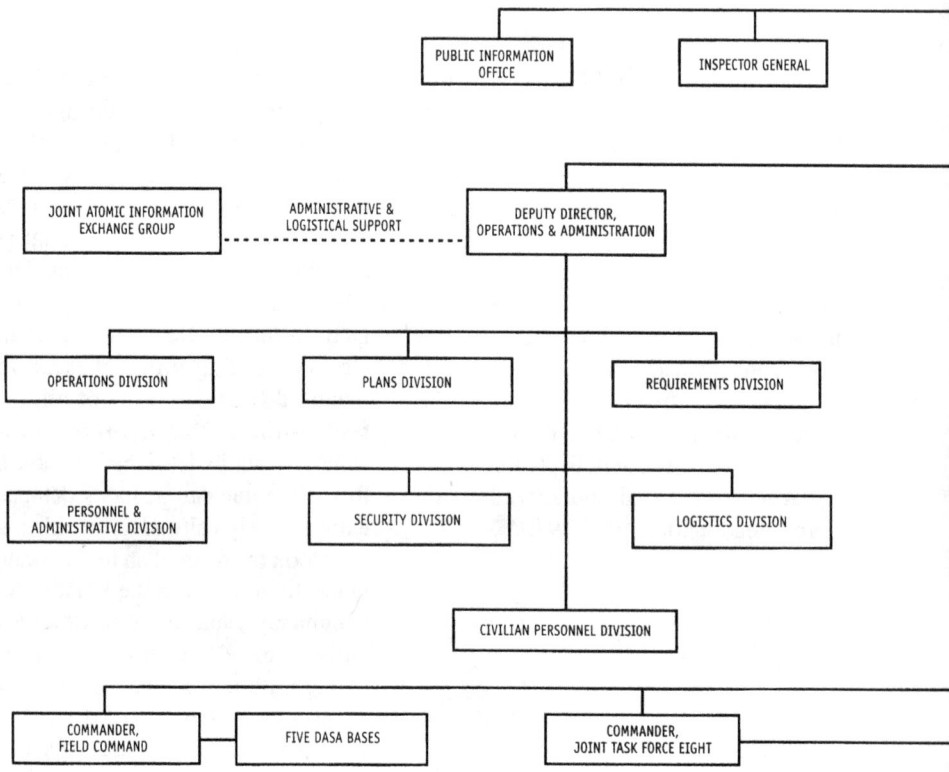

Headquarters Defense Atomic Support Agency Organizational Chart, 1966.

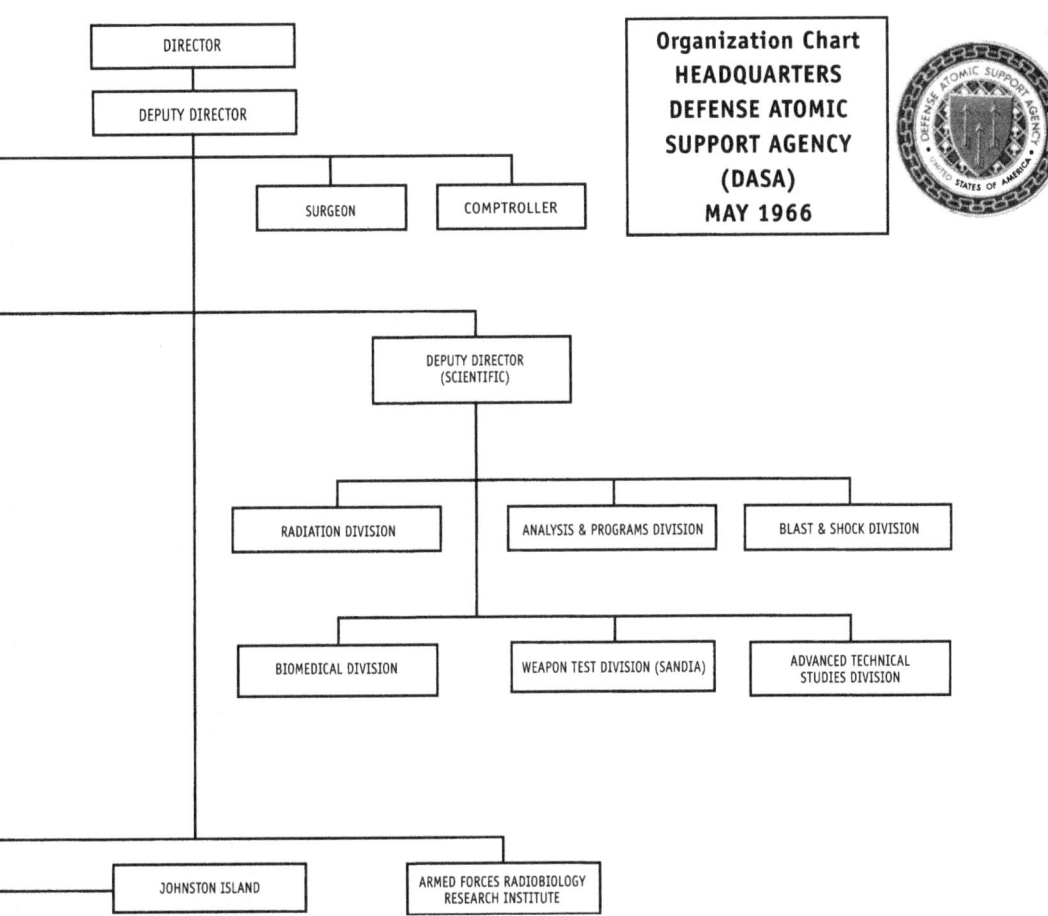

ence DASA and the AEC had with underground tests; in fact, the first test DASA managed underground was shot HARD HAT on February 15, 1962. In 1964 and 1965, the nuclear testing program concerned itself with developing procedures, technologies, and support groups that would acquire the technical knowledge to properly manage the tests and develop means of testing nuclear weapon effects without actual nuclear detonations. Although the division of labor between AEC and DASA was relatively clear, especially after the November 14, 1962, agreement, some areas of concern remained. The AEC operated the NTS, and AEC laboratories that provided the devices to be detonated in DASA effects tests. A set of "safeguards" under the treaty legislation provided guidance to both agencies, but the responsibilities of the two agencies intersected under those safeguards. First of all, both AEC and DASA would conduct tests; second, the AEC would continue to maintain nuclear laboratories; third, under the so-called "Safeguard C," DASA would maintain the ability to restart atmospheric testing in the National Nuclear Test Readiness program; and fourth, both AEC and DASA supported research to detect both atmospheric and underground tests by other nations.[43]

Both AEC and DASA conducted tests over the next decade to improve methods used to detect underground testing around the world, both to monitor Soviet progress in underground testing and to determine if other nations had joined the nuclear club. Tests that aided in this effort were designated "VELA UNIFORM" tests, the initial letters of which stood for "Verification-Underground." "VELA-HOTEL" tests would improve methods of verifying high-altitude testing.

One important test, conducted underground by the AEC in Mississippi in 1964, attempted to verify the theory that the magnitude of a device yield could be concealed from distant seismic sensors by "decoupling" the device from the surrounding geologic strata through detonation in a large space in a cavern. It showed that it was extremely difficult to conceal the magnitude of a nuclear yield in this fashion, contradicting results from an earlier test, RAINIER. Although conducted by the AEC, this test was a crucial event in the VELA UNIFORM program, and many later studies by personnel in DASA focused on its data. MUDPACK, a DASA test conducted in December 1964, tested shock propagation through two different ground strata. DASA scientists reviewed the data from this event over the next several years, concluding that seismic detection of large bursts would allow monitoring of the Soviet testing program.

A leading agenda item of the underground testing program conducted by DASA through these years remained concern with the effect of nuclear weapons on various weapon storage sites, such as structures, silos, "igloos," and hangars. DoD planners assumed that primary targets, during a potential nuclear strike by the Soviets, would be the stockpile of nuclear weapons held by the United States, together with the underground missile silos in which ICBMs were housed.[44]

In the fall of 1965, the DDST concluded that the DASA testing program had been driven by scientific and technical interests rather than by a sense of national weapons priorities. It was evident that the tests had been designed to investigate important technical issues, but lacked clear linkage between the knowledge gained by the scientists and the design of new weapon systems. DASA's testing philosophy was about to transition from the pursuit of studies based on scientific curiosity to a prioritization derived from two considerations laid out in McNamara's nuclear strategy.

The research agenda would, henceforth, be directed by the needs of the end-users, not by the interests of the researchers. Nuclear forces had to be able to survive a nuclear attack, and they had to be capable of retaliation in a second strike. DASA should, therefore, test *every weapon delivery system under development* to be sure it would survive a nuclear environment.[45] Within the DoD, opinions were divided over whether every weapon development program should incorporate such testing. DASA supported the concept, as did Harold Brown. Yet others, more concerned with budgetary issues, felt such testing was unnecessary.[46]

For support, General Donnelly, DASA Director, turned to his classmate and personal friend, General Earl Wheeler, Chairman of the JCS. Soon Wheeler arranged for the Joint Chiefs to prepare and issue a directive establishing the policy that all weapons under development should be tested for survivability in a nuclear environment. Getting the JCS directive drafted and issued, however, was no easy matter. DASA maintained that all strategic missile systems and certain other classes of system development programs had to pass through agency testing as a major milestone. Henceforth, DASA's scientific and technical role was no mere adjunct to DoD policy; it became the core of weapon system acquisition.

With the JCS Directive, the experts at DASA moved to the very center of the nuclear arms race. No new weapon system, including every non-nuclear system, developed by the Army, the Navy, or the Air Force, could be deployed without first *passing technical muster* with DASA. With this change, the administrative as well as the advisory role of DASA had been enhanced, reflecting the concerns of Brown and the McMillan Committee.

The issue of nuclear weapon effects on existing and new weapon systems became an increasingly important concern, driven by the knowledge that EMP and other radiation effects could damage or destroy the electronics in a missile in flight if it was exposed to a nuclear burst. Such scenarios now seemed a heightened danger. Soviet ABM systems, armed with nuclear devices, would intercept incoming missiles while still in space or at very high altitude. As a result, U.S. equipment had to be hardened against x-rays transmitted in a near vacuum.

The concern with EMP dominated DASA's technical programs and test results as early as 1963-64. Although the tests in FISHBOWL and DOMINIC had revealed the significance of EMP effects on communications, radar, and electronic equipment, the ending of atmospheric testing hampered further study. DASA representatives discussed this matter with the Office of Science and Technology on July 30-31, 1963, reviewing concerns regarding EMP effects on hardened military sites. At Oak Ridge, an AEC group that had gathered information on shielding of nuclear reactors was instructed to expand its purview to include information on nuclear weapons and space radiation. The center at Oak Ridge produced the first cumulative bibliography on shielding information in April of 1963.[47]

In order to find out more about high-altitude radiation effects, DASA experimenters faced a major technical challenge: how to structure an underground test to simulate high-altitude conditions. Test personnel developed methods that involved the attachment of a long, sealed pipe to the explosive device. They evacuated the air from the pipe and exposed samples to be tested at the other end of this either vertical or horizontal line-of-sight (VLOS or HLOS) pipe in early tests in 1964. Later, DASA weapon effects testers would develop many improvements to this method of simulating high-altitude conditions.

Through 1964 and 1965, testing continued to focus on high-explosive shock and blast effects on ships, with a new emphasis on high-altitude radiation effects on materials and electric parts. WISHBONE, detonated on February 18, 1965, was the first such test. DILUTED WATERS, conducted on June 16, 1965, tested radiation effects on materials and electrical parts using a VLOS system.

The LTBT did not prevent testing the effects of large explosions of conventional high explosives in the atmosphere. Such tests could prove extremely useful in evaluating methods of detecting underground tests and in further establishing high-explosive blast equivalents. In July of 1964, the DASA test program included SNOWBALL, a joint United States-Canadian test in Alberta, Canada. SNOWBALL participants conducted basic blast, ground shock, and other measurements using high explosives. NASA researchers developed a device installed on an airplane which would determine particle size distribution in a cloud of debris; in Operation SNOWBALL, pilots flew the device through the resulting cloud to validate its technology.[48]

Several other DASA tests during this period, including detonations in the range of 500 tons (0.5 KT) of high-explosive TNT helped address the problem of determining nuclear blast effects. Since a high-explosive detonation releases its energy somewhat more slowly than a nuclear explosion, it was determined that a 0.5 KT high-explosive burst would generally represent a 1 KT nuclear yield in blast effect. Such tests included the 1965 SAILOR HAT test. Blast effects on ships, aircraft, buildings, and underground structures could all be examined through the use of high explosives, once reliable scaling principles had been discovered, thoroughly developed, and validated.[49] In 1966, the Naval Ordinance Laboratory tested the concept of exploding stacked ammonium nitrate and fuel oil (ANFO), instead of TNT, to simulate nuclear weapon blast effects. Later, the Navy, and in turn DASA, utilized the same procedure for high-explosive testing since it was less expensive and more readily available than TNT, and that ANFO was much safer to handle and stack.

DASA adjusted to the conditions imposed by the LTBT by developing several above-ground research facilities that could simulate radiation effects of weapons without requiring a nuclear detonation. Neutron emission and x-ray testing stations, although operating on a small scale, could help establish measurement tools and anticipate some effect issues which could then be further tested underground, with the exception of EMP. Because no weapon had to be detonated, such tests could also prove more economical and much easier to repeat frequently. In 1965, DASA reported several accomplishments in the field of transient radiation effects on electronics (TREE) using one such piece of nuclear simulation equipment. The agency tested and proved feasible the accelerator pulsed fast assembly (APFA), a bare, unshielded nuclear reactor. It produced neutrons in very short pulses, a few microseconds in length. Although pulsed neutron sources had been developed earlier, none had been capable of producing such short-duration bursts necessary for nuclear simulation. In order to study such effects as short-lifetime annealing of materials that might occur in a nuclear explosion environment, experimenters had to direct very short bursts at targets.[50] In all such areas, DASA work flowed steadily to the weapons designers, leading to improvements and modifications of the new systems.[51]

During the mid and late 1960s, as the agency made its first adaptations to the new world of the Limited Test Ban Treaty, the specialists at DASA worked out three basic new approaches to the testing of nuclear weapon effects on the weapons, structures, and communications equipment of the military Services. These three methods would continue to be used over the next decades, making progress in defending weapons systems against nuclear weapons without once setting off a nuclear device in the atmosphere.

The first method involved improvements in underground testing techniques, particularly in highly evacuated line-of-sight (LOS) pipes to simulate high-altitude conditions, improvement of data gathering methods and safety features. The second method involved the use of high explosives. Setting off very large above-ground detonations allowed exploration of effects such as airblast, shock waves in ground or water, and the resultant impact of such effects on weapon systems. By working out the scaling relationships between high-explosive detonations and nuclear detonations, it was possible to develop methods to protect weapon systems and equipment against nuclear weapon effects without actually setting off a nuclear weapon in the air, at the surface, or under water. The third method used simulators to achieve particular radiation effects, with some of the first efforts involving the use of unshielded reactors to expose target materials to bursts of neutrons.

More sophisticated underground testing, high-explosive tests above ground or under water, and the development and use of effects simulation facilities became the hallmarks of DASA testing. Improvements and modifications in testing, and addressing some of the technical problems encountered in the underground testing work, became a major push for DASA during the 1960s.

1965 SAILOR HAT high-explosive test stack prior to detonation.

TEST MANAGEMENT

Once the underground testing of nuclear weapons was running on a full schedule in the mid-1960s, the test series designation names simply referred to all the tests, whether AEC or DoD, planned for a fiscal year, as shown in Table 5-3. From 1964 through 1968, the AEC conducted the vast majority of the 40 to 50 underground nuclear tests per year in these series, while DASA scheduled a maximum of five such tests each year. While the AEC usually designed its tests to evaluate a single weapon design, DASA tests often evaluated 20 to more than 70 experiments simultaneously, incorporating a wide variety of equipment from different weapons, weapons systems, and structures. There were two major problems; initially, the percentage of tunnel tests that leaked radioactivity was unacceptably high to the AEC, which ran the test site. Of the five FLINTLOCK effects tests, three were in tunnels and all three leaked radioactivity. Second, the equipment that required testing was becoming physically larger, and at the same time had to be exposed to ever-increasing intensities of radiation, both of which pushed tunnel designs in a direction that made radioactive containment more difficult. These factors demanded a reduction of testing while major efforts were made to understand more thoroughly and improve on containment design. As the tests became larger and more complex their costs rapidly increased, causing budgetary consideration and some later limitations on test scope.

In the late 1960s, methods were perfected for getting ever more systems tested during the same shot. PILE DRIVER, in June 1966, included ground motion phenomena in granite with a total of 73 test chambers constructed in tunnel segments to check effects on structures and other experiments. With such "piggy-backed" and multiple test projects, both technical demands and budgetary pressures were stressed.[52]

DASA staff worked hard to ensure that the testing of weapons systems under development fit into the development schedule of the Services' program offices. Test directors designated one Service as lead for a particular test, devoting the main priority on a particular event to evaluating one particular weapon system. The other Services would then be allowed to "piggy-back" their experiments with those of the lead Service.[53]

Weapon effects tests provided opportunities to examine the radiation response of the Nike-Zeus, the Minuteman III, and other weapons systems. A 1965 underground test, TAPESTRY, established the threshold for permanent damage to electronic parts due to the thermal shock produced by the absorption of x rays. The underground tests allowed for the correlation of data from such detonations with data from flash x-ray machines, encouraging experimenters to consider additional experiments to test x-ray effects on a wide variety of electronic parts, and to determine remedial action to be taken to raise the threshold for damage.[54]

In 1965 DASA updated the TREE handbook, first issued in 1964, and planned a completely new edition that would incorporate the results of the extensive testing program conducted both in the above-ground facilities and the underground tests. This handbook, a pioneering effort, assisted the Services to develop hardened systems more quickly and effectively. DASA held a TREE symposium at Albuquerque in December of 1965, attracting more than 200 specialists who exchanged information concerning the concept, execution, and results of their TREE-related research.[55]

Still another means DASA used to gather information after the test ban was to collect data from tests conducted by the French or other nations that had not joined the test ban treaty. Such work had to be

Table 5-3. DASA Test Series, 1964-1969.

Series	Period	Total Tests	Total Effects Tests
WHETSTONE	1964-65	51	5
FLINTLOCK	1965-66	50	5
LATCHKEY	1966-67	38	4
CROSSTIE	1967-68	56	4
BOWLINE	1968-69	58	5

done without the cooperation of the testing nation by stationing staff and detection equipment at some distance to gather data. As early as 1965, the agency developed tentative plans to conduct such observations in 1967 and 1968.

Increasingly through the 1960s, DASA's tests shifted from using shafts drilled vertically from the surface to emplacing devices in tunnels mined horizontally into the base of a mountain to a point where the amount of rock and soil directly above the test chamber, the overburden, exceeded 1,000 feet, adequate to preclude venting. DASA shifted from shafts to tunnels for several reasons. Shafts created problems of closure and emission, as PIN STRIPE demonstrated with the leakage of a radioactive cloud in April of 1966. When using shafts, experimenters had to mount test materials on towers at the surface over the shaft, moving samples or the tower itself before the subsidence crater collapsed (sometimes within less than a minute). This awkward procedure for the shaft shots made tunnel methods far more preferable for effects tests. Tunnels would allow for big rooms to be mined out, where test arrays could hold collections of target samples for the many experiments simultaneously mounted by the different Services.

One of the major difficulties that developed was that experimenters needed to find ways to expose the test samples to the radiation burst of a nuclear device but prevent damage to the samples from debris coming through the evacuated LOS pipe. DASA addressed the problem by installing a system of fast-closing gates that closed off the pipe immediately after the radiation passed, blocking debris from

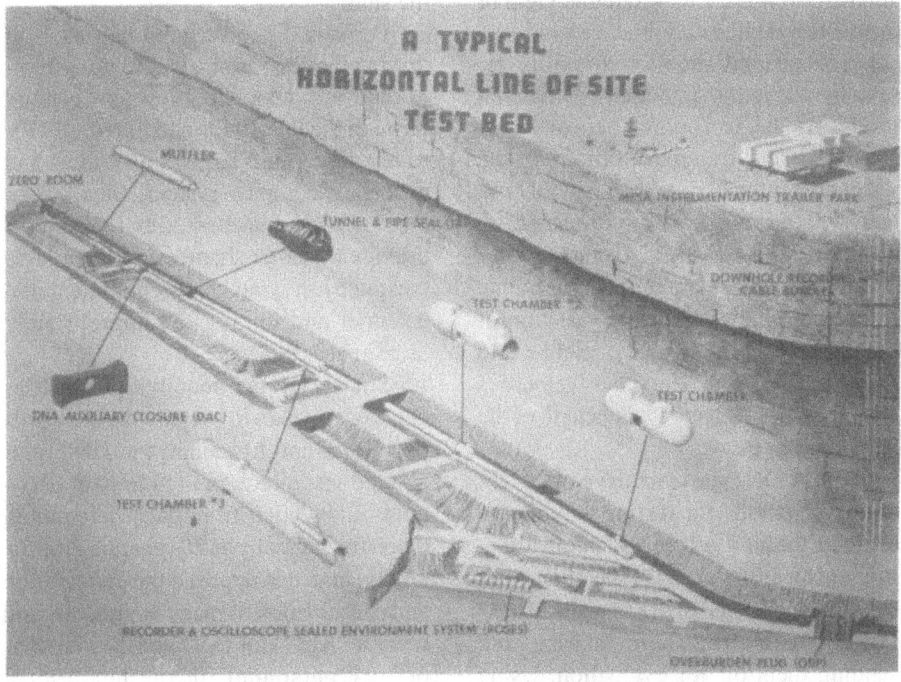

A typical underground horizontal line-of-sight (HLOS) test bed.

reaching the target arrays. However, even thick doors constructed of heavy steel failed to protect the samples, and better closure methods had to be developed.

DASA discovered that as the shock wave traveled through the tuffaceous soil under *Rainier Mesa* test site at NTS, the ground shock itself could be used to collapse the evacuated pipe, closing it thoroughly. However, as a means of protecting the samples from debris, such stemming or collapse of the LOS pipes induced by ground shock was not always reliable and not adequately predictable. Many times the pipe collapsed very close to the detonation point, after debris had escaped and damaged the experiment samples.

Dr. John Northrop, as DASA Deputy Director (Science and Technology), tasked John Lewis, who managed the agency's research work on ground shock, to find out why the timing of the ground shock induced closure of the LOS pipes varied so greatly from one test event to another, even in cases where the yield of the nuclear device was practically identical. The ground shock community researchers developed a numerical material model of the test-event geology that would be sensitive to variations in the water content, and thus the air-void content, within limits of those properties as observed in *Rainier Mesa*. Using the model in a spherically symmetric point source calculation, they found that variation of several percent in air-void content could dramatically influence shock velocities and range-to-effect along the length of the LOS pipe.

DASA's test site team developed laboratory methods for testing samples to evaluate the air-void content of the tuff at forward locations ahead of the mined tunnels. This consisted of drilling ahead, taking cores, sealing them in wax, and sending them off for evaluation. Using these data, the team could then pick locations for emplacement of nuclear test devices that would provide optimum geologic conditions for rapid transmission of the ground shock to collapse the LOS pipes. After adoption of these methods, ground shock stemming of the pipes succeeded in essentially every case in preventing debris damage to the sample arrays. This collaborative research served as a memorable example of how scientific deduction from first principles, coupled with newly gathered test data, could yield a practical solution to an engineering problem of national significance.[56]

Although more expensive, DASA found tunnel emplacement safer both in sealing against radiation emission and in protecting test personnel during re-entry to examine the exposed sample materials. DASA could conduct more experiments simultaneously through a network of horizontal tunnels than would be possible with a shaft system, with its test arrays mounted above the ground at the top of the shaft.

Perhaps the most important element driving the shift from shaft to tunnel emplacement was the increasing need through the late 1960s and into the 1970s to test larger and larger subsystems and eventually complete systems. Shafts, even those of wide diameters, simply could not provide the large chambers that could be created by moving heavy equipment into a tunnel and mining out appropriately large spaces.[57]

Since each test required as much as one to two years to prepare and upwards of $40 million to mount, the DDST-appointed test directors tried to gain maximum knowledge from each detonation. Operating as many as 20 separate projects on the same test required the cooperation and participation of many contractors and separate AEC and DoD and civilian laboratory personnel. In the late 1960s, DASA researchers developed safety and

Instrumentation trailers on *Rainer Mesa* in advance of underground nuclear weapons test at NTS.

security procedures early in the test period to ensure that personnel did not receive radiation exposure that exceeded allowed prescribed limits, to eliminate noxious or explosive gases after an explosion, and to preserve the physical safety of personnel working in the tunnels.[58]

The two agencies used some identical techniques and many of the same contractors. Holmes and Narver performed architect/engineer services for the test site and acted as the principal support contractor for AEC off-continent operations. Reynolds Electrical and Engineering Company, Incorporated, served as the principal AEC and DASA operational and support contractor for the test site, providing electrical and architectural engineering, large diameter and smaller conventional shaft drilling, heavy-duty construction and excavation, mining and tunneling, occupational safety and fire protection, and many other support functions. Beginning in 1963, Fenix and Scisson, Inc., of Tulsa, Oklahoma, took a lead role in designing many underground structures and specialized in the field of deep, large-diameter hole drilling, working for both AEC and DASA.[59]

The Nevada Operations Office of the AEC oversaw both AEC and DASA construction phases and, during construction, collected containment-related information. During either drilling or mining operations, the Nevada Operations Office ordered analysis of rock cores for moisture content, porosity, carbon dioxide content, and many other conditions. The AEC contractors examined and mapped the geologic features of the tunnels several months prior to a planned event.[60] AEC's local Nevada office arranged for required instrumentation and recording facilities, office space and equipment, communications equipment, vehicles, photography, and other support facilities. Contractors provided food services and housing at the test site.[61]

Through the 1960s, as DASA tests grew more sophisticated, they took on a character and developed a degree of technological culture of their own due to the unique testing methods involved. Although DASA test crews began to switch from shafts to tunnels, the AEC only rarely adopted the more expensive tunnel emplacement. To reduce costs, DoD test managers began to employ a number of ingenious means to re-use equipment and even to re-bore and re-use tunnels. By the late 1960s, DASA developed methods of re-using long lengths of LOS pipe and other equipment, resulting in reduced cost of operations.[62]

DASA leadership developed organizational or cultural approaches that, like the technological developments, stayed with the agency as part of its "way of doing business." DASA's staff would select a prime or lead project, giving that particular project office or program office within one of the Services the advantage of being able to set the schedule. Then, DASA would accept applications from other offices and programs needing items or materials tested. The "piggy-backed" projects competed for space, much like grant applicants in an academic setting. In some cases, DASA would provide funding and support and in other cases the project offices would fund their own operations. Early in the planning for the shot, the project officers would travel to the DASA Field Command office in Albuquerque. Meeting in a large hall, in a process similar to college registration, the project officers would go from table to table, filling out applications for the services they would need. For example, DASA staff asked each program officer, as one of the first considerations, how much cabling they would require. Even before emplacement, the cable to relay data would cost over a dollar a foot "on the reel" of spooled cable. With hundreds of data-gathering cables, some stretching thousands of feet, the total cable cost could become a major consideration.[63]

When executing an experiment, the experimenters recorded data from the test stations underground through a system of remote detectors and cabling that sent signals to recording facilities located in trailers on the surface. Prior to a test, operators would maintain electronic equipment, film, and magnetic recorders in the trailer parks to capture the data. Capturing data required the most advanced electronic technology since a test transmitted data for only an instant before the sensors were destroyed. The equipment operated automatically, and crews could not enter the trailer area to recover equipment and data sheets until monitors had declared the area safe.

Most of the early DoD shaft emplacements included LOS pipes from the device emplacement chamber directly to the surface. However, these pipes required systems to prevent release of radioactive debris to the atmosphere. In the mid-sixties, several such releases gave added incentive to switch to tunnel emplacement. Work continued to improve closure techniques for the LOS pipes to allow radiation, but not blast or debris, to reach the test samples. Fast gate closure systems driven by high explosives or compressed air sealed the openings in LOS pipes, but some of these early systems did not prevent releases.

Cables presented further containment problems. Test crews embedded the cables in concrete and epoxy to prevent leakage from venting. Even so, they found that radioactive gases under high pressure traveled along the inside of cables as a conduit. DASA solved this problem by embedding the inner components of cables in epoxy at appropriate intervals, calling the technique "gas blocking."[64] The most serious containment problems, however, resulted from unanticipated geologic conditions at particular test locations. Sometimes a formation would contain more water than anticipated near the detonation point. The nuclear explosion turned the water to steam under pressure. The resulting pressure was sufficient to occasionally break through the surface, despite containment methods.[65]

DASA test staff encountered such a serious difficulty with PIN STRIPE, a vertical LOS test in April of 1966. The test crew emplaced the device in a mined shaft at a depth of approximately 970 feet. Experimenters had mounted a mobile tower, with samples to be tested, directly over the underground emplacement. A vertical LOS pipe with a maximum diameter of 36 inches extended to the surface. Venting from the underground explosion began one minute after detonation and continued until the cavity collapse that occurred about five minutes after the detonation. Further seepage from the ground zero area began seven hours after the detonation and continued for another 21 hours.[66]

At one minute after the detonation, crews began to winch the mobile tower away from the expected subsidence area. At about that time the first effluent emerged from the ground about 150 feet away from the tower. Soon the gases began to seep from a crack that extended both towards the shaft and away from it. A grey cloud formed, growing steadily until the cavity collapsed. The cloud rose to an altitude of about 2,000 feet over the test area, and then was blown in a north-northwest direction at about ten miles an hour.[67] Even though the direction of the wind did not draw the cloud directly over the area where trailers with recording instruments were parked, "gamma shine," or radiation from the cloud, did expose the trailers and the recording equipment.[68]

The radiation count in the trailer park rose to 400R/hour for two to three minutes; in about twenty minutes the radiation fell off to 15 to 20R/hour. The test manager gave permission to proceed with recovering high priority data from the trailers but instructed the crews not to enter areas with exposure rates greater than 17R/hour. They entered the trailers and were able to recover all film within a few minutes. Over a period of six or seven hours, the level of radioactivity dropped as the cloud drifted from the shaft. Soon the crew removed the mobile trailers and began recovering the experiment packages.[69]

The cloud ultimately rose to approximately 5,500 feet, moving to the east at about twenty miles per hour.[70] Both the Public Health Service and the Air Force Technical Applications Center (AFTAC) sent aircraft to track and sample the cloud during the night. VEGAS-8, a Public Health Service twin-turboprop Beechcraft, overflew the cloud and then entered the cloud path to get information on the nature of the release and to collect samples. The next day, however, researchers found it much harder to track the cloud as it headed over Utah and Colorado.

The Public Health Service already had established a milk sampling network, and the Service placed it in operation throughout Utah, Colorado, Wyoming, and southern Idaho. On April 26, a search plane made a positive contact with the cloud about 300 miles due east of the NTS, and a larger, slightly radioactive air mass extended from southern Wyoming south to southwestern Kansas. Late on the night of the 26th, the air mass shifted to a wide area between central Minnesota and central Kansas. Rain and snow in the upper Midwest had a leaching effect. The aircraft tracking the cloud lost all contact with it on the April 27.

Monitors measured their highest radiation level of a populated area near the

PIN STRIPE test tower at D-1 hour (prior to detonation), April 18, 1966.

test site at Hiko, Nevada. There at 4:00 p.m. on the day of the test, outdoor radiation levels reached 1.45mR/h. A higher level of 8mR/h was detected at Coyote Summit, an unpopulated area. The Public Health Service moved a mobile medical trailer to the Hiko area, and 134 cows at one dairy in Hiko were placed on dry feed rather than being allowed to graze.[71]

Careful measurement of exposures at the site and offsite indicated that none of the exposures of individuals exceeded the AEC guideline level of 5 rem per year or about .5mR/h for industrial personnel exposure. Nevertheless, the PIN STRIPE event had revealed that underground nuclear weapon effects testing, particularly in shafts, entailed a risk of offsite radiation exposure.

During the next test, DISCUS THROWER, managers established a more extensive "radsafe" system, complete with monitoring teams and supervisory personnel, for initial radiation surveys on the surface and aerial surveys by helicopter.

They detected no onsite or offsite radiation from this test.[72]

PERMISSIVE ACTION LINKS AND BROKEN ARROWS

While the DASA experimenters perfected testing that provided the maximum data from the tests at acceptably low risks to personnel and/or radiation releases, the scientific, technical, and military jurisdiction of DASA continued to require other adjustments and new ways of conducting business. DASA researchers needed to deal with safety and security of the weapons and response to weapons as hazardous devices.

The AEC's development of Permissive Action Links* (PALs), first installed outside the United States in 1962 at the direction of President Kennedy, derived from an international policy consideration that affected DASA's mission. In 1966, the United States began to locate nuclear weapons with PALs in other NATO countries. This development added to existing concerns about the security of weapons which might be stored in overseas locations. The United States had to extend the PAL system so that the weapons deployed in these countries could not be used if stolen, or could not be improperly employed by local personnel in units to which they had been assigned. The goal was to ensure that U.S. personnel would remain physically in control of the weapons.[73]

Sandia National Laboratory and Lawrence Livermore Laboratory developed PALs in response to concerns expressed in a January 1960 JCS report on the safety of atomic weapons.[74] After investigating joint custody arrangements in Britain, Germany, and other locations outside the United States, Congressmen on the Joint Committee on Atomic Energy grew concerned that relaxed procedures might allow foreign military officers to seize and possibly employ weapons.[75]

Herbert York served at Lawrence Livermore Laboratory as director and then as director of DDR&E in the last days of the Eisenhower administration. In that position, he established a Safety Steering Group, in January of 1961, that focused on safety issues surrounding nuclear weapons. DASA supported the Group with technical staff, adding a major new aspect to its agenda of nuclear military responsibilities.[76] PALs supplemented the dual-key approach by requiring that launching codes be given from higher authority in the chain of command.

The DoD installed the first PAL in 1962, designating them as "Category A," on the Quick Response Aircraft in Germany. DoD later installed "Category A" PALs on the Jupiter strategic missile and a range of tactical nuclear missiles.[77] To reassure Allies that the locks did not imply distrust of Allied officers, DoD installed the same system on weapons in strictly U.S. facilities stationed in Europe.

The AEC made a series of improvements to the PALs through the 1960s, including moving the location of the system from external to the weapon to deep inside to prevent anyone from "wiring around" the link. A "Category B" PAL involved setting a four-digit code with a limited-try system so that after a few incorrect attempts, the system could not be activated. "Category C", introduced in the late 1960s, required a six-digit code, again with a limited-try feature. Production of the "Category B" PALs began in 1966.[78] The United States made the Soviets aware of PAL technology and, as early as 1963, the Soviet Union appeared to have developed and installed the systems on their own nuclear weapons.[79]

In 1964, the Johnson administration began to extend the PAL concept beyond NATO to other aircraft-delivered and ground-launched nuclear weapons. In the late spring of 1966, the Secretary of the Air Force authorized a panel made up of outside experts to review recent "Broken Arrow" incidents and develop recommendations. Although the forthcoming recommendations focused on safety procedures, the panel also urged more assertive protection be exercised over all nuclear weapons carried aboard B-52 aircraft. Secretary Brown accepted the recommendation and extended the use of devices based on the PAL concept to all SAC weapons.[80]

In late 1966 and early 1967, Carl Walske, ATSD(AE) initiated a comprehensive study of use-control devices for nuclear weapons. The new policy, unlike the earlier PALs put in place in Europe, focused on American military personnel.

---

* *Permissive Action Link:* a device included in or attached to a nuclear weapon system to preclude arming and/or launching until the insertion of a prescribed discrete code or combination. It included equipment and cabling external to the weapon or weapon system to activate components within the weapon or weapon system.

In particular, the Air Force installed a system of use-control on planes headed for the failsafe point so that officers on recalled planes would not be able to unilaterally decide to attack.[81] From a military point of view, the advantage of the system was that it would allow the deployment of a greater number of weapons at a high state of readiness. SAC commanders assumed less risk by putting armed but "locked" weapons aboard planes in the air than by using fully armed weapons. This policy vastly increased the number of weapons available at a moment's notice.[82]

The DoD exempted the Navy from the new system of controls, partly because of the difficulty of communicating with submarines under way with only a few minute's time for notification, and due to the inherent safety of nuclear weapons aboard ships, that would insulate them from outside interference or capture. A system of dual keys aboard the submarines required concurrence of two officers in a launch decision. Nevertheless, the Navy adopted PAL systems for some of its nuclear depth charges stored on land.[83]

As a consequence of the policy of remaining in a state of high readiness, SAC began operation "Chrome Dome" in 1961. B-52s, loaded with nuclear weapons, flew airborne alert patrols near the Soviet Union, fully ready to attack with only a few hours' flight time to their ultimate targets.[84]

On January 17, 1966, a B-52 bomber returning from a flight near the Soviet border collided with a KC-135 tanker while refueling over Spain. Both planes disintegrated in the air high over Palomares, a small fishing village on the country's Southern Mediterranean coast. The bomber's four hydrogen bombs fell through the flaming debris, automatically deploying safety parachutes. However, some of the parachutes did not fully open.

Three of the four weapons landed among the fields and houses of the village. One broke open and another suffered a high-explosive detonation, scattering plutonium. Within days, Air Force crews located the three grounded weapons and began an extensive program of decontamination and soil removal to prevent risk to the population from the alpha-emitting plutonium. While the crews worked to cut down vegetation and remove soil, public attention began to focus on the fourth, lost weapon that had fallen into the sea.[85]

The Navy concentrated an assemblage of deep-diving underwater and exploring equipment, including *Alvin* and *Aluminaut*, to locate and recover the fourth weapon, a process that lasted several months. Finally the Navy recovered the missing bomb on April 7, 1966. In general, the DoD followed a policy of not discussing the procedure with the press, creating, in the eyes of some observers, more suspicion and public hysteria than if the department had more frankly discussed the risks and problems.[86]

By focusing on the "lost" bomb at sea, the international press partially ignored the immediate danger from the scattered plutonium on the ground, and such a focus may have helped limit hysteria. Without disclosing classified technology or procedures, U.S. officials had to reassure host country officials, and the general European public to an extent, that the weapons aboard B-52s did not pose a high risk. The public relations and diplomatic tasks proved as difficult as the cleanup itself. No villagers suffered any radiation injury, and the United States compensated all with justified damage claims for lost crop and fishing revenue.[87]

The 16th Air Force, and specifically the commander of the 16th Air Force, Major General Delmar Wilson, retained responsibility for coordinating all recovery efforts. Field Command, DASA, and the Joint Nuclear Accidents Coordinating

Aboard the *USS Petrel*, Major General D. E. Wilson, Commander of the 16th Air Force and Rear Admiral W. S. Guest, Commander of Navy Task Force 65, look over MK28 bomb retrieved from 2,800 feet of water off Palomares, Spain, in 1966.

Center (JNACC), located at Sandia Base in Albuquerque, provided technical assistance. Later, the agency would take a direct interest in studying the whole Palomares episode for "lessons learned," generating a "Summary Report" in 1975 that provided a detailed account of the event.[88]

A series of Broken Arrow incidents in the United States and at sea during the same years received far less publicity than the Palomares incident, but like that event, they required DASA advisory participation in search, cleanup, decontamination, and after-incident reports. Publicly disclosed incidents included several involving SAC aircraft. On January 13, 1964, response teams recovered two weapons relatively intact after an aircraft accident near Cumberland, Maryland.[89]

Another B-52, taking part in the Chrome Dome exercises, caught fire over Greenland on January 21, 1968. The pilot diverted the craft to Thule where the United States maintained a key part of its North American early warning radar system. The plane crashed seven miles short of the runway. The crew ejected and six of the seven airmen survived. Four bombs were destroyed by fire. A four-month decontamination effort followed, which required the removal of contaminated ice and snow.[90]

DASA personnel from the JNACC participated in the emergency. Response teams assembled for both the Palomares

DoD and JNACC personnel participating in the ice cleanup after Broken Arrow incident at Thule, Greenland, 1968.

incident and the Thule incident. JNACC personnel assisted in the recovery of contaminated debris and provided technical assistance and advice to the troops on the ground. DASA established an emergency response team for future accidents as a result of the Palomares accident.[91]

In the wake of Palomares and Thule, Secretary McNamara ordered SAC to discontinue its policy of full peacetime airborne alerts, with its near-border flights of nuclear-armed aircraft. He also discontinued the Chrome Dome exercise a few days after the Thule Broken Arrow incident.[92] Nevertheless, refueling B-52s from KC-135 tankers remained an extremely dangerous procedure. Earlier, on October 15, 1959, a B-52 bomber collided with a KC-135 tanker near Hardinsberg, Kentucky, resulting in the death of eight crewmen aboard the two aircraft and two nuclear weapons falling to earth. The two unarmed weapons were recovered intact. One had been burned, but this did not result in dispersion of nuclear material or other contamination.[93]

The high state of nuclear readiness that resulted from the national defense policy of the Kennedy, Johnson, and Nixon administrations through this period had reshaped DASA's responsibilities. Operation Chrome Dome was only the most dramatic and best known program requiring that nuclear weapons be kept aloft. It was almost inevitable that accidents would occur; when they did, DASA-led teams flew to the spot to assist. Locating weapons overseas to put them credibly close to their probable targets for use in a nuclear war also engaged the agency in designing and testing viable permissive action systems to prevent misuse of the weapons.

REPORTING AND TRAINING

DASA's responsibilities for keeping cadres well informed expanded greatly because of the high state of nuclear preparedness and the involvement of all the military Services in managing and transporting nuclear weapons. Literally thousands of people had a genuine "need to know" about nuclear weapons technology, policy, safety, and handling.

DASA scientists convened symposia and conferences that individuals from all over the American nuclear establishment attended. Some conferences that involved non-classified material even met on an international basis. For example, in October of 1963, DASA personnel participated in the Nuclear Detonations and Marine Radioactivity Conference held in Norway, in another conference on the Biological Effects of Neutron Irradiation held at Brookhaven Laboratory in New York, and in a Tripartite Technical Cooperation Program meeting in London.[94]

Personnel from DASA regularly conducted classified "briefings" for groups including SAC, the President's Scientific Advisory Committee, and the Office of Science and Technology Policy of the Executive Office of the President.[95]

The establishment of the Limited Test Ban demonstrated the importance of a thorough review of already-conducted tests, although such a historical or retrospective study of data ran counter to the experimental culture of the nuclear scientific community. Yet, without the ability to conduct further atmospheric tests, the data from the last tests had to be carefully and thoroughly reviewed. Accordingly, in early November 1963, DASA held an "Operation FISH BOWL Review Symposium" in Chicago attended by 500 visitors from military organizations and the nuclear industry. Its purpose was to summarize the latest results and theories derived from Operation FISH BOWL, the series of tests conducted in 1962-63. The symposium was composed of five separate sessions: phenomenology; trapped radiation in the Van Allen belt; disturbed ionosphere, and its implications on communications; radar blackout; and thermal and blast effects.

Along the same lines, project officers and technical people prepared reports from other prior experiments and sent them to DASA headquarters. A conference on measurements of a 1962 test, SMALL BOY, focused on questions involving interpretation and analysis measurements of the time dependence of the gamma ray intensities.

Tests at Tonopah, Nevada, had included Operation ROLLER COASTER, a series of three one-point safety detonations conducted in May and June of 1963. ROLLER COASTER's objective was to define plutonium dispersal after an accidental explosion of the high explosive in a weapon, information that proved useful later at both Thule and Palomares.[96]

Through 1964 and 1965, DASA scientific and technical personnel issued a dramatically increasing number of reports, scientific papers, and other publications devoted to radiation effects. Subjects ranged from studies of x-ray spectra of shots in prior tests, to studies of electromagnetic blackouts, simulation of EMP, studies of effects on radar, missiles, semiconductors, satellites, and other equipment, and the effects of various kinds of shielding. The agency issued many reports quantifying non-radiation nuclear phenomena, to include fire propagation, debris scattering, ground shock measurement, blast effects on concrete and other structures, and a wide range of retrospective studies of the last atmospheric tests. Such selective subjects only hint at the extensive and intensive work being conducted through the mid-1960s on these and other effects.

DASA's reports demonstrated that its responsibilities in scientific and technical areas had grown to include a range of specializations in a very short period. These reports concentrated on a combination of basic scientific and measurement information on the one hand, and on very practical technological information about the effects of weapons on materials, equipment, weapons, communications systems, and structures on the other hand. Like the symposia and the briefings, the reports served to disseminate knowledge and findings to a broader audience.[97]

By the late 1960s, the training programs that AFSWP had initiated years before had burgeoned into a large-scale school with hundreds of faculty and thousands of graduates. The training programs were conducted within the Atomic Weapons Training Group building at Field Command, which was later renamed Interservice Nuclear Weapons School and more recently, Defense Nuclear Weapons School. The subject matter taught eventually expanded into the fields of nuclear weapon assembly, maintenance, nuclear hazards, safety, emergency demolition, post-graduate scientific courses, and DoD orientation and familiarization courses. Equally important were the courses sponsored by DASA at many of the Service schools, particularly the Naval Post-Graduate School in Monterey and the Air Force Institute of Technology in Dayton. In addition, the Air Force Weapons Laboratory in Albuquerque became an important source of highly trained technical Air Force officers who frequently continued on to staff positions in Headquarters and Test Command.

The training program conducted by the Field Command expanded greatly, burgeoning into an institution the size of a major vocational school or community college, variously nicknamed by its students as "Nuclear U.," "The Vault," or, even more ironically, "the Kremlin." Lodged in a heavily guarded, windowless building with only one door, the students faced intensive work schedules. No classroom notes could be taken away, and all course materials and notes would be locked in classified-material safes overnight. By the mid-1960s, the school had a curriculum of specialized courses, some 3,500-4,000 graduates per year, and a staff of about 300 instructors and administrative personnel to handle the teaching, registration, security, and logistics side of the courses.[98]

By far, the 37-hour Weapons Orientation-Advanced (WOA) program proved itself the most important and largest single course. This course graduated about 500 students per six-month period and engaged officers with the rank of major or above in the Army or Air Force, or lieutenant commander or above in the Navy. The WOA course brought these officers together with senior civil servants and provided them an intensive briefing on nuclear weapons and their effects. Using a program of lectures and DoD-developed motion pictures, students reviewed national weapons policy and strategy, the history of nuclear weapons and their effects, and the types of weapons deployed. This "big picture" course, in a fairly typical six-month period (July-December 1966), ran five separate times, graduating more than 300 officers and 190 civilians.

The school also offered many technical courses, including these specializations: Army Nuclear Weapons Officer, Army Nuclear Weapons Electronics Specialist, Calibration and Electronics, Nuclear Emergency Team, Navy Nuclear Weapons Electronic Calibration and Maintenance, and Nuclear Weapons Maintenance.

The technical courses included classroom instruction on detector fundamentals, dosimetry, radiation detectors, and nuclear weapons fire fighting. Field work included detection exercises for beta-gamma detection, as well as nuclear emergency team exercises.[99]

In addition to Army and Navy Military Occupational Specialty (MOS) courses in these nuclear areas, the weapons school established a number of "transitional" courses that provided a holding class while students awaited arrival of their security clearances. Other transitional courses served as preparatory classes to bring students up to the entry-level technical expectations of the more advanced work.[100] Although the school modified the curriculum through the 1960s, it consistently offered the core of material for technical qualification of enlisted servicemen and of some civilians through the later years of the decade. Military demands of responding to accidents, managing the stockpile, testing weapons, and maintaining a headquarters staff with a good understanding of policy required a steady flow of about 3,000 trained individuals every year from the school.

The nuclear weapons school also operated a Motion Picture Production Division that engaged in constant development of a variety of training and documentary films in conjunction with personnel from Sandia Base. In addition, the school ran a publications and visual aids department that generated slides and prints for instructional purposes and that printed and bound its own technical manuals. A small staff kept up a technical reference library that instructional staff and students used.

By the end of the decade, DASA had become a large enterprise, serving the nuclear weapons establishment not only

Entrance to Field Command's Atomic Weapons Training Group building (*Nuclear U*), later renamed Defense Nuclear Weapons School (DNWS) at Kirtland AFB, Albuquerque, New Mexico.

with research and development and effects testing but also with a significant educational infrastructure to ensure that the information flowed to those with a need to know. Harold Brown's and Robert McNamara's support for invigorated communication of knowledge had resulted in channeling expert nuclear knowledge not only up through the chain of command to policy makers but down through the chain of command to the civilian technical specialists and the enlisted men who took care of the day-to-day mechanical aspects of the weapons program.

ARMED FORCES RADIOBIOLOGY RESEARCH INSTITUTE

By DoD Directive 5154.16, issued May 12, 1961, McNamara established the Armed Forces Radiobiology Research Institute (AFRRI). The Directive came to be regarded as the Institute's "charter." The basic mission of the Institute was to conduct scientific research in the field of radiobiology in support of the U.S. military and for national welfare and general human well being. The rationale for the establishment of AFRRI was based on two realities of the late 1950s and early 1960s; one: the threat scenario of numerous Soviet infantry divisions overcoming the German Fulda Gap defenses and overtaking Europe, and two: the use of nuclear weapons, particularly enhanced weapons rich in neutron output, to halt such a European invasion force. Since there was no DoD or DOE research laboratory at that time that had reactor or other neutron sources as an integral part of its research facilities, AFFRI was constructed around an existing, state-of-the-art Training, Research, Isotopes, General Atomic (TRIGA) nuclear reactor, which had the capability of pulsing and thereby partially simulating the radiation characteristics of a nuclear weapon. The institute was located at the National Naval Medical Center in Bethesda, Maryland, and governed by a Board of Governors consisting of the Chief of DASA as Chairman, and the three Surgeons General of the military Services.

In July of 1964, by DoD Directive 5105.31, DASA was charged with command and administrative control over AFRRI, a role it and its successor agencies continued to play over the next three decades, until 1993 when it came under the control of the Uniformed Services University of the Health Sciences. AFRRI officially became an operational field element of DASA by a further directive in November of 1964.[101]

On a budget which ran in the range of $2 to $3 million per year through the 1960s, the Institute built on its original base. In addition to administrative and support departments, five research departments carried on basic scientific and medical research. The Experimental Pathology Department studied the pathologic effects of ionizing radiation. The Behavioral Sciences Department worked in several areas of fundamental research with special emphasis on the applied area of psychological effects of radiation and noxious agents. The Physical Sciences Department contained several divisions. One worked with the TRIGA experimental reactor, and another with linear accelerators. A Chemistry Division, a Radiological Physics Division, and a Theoretical Division, all formed the basis for later expansion. The Radiation Biology Department worked on both basic and fundamental research, with a core of principal investigators focusing on several research projects. The primary emphasis of the Department was to provide information to the Department of Defense on the deleterious effects of ionizing radiation.[102]

AFRRI made many contributions in the open literature through the 1960s in the area of the biological effects of ionizing radiation of different types and doses. The Institute investigated the incapacitating doses of radiation and the biological responses to radiation. Studies with rats, monkeys, dogs, mice, and other animals helped establish the effects of radiation on nerves, the central nervous system, the blood system, and other tissues and organs.

The Board of Governors of AFRRI usually met twice a year. With turnover of Surgeons General and Directors of DASA, staff at AFRRI would conduct tours and familiarize the new board members with the research activities of the Institute. A 1965 review, for example, covered four research program areas: role of bacteria in radiation injury; radiation studies; depth dose evaluation, and "behavioral incapacitation following lethal radiation exposure."[103] Through papers at conferences, published journal articles and AFRRI reports, investigators disseminated their findings.[104]

AFRRI signed Memoranda of Understanding with several universities, working with the Catholic University of America in Washington and with the University of Pennsylvania School of Medicine in radiobiology and cancer research. AFRRI also entered into inter-agency agreements with a number of government agencies, colleges, and corporations, sharing resources and equipment on a variety of research projects related to radiation, exposure, and basic medical research.[105]

By the late 1960s, the staff size had stabilized at 241 authorized positions, and the research program had become quite varied. Although AFRRI remained structured as a field activity of DASA, it continued to operate as an independent Institute, sponsoring research on the radiation effects on biological systems.

CHANGES ON THE HORIZON

For DASA, 1968 witnessed another command change; Vice Admiral Lloyd M. Mustin, former Navy Deputy and Commander of Joint Task Force 8, replaced General Donnelly as DASA Director on August 1, 1968. There were also changes on the national horizon. The inauguration of President Nixon in January of 1969 marked significant change in policies established during the Johnson administration. However, much of the practice and structure that the DoD had established for DASA in the 1960s continued into this next period. Yet, increasingly in the late 1960s, the Services rankled at the loss of control over nuclear testing, nuclear training, and the nuclear stockpile that had been within their grasp in 1959 when the JCS had established DASA. McNamara and Brown had wrested away that control, and the Services had some practical reasons to be concerned.

In particular, officers in the separate Services appeared to resist DASA's con-

Vice Admiral Lloyd M. Mustin, USN, DASA Director 1968 to 1971.

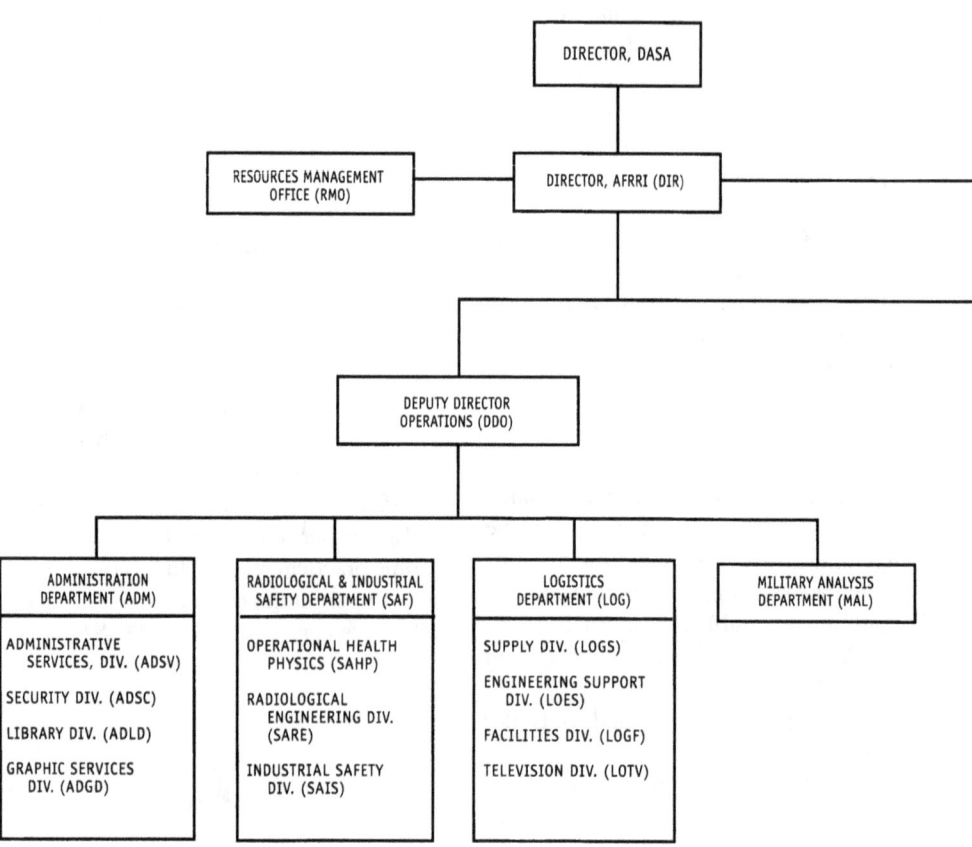

Organizational Chart of Armed Forces Radiobiology Research Institute (AFRRI), July 1969.

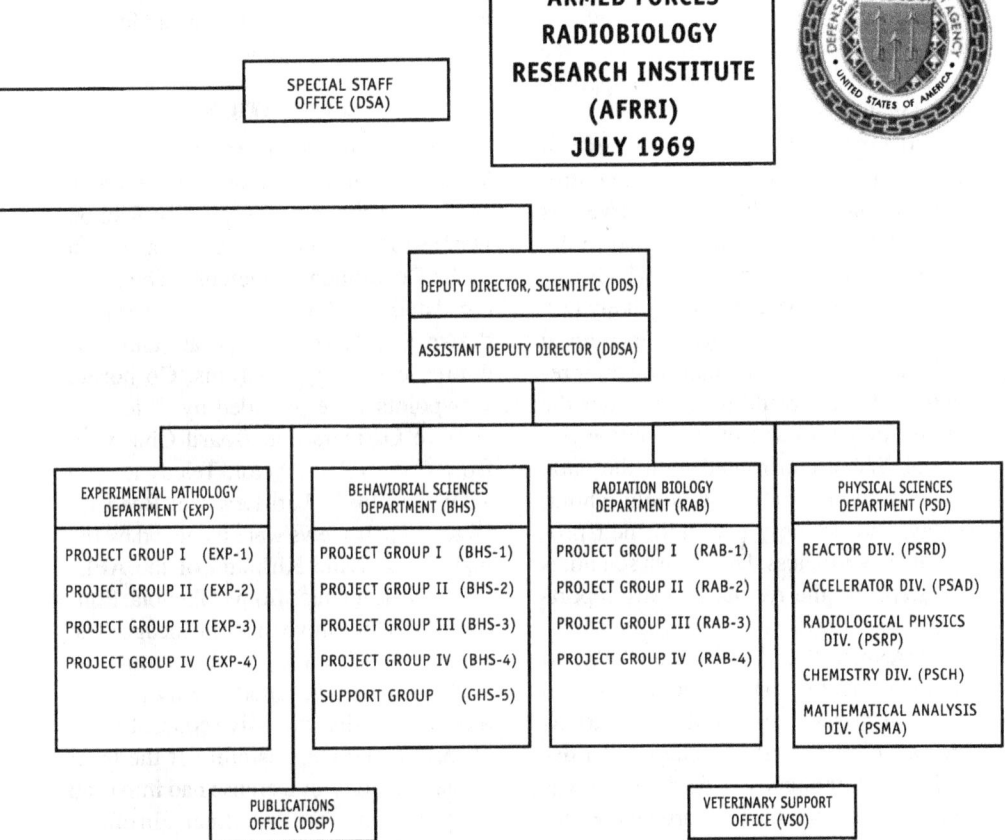

trol over weapon development programs that the Services initiated. Every weapon program had its project or program office that focused on the development of that particular weapons system. Officers would devote years of their lives to overseeing a weapon system through the pitfalls of technology, testing, funding, and opposition. Any obstacle in the way of a weapon's development could play into the hands of the "Antis," those who opposed the development.

At DASA, the officers in charge of testing had a difficult, and even controversial, role. Once the JCS directive was promulgated in 1966, DASA had to determine the conditions under which particular weapon systems would likely fail. For example, some Naval officers refused to believe that the nose cones on their reentry vehicles would degrade under the effects of x rays and other radiation fluences. When confronted with the data, they could only believe it would inhibit, delay, and possibly even kill their program. Nevertheless, DASA test scientists insisted that the results be fully reported.[106]

DASA testing through the 1960s had yielded what the test community came to call "surprises," that is, determinations that a weapon or other system under development or already in deployment was extremely vulnerable to a particular weapon effect and would need to be re-engineered. A RAND study of DASA noted that although the specific nature of the "surprises" remained classified, it was a general fact that a "high rate" of such surprises characterized DASA work in the 1960s. Weapons systems were constantly hardened and upgraded to address the findings of the tests.[107]

Several specific yet unexpected results requiring follow-on action turned up in the Minuteman III, its Mark 12 and Mark 12A reentry vehicles, the Spartan ABM system, the Polaris Mark 2 Mod 2 reentry body, the Poseidon C3 Mark 3 reentry body, and the Trident C4 Mark 4 reentry body. The "unexpected results" in some of these weapon systems would have constituted major system failures if occurring operationally. Before these systems were deployed, however, the Services addressed the issues through additional hardening and retesting.[108]

TRANSITION

Early in his administration, President Nixon and his Secretary of Defense, Melvin Laird, appointed a Blue Ribbon Defense Panel to examine the operation of the Department of Defense. The panel consisted of 16 prominent individuals, drawn largely from corporate and academic leadership positions. Corporate viewpoints were provided by Chief Executive Officers and Board Chairmen from Caterpillar Tractor, Teledyne, and TRW, and by Hobart Lewis of Reader's Digest. Their views were balanced by the insights of Lane Kirkland of the AFL-CIO, and academics from Columbia, Princeton, and the University of Chicago. The panel began its study in the summer of 1969 and issued its report on July 1, 1970. It concluded that excessive concentration of managerial responsibility at the level of the Secretary of Defense had impaired the operation of the department. In effect, the panel offered a stinging criticism of McNamara and the widely resented development of "Whiz Kid" control that had taken place over the 1960s, both in budgetary and technical areas. The panel explicitly criticized the growth of large civilian and military staffs, and much of the report focused on undoing many of Harold Brown's accomplishments.[109]

In reference to DASA, the report became quite specific and biting in its charges and recommendations, suggesting that its extensive headquarters and staffing would no longer be required. With each of the new weapon systems being developed by the Services now being designed to meet nuclear weapon effects specifications, and with each Service developing its own cadre of nuclear experts, times and conditions had changed. "The conditions," the Panel noted, "which led to the assignment of most of the functions initially assigned to DASA no longer exist." Two functions remained relevant in 1970, the Panel admitted: stockpile oversight and weapons effects test coordination. "The scope of the two unique functional capabilities of DASA," the report concluded on this point, "no longer justifies the continuation of the administrative overhead load inherent in a Defense Agency." In effect, it seemed to some reviewers, that the panel was calling for the disbanding of DASA, or at least its downgrading from defense agency status.[110]

Many within the agency agreed that DASA had become top-heavy with administrative overhead. Some military personnel stationed at the Field Command had begged for reassignment, frankly admitting that they reported to work with nothing to do.[111] Clearly, DASA could cut some of the fat without endangering the central mission. Once again, as the agency entered a new decade, it would face the challenges of reorganization and clarification of mission.

ENDNOTES

1. Dr. Frederick Wikner, interview by Rodney P. Carlisle, September 25, 1997.
2. Charles P. McCormick, *The Power of People*, New York: Harper and Brothers, 1949. McCormick's work was an influential management book through the 1950s, advocating that older models of management as top-down enforcement of rules be abandoned in favor of various methods of tapping the talents of lower ranking individuals in organizations.
3. Luttwak, *Strategic Power*, pp. 20-21.
4. *Ibid.*, p. 36.
5. Figures from Luttwak, *Strategic Power*, p. 20.
6. The expansion of weapons and delivery systems during the 1960s as the greatest of the cold war is asserted in the official publication: Donald P. Steury, *Intentions and Capabilities: Estimates on Soviet Strategic Forces, 1950-1983* (Washington, DC: 1996, Center for the Study of Intelligence, Central Intelligence Agency), p. 223.
7. Moulton, *From Superiority to Parity*, p. 151.
8. *Ibid.*, p. 164.
9. *Ibid.*, p. 165.
10. Luttwak, *Strategic Power*, pp. 20-23.
11. Moulton, *From Superiority to Parity*, pp. 168-69.
12. For a discussion on the Nike-X, see Moulton, *From Superiority to Parity*, pp. 177-79.
13. Robert McNamara, *Blundering into Disaster: Surviving the First Century of the Nuclear Age*, New York, 1986, p. 57.
14. *Ibid.*, p. 58.
15. *Ibid.*, p. 65.
16. *Ibid.*, p. 66. Henry Kissinger, President Nixon's National Security Officer, also shared the same regret at the development and deployment of MIRVed missiles.
17. Edgar M. Bottome, *The Balance of Terror: A Guide to the Arms Race*, 1st ed., Boston, Massachusetts, 1971, p. 128.
18. *Ibid.*, p. 132.
19. As quoted in William R. Harris, *Defense Nuclear Responsibilities: From the Armed Forces Special Weapons Project to the Defense Nuclear Agency, 1947-1971*, RAND Study draft: DRR-1285-DNA, February 1996, p. 125.
20. Peter D. Feaver, *Guarding the Guardians: Civilian Control of Nuclear Weapons in the United States*, Ithaca, New York, 1992, p. 210; Harris, *Defense Nuclear Responsibilities*, p. 125.
21. Feaver, *Guarding the Guardians*, p. 211.
22. Freeman J. Dyson, *Weapons and Hope*, 1st ed. New York, 1984, pp. 272-73.
23. W. B. Foster, "Introduction to Panel of 8th Institute on Research Administration at the American University in April 1963," Records of the Office of the DNL, R.C. 3-1, Series 4, Acc. #82-18, Box 14, folder entitled Task 97: Enhancement of DoD In-House R & D, Naval Historical Center.
24. U.S. Congress, Senate, *Report to the President on Government Contracting for Research and Development*, S. Doc. 94, 87th Cong., 2d sess., 1962, Bureau of the Budget, Washington, D.C.: GPO, 1962, pp. 21-22.
25. Wikner interview; Harris, *Defense Nuclear Responsibilities*, p. 91. Other internal agency documents from the period and from later stress the McMillan Committee as providing the intellectual framework for reform, ignoring the broader push of Harold Brown to affect such reforms throughout the Defense establishment. See, for example, *Defense Special Weapons Agency, 1947-1997*, The First 50 Years of National Service, DSWA Printing (FCDSWA), Albuquerque, New Mexico, 1997, p. 15.
26. Harris, *Defense Nuclear Responsibilities*, pp. 100-101.
27. Defense Atomic Support Agency, History of the Defense Atomic Support Agency, 1959-1969, Part 2 - Headquarters, Chapter 6 - Plans and Operations, pp. 53-63.
28. Harris, *Defense Nuclear Responsibilities*, p. 81.
29. A copy of this charter is reproduced in *RAND Corporation, Charters and Directives for the Defense Nuclear Agency and*

Predecessor Organizations, 1947-1971, RAND Study draft DRR-xxxx-DNA, April 1994, document number 10.
30. *RAND Corporation, Charters and Directives, Documents 10 and 12;* Harris, *Defense Nuclear Responsibilities*, p. 103.
31. Admiral Robert Monroe, interview by Rodney P. Carlisle, September 24, 1997, p. 4.
32. Harris, *Defense Nuclear Responsibilities*, p. 91.
33. *Ibid.*, pp. 91, 10; H. L. Brode, "Partial History of the DNA Scientific Advisory Group on Effects (And Its Predecessors)" (Los Angeles, July 1989), Pacific Sierra Research Corporation report 197, as cited in Harris, *Defense Nuclear Responsibilities*, p. 91.
34. Wikner interview.
35. Harris, *Defense Nuclear Responsibilities*, p. 104.
36. The text of 5105.31 giving authority over AFRRI and JNACC is found in DASA, *History of DASA, 1959-1969,* as an appendix to Vol. 1.
37. DASA: *History of DASA, 1959-1969,* appendix to Vol. 1; Robert Brittigan, interview by Rodney Carlisle, October 24, 1997.
38. For a description of Taylor's varied interests and his changing positions on nuclear issues, see John McPhee, *The Curve of Binding Energy*, New York, 1973.
39. Wikner interview.
40. Biography, U.S. Air Force, DTL 070 289.
41. *Ibid.* The test record during this period reflects many of the reforms Wikner discussed. See Defense Nuclear Agency, *Operations Flintlock and Latchkey,* Events Red Hot, Pin Stripe, Discus Thrower, Pile Driver, Double Play, Newpoint, Midi Mist, March 5, 1966 - June 26, 1967, DNA Report 6321F, Kirtland AFB, New Mexico.
42. Wikner interview.
43. *Defense Special Weapons Agency, 1947-1997*, p. 15.
44. Purposes of tests through this period are summarized in DNA operations reports 6321F, 6322F, and 6325F.
45. Wikner interview.
46. *Ibid.*
47. DASA, *History of DASA, 1947-1971,* Part 2, Headquarters, Chapter 8–Weapons Effects and Tests, Section 8-3–Radiation, DSWA Technical Resource Center, 34 (hereafter: DASA: *History of DASA,* Part 2, Chapter 8).
48. DASA: *History of DASA,* Part 2, Chapter 8, p. 32.
49. Dr. Marv Atkins, interview by Rodney P. Carlisle, October 10, 1997.
50. DASA: *History of DASA,* Part 2, Chapter 8, pp. 45, 66.
51. *Ibid.*, pp. 67-68.
52. Operations Flintlock and Latchkey, p. 127; Wikner interview.
53. *Ibid.*; Monroe interview, pp. 8-10.
54. DASA: *History of DASA,* Part 2, Chapter 8, p. 68.
55. *Ibid.*, p. 69.
56. Telephone conversation, R. Carlisle with John Lewis, September 25, 1998.
57. Atkins interview.
58. General observations regarding the evolution of testing and testing procedures through the period derived from review of DNA operations reports 6321F, 6322F, and 6325F.
59. Defense Nuclear Agency, Operations *Anvil, Cresset, Tinderbox,* and *Guardian,* Events *Husky Pup, Mighty Epic, Hybla Gold, Diablo Hawk, Huron King,* and *Miners Iron*, October 24, 1975 - October 31, 1980, DNA Report 6325F (Kirtland AFB, New Mexico, 1989), pp. 20-21.
60. Operations *Anvil* and *Cresset*, pp. 10-11.
61. *Ibid.*, p. 12.
62. See Defense Nuclear Agency, Operations *Crosstie and Bowline*, Events *Door Mist, Dorsal Fin, Milk Shake, Diana Moon, Hudson Seal,* and *Ming Vase*, August 31, 1967 - November 20, 1968, DNA Report 6322F, Kirtland AFB, New Mexico, 1985, pp. 43-44. For reasons that DoD test crews switched to tunnels and for information on how pipe and other equipment were reused, see Operations *Crosstie* and *Bowline*, p. 140.
63. Atkins interview.
64. *Operations Flintlock and Latchkey*, p. 46.
65. Wikner interview.

66. *Operations Flintlock and Latchkey*, p. 96.
67. *Ibid.*, pp. 103-104.
68. *Ibid.*, pp. 103-110.
69. *Ibid.*
70. *Ibid.*, p. 105.
71. *Ibid.*, p. 110.
72. *Ibid.*
73. Shaun Gregory, *The Hidden Cost of Deterrence: Nuclear Weapon Accidents*, Washington, D.C., 1990, pp. 27-30.
74. Harris, *Defense Nuclear Responsibilities*, p. 90.
75. Gregory, *Hidden Cost of Deterrence*, pp. 27-30; Harris, *Defense Nuclear Responsibilities*, pp. 63-64, 90.
76. Harris, *Defense Nuclear Responsibilities*, p. 90.
77. Gregory, *Hidden Cost of Deterrence*, pp. 27-28.
78. *Ibid.*, pp. 28-29. PAL Category B production is discussed in DASA, History of DASA, 1959-1969, Part 1, Chapter 3, pp. 113-14, 134, 157-58, and 186.
79. Gregory, *Hidden Cost of Deterrence*, p. 30.
80. Feaver, *Guarding the Guardians*, p. 207.
81. *Ibid.*, p. 208.
82. *Ibid.*
83. *Ibid.*, p. 39; Gregory, *Hidden Cost of Deterrence*, p. 33.
84. *Ibid.*, p. 26; Defense Nuclear Agency, *Palomares Summary Report*: Field Command, Defense Nuclear Agency, Technology and Analysis Directorate, Kirtland Air Force Base, New Mexico, Accession #NV0067458, Department of Energy, Nevada Coordination and Information Center, p. 13.
85. *Ibid.*, pp. 13-24.
86. *Ibid.*, p. 191.
87. For a full narrative account of this accident, see Tad Szulc, *The Bombs of Palomares*, New York, 1967. For details on the public relations situation, see pp. 168-77, 214-18.
88. Defense Nuclear Agency, *Palomares Summary Report*, p. 17.
89. Gregory, *Hidden Cost of Deterrence*, p. 26.
90. *Ibid.*, p. 164.
91. Harris, *Defense Nuclear Responsibilities*, p. 70.
92. Gregory, *Hidden Cost of Deterrence*, pp. 163-64.
93. *Ibid.*, p. 167.
94. History of DASA, Part 2, Chapter 8, p. 33.
95. *Ibid.*, p. 34.
96. *Ibid.*, p. 31.
97. DASA: *History of DASA*, Part 2, Chapter 8, pp. 74, 77-79, 97-99.
98. William Harnin, "Privates and Generals Study A-Bomb," *Popular Mechanics*, August, 1956, pp. 110-12, 210.
99. *Defense Atomic Support Agency, Semi-annual Historical Report of Atomic Weapons Training Group, July 1 - December 31 1966*, DSWA Technical Resource Center (unpaginated).
100. DASA, Semiannual Historical Report, p. 30.
101. DoD Directive 5105.33, dated November 20, 1964, as cited in Armed Forces Radiobiology Research Institute, Command Historical Report for calendar year 1964, dated January 28, 1965.
102. AFRRI, "Functional Statements," no date, c. 1965.
103. "Historical Report," July 1 - December 31 1965, AFRRI SP66-18, January 1966, p. 1.
104. "Historical Report," AFRRI, SP66-22, July 1966, p. 26.
105. "Historical Report" July 1 - December 31 1967, AFRRI SP68-1.
106. Wikner interview; Monroe interview.
107. Harris, *Defense Nuclear Responsibilities*, pp. 109-11.
108. Harris, *Defense Nuclear Responsibilities*, pp. 110-13, 115.
109. Gilbert W. Fitzhugh, et al., Report to the President and the Secretary of Defense on the Department of Defense by the Blue Ribbon Defense Panel, July 1, 1970 (Washington, D.C., 1970), iii, 1 (hereafter Blue Ribbon Defense Panel Report).
110. Fitzhugh, Blue Ribbon Defense Panel Report, 43-44; Atkins interview.
111. Atkins interview.

CHAPTER SIX

ANOTHER WAY, 1970 TO 1980

"*We shall continue, in this era of negotiation, to work for the limitation of nuclear arms, and to reduce the danger of confrontation between the great powers. Let us build a structure of peace in the world..."*

President Richard M. Nixon,
Second Inaugural Address,
January 20, 1973

CRISIS OF CONFIDENCE

The basic changes in American popular values in the late 1960s and the early 1970s affected many questions central to the very existence of the Department of Defense and DASA. Americans changed their views of the federal government in general, of the Executive branch, of the conduct of international affairs, and of the military Services. Americans had even come to mistrust the triumphs of "Yankee ingenuity," long a mainstay of American pride and self-confidence. That confidence in technology had reached a culmination in the early Apollo project of the 1960s, a confidence that quickly waned by the mid-1970s.

This *crisis of confidence* had been mounting for several years. But for agencies of government attempting to meet their established missions, the change in public perception and in Congressional attitude occurred in a very short span of years, and the change would directly affect the mission of DASA. In 1969, Congress had rallied to support a wide variety of national defense and technology-related efforts; whereas by 1974, after Vietnam and Watergate, there was a different Congress, with new demands and expectations.

A host of new public issues impinged on the agency's areas of responsibility. Clearly, DASA would have to find "another way" of doing business in this decade of change. Concern with the exposure of individuals to radiation, that sprang from the new levels of suspicion of government and from new levels of concern with the impact of science and technology upon public health and the environment, led to examination of radiation exposure experienced by the "downwinders," residents in Utah and Nevada affected by fallout from early atmospheric testing at NTS. However, the AEC, not DASA, bore the brunt of most of those particular nuclear-related concerns.

Congress reorganized the AEC in 1975, partly in response to such issues. To many in Congress it seemed no longer appropriate that the agency promoting nuclear power should engage in regulating it. As a consequence, the research and development side of nuclear weapons and nuclear power became the core of one new agency, the Energy Research and Development Administration (ERDA), while another new agency, the Nuclear Regulatory Commission (NRC) took on the function of regulating nuclear energy. In 1978, Congress established the Department of Energy (DOE), which took over the functions of ERDA.

PACKARD COMMISSION AND AGENCY REORGANIZATION

As controversies related to nuclear weapons and nuclear research mounted, DASA did not emerge entirely unscathed. Initially, DASA's functions had been slightly reduced as a result of the Blue Ribbon Defense Panel (BRDP) recommendations contained within the Packard Commission report. On March 29, 1971, to be effective on July 1, 1971, the Deputy Secretary of Defense, David Packard, directed that DASA be reorganized. He retained DASA, with reduced responsibilities and a new title, the Defense Nuclear Agency (DNA). On January 1, 1972, DNA disestablished the Test Command and transferred its personnel to Field Command, in Albuquerque, New Mexico. The Test Directorate at Field Command took over direction of field operations for nuclear weapon effects tests, with Headquarters, DASA, retaining test planning activities.[1]

Packard spelled out the specific changes that would accompany the transformation of DASA into DNA. Initially, DNA functions would be limited to nuclear weapon management, nuclear weapon testing, and nuclear weapon effects research; second, in Albuquerque, the Kirtland Air Force Base, the Sandia Base and the Manzano Base would be consolidated under Air Force control; third, the military Departments would take full responsibility for nuclear training; and fourth, host-manager responsibilities at Johnston Atoll would remain with the Air Force.[2]

Even though the Packard Commission had suggested transfer of the Armed Forces Radiobiology Research Institute, the agency retained the medical research facility. As Admiral Mustin pointed out, AFRRI began to make more progress under DASA administration, in terms of research and development results, than it had under Navy administration prior to 1964. After presenting this argument to David Packard, Mustin claimed, the Deputy Secretary decided to retain AFRRI under DNA control. Mustin argued that the "Mansfield Amendment," that prohibited the Armed Services from sponsoring research that did not have a military application, precluded AFRRI from undertaking broad-based radiological basic research. With a focus on military applications under DNA, AFRRI would con-

Lieutenant General Caroll H. Dunn, DNA Director 1971 to 1973.

form to the letter and spirit of the Mansfield Amendment.[3]

Stockpile responsibility of the agency now consisted of inspection of units of the Services that actually held the weapons to ensure safe practices. Conduct of nuclear effects tests, in the range of one or two per year, continued as another DNA responsibility. However, with the ability to mount numerous effects tests at the same time, and with the increase in technical know-how, underground testing became more routine. As weapon system engineers developed experience and understanding of nuclear weapon effects, designing various forms of hardening also became more routine. The Joint Service training function of DNA had been transferred to the individual Services, further reducing the scale of the agency's operations. The Joint Service training activity at Field Command was transferred to the Air Force.[4]

The changeover from DASA to DNA took place in several steps. In fiscal year 1970-71, the Sandia Base Hospital transferred from DASA to the Department of the Army, and JTF-8 was dissolved. JTF-8 had maintained a staff of 55 military personnel at Johnston Atoll to manage the facility. Johnston Atoll, which was held in readiness by the Air Force for possible use if atmospheric testing were to be resumed, would continue under Air Force control. Administration of the Atoll was assumed by DNA in 1973 primarily due to "Safeguard C" testing requirements.

The reorganization plan for DASA—developed during the 1970-1971 timeframe—went into effect in 1971-1972. The official establishment of DNA took place in a charter issued November 3, 1971. With the transfer of stockpile, training, and other responsibilities from DASA to the Services, the agency staff fell from about 6,500 in 1969 at DASA, to about 1,200 in 1973 at DNA.[5] The rapid drop in personnel largely resulted from the transfer of the responsibility to provide guards and personnel at each of the stockpile sites. As Admiral Mustin pointed out to Congress in 1971, the agency staff had been drastically reduced from its peak year in 1959, as shown in Table 6-1. The transfer of stockpile responsibility alone had reduced DASA by half by 1970-1971, even before the conversion to the new organization of DNA.[6]

DNA: THE NEW POLICY CLIMATE

DNA thus became a leaner agency with a lower profile in the Services than DASA. The changing climate of values and policies affected the mission and agenda of the agency in a number of other major ways through the decade. Early in the 1970s, concern with the effect of nuclear weapon tests on public health, arising from the "downwinder" cases, increased public concern for two other groups of individuals: the Pacific Islanders who had been displaced during nuclear weapon testing on Bikini and Enewetak, and the military and civilians who had attended the above-ground tests in the Pacific and in Nevada.

Table 6-1. Agency Staffing, Civilian and Military, 1959 to 1973.

1959	1969	1970	1973
8,760	6,500	4,081	1,200

As the organizational heirs of the Joint Task Forces that operated the Pacific and Nevada tests, DNA inherited the task of addressing the concerns of test participants. The changing international attitudes toward nuclear weapons also affected the responsibilities of DNA. With detente came a series of arms control agreements, limiting the scale of underground nuclear testing, the deployment of ABM systems, the proliferation of nuclear weapons to new countries, and the emplacement of nuclear weapons in new environments by the existing nuclear-armed countries. The ABM Treaty of 1972 achieved the limitation on ABM systems that McNamara had sought in the mid-1960s. Without an anti-missile defense of fixed U.S. strategic missile sites, alternate forms of protecting American missiles by making them more survivable became attractive, leading planners to work on alternative basing systems.

Continued pressure for nuclear arms limitation and for limitation on testing generated a movement for a comprehensive test ban. Leaders at DNA and elsewhere in the defense establishment questioned whether the United States should enter a comprehensive test ban; many believed such a ban could place the whole weapon development program in jeopardy. Vice Admiral Monroe later argued that the United States would be unable to maintain a credible nuclear deterrent without a sustained weapons' improvement and test program. Peter Haas and Ed Conrad, both Deputy Directors (Science and Technology) under Monroe, and responsible for the preparation of the agency's Congressional testimony, developed arguments for weapon effects testing of strategic systems and forwarded them to the DDR&E and Congressional staffs. Advocates of continued testing within and outside the agency believed that a comprehensive test ban

Lieutenant General Warren Johnson, DNA Director 1973 to 1977.

would represent unilateral nuclear disarmament and placed U.S. strategic systems at unacceptable risk. Their efforts to forestall the test ban prevailed and, in part, made possible the validation of the nuclear hardness of U.S. strategic systems.

Despite adjustment to new national priorities, continuing responsibilities and established trends still drove DNA's policy. Technological progress, particularly due to integrated electronic circuitry and the development of faster and smaller computer components, aided the development of new and enhanced weapons. Although the number of nuclear weapons developed in the 1970s declined from the previous decade, two new warheads and a new missile went from the development laboratories to DNA for effects and vulnerability testing before entering the arsenal. The move to mobile launching system concepts spawned a series of tests of underground structures, tunnels, trenches, and communication systems. The advent of the B-1 manned bomber prompted EMP hardness testing of aircraft designs.

The adoption of a computerized inventory system allowed DNA to instantly check on the location of critical weapon parts and their currency. Computer simulation of the effects of nuclear weapons detonated over land brought the realization that unanticipated dirt and dust lofted into the atmosphere could create a new class of weapons effects that required further study.

THEATER DETERRENCE AND DEFENSE

The emergence of Soviet nuclear forces in the 1950s shaped a nuclear force policy and strategy in the U.S. that persisted for decades. Influencing these developments were the operational experiences of World War II, the unfavorable conventional force balance in postwar Europe, and the leadership required of the United States for the free world which was slowly recovering from the ravages of that war.

The 1950s saw the formulation of offensive nuclear forces for the nation and its friends and allies, manned aircraft were the principal means. These strategic forces were created and matured with the development of new aircraft and new bombs; later augmented with long-range ballistic missiles. The U.S. also developed a nuclear-armed, strategic defense force made up of manned interceptors and surface-to-air missiles. With the establishment of NATO came the decision on the use of U.S. strategic forces. This policy, in the late 1950s, was given the name of massive retaliation, although terms like brinksmanship were used earlier.

Early in NATO's history, General Eisenhower, as Supreme Allied Commander Europe (SACEUR), along with his staff, conducted studies to address the conventional (non-nuclear) defense of Europe in the face of substantial Soviet ground forces. In the most comprehensive of these studies, the Lisbon Planning Conference surfaced the need for at least 90 Army divisions, and approximately 10,000 aircraft, for the conventional defense of Europe. For the most part, the nations of Europe were largely destroyed by the war fought there from 1939 to 1946, and Great Britain, although suffering less in the way of physical destruction, had been largely bankrupted by the war. It was clear that there was a significant gap between the desires of the military planners and what the nations could provide. When elected President, Eisenhower came to office with these blunt and disturbing facts in mind.

In his early presidency, Eisenhower effected a compromise, which included creating theater nuclear forces. A lower NATO objective, of approximately 26 ready divisions and 1,400 aircraft, were set as goals. These would result from the buildup of national forces, including those of the Federal Republic of Germany. In addition, there would be a theater nuclear force, whose composition would be underwritten entirely by the United States. This force would be based upon a firepower replacement concept to make up, with destructive power, the shortfall in conventional numbers and capabilities. A coupling was to exist between the strategic and theater nuclear force components. The overall strategy was one of massive retaliation. This policy was embodied in a NATO Military Committee document "14/2," sometimes referred to as the NATO Nuclear Strategy. The operational concept for all these forces was one that merged the technical destructive character of nuclear weapons with the successful characteristics of World War II forces.

The 1960s saw substantiated refinements and modernization. These were focused for more than a decade on the

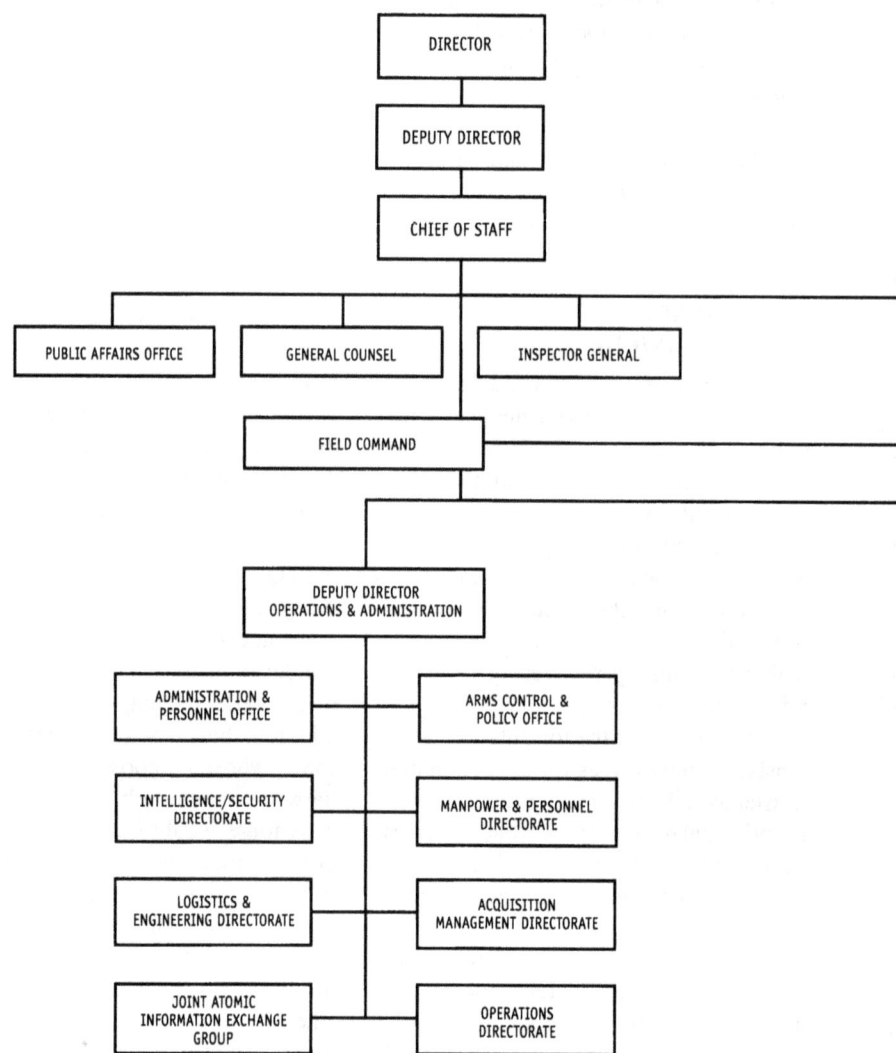

DNA Oganizational Chart, 1971.

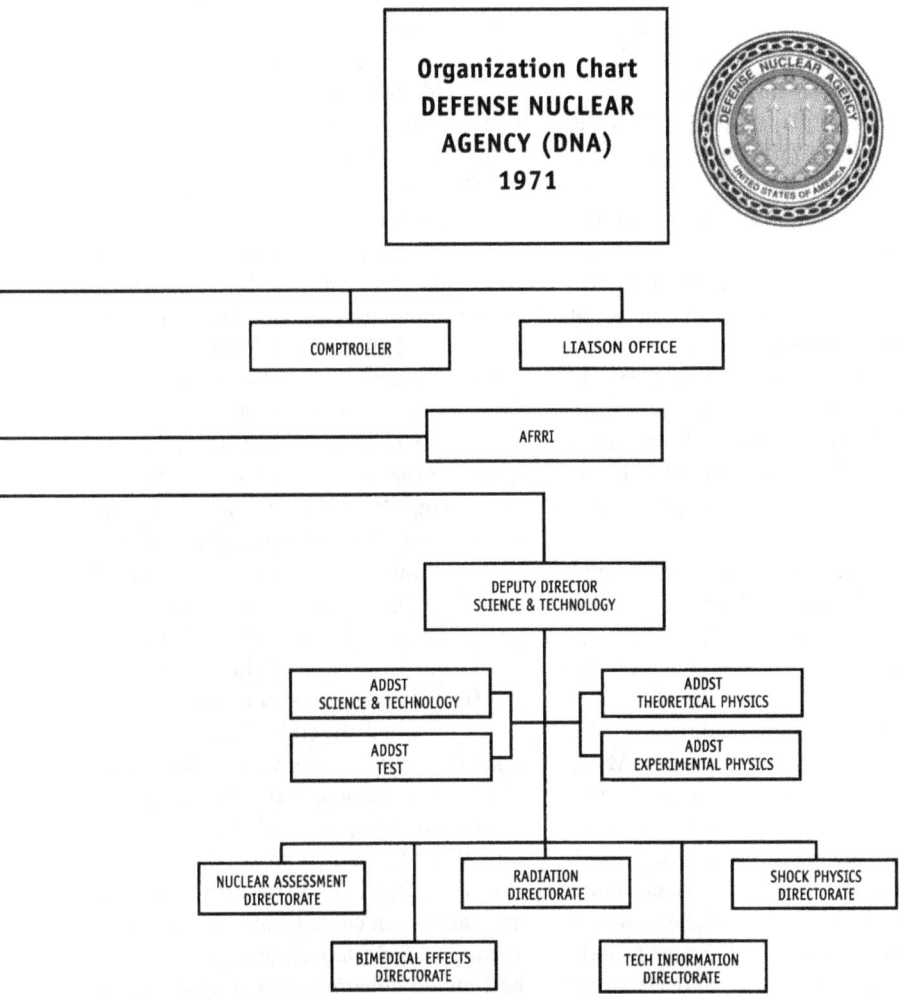

strategic triad, and intelligence and command central improvements such as early warning and attack assessment capabilities. During this period, theater and tactical forces were expanded quantitatively using the previously mentioned firepower replacement concept.

In the late 1960s and early 1970s, the Nixon administration and Congress addressed the need for a more comprehensive strategy to underwrite deterrence and defense should deterrence fail. The signing of the ABM treaty and the termination of the U.S. strategic defense program added additional pressure on this strategy. What emerged over the next decade and a half was profoundly different from the past. It is important to understand the differences and the state of the firepower replacement program as the nation entered the 1970s.

Theater forces, in the late 1950s, could be called firepower replacement forces, since nuclear warheads replaced conventional warheads in conventional combat systems. In the Army, the missile-based air defense forces were nuclearized. The Nike-Hercules and Hawk, the SAM-D, the predecessor of the Patriot missile, was intended to be nuclear but political considerations intervened. All of the Army's artillery missiles were nuclearized, starting with the Pershing and Sergeant, which was followed by Lance. Nuclear rounds were developed for the 280-mm, 203-mm, and 155-mm artillery systems. The Davy Crockett was an infantry crew-launched weapon of low yield, intended to be used in a close battle environment. Atomic Demolition Munitions were provided to the engineers for breaching obstacles and/or creating obstacles.

In the Air Force, nuclear munitions were provided for air-delivered bombs and air-to-air missiles. The Navy experienced a nuclear upgrade in the same sense of changing conventional lethality mechanisms to nuclear for surface-to-air weapons, surface-to-surface weapons, air-to-surface weapons, and anti-submarine warfare weapons. Much of this was accomplished by the late 1950s and early 1960s. Doctrine and concepts were developed, although, in many cases, the concept followed the development of the actual weapons systems.

Doctrinal efforts concentrated on tactical warfighting and were based on the combination of environment effects and physical vulnerabilities. DNA provided response/vulnerability data from field experiments. Efforts to understand the operational and tactical implications took the form of major experiments such as the Army's Oregon Trail, and the reorganization of the Army into a so-called Pentomic Army. At the same time, dispersion of air bases, for both launch and recovery, was implemented by the Air Force. The Navy likewise took measures to improve survivability of the fleet at sea.

Toward the end of the 1960s, the NATO Alliance adopted a new nuclear strategy called Flexible Response, embodied in Military Committee document "14/3." It was not universally acclaimed. Some have argued that it led to the departure of the French from the military element of NATO. When the Nixon administration came to office in the late 1960s, it conducted a thorough review of both threat developments and the policy for nuclear forces for the nation and the Alliance. The initiatives which grew out of this review were developed by Secretary Schlesinger, Senator Nunn, the Services, and by other senior people, including the leadership of DNA. The agency put substantial energy into alternative concepts to provide an adequate deterrent and defense should deterrence fail; where both deterrence and defense might be more viable without an early resort to the use of nuclear forces, but, at the same time, taking advantage of the presence of these forces. DNA led the way in providing the intellectual underpinning for what was demanded by the leadership; not only the DoD but to Congress as well.

Continuing collaboration was effected with OSD, led by Mr. Donald Cotter, as the Assistant to the Secretary of Defense for Atomic Energy, ATSD(AE), the leadership of DNA encompassing its Directors, its DDSTs, and the various CINCs responsible for the regions where nuclear forces were based and might be employed. The basis for this coordination was the development of new concepts. The major change embodied in these ideas was to focus planning, training, and modernization on a combination of both operational and physical considerations. It was a much wider base of consideration than before, and it led to more effective options. As a result, DNA initiated a New Alternatives program with the Defense Advanced Research Projects Agency (DARPA), seeking to improve both conventional and nuclear forces and—in some cases—even decrease dependence upon nuclear forces. Thus, the beginnings of the 1970s was a time of substantial change that affected theater forces as well as strategic forces.

With this as background, the theater developments, that started in the early 1970s, resulted from a four-pronged initiative by DNA on behalf of SACEUR and with CINCPAC. The first point involved characterizing Soviet operations at a level of detail sufficient to understand the strengths, the weaknesses, and the opportunities for new or improved Alliance operations. In a sense, these new initiatives strove to "target" vulnerabilities within Soviet doctrine for the offensive use of Warsaw Pact Forces as well as the forces themselves. Next, the formulation and examination of alternative options, which were political-military, for the use of conventional and nuclear forces. Third, the examination of technologies which could contribute to the alternative options. Fourth, the intersection of these with components of planning, training, and the use of infrastructure such as surveillance assets. Again, DNA made a substantial investment in its activities in understanding the interaction between new policies and strategies with military concepts and new technologies. The dollar value of these efforts was small compared to the overall agency budget, but the yield was very high.

At the same time, the Army and the Air Force were initiating both conceptual and system development activities, which would improve forward defenses in Europe. They borrowed liberally from DNA's work. The Army developed new forward defense concepts based upon the very successful fielding of a new family of highly accurate, highly lethal and very affordable anti-armor weapons to offset the major advantage the Soviets had in armor. The Air Force was developing precision-guided weapons, which would permit them to effectively attack fixed targets and some movable targets in ways which were difficult or impossible beforehand. These developments offered the opportunity to make major changes in the structuring and deployment of forces. They also imposed threats on the Soviet forces, which added to their dispersion requirements in the face of the theater nuclear threat.

In the early 1980s, these efforts by DNA culminated in a series of doctrinal innovations, which included Air-Base and Infrastructure attack programs of the Air Force, the AirLand Battle jointly developed by the Air Force and the Army, and Follow-On Forces Attack (FOFA) promulgated by NATO and agreed to by its member nations. In the U.S., it led to the modernization effort called the Deep Attack Program, a $55 billion acquisition program to underwrite AirLand Battle and Follow-On Forces Attack concepts.

DNA played a key role in the development of the military requirements, for the nuclear Ground-Launched Cruise Missile and the improvement to the Pershing missile, by conducting the key Cost and Operational Effectiveness Analysis (COEA) for the Army. These developments, in turn, led to substantial improvements in conventional capabilities. The new nuclear systems also demonstrated improved nuclear survivability over the previous posture. DNA directly assisted the operational community in understanding new technologies and assuring overall theater nuclear force survivability. The agency, in effect, provided the schoolhouse and subject matter experts for U.S. Commands and their forces, the Multinational Alliance Commands, and materiel commands as well. It also provided substantial technical assistance for the conventional and nuclear improvements undertaken by the DoD acquisition community. Finally, all these efforts, under the Theater Deterrence and Defense umbrella, led to the establishment of a Theater Nuclear Force Survivability, Security, and Safety (TNFS^3) Program, which addressed every threat to Theater Nuclear Forces (TNF). These efforts were the "crown jewels" of the agency's TNF mission thrust during the decade and ultimately, led the Army and Air Force, "kicking and screaming," into accepting new doctrine.

ENVIRONMENT AND EXPOSURE: JOHNSTON ATOLL

At Johnston Atoll, DNA took on a variety of relatively low profile administrative duties during the 1970s, which touched on the issues of environment and exposure resulting from its administrative role as the DoD's central agency for dealing with nuclear issues. On the Atoll, where DNA's Field Command served as the local government following transfer from the Air Force in July 1973, administrators took up such prosaic issues as mail delivery and demolition of fire-hazard wooden structures and laundry facilities. These duties were minor compared to the issues of environment and exposure.[7]

Retroactive records of radiation exposure of military and contractor personnel at Johnston Atoll continued to be a major issue. In June of 1978, McDonnell Douglas Corporation requested that DNA provide Johnston Atoll radiation exposure data in connection with a workman's compensation claim alleging death due to plutonium exposure. Local DNA staff retrieved the data from historical files and forwarded it to DNA Headquarters for distribution to McDonnell Douglas through the Public Affairs Office.[8]

In 1976, DNA Director Lieutenant General Warren Johnson urged the JCS to modify the language surrounding "Safeguard C," that is, the stipulation that the United States remain ready to "promptly resume atmospheric testing." Johnson recommended that the term "promptly" be deleted. With the implementation of this change in 1977, Johnson reduced the readiness stature at the Atoll, declaring much testing equipment as surplus and reducing the operating and maintenance budget there by about $5 million per year.[9]

In 1972, following the Vietnam War, more than 10,000 tons of Agent Orange had been stored in some 27,000 fifty-five gallon drums on Johnston Atoll, and DNA Field Command was given the responsibility for its destruction. During 1977, Field Command coordinated Agent Orange incineration at sea. The incineration method used diesel fuel to rinse the herbicide drums and the loading and dedrumming equipment, which was then mixed with the herbicide for burning. The burning took place on the open sea, about 120 miles west of Johnston Atoll. The motor tanker *Vulcanus* took 3,300 tons of the Agent Orange aboard, mixed it with diesel fuel, then spent ten days on station, burning the mix in three separate voyages in the period July-September of 1977. The Air Force monitored the atmosphere and stated that the disposal met all Environmental Protection Agency (EPA) standards. Extensive analysis of samples of water from Johnston Atoll and adjacent areas found no contamination as a result of the disposal.[10]

However, during the testing of the drinking water on Johnston Atoll for Agent Orange residue, the Air Force Environmental Health Laboratory discovered measurable quantities of polychlorinated biphenyls (PCBs), a chemical regarded as potentially carcinogenic. Tests revealed the concentration in the drinking water at 1 to 3 parts per billion (ppb). Engineers suspected the plastic liners of the reservoirs as the source of the PCBs, which was verified when administrators took both reservoirs off the water system. The PCB concentration then fell below the detectable level of .2 ppb. With the reservoirs off the system, the water production costs from desalinization doubled, so Field Command ordered the larger of the two reservoirs water-blasted to remove residues. Unfortunately, when engineers returned the reservoir to the water system, the PCB level once again climbed. Field Command decided to sandblast and recoat the reservoir, which corrected the problem.[11]

As the administrator for Johnston Atoll, DNA became involved in many civil government responsibilities, going well beyond environmental concerns, maintenance issues, and security operations. For example, even though no commercial shipping or aircraft routinely served Johnston Atoll, its remote location itself made the island important to travelers in the Central Pacific. The Atoll is the only land in several hundred square miles of ocean, and as a result, it became an emergency haven for both ships and aircraft. During 1977-1978, it served as the refuge or medical evacuation point for 114 people, of whom 42 had been rescued by a Japanese fishing boat, *Taiki Maru*, from the sinking Philippine-registered ship *La Carlotta*.[12]

BIKINI CLEANUP

When DASA took on the cleanup of Bikini Atoll in 1969, it was the first such effort in the world to repair a landscape damaged by nuclear tests. The Atoll had been the site of 23 atmospheric and underwater nuclear detonations in four series: two shots in Operation CROSSROADS in 1946, five shots in Operation CASTLE in 1954, six shots of Operation REDWING in 1956, and ten shots of the series Operation HARDTACK in 1958. The BRAVO shot of the CASTLE series at Bikini received perhaps the most public attention of all the Pacific nuclear tests. Fallout from this 15 MT detonation, carried to the east rather than to the north, as predicted, contaminated the atolls of Rongelap, Alinginae, and Rongerik, where U.S. authorities had resettled residents from Bikini. The public response concerning BRAVO spurred a world-wide movement for a limited nuclear test ban treaty.[13]

In December of 1966, Secretary of the Interior Stewart Udall made two inquiries to the AEC regarding Bikini. He asked if the island was safe for habitation and when the inhabitants might have hazard-free use of the resources of the Atoll. After several radiological surveys of the island, in August of 1968, President Lyndon Johnson announced that the United States no longer required Bikini for nuclear testing. In January of 1969, the JCS designated the Director of DASA as the project manager for the Defense Department to cooperate with the AEC in the first phase of the Bikini cleanup.[14]

In the nine-month cleanup operation in 1969, DASA worked with the AEC in the first phase of the cleanup of the Atoll, dismantling abandoned nuclear test facilities and disposing of radioactive debris on the islands of the Atoll. The U.S. State Department then turned the island over to the Trust Territory of the Pacific Islands (TTPI), for completion of five more years of rehabilitation of the islands preparatory to the return of the Bikini natives to the island from Kili island, an isolated and inhospitable spot over 400 miles away, where they had to subsist almost entirely on imported food.[15]

Bikini had been abandoned for 11 years, and it included not only the remains of the nuclear weapon tests, but wreckage and debris from World War II. A sealift opportunity came with transport by the Navy of troops and equipment to Vietnam, and using the Navy ship *Belle Grove*, a DASA work force landed on February 17, 1969, to begin cleanup efforts.

Forces under the command of JTF-8 conducted the operation, including both DoD and AEC personnel stationed in Honolulu and on Johnston Atoll. Immediately after landing on the island, crews went to work clearing overgrown vegetation from an old airstrip on the island of Eneu.[16] Within five days, a team cleared, graded, and compacted a 4,600 foot coral runway. A Military Airlift Command C-54 landed five days after the first landing, and began making weekly support deliveries of personnel, food, equipment, mail, and movies. Later, C-124s delivered over 300 tons of cargo through this airstrip.[17] During the course of the cleanup, over 40,000 tons of scrap and rubble were buried.[18]

The project continued from February to June of 1969, using JTF-8 provided landing craft and barges.[19] Crews buried thousands of tons of concrete rubble, and used some 800 tons of concrete rubble to provide riprap to protect the runway from wave damage. Many salvageable buildings were cleaned out and left intact.[20]

At the time of the Bikini administration turn over on October 12, 1969, an agency report noted the project ahead of schedule and $300,000 under budget. Contractor crews soon followed to lay out housing sites, plant trees, and prepare for the return of the islanders.

Shortly after the successful cleanup of Bikini, just as native peoples were beginning to return, the issue arose of cleaning up the Pacific Atoll that had been used for even more testing than at either Bikini or Johnston.

CLEANUP AT ENEWETAK

The testing program at Enewetak, as at Bikini, had left a legacy of damage and radioactivity, but the contrasts and differences between the two projects warrant close inspection. Enewetak, in the western region of the Marshall islands some 200 nautical miles from Bikini, had been occupied by the Japanese during World War II. Enewetak had been temporarily evacuated during the first Pacific nuclear tests of the CROSSROADS series at Bikini in 1946. The AEC established the Enewetak Proving Ground in 1947, and in October of that year, Joint Task Force-7 (JTF-7) began to prepare the Atoll for the SANDSTONE series of nuclear tests. The native people, the *dri-Enewetak* and *dri-Engebi*, after a brief return to their island following the CROSSROADS tests, were again evacuated to Ujelang in December of 1947, where they remained for over 30 years. The 136 evacuees and their descendants made clear their desire to return to their homeland.

Bikini natives loading their gear into LST-1108 in preparation for evacuation, 1946.

Over the decade 1948-1958, the United States detonated 43 nuclear and thermonuclear devices on the islands of the Enewetak Atoll, in the Atoll lagoon, on barges, and on towers. A few detonations were very high yield hydrogen-fusion devices, such as the MIKE shot at 10.4 megatons on October 31, 1952, and the 8.9 megaton OAK shot in the HARDTACK series on June 28, 1958. Table 6-2 details the test series on Enewetak during the 1948-1958 period.[21]

As a consequence of the tests, two islands, Elugelab and Lidibut, were completely obliterated along with most of two others. Nine of the shots had taken place on or near Runit, and the surface-emplaced CACTUS shot of May 5, 1958 had created a wide crater at the northern tip of the island into which the sea flowed. Even on island areas with slight radiological damage, ruined habitat and waste scarred the few livable acres of land.[22]

The agreement between the DoD and the DOI under which Enewetak Atoll had been used for nuclear testing came under review by the parties June 30, 1961 and every five years afterwards. During the 1971 review, the DoD agreed to terminate the use of Enewetak as a test range and to return it to the Trust Territory. Under the original agreement between the DOI, as the Trust Territory representative, and the DoD, upon the decision to leave, the U.S. would have 30 days to remove any improvements and structures it wished to take, and then to leave everything else for the Trust Territory government. However, as the DNA official report later noted, "the United States recognized a moral, if

Table 6-2. Enewetak Tests, 1948 through 1958.

Year	Series	Number of Shots
1948	SANDSTONE	3
1951	GREENHOUSE	4
1951	IVY	2
1954	CASTLE	1
1956	REDWING	11
1958	HARDTACK I	22

not legal, obligation to restore the Atoll to a more habitable condition."[23] An immediate departure would leave debris, ruined buildings, and numerous radiologically contaminated areas.

Following an interagency conference in February of 1972, Interior officials notified the U.S. Ambassador to the Micronesian Status Negotiations, Franklin H. Williams, that the United States would begin cleanup and restoration of the Atoll and planned to return it to the Trust Territory. Although the DOI anticipated return of the atoll in 1973, planning, funding, and a series of administrative and jurisdictional issues delayed completion of the process for seven years.[24]

Lieutenant General Caroll H. Dunn, Director of DNA, went to Enewetak in September 1972 to personally survey the situation. He ordered an immediate start on a pre-cleanup survey. Later that year, Secretary of Defense Melvin Laird formally notified the Joint Chiefs of Staff that DNA would be the responsible agency for the cleanup, and requested that the Director of DNA be designated as Project Manager. The Joint Chiefs accepted the recommendation, and authorized DNA to act for the DoD in planning and operations.[25] The choice of DNA reflected the agency's prior history of involvement in similar, but smaller scale clean-up operations at Palomares, Thule, and, especially, Bikini.[26]

Lieutenant General Warren Johnson, Dunn's successor at DNA, faced a complex new mission, now including the operation of two island groups: Johnston Atoll and Enewetak. The Air Force transferred Johnston Atoll to DNA in July 1973, and Enewetak on January 1, 1974.[27] Suddenly, the agency became, in effect, a temporary governing agent of two remote island territories.

DNA originally planned to subcontract the work of the cleanup of Enewetak. The Pacific Ocean Division of the Army Corps of Engineers, accomplished the actual contracting, including design, preparation, award of contract, and monitoring of contractors' performance. DNA expected to provide only conceptual guidance, leaving the administrative details to the Corps.[28] As it turned out, however, interagency concerns, funding, and logistical problems prevented such a simple solution.

While inspections, planning, and preparation of a Draft Environmental Impact Statement was being developed in 1974 and 1975, DNA worked with Congressional staffs to secure appropriations to cover the cost of the cleanup. During these planning stages, DNA officials considered several alternative plans to dispose of the radioactive waste and scrap from the islands, including ocean dumping, transfer of the materials to the continental United States, and crater entombment.[29]

All the plans seemed to have political or legal impediments. The shipment of waste to the United States proved costly and seemed likely to arouse political opposition. The EPA advised that ocean dumping, the method used legally and properly earlier at Bikini, would violate new domestic law and international agreements, established when the United States ratified the International Ocean Dumping Treaty in 1970. Furthermore, Public Law 92-532, Title I, Section 101c prohibited the dumping of radiological materials intended for warfare. DNA administrators doubted whether the letter of the law prevented dumping of residue from prior weapon tests. The EPA, however, insisted that it would interpret the law to require that any materials contaminated by plutonium, if dumped in the ocean, be housed in containers guaranteed to remain intact for 125,000 years. DNA recognized that ocean dumping would encounter severe legal problems and abandoned that option for any radiologically contaminated materials.[30]

At a number of conferences through 1975 and 1976, ERDA representatives, as the successors to AEC, continued to argue for an ocean-dumping solution on the grounds that the amount of radioactive material from Enewetak would represent a very small fraction of the total radioactive waste already dumped in the ocean. Since ERDA would be responsible for the long-term storage site if crater entombment were chosen, that agency preferred ocean dumping.[31]

350-foot wide CACTUS crater dome on Enewetak Atoll.

In the face of legal opinions and the opposition of both DNA and EPA to the ocean dumping concept, the DNA proposal for entombment prevailed. Under this plan, radiological debris would be transported to the large crater on Runit caused by the CACTUS shot of the HARDTACK series. Workers mixed the debris and contaminated soil with concrete, and pumped the mix into the crater and covered the mass with a thick concrete dome. After rehabilitation of several islands for residence, agriculture, and fishing, the *dri-Enewetak* and *dri-Engebi* would return to live on the southern islands of the Atoll. They agreed to avoid Runit and its domed repository of radioactive waste.

With the project still in the planning stage in 1974, General Johnson estimated that a full cleanup and restoration of all the islands would cost $200 to $300 million. Had the project required making all of the islands completely habitable, Johnson had probably made a reasonably accurate estimate. Considering that Congress had refused to support estimates in the much lower range of $40 million (eventually approving only $20 million for cleanup), Johnson concluded that either DNA would have to recommend less than a complete rehabilitation or the project would have to be declared not feasible. However, General Johnson felt strongly that the Government had a "moral obligation" to do everything within reason to accomplish the cleanup.[32]

Operations on the Atoll began in early 1977 and continued intensively over the next three years. Army engineers constructed a base camp and provided cleanup labor, while Air Force personnel operated communications equipment and aircraft, and the Navy provided military sealift command vessels to bring cargo and equipment. The three-year operation encountered many setbacks and difficulties, including two major typhoons in 1978, vast quantities of non-radiological debris that had to be hauled and dumped at three sites in the lagoon, and a number of difficulties with the construction of the entombment dome.[33]

Bureaucratic concerns led to further delays. For example, even though EPA had approved the environmental impact statement and all the plans, DNA decided that the Corps of Engineers should acquire all the usual permits to proceed with work. As a consequence, the Corps sought permits for disposal of non-radiological debris in the lagoon, for clearance of coral obstructions to channels into the lagoon, and for the main crater containment of contaminated debris and soil.[34]

The permit from the Corps of Engineers for the crater presented difficulties. Since the crater entombment project included levels below water, engineers assumed that water would migrate from the entombed area into the lagoon. Regulations required that anyone constructing a structure that might leach into navigable waterways had to commit to perpetually maintaining the structure. At the last moment, the Corps issued the permit in November of 1977, one week before the "mobilization phase" of entombment in the crater began.[35] The eventual entombment crater on Enewetak was called the CACTUS crater dome, which featured a massive circular concrete cover.

The project involved not only cleanup, but extensive preparation of home sites, agricultural plantings and provision of infrastructure, such as roads, utilities, and common areas.[36] With the completion of all such work, DNA returned the island to the Enewetak people, now numbering about 400, in a ceremony held on April 8, 1980.[37] The full population returned from Ujelang in several trips in early October of 1980.[38]

BIKINI AND ENEWETAK CLEANUPS COMPARED

A contrast between the speed and simplicity of the earlier operation to clean up Bikini and the project taken up by DNA to rehabilitate Enewetak is striking. Whereas the DASA Bikini project took about 9 months and less than $2 million, the DNA operation at Enewetak took nearly seven years and $19 million to bring to completion after three years of preliminary planning. First discussed in 1971, DNA fully completed the project in 1980.

There were similarities. The natural environments of both Bikini and Enewetak Atolls were damaged by the nuclear test program. At Bikini, in addition to the 1946 CROSSROADS test with two weapons, other series in 1954, 1956 and 1958, had resulted in the detonation of a total of 23 devices, ten of them in 1958. The BRAVO 15 megaton-yield thermonuclear device fired in 1954 at Bikini exceeded the yield of any fired at Enewetak.[39] While Enewetak saw 43 detonations and Bikini experienced only 23, the damage, waste, and radiological hazards at the two locations were roughly comparable. The reasoning behind the differences in cost and time can be attributed to several factors. JTF-8, in cleaning up Bikini, had not sought approvals from other agencies. Furthermore, the EPA did not come into existence until December 2, 1970, 14 months after the completion of the Bikini project.

The United States had not adhered to any treaty in 1969 to prohibit the dumping of radioactive waste at sea, nor did domestic law at that time preclude this approach. Thus, at Bikini, DASA never had to face the extensive costs of entombment, characteristic of the Enewetak cleanup undertaken by DNA a few years later. Furthermore, at Bikini, DASA had responsibility for only the very first phase of the cleanup, leaving full rehabilitation of the island for occupation to other agencies after JTF-8 departed. But at Enewetak, the agency prepared the islands for agriculture and residency. Table 6-3 provides further comparisons on the two island's cleanup effort.

Another cause of the broad contrast between the prompt restoration of Bikini in 1969, and the decade-long process at Enewetak, is the change in policy, procedures, and values between the two periods. In the late 1960s, President Johnson could order the cleanup of Bikini, and DASA could then immediately proceed to the task, employing existing JTF forces and relatively small amounts of already-appropriated funds. In the mid- and late-1970s, a similar decision required negotiation

Table 6-3. Enewetak and Bikini Restorations Compared.

	Bikini	**Enewetak**
Government Commitment	August 12, 1968	1971
Start of Work	February 17, 1969	March 1977
End of Work	September 22, 1969	April 1980
Cost	$1,300,000	$18,770,000
Number of Islands in Atoll	26	40
Lagoon Size	20 × 10 st. mi.	23 × 17 st. mi.
Lagoon Size in Miles	240 sq. mi.	388 sq. mi.
Acreage	894 acres	1,761 acres
Total Nuclear Weapons Tested at Atoll	23	43
Waste Disposed: Dumped at Sea	500 tons	125,000 tons (Non-radioactive)
Cubic Yards Removed	100,000	253,650
Population Resettled	100 temporary	450 permanent

through a hostile Congress for funding, considerable inter-agency communication and clearance, and extensive planning and documentation not needed only a few years before. Despite the fact that radiological standards had not changed, those standards were applied much more aggressively in the mid-1970s than they had been five to six years before.[40]

Arising from the different level of expenditure and care in the two cleanups, Bikini proved less safe for the returnees, in the long run, than Enewetak. At Enewetak, the islanders declared some contaminated islands off-limits entirely, and visited others only for food-gathering purposes, rather than settlement. Their settlements on Medren and Enewetak islands, carefully screened for radiological safety, became permanent residences, and those islands most targeted during the testing were simply not resettled.

A similar pattern of settlement had been arranged at Bikini. The Trust Territory government preferred that Bikini settlers return in small groups, allowing time for newly-established plants and trees to mature. Accordingly, between 1974 and 1977, over 100 Bikinians gradually returned to their Atoll. In the spring of 1977, however, regular testing of radiation revealed an alarming increase in radioactive cesium among the Bikinians.[41] Specialists traced the problem to the diet. Since the islanders preferred fresh food to imported supplies, they had exceeded recommended limits on plants and animals grown locally, especially coconuts from new groves. In the summer of 1978, the U.S. government removed the islanders once again. At the Enewetak project, specialists noted that the Bikinians suffered unexpectedly high levels of strontium and cesium from eating locally grown coconuts, and the agricultural and dietary plans for Enewetak natives were adjusted to take account of the news.[42]

The DNA effort to restore Enewetak turned out to be far more successful than the earlier Bikini cleanup by DASA. What appeared to be bureaucratic delay and constant negotiation paid off in the end. Resulting from the additional labor, time, and money expended, and because of more stringent concern with standards, health, and the well-being of the islanders that characterized the mid 1970s, the *dri-Enewetak* and *dri-Engebi* stayed on their islands permanently, while the Bikinians once again returned to exile.

In later years, the Bikinians won a settlement of over $200 million in compensation. While not returning to their island to live, they began to convert the site into a tourist destination. Over 2,300 descendants of the original 186 Bikinians removed from the island in 1946 now live on Kili, other islands in the Marshall islands, and in other countries.[43]

NEW DNA MISSION: NUCLEAR TEST PERSONNEL REVIEW

The Nuclear Test Personnel Review (NTPR) program grew out of one veteran's claim, initiated in 1977 at the Veterans' Administration (VA) office in Boise, Idaho. Retired sergeant Paul R. Cooper, a patient in the VA hospital in Salt Lake City, filed for disability payments, attributing his acute myelocytic leukemia to the radiation exposure he had received as a participant in shot SMOKY, conducted on August 31, 1957 as part of Operation PLUMBBOB. The VA denied Cooper's claim, but an appeals board later reversed the decision, noting that sufficient signs of the disease had been present when Cooper served on active duty to support his claim that his disability grew out of his military service. The appeals board, however, did not establish whether or not the disease stemmed from his radiation exposure at SMOKY.

While Cooper's case proceeded

through the VA, his physician at Salt Lake City contacted Dr. Glynn G. Caldwell, Chief of the Cancer Branch of the Centers for Disease Control (CDC) in Atlanta, expressing concern over the possibility of a connection between Cooper's disease and his exposure at SMOKY. Caldwell, in turn, contacted Colonel LaWayne R. Stromberg, USA, Director of AFRRI, a DNA subordinate organization, located in Bethesda, Maryland.

On the denial of his case in February of 1977, Cooper took his case to the media, and the event became a major news story in March and April. Within a few days, the CDC received letters from several dozen people who had participated in nuclear weapon tests. Within four months, the number increased to 2,000.[44]

Vice Admiral Robert Monroe succeeded Lieutenant General Warren Johnson as Director, DNA, in March of 1977, and found himself in the thick of the issues surrounding the exposure of Service personnel to nuclear detonations. Dr. Caldwell at the CDC notified DNA that he had identified three leukemia cases among personnel who had written to the CDC claiming to have participated in SMOKY. The number of cases exceeded the expectation for a comparable population, and Caldwell conducted a study of everyone who had been exposed at SMOKY. AFRRI representatives agreed that a complete roster of participants should be made available from the DoD. Researchers found information on service personnel participation in nuclear tests incomplete and scattered in archives and repositories across the country. An inter-agency ad hoc group recommended that DNA should function as the DoD executive agency for all matters pertaining to DoD personnel who had participated in the atmospheric nuclear test program.[45]

By the end of 1977, the DoD, and DNA in particular, became deeply committed to gathering the needed information and conducting a study of the relationship between atmospheric exposure at nuclear weapon tests and later evidence of cancer among participants. When the Subcommittee on Health and Environment of the House Committee on Interstate and Foreign Commerce held hearings in January and February of 1978 on actions to collect data on DoD personnel, Admiral Monroe and Dr. Darrell McIndoe, the new Director of AFRRI, were able to testify to the considerable effort already mounted. The hearings spurred the official establishment of the NTPR in January 1978.[46]

The NTPR officially began with two memoranda issued by Assistant Secretary of Defense for Manpower, Reserve Affairs, and Logistics, John P. White. On January 28, 1978, he wrote to Admiral Monroe, assigning several tasks to DNA. He requested that DNA develop a history of every atmospheric nuclear event that

Vice Admiral Robert Monroe, DNA Director 1977 to 1980.

involved DoD personnel, that the agency identify the specific radiation monitoring and control policies in effect at the tests, and assemble a census of personnel at each event. For each individual, DNA should identify their location, movements, protection, and radiation dose exposures. Further, DNA should handle both public relations and Congressional relations in regard to DoD responsibility.[47]

Admiral Monroe led the coordination of the DoD effort for DNA, and beginning in February of 1978, the information gathering started in earnest. In June of 1978, Monroe ordered that the data be consistent for each participant, including name, branch of service or contractor organization, unit or ship, grade or rank, service serial number and social security number, date of birth, shots participated in, as much detail as possible about exposure, and the sources for each of the data elements.[48]

In October of 1979, the database was expanded to include DoD personnel who had been exposed at Hiroshima and Nagasaki, even though these were not "tests."[49] In this fashion, DNA emerged as lead agency for conducting the NTPR, an activity, like the ongoing Enewetak cleanup, devoted not to improving U.S. weapons capability, but to remedying past negative consequences that had grown out of the nuclear side of the Cold War. The shift in emphasis grew naturally out of prior work at the agency. Earlier AFRRI and JNACC responsibilities had established the agency's credentials in the area of monitoring and radiation testing.

The NTPR eventually encompassed a group of separate but related tasks. These included development of a roster of DoD participants in nuclear tests and preparation of a "personnel-oriented" history of the atmospheric test program, that resulted in 41 volumes totaling over 9,000 pages. The agency took on the declassification of over 1,000 publications with data and the development of dose reconstruction to determine exposures of personnel. The agency sought to make personal contact with all DoD personnel who had participated in the tests, to identify those with high exposures, and to provide free medical examinations. DNA sponsored studies on mortality of test participants. The agency also officially undertook the development of a roster of Hiroshima and Nagasaki veterans.[50]

On February 9, 1978, DNA established a toll-free call-in program for participants to report their involvement in atmospheric nuclear tests. Multiple news releases explained the purposes of NTPR and included the toll-free number and the DNA address for postal replies. During the first two weeks after the toll-free lines were established, the program received almost 13,000 calls. The number of calls and letters per week declined thereafter, but by 1985, about 50,000 test participants had called or written to DNA.[51]

Since the toll-free number could not be used in Hawaii, Field Command made arrangement for residents there who participated in testing between 1946 and 1963 to call the Pacific Support Division in Hawaii.[52] Within a week, over 100 calls came in to the Hawaii office, each requiring discussion to record the needed information.[53] Later, DNA arranged that calls from participants in Alaska, Hawaii, and Virginia could be made on a collect basis to a number at DNA Headquarters in Alexandria, Virginia.[54] Researchers entered the information gathered from the phone calls and from the letters into the NTPR database. In addition to the voluntary call and write-in program, DNA sent out direct mailings to participants, continuing the program into the 1980s.[55]

NTPR attracted national attention with interviews and intensive reports appearing on television shows such as *60*

Minutes (September 28, 1980) and *20/20* (March 5, 1981), and in national magazines and newspapers such as *People, National Geographic, New West*, and *The Washington Post*.[56] Admiral Monroe and other DNA representatives testified regarding the NTPR effort frequently through the late 1970s, with several appearances at the Senate Committee on Veterans Affairs.[57]

Considering the active participation of over 200,000 servicemen and civilians in the tests from *Trinity* in 1945 through DOMINIC II and PLOWSHARE in 1962, a rather small number of individuals received significant doses of radiation. A 5-rem exposure in a twelve-month period had been established by the 1980s as an annual whole body dose limit recommended by the National Council on Radiation Protection and Measurements. Using that standard retroactively after examining all of the records, NTPR concluded that, of 202,224 participants, only some 1,299 had received gamma exposures in excess of the limit. About 40 troops who volunteered to move close to ground zero during troop-exposure exercises of UPSHOT-KNOTHOLE (1953), TEAPOT (1955), and PLUMBBOB (1957), received neutron doses of radiation estimated to be as high as 28 rem.[58]

The initial case of Sergeant Cooper had grown out of exposure at shot SMOKY during Operation PLUMBBOB. As a consequence, both the CDC and DNA closely examined the data from SMOKY.[59] DNA helped identify 3,153 individuals who had received film badges during the period of the SMOKY shot and related exercises. DNA found a total of nine leukemia cases (later increased to ten), including the case of Sergeant Cooper. The CDC noted that, among a group of this size and age, one might typically expect three to four cases of leukemia and regarded the excess number of cases as significant. Later, the CDC extended the count to some 3,217 veterans.[60]

The CDC found disease records and mortality causes on over 95 percent of the group. Surprisingly, in a group that size, one might expect over 117 deaths from cancers of all types, consistent with the 112 cancer cases that were found. However, a total of 10 leukemia cases, in a group in which 3 or 4 might normally be expected, remained statistically significant.[61]

Other surprises came from the study: the mean dose received by the military participants in units close to ground zero of SMOKY was higher than others in support groups, although still well under the estimated safe dose of 5 rem per year. Yet the frequency of cancers ran higher among the support units who received the lower doses, rather than among those close to ground zero. If the dosimetry and the dose reconstruction were correct, one would have expected the reverse to be true.[62] After examining these anomalies and the fact that the overall cancer rate fell well within acceptable or normal standards, the CDC concluded that the excess of six or seven leukemia cases could be attributed to chance, to factors other than radiation, or "to a combination of risk factors, possibly including radiation."[63]

PUBLIC PERCEPTION AND STATISTICAL REALITY

To gather the NTPR information required an outreach campaign; inevitably, that outreach campaign had a dual effect. The campaign helped to locate information, but the repeated statements that the government searched for information that might establish a correlation between cancer cases and exposure to nuclear radiation during nuclear testing helped enforce the popular impression that such a correlation existed, whether or not statistics eventually uncovered the correlation.

Another factor compounding the effort to respond to public concerns in this area was the very nature of the statistical reasoning employed by epidemiologists and the ambiguous nature of the statistical results. Even when independent agencies or research groups such as the CDC or the National Research Council applied epidemiological methods to the facts, the results were not reassuring to victims or those who suspected they were victims. When scientists at the National Research Council reviewed the data, the number of leukemia cases (10) in the SMOKY case exceeded the expected number (3.97) from the total. They concluded that radiation could only account for less than 1 case (an increase of 0.2 case), and that the increase was either "a chance aberration" or that the mean radiation doses were several times the doses recorded by the film badges used, which did not seem likely.[64] The National Research Council language was reassuring to DNA officials and to others concerned with the military record of handling radiation exposure and the consequences of exposure. Yet to the public, an assertion that the facts could not "affirm or deny" a correlation, or that excess numbers of cases of cancer might be due to "chance" seemed hardly reassuring, especially coming from official sources that might, in the public's eyes, be associated with officialdom in general.

Admiral Monroe explained one aspect of the statistical problem in his 1979 testimony before the Senate Committee on Veterans' Affairs. After collecting information for one and a half years, Monroe noted that the agency had reached some preliminary conclusions. He pointed out that the DoD estimated some 250,000 personnel had participated in the nuclear tests. According to national statistics regarding distribution of various kinds of cancer among populations, one might expect 40,000 of the 250,000 people to die of cancer of one form or another. After studying the best estimates of radiation exposure during the tests, one might expect that among the 250,000 individuals there would be 12 cancer deaths that could be attributed to radiation. However, he pointed out, "Medical science is not able to distinguish the 40,000 deaths not related to radiation from the 12 deaths that are."[65]

Another problem arose from the fact that in the 1950s, scientific authorities on radiation believed that low levels of ionizing radiation posed no likelihood of permanent danger or risk to individuals. Thus, health officials set permissible exposure levels of 3 or 5 rem, and test administrators accepted such limits as operational. Because so many exposure records were in the low and safe range, many film badges and film badge records were discarded. Only later did the suspicion arise that very low levels of ionizing radiation might cause permanent effects, long after the records had been destroyed or discarded.[66]

The problem of dealing with classified documents led to anxiety and complaint among veterans seeking information. As Admiral Monroe pointed out, both in testimony and in correspondence with members of Congress, classification of documents in no case stood in the way of an individual receiving information about personal exposure during a test. However, sometimes veterans would request a whole document that remained classified and it could not be supplied; sometimes the person would suspect that officials were hiding something that contained relevant information.[67]

VETERANS' ADVOCATES AND DNA

Stewart Udall, who had served as Secretary of Interior under Presidents

Kennedy and Johnson, authored an introduction to one atomic veteran's memoir, *Countdown Zero*. The work, noted Udall, was "an exposé of a systematic thirty-year cover-up by high officials in the U.S. government of the plague of cancer and other illnesses they needlessly inflicted on the soldiers and civilians who were unwitting participants in their experiments."[68] Udall linked the concern of the atomic veterans to other issues: "This book is part of a search for justice which Orville Kelly started in 1977, a search which now includes not only the atomic veterans who were sacrificed, but the Marshallese and the civilians who were downwind from the Nevada tests, the test-site employees whose workplace was the poisoned pit at Yucca Flat in Nevada, and the early uranium miners who were allowed to work underground in air impregnated with long-lived radiation emanations."[69] Udall, after his retirement from government, served as an attorney representing several such groups, including some "downwinders" and some uranium miners who had filed claims for compensation for illnesses that they believed derived from their exposure to radioactive mine tailings.

At the time he wrote the introduction to the work on atomic veterans, Udall served as co-counsel on the case of *Irene Allen v. the United States*. The Allen case, filed in August of 1979 by 24 plaintiffs, served as the lead case representing the plight of the "downwinders." [70] DOE attorney Henry Gill argued that there was no scientific evidence that any exposure to radiation caused the illnesses or death. Udall fought to establish a correlation between dosages from the weapon tests and illness in both the courts and in the more public forum of the press and literature.[71] The Allen case went to trial, after various efforts by government attorneys to dismiss the case, on September 20, 1982. After ruling on a variety of complex issues of law and responsibility, Judge Bruce Jenkins awarded the plaintiffs some $2.66 million in damages, almost all to the surviving family members of eight leukemia victims.[72]

Authors like Saffer and public figures like Udall used the same facts that the CDC epidemiological study had suggested were statistically significant, but not conclusive. Udall and Saffer gave those statistics a different flavor of importance, sometimes based on little more than a general suspicion that an extensive conspiracy had worked to suppress evidence.

Atomic veterans like Cooper, Kelly, and Saffer did not believe the experts. The leading experts on the issues of greatest concern to them were employees of the CDC, of the DNA, or government contractors. It seemed unlikely to Saffer that such an organization "would bite the hand that feeds it."[73] The Secretary of Defense in this period was Harold Brown, former director of Lawrence Livermore Laboratory, the laboratory that had designed the very weapons tested during some of the subject exposures. This fact seemed to the atomic veterans to place all evidence or testimony by current defense department employees or contractors under suspicion of conflict of interest.[74]

Because the conclusions derived from the NTPR data were ambiguous, veterans and their advocates found it extremely logical to question the objectivity of employees of the agency ultimately responsible for organizing military participation in nuclear weapon tests. Most of the experts suggesting that the lack of correlation between radiation exposure dosages and cancers prevented assigning causality were indeed "hired guns" of the government.[75]

A balanced treatment of the issue by Barton Hacker, a historian, suggests that AEC policy makers made a series of conscious decisions early in the testing program to "reassure rather than inform."[76] He went on to comment, "Reluctance to acknowledge any risk, the policy that mainly prevailed in the 1950s, undercut the AEC's credibility when the public learned from other sources that fallout might be hazardous."[77] Part of the unraveling of that policy of reassurance led to the decision to conduct a full and open investigation that eventually produced the NTPR. In effect, the function of the NTPR, despite criticisms of statistical conclusions and the ease of communication over the complex issues, eventually became clear.

Work on the NTPR program continued. The problems which had surfaced in the first years of the program persisted. DNA proceeded to gather information and to attempt to report it in a balanced fashion. Dealing with deep-seated suspicions of the veracity of the government remained an issue to haunt the agency for years to come.

CONTINUING TESTING

The inability to gather test data from atmospheric nuclear detonations and the expense and relative immaturity of underground nuclear effects testing prompted DASA and the Service laboratories, in the late 1960s, to seek additional laboratory facilities to simulate the effects of nuclear weapons. These were sorely needed for studying the effects of nuclear radiation on military electronic systems such as fuzing, guidance, and control. Linear accelerators, pulsed critical nuclear assemblies, a pulsed nuclear reactor called TRIGA, and flash x-ray (FXR) generators were vying for funding.

The FXR generator is an interesting case in point. It consists of either a Van de Graaff machine that charged a large capacitor or a Marx generator to store energy. The high electric fields were a source of cold field emission of electrons that impinge on an x-ray-emitting target. The suggestion to use this technique came from a highly imaginative staff member, Charley Martin, at the Atomic Weapons Research Establishment in the United Kingdom. He had been using this technique for high-speed FXR photography and thought it would be useful for studying radiation effects. This innovation gave birth to a family of x-ray and gamma-ray simulators developed at the Naval Research Laboratory and other commercial laboratories that became the backbone of laboratory nuclear weapon effect (NWE) radiation simulators. Similar machines were developed to conduct the stored energy into radiating antennas to study EMP effects.

One of the great services performed by DNA in the 1970s was to erect these simulators at the Service laboratories and to staff them with the resident experts. This was done without regard to just those radiation problems peculiar to that Service. The result was that the experimental staffs of these simulators became familiar with the radiation effects problems of their sister Services thereby enhancing the national resource of expertise. Correspondingly, the staffs at the Service laboratories played a key role in assisting DNA on the development of new and better facilities.

The requirements for NWE radiation testing by DASA were different than those for nuclear weapon development and validation testing by the AEC. Radiation effects testing required a vertical pipe through which the radiation from an underground device could be transported up to the surface and impinge on the experiments placed directly above, in cassettes that were mounted in a multi-story tower above the pipe. Monitor cables ran from the experimental cassettes to an instrumentation park about a thousand feet from surface zero. The trick was to let the radiation out and close off the pipe before debris could escape. Many closure techniques, including ball valves, clamshells, explosively driven steel gates and spoilers were tried.

Recovery of the experimental cassettes was essential. Since the tower was destined to fall into the subsidence crater, a number of techniques were investigated to recover the cassettes before this happened. At first, the cassettes were mounted on sleds and pulled away a few minutes after zero time by cables. Ultimately, they were mounted on a wheeled mobile tower that was pulled away by large winches. Until the techniques could be sufficiently refined there was a high incidence of effluent leakage. Closures would fail or escape would occur from the pipe at a deep location and travel up a fault or fissure in the soil. Since much of the data was recorded on high-speed (up to ASA 10,000) Polaroid film cameras affixed to oscilloscopes, they were at risk from being fogged by the radioactive effluence. The film could not be developed until it was safe to enter the trailer park. This necessitated a speedy reentry shortly after the detonation to avoid fogging of the film. In particularly risky environments it was decided to remove the whole camera and deliver it to the Polaroid Corporation, where it was hoped that they could provide a more optimized development.

The first time this was done, after the 1965 DILUTED WATERS event, the experimenters brought the box of cameras to Polaroid's chief engineer and said that they had some film that was fogged, but they couldn't tell him how and where. On the next event, PIN STRIPE, the shot vented again and the experimenters returned to Polaroid with the same clandestine posture. The chief engineer was much more scientifically acute than they thought. He remarked, "Oh, you guys out in Nevada did it again." As time went on it became generally much more practical to utilize horizontal tunnels that, with some exceptions, provided greater reliability and economy.

Through the 1970s, DNA mounted an average of two tests per year, each with a large number of projects scheduled for testing. The patterns set up during the 1960s became routine. Yet the tests ventured into new areas, testing radiation effects on satellites and on new systems, testing effects previously unexplored, and researching problems associated with deployment and protection of the proposed MX* or mobile missile system.

SIMULATORS

Simulators provided an alternative to direct testing using nuclear devices as sources in underground tunnels and shafts. In fact, by the early 1970s, DNA had become quite successful in simulating nuclear radiation phenomena using large simulation machines. AURORA was a FXR machine located at the U.S. Army's Harry Diamond Laboratories, in Adelphi, Maryland. It simulated the effects of gamma rays from nuclear weapons. This six-story high, 100-foot long FXR simulator could provide radiation of up to 30,000 rads, over a volume of one cubic meter, in one ten-millionth of a second. With this volume, the system could test whole electronic systems and subsystems. This system had the advantage that it would allow repeated testing of electronic equipment in various stages of operation, with up to ten separate tests per day. Compared to the difficulty of exposing electronic equipment in tunnels, the AURORA FXR offered a much more efficient and economic arrangement for testing gamma ray effects

---

* MX (Peacekeeper) missile also referred to as M-X in technical reference.

than underground nuclear tests.[78] The agency supplemented the AURORA facility with another at Adelphi built over a five year period ending in 1978, at a cost of about $2.5 million. Nicknamed "CASINO", it was operated by Naval Surface Warfare Center, Silver Spring, Maryland. It was originally built to test the response of Pendulous Integrating Gyro Accelerometers (PIGAs) to x-ray induced heating and to test accelerometers of missile systems. Later, as these requirements faded, CASINO was used to test the effects of x rays on critical materials such as military satellites. Since so much critical military communication was carried by satellite, DNA focused attention on the problem of improving the ability of satellites to withstand nuclear effects during a nuclear weapon exchange.[79]

Exposing a full-scale satellite in a test chamber presented difficulties of expense and arrangement. While feasible to use scaled-down simplified models, it would have been extremely expensive to test full-size satellites in an underground nuclear test because of their size, fragility, and the requirement that the satellite be inside a vacuum chamber two to three times its size. For this reason, work on CASINO continued through the 1970s, with the expectation that it would go on line by 1983.[80]

Through the 1970s, scientists developed an increasing variety of means of simulating nuclear weapon effects, going well beyond the use of high explosives and radiation machines. In 1977 DNA launched a special transmitter on a dedicated Navy transit satellite. The transmitter provided a means for evaluating the propagation of data formats through the atmosphere when disturbed by natural phenomena such as the Aurora Borealis. Using computer codes, the natural phenomena could be compared with nuclear effects. Receivers located in Lima, Peru and Fairbanks, Alaska, recorded the degree of interference in the data transmission. DNA also participated in missile launches in Alaska to measure the blackout effect of the aurora on radio and radar reception. Large, pulsed transmitters, some of which were transportable, with

Missile x-ray test by CASINO simulator, Adelphi, Maryland.

AURORA flash x-ray simulator under construction at Harry Diamond Laboratory in 1978.

specially designed antenna, were used to simulate nuclear weapon high altitude EMP. This capability enabled DNA engineers to test military equipment and strategic land-line facilities. In another experiment, DNA engineers arranged for the release of barium at a high altitude between an existing Air Force satellite and several ground and airborne receivers. The barium release provided a simulation of a nuclear disturbance in the atmosphere. Using the results from this experiment, engineers could test the reliability of the computer codes, and extrapolate the results to nuclear tests.[81]

DNA found another opportunity to learn about nuclear effects by observing French testing of nuclear weapons in the Pacific during 1973. The Test Ban Treaty prohibited the United States from cooperating in the French tests, but it did not prohibit the U.S. from observing or detecting the weapon effects on their own. Accordingly, DNA arranged for 784 observers on two ships, the *Wheeling* and the *Corpus Christi Bay*, several helicopters, and at least two other aircraft, working out of Hickam AFB in Hawaii and supported by Field Command offices. The teams recorded effects from remote locations, gathering data unobtainable in any other fashion.[82] A similar operation was fielded during the French tests of 1974, but used only one ship and considerably fewer observers.

Experiments during the 1970s continued to involve ingenious adaptations to new challenges. MINT LEAF, in May of 1970, was a HLOS test of the vulnerability of the Army Spartan missile system. Due to the size of the device to be tested and the number of HLOS tests being prepared simultaneously, engineers constructed the largest tunnel system ever used at NTS. In July 1970, DASA ran DIAL PACK, a joint U.S. and Canadian high explosives test at the Defence Research Establishment, Suffield, in Alberta, Canada to determine loading and response of various systems to airblast and ground shock. The primary objective of this test was to obtain loading and response data for a variety of military targets such as missiles, communications and field equipment, shelters, and various structural parts. A secondary objective was to obtain data on air blast and ground motion, both direct and air blast-induced. Another test would use a method of directing blast to produce effects with characteristics similar to those produced by much larger charges than actually used.[83]

At the NTS and at other test facilities DNA conducted a series of underground effects tests. DIAMOND MINE was a cavity shot to evaluate seismic effects under various conditions in July of 1971. DIAGONAL LINE, conducted in November of 1971, was a VLOS test of Poseidon missile components, including a study of internal effects of EMP. DIAMOND SCULLS, conducted in July of 1972, used the largest LOS pipe system, with a large, 26-foot diameter test chamber to test the vulnerability of Spartan missile components. MIXED COMPANY was a series of 1972 high explosive tests in Colorado to investigate blast, cratering, and shock effects of a simulated 1-KT airblast. DIDO QUEEN, in June of 1973, and HUSKY ACE, in October of 1973, tested several weapons systems, each using new test equipment. DIDO QUEEN made successful use of a new closure system, while HUSKY ACE made use of a self-contained recorder and oscilloscope system. Like a few other tests through this period, HYBLA FAIR, in October of 1974, was designed to improve testing equipment.

A few tests illustrate the range of effects being studied by DNA in this period. HYBLA GOLD, executed on November 1, 1977, was a specialized investigation of some of the physics of a nuclear detonation in or near a buried trench, to gather data that might be used in a particular missile basing scheme. Although prior tests had focused on nuclear weapon effects on weapon systems, engineers designed this test primarily to gather information about the effect of weapons on tunnels and trenches that could be used to house an MX system. In particular, experimenters measured such effects as scoring and breaking of pipe walls, and magnetic and EMP effects on cables and electronic instrumentation. Extensive grounding and shielding of equipment resulted in accurate readings and such methods were established as mandatory on future tests.[84]

Through the 1970s, DNA arranged tests to evaluate three separate concepts of the MX system, with many high explosive tests through the decade providing assistance in evaluating the concepts. The three different concepts being tested included trench systems, shelter systems, and a liquid-pool system. The pool system involved a concept of 20' x 20' x 100' liquid shelters that would be designed to survive the effects of a nearby 5-MT nuclear surface burst. During the MIXED COMPANY tests in November of 1972, various plastic-lined "pans" or holes filled with liquid were situated in different orientations at varying distances from the blast, to determine how much liquid would "slosh" out the containers due to airblast. Using scaling laws, the effectiveness of the full scale system as a means of sheltering nuclear missiles could be determined.[85]

DIAL PACK high-explosive test; dummy in foxhole facing 500-ton TNT test stack, July 1970.

The test ran into a great number of difficulties. Researchers found it impossible to simultaneously scale ground motion, airblast, and debris effects. Debris tended to mix with the fluid, making fluid loss impossible to determine. Even so, experimenters determined that construction of berms around the pools would reduce fluid loss.[86]

Another experiment, the (PRE) DICE THROW II event with 100 tons of TNT, measured the effects of a pressure environment inside a collapsing MX trench. Two small steel trenches were constructed, one with a two-foot diameter and the other, a half-foot in diameter. To isolate the pressure effect from other effects, technicians covered surrounding dirt with dust-suppressing material. The test allowed verification of the strength of roof panels. Another part of the test studied the way in which ground debris mounded around an explosion and how it might entrap shelters and tunnel opening. The motion of debris as it moved from ground zero had always been hard to determine as fireballs and dust clouds during atmospheric nuclear tests obscured the debris motion in the first seconds after a blast. The latter test produced a surprise, with debris mounding five to ten times the amount predicted. Still another test determined how concrete cylindrical tunnels compacted, and how they might be made strong enough to withstand multiple detonations. Such tests built up a base of information that could be used to evaluate future MX missile designs.[87]

By 1977, the development of the MX missile was the "largest single driving function" behind DNA's work in developing strategic structures that could better withstand nuclear weapon effects. Supporting the general MX concept were a number of specific basing concepts, with different types of tunnels, tracks, roadways, and connecting systems. For each proposed basing concept, simulation testing methods had to be developed and validated to evaluate and overcome potential weak points.[88]

Nuclear radiation experimenters had been concerned with the accuracy of their data because of the large currents induced on cables in earlier tests. They determined

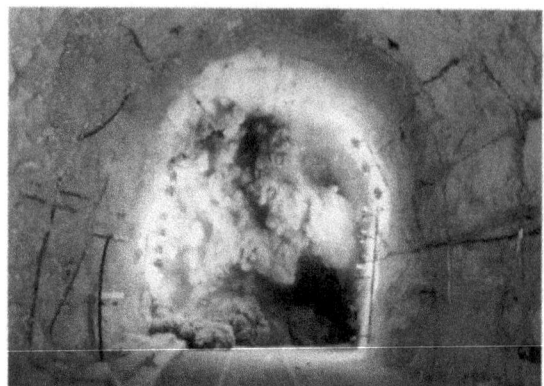

NTS underground test tunnel the moment after detonation. Note cabling and sensor devices mounted on tunnel walls.

that with proper shielding of cables close in to the detonation, such currents could be successfully suppressed. They planned to incorporate the grounding and shielding techniques on future tests.[89] Using the principle of dual use developed in the 1960s with equipment, experimenters extended the concept to using whole drift and tunnel complexes used from the earlier, May 1976, MIGHTY EPIC test.

Although the primary experiment on DIABLO HAWK had been an Air Force reentry system, a nine-month delay in schedule allowed the addition of a wide range of other tests. For example, an EMP phenomenology experiment, and a major Navy Trident missile body electronics experiment, became part of the final test. The EMP phenomenology experiment required several modifications, including a completely separate drift. The Navy project required a very large vacuum chamber. Other materials being tested required underground air-conditioning. One of the largest tests, DIABLO HAWK, required 16 instrumentation trailers which were supported by nine contractors.[90]

Along with the continuing program of underground nuclear tests, DNA continued to use high-explosive simulation tests to investigate ground motions generated by single and multiple nuclear detonations. DNA designed the MISERS BLUFF test to determine the effect of several near-simultaneous bursts directed at the proposed MX system of weapons situated in underground tunnels.[91]

DNA conducted MISERS BLUFF in two phases, the first at the White Sands Missile Range in New Mexico, and the second at Planet Ranch in western Arizona. The White Sands series consisted of eight high-explosive events using small TNT spheres in the range of 265 pounds to 1,000 pounds, over the period from June to December of 1977. The second phase in Arizona, in April to August, 1978, included two multi-burst events using 120-ton charges of ANFO mixtures. These experiments provided data from which analysts could refine and prove a model for nuclear effects in different geological settings in which the MX missile might be deployed.[92] These tests, required a high number of data channels and recording equipment, resulting in a shortage of gear for the DIABLO HAWK nuclear test being set up at the same time. The tests at White Sands required 850 channels for recording airblast and ground motion data. In the high-explosive tests at Planet Ranch, the first event required 470 data channels, while the second event required 370 channels. As a result, Field Command had to rent and borrow equipment to meet its test obligations through 1978.[93]

Like the nuclear tests, the high-explosive tests made maximum use of the event by scheduling multiple experiments and engaging various projects. MISERS BLUFF involved over 180 different users. Facing the heat of Arizona in August was also a serious problem for the trailers and the power distribution systems.[94]

Another two-event high-explosive test, MIGHTY MACH, was held near Alberta Canada in August and September of 1978.[95] Each of these two events involved a 1,000 pound sphere of Pentalite explosive suspended 15 feet above a flat surface. Experimenters gathered data on static and dynamic pressures from the surface up to 40 feet, out to a range of 245 feet.

The urgent need to determine exactly what sort of underground emplacement would be safe for MX missiles led to a compressed schedule of testing. With MISERS BLUFF and MIGHTY MACH, both high-explosive tests, and the nuclear DIABLO HAWK test all running at nearly the same time, some of the equipment that test managers used did not measure up to the usual standards of quality. Taking equipment to the Canadian site, and variations in weather conditions presented further difficulties.[96] Since the schedule through this period resulted in four ongoing tests during the summer of 1978, DNA dealt with a severe shortage of equipment by borrowing equipment from the National Security Agency (NSA), from NASA, from the Air Force Weapons Laboratory, and from several smaller agencies. Altogether, the borrowed equipment had a value over $2,000,000. DNA also purchased some new equipment and modified existing equipment to help meet its needs.[97]

DNA conducted thermal radiation simulation tests using arrays of oxygen-filled polyethylene bags injected with aluminum powder that were then ignited. The thermal output could be varied by arranging the array in different geometric patterns, presenting scaled simulation of the thermal flux, fluence, and waveform of

Workmen construct high-explosive TNT test sphere.

the thermal pulse from nuclear explosions in the 1KT to 1MT range. DNA used these tests in conjunction with the airblast tests to determine the characterization of the dusty thermal layer formed over many soil surfaces in the vicinity of a nuclear blast. The agency scheduled four of these tests starting in August of 1978.[98] Such tests allowed DNA to examine phenomena not originally studied during the atmospheric testing program. The United States had conducted no atmospheric tests of thermonuclear devices over a large land mass. Furthermore, when atmospheric testing had been terminated in 1963, nuclear warfare scenarios had not incorporated the possibility that multiple weapons would be detonated near each other over targets within seconds of each other. As a consequence, earlier experiments had not examined such effects as the interference of massive amounts of dust with incoming weapons or weapon systems. By combining scaled non-nuclear test results with data from the older atmospheric tests, researchers could extrapolate some of the new effects they needed to know.

In 1971, Admiral Mustin testified to Congress that a rising fireball of a one-megaton burst would probably loft up to 500,000 tons of dust into the atmosphere, with

MIXED COMPANY: 500-ton TNT test stack, November 1972.

particles ranging from boulder size down to powder size. Such a cloud would rise tens of thousands of feet, spread out for tens of miles, and last for as long as a half-hour. The effect on a B-1 bomber would be "erosion" of the structure. "It just gets sandpapered," concluded Mustin.

Table 6-4 summarizes the tests conducted during the 1970-1980 period.[99] The decline in testing rate from the 1960s, when DASA had fielded five or more tests a year, derived from several factors. On one hand, in the 1970s, the Services introduced fewer new systems. In addition, because of the increasing complexity and cost of the experiments fielded by DNA, the number of tests had to be reduced. By the late 1970s, the cost for a single underground nuclear test was on the order of $30 million. As a consequence, managers extended the practice of combining (*piggy-backing*) experiments as well as reusing older LOS pipes and chambers. By 1978, the Director of DNA could tell Congress that in a single underground test, the agency would field as many as 400 separate experiments, for all three Services, other defense agencies, and DOE laboratories.[100]

By the early to mid 1970s, the individual Services were not only incorporating the results of DNA tests into their new weapon systems, they were beginning to respond in other ways to the knowledge gained from DNA work. Planned military satellites were being hardened against radiation effects as a regular part of the design process. The Navy had incorporated new methods of strengthening ship structures as a consequence of data provided by DNA about airblast and underwater nuclear blast and shock effect in the 1950s. The Navy constructed its own EMP simulator operated off of Solomons, Maryland, and conducted its underwater shock tests against ship structures at Norfolk and Portsmouth. By 1974, DNA Deputy Director (Science and Technology), Peter Haas, reported that the Navy had made substantial effort incorporating EMP hardening technology and other radiation effects programs.[101]

TEST BAN NEGOTIATIONS AND DNA

When Averill Harriman negotiated the LTBT with the Soviet Union in 1963, President Kennedy faced a difficult time ensuring that it would be ratified by the Senate. In order to win the support of the JCS for the treaty, Kennedy had agreed to four safeguards: comprehensive and aggressive underground testing program; maintenance of modern weapons laboratories; maintenance of the ability to resume atmospheric testing on short notice; and improvement of the means to verify compliance with the treaty.[102]

DASA, and then DNA, played important parts in three of the safeguards. DNA's nuclear testing of weapon effects on military systems, DOE's program of underground development testing of the

Table 6-4. DNA Tests, 1970-1980.

Test	Date	Function
ROCKTEST II	March 1970	HE test silo structures
DIAMOND DUST	May 1970	Cavity shot, seismic effects
MINT LEAF	May 1970	HLOS to test Spartan missile
DIAL PACK	July 1970	HE airblast/ground shock
DIAMOND MINE	July 1971	Cavity shot, seismic effects
DIAGONAL LINE	November 1971	VLOS to test Poseidon Missile
DIAMOND SCULLS	July 1972	HLOS to test Spartan missile
MIXED COMPANY	November 1972	HE blast, cratering, shock
DIDO QUEEN	June 1973	HLOS effects on weapon systems
HUSKY ACE	October 1973	HLOS effects on weapon systems
MING BLADE	June 1974	HLOS effects on weapon systems
HYBLA FAIR	October 1974	Evaluate short LOS & low yield
DINING CAR	April 1975	HLOS tests Trident, Minuteman missile
HUSKY PUP	Oct. 1975	HLOS tests Navy reentry vehicles
MIGHTY EPIC	May 1976	HLOS test Air Force/Navy reentry vehicles
DICE THROW	1975-1977	HE events, White Sands
HYBLA GOLD	November 1977	HLOS airblast on MX
MISERS BLUFF	1977-1978	HE events, NM and AZ
DIABLO HAWK	September 1978	HLOS certify reentry vehicles
HURON KING	June 1980	VLOS test satellites
MINER'S IRON	October 1980	HLOS test MX components

new nuclear warheads, and the operation of Los Alamos and Lawrence Livermore laboratories fulfilled the first and second safeguards. DARPA and AFTAC work on means to verify compliance met the fourth safeguard. The third safeguard, or "Safeguard C," to maintain readiness for resumption of above-ground testing required that Johnston Atoll be retained as a possible site for resumption of atmospheric testing, especially with the rehabilitation of Enewetak and the cleanup of Bikini. Despite fears that the end of atmospheric testing would impede weapon development, observers noted that the vigorous underground testing program of

Peter Haas, DNA Deputy Director (Science and Technology), 1974 through 1979.

the 1960s and the 1970s allowed weapon development to proceed almost unimpeded. The LTBT did very little to impede the development of modern nuclear weapons.[103]

The goal of negotiating a Comprehensive Test Ban (CTB) treaty remained part of the official agenda of the Johnson and Nixon administrations, although neither one vigorously pursued such a test ban. Rather, Lyndon Johnson sought to arrest nuclear proliferation, and to slow the production of fissile materials by cutting back on production facilities. Since the United States already had a surplus, closing seven production reactors over the period 1964-68 was a peace gesture that did not adversely impact the nation's nuclear preparedness. Johnson also began the process that led to a strategic arms limitation agreement, and achieved international agreement on a non-proliferation treaty.[104]

The increasing tempo of arms control talks and resultant arms limitation treaties through this period demonstrated that the thaw was not simply a one-sided illusion on the part of the United States, but that the Soviet Union reciprocated with concessions and negotiation. Not incidentally, other nuclear powers, especially Great Britain, also joined in the spirit of negotiating nuclear arms settlements.

The Non-Proliferation Treaty was opened for signature July 1, 1968 and it entered into force on March 5, 1970. This treaty prohibited the nuclear-weapon nations from transferring to or assisting in the acquisition or manufacture of nuclear weapons or other nuclear devices by non-nuclear nations. It also prohibited non-nuclear nations from manufacturing or acquiring nuclear devices.

The United States and the Soviet Union agreed to two new treaties on September 30, 1971. One improved the existing hot-line telephone link between the two countries by setting up a satellite phone connection. The second treaty, an agreement on measures to reduce the risk of nuclear war through accidents, required each party to give immediate notification of any unauthorized incident involving the possible detonation of a nuclear weapon. It also required immediate notification of the detection of an unidentified object by either country's missile warning system, as well as notice of any interference with the warning systems. Both countries agreed to notify each other in case of any planned missile launches beyond their own borders in the direction of the other country.[105]

A new multilateral treaty on the prohibition of the emplacement of nuclear weapons on the seabed of the ocean entered into force on May 18, 1972. Although a minor treaty, readily agreed to, it prevented the deployment of nuclear weapons on the bottom of the sea for any purpose, including mining of straits and access channels.

While these specialized treaties did much to lessen tensions between the two countries, the ABM agreements, signed in 1972, limited permissible ABM systems to the defense of the capital of both the

United States and the Soviet Union, together with a system at one other site housing ICBMs. The ABM treaty captured the long-held view of Robert McNamara, to which Henry Kissinger and the Nixon administration adhered, that these new missiles, although defensive, represented an incentive to an another arms race. Although the public had difficulty understanding or accepting the concept of assured destruction, by prohibiting the emplacement of ABM systems around population centers and by protecting weapons instead of people, the threat of population destruction would serve to deter each country from embarking on a nuclear first-strike. The protection of the capital cities, it was thought, would allow decision making to proceed in the unlikely event of an accidental war, with the hope that escalation might be limited by the surviving leadership. A protocol added to the ABM treaty in 1974, that went into force in 1976, reduced the sites to be protected by ABMs to one site each.

The Strategic Arms Limitation Treaty (SALT) Agreement of 1972 limited the number of missiles each country would deploy, for a period of five years, as an interim measure while the two countries worked out further details. Between 1972 and the completion of the SALT II Treaty in 1979, several other arms control treaties went into effect. The general thrust of these treaties during the 1970s extended the area of agreement between the United States and the Soviet Union, and put the various testing programs of DNA into a new international context. Table 6-5 lists the treaties and agreements in effect during this period.

DNA was particularly governed by the Threshold Test Ban Treaty (TTBT) of 1974, which prohibited underground nuclear tests over 150-KT yield and specified the sites at which the tests would be conducted. For the U.S. test program, this limitation did not represent a change in policy, as the vast majority of weapon tests were well under the limit. For example, the DoD weapon effects tests arranged by DNA through the period were all in much lower ranges of yield.

President Carter was the first president since John Kennedy to make a serious effort to negotiate a CTB treaty. In two speeches, in January and March of 1977, Carter announced that he would seek an end to all nuclear testing. Secretary of State Cyrus Vance and Soviet Foreign Minister Andrei Gromyko met in March of 1997, and agreed to work toward a treaty that would involve Great Britain in a comprehensive treaty to ban all nuclear tests, including those underground. Negotiations began in earnest toward a new treaty in October 1977 at Geneva.[107]

The negotiations with the Soviet Union made relatively rapid progress in 1977-78. Two negotiating obstacles were easily overcome. The Soviets agreed to a moratorium on peaceful nuclear explosions for the duration of the discussions and Premier Brezhnev took a more lenient attitude towards the question of on-site inspections than had characterized the Soviet negotiating positions since early in the 1960s.[108]

The Soviets agreed to a fixed number of tamper-proof seismic stations to supplement observation by satellite and remote seismic stations outside of the Soviet Union. Both the United States and the Soviets agreed to a system of voluntary on-site inspections.[109]

While these issues were being discussed at Geneva, opponents to a CTB treaty mounted a campaign in both Britain and the United States. In hearings before Congress in August of 1978, representatives from the DoD, the weapons laboratories, and the Joint Chiefs all indicated that continued testing would be required to identify and correct problems

Table 6-5. U.S.-Soviet Treaties and Agreements, 1973-79.[106]

Basic Principles of Negotiation	Signed June 1973
Agreement on Prevention Nuclear War	In Force June 1973
Threshold Test Ban Treaty	Signed July 1974
Vladivostock Accord	Signed Nov 1974
Peaceful Nuclear Explosions Treaty	Signed May 1976
SALT II	Signed June 1979

that might develop in new warheads or bombs. Such issues could not be addressed with confidence without underground testing. Continued reliability of the stockpile of weapons simply required some form of testing. In making arguments to oppose the CTB treaty, far more public support was mustered for the concept of maintaining the stockpile and its deterrent capability, than for modernizing and developing new weapons.[110]

Admiral Monroe testified before Congress, carefully marshalling the arguments against a CTB. After detailing the current underground test program, he pointed out that scientists at the agency had been using simulation methods and a decreasing number of underground tests. Nonetheless, moving entirely to simulators presented several scientific issues. "We are dealing," he said, "in power levels of trillions of watts, and time spans of billionths of a second." With intensive priority and funding, and some luck, he pointed out, it might be possible in five or ten years to accomplish most, but not all of the experimentation with simulators.[111]

Some members of Congress agreed that limiting testing in the 1960s had already posed a danger to the strategic safety of the United States. Representative Bob Wilson, a long-time Republican Congressman from California, led his witness. "We were caught flat footed. Is that a pretty accurate statement?" DNA Deputy Director for Science and Technology, Pete Haas, referred the question to the intelligence community, but had to admit that he agreed.[112]

However, when the Chairman of the Committee, Representative Dan Daniel, asked Monroe if DNA had "...officially gone on record as opposed to a comprehensive test ban treaty," the Admiral clearly stated that the agency had not taken such a position. To clarify his own position, as distinct from that of his predecessor, he chose his words carefully. "This country's security can be enhanced by arms control measures, including test ban treaties, that are symmetrical, verifiable, and take into account other national security needs."[113]

The committee members encouraged Admiral Monroe to make a clear statement opposing the CTB. Clearly, from a military point of view, such an issue involved a broad policy question not within DNA's purview. On the other hand, as members of Congress saw it, Monroe was the best-qualified expert to speak to whether such a treaty would harm U.S. defense readiness. Congressman Stratton attempted to elicit more direct opposition.

"I assume," asked Stratton, "you agree with your predecessor that there are military disadvantages in a Comprehensive Test Ban Treaty?" "Absolutely, sir," said Monroe.[114] When recounting his experiences later, Monroe remembered that he had taken a very firm tone, in his opposition.[115] Monroe went on to make it clear that he believed that with current methods of verification, it would be possible for the Soviets to conduct tests below the level of verification and to obtain a military advantage from such testing.[116]

With seismic sensing representing the primary means of detecting nuclear explosions, verifiers confronted a serious problem. Literally thousands of natural seismic events per year exceeded in force very low yield nuclear devices. A great deal of experimentation could proceed with nuclear devices with a yield of under five kilotons, and it would be difficult to determine if any of the seismic events in that range derived from testing or not.[117]

The Arms Control and Disarmament Agency (ACDA) continued to argue through this period that detection and verification could be achieved. The JCS did not agree. A substantial body of members of Congress, together with a conservative sector of the press, also doubted the assurances of ACDA.[118]

President Carter changed his tactics in May of 1978, negotiating with the Soviets for a CTB of five-year, limited duration, and then asking for an agreement for a three-year treaty in September. Again, in October of 1978, Congressional committees provided forums for military objections to the treaty.

Negotiations addressed the issues of a renewable three-year CTB treaty through late 1978 and early 1979. Both Brezhnev and Carter turned their negotiation toward the issue of SALT II, a treaty that would limit the total number of nuclear weapons in the arsenals of the two major powers. By 1978, negotiators had worked out the terms of SALT II, and President Carter signed the new treaty. It was withheld from Senate ratification due to the Soviet invasion of Afghanistan in December of 1979. Along with SALT II, the CTB appeared dead. Testing would continue.[119]

TRANSITION

Throughout the 1970s, DNA continued to meet its core mission of weapon effect testing, while adding new missions that grew out of the new, more environmentally conscious sensitivities of the decade. Cleaning up Enewetak in the 1970s, in comparison to the clean up of Bikini in a few months in 1969, took much longer and a much higher order of expenditure and time. Yet bureaucratic delays, coordination with other agencies, and the effort to respond to the concerns of the *dri-Enewetak* all paid off in the long run. While Bikini had to be evacuated, over 400 native people returned to Enewetak, no longer living as refugees, readjusting to a new life in their ancestral homeland.

The NTPR absorbed a significant part of DNA's efforts in the late 1970s and early 1980s, but in this area, as in the Enewetak cleanup, the agency's care in dealing with veterans, its patience in developing information, and the detailed and careful responses, produced a body of data that bounded the problem. In the end, federal compensation to a handful of leukemia victims and their families appeared to represent a just solution to a intricate problem with legal, epidemiological, scientific, and administrative complications.

The focus of testing itself changed, as Presidents Nixon, Ford, and Carter considered building the MX (Peacekeeper) missile. Proposed designs required that a wide variety of weapon effects be understood, including the effect of nuclear near misses on tunnels and trenches, on the propagation of effects through tunnels, and on the effect of weapons on liquid missile emplacement systems. By using a wide variety of high-explosive simulation testing, radiation equipment, evaluations of foreign tests, and study of natural phenomena, DNA contributed volumes of information to each of these defense concerns.

When the Carter administration considered a CTB treaty as a capstone to its negotiating efforts with the Soviet Union, DNA administrators found themselves in an awkward position. As Admiral Monroe made clear to Congress, the agency had to carry out its mission and it would be inappropriate to offer political opinions, especially when those opinions ran counter to a plan supported by the Commander in Chief. On the other hand, as the agency within the military closest to the subject of nuclear testing, DNA had the expertise to be able to comment on the effect that such a test ban would have. So, without stepping out of bounds, representatives of the agency made clear to Congress and to the Joint Chiefs, that in their opinion, a CTB would adversely affect U.S. preparedness.

With the decline in Soviet-American relations during the decade, the issue of a CTB became moot, at least for the time being. Disarmament and a nuclear testing accord would have to wait until the wheel of time turned a few more rotations.

ENDNOTES

1. Defense Nuclear Agency, *Operations Mandrel and Grommet,* Events Minute Steak, Diesel Train, Diana Mist, Mint Leaf, Hudson Moon, Diagonal Line, and Misty North, September 12, 1969 to May 2, 1972, DNA Report 6223F (Kirtland AFB, NM, 1987), p. 7.
2. Packard to Sen. Thomas McIntyre, cited in hearings, U.S. Congress, Senate, Hearings, Committee on Armed Services, *Fiscal Year 1972 Authorization for Military Procurement, Research and Development, Construction and Real Estate Acquisition for the Safeguard ABM and Reserve Strengths* (herein referred to as *Fiscal Year 1972 Authorization*), Part 3 of 5 Parts, 92nd Congr., 1st Session, 1971, (Washington, D.C.: GPO, 1971), pp. 2427-2428.
3. U.S. Congress, Senate, *Fiscal Year 1972 Authorization*, p. 2449.
4. Admiral Robert Monroe, interview by Rodney P. Carlisle, September 18, 1997, 20-21; Dr. Marvin Atkins, interview by Rodney P. Carlisle, October 10, 1997.
5. Defense Nuclear Agency, *Field Command, DNA–Special Historical Report, 1946-1985*, DSWA Technical Resources Center, 15-20. U.S. Congress, Senate, *Fiscal Year 1972 Authorization*, p. 2448.
6. U.S. Congress, Senate Committee on Armed Services, Hearings, *Fiscal Year 1972 Authorization*, p. 2448.
7. Defense Nuclear Agency, *Annual Historical Summary, Field Command, Defense Nuclear Agency, October 1, 1977 to September 30, 1978, RCS: HQDNA(A) -1M,* (herein referred to as *1978 Field Command Historical Summary*) DSWA Technical Resources Center, pp. 21, 88.
8. Defense Nuclear Agency, *1978 Field Command Historical Summary*, p. 91.
9. U.S. Congress, House, Hearings, Committee on Armed Services, *Military Posture and H.R. 11500; Department of Defense Authorization for Appropriations for Fiscal Year 1977*, Part 5 of 5 Parts, 94th Congr., 2nd Session, 1976, (Washington, D.C.: GPO, 1976), p. 1256.
10. Defense Nuclear Agency, *1978 Field Command Historical Summary*, pp. 240-241.
11. *Ibid*, p. 241.
12. *Ibid*, pp. 244-245.
13. Defense Nuclear Agency, *The Radiological Cleanup of Enewetak Atoll*, (Washington, DC: Defense Nuclear Agency, 1981), 45-55. Steve Fetter, *Toward a Comprehensive Test Ban*, (Cambridge, MA: 1988), p. 3.
14. Defense Atomic Support Agency, *Cleanup of Bikini Atoll*, (Washington, DC: Defense Atomic Support Agency, 1971); Stewart L. Udall to Seaborg, December 7, 1966, cited in Barton Hacker, *Elements of Controversy*, (Berkeley, CA, 1994), p. 256.
15. Hacker, *Elements of Controversy*, p. 256.
16. Defense Atomic Support Agency, *Cleanup of Bikini Atoll*, pp. 10-11.
17. *Ibid*, p. 11.
18. *Ibid*, pp. 12, 9.
19. *Ibid*, p. 12-13.
20. *Ibid*, p. 13.
21. Defense Nuclear Agency, *Radiological Cleanup of Enewetak Atoll*, pp. 51, 56.
22. *Ibid*. p. 51.
23. *Ibid*. p. 63.
24. *Ibid*. p. 64.
25. *Ibid*, p. 68.
26. *Ibid*, pp. 63, 98.
27. *Ibid*, p. 80.
28. *Ibid*, p. 82.
29. *Ibid*, p. 93.
30. *Ibid*, p. 94.
31. *Ibid*, pp. 97-98.
32. *Ibid*, p. 99.
33. *Ibid*, p. 158.
34. *Ibid*, p. 175.
35. *Ibid*, p. 176.
36. *Ibid*, p. 523.
37. *Ibid*, p. 548.
38. *Ibid*, p. 557.
39. Defense Atomic Support Agency, *Cleanup of Bikini Atoll*, pp. 2-3.
40. Hacker, *Elements of Controversy*, p. 258.
41. *Ibid*, p. 257.
42. Defense Nuclear Agency, *Radiological Cleanup of Enewetak Atoll*, p. 532.

43. John Noble Wilford, "For Pacific's Atomic Nomads, A Symbolic Ground-Breaking," *New York Times*, April 10, 1988. The Bikinians maintain a web page at www.bikiniatoll.com that contains statistics and current news about Bikini Atoll.
44. Abby A. Johnson, Jerald L. Goetz, and William K. McRaney, *For the Record–A History of the Nuclear Test Personnel Review Program, 1978-1986* (herein referred to as *For the Record*), (McLean, VA: 1986), pp. 1-2.
45. Johnson et. al., *For the Record*, pp. 4-5.
46. *Ibid*, p. 5.
47. *Ibid*, p. 6.
48. *Ibid*, p. 8.
49. *Ibid*, p. 9.
50. The eight NTPR tasks are noted in the 1996 updated edition of the NTPR report. See *For the Record: A History of the Nuclear Test Personnel Review Program, 1978-1993* (McLean, VA: 1996), pp. 11-16.
51. Johnson et. al., *For the Record*, 1986 edition, pp. 11-13.
52. Details of which news media were contacted are noted in Defense Nuclear Agency, *1978 Field Command Historical Summary*, p. 36.
53. Defense Nuclear Agency, *1978 Field Command Historical Summary*, p. 36.
54. Johnson et. al., *For the Record*, p. 13.
55. *Ibid*, p. 14.
56. Media coverage cited in Johnson et. al., *For the Record*, p. 14. Also, David Kaplan, "Where the Bombs Are," *New West*, April 1981, pp. 76-83.
57. Johnson et. al., *For the Record*, pp. 15-16. Over an eight-year period, DNA officials gave testimony regarding the NTPR in front of: the Subcommittee on Health and Environment, House Committee on Interstate and Foreign Commerce January 24-26, and February 14, 1978; the Subcommittee of the House Committee on Government Operations, July 13, 1978; the Subcommittee on Energy, Nuclear Proliferation, and Federal Services, Senate Committee on Government Affairs, May 8, 1979; the Senate Committee on Veterans Affairs, June 20, 1979; the Senate Committee on Labor and Human Resources, October 27, 1981; the Senate Committee on Veterans affairs, April 18, 1983; the Subcommittee on Oversight and Investigations, House Committee on Veterans' Affairs, May 24, 1983; and the Senate Committee on Veterans' Affairs, December 11, 1985.
58. Johnson et. al., *For the Record*, p. 21.
59. *Ibid*, p. 28.
60. Glyn G. Caldwell, Delle B. Kelley, Clark W. Heath, Jr., "Leukemia Among Participants in Military Maneuvers at a Nuclear Bomb Test: A Preliminary Report," *Journal of the American Medical Association*, v. 244, no. 14, p. 3, October 1980.
61. Johnson et. al., *For the Record*, p. 183.
62. *Ibid*, p. 183; Caldwell et. al., "Leukemia among Participants in Military Maneuvers at a Nuclear Bomb Test."
63. Caldwell et. al., "Leukemia among Participants in Military Maneuvers at a Nuclear Bomb Test," pp. 620-624.
64. C. Dennis Robinette, Seymour Jablon, and Thomas L. Preston, *Studies of Participants in Nuclear Tests*, NRC Medical Follow-Up Agency, (Washington, DC: 1985), as cited in Johnson et. al., *For the Record*, pp. 187-88.
65. U.S. Congress, Senate, Hearings, Committee on Veterans' Affairs, *Veterans' Claims for Disabilities from Nuclear Weapons Testing* (herein referred to as *Veterans' Claims*), 96th Congr., 1st sess., June 20, 1979 (Washington, DC: GPO, 1979), p. 19.
66. Admiral R.R. Monroe to Cranston, June 18, 1979, 2, in U.S. Congress, Senate, *Veterans' Claims*, p. 353.
67. Admiral R.R. Monroe to Cranston, June 18, 1979, 4, in U.S. Congress, Senate, *Veterans' Claims*, p. 355.
68. Thomas H. Saffer and Orville E. Kelly, *Countdown Zero*, (New York: 1982), p. 13.
69. *Ibid*, p. 14.
70. Howard Ball, *Justice Downwind*, (New York: 1986), p. 148.
71. *Ibid*, p. 147.
72. *Ibid*, p. 161.

73. Saffer and Kelly, *Countdown Zero*, p. 275.
74. *Ibid.*
75. Ball, *Justice Downwind*, p. 118.
76. Hacker, *Elements of Controversy*, p. 278.
77. *Ibid.*
78. U.S. Congress, House, Hearings, Subcommittee of the Committee on Appropriations, *Department of Defense Appropriations for 1973*, Part 4, 92nd Congr., 2nd Session, 1972, (Washington, DC: GPO, 1972), p. 1229.
79. U.S. Congress, Senate, Hearings, Subcommittee of the Committee on Appropriations, *Department of Defense Appropriations for Fiscal Year 1973*, (herein referred to as *FY 73 DoD Appropriations*) Part 1, 92nd Congr., 2nd Session, 1972 (Washington, DC: GPO, 1972), p. 1022. Also see U.S. Congress, House, Hearings, Committee on Armed Services, *Hearings on Military Posture and H.R. 10929, Department of Defense Authorization for Appropriations for Fiscal Year 1979* (herein referred to as *FY 79 DoD Authorization for Appropriations*) Part 3 of 7 Parts, Book 2 of 2 Books, 95th Congr., 2nd sess., 1978, (Washington, DC: GPO, 1978), pp. 1648-1650.
80. U.S. Congress, House, *FY 79 DoD Authorization for Appropriations*, pp. 1656-57.
81. U.S. Congress, House, Committee on Armed Services, *Hearings on Military Posture and H.R. 11500, Department of Defense Authorization for Appropriations for Fiscal Year 1977* (herein referred to as *FY 77 DoD Authorization for Appropriations*), Part 5 of 5 Parts, 94th Congr., 2nd sess., 1976 (Washington, DC: GPO, 1976), pp. 1248-1249. Regarding barium release, see also U.S. Congress, House, *FY 79 DoD Authorization for Appropriations*, p. 1655. Regarding missile launches, see U.S. Congress, Senate, *FY 73 DoD Appropriations*, pp. 1027-1029.
82. U.S. Congress, House, Hearings, Committee on Armed Services, *Hearings on Military Posture and H.R. 12564, Department of Defense Authorization for Appropriations for Fiscal Year 1975*, Part 4 of 4 Parts, 93rd Congr., 2nd Session, 1974 (Washington, DC: GPO, 1974), pp. 3624-3625.
83. "History of the Shock Physics Directorate", 21, in Defense Nuclear Agency, *DNA Semi-Annual Historical Reports, January 1, 1970-June 30, 1970*, Volume I, DSWA Technical Resources Center.
84. Defense Nuclear Agency, *1978 Field Command Historical Summary*, pp. 213-214.
85. U.S. Congress, House, *FY 77 DoD Authorization for Appropriations*, p. 1261.
86. *Ibid*, pp. 1262-1263.
87. *Ibid*, pp. 1266-1267, 1269, 1270.
88. *Ibid*, pp 1251-1252. Also, see John Edwards, *Superweapon: the Making of M-X*, (New York: 1982).
89. Defense Nuclear Agency, *1978 Field Command Historical Summary*, p. 215.
90. *Ibid*, pp. 217-218.
91. *Ibid*, p. 219.
92. *Ibid.*
93. *Ibid*, pp. 218, 220.
94. *Ibid*, p. 220.
95. *Ibid*, p. 221.
96. *Ibid*, pp. 221-222.
97. *Ibid*, p. 225.
98. *Ibid*, p. 224.
99. U.S. Congress, Senate, *Fiscal Year 1972 Authorization*, pp. 2438-2439, 2447.
100. U.S. Congress, House, Hearings, Committee on Armed Services, *Current Negotiations on the Comprehensive Test Ban Treaty*, 95th Congr., 2nd sess., March 15 and 16, 1978, (Washington, DC: GPO, 1978), p. 55.
101. U.S. Congress, House, Hearings, Committee on Armed Services, *Hearings on Military Posture and H.R. 12564, Department of Defense Authorization for Appropriations for Fiscal Year 1975*, Part 4 of 4 Parts, 93rd. Congr., 2nd Session., 1974, (Washington, DC: GPO, 1974), p. 3638.
102. Steve Fetter, *Toward a Comprehensive Test Ban*, (Cambridge, MA: 1988), p. 10.
103. *Ibid*, p. 11.

104. *Ibid.*; Rodney P. Carlisle and Joan M. Zenzen, *Supplying the Nuclear Arsenal*, (Baltimore: 1996), p. 152.
105. Julie Dahlitz, *Nuclear Arms Control, With Effective International Agreements*, (Boston: 1983), p. 29.
106. As described in United States Arms Control and Disarmament Agency, *Arms Control and Disarmament Agreements*, 1990 edition, (Washington, DC: 1990).
107. Fetter, *Toward a Comprehensive Test Ban*, p. 15.
108. *Ibid*, p. 16.
109. *Ibid*.
110. *Ibid*.
111. U.S. Congress, House, *Comprehensive Test Ban Treaty*, p. 55.
112. *Ibid*, pp. 56-57.
113. *Ibid*, p. 63.
114. *Ibid*, p. 65.
115. Monroe interview, p. 34.
116. U.S. Congress, House, *Comprehensive Test Ban Treaty*, pp. 66-67.
117. *Ibid*, p. 72.
118. Rowland Evans and Robert Novak, "NO Rubber Stamping," *Washington Post*, March 16, 1978.
119. Fetter, *Toward a Comprehensive Test Ban*, p. 17.

CHAPTER SEVEN

A REBIRTH OF CONFIDENCE, 1980 TO 1988

"If history teaches anything, it teaches self-delusion in the face of unpleasant facts is folly... we see totalitarian forces in the world who seek subversion and conflict around the globe to further their barbarous assault on the human spirit... let us move toward a world in which all people are at last free to determine their own destiny."

President Ronald Reagan,
Speech to House of Commons, London, England
June 8, 1982

REAGAN DEFENSE BUILDUP

The inauguration of Ronald Reagan in 1980, his landslide reelection in 1984, and the subsequent dramatic increase in defense spending—euphemistically referred to as the "Reagan Defense Buildup"—were a direct result of public disenchantment of the Carter administration in the late 1970s. Double-digit inflation, the Iran hostage debacle, the Soviet Union's invasion of Afghanistan, Olympic boycotts by the U.S., and later the USSR, and the rearmament of Soviet strategic forces created a sense that the nation faced a "window of vulnerability." Indeed, part of Reagan's election strategy hinged on his theme of closing this window of vulnerability and achieving a "rebirth of confidence" in American technical and military superiority.

In 1980-1981, Reagan and Secretary of Defense Caspar Weinberger sought several broad defense spending initiatives to counter the Soviet rearmament. Their spending initiatives were a dramatic de-

Ronald Reagan, President, 1981 to 1989.

parture from prior military policies espoused by President Carter. Military spending under the Reagan administration rose from $171 billion in 1981 to more than $300 billion in 1985, the largest peacetime defense appropriation in U.S.

history. Approximately 10 percent of that total, or $180 billion, was earmarked for the development and procurement of new strategic systems. Congress approved the construction of 100 long-range B-1 bombers, the development of totally new fighters and bombers employing Stealth technology, the stockpiling of tactical nuclear and neutron bombs, the acquisition of 400 air-launched and ground-launched cruise missiles (ALCMs and GLCMs), 100 MX (Peacekeeper) ICBMs, the development of the Trident submarine program, and a variety of other defense programs and initiatives.[1] Additionally, Reagan also began planning for the controversial Strategic Defense Initiative (SDI) or Star Wars, a space-based system designed to intercept Soviet missiles headed toward American targets.

Lieutenant General Harry A. Griffith, USA, DNA Director 1980 to 1983.

DNA PROGRAMS IN THE EARLY 1980S

President Reagan's "defense buildup" had a direct effect upon DNA's programs and policies in the 1980s, and dictated the course of agency support to DoD. The resurgence of the Cold War and the shift in America's nuclear strategy also had a profound effect on DNA's mission. The agency's activities turned to enhancing the endurance and destructive superiority of the country's strategic and conventional forces in the event of nuclear war; a war that U.S. planners now believed the country must be prepared to fight and win. This policy was shared by the agency's new director in 1980, Lieutenant General Harry A. Griffith, USA.

Shortly after taking office in 1976, President Carter signed Presidential Directive 18 (PD-18), which directed the defense establishment to conduct three studies: an ICBM Force Modernization study, a study on the maintenance of the country's military reserve structure, and a third, the Nuclear Targeting Review (NTR), which dealt with Soviet strategic doctrine, perceptions of U.S. nuclear strategy, and means for the destruction of the Soviet governmental infrastructure. In this last connection, the review recommended the adoption of an expanded set of targets in the Soviet Union, including some 700 underground shelters earmarked for top Soviet officials, 2,000 strategic targets, hundreds of critical factories, communications installations, airfields, fuel depots, and more. These recommendations formed the basis of another directive: PD-59.[2]

Even before President Carter approved PD-59 and the changes in strategic policy it implied, Defense Secretary Harold Brown ordered DNA to get a head start on its implementation in case it *was* approved. In contrast to the earlier theater nuclear force evaluation, the Strategic Nuclear Implications and Assessments program launched by DNA in 1979 had a decidedly offensive character. It evaluated and prioritized the new target list, defined damage objectives, considered alternate nuclear weapon employment strategies, and developed improved targeting tools. It was a critical step in acquiring the techniques, the hardware, and the expertise needed to carry out the PD-59 nuclear strategy.[3]

DNA played a critical role in virtually every phase of the buildup of U.S. strategic and theater forces in the early 1980s. Survivability—of shelters, weapons, and the communication, intelligence, and control systems that would tie them all together—became the linchpin of its programs in the early 1980s, consuming a substantial share of DNA's RDT&E budget.

Like the strategy itself, the shift by DNA to a more proactive footing, in which nuclear exchange was considered a legitimate option, actually began during the Carter administration. As discussed earlier, in 1977 the agency was assigned the task of establishing a Theater Nuclear Force Survivability, Security, and Safety program to assess the degree to which U.S. nuclear forces in Europe would be vulnerable to a Soviet first strike and how much warfighting capability would remain. It went far beyond the issues of nuclear survivability. This study addressed every threat in Europe, including sabotage, special forces, conventional forces, hostile environments and safety. This program reflected heightened sensitivity to the insecurities of the global political climate and the weakening of the U.S. force structure of the post-Vietnam era. It also represented a departure from DNA's traditional focus on strategic systems. Its orientation, however, was strictly defensive.[4]

As part of the study, DNA conducted a series of specific, Service-related studies. For the Navy, DNA conducted tests on the survivability of submarines to nuclear blast. Building on existing knowledge about how shock is transmitted through water, DNA began intensive investigations, utilizing conventional high explosives, of how shock is conveyed through the hull to the critical subsystems of the submarine. These experiments led to improved shock hardening and resistance techniques that were integrated into future submarine designs. For the Air Force, DNA conducted groundbreaking work on the survivability of tactical and strategic aircraft in the face of EMP threats. The aging B-52 bomber fleet was retrofitted with advanced avionics capability to give it enhanced survivability against Soviet air defenses. Direct support to the Army included assistance in conducting a Cost and Operational Effectiveness Assessment in the choice between the nuclear capable 155-mm howitzer and the 8-inch alternative, and the construction of a Large Blast-Thermal Simulator (LB/TS). This simulator, eventually constructed at White Sands Missile Range (WSMR) in New Mexico, would be the world's largest shock tube, capable of full-scale thermal and blast testing of military systems.

Department of Defense Instruction (DoDI 4245.4), Acquisition of Nuclear-Survivable Systems, issued in September of 1983, tasked the ATSD(AE) with assuring the nuclear survivability of major weapon systems. This senior official, in turn, tasked DNA with this effort and beefed up the agency's budget and manpower resources. DNA formed the Survivability Technology Division and produced courses, publications, and guidelines to assure that the weapon system development plans would pass Defense Systems Acquisition Review Council (DSARC) reviews. DNA wanted its program managers to include hardening techniques as early as possible in weapon system development to assure minimal cost impact. This program fit well with the agency's overall nuclear survivability mission.

All the Services, especially the Army, were beneficiaries of DNA's increasing research on tactical issues. Based on its growing operational experience at the theater level and working with ground commanders, initially in Europe and then in the Pacific as well, DNA was able to make significant contributions to the design and employment of tactical weaponry. To provide support for these improvements, DNA developed hand-held calculators designed to allow unit commanders to rapidly calculate nuclear weapon effects, thus speeding targeting decisions. This was extended to a much more sophisticated Target and Analysis Planning System (TAPS) for desktop computers. As with its strategic testing program, technical evaluation of Soviet capabilities, and identification of potential vulnerabilities constituted a major portion of its theater-level mission. Having evaluated enemy weapons capabilities, DNA advisers were able to help theater commanders better match nuclear weapons with targets by providing information on damage criteria and weapon effects.[5] In 1980, DNA assisted in the deployment of the new systems at U.S. commands and NATO headquarters in Europe.

The close support by DNA to SACEUR, CINCPAC and CINCSAC was not just an in-name only function. It was a first name personal relationship with the CINCs and their staffs. It was a tradition started by Fred Wikner, strongly enhanced by Peter Haas, and arduously maintained by his successor, Ed Conrad. Haas opened a DNA support office in Munich, Germany. Ed Conrad institutionalized the DNA support role by creating a dedicated nuclear support directorate within the agency. The PACOM Tactical Nuclear Force improvement program was implemented in the early 1980s. In recognition of the key role played by DNA, the Undersecretary of Defense for International Security Policy, Richard Perle, appointed the DDST as a permanent U.S. team member of the NATO High Level Group that dealt with TNF modernization. In 1985, the ATSD (AE), with the support of DNA, implemented the recommendation of the Secretary of Defense to the Secretary General of NATO to form and lead a Senior Level Weapons Protection Group (SLWPG) to address the security and survivability of nuclear weapons deployed to NATO countries. The DNA Deputy Director for Operations headed the U.S. delegation to the new group, which was instrumental in the installation of the Weapons Security and Survivability System (WS3) throughout NATO. It significantly enhanced weapon security.

Dr. Ed Conrad, DNA Deputy Director (Science and Technology), 1979 to 1983.

STRATEGIC MISSILE MODERNIZATION

The MX missile (Peacekeeper) program began in the early 1970s and entered advanced development by the U.S. Air Force in the mid-to-late 1970s. Prompted by the realization that new Soviet ICBMs posed a serious threat to Minuteman missiles in their silos, and the fact that Minuteman technology approached 20 years of reliance, the MX missile was designed and developed with advanced components and technology in its missile booster, guidance and inertial control system, post-boost vehicle, reentry system, and warhead. These enhancements were expected to be a significant improvement over the Minuteman III capabilities. Additionally, the MX missile was designed to address key survivability concerns through an elaborate basing program, which stressed survivability of a Soviet first-strike nuclear attack.

The MX was to be a whole new ICBM, with multiple basing options. The basing "modes" for the MX involved contentious military and political consideration of numerous alternatives to include underground "racetrack" deployment in massive closed-loop road systems; underground shelter or "trench" deployment; rail deployment; closely-spaced or "dense-pack" hardened-shelter deployment; or, at very least, deployed in revamped Minuteman silos. Probably no project absorbed more of DNA's attention and resources than the MX missile.

DNA's role in the MX project was three-dimensional. First, it focused on the survivability of the missile proper in what was expected to be an unprecedented hostile operational environment. For the MX, the alternative to fixed basing (silos) was mobility, which required large land areas, presumably in the midwestern part of the country. To address limited land usage, MX proponents countered with the idea of mobility with deception; i.e., a sufficiently large number of fixed targets with only a few containing real missiles, so the enemy couldn't afford to attack all threats. The feasibility of such a basing solution rested on avoiding multiple kills with a single weapon; the harder the facility (blast resistant, EMP resistant, etc.) the less the required separation between possible targets, thus the smaller land area required. This survivability rested on nuclear hardness, which DNA confirmed in one research study after another.

Shelter hardness was the second role of DNA's MX involvement. MX basing had proved almost as controversial as the missile itself. Environmentalists and ranchers from largely Republican western states, who rarely agreed on such things, were infuriated by the proposition that vast unsettled tracts of land should be earmarked for the mobile missile's underground complexes. The subject of land withdrawal was particularly frustrating for both the Carter and Reagan administrations because the basing scheme originally required a spacing of approximately one mile to preclude an attacker from targeting two silos with the blast from one warhead. Richard Latter, who sat on the Defense Science Board, warned that a mile separation wasn't adequate because a detonation on one site would place the adjacent silos in the EMP source region, which could potentially create burnout in the electronics of the two neighboring silos. To resolve the issue DNA conducted a study to stipulate construction guidelines to mitigate the vulnerability. Ultimately, the problem became moot with a change in basing scheme, but the study was important in that it impressed the DDR&E with the agency's responsiveness.

The MX quickly became a major stumbling block in the START negotiations. The Soviets saw the solid-fuel, multiple-warhead MX as a potent first-strike weapon and insisted that the Americans drop their deployment plans in order for the arms limitation talks to proceed. In addition, the MX system requirements called for the ability to withstand extraordinarily high levels of radiation. This required harder materials than ever, especially for the protection of motor cases, interstage cablings, and other external booster components.

An early MX basing option, the so-called multiple aim point "racetrack" concept, was favored by the Carter administration and entered engineering development in 1981 when Reagan was elected. Shortly thereafter, the "racetrack" basing option was abandoned, partly due to land requirements and other restrictive limitations.

Domestic and foreign concerns led to growing opposition to the MX program in Congress. The suspicion that MX stood in the path of progress on START and that the administration was insincere in its commitment to the negotiations led to Congressional rejection of another MX basing scheme, known as the closely-spaced basing or "dense-pack." Dense pack plans called for launch sites 1,800 feet apart in a column 14 miles long near Cheyenne, Wyoming. The rationale for this basing scheme assumed that, by placing the MX silos virtually atop each other, incoming Soviet warheads would disable each other, improving the odds that multiple MX missiles would survive an attack. In rejecting this plan, Congressional opponents cited both political and technical problems with the plan. But it was also putting the administration on notice that its premise of Soviet negotiating intransigence would no longer be accepted at face value.

While the "dense pack" basing option was founded upon viable scientific research, its rejection by Congress led to a follow-on basing scheme: the development of a "superhard" silo which would be hard enough to survive an incoming missile detonation up to the silo crater's edge. The Air Force became the proponent for this concept and DNA conducted numerous cratering and site geology tests, as part of the "superhard" basing scheme. Despite initial promise, this "superhard" silo option was later rejected, due to widespread belief that Soviet missile accuracy was too great for the development of any fixed silos, no matter how much they were hardened or deemed survivable.

There were several interesting DNA scientific efforts undertaken in connection with the "superhard" silo-basing concept. According to the accepted method of estimating the size of megaton-yield craters and the intensity of crater-induced ground motions, silo survivability was controlled by these effects rather that hardness to airblast. Further, there was considerable debate within the scientific community regarding the accuracy of crater estimates based, as they were, on the megaton craters in the coral atolls of the Pacific missile range. DNA thus funded an extensive scientific exploration, by the United States Geological Service (USGS), of several Pacific crater sites. This exploration,

One-eighth scale MX silo model after being subjected to a large TNT blast during DNA testing.

called the Pacific Enewetak Atoll Cratering Experiments (PEACE) program, completely rewrote the accepted data on large yield crater estimates. Additionally, the concept of beneficial site geology was first introduced as an essential aspect of the "superhard" silo design.

To break the basing logjam, in January 1983, President Reagan established a Commission headed by former national security adviser Lieutenant General Brent Scowcroft. Although the Commission was dominated by one-time MX supporters, its report, prepared with input from DNA, was a disappointment to the administration. While the report endorsed MX deployment, it recommended placing the new missile in existing Minuteman missile silos, thus eliminating mobile characteristics that constituted the MX program's chief attribute. Even then, the Scowcroft report suggested that the nation's security could be better safeguarded with small, mobile, single-warhead "midgetman" missiles, which were less threatening to the Soviets. In conclusion, Scowcroft delivered a mild rebuke to the administration for insufficient zeal in pursuing a strategic arms agreement.[6]

The controversy over MX basing brought complications for DNA. At one time or another in the MX controversy, no fewer than 34 separate basing schemes were advanced, and all were candidates for DNA evaluation. The concepts required the agency to repeatedly reorient its hardening program to identify the relevant survivability issues. DNA built scale model mock-ups of proposed hard silo designs and subjected them to tremendous overpressures to validate their survivability, and then, when the basing modes changed, went through an iterative process.[7]

DNA data and estimates of the hardness of the proposed Peacekeeper and the Soviet missile silos brought the agency to the attention of the Administration and Congress. The Deputy Director (Science and Technology) and members of his staff had to personally brief the Secretary of Defense on this hardness and survivability data. When some of the DNA recommendations were ignored, the DDST was called to testify before the full House Armed Services Committee and the Senate Select Committee on Intelligence.

Even as treaty negotiations moved forward, the administration strengthened the strategic missile armament of the United States. Fifty MX launchers, each carrying ten MK-21 MIRVS, deployed

Peacekeeper (MX) missile transporter at Vandenberg Air Force Base, California.

starting in 1986. Following the Scowcroft Commission Report, Reagan approved basing the MX missiles in silos. More advanced deployment options, like the forthcoming SDI initiative, would mean increased agenda items for DNA.

DNA provided a number of studies and other support to the Commission. Once Reagan had approved the basing decision, the agency mined its databases and other resources to assist in the design of the silos. DNA evaluated existing craters and historical data to assess the survivability of various silo designs. DNA's Structural Dynamics Division continued several projects through the 1980s with a focus on silos. The Silo Test Program (STP) included studies of silo hardness and survivability, airblast hardness of Soviet silos, and tests of innovative methods of attacking silos within varied site geology.[8]

The Special Projects Office coordinated the interdisciplinary work on both the hardened mobile launcher (HML) and the rail-garrison basing of the MX missile systems. Under the memorandum of agreement with the Ballistic Missile Office, the work focused on site characterization, definition of the airblast and thermal radiation environment, developing airblast simulation methods, developing instrumentation, and field testing the entire system for loads and blast. Researchers scheduled a full-scale test of the new mobile missile system for the MISERS GOLD high-explosive test in 1988. For the rail-garrison basing method considered for the MX missile, the Special Projects Office worked on a research program to define the nuclear effects environment that would apply to a rail garrison system at existing missile bases.[9]

COMMAND, CONTROL, COMMUNICATIONS AND INTELLIGENCE

The third role of DNA's strategic initiative involvement, which actually started in the early 70s, concerned the survivability of DoD's command, control, communications, and intelligence (C^3I) systems. DNA's C^3I program illustrated the increasingly complex, fast-moving, and interrelated nature of DNA's work. The new emphasis on interoperability within the military Services meant that findings gathered for one system had application to others. Any easing of DNA's workload associated with the more generic weaponry, however, was offset by the accelerating pace of technological development, which in turn meant a more sophisticated threat to be defended against. The long lead time for testing and evaluation meant that solutions were often obsolete before they were introduced. For example, after decades of studying the physical behavior of metals in a nuclear

Peacekeeper (MX) missile launch.

environment, the introduction of synthetic and composite materials, like graphite epoxy, for aircraft and missile construction raised entirely new survivability issues. Projects were launched with great fanfare only to be abandoned when design parameters changed.

The largest breakthroughs occurred in computer technology. For weapon testers, computerization was both a blessing and a bane. DNA increasingly found that computer memory and speed was the solution to some of its own long-standing technical and analytical problems. On the other hand, densely packed microcircuits proved unusually susceptible to radiation and other nuclear weapon effects. The more missile guidance systems depended upon microcircuitry, the more critical it became to protect and harden them.

A particular focus of C^3I vulnerability, which consumed an average of about 15 percent of DNA's RDT&E budget through the early 1980s, was on satellite links. Like ground-based components of the military communications network, satellites were ultimately as important as the survival of the weapon itself in a nuclear conflict; they were also a potential critical vulnerability. While satellites were not subject to blast waves, which do not propagate outside of the atmosphere, they were highly sensitive to x rays and other radiation. And while ground-based equipment could be physically relocated and protected in the event of hostilities, satellites were essentially sitting ducks in predictable orbits, exposed to physical damage from radiation as well as to disruption of their communication, infrared, and optical paths. This inherent vulnerability, and their growing indispensability to the whole C^3I framework, made satellites a major focus of DNA's total C^3I effects program.[10]

Thus, DNA undertook a major test program to address radiation and plasma effects on satellites. The whole satellite program was designed to achieve three objectives: use of shielding to reduce the amount of x rays bombarding the satellite; using internal enclosures for sensitive components to reduce exposure; and improving circuit design to reduce susceptibility to the radiation that did reach the electronics.

The major challenge in the testing program was constructing a power generator capable of delivering the necessary ionization fluence to adequately simulate the nuclear environment. DNA turned to its stable of government laboratories and contractors for help. Under the terms of a new memorandum of understanding between the two agencies, DNA worked closely with the DOE to accomplish the mission. With DOE-developed technology to increase radiation output, DNA developed a new generation of pulse power generator and primary radiating sources—known as PITHON and BLACKJACK

BLACKJACK radiation simulator under development.

V—to augment AURORA and CASINO simulators.[11]

MICROELECTRONICS HARDENING

Following the DoD Nuclear Survivability Directive in 1983, DNA reinforced its role in encouraging Service System Program Offices (SPOs) and Program Managers to adopt radiation-hardened microelectronic components. Re-analysis of system-generated electromagnetic pulse (SGEMP) effects led to early consultations with system designers to assure operability without large system retrofit costs. As the semiconductor industry increased processing speeds within smaller silicon chip packages, miniaturized circuits exhibited reduced tolerances to radiation. DNA sponsored development of radiation tolerant satellite and computer microelectronics, which subsequently demonstrated their endurance through solar flares that disrupted unhardened satellites. DNA's microelectronics hardening program contributed to U.S. preeminence in long-lived reconnaissance, space exploration, and communication satellites.

Deficiencies in understanding of certain radiation effects, in terms of environment characterization of source region EMP, led DNA in the 1980s to design an underground test as part of the DISTANT LIGHT program and to correlate results with above ground test simulations and computer models.

DNA RESOURCES DURING THE DEFENSE BUILDUP

Testifying before the House Armed Services Committee in the spring of 1983, DNA Director Griffith, warned that "...facilities have been allowed to erode to an unacceptable condition." Griffith was referring to the fact that over 75 percent of DNA's test instrumentation was over 10 years old. The cable plant had been installed in 1965 and had not been expected to last for more than five years. Instead, after nearly two decades of use, fewer than half the test cables were fully functional. "Not only is repair becoming difficult and increasingly expensive," Griffith said, "but the majority of this equipment (at NTS) is not suited for the increasing sophistication of the underground experiments." Indeed, only one of the tunnel complexes was operational, which was the major reason why the program had been reduced from four to five underground tests per year during the 1960s to two or three shots per year during the 1970s to less than one per year in the early 1980s. The result was not only a decline in nuclear readiness but also erosion in the technical skills of the NTS personnel. "We are on the ragged edge now," Griffith warned.

The agency's primary objective, clearly, was to repair the damage sustained by use and decay of its testing facilities. One way DNA went about this budgetary rehabilitation was by enlisting the support

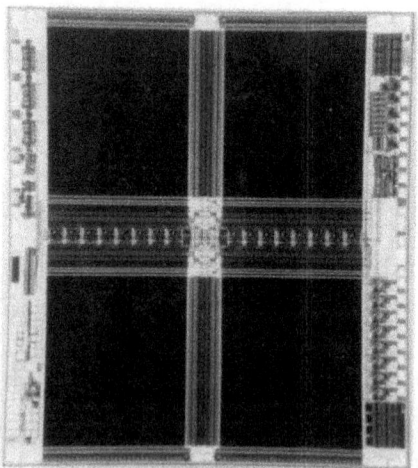

Radiation hardened 64-kilobit static random access memory chip from the early 1980s.

of outside experts. Early in 1981, Director Griffith asked Under Secretary of Defense Richard DeLauer to commission a study by the Defense Science Board on how well DNA was meeting its responsibilities in the post-PD-59 era. DeLauer agreed. The Board, headed by Professor John Deutch of the Massachusetts Institute of Technology, submitted its report in December of 1981. It concluded that DNA's mission was more crucial to national security than ever before, and essentially all of the agency's endorsed current programs and priorities. It found that the agency was doing an admirable job with its constrained resources, but, because of budget limitations, "signs of weakness" were evident, most glaringly in the underground testing facilities. The Defense Science Board therefore recommended that DNA should receive an immediate increase of 20 civilian personnel slots and an increase in resources "...in proportion to the cost of living and new near-term system requirements."[12]

With this vote of confidence, DNA was able to make a persuasive case for its budgetary needs to the Pentagon budget analysts, to the Administration, and to the Congressional authorization and appropriations committees. As a result, DNA's fiscal year 1983 budget reflected a nearly 19 percent real dollar increase in its spending authority. Already under way was a $30 million program to upgrade the NTS underground facilities to provide digital recording systems, fiber-optic data transmission, physical restoration of the tunnel complexes, and the acquisition of modern mining equipment.[13] Although fiscal year 1984 witnessed another budgetary setback in real terms, the agency soon recouped those losses as well.[14]

Soon after the 1983 House Armed Service Committee hearings concluded, DNA Director Griffith retired and was replaced by Lieutenant General Richard K.

Lieutenant General Richard K. Saxer, USAF, DNA Director 1983 to 1985.

Saxer, USAF, who served the agency through 1985.

UNDERGROUND AND HIGH-EXPLOSIVE TESTING

The development of new and more powerful simulators did not eliminate the necessity of maintaining a robust underground nuclear test capability for confirming satellite hardening against x rays, although, to hear DNA managers discuss it, they would have preferred to use simulators exclusively if it were possible. In addition, given DNA's mounting responsibilities, both underground nuclear testing and above ground testing had to be stepped up in the late Carter and early Reagan years to meet satellite survivability needs.

In June of 1980, DNA conducted test HURON KING, a vertical Line of Sight test to investigate the radiation hardening technology of satellites. A large evacuation chamber located at the surface contained a full-size mockup of the satellite. MINERS IRON, a horizontal LOS test in October of

1980, was designed to evaluate the nuclear hardness of MX components such as the motor case, control section, and laser gyro. A fiber-optic data transmission system, replacing the hard wiring that was itself susceptible to radiation, was successfully tested for the first time to improve data recovery.[15]

HURON LANDING, conducted in September of 1982, was an HLOS test to validate hardness of MX components that were unavailable for MINERS IRON. In addition, the event included a test of fiber-optic data transmission and a portal recording system to reduce the number of recording systems on the mesa above the tunnel. DIAMOND ACE was fired simultaneously with HURON LANDING and designed to evaluate the low yield test bed design being developed by DNA. MIDNIGHT ZEPHYR, conducted in September of 1983, had the primary objective to evaluate the performance of the low-yield test bed concept. For the first time on a DNA event the data was totally recorded underground, putting to work the ideas developed in HURON LANDING.[16]

The increased reliance on high-explosive testing for blast and shock hardening of equipment and structures was the result of several factors. Underground tests are extremely expensive and inappropriate for use in evaluating blast effects of free air nuclear bursts. There are significant limitations to the size of test objects that can be exposed in underground tests, while results from small-scale models are frequently uncertain. In addition, expensive test equipment frequently cannot be recovered for reuse. In high-explosive tests like DISTANT RUNNER in November of 1981, high-explosive charg-

Satellite test chamber recovery apparatus utilized for June 1980 HURON KING test.

es were detonated inside and outside hardened aircraft shelters to evaluate their vulnerability to external air blast and to the accidental explosion of stored aircraft weapons. With the data collected from DISTANT RUNNER, the Air Force was able to establish the proper shelter spacing and construction ratios; specifically, the right quantity of reinforced concrete to achieve specific thresholds of survivability, for its new generation of shelters, runways, and taxiways in the tactical theaters.[17]

Another test in the Distant Runner series validated the survivability of the under ground weapon storage vault and the Weapon Security and Survivability System (WS3), leading to the elimination of above ground storage of weapons in Europe during the 1990s.

The agency's Structural Dynamics Division continued work through the 1980s on studies of shallow and deeply-buried underground structures, using high-explosive simulation techniques. One test revealed that concrete structures coated with teflon to reduce friction with the surrounding soil survived better than uncoated structures. The deep underground structure work included evaluation of issues surrounding construction operation and maintenance. Researchers tested tunnel sections and scaled tunnel intersections at the MIGHTY OAK test in 1986.[18] Work on improving the DNA-designed HML for strategic missiles continued through many agency studies in the mid-1980s. A Memorandum of Agreement between the BMO and DNA in 1983 led to a series of survivability tasks. During 1986, studies of a large-scale airblast test validated models used in survivability assessments of HML designs.[19]

In order to conduct experiments in which tactical and strategic weapon systems, communications, vehicles, and structures would be subjected to a high airblast and ground shock environment, DNA successfully detonated a 4,800 ton high-explosive charge. This June 27, 1985

DISTANT RUNNER high-explosive above-ground test conducted in November 1981, at White Sands Missile Range.

test, MINOR SCALE, was the largest non-nuclear explosion ever detonated by the U.S. or its Allies. Twenty U.S. agencies and six foreign governments sponsored about 200 separate experiments. One of the experiments, sponsored by the Norwegian government, included the construction of a reinforced concrete tactical shelter not far from the fiberglass hemisphere housing the explosive charge.[20]

DNA continued work on the survivability of underground structures in other ways. To increase the survivability of U.S. bunkers, as well as to determine how to make Soviet bunkers vulnerable, weapon designers turned to enhancing the ground shock produced by nuclear weapons. Existing weapons, aimed at producing surface blast effects, had not been optimized to propagate the force into the ground. Moreover, the larger atmospheric tests in the 1950s provided information on ground effects in a Pacific coral geology and the smaller Nevada tests of the same period in a desert geology. Extrapolating these results to very different underground soil and rock configurations was risky. Underground tests included excavations containing constructed model silos and other structures, to be subjected to ground shock. In effect, DNA had been able to move an atmospheric test setup into a large cavern, keeping the test underground.[21]

In 1986, DNA Director Lieutenant General John L. Pickitt, USAF, transferred the Field Command Test Directorate to DNA Headquarters.

TITAN II
EXPLOSION AND NUCLEAR SAFETY

The issue of the aging land-based deterrent was dramatized in an accident at a Titan II missile site near Damascus, Arkansas. On September 19, 1980, a maintenance worker dropped a heavy socket wrench, which rolled off a work platform and fell toward the bottom of the silo. The wrench bounced and struck the missile, causing a leak from a pressurized fuel tank. The missile complex and the surrounding area were immediately evacuated and a team of specialists were called in from Little Rock Air Force Base. About eight and a half hours after the initial puncture, fuel vapors within the silo ignited and exploded, injuring 22 Air Force personnel, one fatally. The force of the blast sent pieces of debris, some weighing several tons, as far as a half-mile away.

Initially, in accordance with established DoD policy, the Air Force refused to confirm or deny that the missile carried a nuclear warhead. However, after public and behind-the-scenes protests from then Arkansas Governor Bill Clinton, it was finally acknowledged that the missile had indeed borne a 6,000-pound warhead, which had survived the disaster with only a few dents and no leakage of radioactivity.[22] As a consequence of this incident, the policy of "neither confirming nor denying" the presence of nuclear weapons was changed with respect to nuclear accidents.

Titans used extremely corrosive liquid fuel and oxidizers which ignite on contact. After years of storage the missiles were showing their age. Between 1975 and 1981, there had been numerous accidents or incidents at Titan sites, including several with fatalities.[23] As a result, procedures were devised to deal with emergencies such as the Damascus incident. A DNA Nuclear Weapons Accident Advisory Team, trained to control the radiological hazards from fissionable material, conduct radiation surveys, and organize cleanup of the site, was rushed to the scene.[24]

The Arkansas accident had two significant results. It was in some ways the final straw for the increasingly accident-prone Titan II and became a persuasive argument in favor of the MX program to replace it. A program was initiated to retire the Titan missiles; the last one was decommissioned in the fall of 1987.[25] Second, the accident accelerated plans to systematize the Armed Services' response to nuclear incidents, accidental or deliberate. In the latter regard, in January 1982, the Departments of State, Energy, and Defense signed a memorandum of understanding "...for responding to malevolent nuclear incidents outside U.S. territory," which assigned responsibilities for dealing with possible acts of nuclear terrorism and sabotage.[26]

Concern about the aging ICBM force had prompted DoD in 1979 to assign DNA the task of organizing and conducting a joint DoD/DOE nuclear weapons accident training exercise (NUWAX). It was designed to determine the effectiveness of the existing capacity to deal with an accident, and the results of the 1979 exercise gave the organizers pause. NUWAX-79 "...clearly demonstrated the need for significant changes in DoD's organization, training, equipment, and procedures to ensure effective response to a real nuclear accident."[27] The coordination of military and civilian authorities in U.S. localities, initially through the Federal Emergency Management Agency (FEMA), was deemed problematic and inter-Service communications were not much better. Clearly there was work to be done. In 1981, therefore, DNA received the mission to carry out a ten-year series

Joint DoD (DNA), DOE, and FEMA personnel participating in NUWAX exercise (simulated crash of Navy helicopter) at Nevada Test Site on May 5, 1983 as part of NUWAX '83.

of biennial field exercises and annual command post exercises to upgrade the response capability. Lessons learned from the exercises were compiled into formal Nuclear Weapons Accident Response Procedures.[28]

Not unexpectedly, NUWAX-81 and NUWAX-83 were more successful. The latter was held in early May at NTS, which had been set up to simulate an urban environment. The scenario was an accident on a Navy base, that rapidly spilled over into the surrounding communities. DNA's job, specifically, its Emergency Actions Division, was to coordinate the 7 DoD and 10 non-DoD agencies involved in the exercise, as well as the 150 official visitors, 71 observers from other NATO countries, and dozens of media representatives who witnessed the exercise.[29]

BIOMEDICAL AND ENVIRONMENTAL ISSUES

By fiscal year 1984, the NTPR program was entering what most of those involved believed would be a wind-down phase. Total spending during that period amounted to just under $4 million, less than half of what the program cost at its peak, even before adjusting for inflation. The number of man-years devoted to the project showed an even steeper decline: from a peak of just over 200 in fiscal year 1981 to 60 in fiscal year 1984. By September of 1986, the catalog of NTPR's accomplishments included a 41-volume history of the U.S. atmospheric testing program; the identification of 198,000 of the estimated 200,000 American Servicemen and civilians who had participated in atmospheric tests; the sponsorship of a large number of scientific, medical, and other studies; and correspondence with over 50,000 veterans to provide them with relevant information. All that was presumably left to do was to maintain contact with these veterans and handle the trickle of new inquiries. The basic research, declassification, and release of information that was NTPR's objective was complete.[30]

With NTPR's original goals essentially met, DoD and DNA believed they could safely curtail the program. In 1985, Air Force Lieutenant General John L. Pickitt, who had just taken over leadership of DNA from Lieutenant General Saxer, proposed to change the existing NTPR structure, under which DNA had served as executive agent and separate teams from each of the military Services had carried out the work dealing with their own respective personnel. Under Pickitt's proposal, DNA would assume all remaining NTPR responsibilities. He projected annual savings from this consolidation of as high as $1 million. The Service Chiefs readily agreed. By the middle of 1988, consolidation had been accomplished.[31]

Despite the findings from a succession of independent analyses concluding that exposure to low level radiation was not responsible for any statistically significant increase in health problems among former Servicemen, suspicion remained widespread that the government was engaged in a cover-up to hide a more damning truth. The administration was believed to be doing everything in its power to limit the government's liability to lawsuits, and this belief exposed it to allegations of indifference to the plight of the sick and dying veterans.[32]

As the executive agent for NTPR, DNA frequently found itself in the hot seat, having to defend not only its own handling of the project but also the administration's opposition to legislative proposals to compensate veterans for illness related, to a greater or lesser degree, to their exposure to radiation as participants in the testing program. Often these appearances, taking the form of Congressional testimony, turned rancorous, as administration opponents used the issue as a wedge to attack the Reagan military build-up. A number of later laws did pass, which permitted claims by several new groups of veterans, the largest being those who had participated in the occupation of Hiroshima and Nagasaki after World War II. Thus, DNA's NTPR responsibilities were marginally reduced in the mid- to late-1980s, and the resources allotted to DNA for the purpose were also reduced.[33]

NUCLEAR WINTER

"Nuclear Winter" is a term generally applied to a hypothetical climatic consequence of nuclear war. The theory was first written and published in 1982 in Europe as "The Atmosphere After a Nuclear War: Twilight at Noon," by German researchers Paul Crutzen and John Birks. It was later reworked and advanced, in 1983, by Richard Turco, Brian Toon, Tom Ackerman, and Jim Pollack, who were joined by Cornell University scientist, Carl Sagan, (research team colloquially named TTAPS). This team, drawing heavily on the research by Crutzen and Birks, conceived that Martian dust storms might be an example of the climatic phenomena on earth following a nuclear exchange. Sagan's role in TTAPS largely involved popularization of the "nuclear winter" theory; he published this theory in *Parade* magazine in November of 1983, and later developed it in other journals and symposia. If the theory were true, no shelter, no weapon and, no existing technology could protect the world from a catastrophe infinitely more damaging and more widespread than anything that might occur as a direct consequence of blast, fire, or radiation.

Follow-up studies and computer modeling on the "nuclear winter" hypothesis suggested that its proponents were wrong or, at best, half right.[34] Some of these studies were conducted or commissioned by DNA, which was assigned to be DoD's agent on the subject. Perhaps the most significant of the DNA-sponsored studies was the one published by the National Academy of Sciences in 1985. It confirmed that the phenomena Sagan and associates described *could* conceivably occur, but urged caution in drawing such sweeping conclusions from unknown and unknowable circumstances. Other independent studies found TTAPS's methodology was badly flawed, its conclusions based on unreliable sources, works "in preparation," and speculation. A 1987 study by the National Center for Atmospheric Research, based on a state-of-the-art computer model, found that, in the worst case, most of the world would experience "...a mild nuclear winter, not a deep freeze." Such a "mild" winter might, however, cause a dramatic drop in food production.

In short, the "nuclear winter" debate was inconclusive and deeply frustrating to Congress, which in 1984 had ordered

Lieutenant General John L. Pickitt, USAF, DNA Director 1985 to 1987.

the Pentagon to study the implications of all of this theorizing for U.S. nuclear policy and to come up with recommendations. But it proved impossible for DNA to come out squarely on one side or the other of a debate that was as much about the politics of nuclear weapons as it was about much-disputed scientific facts. In the end, as one analyst put it, the threat of nuclear winter became "…but one more item on an already lengthy list of convincing reasons to avoid a nuclear holocaust."[35]

DEALING WITH TECHNOLOGICAL RISK

The late 1970s and mid-1980s brought a number of mishaps that cast public doubt on America's technological competence. The Harrisburg, Pennsylvania Three Mile Island accident in March 1979 was a major setback for proponents of nuclear power. Then, on January 28, 1986, seconds after liftoff, the Challenger space shuttle exploded, killing all seven astronauts aboard. Throughout the country, the grief was profound, and so was disillusionment with the space program. Concern about hidden technological problems in space and defense systems prompted numerous investigations. Worse, with the shuttle fleet grounded and the military dependent on the shuttle to partially support critical satellite launches, access to space was limited. Later, in 1986, a Titan III missile carrying a major classified defense satellite exploded over the coastal California launch site, grounding the expendable launch vehicle fleet and thus effectively cutting off the United States from space.

DNA was not immune to failures of U.S. advanced technology. In April of 1986, the MIGHTY OAK underground test went awry, contaminating the tunnel and damaging critical test equipment. Although this test was successful, the test was the final MK-21 reentry vehicle validation for the MX missile as well as the Trident II D-5 missiles. Downstream tests were jeopardized, and DNA had to hastily reprogram funds to replace equipment.

Each of these disasters took its toll on public confidence. In February of 1984, an HLOS test, MIDAS MYTH, had damaged the NTS underground chambers containing sensor equipment. The slumping of the subsidence crater after the test injured a number of people, causing one death. Americans and their representatives in Congress wondered whether the string of mishaps was coincidental or related to common managerial or technical deficiencies.[36]

At Johnston Atoll, DNA developed a radiation-monitoring and waste-sorting robot to aid cleanup operations. Plutonium had been scattered when a Thor missile exploded on the launch pad in 1962. Similar machines were later used at NTS. The U.S. Army began constructing a

Thor missile at DNA's Johnston Island launch site.

A REBIRTH OF CONFIDENCE, 1980 TO 1988

Strategic Defense Initiative laser test.

STRATEGIC DEFENSE INITIATIVE

Throughout his administration, President Reagan spoke with a number of scientists and administrators in the weapons laboratories regarding new developments that might change the nuclear balance. Among them was Edward Teller, who claimed that a technological breakthrough promised to cut the arms control "Gordian knot" and simply make the United States immune to any Soviet attack. Specifically, Teller and his team at Livermore claimed to have moved a nuclear-pumped x-ray laser from speculative concept to feasibility.

Reagan had known Teller since his time as governor, and it had been Teller who recommended George Keyworth for the post of science advisor. Teller's advice and ideas impressed Reagan. In a nationwide March 1983 broadcast address, Reagan recalled the Manhattan Project and announced for a similar effort to develop a defensive shield that would intercept nuclear missiles, the Strategic Defense Initiative (SDI). Dubbed by its opponents "Star Wars," after the popular 1977 science fiction film, SDI led to a variety of research investigations that would involve DNA for several years.

SDI touched off vigorous and protracted debates among scientists, policy makers, journalists, and the public. Critics claimed that the SDI systems would violate the 1972 ABM Treaty. Supporters noted that SDI only called for exploratory and conceptual development, while both the ABM treaty and the Outer Space Treaty addressed deployment of full systems. If a promising technology developed from the research, modification of the treaties would then be necessary. For example, Article XIV of the ABM treaty specifically allowed for amendment and review, at which time, modifications to the treaty could be discussed.[40]

chemical agent incineration system on the atoll, which, when operational in 1990, began destruction of nerve and mustard gas stocks from the United States and Germany.[37] DNA Field Command coordinated the improvements to accommodations, utilities, and food service to support the tripling of the island population in support of the Johnston Island chemical demilitarization operations.

The agency's expertise in dealing with accidents, hazardous materials, and the problems of radiological cleanup also played into the newly emerging spirit of improved relations with the Soviet Union. After the catastrophic 1986 Chernobyl reactor fire in the Ukraine, DNA staff from AFRRI formed part of an International Chernobyl Site Restoration Assistance Team.[38] DNA later provided assistance to environmental cleanup efforts at the closed Soviet test site at Semipalatinsk, Kazakhstan.[39]

The largest area of disagreement, however, concerned definition and technical feasibility. As initially conceived, it would have consisted of a layered defense umbrella of various weapons covering the entire United States. Space-based sensors would detect the launch and boost phase of offensive missiles, track them, and relay data to various defensive systems. The defensive systems would include space- and ground-based nuclear-pumped x-ray lasers, particle beam weapons, and so-called kinetic "kill" or "hit to kill" weapons, all of which would be computer-controlled to attack and destroy any hostile missiles during the boost or midcourse phases. Previous ABM concepts had targeted the incoming warheads during re-entry, a difficult enough task with single warheads, but made increasingly complex in the case of multiple warheads.

In the slower boost phase, or while coasting at the edge of space, the vehicles would be easier to target and hit. Advocates of the SDI approaches pointed out that to interdict missiles during their launch phase, and to use non-nuclear devices to destroy them, provided clear advantages over previous ABM systems. Traditional ABM systems depended upon detonation of nuclear defensive missiles high over the target country, that would almost certainly lead to some collateral effects. With such ABM systems, the United States would face the prospect of detonating hundreds, perhaps thousands, of nuclear weapons over its own territory to defend itself. This was an unpalatable approach that had been more or less abandoned with the ABM treaty limiting anti-ballistic missile installations in both the U.S. and the Soviet Union. The United States had deployed one of the two installations allowed under the ABM treaty and then had shut it down.[41]

A committee led by NASA administrator James Fletcher worked during the summer of 1983 to define the technical scope and architecture of the proposed SDI program and the committee sought information from DNA. Both the Fletcher Committee that studied the technical feasibility of such concepts, and another group working under Dr. Fred Hoffman to study policy matters concluded that these new possibilities for defense should be further explored. The two committees served to validate, both from a technical feasibility and a policy viewpoint, the SDI program put forward in Reagan's March 1983 speech.[42]

In 1982, the DDST elected to expand the scientific activities of the agency beyond its nuclear domain. It was apparent that the expertise in x-ray thermomechanical effects could be applied to issues of laser lethality and survivability. The counter argument offered against this initiative was that the Congressional staffs might object to the diversion of research resources to this new activity. The DDST was able to capitalize on his amiable relationship with the Congressional staff members and win approval. By the time the Strategic Defense study was initiated, the broader expertise within the agency was recognized and cognizant agency staff were invited to participate in the summer study.

The DoD tasked DNA, after its work with the Fletcher Committee, as Executive Agent for Directed Energy Lethality and Target Hardening research, testing, and evaluation. With a special budget infusion, DNA took over management of all Defense Department activities in this area, identifying military requirements, assessing technologies, and identifying potential countermeasures available to the Soviets.

SDI, however, faced continuing political obstacles. On one hand, a range of scientists and policy specialists, who overlapped with those publicizing the nuclear winter theory, opposed the concept. Opponents included a group headed by Hans Bethe and Carl Sagan, working through the Union of Concerned Scientists. Raising technical issues about the limited range of lasers, and the ineffectiveness of railgun projectiles, such experts claimed that most, if not all, the concepts under discussion would never be brought to fruition.[43]

Even one of the most staunch advocates of such a system, retired General Daniel O. Graham, who headed *High Frontier*, a group devoted to supporting a space-based defense system, argued by 1986 that a program so heavily dependent on research, rather than deployment, would be difficult to support for a long period. Another political difficulty, even for supporters, was that neither the Air Force nor the Navy had a vested interest in developing such a system and viewed SDI as a drain on their budgets. Even members of Congress generally on the side of increased defense expenditure balked when estimates of the cost to deploy even a partially effective system became astronomical. Cost estimates ran from $160 billion for a partial system, to $770 billion for a comprehensive system as envisioned by Reagan in his original speech.[44]

Even so, through the mid-1980s, several billion dollars per year became available for studies and research into the feasibility of SDI systems and methods that might be employed to foil them. An additional long-range benefit to the military Services might be transfer of technology from SDI projects to other applications in weaponry and defense. DNA's SDI work on directed energy weapons, as well as its existing expertise in pulsed power generators for nuclear radiation simulators, for example, found ready application in improving muzzle velocity and range of artillery.[45]

SDI projects ranged from a few with immediate and practical results, to more speculative work. Some generated promising progress very quickly, such as DNA-sponsored research in the field of electromagnetic launchers. By 1987, the agency could report the achievement of a velocity of 6 kilometers/second with a six-gram projectile, using the Scientific Ultravelocity Accelerator (SUVAC) built by Westinghouse. The Strategic Defense Initiative Organization's (SDIO) Innovative Science and Technology office sponsored the construction of SUVAC in Pittsburgh, Pennsylvania. Westinghouse researchers designed, built and tested the pulse power systems for both THUNDERBOLT, an early system constructed in California, and SUVAC, however, they reported continuing technical challenges in the barrel design. Researchers anticipated an early high payoff from this work in the Army's Armor/Anti-Armor effort.[46]

A wide variety of studies and technical evaluations in support of different types of SDI weapon systems proceeded under DNA auspices. In 1986 DNA studied Thermal Laser Lethality, focused not only on validation of analytic predictive failure models, but on effective hardening systems. Studies of impulse laser lethality investigated improving the efficiency of the system and at the same time, developing effective hardening materials. On particle beam lethality studies, technical issues included target/decoy discrimination capability, failure modes for electronic components and subsystems, and again, development of hardening and mitigation techniques.[47]

SDI work altered the agenda of the communications degradation specialists at DNA. By 1986-1987, researchers used the Pharos II facility at NRL to study different kinds of "collisionless" processes in high altitude regimes. One earth-orbiting satellite, HiLat, launched in 1983 provided a better physical understanding of

Dr. Marvin C. Atkins, DNA Deputy Director (Science and Technology), 1983-1989

ionospheric dynamics at high altitudes. The Polar BEAR satellite, launched in 1986, carried a radio beacon, a magnetometer, and a four-color imager. High-altitude rockets provided data on infrared light over a wide range of altitudes and intensities.[48] The infrared data was crucial to evaluations of the space-based SDI detection and identification systems.

Among the many projects in new areas that SDI spawned, DNA conducted innovative experiments to evaluate infrared sensors, using the natural Aurora Borealis as a simulated nuclear environment that might confuse sensors with an intense background. SPIRIT I, launched April 8, 1986, received the SDI Laboratory Award from the American Defense Preparedness Association in recognition of the results received. SPIRIT I measured a bright aurora, studying the "window-filling" infrared emissions, that appeared to result from earthshine, scattered into the receiver from gases that accompanied the rocket or from problems with the optics.[49]

Researchers tested reentry vehicles and components for the Trident II and Peacekeeper weapons for survivability, and evaluated SDI-related electronics. The increasing miniaturization of electronics and the extreme tolerances and operational environments expected for SDI systems, especially those that would be based on orbiting satellites, required constant improvements in hardening of electronics.[50]

As conceptual development and research proceeded on various SDI systems, the issue of survivability of space-based systems became ever more important and more complex. SDIO sponsored studies to increase tracking, battle management, engagement, and other features of satellites planned as part of the new defensive shield systems. Working with DNA, SDIO developed the concept of "Operate Through," in which systems would be able to operate without interruption following a burst of harmful radiation. Consequently, information flow to parts of a system could be disturbed or interrupted without loosing the mission. Studies examined such issues as how outage and recovery times would affect the tolerance of a system to a radiation dose rate. During key portions of the system's mission, the outage requirements might be more restrictive than at other times. Researchers explored various techniques of allowing systems to work smarter and faster. The Operate Through program worked on developing an integrated test module that contained processors, hard memories, input/output logic and other subsystems that could be used to gain experimental insight into the effect of combined hardness techniques. Operate Through sought to identify and solve individual technology difficulties prior to deployment of SDI systems.[51]

The various scenarios of warfighting considered under SDI planning included the possibility of massive multiple nuclear bursts at high altitude. Studies by Los Alamos National Laboratory (LANL) and other researchers showed the potential for serious degradation of command and control abilities, of radar, and of other sensor systems. Plans focused on a theoretical effort to "bound the uncertainties" in the predictions of such effects through 1987.[52]

Groups working on Transient Radiation Effects on Electronics (TREE) and other radiation effects phenomena naturally found their work schedule, the number of contracts monitored, and the activity of related scientists at other facilities vastly increased as a result of the SDI effort through the mid-1980s. Work on a protective film, SIMOX, proved dramatically successful, and opened the way to protection of high-performance integrated circuits. DNA let contracts to develop high-performance radiation hardened computer components. Meanwhile, studies produced new codes, standards, and detailed documentation. The Electromagnetic Applications Division coordinated SDI activities associated with space power, and worked with the Air Force in developing radiation hardened optical sensors and mirrors for space-based systems.

The degree to which x-ray lasers, kinetic energy weapons, neutron particle beams, and microwave defensive weapon systems could effectively destroy missiles was also a central problem. The Electromagnetic Applications group of DNA's Radiation Sciences Directorate worked to determine the ability of such proposed new defensive weapon systems to damage strategic missile systems. For kinetic energy lethality studies, the issues included modeling predictions, development of kill criteria for re-entry vehicles and booster targets, and development of hardening materials.[53]

Admiral Parker noted that work on nuclear survivability would increase if any of the SDI systems moved from concept to deployment. To the extent that SDI systems would depend on easily targeted satellites, every effort had to be made to protect the electronics aboard from radiation. Parker pointed out that the agency had already done some testing of satellite components. As SDI systems became part of the strategic deterrent, much more extensive testing would be required to ensure survivability of the new systems. Increased testing of all such pieces of proposed new systems would necessarily add to the agency's workload.[54] SDI participants had exploited the agency's underground tests to expose the components and subsystems to radiation. A notable example was the ex-

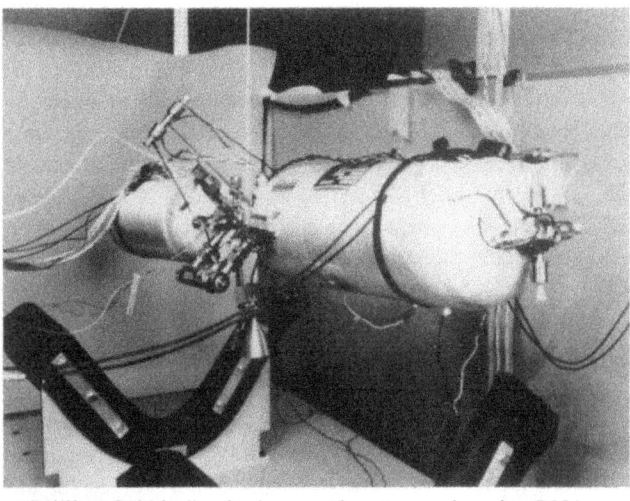

"Brilliant Pebbles" attitude control system undergoing DNA radiation hardening test.

Space Power Experiments Aboard Rockets (SPEAR) II, sponsored by the Strategic Defense Initiative Office (SDIO) and DNA, was a 1988 technology experiment to operate strategic power components in space environment.

periments involving the structural response of the highly sensitive components used for SDI detection, tracking, and aiming functions. Radiation induced structural response was of prime concern. In the late 1980s, the "Brilliant Pebbles" concept became the leading interceptor option for SDI, with the space-based infrared system as the leading detection and tracking candidate. The developers of these systems articulated substantial requirements for DNA products, including a substantial number of underground nuclear effects tests. These requirements never fully materialized because the Clinton administration, in the 1990s, de-emphasized SDI. A new Ballistic Missile Defense Office (BMDO) was set up, with most of its research activities aimed at Theater Missile Defense and preserving options for National Missile Defense.

During the mid-1980s, as negotiations moved toward more comprehensive reductions in nuclear forces with the Soviet Union, and as SDI and continuing DoD research into new defensive systems progressed, the agency explored a wide variety of hardening techniques, for satellites, for ground facilities, for aircraft, and for missile launching equipment. DNA publications between 1984 and 1987 included new approaches to hardening aircraft, an assessment of satellite survivability, studies of hardening ground based facilities, including mobile launchers, against EMP, and studies on the use of thin metal films as a hardening shield against x-ray laser effects. The subjects of the reports show the direction of DNA-sponsored research during the mid-1980s, as the agency continued to focus on the hardening of defensive weapon systems against the effects of nuclear weapons.[55]

As in the past, DNA's technical contractors generated many of the research studies and reports. A study of EMP guidelines for Navy ship platform hardening in 1983 was produced, along with research on communication facility design practices for protection against high-altitude electromagnetic pulse (HEMP) in 1984. Other DNA-sponsored research included a multi-volume EMP engineering handbook in 1986 and a guide to some 1,900 citations pertinent to the effects of EMP on communications in 1987. These represent only a few of several dozen studies generated through the mid-1980s reflecting similar emphasis.[56]

With the possibility that a comprehensive test ban would prohibit all nuclear testing, including underground detonations, the importance of simulation increased. One publication reflected the effort to develop methodologies for the use of nuclear simulators to integrate several types of effects. Equipment that would suffer near simultaneous effects from blast, heat, radiation, and shock, such as ground mobile electrical equipment, be needed for such an integrated approach to testing.[57]

During the mid-1980s, DNA also expanded its research into conventional explosive weapons. Its expertise in high-explosive modeling of blast effects fed directly into new programs and new authority to investigate much more effective conventional munitions. In October of 1983 a car bomb killed nearly 250 marines at their Beirut headquarters. DNA applied its expertise in analyzing the terrorist bombing of the barracks, thereby developing an application for conventional high-explosive analysis that it would use in the future.

POLITICAL CONTINUITY AND CHANGE: MID-1980S

In the United States, the 1984 presidential elections reaffirmed the choices made by Americans in 1980. President Reagan and Vice President George Bush defeated the Democratic nominees, Walter Mondale and Geraldine Ferraro, in a landslide election. Meanwhile, in the Soviet Union, political changes began to drastically change the international security context, with direct impact for the agency. Premier Leonid Brezhnev died in 1982, succeeded by aged Yuri Andropov for fifteen months, and then by a similarly ailing Konstantin Chernenko. During this period, a younger Communist Party Secretary, Mikhail Gorbachev, began to emerge as a leader of Soviet Union. He won election as the Secretary General of the party in March 1985. He would be the leader with whom President Reagan began to deal on a face-to-face basis in arms control negotiations.

Reagan began his second term in the same month that Gorbachev won the post of Party Secretary. Gorbachev, urbane, affable, young, and vigorous, with impeccable Soviet credentials and portfolio, found that despite many differences with Reagan they shared much in common. Both men wanted to make an impact; both brought vigor and energy to public presentations; both tried to think outside the framework of strategic thinking that had put both great powers into the "two scorpions in a bottle" model. However, by 1985, relations between the two nations had brought strategic arms control talks to a standstill.[58]

Summits in Geneva (1985) and Reykjavik (1986) brought Reagan together with Gorbachev. Unlike his predecessors, who had been suspicious and hostile toward the United States, Gorbachev sought a lessening of tensions, and he had the good health and energy to pursue that goal vigorously. The breakthrough came in the personal *tête-à-tête* of the 1985 Geneva summit. Reagan discovered, in place of the standard cartoon caricature of a grey and unyielding Soviet man, a reasonable person with whom he could get along. Gorbachev, in turn, found Reagan to be far more open to new ideas than his rhetoric implied.[59]

In July of 1985 Gorbachev unexpectedly had halted Soviet underground nuclear testing. Six months later he stunned Russians and Americans by calling for abolition of all nuclear weapons by the year 2000. He backed up what might have been perceived as a rhetorical ploy with a credible, staged plan. As an early step, he proposed dismantling and removing all mid-range weapons in Europe, verified by on-site inspection. Some observers thought it ironic that the Soviet leadership appeared to endorse a position taken by American conservatives; perhaps Gorbachev had called an American bluff. "The famous zero-option," noted one, "handiwork of hard-liners, non-negotiability its charm—had been embraced by this alarmingly original Soviet leader."[60] The 0/0 option is defined succinctly as "...the arms control proposal to reduce land based intermediate range nuclear capable missiles in Europe to zero."

As plans developed for the next summit, Gorbachev seemed eager to come away with a signed agreement. In pre-negotiations, the Soviets and Americans agreed to meet in Reykjavik, Iceland. The agenda, for the first time, put all tactical, and strategic offensive weapons, and strategic defensive weapons, on the table.[61]

In Iceland, the two leaders thought that they had made a breakthrough agreement. In a way they had, for they had forged a personal bond of trust even if the agreement itself fell to pieces almost immediately. The two leaders' senior staffs found it difficult to determine just what had been agreed. The verbal agreement to work toward the elimination of all nuclear weapons appeared ideal in many ways, yet unworkable in other ways. Reagan's senior staff, Congressional leaders, and the European allies all challenged pieces of what Reagan and Gorbachev so spontaneously fused together. Reagan himself did not feel totally optimistic after the talks, however, disturbed by Gorbachev's insistence that SDI be part of the bargaining process. Back in Washington, where SDI had already outgrown its "bargaining chip" status and had become an established set of research programs, the Defense establishment did not care to risk bargaining away the progress for Soviet promises that might prove empty.[62]

Even though the Reykjavik agreements did not win wide support, the spirit of cooperation that emerged at the meeting provided a basis for further negotiations between the two leaders. Gorbachev seized the initiative. He removed Soviet linkage of the Intermediate Nuclear Forces (INF) agreement with a strict interpretation of the ABM treaty and accepted on-site verification and inspection "anytime, anywhere" as the Reagan administration had proposed. The position that American arms control negotiators had assumed would never be accepted by the Soviets, called for both sides to achieve absolute reductions in weapons, to be confirmed and verified with extensive systems of on-site inspection, including unannounced visits. Suddenly, the zero/zero option or "0/0," as the option was identified in military reports, became feasible. By the fall of 1987, a new, significant treaty seemed possible.[63]

The INF treaty, signed on December 8, 1987 at the Washington Summit, for the first time eliminated an existing set of deployed missiles rather than setting limits on future deployments. It called for the destruction of existing Intermediate-Range Missiles (IRMs), Short-Range Missiles (SRMs), and associated launchers, bases, support equipment, and other infrastructure. It even called for control on the production of such technology. The land-based nuclear missiles of intermediate and short range constituted only a small fraction of the two powers' nuclear arsenals, but the treaty represented a solid step forward by requiring that those weapons be physically dismantled. Perhaps even more precedent-setting than the destruction of missiles, both sides agreed to a wide range of verification measures, including for the first time, extensive on-site inspections.[64]

If the INF treaty were not coupled with a wider easing of U.S.-Soviet relations, DNA personnel worried that it might have ironic implications, heightening rather than alleviating certain aspects of the nuclear arms race. DNA Director Parker told the House Committee on Armed Services that "...if the INF treaty is ratified and we move into a START environment where we have to remain dependent upon our deterrent, but with

Soviet General Secretary Mikhail Gorbachev and President Ronald Reagan signed the INF Treaty on December 8, 1987.

smaller forces, then each part of that force bears a greater burden of the deterrent, and each part of our remaining force would have to be more inviting to attack, would have to be better protected, would have to be more survivable...." With intermediate and short range deterrent missiles gone from Europe, if the policy of Assured Destruction were to continue to apply, the U.S. strategic triad would be even more crucial and important than it had been before.

In short, the INF could increase DNA's workload, especially in providing testing for the survivability of C^3I and the remaining weapon systems. Over the short term, events began to bear out agency predictions, as new planning had to be formulated to deal with the new situation.[65]

In a triumphant and hopeful visit to Moscow in late May 1988, after ratification by the U.S. Congress and the Soviet Presidium, President Reagan and Premier Gorbachev exchanged the instruments of ratification of the INF treaty on June 1, 1988, in Moscow.

DNA AND THE NUCLEAR WEAPONS COUNCIL

The formation of the congressionally-mandated Blue Ribbon Task Group in 1985 led to the recommendation to disestablish the Military Liaison Committee and to establish the joint DoD-DOE Nuclear Weapons Council (NWC). These actions were legislated in 1986, with the intent of improving the coordination on nuclear weapon programs between DoD and the DOE. DNA played an important role in the early formation activities of the NWC and continues to be an active member of the supporting Standing and Safety Committee by providing staff members to the NWC Staff.

ARMS CONTROL IMPACT ON DNA

With momentous changes already under way and the prospect of even more in the future, DNA confronted a new context. But agency leaders could not clearly read the implications of that context. In 1986-87, as Reagan and Gorbachev moved through negotiation to agreement,

American defense analysts and planners anticipated that the Soviet threat to the NATO alliance would remain as strong as it had been in the past. Political scientists, defense department personnel, cabinet officers, and journalists alike simply could not foresee the dissolution of the Soviet Union and the breakup of the Warsaw Pact, events that lay a few years in the future. DNA and defense planners faced the reality that INF would mean that the United States had fewer missiles as part of its deterrent, but that U.S. strategic forces still had to keep up deterrence as essential to maintaining the balance of peace.

The movement toward INF appeared to promise a reduction in tension and reduced armaments. Yet its implementation could have two almost contradictory effects, both of which could add to the tasks undertaken by of DNA. To implement the treaty would require lots of work by experts in inspection and dismantling of weapons, clearly in an area close to the specialties of DNA staff and contractors. And as both sides implemented the treaty, the United States would rely ever more heavily for deterrence on remaining nuclear weapons. Meanwhile, SDI programs continued, with no requirement in the INF treaty that the proposed new systems be abandoned or cut back. Therefore, the years 1987 and 1988, represented a continuation and expansion for the agency, not a diminution of responsibilities and activities.

The agency reorganized in February 1987, with the changes officially in place March 2, 1987. A Directorate for Operations took over former directorates, such as Nuclear Assessment, which became a subdirectorate within Operations. DoD Directive 5105.31 repromulgated a mission statement that incorporated the "taskings" DNA had received from the Secretary of Defense subsequent to the previous agency mission statement. Still in the midst of the Cold War, the new mission affirmed the requirement to assist NATO commands in areas relative to nuclear warfare.[66]

The old Nuclear Assessments Theater Forces division became the Nuclear Assessments Nonstrategic Forces division, recognizing the withdrawal of nuclear strategic forces from the European theater under INF. The new division would now be concerned with protecting European military assets of a non-nuclear nature. The agency had to focus on the 0/0 option. Research projects for the division, however, continued to reflect some of the same issues: how would command and control facilities in theater operations, both in Europe and the Pacific, survive under nuclear attack? Studies focused on USPACOM's Enhanced Management Capability, the NATO's Central Region Battlefield Information and Targeting System (BITS) and Allied Tactical Operations Center Automation. New projects included studies of the effect of the INF Treaty, and the development of a mobile electrical power generation system.[67]

While the INF Treaty option changed the work of the groups charged with assessing nuclear survivability issues in the European theater, other groups continued with ongoing studies that appeared little changed by the developing treaty negotiations. Analysts were not ready to declare the Cold War over, nor to wave aside concern with the Soviet threat in 1986 and 1987. Thus, for example, the Strategic Forces Division continued to work on enhancing the computer programs used by SHAPE and worked to interface those programs with the Nuclear Planning System being developed for the JCS. They also worked on a continuing, five-year effort to improve the SIOP planning process.[68]

The studies conducted by DNA reflected the changing priorities in European nuclear survivability, with the diminished concern for protecting strategic assets, and for protecting command and control systems. DNA contractors, as well as computer hardware/software firms, provided much of the detailed work for the nuclear assessment groups. The Nuclear Security and Safety Division worked with Sandia National Laboratory, with the Waterways Experiment Station of the Army Corps of Engineers at Fort Polk, Louisiana, and other DNA contractors. Much of the research conducted for the Security and Safety Division through the mid- to late-1980s focused on development of techniques for automatic control of sensor equipment and on improvement of intruder-detection systems.[69]

The depth of experience of DNA and its contractors in dealing with security and protection of the nuclear stockpile would have clear applications under the new arrangements evolving in the arms control discussions. DNA had years of background in dealing with monitoring the nuclear stockpile, both visually and through automated methods. The methods of inspection agreed to under the Memorandum of Understanding associated with the INF treaty included on-site inspections of listed military facilities on short notice. Inspections included the insides of buildings, vehicles, boxes, containers, and other covered objects the size of missiles or launchers. Between 1988 and 2001, both sides had the right and conducted annual short- notice inspections at the sites named in the Memorandum of Understanding. Other methods included automatic monitoring, and national technical means, such as satellite imaging and ground and sea-based radars and listening devices. Furthermore, each side agreed to notify the other of movement of missiles and launchers. DNA had the contacts, the capability, and the experience to be the DoD agency for procurement of personnel, systems, and the management of such activities.[70]

In addition, under the INF Treaty, both sides could establish a monitoring center on each other's territory. The U.S. site would be established at the Votkinsk Machine Building Plant east of the Ural Mountains in Udmurt. The Soviets set up their matching monitoring facility at Hercules Plant Number I, in Magna, Utah, near Salt Lake City. The Hercules plant manufactured the Pershing II missile. At each of these plants, inspectors would monitor three plant exits with weight sensors, x-ray equipment and other measuring devices.[71] To implement the wide variety of on-site inspections and to monitor the stationary equipment, DoD established the On-Site Inspection Agency (OSIA). In accordance with DoD emphasis on holding down overhead costs, the Department created OSIA with DNA providing essential administrative services, such as legal, procurement, and personnel work.[72]

REDUCTION IN GOVERNMENT

Early in his administration, Reagan had stressed the policy of contracting many government functions to the private sector. This policy carried forward a concept developed in prior administrations, which had resulted in an order from the Office of Management and Budget (OMB Circular A-76) that required every federal agency to examine whether it was more cost effective to contract work than to conduct it in-house. In December of 1983, the Grace Commission, appointed by Reagan, issued the "President's Private Sector Survey of Cost Control, Task Report on Research and Development." In addition to asking for more strategic planning within in-house government laboratories and other efficiencies, the report urged the federal government to contract its research and development work, whenever possible.[73]

This new policy harmonized with DNA's long-standing administrative style that depended on substantial use of contractors for scientific work, policy analyses, database development, engineering and technology, procurement, and a wide variety of classified and unclassified documentary report writing. Considering the number of personnel in the agency and the vast amounts of intellectual products generated by its contractors, the proportion of in-house to outside work came close to the ideal recommended by OMB.[74]

As the entire federal government shifted during the 1980s and 1990s away from reliance on in-house facilities and research to procurement of services from contractors, DNA's heritage in this regard would help defend it against those who sought to cut government spending. During the Reagan administration, while defense budgets climbed, DoD remained under constant pressure to reduce in-house expenditures. Ironically, during the period of Defense budget expansion from $171 billion in 1981 to $303 billion by 1989, the military and the civil service side of the defense establishment faced budgetary restraint, personnel ceilings, and grade limitations. DNA, however, had little obvious "fat" to be cut.

In 1987, the agency put in place a new charter reflecting the mid-1980s mission changes. The new organizational structure incorporated other reforms suggested by the Grace Commission, such as eliminating layers of bureaucracy within agencies. The new DNA charter altered the structure of the agency, eliminating the positions of Deputy Director Science and Technology (DDST) and Deputy Director for Operations, in accordance with Grace Commission recommendations to cut down on intermediate level personnel.

The civilian incumbent of the DDST position became the Deputy Director. The agency created a Plans and Programs function and administratively transferred Field Command's underground test functions to headquarters, reflecting the Director's concern that Field Command's expertise and management activities had grown too remote from headquarters. This change also coincided with DoD attempts to streamline its agencies and to reduce administrative overhead in accordance with shifting national priorities.[75]

A 1986 review by a Defense Science Board Task Force concluded that DNA "...is, and has been, operating effectively across a wide range of national nuclear weapons, operational and research missions."[76] The new charter recognized, to an extent, the shift in missions of the agency that had evolved out of the rapidly changing world situation. The new responsibilities, which had very quickly emerged under the INF treaty, had been captured in the new charter. DNA under-

Vice Admiral John T. Parker, DNA Director 1987 to 1989.

took treaty verification technology development, including perimeter monitoring systems and unique identifiers for missile and reentry vehicle inventories.[77]

In April of 1984, Secretary of Defense Weinberger authorized DNA to begin research on advanced conventional weapons, a role later reinforced by an agreement with the Energy Department for joint studies on conventional weapons. The 1987 charter also explicitly made this area, ongoing for some time, a part of the agency's revised mission.[78]

The Defense Department's directive of March 18, 1987 more clearly defined DNA's mission, functions, and responsibilities in line with changes that had taken place in the interim. The reorganization had been carried out March 2, 1987 and the directive captured the effort to provide better management structure and assure the maintenance of a broad technology base to support defense needs.[79] The new charter also brought about a change in DNA's director in 1987, from Lieutenant General John L. Pickitt to Vice Admiral John T. Parker, who served from 1987 to 1989.

TRANSITION

While no one could foresee the momentous events yet to come with the Soviet Union, policy makers knew that the START treaty would lead to a stockpile drawdown. With lessened U.S.-Soviet tensions, and the unilateral Soviet decision to suspend nuclear testing, it seemed likely that a comprehensive test ban would be discussed once more. The two nations had already begun the INF elimination of weapons, exchanging site visit delegations, and monitoring compliance.

In 1988, Vice President George Bush defeated the Democratic candidate Michael Dukakis. President Bush eagerly looked forward to addressing festering domestic and economic troubles that had continued in the background, obscured by the dramatic breakthroughs in Soviet-American relations. Little did he know, however, that he would preside during even more tumultuous international events that would bring the Cold War to an end and possibly represent a beginning of the end of the delicate nuclear balance that had dominated international relations for decades.[80] Other precipitous world events— Soviet troops leaving Afghanistan, the end of the Warsaw Pact, the fall of the Berlin Wall, and the Gulf War— would herald the beginning of the "nineties" and signal a *new world order* under which DNA's mission would evolve once again.

Endnotes

1. Ronald E. Powaski, *March to Armageddon: The United States and the Nuclear Arms Race, 1939 to the Present*, New York, 1987, p. 188.
2. DNA, *For the Record: A History of the Nuclear Test Personnel Review Program, 1978-1993*, March 1996, pp. 41.
3. DNA, *Program Objective Memorandum* [hereafter *POM*], May 1979, I-2; DNA, *POM*, May 1983, pp. V-10 - V-11.
4. DNA, *POM,* May 1979, pp. 3, I-3 - I-4.
5. DNA, *POM,* June 1981, I-2 - I-5; Prepared statement of Vice Admiral R.R. Monroe, USN, Director, DNA, Senate Subcommittee on Appropriations, *Department of Defense Appropriations for Fiscal Year 1981,* Washington, D.C., 1980, pp. 707-8, 709-710.
6. Powaski, *March to Armageddon*, pp. 205-6; Michael R. Gordon, "The Midgetman Missile—A Counterpoint to the Giant MX, But Will It Work?," *Defense* 15, October 1, 1983, p. 2000.
7. Historical Report, Oct. 1, 1981 - Sept. 30, 1982, Electromagnetic Pulse Effects Division, Radiation Directorate, 8; "Defense Nuclear Agency Nurtures A Surging Budget," *Defense Week*, April 12, 1983; House Subcommittee on Appropriations, *Department of Defense Appropriations for 1984*, Washington, D.C., 1983, pp. 423-25.
8. Annual Historical Report, FISCAL YEAR 1987, Structural Dynamics Division.
9. Annual Historical Report, FISCAL YEAR 1987, Special Projects Office Section.
10. "Satellite Vulnerability," Senate Committee on Appropriations, *Department of Defense Appropriations for Fiscal Year 1980,* Washington, D.C., 1980, pp. 74-76.
11. "Satellite Vulnerability," Senate Committee on Appropriations, *Department of Defense Appropriations for Fiscal Year 1980,* Washington, D.C., 1980, pp. 74-76; House Subcommittee on Appropriations, *Department of Defense Appropriations. for 1985,* Washington, D.C., 1984, pp. 547-48; House Armed Services Committee, *Defense Department Authorization and Oversight for FISCAL YEAR 1984*, Washington, D.C., 1983, pp. 964-68; "Memorandum of Understanding Between the Department of Defense and the Department of Energy on Objectives and Responsibilities for Joint Nuclear Weapons Activities, Jan. 1983."
12. "Defense Science Board Task Force Review on the Defense Nuclear Agency Technology Base Program, July - December 1981," pp. 1-8.
13. House Armed Services Committee, *Hearings on Military Posture*, Washington, D.C., 1982, pp. 201-13.
14. Memorandum for the Secretary of Defense, May 6, 1983, Subject: Program Objective Memorandum, FISCAL YEAR 1985-1989," in DNA, *POM Fiscal Year 1985-1989.*
15. Senate Subcommittee on Appropriations, *Department of Defense Appropriations for Fiscal Year 1981*, Washington, D.C., 1980, pp. 712-713; on MINERS IRON, see Field Command, *Annual Historical Summary, October 1, 1979 to September 30, 1980*, pp. 99-100.
16. "Field Command Chronology," n.p.; on HURON LANDING, see Field Command, *Annual Historical Summary October 1. 1982 thru [sic] September 30, 1983*, pp. 86-87.
17. "Field Command Chronology," n.p.; K. E. Gould and Kaman Tempo, "High-Explosive Field Testing (1945-1987): A DNA Historical Perspective," December 1, 1987, p. 11; David Kennedy, "Big Bang in the Desert," *Science* 17, July-August 1986, pp. 35-36.
18. *Ibid.*
19. Annual Historical Report, FISCAL YEAR 1986, Aerospace Systems Division.
20. *Nuclear Survivability*, August 1985, p. 7; September 1986, pp. 5, 11.
21. *Hearings on National Defense Authorization Act for Fiscal Year 1989—HR 4264 and Oversight of Previously Authorized Programs Before the Committee on Armed Services, House of Representa-*

tives, 100th Cong., 2d sess., Title II—Research, Development, Test and Evaluation, 1988, 169; House Committee on Armed Services, *Defense Department Authorization and Oversight, Hearings on H.R. 2287, Department of Defense Authorization of Appropriations for Fiscal Year 1986 and Oversight of Previously Authorized Programs*, 97th Cong., 2d sess., pt. 2, pp. 80-85.

22. DoD: Narrative Summaries of Accidents Involving U.S. Nuclear Weapons, 1950-1980, 1; *New York Times*, September 22, 1980, pp. 1, 16.
23. *Defense Monitor* 10, No. 5 (1981), p. 11.
24. Armed Forces Radiobiology Research Institute, *Historical Report October 1, 1986 - September 30, 1987*, p. 8.
25. *Defense Special Weapons Agency, 1947-1997: The First Fifty Years of National Service*, 50-Year Commemorative Document, FC DSWA Printing, Kirtland AFB, NM, 1997, p. 23.
26. As cited, January 28, 1982.
27. DNA, *POM Fiscal Year 1981-1985*, p. 4.
28. DNA, *POM Fiscal Year 1983-1987*, p. I-9.
29. DNA, Emergency Action Division, *Annual Historical Review Oct. 1, 1981-Sept. 30, 1982*; Ibid., Oct. 1, 1982-Sept. 30, 1983.
30. DNA, *For the Record: A History of the Nuclear Test Personnel Review Program, 1978-1993* (March 1996), pp. 10, A-6.
31. DNA, *For the Record: A History of the Nuclear Test Personnel Review Program, 1978-1993*, March 1996, pp. 40-42.
32. In 1984, at the administration's behest, Senator John Warner (R- VA) attached an amendment to a bill that protected federal contractors from claims for injuries arising out of atomic weapons testing programs. The Warner amendment provided that in such suits involving the employees of contractors, the Federal government should be substituted for the contractor as the defendant. But, as Warner seemed not to know, the Federal government was immune from such lawsuits under a Supreme Court ruling known as the Feres Doctrine. In effect, the Warner Amendment was a complete bar to suits by atomic veterans who had been employed by contractors. The veterans sought to have their rights reinstated through passage of a new law. See Sandra Sugawara, "Bomb Testing Victims Seek Right to Sue U.S.," *Washington Post*, October 3, 1985, p. A8.
33. F. Gladeck and A. Johnson, *For the Record: A History of the Nuclear Test Personnel Review Program, 1978-1993*, DNA 6041F, Washington, D.C., Defense Nuclear Agency, 1996, see especially "Chronology." For examples of DNA and NTPR under fire, see House Veterans Affairs Committee, Review of Federal Studies on Health Effects of Low Level Radiation Exposure and Implementation of Public Law 97-72, 6-24; DNA, *For the Record: A History of the NTPR*, pp. 41-44.
34. Garcia Marquez quoted in "Nuclear Winter Debate Heats Up," *Science* 235, January 16, 1987, p. 27; *Defense Special Weapons Agency, 1947-1997*, p. 23; Larry Badash, "Nuclear Winter Research: Science and Politics," paper presented at the 1993 History of Science Society Annual Meeting.
35. House Committee on Armed Services, *Defense Department Authorization and Oversight, Hearings on H.R. 2287, Department of Defense Authorization of Appropriations for Fiscal Year 1986 and Oversight of Previously Authorized Programs*, 98th Cong., 2d sess., pt. 4, p. 284; David C. Morrison, "Nuclear Winter," *Defense* 18, June 21, 1986, p. 1570.
36. *Department of Defense Appropriations for 1988, Hearings Before a Subcommittee of the Committee on Appropriations*, U.S. Senate, 100th Cong., 1st sess., 1987, p. 1003.
37. Vice Admiral R. R. Monroe to Hon. Philip Burton, House of Representatives, 28 March 1980, in *Department of the Interior and Related Agencies Appropriations for Fiscal Year 1981, Hearings Before a Subcommittee of the Committee on Appropriations*, U.S. Senate, 96th Cong., 2d sess., 1981; "Marshall Islands

Stagger from Ravages of U.S. Control," *Baltimore Sun*, October 26, 1997, pp. 1A, 14A; "Defense Special Weapons Agency, 1947-1997," pp. 24-25.

38. Transcript of Mr. Paul Carew, *Oral History*, November 13, 1997, DSWA Headquarters, pp. 19-20.

39. *Defense Special Weapons Agency, 1947-1997*, pp. 24-25.

40. Richard N. Perle, "The Strategic Defense Initiative: Addressing Some Misconceptions," *Journal of International Affairs* 39, Summer 1985, p. 28.

41. Hans Mark, "War and Peace in Space," *Journal of International Affairs* 39, Summer, 1985, p. 12.

42. Richard Garwin, "Star Wars: Shield or Threat," *Journal of International Affairs* 39, Summer, 1985, pp. 33-34.

43. Richard Ned Lebow, "Assured Strategic Stupidity: The Quest for Ballistic Missile Defense," *Journal of International Studies* 39, Summer, 1985, pp. 57-79. Lebow reviews the critiques in detail, including those by Bethe and Sagan.

44. David C. Morrison, "Shooting Down Star Wars," *Defense* 18, October 25, 1986, p. 2544 ff.

45. *Defense Special Weapons Agency, 1947-1997*, p. 25; Vice Admiral John Parker, interview by Joseph N. Tatarewicz, September 18, 1997.

46. Annual Historical Report, FISCAL YEAR 87, Electromagnetics Division, DNA Radiation Sciences Directorate.

47. Annual Historical Report, FISCAL YEAR 1986, p 3-5, Lethality and Hardening Division.

48. Annual Historical Report, FISCAL YEAR 1987, Atmospheric Effects Division, Radiation Directorate, pp. 4, 5.

49. House Committee on Armed Services, *Defense Department Authorization and Oversight, Hearings on H.R. 2287, Department of Defense Authorization of Appropriations for Fiscal Year 1985 and Oversight of Previously Authorized Programs*, 98th Cong., 2d sess., pt. 4, p. 983; Annual Historical Report, FISCAL YEAR 1987, Radiation Directorate, p. 6.

50. *Defense Special Weapons Agency, 1947-1997*, p. 23; Harold L. Brode, *Partial History of the Defense Nuclear Agency Scientific Advisory Group on Effects (And Its Predecessors)*, Santa Monica, (California: Pacific Sierra Research Corp., December 13, 1985). The changing composition of topics discussed at SAGE reflected the impact of the Strategic Defense Initiative.

51. Charles Hill, "Operate Through, A New DNA/SDIO Program," *Nuclear Survivability*, July 1988, p 3, 4, 9.

52. Annual Historical Report, FISCAL YEAR 1987, Atmospheric Effects Division, Radiation Directorate, p. 7.

53. Annual Historical Report, FISCAL YEAR 1986, p. 3-5, Lethality and Hardening Division; Annual Historical Report, FISCAL YEAR 1987, Electronics Effects Division, Radiation Sciences Directorate.

54. "Nuclear Survivability Interviews VADM Parker, Director, DNA, "*Nuclear Survivability*, July 1989, p. 2.

55. The reports, referenced in *Nuclear Survivability*, July 1988, p. 10, included: DNA-TR-86-33, "HARDTAC Program Summary and Test Bed Aircraft Hardening Approach," AD B177691L; DNA-TR-86-154, "DSP-1 Satellite Survivability Assessment," AD CO 41977L; DNA-H-86-60-V1, "DNA EMP Engineering Handbook for Ground Based Facilities, 3 Volumes." AD B114878 (V3), AD B116353 (V2), AD B115101 (V1); DNA-TR-87-100, "EMP Coupling to Hard Mobile Launcher," AD C041752L; and DNA-TR-87-51, "Thin-Film Standoff Radiation Shields," AD B114956.

56. Donald C. Sachs, *A Guide to Nuclear Weapons Phenomena and Effects Literature*, (1993 Edition), Kaman Sciences-DASIAC SR-92-004, lists these citations on EMP on pages 10-7 through 10-9.

57. DNA-TR-87-94 "A Strategy of Integrated Use of Nuclear Weapon Effects Simulators," AD B117664L, cited in *Nuclear Survivability*, August 1988, p. 10.

58. Newhouse, *War and Peace*, pp. 377-79.

59. *Ibid.*, p. 387.
60. *Ibid.*, p. 389.
61. *Ibid.*, pp. 395-98; Don Oberdorfer, *The Turn: From Cold War to the New Era: The United States and the Soviet Union, 1983-1990*, New York: Poseidon Press, 1991.
62. Newhouse, *War and Peace*, p. 394.
63. *Ibid.*, p. 401.
64. *Defense Special Weapons Agency, 1947-1997*, p. 25; Admiral Parker interview; *Understanding the INF Treaty*, Washington: U.S. Arms Control and Disarmament Agency. 1989, pp. 1, 13-15.
65. *Hearings on National Defense Authorization Act for Fiscal Year 1989—HR 4264 and Oversight of Previously Authorized Programs Before the Committee on Armed Services, House of Representatives*, 100th Cong., 2d sess., Title II—Research, Development, Test and Evaluation, 1988, p. 159.
66. Annual Historical Report, FISCAL YEAR 1987, Nuclear Assessments and Applications (OPNA) Section, p. 2.
67. *Ibid.*, p. 3-4.
68. *Ibid.*, p. 6.
69. Annual Historical Report, FISCAL YEAR 1987, OPNA Section, passim; Annual Historical Report, FISCAL YEAR 1987, Nuclear Security and Safety Division.
70. *Understanding the INF Treaty*, pp. 26-28.
71. *Ibid.*, p. 28.
72. Robert Brittigan, interview with Rodney Carlisle, 1998.
73. "President's Private Sector Survey of Cost Control, Task Report on Research and Development," December 8, 1983, pp. 16-17, 61-65.
74. *An Assessment of Defense Nuclear Agency Functions: Pathways Toward a New Nuclear Infrastructure for the Nation*, Santa Monica, California: RAND Corporation, 1994, budget graph on p. 30 and commentary; William M. Arkin, "Beltway Bandits," *Bulletin of the Atomic Scientists* 41, No. 8, September 1985, pp. 5-6; Harold Brode, interview by Joseph N. Tatarewicz, October 17, 1997.
75. Department of Defense Directive 5105.31, 18 March 1987, reproduced in William Harris, ed., "Charters and Directives for the Defense Nuclear Agency and Predecessor Organizations, 1947-1993, RAND Review of the Defense Nuclear Agency," draft, April 1994; Parker interview.
76. Memo, June 18, 1986 from Fowler.
77. Harris study, RAND, February 1995, p. xxv.
78. *Defense Special Weapons Agency, 1947-1997*, p. 23.
79. Study team report, draft Sept. 1, 1987. In 1987, the OSD Reorganization Study Team, confirmed the conclusion of the task force and concluded that DNA should be named a Combat Support Agency.
80. John Lewis Gaddis, "The New Cold War History," in Gaddis, *We Now Know: Rethinking Cold War History*, Oxford University Press, 1997, pp. 281-95.

CHAPTER EIGHT

POST-COLD WAR ERA: NEW MISSIONS, 1989 TO 1997

"The Cold War is over... and we no longer live in the shadow of nuclear annihilation... yet we still have to finish the work of reducing the Cold War nuclear stockpiles. We cannot afford to ignore these challenges."

President William J. Clinton,
Radio Address, January 15, 1994

NEW WORLD ORDER: COLLAPSE OF COMMUNISM

The Cold War, centered in Europe, ended in 1989, far more suddenly than anyone anticipated. In the summer of 1989 major political changes occurred in Poland and Hungary. Then, into the fall of 1989, national revolutions swept across Eastern Europe, Czechoslovakia, Bulgaria, and Romania. The Berlin Wall—the quintessential symbol of the Cold War—fell in November 1989. Less than a year later, Germany had been unified by treaty and the Soviet Union was carrying out its declared commitment to withdraw, within four years, all of its 680,000 stationed troops from East Germany and other Eastern European states.

Against this background of political revolution, German Unification, and massive military withdrawals, the leaders of the European States, the United States, Canada, and the Soviet Union met in France in November of 1990 to sign the Peace of Paris treaties. Two arms control treaties constituted the heart of that peace conference: the Conventional Armed Forces in Europe Treaty and the 1990 Accords for the Conference on Security and Cooperation in Europe. At the same time a major nuclear arms control measure, the Strategic Arms Reduction Treaty (START), was in the final stages of negotiation. This treaty would reduce U.S. and Soviet nuclear arsenals, while establishing a comprehensive system to monitor all nuclear forces in the future.

Then, early in 1991, U.S. leaders declared that within three years, by 1994, nearly 2/3 or 160,000 American troops from Western Europe would be withdrawn. As 1991 progressed, demonstrations for national independence occurred across Europe further and further to the east. Mikhail Gorbachev, the last leader of the Soviet Union, hoped that his reform programs of *glasnost* and *perestroika* would breathe new life into the increasingly stagnant Soviet system. Instead, by removing the rigid controls that had kept the system together for decades, he brought about its dissolution. In April,

President Gorbachev and other Soviet Republic leaders signed a new treaty of union. That measure proved insufficient to stem the tide of nationalism sweeping across the Eurasian continent. Soviet-led Communism had failed; new nations were emerging.

Following an abortive coup attempt against the Soviet Union's government in August by "hard-line" Communists, the parliaments of Ukraine and Belarus declared independence. At the same time, newly-appointed Russian President Boris Yeltsin and his government banned the Communist Party.

In September of 1991, less than a month after the failed coup, President George Bush announced a series of unilateral reductions in U.S. strategic and tactical weapons. A week later Gorbachev responded, canceling Soviet nuclear weapons programs, withdrawing tactical nuclear weapons, and extending a moratorium on underground nuclear testing indefinitely. Then, on December 25, 1991, as the world watched in amazement, the Soviet Union collapsed as a nation and 15 new nations emerged, along with a new international organization, the North Atlantic Cooperation Council. New arms control treaties were promptly negotiated and signed, including the Open Skies Treaty, the START II Treaty, and the Chemical Weapons Convention. Adding to the political complexity and fueling later unrest, three new nations split away from the former Yugoslavia: Slovenia, Croatia, and Bosnia-Herzegovina. By the end of President Bush's administration in January 1993, a post-Cold War peace had emerged across Europe.

With the signing of the START I and START II treaties came a dramatic change in direction for nuclear forces and nuclear weapons. New questions arose regarding nuclear testing, force modernization, technologies for treaty verification, and the future of nuclear deterrence. Existing Department of Defense agencies whose missions had focused on nuclear weapons found their existence suddenly challenged. Defense panels, Congressional studies, and internal examinations raised hard questions through the decade.

AGENCY REACTION

The question of exactly how DNA should adapt to the cessation of Cold War conflict and the broader international changes generated much discussion inside and outside the agency during the late 1980s and early 1990s. At first, DNA leadership asserted several roles that they believed would continue or would expand in the new world situation. DNA's director, Vice Admiral John T. Parker, evaluated the situation as early as mid-1989, well before the fall of the Wall. "Superficially," he noted, it might "be reasonable to conclude that DNA's role was to be reduced," with the INF treaty, START negotiations, and U.S. and Soviet unilat-

Major General Gerald Watson, DNA Director, 1989-1992.

General Colin Powell, Chairman, Joint Chief of Staff, briefs reporters at the beginning of Desert Storm air campaign.

eral initiatives, all of which would lead to substantially reduced total number of nuclear weapons. Admiral Parker believed the agency would continue to play a major role in maintaining deterrence and ensuring the survivability of existing deterrent systems. Furthermore, if the nation came to rely on space-based SDI systems, the agency would be responsible for helping the Strategic Defense Initiative Office (SDIO) ensure that these systems were survivable. Testing of satellite components had already become a part of DNA's agenda, and that work would only expand if the nation planned to rely on such systems.[1] In May of 1990, Major General Gerald Watson, Parker's successor as Director of DNA, concurred with his predecessor's earlier assessment. "As treaties are signed that limit the number of offensive weapons, DNA's lead role in developing the technology necessary to verify treaty compliance increases in importance."[2]

PERSIAN GULF WAR

Following the Iraqi invasion of Kuwait in August of 1990, a U.S.-led coalition of nations deployed forces to Saudi Arabia and surrounding areas to help prevent further Iraqi offensive incursions. In January of 1991, coalition air power began executing a massive air campaign, Operation Desert Storm, against Iraq's military and supporting infrastructure. The effectiveness of precision-guided munitions and stealth aircraft was quickly demonstrated. Coalition air power attacked facilities suspected of housing Iraqi weapons of mass destruction (WMD) in hardened bunkers. Coalition forces launched a ground offensive in late February of 1991 that expelled Iraq's forces from Kuwait 100 hours after the offensive began.

DNA's expertise in weapon lethality and modeling of atmospheric dispersion of hazardous materials supported target planning and consequence assessments during the Gulf War. The agency deployed expert teams to a DNA assessment facility, to Defense Intelligence Agency (DIA) Headquarters, and to the Pentagon in support of operational target planning from the start of the air campaign through the expulsion of Iraqi forces from Kuwait. The agency also set up a 24-hour command center to assess the consequences if Iraq launched Scud missiles, armed with WMD warheads, against Saudi Arabia and Israel. DNA provided the results of these assessments to U.S. Central Command. Agency officers also participated in post-war inspections of coalition-struck targets to validate DNA's lethality and survivability models in comparison to wartime experience. Battle damage assessments suggested new damage indicators, such as the temperature of target smoke. The agency incorporated data from the Persian Gulf War in lethality, survivability, and collateral effects modeling, especially for hardened targets. Another Gulf War-related effort, initiated by DNA, was the development and militarization of an anti-emetic compound named *Kitral*, which was used for military applications to treat nausea and vomiting in nuclear, chemical, and biological environments. The agency sponsored *Kitral's* later FDA approval. Later, this compound acquired commercial use for controlling nausea and vomiting following cancer treatment.

Underground connection tunnel prior to detonation of HUNTERS TROPHY test, NTS, September 18, 1992.

FUTURE OF NUCLEAR DETERRENCE

In September 1991, President Bush announced nuclear posture changes reflecting the end of the Cold War. These changes included the withdrawal of tactical nuclear weapons from overseas Army bases, surface ships, and attack submarines; cancellation of mobile basing programs for the Peacekeeper missile; cancellation of the Short Range Attack Missile-II (SRAM-II) and the Small ICBM; and stand down from alert of strategic bombers and Minuteman ICBMs. In January 1992, another Presidential decision set the groundwork for the eventual elimination of all fifty Peacekeeper missiles, the reduction of MIRV deployments, and the shift of bombers to conventional missions.

September of 1992 brought about an end of an era in nuclear testing. HUNTERS TROPHY, a weapon effects test of less than 20 KT, was detonated in a HLOS shaft under Rainier Mesa at NTS on September 18, 1992. It was the last nuclear effects test executed. After the HUNTERS TROPHY test, NTS and its facilities served as a testbed for experiments to develop and validate the use of non-nuclear munitions for defeat of facilities located within tunnels or hardened installations.

The inauguration of President Bill Clinton in 1993 brought further change throughout the U.S. government. The Nuclear Posture Review (NPR), chartered in 1993 and led by the Office of the Secretary of Defense and the Joint Staff, sought to determine the role of nuclear weapons in U.S. security strategy and resultant military consequences. Among the findings of the 1993 NPR was a new definition of an "enduring stockpile" of nuclear weapons. DNA staff supported the NPR study, coordinating requirements with agency analyses and other activities, and provided products to meet the NPR needs. In September of 1994, President Clinton approved a reduced strategic force. That force consisted of significantly reduced arsenals of Minuteman ICBMs, Trident submarines (all with D-5 missiles), B-2 and B-52 strategic bombers, and a non-nuclear role for the B-1 bomber.

With the 1993 decision to conditionally cease U.S. nuclear testing, questions arose concerning how to maintain the reliability of the enduring nuclear stockpile. The Department of Energy advocated "Science Based Stockpile Stewardship," in which reliability would be preserved through stockpile surveillance, laboratory experiments, and improved computational software and hardware. Subsequently, a DoD-DOE agreement called for "dual revalidation" of weapons remaining in the inventory through a process in which each DOE weapon laboratory independently and periodically examines all data relevant to a specific weapon type. The results are reviewed by DOE Headquarters staff and provided to the Joint Nuclear Weapons Council for final action. DNA participated in the process, stationing agency military officers at all three national laboratories. These officers contributed to the dual revalidation process and annual recertification of the stockpile. In 1995, the President instituted an annual certification program to certify the safety and reliability of the nuclear weapons stockpile as part of his decision to eliminate underground testing. DNA is a full participant in this process that involves the full spectrum of the nuclear weapons community.

DNA ADJUSTS TO THE POST-COLD WAR ERA

The post-Desert Storm revelations of the breadth and scope of the Iraqi quest to obtain nuclear, chemical, and biological weapons spawned a heightened awareness of WMD proliferation. DNA began a series of initiatives in 1991 to address the proliferation of WMD by terrorists and third-world countries. In a briefing on the "Implications of Nuclear Proliferation" to the American Nuclear Society in Orlando, Florida, on June 5, 1991, DNA Deputy Director, Dr. George W. Ullrich summarized the pertinent issues surrounding nuclear and WMD proliferation and the difficult questions such proliferation presented to U.S. defense and security policy.[2] His briefing painted a picture of ongoing rogue nation "threat containment" in order to control what Dr. Ullrich deemed the "proliferation genie." Such technical briefings contributed general understanding toward later counterproliferation measures and raised the national consciousness on this issue. Later counterproliferation conferences, the first at the Air Force Academy in Colorado in May of 1994 and the second at the National Defense University (Fort McNair) in Washington, D.C., in October of 1995, focused national attention on counter-proliferation concerns. President Clinton highlighted the growing crisis in the proliferation of WMD in his 1994 speech to the United Nations General Assembly, "One of our most urgent priorities must be attacking the proliferation of weapons of mass destruction whether they are nu-

Major General Kenneth Hagemann, DNA Director, 1992-1995.

clear, chemical or biological, and the ballistic missiles that can rain down on populations hundreds of miles away... If we do not stem the proliferation of the world's deadliest weapons, no democracy can feel secure." Later in 1995, at a Fort McNair conference, Dr. Harold P. Smith, Assistant to the Secretary of Defense (Atomic Energy), echoed the President's earlier message that "...the number one challenge facing the United States now, and probably for the years ahead, is to prevent the proliferation of these weapons of mass destruction, whether chemical, biological, or nuclear, and the scientific knowledge of how to make them." The clear message was that DNA's central focus, for the foreseeable future, would be counterproliferation concerns.

The agency supported a review of all U.S. non-proliferation and counterproliferation activities that were the responsibility of the (then) Deputy Secretary of Defense, Dr. John Deutch. DNA supported counterproliferation planning by the Assistant to the Secretary of Defense (Atomic Energy), later renamed the ATSD (Nuclear and Chemical and Biological Defense Programs, or NCB). That office was assigned centralized responsibility for DoD counterproliferation research and development activities. DNA's tasks within the counterproliferation mission area, under the DoD Defense Counterproliferation Initiative, addressed critical technology base support to the emerging DoD counterproliferation strategy.

DNA's research focused specifically on military response options to develop and provide new weapons that used discriminant lethality against counterproliferation targets and could minimize unwanted or collateral effects. The agency's Counterproliferation Technology Base Support program emphasized collateral effects definition and prediction analysis; chemical weapon/biological weapon (CW/BW) agent neutralization; hardened/underground structural analysis; enhanced conventional weapon payload concepts; targeting technical assistance; and target signature evaluation.

In response to the dangers associated with the potential breakdown of nuclear controls in the new nations of the former Soviet Union in late 1991, the U.S. embarked on an innovative program of cooperative assistance. Until 1993, the Cooperative Threat Reduction (CTR) Program was called the Safe, Secure Dismantlement Program; it was also known as the "Nunn-Lugar Program." The program's fundamental objectives were to help all of the new nations, except Russia, to become non-nuclear, to accelerate START arms reductions, to enhance nuclear safety, security, and control, to initiate FSU chemical weapon destruction, to encourage demilitarization, and to extend contacts between the U.S. and FSU defense establishments.

In January of 1993, Dr. Harold Smith, ATSD(AE), assigned DNA the task of implementing the CTR program, on a cradle-to-grave basis, for each of the program's elements. As of mid-1996, the agency was executing over 50 CTR projects, ranging from supplying Russia with secure containers for transport and storage of fissile material, to projects in demilitarization designed to ensure that threat reduction efforts led to enduring, peaceful, and commercially viable endeavors. Specifically, the CTR program achieved the removal of over 1,200 warheads from deployed systems in Russia; realization of nuclear-free status in Ukraine, Kazakhstan, and Belarus; and elimination of many FSU strategic nuclear delivery systems.

U.S.-Soviet cooperation in scaling down their nuclear arsenals under such treaties as the INF signaled a changing role for the agency. In December of 1987, a ten-member task force set up offices in the Coast Guard headquarters at Buzzards Point in Washington, D.C. The group was to develop a plan for carrying out the on-site inspection provisions of INF. One of the original cadre of military personnel assigned to the work maintained that the original concept for this new agency was as a DNA component that would handle baseline (initial inspections) only. Later inspections were originally envisioned to be contracted out and the agency dissolved.[3]

The On-Site Inspection Agency (OSIA), formed with budgetary and administrative support from DNA, became a separate and more permanent inspection agency.[4] The mission of OSIA increased with the growth of several further treaties over the next few years, each requiring on-site inspection capability. In particular, the Threshold Test Ban Treaty (TTBT) and the Conventional Forces in Europe (CFE) Treaty, both signed in 1990, and START in 1991, required further inspection teams. In July of 1991, OSIA became the DoD executive agent for supporting the United Nations Special Commission (UNSCOM), the organization conducting inspections of Iraq to determine treaty compliance regarding elimination of Iraqi WMD threats. Over the decade 1989-1997, for all treaties and inspections, OSIA deployed more than 9,600 inspectors.[5]

As OSIA split from DNA and performed the direct inspection role, DNA itself appeared at first to have only a very minor part to play in the new arms control regime. This changed, however, following the breakup of the Soviet Union in 1991. Arms control and verification, and the ongoing destruction of missiles as dictated by treaty, were too expensive for the states which emerged from the former Soviet Union, and the work lagged. Throughout the new decade, as a primary mission thrust, DNA staff would address elements of this arms control and verification need in the new republics.

The "nuclear club" suddenly had four new nations: Russia, Belarus, Ukraine, and Kazakhstan, where the Soviet Union had been only one member before 1991. The impact of the dissolution of the Soviet Union on the issue of proliferation was worrisome and unpredictable. Then, in 1991, Belarus, Kazakhstan, and Ukraine all announced their plans to send to Russia for storage and dismantling thousands of Soviet-produced nuclear weapons that were housed on their territories. Intentions were one thing, action another. Leonard Spector, Director of the Carnegie Endowment for International Peace's Nuclear Non-Proliferation Project, noted that "...it is increasingly difficult to judge whether proliferation is on the wane or on the rise." He speculated that the protests from the republics of the FSU against the spread of nuclear weapons might be a "...thin veneer" over more sinister intentions. Concern about smuggling of nuclear materials and possibly whole missile systems from the new nuclear states was voiced in the press.[6] Although Ukraine, Belarus, and Kazakhstan stated their willingness to eliminate missiles on their territories, they claimed they were unable to pay for the effort.

In response to this problem, Congress in November of 1991 funded assistance to the new republics to destroy nuclear, chemical, and biological weapons and to transport, store, disable, and safeguard weapons in conjunction with their destruction. The funding established safeguards against the spread of the weapons to new countries. The initial legislation, known as the Nunn-Lugar Act, authorized the transfer of up to $400 million from DoD accounts to this program. An additional $400 million was authorized under the fiscal year 1993 Defense Appropriations Act (Public Law 102-396). In a practical sense, the CTR effort would require the procurement of tools and equipment and the sending of teams to do the actual work of missile dismantling, safeguarding, storing, and transporting nuclear warheads. OSIA, a small agency made up of technical people engaged in actual inspections, was not capable of mounting a major contracting/procurement effort.

In March of 1992, the Secretary of Defense delegated responsibility for executing the CTR Program to the ATSD(AE). The considerable responsibilities under CTR required an agency capable of contracting, providing logistics, support, and management on a vast scale. DNA was a logical choice. On January 11, 1993, DNA was delegated responsibilities for program management and execution, including project and acquisition planning, procurement, financial management, and performance oversight. DNA's ability to quickly contract out this work soon paid off. The CTR Program included a number of proposed projects that supported the umbrella agreement and fourteen implementing agreements signed between the United States and Russia, and another group of eight agreements between the United States and Belarus. On September 24, 1993, an additional umbrella agreement was initiated between the United States and Kazakhstan, with five draft implementing agreements. In addition, a number of agreements between the United States and Ukraine went through preliminary drafting before being tabled in 1993.

In late 1993, DNA's CTR Program completed its first project with the delivery of 2,500 soft armored blankets, used to protect nuclear devices from small arms fire or from spreading hazardous debris in case of accident during transportation, to the Russian Ministry of Atomic Energy. Belarus, Russia, and Ukraine also were planning "Defense Conversion"

Secretary of Defense William Perry, Colonel-General Volodymy Mikhtyuk, and Ukrainian Defense Minister Valeriy Shmarov at Silo #8 at Pervomaysk supervise removal of SS-19 missile in compliance with START under the Cooperative Threat Reduction (CTR) Program.

projects. Specialized projects included Russian containers to store fissile materials and construction of a new Science and Technology Center in the Ukraine.[7] A later initiative under Nunn-Lugar allowed the purchase and transfer of a limited amount of highly enriched uranium from Kazakhstan to storage in the United States. In addition and collaterally related to the CTR Program, more than 5,000 warheads were removed from missiles in Belarus, Ukraine, and Kazakhstan and returned to Russia.[8]

By 1994, DNA set up a "Defense Conversion Division" to implement specific agreements between the United States and four new republics directed at conversion of the defense industrial base in those republics to peaceful purposes. For example, DNA awarded contracts for industrial partnerships for a hearing aid factory, an air traffic management system, a bottling plant, and a dental equipment production firm. Other industrial partnership contracts involved work on automobile battery chargers, integrated circuits, antennas, and other non-defense related items. Part of the focus of the division's activities was to provide assistance in building pre-fabricated housing for demobilized Strategic Rocket Force personnel in the former Soviet Union.[9] The division also took on a variety of complementary projects within the CTR Program including setting up the international science and technology centers, conducting environmental restoration of former strategic rocket force bases, and assisting in the disposal of such non-nuclear, conventional weapons systems as radar arrays and tanks.[10]

DNA's Verification Technology Programs, conducted under the agency's Arms Control Verification Technology Research and Development Program, expanded during the 1990s to include support to virtually every arms control and bilateral agreement to which the U.S. was a party. Technology verification achievements and activities during this period included sensors for *Open Skies* aircraft, unified databases relevant to arms control, analytical techniques and sensors for chemical and biological agents, gravity gradiometers to characterize START Treaty Limited Items, and improved seismic sensing capabilities to verify provisions of the Comprehensive Test Ban Treaty (CTBT).

DNA sponsored annual conferences and symposia showcasing arms control and verification technologies, which typically attracted domestic and international participants from a wide variety of government, industry, and academic institutions. These conferences highlighted important lessons learned from previous and existing treaty verification technology, cost-effective strategies of verification assurance, and illustrated arms control verification technologies in development.

In his 1995 annual report to Congress, Secretary of Defense William Perry pointed out that American military forces deployed to defeat aggression "will likely face the use or threat of use of weapons of mass destruction (WMD)." Shortly after this speech, DNA was designated by DoD a Center of Excellence for WMD Counterproliferation. To provide technical analyses to assist decisionmakers in countering the WMD threat, the agency developed a wargame support process that allowed DoD participants to use analytic tools to access WMD impact in a training environment.

In 1995, the agency provided wargame support in eight sessions. The Air Force Wargaming Institute sponsored five of the sessions, held at Maxwell Air Force Base in Alabama. The Naval War College sponsored Global War Games 1995 at Newport, Rhode Island, and cosponsored another session in Hawaii with the Commander in Chief, Pacific. The U.S. Army Chemical and Biological Defense Command sponsored a Counterproliferation Research Development Seminar Wargame in McLean, Virginia. The DNA support package included pre-packaged presentations and briefings, seminars, and training sessions to familiarize decisionmakers with the use of analytic tools developed by technical directorates within DNA: Shock Physics, Radiation Sciences, Technology Applications, and Test, and Field Command. Feedback from the sessions was used to validate and refine the models and simulations.[11]

TECHNOLOGY APPLICATIONS FOR COUNTERTERRORISM

As the breadth and scope of terrorism expanded in the 1990s, it became apparent that much of the DNA Cold War expertise was applicable to efforts to counter this terrorism. In particular, DNA expertise in Command, Control, and Communications (C^3) facility survivability had direct application to the safeguarding of U.S. and allied facilities that were potential terrorist targets. Through the 1990s, DNA performed numerous Balanced Survivability Assessments of critical DoD and federal agency facilities. Chief among the findings of these survivability assessments were judgments regarding a facility's vulnerability to terrorism as virtual roadmaps to risk reduction measures. DNA applied blast response calculations to structures using calculational codes and models originally developed for nuclear applications. This analytical support was provided to law enforcement agencies during forensic investigations of terrorist events, including the World Trade Center (1994) and Oklahoma City (1995) bombings.

The agency's culture had centered around the study of catastrophic scenarios with a rational approach, building data to deal with nuclear weapon effects so as to mitigate them. Thus, its institutional culture was well suited to dealing with new terrorist scenarios. The accumulated databases available through DNA, the agency-sponsored Nuclear Information Analysis Center (DASIAC), and its other contractors, were highly pertinent to the issues of proliferation and terrorist use of high explosives, chemical or biological weapons. New threats by non-state-sponsored and state-sponsored terrorists, now armed with more powerful explosive devices and WMD, required technical understanding of such weapons on civilian populations. The attack on Khobar Towers in Dharhan, Saudi Arabia, in 1996, and the release of Sarin gas in the Tokyo subway in 1996 hammered home the need for the U.S. to be prepared for such terrorist acts within its homeland.

DNA's background in dealing with scenarios involving catastrophic attacks with nuclear weapons upon civilian populations gave it techniques and tools for assisting in evaluating such threats and events. Work on countering civilian terrorism led to a high-profile task in an era when small groups of terrorists were armed with extremely powerful weapons.[12] Following the terrorist bombing of the Khobar Towers military housing area in Dhahran, Saudi Arabia, the Defense Department turned to DNA to assess the yield and makeup of the bomb used to destroy Khobar Towers.

With its models and expertise, DNA estimated the likely yield of the bomb. The exact size of the yield would be very important in reviewing security precautions. A low-yield device, say in the range of 5,000 pounds or less, would indicate that traditional security precautions should have prevented extensive damage; a much larger yield would suggest that terrorism had reached a new scale and that entirely new security precautions would be required henceforth to protect personnel exposed in such locations. Using cratering data from the DIPOLE MIGHT tests of 1995, and calculating for a height-of-burst of 5.3 feet, based on the Dhahran tank truck design, DNA estimated that the yield had been approximately 11.5 tons, or 23,000 pounds of TNT-equivalent, in sharp contrast to press reports that had set the yield at about 5,000 pounds.

To confirm that this yield estimate was accurate, DNA examined several other effects of the bomb. Using a variety of methods, DNA generated estimated yields that varied somewhat but all much higher than the press reports. By using glass breakage as an indicator, and acknowledging that the blast wave was shielded by buildings, it was apparent there were varying high and low pressure zones. DNA ran a computer study of the 243 broken windows in the vicinity. This study produced an estimated yield of 31,000 pounds of TNT-equivalent blast.

Another DNA study focused on the deformation and displacement of the concrete facade leading into the building, resulting in a yield of at least 15,000 pounds. Computer studies, assuming the charge to have been roughly cylindrical in the tank truck, indicated a yield of 20,000-25,000 pounds of TNT-equivalent. A number of anomalies in the event were explained by the computer studies. An individual standing near an Army High Mobility Multipurpose Wheeled Vehicle (HMMWV) or Humvee, which was positioned approximately 125 feet from the blast, survived and foliage relatively near the explosion center was still on the trees. The Fort Polk tests, conducted by the U.S. Army Corps of Engineers for DNA along with computer analysis, showed that a blind area existed at a 45-degree angle from the main axis of the truck were the individual stood, with greatly reduced pressures. DNA concluded with a high degree of confidence that the charge used was between 20,000 and 30,000 pounds of TNT-equivalent. To confirm the findings, a 21,000-pound truck bomb was detonated at Fort Polk, Louisiana, on August 27, 1995, which satisfied investigators and confirmed DNA's findings.[13] The conclusion of DNA's Khobar Towers study was no mere technical fact but a finding that would influence safety considerations and facility improvements to withstand possible future attacks.

Such improvements, designed around an understanding of the Khobar Towers explosion, would lead to redesign of office and room layouts, new installation-wide warning systems, new battery-operated lighting, better training for personnel, procedural changes to minimize visits of trucks to areas with large numbers of personnel, and the creation of safe-haven areas to be used in cases of early warning. Earthen barriers and blast-resistant windows could reduce glass fragment injuries. The use of earthquake-proofing technologies in building construction could also increase resistance to terrorist attacks by such weapons.[14]

The 300-page Khobar Towers report by the DNA bomb-damage survey team concluded that the 20,000+ pound bomb had overwhelmed existing security mea-

Fort Polk cratering phenomenology test conducted by DNA and U.S. Army Corps of Engineers to determine accuracy of Khobar Towers bomb damage assessment; upper photo is tank loaded with explosives, lower photo is resultant crater.

sures at the facility. In an investigation led by retired Army General Wayne Downing, former commander of the U.S. Special Forces, Downing criticized the security measures and placed responsibility for inattention to security problems on the commander of the 4404th Air Wing at Dharhan. Downing estimated the truck bomb at 3,000-8,000 pounds. Downing disagreed with the DNA study, noting that "...there is no way a bomb could have been 20,000 pounds and have that man survive," referring to the individual near the Humvee. He also doubted that the leaves could remain on nearby plants if the blast had been over 20,000 pounds of TNT-equivalent.[15] However, Deputy Secretary John White and Chairman of the Joint Chiefs General John Shalikashvili emphasized security improvements rather than placement of blame. White stressed that "Americans didn't kill these airmen. Terrorists killed these airmen. And our focus is on what we can do in order to make sure that we minimize and protect against these kinds of enormous, complicated and sophisticated threats in the future."[16]

Thus, the DNA study was at the heart of the controversy surrounding the question of responsibility and security precautions. General Shalikashvili and Secretary of Defense William Perry accepted the DNA findings and the agency's technical assessment both as to the size of the blast and its anomalous effects. As an indication of support, the DNA report on the Khobar bomb survey was attached to the Downing report prior to submission to the President.[17]

END OF NUCLEAR TESTING–EFFECTS TEST AND SIMULATION

The U.S. underground nuclear testing program ended in September 1992, when the President signed a funding bill that contained an amendment introduced by Senator Mark Hatfield imposing a nine-month nuclear test moratorium. When President Clinton took office in 1993, he extended the moratorium for one year and repeated the extensions after that. In September of 1996, Clinton signed the Comprehensive Test Ban Treaty (CTBT), which was sent to Congress but not ratified. The United States had stopped production of new nuclear warheads in 1989, and the stockpile aged more rapidly than when new weapons were being introduced. Scientists at the weapons laboratories argued that tests remained the best way to determine whether nuclear weapons remained safe and stable, and they argued for as many as 15 full-scale tests in the early 1990s.

DNA had responsibility for two nuclear effects simulators as part of the Centralized Test and Evaluation Investment Program (CTEIP). That program had been approved in November 1988, providing a centrally funded RDT&E program for executing high-priority improvements to the Major Range and Test Facility Base. This $1.3 billion program funded 29 different projects, running from fiscal year 1990 through 1994. CTEIP included support of two DNA nuclear simulator programs that focused on survivability: the Large Blast/Thermal Simulator (LB/TS) and the DECADE radiation effects simulator.

Munitions effectiveness assessment modeling used empirical data obtained, in large measure, from DNA's Permanent High Explosives Test Site (PHETS) at White Sands Missile Range, New Mexico. Since 1988, there had been more than a 30-fold increase in conventional effects tests. DNA's White Sands test facilities were also employed by the Bureau of Alcohol, Tobacco and Firearms to create a computerized database and investigative protocol for law enforcement agencies to use in large-scale vehicle bomb investi-

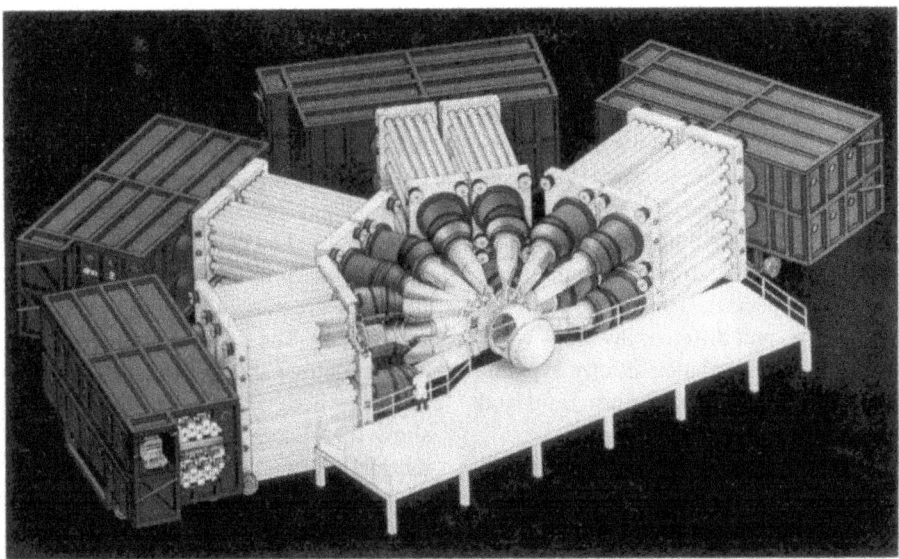

Drawing of DNA DECADE Radiation Test Facility at Arnold Engineering Development Center.

gations. The LB/TS, operated jointly since 1994 by DNA and the Army at White Sands, is the largest shock tube in the world. The simulator replicates the blast and thermal environments of nuclear weapons with yields from one to 600 kilotons. The LB/TS conducted rapid turnaround testing of full-scale systems in a simulated nuclear blast and thermal environment, evaluating hardness to the effects of these nuclear weapons. By 1990, over 200 untested systems were in the backlog that would be addressed by the LB/TS.

Another simulator, DECADE, was operated by the Air Force's Arnold Engineering Development Center. It was designed to simulate x-ray radiation effects of a nuclear detonation in space for testing hardness of space systems and their components. The name implied the fact that the facility would lead to a tenfold increase in capabilities to provide a high-level radiation source that could support hardness validation testing for space subsystems, including communications, navigation satellites, missile electronics, and seeker and surveillance systems.[18] The relationship between the testing equipment that represented one of the agency's core capability and its continued role under a test ban regime was apparent to the staff at DNA at the time. DNA's Director for Test claimed that, "Expertise, coupled with a sound architecture, test methodology, and smarter use of simulator capabilities can be the response to a CTBT. We need to preserve and build upon our existing capabilities and expertise if a CTBT comes along. DNA provided this core of expertise in nuclear weapons effects... We are the honest broker in advising our senior leadership as to whether or not system requirements have been met."[19]

Recognizing the lead that the agency had in the area of simulation, DNA decided to devote three special editions of its *Nuclear Survivability* newsletter, to broadcast its capabilities within the defense community. The August, 1990 edition focused on "Testing in Nuclear Hardness Validation," the February, 1991 issue on "Nuclear Weapons Effects Simulation," and the September, 1991 issue on "Nuclear Weapons Effects Codes and Analysis." Contributors to the issues spanned the nuclear effects community, including specialists from the national laboratories and different divisions within DNA. All contributed articles explaining a variety of simulator programs and equipment.

The aboveground testing Radiation Simulator Program continued to support testing while developing simulator improvements. BLACKJACK 5, DOUBLE EAGLE, PITHON, CASINO, PHOENIX, and AURORA continued as the workhorse simulators and were fully booked throughout the 1990s. These simulators tested the Air Force's Peacekeeper missile, the Navy's Trident II SLBM, the Milstar satellite, the Army Tactical Shelter, and Instrumentation Command and Control Programs, several NSA components, and satellite optical coatings and materials.[20]

With the reorganization of DNA in the 1990s, administration of the agency's testing program was transferred to Field Command, including the Test Operations Directorate that took over the testing functions formerly conducted out of the Test Directorate at Headquarters in Alexandria, Virginia. With the elimination of underground nuclear testing, more emphasis was placed on nuclear effects simulations and conventional weapon testing. Facilities were located not only at WSMR and the NTS, but at other locations and contractor facilities. At White Sands, stacks of high explosive were detonated to simulate nuclear airblast up to the 8 kilotons. The test site itself included hardened targets, instrumentation bunkers, and test control facilities. Tests and targets were also designed to evaluate advanced conventional penetrating weapon performance, new types of penetrating weapon fuzes, and structures themselves. The PHETS at White Sands allowed both live air-drop and static testing of conventional weapons. The new large simulators at White Sands provided ideal airblast wave forms of pressures up to 35 pounds per square inch. The thermal simulator could be operated separately from the blast simulator, or both could be used together to show the synergistic effects from both thermal and blast effects. Aircraft and ship parts, missiles, and other new weapon systems and subsystems developed since the ending of underground nuclear testing could be evaluated for nuclear hardness in this facility.[21]

During the period of underground nuclear testing, experiments to determine gamma-ray and x-ray radiation hardness were conducted in several stages, with limited testing of components in the laboratory and testing of sub-assemblies conducted in underground tests. Prior to the cessation of underground nuclear testing, the investigation of radiation effects and the validation of hardening procedures was conducted through a protocol of aboveground laboratory simulation testing or above-ground testing, computer analysis, a final underground test, and an analytical extrapolation to an operational environment. It had long been established that aboveground test simulations were adequate for investigation of neutron and gamma effects.[22] The underground test provided the proper fluence and spectrum of x rays that were not available aboveground and an interesting mixture of radiations that proved informative, albeit not a true representation of an operational environment. The underground test was always considered a less than optimal simulator for effects testing. It was expensive, risky, difficult to instrument and it required a very long lead time for preparation. Recognizing this fact, DNA, in the 1960s, began an extensive program to develop an aboveground simulator for x-ray testing. The progress of this program was expensive and slow because of the enormous amounts of energy required to generate a proper fluence over a sufficiently large area and of the proper energy spectrum.

When the U.S. entered an underground test moratorium in 1992, the time-proven test methodology was no longer available. All research and validation testing was relegated to aboveground testing and computer simulation. Despite the aggressive programs carried on by DNA, as well as the Department of Energy laboratories, to develop an aboveground test simulator for x rays, the realization of the goals remained many years away. There were suitable simulators for the upper end of the required energy spectrum, the "hot" x-rays. However, the inherent efficiency of the machines for producing the lower portion of the energy spectrum, the "cold" and "warm" part, was a daunting task. Designing the power storage systems and the radiation output sources would have to await the development of a fusion source, such as those later researched at the National Ignition Facility of Lawrence Livermore National Laboratories.[23]

Older facilities also proved useful with the new, heavier reliance on simulation and high-explosive testing. At Kirtland Air Force Base, the Advanced Research Electromagnetic Simulator (ARES) was upgraded in 1995 to allow for up to 20 simultaneous data channels from any particular test object, with up to 36 simulated high-altitude EMP events tested on a single day. ARES was designed as a vertically polarized HEMP simulator to provide an EMP environment compliant with any military or commercial environment. System upgrades gave the ARES facility the capability to produce pulses similar to those generated by a high-altitude nuclear detonation. At NTS in Nevada, using surplus tunnels, the agency conducted high-explosive tests to develop and improve understanding of the response of tunnels and deeply buried structures to nuclear explosions.[24]

In September of 1996, one week after signing the CTBT, President Clinton authorized an expenditure for testing nuclear weapons, not through nuclear explosions but through simulation with high explosives and computers and through the use of above-ground, non-nuclear facilities. Among the facilities was a proposed $1.1 billion National Ignition Facility (NIF) to be constructed at Lawrence Livermore National Laboratory. The NIF would consist of a 192-beam laser to converge the beams on deuterium and tritium pellets, causing them to implode and ignite by nuclear fusion. The NIF represented one small fraction of a planned stockpile stewardship program of $41 billion proposed by the Department of Energy.

DNA made use of facilities maintained by the national laboratories of DOE, including Los Alamos' Dual Axis Radiographic Hydrodynamic Facility that generates flash x-ray images of shock waves, simulating the first-stage detonation of a nuclear weapon. Livermore also maintained a Contained Firing Facility for high-explosive experiments, while Los Alamos housed Atlas, a pulsed power machine to simulate a nuclear weapon trigger implosion.[25]

Additionally, DNA assumed further responsibilities at Johnston Atoll. A state-of-the-art chemical agent incineration facility, the Johnston Atoll Chemical Agent Disposal System (JACADS), was completed by the Army in 1990. The transfer of chemical munitions from Europe to

Johnston Atoll took place in November 1990. These munitions were later destroyed in the JACADS facility.

AGENCY IN CRISIS

From 1989 through 1994, DNA was subjected to numerous official reviews, both internal and external, that examined how the agency functioned and the services it provided. The fiscal year 1993 Congressional Authorization called for the Defense Science Board (DSB) and Office of the Secretary of Defense (OSD) to review the agency's roles and missions. After the DSB and OSD reports were issued, in June 1993, Secretary of Defense Les Aspin responded back to Congress that, "I am satisfied with the comprehensiveness and effectiveness of the DNA program and the manner in which it is adapting to post Cold War realities." In short, Secretary Aspin endorsed DNA's mission as well as the findings of the DSB and OSD reports.

Later in 1993, a Strategic Air Command report recommended the abolishment of DNA as a separate defense agency, with its functions transferred to the Services and ARPA. Later in the same year, Secretary of Defense William Perry wrote to Senator Ted Stevens, claiming "We need the expertise of DNA and the unique technical and operational capabilities of the current [DNA] programs." This action was followed by OSD and the nuclear community rallying in support of the agency. Congressional support soon followed. In turn, Senators Nunn, Thurmond, Exon, and Lott urged reconsideration of DNA as a separate defense agency and reexamination of the agency's proposed (fiscal year 1994) budget.

In order to develop a logical and planned response to Congressional interest for these agency reviews, Victor Reis, the DDR&E, requested the DSB to establish a task force to conduct a thorough review of DNA's science and technology programs and to recommend changes by May 1993. In particular, Reis asked the task force to review the technology base program and the technology application programs of the agency to assess the impact of a comprehensive test ban as well as a reduction in the total number of new weapon systems in which nuclear survivability would be a high priority. "Specific consideration," he said, "should be given to continuing DNA in its historical role as the focal point within the DoD for nuclear weapons expertise." Furthermore, he wanted the task force to examine how DNA's role could be expanded "in the non-nuclear areas where its unique expertise can contribute" to defense requirements.[26]

John Cornwall of UCLA served as chairman of the DSB Task Force, which focused on agency scientific and technical issues. At the same time, a separate review group made up of a team from the Office of the Secretary of Defense and the Joint Staff (OSD/JS) considered the organization, management, and funding of DNA. Both the DSB Task Force and the OSD/JS review group delivered their reports in 1993. These two reports captured the rapid evolution of missions which had already taken place within the agency, but which had not yet been incorporated into its charter.

Cornwall, reporting for the DSB Task Force, noted that "...because of the noticeable and distressing tendency of the Services to reduce their nuclear related expertise," the task force conducted its review in a broader context, rather than simply providing a narrow consideration of science and technology issues. Cornwall placed the review in the larger setting of the future of United States nuclear and conventional weapons technology strategy. With this perspective, the issues became slightly changed from those the task force had originally been charged to examine. In particular, the DSB Task Force looked at how the "DoD in total," not just DNA, "will meet its nuclear responsibilities in this uncertain world." Furthermore, the task force examined the question of how the DoD could make use of advanced technology which had been originally developed for nuclear purposes and now might be used to meet future non-nuclear needs, particularly in the area of countering chemical and biological WMD.[27] The detailed report of the DSB examined many facets of the issue, but its primary thrust was to recommend that the DNA charter be modified to provide focus for non-nuclear activities of critical importance to the DoD. These areas included developing the technology base for advanced conventional munitions, and becoming a focal point for technologies related to counterproliferation of WMD. In addition, the task force expected DNA to continue with major responsibility in warhead stockpile management, military radiobiology research, and new methods of testing in the light of the cessation of underground testing.[28]

The OSD review group slightly overlapped in membership with the DSB Task Force working at the same issue. The overlap allowed the two policy groups to be current on each other's deliberations. The OSD review group received a series of briefings from DNA personnel and conducted interviews and panel discussions. The review group contacted DNA's customers in the military Services, DNA's "performers" such as contractors and service and DOE laboratories, and officials in ARPA and DOE, as well as former DNA directors and civilian leaders.[29]

The OSD review group made its assumptions explicit, and those assumptions provide a good indication of viewpoints and observations common among Defense Department planners in 1993. The group assumed that the United States would maintain nuclear forces into the future and that several nations would continue to have nuclear arsenals larger than 100 weapons. Despite efforts at non-proliferation, the review group assumed the number of nuclear powers would increase in the period 1993-2003. It would remain plausible that various warfighting scenarios for the United States would involve nuclear weapons and that adversaries might employ nuclear weapons. The public would continue to insist on high standards for safety, security, and personnel competence in nuclear matters. Underground testing would diminish, downsizing of nuclear arsenals would require dismantling, destruction, and verification technologies, and budgets for nuclear matters would further diminish.[30] Working from these assumptions and examining the mission of DNA, the review group concluded that "DNA is the only logical focal point in DoD for nuclear competencies." Dispersing the expertise to various other groups within DoD would run the "danger of dilution/loss" of the expertise.[31]

The two reports reflected changes already afoot at the agency. Yet each report gave a different emphasis—one suggesting that the new missions would help ensure that DoD maintained its core of nuclear expertise, while the other stressed the new missions as important in themselves. The DSB report stressed the need for the agency to focus nuclear weapon effects work and continuing stockpile management. The DSB report regarded several new missions in countering non-nuclear weapons of mass destruction and in dealing with advanced conventional munitions, as a means to "...ensure maintenance of nuclear-related core competencies." The DSB, with its more scientific and technical orientation than the administrative OSD report, viewed the nuclear issues as paramount, and saw the new programs taken on by the agency primarily as useful to maintain its ability to serve as the DoD's "continuing repository of certain essential nuclear expertise." Essentially the DSB treated DNA as a nuclear agency that would survive better if it took on some non-nuclear functions.[32]

The OSD report stressed the new missions as crucial in themselves in a world that was drastically changed. The report gave a close analysis and comparison of the programs at DNA in 1985 with those in 1993, capturing the details of the "changing focus of DNA's key programs from a time of the Cold War to the present." By asserting that the changes had occurred from "a time of the cold war," the OSD report made clear that its participants regarded the Cold War as over and that a new era was already well under way. The changes in program emphasis included such new elements as "Dismantlement in the Former Soviet Union," "Counter-proliferation," and "Verification Technology."[33]

Pointing to these last three programs, the OSD report noted that such programs were "consistent with geopolitical trends to denuclearize and curb nuclear ambitions throughout the world." Other programs such as Adaptive Targeting represented a broadening of DNA's weapon system lethality mission to encompass conventional weapons, as applied to hardened targets, such as the deeply buried bunkers encountered during the Gulf War. Still other programs represented the search for "high fidelity testing alternatives" in anticipation of a comprehensive underground test ban. In short, the report stated, "all current DNA programs have been reoriented to meet the emerging needs of the post-Cold War era."[34] The language of the OSD report made it clear that the review group saw its charge as documenting and capturing what had already begun to happen within the agency, and recommending that it be more formally recognized. Despite the fact that the two groups overlapped to some extent in membership, the tone of the two reports represented two shades of opinion. However, they did agree on certain essentials. Both the DSB Task Force and the OSD review group agreed that DNA was doing the right thing to adapt. With more emphasis on DNA's nuclear heritage, the DSB Task Force saw the changes and new programs as essential in justifying and helping to maintain that core heritage. The OSD recognized that the new programs at the agency represented the beginnings of an adaptation to a different world, one in which nuclear weapons were only one of several types of WMD, and a world in which "denuclearization" was the order of the day. While nuclear threats remained part of that new world, new issues regarding other weapons of mass destruction would occupy the agency, and those new programs were not supportive of the nuclear function but were important in themselves.

The two reports, differing in emphases, gave the DDR&E two different justifications for continuing and redefining the mission of the agency—one that echoed Cold War assumptions about a continuing nuclear stand-off with one or more nuclear powers and another based on post-Cold War assumptions. By either rationale, DNA would continue to exist and have a crucial mission.

Even as the mission and program emphasis evolved, further studies focused on DNA's role in stockpile stewardship and on the nature of weapons research and weapon effects research in a post-Cold War world where international agreement prohibited underground testing of nuclear weapons. In May of 1993, the Scientific Advisory Group on Effects (SAGE) conducted a meeting that reviewed the

OSD and DSB reports. The meeting of the SAGE included a number of classified briefings, as well as a concluding executive session held as a closed meeting. The objectives of the May 1993 meeting of the SAGE Panel, held at Tyndall Air Force Base in Florida, were to review the reports produced by OSD and DSB, to discuss an investment strategy for the next generation of radiation effects simulators, and to develop planning regarding nuclear non-proliferation. Reiterating points made in the two prior studies, the published report of the SAGE meeting stressed the fact that DNA was uniquely qualified to provide the research and development needed to develop effective counterproliferation capabilities. Specifically, the agency could "play a particularly important role as the technical agent (and advocate)" for military responses to proliferation threats. However, the SAGE group recommended, "...the agency must develop a clear vision and anticipation of what [the agency] is and what it should do."[35]

Among the recommendations raised at the meeting was the agreement that strategic thinking should focus on the increased threat of proliferation in a world in which both the former Soviet Union and the United States vastly reduced their nuclear arsenals. To study the question would require the integration of military, political, and diplomatic considerations, and these different responsibilities should be housed in a single command. For this reason, DNA would need to work with the intelligence community and the Services to ensure that all parties understood nuclear weapon effects, especially on those crucial military systems that had never been hardened. Thus, considerable attention should focus on developing Command and Control, Communications, Computers and Intelligence (C^4I) systems as the organizing principle and framework for DNA.[36] As in the earlier studies by DSB and OSD, the SAGE Panel simultaneously recognized what was already happening at the agency and recommended that it be made explicit. Shortly after the group delivered its findings in 1993 the SAGE Panel was disbanded, as part of a government-wide move to reduce the number of federal advisory groups.

The Congress 1994 Appropriations Conference Report retained DNA, but called for independent review, by the RAND Corporation, to further investigate the agency's functions. The RAND review would be utilized by the Secretary of Defense in his 1995 Quadrennial Defense Review (QDR) of roles and missions. The RAND review presented an opportunity to gain support for DNA's course of change. All of these official reviews focused attention on not just DNA but how the DoD, in total, would meet its continuing nuclear responsibilities in the uncertain world. Additionally, the reviews addressed not just nuclear responsibilities, but how DoD could best use advanced technology, originally developed for nuclear purposes, to meet future non-nuclear needs, particularly in countering WMD threats looming on the horizon.

The first RAND study on the agency's future mission, presented as a briefing in March of 1994, assessed the options facing DNA. Agency personnel provided the RAND group with extensive briefings, including one presented in February of 1994, that opened with the assertion: "DNA is a highly dynamic organization, still evolving, whose technical and operational expertise is vital to our national security."[37] This RAND study identified several trends under way during the early 1990s, including the likelihood that the United States would only require minimum nuclear deterrence in the future, and that arms control, non-proliferation and counterproliferation agreements, backed by security guarantees, would tend to address regional instabilities. In the future, the study asserted, there would be increasing demand for innovative non-nuclear solutions to nuclear problems, and such solutions would only marginally involve nuclear "core competencies" as discussed in the 1993 reports.

The sense of having moved to a new era was pervasive: the RAND study pointed out that fiscal constraints would force a competitive search for the least expensive way to achieve the non-nuclear work done by DNA. The pressure would not necessarily lead to the "...conversion of Government agencies." Rather, work would be shifted on the basis of "value added" and on the basis of the value of the products of agencies. On both counts, DNA was highly respected in the defense community, the report asserted, with "almost universal support for DNA continuing" its nuclear weapon effects and stockpile functions. Various agencies utilizing DNA's services praised the agency's contributions and responsiveness, particularly DNA's flexible resources both in handling funding and in getting access to contractors and to government and Service laboratories performing the technical work. Most of the findings of the March, 1994 study were presented as "preliminary," but it was clear that the study had identified some of the major strengths of the agency, especially its reputation for excellence and responsiveness and its ability to work with very low direct budget costs. The agency's reliance on contractors to serve its clients in the services meant that the cost of running the agency itself was relatively low, considering its variety of services and products.[38]

Philip E. Coyle, Victor Gilinsky, and Harold M. Agnew authored a second RAND report. Their study, published in December, took a different perspective on the changes than did the 1993 OSD and DSB reports and went beyond the March 1994 study to address how DNA might fare under consolidation of nuclear work from both DoD and DOE.[39] Coyle, Gilinsky, and Agnew addressed the post-Cold War environment of smaller defense budgets, declining nuclear weapon stockpiles, and changing missions. In light of these changes, they wrote, the United States nuclear weapons establishment was already beginning to consolidate its activities, and it would continue in that direction. They saw three possible pathways for further consolidation: consolidation within DoD, consolidation of all non-military nuclear functions in DOE, or possibly establishing a separate independent agency for nuclear-weapons related functions. They reviewed the three possibilities, institutional obstacles, and the possible role of DNA within a larger realignment of United States nuclear weapons policy.[40] Their study concluded that, for the first time in five decades, there

Dr. George W. Ullrich, DNA/DSWA Deputy Director, 1990-1997.

were no military requirements for any new nuclear warheads or bombs. The only "unsatisfied needs" were for an earth-penetrating warhead and an air-delivered enhanced radiation bomb. The authors commented that it might be possible to develop both such devices without any nuclear testing, using existing warheads repackaged to meet the objectives.[41]

With reductions in the stockpile, with phasing out of nuclear organizations in the Services, and with reduction in training centers, it was becoming more difficult to attract and retain skilled personnel to handle stockpile maintenance. Furthermore, the character of the work done by DNA, DOE, and their contractors had shifted dramatically from designing and producing new warheads to maintaining the nuclear capability, taking care of a declining number of warheads, dismantling American weapons, assisting in the reduction of the former Soviet stockpile, and cleaning up the nuclear sites.

Consequently, the authors of the December, 1994 RAND study looked at three different alternatives: either creating an enlarged agency within DoD that would encompass DNA as well as related nuclear functions, or creating an independent agency that would incorporate DNA functions along with other nuclear functions, or consolidating its functions within the DOE. After weighing a series of pros and cons, the group recommended the first option: an expanded DoD agency that would take on issues of threat reduction, nuclear weapons effects, and technology applications, as well as centralized stockpile management.[42]

In this conclusion, the December, 1994 RAND study echoed the February, 1994 presentation by DNA in which a series of pros and cons regarding a similar set of options had been weighed. DNA leaders themselves concluded that the "cons" of combining nuclear work in the DOE or in an independent agency like ARPA outweighed the pros. Whereas they thought that the pros outweighed the cons in the option of combining the functions in an expanded DNA.[43] Over the next few years, the suggestions made by OSD, DSB, the SAGE review, and the RAND studies all continued to bear fruit for later agency reorganization.

NUCLEAR WEAPON SAFETY

In 1990 the Drell Committee on Nuclear Weapons Safety submitted a report to the House Armed Services Committee. It led to many new agency responsibilities. DNA played an important role in the implementation of the committee recommendations, to include serving as chair of the Red Team which addressed the design safety of the W-80 warhead, execution of the executive secretary role for the Joint Advisory Committee on Nuclear Weapons Surety, and the development and conduct of the Joint Nuclear Surety Executive Course, as well as carrying out numerous assessments to develop enhanced safety baseline data.

NEW AGENCY CHARTERS

After internal review at DoD, Donald J. Atwood, Deputy Secretary of Defense, issued a revised organizational charter for DNA in January 1991. The new charter, replacing the 1987 charter, strengthened the role of the Deputy Secretary of Defense in oversight management of DNA and reduced the policy-setting role of the Joint Chiefs of Staff. The new charter also changed the administrative structure of the Armed Forces Radiobiology Research Institute, removing it as a subordinate command of DNA. The DNA mission had expanded in 1987. Under that version of the charter, DNA's role in planning non-strategic nuclear force requirements had increased "to improve the ability to plan, modernize and preserve a U.S. and allied global nuclear deterrence strategy."[44] The Office of the Secretary of Defense issued a summary statement in the Federal Register in February of 1991 affirming that the new charter placed the Director of DNA directly under the direction, authority, and control of the Pentagon's Director, DDR&E.[45]

The mission of DNA, however, remained identical in both the 1987 version of DoD Directive 5105.31, the DNA charter, and the 1991 new edition of the same directive and in the changed Code of Federal Regulations, showing the authority of DDR&E over DNA. The revised charter of 1991 seemed to make little adjustment to the end of the Cold War, and policy discussions within the agency and among advisory groups regarding the precise role of DNA continued at a high pace throughout the period of 1989 to 1994.[46]

DNA TRANSITION TO DSWA

As explained earlier, in 1992, and again in 1993, Congress mandated reviews of DNA's roles, missions, and functions. The eventual result was a reaffirmation of the DoD commitment to maintain nuclear competencies with DNA as the *center of excellence* for the Department's nuclear matters, including cooperative threat reduction and activities in Nuclear Stockpile Stewardship. DNA also gained responsibility for non-nuclear development activities that took advantage of the agency's nuclear heritage. The traditional DNA roles, along with the new tasks, were institutionalized in a new charter issued in 1995. Subsequently, the agency reorganized to improve service to its customers, to implement total quality management, to break away from Cold War traditions, and to foster a higher degree of coordination and teamwork.

On June 26, 1996, the Defense Special Weapons Agency (DSWA) was established, replacing the Defense Nuclear Agency. DSWA had a new charter and an explicitly expanded mission. In addition to the missions which the new agency inherited from AFSWP, DASA, and DNA, such as management of the military nuclear weapons stockpile, the agency now was charged with conducting programs associated with the CTR work, with arms control technology, and with counterproliferation support. The 'special weapons' designation was a symbolic return to the agency's roots, yet in accordance to its new missions encompassing both nuclear and advanced conventional weapons support programs. In an August 1996 *Science & Technology Digest* article entitled "DNA Restructuring," DSWA Deputy Director Dr. George Ullrich explained the basis for the new agency name, "We didn't want our old name to preclude us from applying our unique nuclear skills and tools to such new program areas as counterproliferation and hard target kill... we felt strongly that 'weapons' should be

Major General Gary L. Curtin, DSWA Director, 1995-1998.

part of the name to convey the fact what we deal with warfighting issues."

DSWA was also charged with researching and developing technologies to enable the United States to implement, comply with, and verify nuclear, strategic, chemical, biological, and conventional arms control treaties and agreements. With an authorized personnel level of slightly over 1,000 and a budget for fiscal year 1996 of $361 million, the agency appeared to have found a solid place in the post-Cold War environment.[47] Subsequent events would modify that appearance.

DSWA Director Major General Gary L. Curtin, who succeeded Major General Hagemann in 1995, expressed the reasoning behind maintaining DSWA in the post-Cold War environment: "DSWA has been evaluated by a number of different review groups... to determine how the agency could be best employed today and in the future. After careful investigation, every one of those studies concluded that there was a need for a *center of nuclear excellence* within DoD, because of the curtailment of these activities within the Services and many CINC Headquarters."

AGENCY PROGRAMS IN THE 1990S

In addition to DSWA's overall counterproliferation, ACTD, and CTR mission emphasis in the 1990s, a number of smaller, yet critically important programs and mission tasks emerged that built upon the agency's legacy nuclear experience. Among these programs were the following:

JOINT SCIENCE PROGRAMS

DSWA sponsored joint science programs with scientific institutions in Russia, Ukraine, and Kazakstan through the 1990s. These programs included an evaluation of the Russian Topaz reactor for thermionic energy, applications of energetic materials, comparative findings on nuclear weapons effects, and the use of advanced computational techniques. The Topaz program was unique, involving the acquisition and subsequent non-nuclear testing of a power system that served as the means to evaluate Russian technology and to find peaceful civilian applications. Topaz research began at Phillips Laboratory in May of 1992, after two unfueled nuclear reactors were delivered to Kirtland AFB following a statement by President Bush to allow the purchase. Nicknamed Topaz, the reactors used a nuclear power system for non-nuclear testing and technology spin-off applications. This technology was ahead of what the United States or any other country had yet developed. Topaz was an international technology cooperation program involving DSWA, Phillips Laboratory, Sandia

A Russian-built Topaz II nuclear reactor sits in a DSWA laboratory at Kirtland AFB, New Mexico.

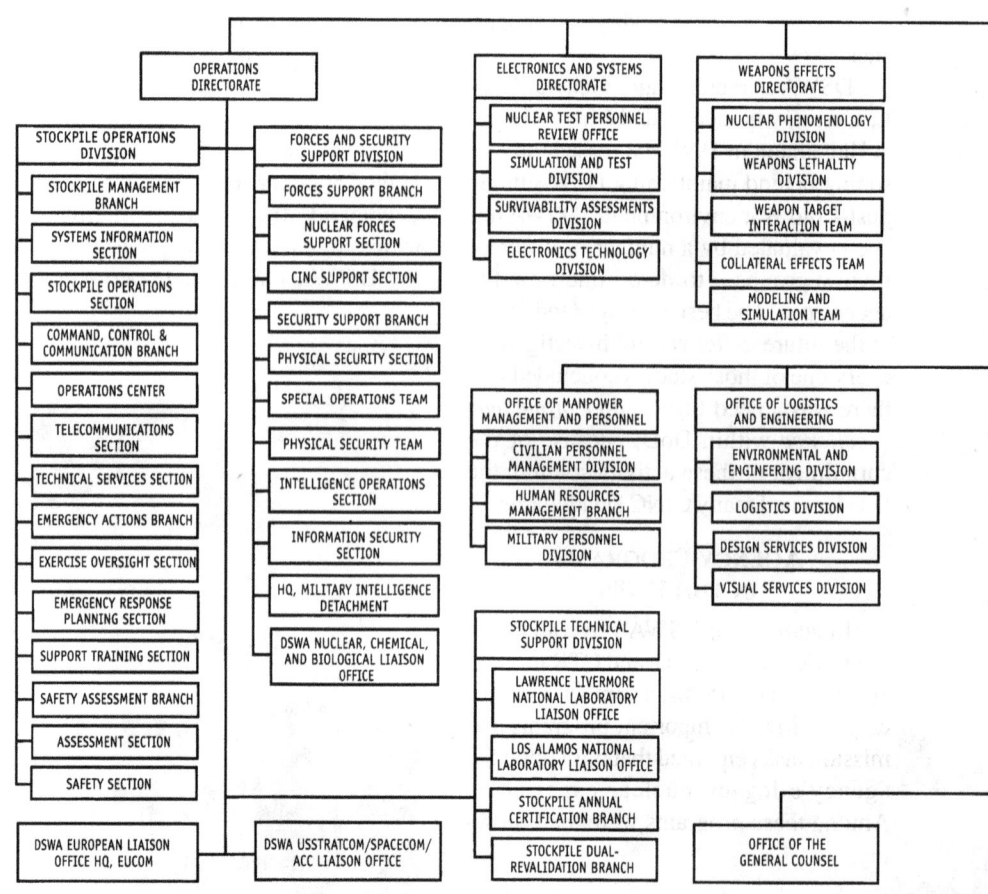

DSWA Organizational Chart, July 1996.

POST-COLD WAR ERA: NEW MISSIONS, 1989 to 1997

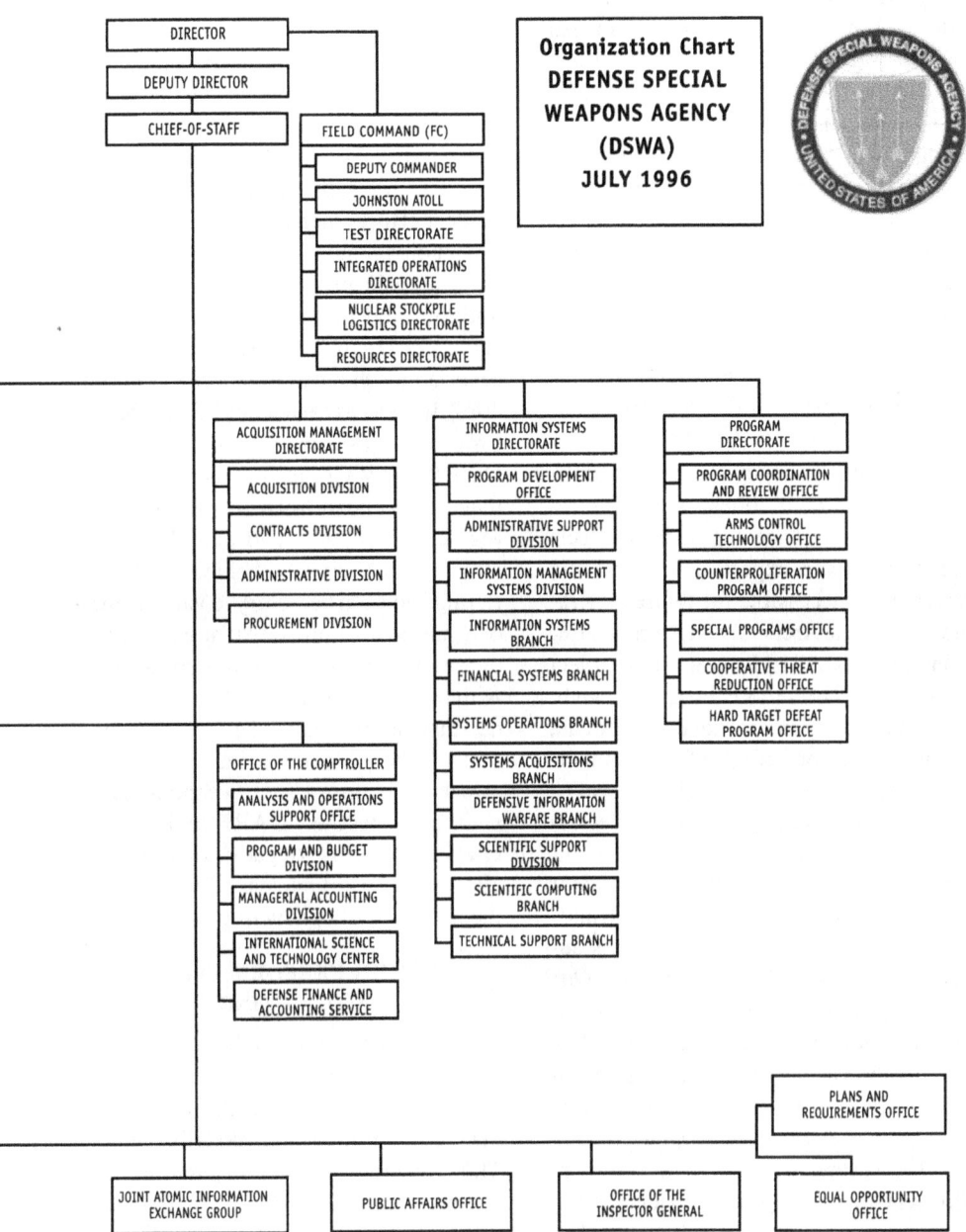

National Laboratories, the University of New Mexico in Albuquerque, and Los Alamos National Laboratory, all managed by the Ballistic Missile Defense Office. Originally, Topaz was Russia's answer for a space nuclear reactor capable of delivering power to its orbiting or long-range satellites and spacecraft. The Russians fabricated 26 complete Topaz II systems from 1970 through 1990 for system testing, but research cutbacks ended the program.

GRAYBEARDS/DARE: DATA AND KNOWLEDGE PRESERVATION

Two linked agency efforts were initiated in 1993 as a cohesive program to ensure that irreplaceable nuclear effects information and expertise survived and was readily accessible for future generations: the Data Archival and Retrieval Enhancement (DARE) Program and Project Graybeard. The DARE Program sought to locate, store, and retrieve effects data from its inventory of waveforms, numeric tables, diagrams, reports, photographs, and video media. Integration and declassification of effects knowledge was underway in the new *Handbook of Nuclear Weapon Effects* (Calculational Handbook), that drew upon the agency's authoritative 22-volume *Effects Manual One* (EM-1). The agency broadcasted community technology advancements and data preservation achievements in the publications *Nuclear Survivability* and its successor, *Science & Technology Digest*.

The second DNA archival program, Project Graybeard, planned to identify, locate, interpret, and comment on test data and lessons learned, and integrate the information into the DARE database for archival storage. Project Graybeard had, as its goal, the documentation of the technical history of atmospheric and underground nuclear weapon effects testing. It was originally organized into four technical area domains of shock physics, ionizing and electromagnetic radiation, thermomechanical effects, and biological effects. A fifth domain, nuclear sources, was added later. The early shock physics emphasis of Project Graybeard built the template for subsequent study of other nuclear effects such as high-altitude phenomenology, nuclear radiation, and electromagnetic effects, underwater and underground effects. John Lewis, who served as DASA's program manager for seven atmospheric tests between 1958 and 1962, worked as a leader in the Graybeard Project and as a member of the DARE Data Review Group. Lewis recognized that he was one of "relatively few remaining scientists" who had participated in atmospheric testing. He believed that such testing had been necessary to validate theory, but he also prayed "that world conditions will never again present anyone with the same dilemma" of having to understand all the potential effects of weapons of mass destruction in order to effectively control such weapons. Like simulation testing, DARE and Project Graybeard, using "legacy" data, would allow for study of nuclear effects without the necessity of conducting new tests.[48]

HIGH PERFORMANCE COMPUTING

The underpinning of the agency's nuclear expertise and advanced conventional weapon applications was its high performance computing and modeling work. The High Performance Computing and Communications (HPCC) program provided advanced scientific computing resources to the nuclear effects community since the mid-1970s. In the early years, this was accomplished by buying large blocks of computer time from the AEC and Service laboratories. From 1980 to 1983, DSWA (then DNA) operated its own CDC 7600 supercomputer at Kirtland AFB. In 1983, the agency entered into an arrangement with Los Alamos National Laboratories to provide high performance computing resources. Since then, Los Alamos has integrated a series of DSWA supercomputers (CDC CYBER 176 in 1984 and Cray M98 in 1994) into its computational environment and operated a private communications network providing classified and unclassified computing to DSWA's geographically distributed support sites. In 1995, DSWA augmented its high performance computing capability with a Cray J90 operating at its headquarters.

Arguably the most important "product" of DSWA and its predecessors over the years had been information. The results of the 1993 SAGE meeting had confirmed this point: information was perhaps the most crucial product of the agency in the fast-changing strategic environment. With the development of more and more powerful desktop computers, and with protection of them so that classified databases and programs could be operated, the agency's production of a wide variety of information sets and programs for customers in the Defense community flourished. As "Windows" and "hypertext" programs became available, DSWA adapted and updated programs to make this technology even more usable.

COMBAT SUPPORT

One example of a high-performance computing effort was the agency's work on the Joint Munitions Effectiveness Manual. This manual was developed by the Joint Technical Coordinating Group for Munitions Effectiveness. The agency worked with the group to bring together effectiveness evaluations of air-to-surface weapons with analysis methods for prediction of weapon effects into a single software application. The system, dubbed Joint Munitions Effectiveness Manuals/Air-to Surface (JMEMM/AS or JAWS), brought together the contents of more than a dozen different air-to-surface manuals, dealing with such topics as weapon characteristics and effectiveness, target vulnerability, and delivery accuracy. One of the major goals of the system designers was to enable weapon planners to immediately and effectively access and use the information in the assorted manuals. By June of 1994, designers had prepared a version of the computer program for testing. They believed that with its system of links and intuitive presentation, it would make the data far more usable than the older paper manuals, some of which, designers discovered, had become either redundant or obsolete. The new JAWS software package held out the promise of serving as a model for future cross-platform weaponeering analysis packages.[49]

Early in the 1990s, DNA, with Service headquarters and laboratory participation, and support from the agency's Information Analysis Center, established the Joint Services Conventional Weapons Effects Advisory Group. It managed the consolidation and technology update of Service conventional weapon effects protective design manuals, with the support and participation of NATO International Staff. Drawing upon the technical expertise of conventional weapon experts across the DoD, DSWA integrated the fruits of its research and test results and with those of the Services to publish, in August of 1998, an authoritative, state-of-the art technical manual, *The Design and Analysis of Hardened Structures to Conventional Weapons Effects* (DAHS CWE Manual). A hyperlinked version of the design manual, developed in parallel, and complete with executable analytic codes for both design and analysis use, was published in September of 1998. It was known as the *Protec-*

tive Structures Automated Design System.

With the advent of both floppy and compact disk media readers on personal computers, DSWA published a wide range of powerful desktop computer aids or *"comp aids,"* designed to benefit the nuclear and conventional weapon effects communities. The variety of such computational aids ranged from methods of calculating airblast phenomena and ocean basin acoustic reverberation from nuclear blasts, to the response of satellite subsystems to x-ray induced fields. Newly developed aids reflected the changing and evolving mission of DSWA to deal with new threats. *High Explosive Blast* calculated effects produced by above-ground detonations of high-explosive charges, providing scaling models from ANFO and TNT for other explosives. *Fireball Radiation* modeled radiated infrared, visible, ultraviolet power, and energy time histories and distributions for the first ten seconds following a nuclear detonation. Developers subjected each updated or republished computational aid to an intensive three-month period of testing by technical and operational users.[50] These computational aids were distributed extensively throughout DoD, DOE, the contract community, and among Allied countries.[51]

To an extent, DSWA became the beneficiary of consolidation of a variety of informational sources. In 1981, the agency's Information Analysis Center, DASIAC, became the point of contact for the Electronics Radiation Response Information Center (ERRIC), previously operated by the U.S. Army's Harry Diamond Laboratories as the Component Response Information Center. By the late 1990s, ERRIC contained a large database of over 11,000 data sets detailing the response of electronic parts to nuclear radiation. ERRIC made information readily available re-

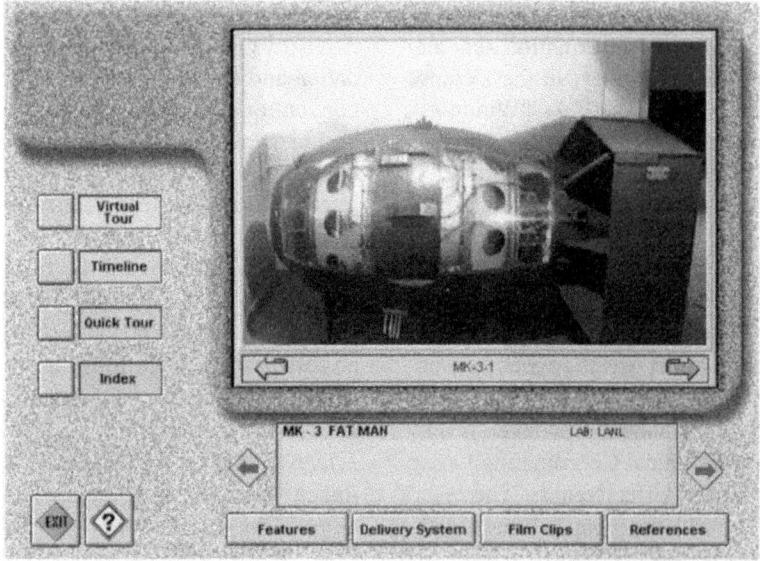

Defense Nuclear Weapons School Virtual Tour Interface, part of DSWA's nuclear weapons training multimedia technology.

garding the transient radiation effects on electronics to the "hardening community" in DoD, the Services, other government agencies, and government contractors. To facilitate technical access, ERRIC was later distributed via server access on the Internet/World Wide Web.[52]

Another combat support initiative that DSWA enthusiastically pursued was the Hard Target Defeat program. Acknowledging that the U.S. and its Allies face a growing threat related to critical military targets hidden within and shielded by hardened, deeply-buried tunnel complexes, the Office of the Under Secretary of Defense for Acquisition and Technology's Hard and Deeply Buried Target Defeat Capability Initiative was commissioned. It set the priorities for DSWA's Hard Target Defeat program. The objective of the agency's support was to examine existing U.S. and Allied capabilities to target hardened, deeply-buried complexes and to pursue new technologies to mitigate shortfalls in such targeting. Responding to the challenge of characterizing hard targets to exploit specific weapons, DSWA identified areas of focus, to include examination of operational signatures of tunnels or underground development; scale testing of target subsystem vulnerabilities; utilization of geological models for weapon defeat; and intelligence and surveillance assessment to provide targeteers with information required to defeat hard targets with conventional weapons.

DEFENSE NUCLEAR WEAPONS SCHOOL

When DASA was reorganized and became DNA in 1973, the nuclear school that had flourished in the 1960s was turned over to the Air Force for operation as the Interservice Nuclear Weapons School. Twenty years later, Deputy Under Secretary of Defense John Deutch directed the transfer of the school back to DNA, effective October 1, 1993. Deutch designated the agency as the DoD Executive Agent "...for sustaining general interest nuclear weapons training expertise."[53] Renamed the Defense Nuclear Weapons School, the training facility remained at Kirtland Air Force Base in Albuquerque, New Mexico. In the 1990s, many of the courses taught at the school reflected the same topics taught thirty years earlier, although they had been regularly updated with new information. For example, the Senior Officers Nuclear Accident Course and the Nuclear Weapons Orientation Course served as introductions for military officers and civilians who would serve at DNA or in other organizations requiring familiarity with nuclear weapons and policies.

At the request of the joint DoD-DOE Nuclear Weapons Council and the Secretary of Defense for Atomic Energy, new courses were added, including a one-day executive course on nuclear weapons surety for senior DoD and DOE officials with nuclear weapons-related responsibilities. Other new courses included a one-day Nuclear Weapons Technical Inspection course and a four-day Counterproliferation Awareness Course. The latter provided a mix of historical and current information to ensure that decisionmakers, action officers, and operators would have a common frame of reference. It examined all weapons of mass destruction, including nuclear, chemical, and biological missiles. Through the school's long history, attendance at such a course required a high-level security clearance. Additional classes, reflecting the growing assortment of new missions of the agency, included Environmental Management of Radioactive and Chemical Contamination. This course was designed to train federal and support personnel who would manage or lead the cleanup and restoration of contaminated sites. The course included topics on chemical and nuclear materials, the effects of the material on the environment, site characterization, and issues involving transportation of hazardous materials. Other lessons included a two-day course to train flag officers in dealing with nuclear weapon accidents, an eight-day course for nuclear emergency team members, a four-day course on nuclear hazards, and a five-day ordnance disposal course. The courses not only met significant continuing and new needs but also adapted new technologies of distance learning. Using video teleconferencing equipment, for example, a lecturer on the "Tokyo Subway Gas Attack" presented his material from DSWA headquarters in Alexandria, Virginia, to attendees at the school in Albuquerque, New Mexico, during a 1996 snowstorm that prevented him from flying out of Washington.

TRANSITION

Throughout 1989 to 1997, the agency had responsibly adapted to the changing defense environment. DSWA represented an investment in intellectual capital that many of its supporters within DoD and on Capitol Hill recognized and did not want to see dispersed. Through the DoD, a wide variety of customers for DSWA's services and knowledge had come to rely on the organization. The agency had a good reputation both for technical competence as well as timely and responsive service. The new international environment suddenly became alive with potential threats from new directions, to which the agency was capable of responding with expertise, experience, and dispatch; when DoD "customers" sought repositories of talent and knowledge, many of them reflexively turned to DSWA. The very nature of the technical work and the body of data and knowledge that DSWA and its predecessor agencies had assembled over fifty years became even more pertinent in the post-Cold War world. The nature of its structure as a Joint Service organization gave it flexibility not present in line organizations. Thus, DSWA was well positioned for the emerging post-Cold War military structure and policy.

The effort to reduce the size of government bureaucracy which had characterized the administrations of Presidents Jimmy Carter, Ronald Reagan, George Bush, and William Clinton did not undermine or destroy the agency. Since DNA operated efficiently, with a small, responsive, and technically competent core of civilian employees, augmented by a talented array of military staff, and since it had well-established relationships with the contractors who had expertise in many areas related to WMD, the agency demonstrated that it was quite capable of adapting to changing priorities as the Cold War ended. DSWA emerged from DNA as a strong and important resource for the Defense Department to meet its continuing and new responsibilities.

As the heir of the Manhattan Engineer District, DSWA became the natural and efficient choice of an agency to house the DoD's response to the WMD technological dangers of the coming 21st century.

EPILOGUE: DTRA

On October 1, 1998, the Defense Special Weapons Agency, the On-Site Inspection Agency, the Defense Technology Security Administration, along with selected elements of the Office of the Secretary of Defense staff, were merged to form the Defense Threat Reduction Agency (DTRA), a new combat support agency. Like its predecessor, the new agency would exist, and its missions would be rewritten, to focus on "special" or perceived threats while its traditional role of "nuclear" stewardship remained. Veteran nuclear phenomena and effects "Graybeards" were phased out of agency employ while a new breed of young threat analysts assumed control of the agency. Agency contracts were rewritten to focus upon new defense threats.

Secretary of Defense William S. Cohen formally established DTRA in a ceremony at Dulles International Airport in Northern Virginia, where DTRA was initially headquartered. Secretary Cohen outlined the agency's mission areas as maintaining current nuclear deterrent capability, reducing threats from nuclear, chemical, and biological weapons, and countering WMD threats, in order "...to help catapult America, safe and secure, into a new century."

The initial DTRA Director, Dr. Jay Davis, reported directly to the Under Secretary of Defense for Acquisition and Technology (USD(A&T)). Dr. Davis' advisors included senior officials from the Department of State, the Department of Energy and the Federal Bureau of Investigation. DTRA's Advanced Systems and Concepts Office (ASCO), was charged with analyzing emerging WMD threats and the future technologies and concepts needed to counter them. DTRA's Threat Reduction Advisory Committee (TRAC), comprised of senior experts in policy, science, and defense, considers and assesses emerging WMD threats. The agency's personal and special staff and business management offices performed key support functions for the Director and the agency. DTRA's six directorates—On-Site Inspection, Chemical-Biological Defense, Cooperative Threat Reduction, Technology Security, Nuclear Support and Operations, and Counterproliferation Support and Operations, carry out DTRA's critical mission elements. In October 1998, DTRA was authorized 2,110 military and civilian personnel and a fiscal year 1999 budget authorization of $1.9 billion. The agency operated field offices in Alexandria and Arlington, Virginia; Albuquerque, New Mexico; Magna, Utah; and San Francisco, California; along with numerous overseas locations.[54]

On October 4, 1998, Deputy Secretary of Defense John Hamre, writing in an editorial for the Armed Forces Information Service's *Defense Viewpoint*, expressed DTRA as " ...a coherent, focused organization that will create the intellectual infrastructure for a new approach to deal with weapons of mass destruction."[55] DTRA's mission statement was to reduce the threat to the United States and its allies from nuclear, biological, chemical, conventional and special weapons through the execution of technology security activities, CTR programs, arms

DTRA Inspectors examining missile warhead as part of treaty compliance in the Former Soviet Union.

control treaty monitoring and on-site inspection, force protection, nuclear, biological and chemical defense, and counterproliferation; to support the U.S. nuclear deterrent; and to provide technical support on WMD matters to the DoD components.

The nation's oldest defense agency thus lives on; *MED to AFSWP to DASA to DNA to DSWA to DTRA.*

ENDNOTES

1. "*Nuclear Survivability* interviews VADM Parker, Director, DNA," *Nuclear Survivability*, July 1989, pp.1, 2.
2. "DNA Director Shares Expectations, May 22, 1990," *Contact* (DASIAC newsletter), June 1990, p. 2.
3. Joseph P. Harahan, *On-Site Inspections Under The INF Treaty*, Chapter 1, U.S. General Printing Office, Washington, D.C., 1993.
4. *On Site Insights*, January 1998, Pat Snyder, "Humble Beginnings for the Inspection Professionals at Buzzard Point," p. 7.
5. Joseph P. Harahan, "Ten Years, Twelve Treaties and Agreements, Hundreds of People: One Agency," *On Site Insights*, January 1998, pp. 18, 19.
6. "Using the Tools of Diplomacy," *Carnegie Quarterly*, Spring-Summer 1996, pp. 8-11.
7. Annual Historical Report (AHR), 1992-93, section on Cooperative Threat Reduction Office (no pagination).
8. "Using the Tools of Diplomacy," *Carnegie Quarterly*, Spring-Summer, 1996, p.13, note 5.
9. AHR, 1993-94, section on Defense Conversion (no pagination).
10. *Ibid.*, section on Safe Secure Nuclear Weapons (no pagination).
11. DNA, *The Course of Change,* presented to RAND review panel, February 7, 1994, viewgraphs not numbered.
12. RAND: Defense Nuclear Agency (DNA) Functions, An Assessment of Future Options, Senior Review Board, March 1994, Slides 22, 23.
13. *Ibid.*, Slide 7.
14. Philip E. Coyle, Victor Gilinsky, and Harold M. Agnew, *A Perspective on the U.S. Nuclear Weapons Infrastructure Evolution* (PM302-DNA), RAND, December 1994.
15. Rand, pp.2-3.
16. *Ibid.*, p. 7.
17. *Ibid.*, p. 24.
18. See February 1994 *The Course of Change* viewgraphs weighing "Mandated Study Options."
19. AHR, 1990-91, OPNA section, p. 2.
20. Noted 15 February 1991 *Federal Register*, 32 CFR 361, pp. 6273-77.
21. Comparison of 5105.31 of 1987, with 5105.31 of 1991, both in Harris Materials.
22. Victor Reis, DDR&E, to Chairman, DSB, January 21.1993, Harris Materials.
23. John Cornwall (Chair, DSB task force) to John S. Foster, Jr. (Chair, DSB), May 3, 1993, DSB Report.
24. Cornwall to Foster, May 3, 1993.
25. OSD-JS Report, p. 5.
26. *Ibid.*, p. 9.
27. *Ibid.*, pp.15,14.
28. DSB Report, pp. 39, 38.
29. OSD-JS Report, pp.19-20.
30. *Ibid.*, p.19.
31. Daun A. Sanders, "DNA Weapons of Mass Destruction Game Support," *Science and Technology Digest*, September 1995, pp. 11-12.
32. Peter H. Thompson, "FCDNA Testing Capabilities Support Anti-Terrorist Programs," September 1995, pp.14-15.
33. Steve Macko, "Report Says Pentagon Failed to Take Adequate Security Measures," EmergencyNet News Service, www.emergency.com/dhaharpt.htm (hereafter "Macko, ENN").
34. Lt. Col. Ken Knox, "Khobar Towers Bomb Damage Survey," *Science and Technology Digest,* May 1997, 7-10.
35. "Macko, ENN".
36. *Ibid.*
37. *Ibid.*
38. John V. Bolino (Director Test Facilities and Resources, Defense Research and Engineering), open letter, June 7, 1990, as published in *Nuclear Survivability*, August 1990, p. 3.
39. "*Nuclear Survivability* interviews Dr. Don A. Linger, Director for Test, DNA," *Nuclear Survivability*, August 1990, p.5.
40. AHR, 1990-91, section on Electromagnetic Applications Division of the Radiation Sciences Director (no pagination).

41. Eric J. Rinehart and Harlan Lawson, "Field Command Becomes Center for DSWA Test Operations," *Science and Technology Digest*, August 1996, pp.15-17.
42. *Ibid.*
43. DSWA, "Radiation Test Facilities and Capabilities," fourth ed., January 1997.
44. Ray Kelley, "ARES Upgrade," September 1995, pp. 21-22.
45. Irwin Goodwin, "Without Explosions to Test the Aging Nuclear Arsenal, Bomb Builders turn to Inertial Fusion and Supercomputers," *Physics Today*, March 1997, pp. 63-65.
46. Redesignation Ceremony, June 26, 1996, DSWA Congressional Affairs Office.
47. John G. Lewis, "Project Graybeard: Preserving Legacy Nuclear Data," *Science and Technology Digest*, August 1996, pp. 31-35.
48. Rob Mahoney, "Overview—May 1993 SAGE Meeting" (DRAFT), June 3, 1993, p.2.
49. SAGE Overview, pp.38-39.
50. Edwin Wolfe, Geoffrey Butler, and Graham Rhodes, "The JMEM Air-To-Surface Weaponeering System (JAWS)," pp. 27-29.
51. Tom Stephens and Stuart Kelly, "DNA Updates Computational Aids," *Science and Technology Digest*, September 1995, pp. 29-30; "Computational Aids Update," *Science and Technology Digest*, August 1996, pp. 42-43.
52. Claude Fore, "New ERRIC Contact at DASIAC," *Science and Technology Digest*, September 1995, p. 30.
53. William B. Daitch, "Nuclear Weapons Training—The Defense Nuclear Weapons School Returns to DNA," *Science and Technology Digest*, September 1995, pp. 8-9; "Defense Nuclear Weapons School Update," *Science and Technology Digest*, August 1996, pp. 40-41.
54. Joseph P. Harahan and Robert J. Bennett, *Creating the Defense Threat Reduction Agency*, DTRA History Series, U.S. General Printing Office, Washington, D.C., 2002, pp. 12-21.
55. John Hamre, Editorial, *Defense's Viewpoint*, U.S. Armed Forces Information Service, November 1998.

APPENDIX A

BIBLIOGRAPHY

PRIMARY SOURCES ~ U.S. GOVERNMENT REPOSITORIES

Army Corps of Engineers, Fort Belvoir, Alexandria, VA

Department of Defense Nuclear Information Analysis Center (DASIAC), Albuquerque, NM and Alexandria, VA

Defense Technical Information Library, Alexandria, VA

Department of Energy, History Office, Germantown, MD

Department of Energy, Nevada Operations Office, Las Vegas, NV

Dwight D. Eisenhower Presidential Library, Abilene, KS

National Archives and Records Administration, Archives II, College Park, MD
Record Group 77 Army Corps of Engineers
Record Group 326 Atomic Energy Commission
Record Group 374 Defense Special Weapons Agency

REPORTS AND PROJECT HISTORIES

American Embassy, Tokyo. *Daily Summaries of the Japanese Press*. Microfilm collection, Periodicals Division, Library of Congress.

Anderson, C.H. et al. *Report of the Study Group on Organization for Future Test Operations*, Defense Nuclear Agency, 1959. DOE/NV, NV94021.

Armed Forces Special Weapons Project. *First History of AFSWP, 1947-1954*. 6 Volumes. Armed Forces Special Weapons Project, 1954. DSWA Defense Technical Library.

———. *History of the Armed Forces Special Weapons Project* (Latter Period, 1955-1958), Parts I and II. Armed Forces Special Weapons Project, 1959. DSWA Defense Technical Library.

Brown, Harold. "Research and Engineering in the Defense Laboratories," *Records of the Office of the Director of Navy Laboratories*, R.C. 3-1, Series 3, Acc. 84-55, Box 61, Naval Historical Center.

Camm, Frank *Chronology of Early Days at Sandia Base*. 1996.

———. "Interview with Lieutenant General Frank A. Camm." Washington, DC: Army Corps of Engineers.

Defense Atomic Support Agency. *Armed Forces Radiobiology Research Institute (AFRRI) Semi-Annual Historical Reports, 1963 Through 1969, Volume I*. DTL 070,052. Defense Atomic Support Agency. DSWA Defense Technical Library.

———. *History of the Defense Atomic Support Agency, 1959-1969*. Parts I and II. Defense Atomic Support Agency. DSWA Defense Technical Library.

Defense Nuclear Agency. *AFRRI Historical Documents*, DTL 070,590. Defense Nuclear Agency. DSWA Defense Technical Library.

———. *Cleanup of Bikini Atoll*, DTL 070,170. Defense Atomic Support Agency, Washington, DC, 1971. DSWA Defense Technical Library.

———. *Field Command, DNA–Special Historical Report, 1946-1985*, DTL 070,204. Defense Nuclear Agency.

———. *Test Command Historical Documents*, DTL 070,589. Defense Nuclear Agency. DSWA Defense Technical Library.

Defense Special Weapons Agency. *Defense Special Weapons Agency: 1947-1997: The First 50 Years of National Service*. Alexandria, VA: Defense Special Weapons Agency, 1997.

"DNA Director Shares Expectations–May 22, 1990." *Contact* (June 1990).

Dorland, Colonel Gilbert M. *Engineer Memoirs: Colonel Gilbert M. Dorland, USA, Retired*. 1987. Interviewed by William C. Baldwin. US Army Corps of Engineers, Alexandria, VA.

For the Record: A History of the Nuclear Test Personnel Review Program, 1978-1993, DNA 6041F. Jaycor, Vienna, VA, 1996. DOE/NV, NV57580.

Gould, Kenneth E. *High-Explosive Field Testing (1945-1987): A DNA Historical Perspective*. DNA 001-82-C-0274. DASIAC-TN-87-3.

Groves, Major General Leslie R. *Now It Can Be Told: The Story of the Manhattan Project*. New York: Harper and Brothers, 1962.

Harris, William R. *Defense Nuclear Responsibilities: From the Armed Forces Special Weapons Project to the Defense Nuclear Agency, 1947-1971*. Rand Corporation Study, 1996.

———. *Functions of the Defense Nuclear Agency and Its Predecessor Organizations, 1947-1994*. Rand Restricted Draft Series, 1995.

Jackson, Robert E. *Guide to US Atmospheric Nuclear Weapon Effects Data*, DASIAC SR-92-007. Kaman Sciences Corporation, Santa Barbara, CA, 1993. DASIAC.

Johnson, Abby A., Jerald L. Goetz, and William K. McRaney. *For the Record– A History of the Nuclear Test Personnel Review Program, 1978-1986*. SAIC, McLean, VA, 1986. DOE/NV, NV51275.

National Security Archives. *US Nuclear Non-Proliferation Policy 1945-91*.

Ogle, William E. *An Account of the Return to Nuclear Weapon Testing by the United States After the Test Moratorium, 1958-1961*. Department of Energy, Nevada Operations Office, Albuquerque, NM, 1993. NVOO291– Nevada Operations Office.

MEMOIRS AND HISTORIES

Alvarez, Luis. *Alvarez: Adventures of a Physicist*. New York: Basic Books, 1987.

Barnard, Chester I., and others. *A Report on the International Control of Atomic Energy* [Acheson-Lilienthal Report]. Washington, DC: Department of State, 1946.

Baruch, Bernard. *The Public Years*. New York: Holt, Rinehard and Winston, 1960.

Brzezinski, Zbigniew. *Power and Principle: Memoirs of the National Security Adviser, 1977-1981*. New York: Farrar, Straus, Giroux, 1983.

Carter, Jimmy. *Keeping Faith: Memoirs of a President*. Toronto: Bantam Books, 1982.

———. "Transcripts of the President's Address on Energy Problems." *New York Times*, 16 July 1979, sec A, p. 10.

Church, Frank. *Strategic Arms Limitation Talks and Comprehensive Test Ban Negotiations: A Report to the Committee on Foreign Relations, United States Senate*. Washington, DC: GPO, 1978.

Clay, Lucius D. *Decision in Germany*. Garden City, NY: Doubleday and Company, 1950.

———. *The Papers of General Lucius D. Clay: Volume II: Germany 1945-1949*. Edited by Jean Edward Smith. Bloomington, IN: Indiana University Press, 1974.

APPENDIX A: BIBLIOGRAPHY

Cole, Alice, et al. *The Department of Defense: Documents on Establishment and Organization, 1944-1978*. Washington, DC: DoD History Office, 1979.

Conant, James. *My Several Lives*. New York: Harper and Row, 1980.

Dean, Gordon E. *Forging the Atomic Shield: Excerpts from the Office Diary of Gordon E. Dean*. Edited by Roger M. Anders. Chapel Hill, NC: University of North Carolina Press, 1987.

Department of State. *Documents on Disarmament, 1945-1959*. Washington, DC: GPO, 1973.

———. *The International Control of Atomic Energy: Scientific Information Transmitted to the United Nations Atomic Energy Commission, June 14, 1946-October 14, 1946*. Washington, DC: GPO, 1946.

Eisenhower, Dwight D. *The Quotable Dwight D. Eisenhower*. Edited by Elsie Gollagher. Anderson, SC: Drake House, 1967.

———. *The White House Years: Mandate for Change, 1953-1956*. Garden City, NY: Doubleday, 1963.

———. *The White House Years: Waging Peace, 1956-1961*. Garden City, NY: Doubleday, 1965.

Elsasser, Walter M. *Memoirs of a Physicist in the Atomic Age*. New York: Science History Publications and Adam Hilger, 1978.

Engineer Memoirs: Lt. Gen. Frederick J. Clarke. Washington, DC: Office of the Chief of Engineers, 1979.

Fitzhugh, Gilbert W., and others. *Report to the President and the Secretary of Defense on the Department of Defense by the Blue Ribbon Defense Panel, July 1, 1970*. Department of Defense. Blue Ribbon Defense Panel Report. Washington, DC: GPO, 1970.

Ford, Gerald R. *A Time to Heal: The Autobiography of Gerald R. Ford*. New York: Harper and Row, Publishers, 1974.

Forrestal, James. *The Forrestal Diaries*. Edited by Walter Millis. New York: Viking Press, 1951.

Gates, Mahlon E. *The Nuclear Emergency Search Team–Preventing Nuclear Terrorism*, The Report and Papers of the International Task Force on Prevention of Nuclear Terrorism. Edited by Paul Leventhal and Yonah Alexander. Lexington, MA: D.C. Heath and Company, 1987: 397-402.

Haas, Peter H. *Some Observations on the Design and Use of Simulation for Nuclear Weapons Effects*. Defense Nuclear Agency. RDA Logicon, April 1984.

Human Survivability. 2 vols. Alexandria, VA: DoD Nuclear Information Analysis Center (DASIAC), 1993, 1994.

Joint Committee on Defense Production. *Deterrence and Survival in the Nuclear Age, (The "Gaither Report" of 1957)*. For the Joint Committee on Defense Production. Washington, DC: GPO, 1976.

Kennedy, Robert F. *Thirteen Days: A Memoir of the Cuban Missile Crisis*. New York: W.W. Norton, 1969.

Killian, James R., Jr. *Sputnik, Scientists, and Eisenhower: A Memoir of the First Special Assistant to the President for Science and Technology*. Cambridge, MA: MIT Press, 1977.

Kissinger, Henry A. "Secretary Kissinger Discusses US Nonproliferation Strategy." *Department of State Bulletin* 74 (March 29, 1976): 405-11.

———. "Secretary Kissinger's News Conference of December 9." *Department of State Bulletin* 74 (5 January 1976): 1-12.

———. "Secretary Kissinger's News Conference of January 14." *Department of State Bulletin* 74 (February 2, 1976): 125-32.

LeMay, General Curtis E., et al. *Strategic Air Warfare: An Interview with Generals Curtis E. LeMay, Leon W. Johnson, David A. Burchinal, and Jack J. Catton.* Edited and Introduction by Richard H. Kohn and Joseph P. Harahan. Washington, DC: Office of Air Force History.

Lilienthal, David. *The Atomic Energy Years, 1945-1950,* Vol. 2: The Journals of David Lilienthal. New York: Harper and Row, 1964.

Nitze, Paul H. *Paul H. Nitze on National Security and Arms Control.* Editor Kenneth W Thompson, and Steven L. Rearden, Vol. XIV. W. Alton Jones Foundation Series on Arms Control. Lanham, MD: University Press of America, 1990.

Nixon, Richard M. *The Memoirs of Richard Nixon.* New York: Grosset and Dunlap, 1978.

"NSC 162/2." In *Foreign Relations of the United States, 1952-1954.* Vol. 2, National Security Affairs. Washington, DC: GPO, 1984: 577-97.

Public Papers of the Presidents of the United States, 1953: Dwight D. Eisenhower. Washington, DC: GPO, 1960.

RAND Corporation. *Charters and Directives for the Defense Nuclear Agency and Predecessor Organizations, 1947-1993.* Santa Monica, CA: RAND Corporation, 1994.

Schlesinger, James R., *Selected Papers on National Security, 1964-1968,* Santa Monica: Rand Corporation, 1974.

Seaborg, Glenn Theodore. *Kennedy, Khrushchev, and the Test Ban.* Berkeley: University of California Press, 1981.

———. *The Atomic Energy Commission Under Nixon: Adjusting to Troubled Times.* New York: St. Martin's Press, 1993.

———. *The Plutonium Story: The Journals of Professor Glenn T. Seaborg, 1939-1946.* Edited and annotated by Ronald L. Kathren, Jerry B. Gough, and Gary T. Benefiel. Columbus, OH: Battelle Press, 1994.

———. *Stemming the Tide: Arms Control in the Johnson Years.* Lexington, MA: Lexington Books, 1987.

Shelton, Frank H., *Reflection on the Big Red Bombs.* Colorado Springs, CO: Shelton Enterprises, 1995.

Shelton, Frank H., *Reflections of a Nuclear Weaponeer.* Colorado Springs, CO: Shelton Enterprises, 1988.

Shurcliff, W.A., *Bombs at Bikini: The Official Report of Operation Crossroads.* US Joint Task Force One. New York: William H. Wise and Company, 1947.

Smyth, Henry De Wolf. *Atomic Energy for Military Purposes: The Official Report on the Development of the Atomic Bomb Under the Auspices of the United States Government, 1940-1945.* 1946. Stanford Nuclear Age Series. Stanford, CA: Stanford University Press, 1989.

———. *A General Account of the Development of Methods of Using Atomic Energy for Military Purposes Under the Auspices of the United States Government, 1940-1945.* August 1945 ed. Washington, DC: War Department, 1945.

Suid, Lawrence H. *An Army Engineer: A Career and A Great Calling.* Interview With Lieutenant General Lawrence J. Lincoln. Fort Belvoir, VA: Office of History, US Army Corps of Engineers, 1993.

Truman, Harry S., *Memoirs by Harry S. Truman: Volume I: Year of Decisions.* Garden City, NY: Doubleday and Company, 1955.

Truman, Harry S., *Memoirs by Harry S. Truman: Volume II: Years of Trial and Hope.* Garden City, NY: Doubleday and Company, 1956.

APPENDIX A: BIBLIOGRAPHY

———. *Where the Buck Stops: The Personal and Private Writings of Harry S. Truman*. Edited by Margaret Truman. New York: Warner Books, 1989.

United Nations Secretary General. *Nuclear Weapons: Report of the Secretary-General*. Brookline, MA: Autumn Press, 1980.

US Armed Forces, Joint Task Force One, Office of the Historian. *Operation Crossroads: The Official Pictorial Record*. New York: William H. Wise, 1946.

US Arms Control and Disarmament Agency. *Arms Control and Disarmament Agreements: Texts and Histories of the Negotiations*. 6th ed. Washington, DC: United States Arms Control and Disarmament Agency, 1990.

Vance, Cyrus R. "Arms Control: Secretary Vance's Testimony on SALT II." *Department of State Bulletin* 79 (August 1979): 30-37.

———. *Hard Choices: Critical Years in America's Foreign Policy*. New York: Simon and Schuster, 1983.

Vandenberg, Arthur H. Jr., with Joe Alex Morris, *The Private Papers of Senator Vandenberg*. Boston: Houghton, Mifflin, 1952.

Weinberger, Caspar, *Fighting for Peace: Seven Critical Years in the Pentagon*. New York: Warner Books, 1990.

York, Herbert F., *Making Weapons, Talking Peace: A Physicist's Odyssey From Hiroshima to Geneva*. The Alfred P. Sloan Foundation Series. New York: Basic Books, 1987.

———. *Race to Oblivion: A Participant's View of the Arms Race*. New York: Simon and Schuster, 1970.

York, Herbert F., and Harry Kreisler. *Reminiscences From a Career in Science, National Security and the University*, With Herbert F. York. 1 videocassette (60 min.) Berkeley, CA: Institute of International Studies. A production of *The Television Service*, U.C. Berkeley, 1988.

CONGRESSIONAL HEARINGS AND REPORTS

US Congress. House. *Committee on Appropriations. Department of Defense Appropriations for 1958*. 85th Cong. 1st Session. Hearings Before the Subcommittee of the Committee on Appropriations. GPO, Washington, DC, 1957.

———. *Department of Defense Appropriations for 1972*. Ninety-second Congress. First Session. Hearings Before the Subcommittee of the Committee on Appropriations. Washington, DC: GPO, 1971.

———. *Department of Defense Appropriations for 1973*. Ninety-second Congress. Second Session. Hearings Before the Subcommittee of the Committee on Appropriations. Washington, DC: GPO, 1972.

———. *Department of Defense Authorization for Appropriations for 1979*. Ninety-fifth Congress. Second Session. Hearings Before the Subcommittee of the Committee on Appropriations. Washington, DC: GPO, 1978.

———. *Department of Defense Appropriations for 1985*. Ninety-eighth Congress. Hearings Before a Subcommittee of the Committee on Appropriations. Washington, DC: GPO, 1984.

US Congress. House. Committee on Armed Services. *Current Negotiations on the Comprehensive Test Ban Treaty*. Ninety-fifth Congress. Second Session. Hearings Before the Committee on Armed Services. Washington, DC: GPO, 1978.

———. *Defense Department Authorization and Oversight for Fiscal Year 1984*. Ninety-eighth Congress. First Session. Washington, DC: GPO, 1983.

———. Defense Department Authorization and Oversight, Hearings on H.R. 2287, *Department of Defense Authorization of Appropriations for Fiscal Year 1986 and Oversight of Previously Authorized Programs*. Ninety-eighth Congress. Second Session. Washington, DC: GPO, 1985.

———. Defense Department Authorization and Oversight, Hearings on H.R. 4264, *Department of Defense Authorization of Appropriations for Fiscal Year 1986 and Oversight of Previously Authorized Programs*. One-hundredth Congress. Second Session. Washington, DC: GPO, 1985.

———. Military Posture and H.R. 10929, *Department of Defense Authorization for Appropriations for Fiscal Year 1979*. Ninety-fifth Congress, Second Session. Hearings Before the Committee on Armed Services. GPO, Washington, DC, 1976.

———. Military Posture and H.R. 11500 [H.R. 12438], *Department of Defense Authorization for Appropriations for Fiscal Year 1977*. Ninety-fourth Congress, Second Session. Hearings Before the Committee on Armed Services. GPO, Washington, DC, 1976.

———. Military Posture and H.R. 12564, *Department of Defense Authorization for Appropriations for Fiscal Year 1975*. Ninety-third Congress, Second Session. Hearings Before the Committee on Armed Services. GPO, Washington, DC, 1974.

———. Military Posture, H.R. 5968, *DoD Authorization for Appropriations for FY 1983*. Hearings Before the Committee on Armed Services. GPO, Washington, DC, 1982.

US Congress. Senate. *Report to the President on Government Contracting for Research and Development*. Eighty-seventh Congress. Second Session. Washington, DC: GPO, 1962.

US Congress. Senate. Committee on Appropriations. *Department of Defense Appropriations for Fiscal Year 1973*. Ninety-second Congress. Second Session. Hearings. Subcommittee of the Committee on Appropriations. Washington, DC: GPO, 1972.

———. *Department of Defense Appropriations for Fiscal Year 1979*. Ninety-fifth Congress. Second Session.

———. *Department of Defense Appropriations for Fiscal Year 1980*. Ninety-sixth Congress. First Session. Washington, DC: GPO, 1980.

———. *Department of Defense Appropriations for Fiscal Year 1981*. Ninety-sixth Congress. Second Session. Washington, DC: GPO, 1980.

———. *Department of Defense Appropriations for Fiscal Year 1984*. Ninety-eighth Congress. First Session. Washington, DC: GPO, 1983.

———. *Department of Defense Appropriations for Fiscal Year 1988*. Hearings Before the Subcommittee of the Committee on Appropriations. One-hundredth Congress. First Session. Washington, DC: GPO, 1987.

———. *Department of the Interior and Related Agencies Appropriations for Fiscal Year 1981*. Hearings before a Subcommittee of the Committee on Appropriations. Ninety-sixth Congress. Second Session. Washington, DC: GPO, 1981.

US Congress. Senate. Committee on Armed Services. *Fiscal Year 1972 Authorization for Military Procurement, Research and Development, Construction and Real Estate Acquisition for the Safeguard ABM and Reserve Strengths*. Ninety-second Congress, First Session. Hearings Before the Committee on Armed Services. Washington, DC: GPO, 1971.

US Congress. Senate. Committee on Veterans' Affairs. *Veterans' Claims for Disabilities From Nuclear Weapons Testing*. Hearings Before the Committee on Veterans' Affairs. Ninety-sixth Congress. First Session. Washington, DC: GPO, 1979.

US General Accounting Office. *Enewetak Atoll–Cleaning Up Nuclear Contamination: Report to the Congress*. Washington, DC: US General Accounting Office, 1979.

APPENDIX A: BIBLIOGRAPHY

———. *The Nuclear Non-Proliferation Act of 1978 Should Be Selective Modified: Report to the Congress.* Washington, DC: US General Accounting Office, 1981.

US Library of Congress, Congressional Research Service. *Facts on Nuclear Proliferation: A Handbook Prepared for the Committee on Government Operations, United States Senate.* Washington, DC: GPO, 1975.

US War and Navy Departments, Armed Forces Special Weapons Project. *Radiological Defense: A Manual Prepared by the Joint Crossroads Committee, Volume I.* Washington, DC: GPO, 1948.

ORAL HISTORY INTERVIEWS

Atkins, Marvin C. Interview by Rodney P. Carlisle. October 1997. DSWA Project Files.

Brittigan, Robert. Interview by Rodney P. Carlisle. 1997. DSWA Project Files.

Brode, Harold Leonard. Interview by Joseph Tatarewicz. October 1997. DSWA Project Files.

Carew, Paul. Interview by Rodney P. Carlisle. November 1997. DSWA Project Files.

Hayward, Colonel John T. Interview by Philip L. Cantelon. September 1996. DSWA Project Files.

Monroe, Vice Admiral Robert. Interview by Rodney P. Carlisle. September 1996. DSWA Project Files.

Ord, Colonel John A. Interview by Philip L. Cantelon. September 1996. DSWA Project Files.

Parker, Vice Admiral John T. Interview by Joseph Tatarewicz. September 1997. DSWA Project Files.

Shelton, Frank H. Interview by Philip L. Cantelon. November 1996. DSWA Project Files.

Wikner, Fred. Interview by Rodney P. Carlisle. September 1997. DSWA Project Files.

Wilhoyt, Brigadier General Ellis E., Jr. Interview by Philip L. Cantelon. February 1981. DSWA Project Files.

SECONDARY SOURCES

"The ABM Debate." *Bulletin of the Atomic Scientists* 23, nos. 5 and 6 (May and June 1967).

Aliano, Richard. *American Defense Policy From Eisenhower to Kennedy: 1957-1961.* Athens, OH: Ohio University Press, 1975.

American Security Council, National Strategy Committee. *The ABM and the Changed Strategic Military Balance: A Study.* 2nd ed. Washington, DC: Acropolis Books, 1969.

Anders, Roger M. *The Office of Military Application.* Revised ed. Washington, DC: History Office, Office of the Secretary, US Department of Energy, 1980.

Arkin, William M. "Beltway Bandits." *Bulletin of the Atomic Scientists* 41, no. 8 (September 1985): 5-6.

Arkin, William M., and Richard W. Fieldhouse. *Nuclear Battlefields—Global Links in the Arms Race.* Cambridge, MA: Ballinger Publishing, 1985.

Badash, Lawrence. "Nuclear Winter Research: Science and Politics." Paper presented at 1993 History of Science Society Annual Meeting.

———. *Scientists and the Development of Nuclear Weapons: From Fission to the Limited Test Ban Treaty, 1939-1963.* The Control of Nature. Atlantic Highlands, NJ: Humanities Press, 1995.

Bailey, Janet. *The Good Servant: Making Peace With the Bomb at Los Alamos.* New York: Simon and Schuster, 1995.

Baldwin, William C. *The Engineer Studies Center and Army Analysis.* Fort Belvoir, VA: US Army Engineers Studies Center, 1985.

Ball, Desmond. *Deja Vu: The Return to Counterforce in the Nixon Administration*. Los Angeles: California Seminar on Arms Control and Foreign Policy, 1975.

———. *Politics and Force Levels: The Strategic Missile Program of the Kennedy Administration*. Berkeley: University of California Press, 1980.

Ball, Howard. *Justice Downwind: America's Atomic Testing Program in the 1950s*. New York: Oxford University Press, 1986.

Baucom, Donald R. *The Origins of SDI, 1944-1983*. Lawrence, KS: The University Press of Kansas, 1992.

Bauer, Theodore W. and Eston T. White. *National Security Policy Formulation*. Washington, DC: National Defense University, 1977.

Baylis, John. *Ambiguity and Deterrence: British Nuclear Strategy, 1945-1964*. New York: Clarendon Press, 1995.

Bebbington, William P. *History of Du Pont at the Savannah River Plant*. Wilmington, DE: E.I. du Pont de Nemours, 1990.

Beckman, Peter R., and others. *The Nuclear Predicament: Nuclear Weapons in the Cold War and Beyond*. 2nd ed. Englewood Cliffs, NJ: Prentice Hall, 1992.

Beede, Benjamin. *Military and Strategic Policy: An Annotated Bibliography*. New York: Greenwood Press, 1990.

Berding, Andrew H. *Dulles on Diplomacy*. New York: D. Van Nostrand Company, 1965.

Beres, Louis Rene. *Mimicking Sisyphus: America's Countervailing Nuclear Strategy*. Lexington, MA: Lexington Books, D.C. Heath and Company, 1983.

Berger, Karl. *America, the Soviets, and Nuclear Arms: Looking to the Future*. Providence, RI: Center for Foreign Policy Development, Brown University, 1989.

"Berlin: The Squeeze on the Corridors." *Newsweek* 32 (1948): 30, 32.

Bernstein, Barton J. "Truman, Acheson, and the H-Bomb." *Foreign Service Journal* 60, no. 6 (June 1983): 20-3.

Bernstein, Jeremy. *Hitler's Uranium Club: The Secret Recordings at Farm Hall*. New York: American Institute of Physics, 1996.

Bertram, Christoph. "SALT II and the Dynamics of Arms Control." *International Affairs (London)* 55 (1979): 565-73.

Beschloss, Michael R. *May–Day: Eisenhower, Khrushchev and the U-2 Affair*. New York: Harper and Row, 1986.

Bethe, Hans. *The Road From Los Alamos*. New York: American Institute of Physics, 1991.

Betts, Richard K. *Nuclear Blackmail and Nuclear Balance*. Washington, DC: Brookings Institution, 1987.

Bissell, Richard M., Jr. *Reflections of a Cold Warrior: From Yalta to the Bay of Pigs*. New Haven, CT: Yale University Press, 1996.

Blumberg, Stanley, and Louis Panos. *Edward Teller: Giant of the Golden Age of Physics*. New York: Scribners, 1990.

Bluth, Christoph. *Soviet Strategic Arms Policy Before SALT*. Cambridge: Cambridge University Press, 1992.

Bobbitt, Philip. *Democracy and Deterrence: The History and Future of Nuclear Strategy*. New York: Macmillan Press, 1988.

Bobbitt, Philip, and others, editors. *US Nuclear Strategy: A Reader*. New York: New York University Press, 1989.

Bolino, John V. "Letter of 7 June 1990." *Nuclear Survivability* (August 1990): p. 3.

Booth, Major General Robert H. "Red Test Fallout Will Double 59's: Interview with Major General Booth, Robert H." *Army, Navy, Air Force Register* 83 (December 16, 1961): 13-14.

Borowski, Harry R. "Air Force Atomic Capability from V-J Day to the Berlin Blockade–Potential or Real?" *Military Affairs* 44, no. 3 (October 1980): 105-10.

———. *A Hollow Threat: Strategic Air Power and Containment Before Korea*. Westport, CT: Greenwood Press, 1982.

Bottome, Edgar M. *The Balance of Terror: A Guide to the Arms Race*. Boston: Beacon Press, 1972.

———. *The Balance of Terror: Nuclear Weapons and the Illusion of Security, 1945-1985*. Revised and updated ed. Boston: Beacon Press, 1986.

———. *The Missile Gap: A Study of the Formulation of Military and Political Policy*. Rutherford, NJ: Fairleigh Dickinson University Press, 1971.

Boyer, Paul S. *By the Bomb's Early Light: American Thought and Culture at the Dawn of the Atomic Age*. New York: Pantheon, 1985.

Bracken, Paul. *The Command and Control of Nuclear Forces*. New Haven, CT: Yale University Press, 1983.

Brands, H. W. *The Wages of Globalism: Lyndon Johnson and the Limits of American Power*. New York: Oxford University Press, 1995.

Britten, Stewart. *The Invisible Event: An Assessment of the Risk of Accidental or Unauthorized Detonation of Nuclear Weapons and of War by Miscalculation*. London: Menard Press, 1983.

Brodie, Bernard. *The Absolute Weapon: Atomic Power and World Order*. New York: Harcourt, Brace, 1946.

Brucer, Marshall. "The Great Fallout Controversy." *Journal of the American Medical Association* 179 (1962): 66-67.

Bundy, McGeorge. *Danger and Survival: Choices About the Bomb in the First Fifty Years*. New York: Random House, 1988.

———. "Early Thoughts on Controlling the Nuclear Arms Race: A Report to the Secretary of State, January 1953." *International Security* 7, no. 2 (Fall 1982): 3-27.

———. *Reducing Nuclear Danger: The Road Away From the Brink*. New York: Council on Foreign Relations Press, 1993.

Burns, Grant. *The Nuclear Present: A Guide to Recent Books on Nuclear War, Weapons, the Peace Movement, and Related Issues*. Metuchen, NJ: Scarecrow Press, 1992.

Burns, Richard Dean, and Susan Hoffman Hutson, compilers. *The SALT Era: A Selected Bibliography*. Revised ed. Los Angeles: Center for the Study of Armament and Disarmament, California State University, 1979.

Buteau, Paul. *The Politics of Nuclear Consultation in NATO, 1965-1980*. New York: Cambridge University Press, 1983.

Caldwell, Glyn G., Delle B. Kelley, and Clark W. Heath Jr. "Leukemia Among Participants in Military Maneuvers at a Nuclear Bomb Test: A Preliminary Report." *Journal of the American Medical Association* 244, no. 14 (1980): 1575-78.

Campbell, Christopher. *Nuclear Weapons Fact Book*. London: Hamlyn Publishing Group, 1984.

———. *Weapons of War: Present and Future Weapons, Systems and Strategies*. New York: Peter Bedrick Books, 1983.

Cantelon, Philip L., Richard G. Hewlett, and Robert C. Williams, editors. *The American Atom: A Documentary History of Nuclear Policies From the Discovery of Fission to the Present*. 2nd ed. Philadelphia: University of Pennsylvania Press, 1991.

Cantelon, Philip L., and Robert C. Williams. *Crisis Contained: The Department of Energy at Three Mile Island: A History*. Carbondale, IL: Southern Illinois University Press, 1982.

Carlisle, Rodney P., and Joan M. Zenzen. *Supplying the Nuclear Arsenal*. Baltimore: Johns Hopkins University Press, 1996.

Carlton, David, and Carlo Schaerf, editors. *The Arms Race in an Era of Negotiations*. New York: St. Martin's Press, 1991.

Carnegie Quarterly. Vol. 16. New York: Carnegie Corporation of New York, 1996.

Carnovale, Marco, *The Control of NATO Nuclear Forces in Europe*. Boulder, CO: Westview Press, 1993.

Cave Brown, Anthony, and others, editors. *The Secret History of the Atomic Bomb*. New York: Dial Press, 1977.

Cernik, Joseph A. "The Current United States Targeting Doctrine of Nuclear Weapons: An Explanation and Analysis." *Presidential Studies Quarterly* 6, no. 1 and 2 (1976-1977): 49-64.

Chandler, Robert W., with Ronald J. Trees. *Tomorrow's War, Today's Decisions: Iraqi Weapons of Mass Destruction and the Implications of WMD–Armed Adversaries for Future US Military Strategy*. McLean, VA: AMCODA Press, 1996.

Charlton, Michael. *From Deterrence to Defense: The Inside Story of Strategic Policy*. Cambridge, MA: Harvard University Press, 1987.

Clarfield, Gerard H., and William M. Wiecek. *Nuclear America: Military and Civilian Nuclear Power in the United States, 1940-1980*. New York: Harper and Row, 1984.

Clark, Ian, and Philip A.G. Sabin. *Sources for the Study of British Nuclear Weapons History*. College Park, MD: Center for International Security Studies at Maryland, University of Maryland, 1989.

Clark, Ronald. *The Birth of the Bomb*. New York: Horizon Press, 1961.

Coates, James, and Michael Killian. *Heavy Losses: The Dangerous Decline of American Defense*. New York: Viking Press, 1985.

Cochran, Thomas B., William M. Arkin, and Milton M. Hoenig. *Nuclear Weapons Databook: Volume I: US Nuclear Forces and Capabilities*. Cambridge, MA: Ballinger Publishing, 1984.

Cochran, Thomas B., William M. Arkin, Robert S. Norris, and Milton M. Hoenig. *Nuclear Weapons Databook: Volume II: US Nuclear Warhead Production*. Cambridge, MA: Ballinger Publishing, 1984.

———. *Nuclear Weapons Databook: Volume III: US Nuclear Warhead Facility Profiles*. Cambridge, MA: Ballinger Publishing, 1984.

Cochran, Thomas B., Robert S. Norris, and Oleg A. Bukharin. *Making the Russian Bomb: From Stalin to Yeltsin*. Boulder, CO: Westview Press, 1995.

Cockburn, Andrew. *One Point Safe*. New York: Anchor Books, 1997.

Cohen, S.T. *US Strategic Nuclear Weapon Policy: Do We Have One? Should There Be One?*, 5127. Santa Monica, CA: RAND Corporation, 1973.

"Computational Aids Update." *Science and Technology Digest* (August 1996): 42-3.

Condit, Doris M. *History of the Office of the Secretary of Defense: Volume II: The Test of War, 1950-1953*. Washington, DC: Historical Office, Office of the Secretary of Defense, 1988.

Condit, Kenneth W. *The History of the Joint Chiefs of Staff: The Joint Chiefs of Staff and National Policy: Volume II: 1947-1949*. Wilmington, DE: Michael Glazier, Inc., 1979.

———. *The Joint Chiefs of Staff and National Policy, 1955-1956*. Washington, DC: GPO, 1992.

Connery, Robert H., and Demetrios Caraley, editors. *National Security and Nuclear Strategy*. New York: Academy of Political Science, 1983.

Critical Mass: America's Race to Build the Atomic Bomb. Bellevue, WA: Corbis Corporation, 1996. CD-ROM.

Dahlitz, Julie. *Nuclear Arms Control, With Effective International Agreements*. Boston: G. Allen and Unwin, 1983.

Dahlman, Ola. *Monitoring Underground Nuclear Explosions*. Amsterdam: Elsevier Scientific Publishers, 1977.

Daitch, William B. "Nuclear Weapons Training–The Defense Nuclear Weapons School Returns to DNA." *Science and Technology Digest* (September 1995): 8-9.

Dallin, Alexander, and Condoleezza Rice, editors. *The Gorbachev Era*. Stanford, CA: Stanford Alumni Association, 1986.

Davis, Lynn E. *Limited Nuclear Options: Deterrence and the New American Doctrine*. London: International Institute for Strategic Studies, 1976.

Davison, W. Phillips. *The Berlin Blockade: A Study in Cold War Politics*. Princeton, NJ: Princeton University Press, 1958.

Dean, Arthur H. *Test Ban and Disarmament: The Path of Negotiation*. New York: Harper and Row, Publishers, 1966.

"Defense Nuclear Agency Nurtures A Surging Budget." *Defense Week* (April 12, 1982): 15.

"Defense Nuclear School Update." *Science and Technology Digest* (August 1996): 40-1.

Del Tredici, Robert. *At Work in the Fields of the Bomb*. New York: Perennial Library, 1987.

Department of Energy. *Plutonium: The First 50 Years*. Washington, DC: Department of Energy, 1996.

Dibblin, Jane. *Day of Two Suns: US Nuclear Testing and the Pacific Islanders*. London: Virago, 1988.

"Did Russia Steal Satellite Secret from US?" *US News and World Report* 43 (October 18, 1957): 44.

Dingman, Roger. "Atomic Diplomacy During the Korean War." *International Security* 13, no. 3 (Winter 1988/89): 50-91.

Divine, Robert A. *Blowing on the Wind: The Nuclear Test Ban Debate, 1954-1960*. New York: Oxford University Press, 1978.

———. "The Cuban Missile Controversy." *Diplomatic History* 18 (Fall 1994): 551-60.

———, editor. *The Johnson Years, Volume Three: LBJ at Home and Abroad*. Lawrence, KS: University Press of Kansas, 1994.

Dockrill, Saki. *Eisenhower's New–Look National Security Policy, 1953-1961*. London: Macmillan Press, 1996.

Dokos, Thanos P. *Negotiations for a CTBT, 1958-1994: Analysis and Evaluation of American Policy*. Lanham, MD: University Press of America, 1995.

Donley, Michael B. *The SALT Handbook*. Washington, DC: The Heritage Foundation, 1979.

Donovan, Robert J. *Tumultuous Years: The Presidency of Harry S. Truman, 1949-1953*. New York: W.W. Norton, 1982.

Drell, Sidney D. *In the Shadow of the Bomb: Physics and Arms Control*. Masters of Modern Physics, Robert N. Ubell, six. New York: American Institute of Physics, 1993.

Drell, Sidney D., Philip J. Farley, and David Holloway. *The Reagan Strategic Defense Initiative: A Technical, Political, and Arms Control Assessment.* Center for International Security and Arms Control, Stanford University. Cambridge, MA: Ballinger Publishing Company, 1985.

Dukert, Joseph M. *Atoms on the Move: Transporting Nuclear Material.* Washington, DC: GPO, 1975.

Dunn, Lewis A. *Controlling the Bomb: Nuclear Proliferation in the 1980s.* New Haven, CT: Yale University Press, 1982.

Dunnigan, James F. *Digital Soldiers: The Evolution of High-Tech Weaponry and Tomorrow's Brave New Battlefield.* New York: St. Martin's Press, 1996.

Durch, William J. *The ABM Treaty and Western Security.* Cambridge, MA: Ballinger Publication, 1988.

Dyson, Freeman J. *Weapons and Hope.* New York: Harper and Row, 1984.

Edwards, John. *Superweapon: The Making of MX.* New York: W.W. Norton, 1982.

Edwards, Paul N. *The Closed World: Computers and the Politics of Discourse in Cold War America.* Cambridge, MA: MIT Press, 1996.

"Eisenhower to Khrushchev: The Real Way to End H-Tests." *US News and World Report* 44 (April 18, 1958): 78.

Else, Jon. *The Day After Trinity: J. Robert Oppenheimer and the Atomic Bomb.* Voyager Multimedia, 1996. CD-ROM based on film.

Enthoven, Alain C, and K. Wayne Smith. *How Much Is Enough?: Shaping the Defense Program, 1961-1969.* New York: Harper and Row, 1971.

Ernst, Colonel Frederick. "Role of the Defense Nuclear Agency in the Persian Gulf Conflict." *Nuclear Survivability* (April 1992): 3, 33.

Evangelista, Matthew. *Innovation and the Arms Race: How the United States and the Soviet Union Develop New Military Technologies.* Ithaca, NY: Cornell University Press, 1988.

Evans, Rowland, and Robert Novak. "No Rubber Stamping." *Washington Post*, March 16, 1978, sec. A, p. 23.

"Factfile: Fifty Years of Nuclear Testing." *Arms Control Today* (1995): 28-34.

Feaver, Peter Douglas. *Guarding the Guardians: Civilian Control of Nuclear Weapons in the United States.* Ithaca, NY: Cornell University Press, 1992.

Feld, Werner J. *Congress and National Defense: The Politics of the Unthinkable.* New York: Praeger, 1985.

Feldbaum, Carl B., and Ronald J Bee. *Looking the Tiger in the Eye: Confronting the Nuclear Threat.* New York: Harper and Row, 1988.

Fermi, Rachel, and Esther Samra. *Picturing the Bomb: Photographs from the Secret World of the Manhattan Project.* Introduction by Richard Rhodes. New York: Harry N. Abrams, 1995.

Ferrell, Robert H. *American Diplomacy: A History.* Revised and expanded ed. New York: W.W. Norton and Company, 1969.

Fetter, Steve. *Toward a Comprehensive Test Ban.* Cambridge, MA: Ballinger Publishing Company, 1988.

Flax, Alexander. "Ballistic Missile Defense: Concepts and History." *Daedalus* 114, no. 2 (Spring 1985): 33-52.

Ford, Daniel. *The Button: The Pentagon's Strategic Command and Control System.* New York: Simon and Schuster, 1985.

Ford, Mary Shelly. *Sowing the Wind: A History of the Manhattan Project.* Washington, DC: Defense Atomic Support Agency, 1961.

Fore, Claude. "New ERRIC Contact at DASIAC." *Science and Technology Digest* (September 1995): 30.

Fradkin, Philip L. *Fallout: An American Nuclear Tragedy*. Tucson, AZ: The University of Arizona Press, 1989.

Freedman, Lawrence. *The Evolution of Nuclear Strategy*. London: Macmillan Press, 1981.

———. *The Price of Peace: Living with the Nuclear Dilemma*. First American ed. New York: Henry Holt and Company, 1986.

Freeman, John Patrick George. *Britain's Nuclear Arms Control Policy in the Context of Anglo-American Relations, 1957-68*. Basingstoke, Hampshire, England: Macmillan, 1986.

Friedberg, Aaron L. "A History of the US Strategic 'Doctrine'–1945-1980." *Journal of Strategic Studies* 3, no. 3 (Dec. 1980): 37-71.

Fritzel, Roger N. *Nuclear Testing and National Security*. Fort Lesley J. McNair, Washington, DC: National Defense University, 1981.

Fuller, John G. *The Day We Bombed Utah: America's Most Lethal Secret*. New York: New American Library, 1984.

Furman, Necah Stewart. *Sandia National Laboratories: The Postwar Decade*. Albuquerque, NM: University of New Mexico Press, 1990.

Futrell, Robert Frank. *Ideas, Concepts, Doctrine: A History of Basic Thinking in the United States Air Force, 1907-1964*. Maxwell Air Force Base: Air University, 1974.

Gaddis, John Lewis. *The Long Peace: Inquiries into the History of the Cold War*. New York: Oxford University Press, 1987.

———. *Strategies of Containment: A Critical Appraisal of Postwar American National Security Policy*. New York: Oxford University Press, 1982.

———. *The US And the Origins of the Cold War*. New York: Columbia University Press, 1988.

———. *We Now Know: Rethinking Cold War History*. New York: Oxford University Press, 1997.

Garwin, Richard. "Star Wars: Shield or Threat." *Journal of International Affairs* 39 (Summer 1985): 31-44.

Gay, William, and Michael Pearson. *The Nuclear Arms Race: A Digest with Bibliographies*. Chicago: American Library Association, 1987.

Gellner, Charles R. "The Reagan Administration: Negotiating Arms Control with the Soviet Union." In *Conflict and Arms Control: An Uncertain Agenda*. Edited by Paul R. Viotti. Boulder, CO: Westview Press, 1986: 24-42.

"General Twining Says: Atomic Tests Are Vital to Safety of US and Allies." *US News and World Report* 44 (April 18, 1958): 66-7.

George, Alexander L., Philip J. Farley, and Alexander Dallin. *US–Soviet Security Cooperation: Achievements, Failures, Lessons*. New York: Oxford University Press, 1988.

Gertcher, Frank L., and William J. Weida. *Beyond Deterrence: The Political Economy of Nuclear Weapons*. Boulder, CO: Westview Press, 1990.

Gilpin, Robert. *American Scientists and Nuclear Weapons Policy*. Princeton, NJ: Princeton University Press, 1962.

Girrier, Catherine. *The No-First-Use Issue in American Nuclear Weapons Policy, 1945-1957*. Geneva: Institut Universitaire de Hautes Etudes Internationales, 1985.

Glasstone, Samuel, editor. *The Effects of Nuclear Weapons*. Washington, DC: US Defense Atomic Support Agency, 1962.

"Go Ahead With Neutron Bomb?" *US News and World Report* 83 (1977): 55-56.

Goin, Peter. *Nuclear Landscapes*. Baltimore, MD: Johns Hopkins University Press, 1991.

Golden, William T. *Impacts of the Early Cold War on the Formulation of US Science Policy: Selected Memoranda of William T. Golden, October 1950 - April 1951*. Edited with an appreciation by William A. Blanpied. Washington, DC: American Association for the Advancement of Science, 1995.

Goldstein, Jack S. *A Different Sort of Time: The Life of Jerrold R. Zacharias, Scientist, Engineer, Educator*. Cambridge, MA: MIT Press, 1992.

Goldstein, Martin. *Arms Control and Military Preparedness From Truman to Bush*. American University Studies, Series X, Political Science, 37. New York: Peter Lang, 1993.

Goodwin, Irwin. "Plutonium, a 'Clear and Present' Legacy of Cold War, Placed by DOE on 'Duel Track' to Eventual Disposal." *Physics Today* 50, no. 2 (February 1997): 53-4.

———. "Without Explosions to Test the Aging Nuclear Arsenal, Bomb Builders Turn to Inertial Fusion and Supercomputers." *Physics Today* 50, no. 3 (March 1997): 63-5.

Gordon, Michael R. "The Midgetman Missile–A Counterpoint to the Giant MX, But Will It Work?" *Defense* 15, no. 40 (October 1, 1983): 2000.

Gosling, F.G. *The Manhattan Project: Science in the Second World War*. Washington, DC: Department of Energy, 1990.

Gottemoeller, Rose. "Presidential Priorities in Nuclear Policy." In *Dismantling the Cold War: US and NIS Perspectives on the Nunn-Lugar Cooperative Threat Reduction Program*. Edited by John M. Shields and William C. Potter. Cambridge, MA: MIT Press, 1997: 61-84.

Goudsmit, Samuel A. *Alsos*. New York: Henry Schuman, Inc., 1947.

Graebner, Norman A. *Cold War Diplomacy: American Foreign Policy, 1945-1975*. Second ed. New York: D. Van Nostrand Company, Inc., 1977.

Grahlfs, F. Lincoln. *Voices From Ground Zero: Recollections and Feelings of Nuclear Test Veterans*. Lanham, MD: University Press of America, Inc., 1996.

Gray, Colin S. *Missiles Against War: The ICBM Debate Today*. Fairfax, VA: National Institute for Public Policy, 1985.

———. "Mystery Tour: From SALT to START." In *House of Cards: Why Arms Control Must Fail*. Edited by Colin S. Gray. Ithaca, NY: Cornell University Press, 1992: 120-159.

———. "Nuclear Strategy: The Case for a Theory of Victory." *International Security* 4 (Summer 1979): 54-87.

———. *Weapons Don't Make War: Policy, Strategy, and Military Technology*. Lawrence, KS: University Press of Kansas, 1993.

Graybar, Lloyd J. "The 1946 Atomic Bomb Tests: Atomic Diplomacy or Bureaucratic Infighting?" *Journal of American History* 72, no. 4 (March 1986): 888-907.

"Great Precautions Taken to Guard Atomic Secrets." *New York Times*, September 26, 1948, sec. 4, p. 5.

Greenwood, John. *American Defense Policy Since 1945: A Preliminary Bibliography*. Lawrence, KS: University of Kansas Press, 1973.

Greenwood, Ted. *Making the MIRV: A Study of Defense Decision Making*. Lanham, MD: University Press of America, 1988.

Gregory, Shaun. *The Hidden Cost of Deterrence: Nuclear Weapons Accidents*. London: Brassey's, 1990.

Hacker, Barton C. *The Dragon's Tail: Radiation Safety in the Manhattan Project, 1942-1946*. Berkeley: University of California Press, 1987.

———. *Elements of Controversy: The Atomic Energy Commission and Radiation Safety in Nuclear Weapons Testing, 1947-1974*. Berkeley: University of California Press, 1994.

Haig, Alexander, M. *Caveat: Realism, Reagan, and Foreign Policy.* New York: Macmillan Publishing Company, 1984.

Hall, Harry S. "Scientists and Politicians." *Bulletin of the Atomic Scientists* (1956).

Hall, R. Cargill. "From Concept to National Policy: Strategic Reconnaissance in the Cold War." *Prologue: Quarterly Journal of the National Archives* 28, no. 2 (1996): 106-25.

Halloran, Richard. *To Arm a Nation: Rebuilding America's Endangered Defenses.* New York: Macmillan Publishing Company, 1986.

Hammond, Paul Y. *LBJ and the Presidential Management of Foreign Relations.* Austin, TX: University of Texas Press, 1992.

Handbook for Radiological Monitors. Washington, DC: Department of Defense, 1963.

Harahan, Joseph Patrick. "Ten Years, Twelve Treaties and Agreements, Hundreds of People: One Agency." *On Site Insights* (January 1998): 18-9.

Harmon, Amy. "For UFO Buffs, 50 Years of Hazy History." *New York Times*, June 14, 1997, sec. A, pp. 1, 6.

Harnin, William. "Privates and Generals Study A-Bomb." *Popular Mechanics* 106 (August 1956): 110-112, 210.

Harvard Nuclear Study Group. *Living With Nuclear Weapons.* Cambridge, MA: Harvard University Press, 1983.

Hawkins, David, Edith Truslow, and Ralph Smith. *Project Y: The Los Alamos Story.* 2 Vols. Los Angeles: Tomash Publishers, 1961.

Herken, Gregg. *Cardinal Choices: Presidential Science Advising from the Atomic Bomb to SDI.* New York: Oxford University Press, 1992.

———. *Counsels of War.* New York: Alfred A. Knopf, 1985.

———. *The Winning Weapon: The Atomic Bomb in the Cold War, 1945-1950.* New York: Alfred A. Knopf, 1980.

Hewlett, Richard G., and Oscar E. Anderson, Jr. *The New World, 1939/1946: A History of the United States Atomic Energy Commission, Volume I.* University Park, PA: Pennsylvania State University Press, 1962.

Hewlett, Richard G., and Francis Duncan. *Atomic Shield, 1947/1952: A History of the United States Atomic Energy Commission, Volume II.* University Park, PA: Pennsylvania State University Press, 1969.

———. *Nuclear Navy, 1946-1962.* Chicago: University of Chicago Press, 1974.

Hewlett, Richard G., and Jack M. Holl. *Atoms for Peace and War, 1953-1961: Eisenhower and the Atomic Energy Commission.* Berkeley: University of California Press, 1989.

Higham, Robin. *Air Power: A Concise History.* New York: St Martin's Press, 1972.

Hill, Charles. "'Operate Through' A New DNA/SDIO Program." *Nuclear Survivability* (July 1988).

Hill, Kenneth L. *Cold War Chronology: Soviet-American Relations, 1945-1991.* Washington, DC: Congressional Quarterly, 1993.

Hines, Neal O. *Proving Ground.* Seattle, WA: University of Washington Press, 1962.

Hirschbein, Ron. *Newest Weapons/Oldest Psychology: The Dialectics of American Nuclear Strategy.* New York: Peter Lang, 1989.

Hitch, Charles J., and Roland N. McKean. *The Economics of Defense in the Nuclear Age.* New York: Atheneum, 1966.

Hoddeson, Lilian, and others. *Critical Assembly: A Technical History of Los Alamos During the Oppenheimer Years, 1943-1945.* New York: Cambridge University Press, 1993.

Hoffman, Ralph. *Missiles Against War: The ICBM Debate Today. An Executive Summary*. Fairfax, VA: National Institute for Public Policy, 1985.

Holloway, David. *Stalin and the Bomb: The Soviet Union and Atomic Energy, 1939-1956*. New Haven, CT: Yale University Press, 1994.

"House Votes Inquiry On War Files Theft". *New York Times*, April 19, 1946, sec. 1, p. 20.

"Into Space." *Newsweek* (October 14, 1957): 38.

"Is Russia Winning the Arms Race?" *US News and World Report* 63 (1967): 36-38.

Israel, Fred L. *The Chief Executive: Inaugural Addresses of the Presidents From George Washington to Lyndon B. Johnson*. New York: Crown Publishers, 1965.

Jackson, Robert. *The Berlin Airlift*. Wellingborough, Northamptonshire, England: Patrick Stephens, 1988.

Jeffries, John. *Wartime America: The World War II Home Front*. Chicago: I.R. Dee, 1996.

Jervis, Robert. *The Meaning of the Nuclear Revolution*. Ithaca, NY: Cornell University Press, 1989.

———. "Why Nuclear Superiority Doesn't Matter." *Political Science Quarterly* 94, no. 4 (Winter 1979-1980): 617-33.

Johnson, Stuart E., editor. *The Niche Threat: Deterring the Use of Chemical and Biological Weapons*. Washington, DC: National Defense University Press, 1997.

"Joint Task Force Eight Moves Ahead." *Army, Navy, Air Force Journal and Register* 94 (March 17, 1962): 20.

Jones, Greta. *Science, Politics, and the Cold War*. London: Routledge, 1988.

Jones, Vincent C. *Manhattan: The Army and the Atomic Bomb*. Washington, DC: Center for Military History, 1985.

Jungk, Robert. *Brighter Than a Thousand Suns: A Personal History of the Atomic Scientists*. Translated by James Cleugh. New York: Harcourt, Brace, 1958.

Kahan, Jerome H. *Security in the Nuclear Age: Developing US Strategic Arms Policy*. Washington, DC: Brookings Institution, 1975.

Kahn, Herman. *On Thermonuclear War*. Princeton, NJ: Princeton University Press, 1960.

Kaku, Michio, and Daniel Axelrod. *To Win a Nuclear War: The Pentagon's Secret War Plans*. Boston: South End, 1987.

Kaplan, David E. "Where the Bombs Are." *New West* 6, no. 4 (April 1981): 76-83.

Kaplan, Fred. *The Wizards of Armageddon*. New York: Simon and Schuster, 1983.

Karp, Regina Cowen, editor. *Security With Nuclear Weapons?: Different Perspectives on National Security*. New York: Oxford University Press, 1991.

Kaufman, William W. *Glastnost, Perestroika, and US Defense Spending*. Washington: Brookings Institution, 1990.

Kegley, Charles W., Jr., and Eugene R. Wittkopf, editors. *The Nuclear Reader: Strategy, Weapons, War*. 2nd ed. New York: St. Martin's Press, 1989.

Kelley, Stuart, Carol Miller, and Geoffrey Walsh. "Data Archival and Retrieval Enhancement (DARE)." *Science and Technology Digest* (September 1995): 32-4.

Kennan, George F. "Cease This Madness." *Atlantic Monthly* 247 (January 1981): 25-8.

Kennedy, David. "Big Bang in the Desert." *Science* 17 (July-August 1986): 35-6.

Kevles, Dan. "Cold War and Hot Physics: Science, Security, and the American State, 1945-56." *Historical Studies in the Physical and Biological Sciences* 20, no. 2 (1990): 240-64.

"Key US Defenses Center in Empire." *Denver Post*, August 24, 1947, sec. 1, p. 1.

Kidder, Ray E. *Maintaining the US Stockpile of Nuclear Weapons During a Low-Threshold or Comprehensive Test Ban*. Livermore, CA: Lawrence Livermore National Laboratory, University of California, 1987.

Kincade, William H., and Jeffrey D. Porro, editors. *Negotiating Security: An Arms Control Reader*. Washington, DC: Carnegie Endowment for International Peace, 1979.

Kinnard, Douglas. *President Eisenhower and Strategy Management: A Study in Defense Politics*. Washington, DC: Pergamon–Brassey's International Defense Publishers, 1989.

Kissinger, Henry. A. *Nuclear Weapons and Foreign Policy*. New York: Harper and Brothers, 1957Kleinman, Daniel Lee. *Politics on the Endless Frontier: Postwar Research Policy in the United States*. Durham, NC: Duke University Press, 1995.

Knox, Lt. Col. Ken. "Khobar Towers Bomb Damage Survey." *Science and Technology Digest* (May 1997): 7-10.

Koch, Scott A., editor. *CIA Cold War Records: Selected Estimates on the Soviet Union, 1950-1959*. Washington, DC: Center for the Study of Intelligence, 1993.

Kofsky, Frank. *Harry S. Truman and the War Scare of 1948: A Successful Campaign to Deceive the Nation*. New York: St. Martin's Press, 1993.

Kohn, Richard H., and Joseph P. Harahan, editors. *Strategic Air Warfare*. Washington, DC: Office of Air Force History, 1988.

Koplow, David A. *Testing a Nuclear Test Ban: What Should Be Prohibited by a "Comprehensive" Treaty?* Aldershot, England: Dartmouth Publishing Company, 1996.

Korb, Lawrence J. *The Joint Chiefs of Staff: The First Twenty-Five Years*. Bloomington, IN: Indiana University Press, 1976.

Kull, Steven. *Minds at War: Nuclear Reality and the Inner Conflicts of Defense Policymakers*. New York: Basic Books, 1988.

Laird, Robbin F. *The Soviet Union, the West, and the Nuclear Arms Race*. New York: New York University Press, 1986.

Lambeth, Benjamin S. *The Evolving Soviet Strategic Threat*. 5493. Santa Monica, CA: RAND Corporation, 1975.

Lapp, Ralph E. "SALT, MIRV and First Strike." *Bulletin of the Atomic Scientists* 28, no. 3 (March 1972): 21-6.

Lawren, William. *The General and the Bomb: A Biography of General Leslie R. Groves, Director of the Manhattan Project*. New York: Dodd, Mead, and Company, 1988.

Lebow, Richard Ned. "Assured Strategic Stupidity: The Quest for Ballistic Missile Defense." *Journal of International Affairs* 39 (Summer 1985): 57-80.

———. *We All Lost the Cold War*. Princeton, NJ: Princeton University Press, 1994.

Leffler, Melvyn P. *A Preponderance of Power: National Security, the Truman Administration, and the Cold War*. Stanford, CA: Stanford University Press, 1993.

Lehman, John F., Jr., "Why Salt II Failed." In *Beyond the Salt II Failure*. Edited by John F. Lehman and Seymour Weiss. New York: Praeger Publishers, 1981: 96-109.

LeMay, General Curtis E., with MacKinlay Kantor. *Mission with LeMay: My Story*. Garden City, NY: Doubleday and Company, 1965.

LeMay, General Curtis E., with Major General Dale O. Smith. *America is in Danger*. New York: Funk and Wagnalls, 1968.

Leslie, Stuart W. *The Cold War and American Science: The Military-Industrial-Academic Complex at MIT and Stanford*. New York: Columbia University Press, 1993.

Leviero, Anthony. "House Debate is on Over Atomic Bill." *New York Times*, July 18, 1946, sec. 1, p. 2.

Levine, Alan J. *The Missile and Space Race*. Westport, CT: Praeger, 1994.

Lewis, Flora. *One of Our H-Bombs Is Missing*. New York: McGraw-Hill, 1967.

Lewis, John G. "Project Graybeard: Preserving Legacy Nuclear Data." *Science and Technology Digest* (August 1996): 31-5.

Lewis, Julian. *Changing Direction: British Military Planning for Post-War Strategic Defence, 1942-1947*. London: Sherwood, 1987.

Lieberman, Joseph I. *The Scorpion and the Tarantula: The Struggle to Control Atomic Weapons, 1945-1949*. Boston: Houghton Mifflin, 1970.

Lockwood, Jonathan Samuel, Kathleen O'Brien Lockwood, and Jonathan Samuel Lockwood. *The Russian View of US Strategy: Its Past, Its Future*. New Brunswick, NJ: Transaction Publishers, 1993.

Longstreth, Thomas K. *The Impact of US and Soviet Ballistic Missile Defense Programs on the ABM Treaty: A Report for the National Campaign to Save the ABM Treaty*. 3rd ed. Washington, DC: Campaign, 1985.

Lord, Carnes. "Verification and the Future of Arms Control." *Strategic Review* 6 (Spring 1978): 24-32.

Luttwak, Edward. *Strategic Power: Military Capabilities and Political Utility*. The Washington Papers, Volume IV. Beverly Hills, CA: Sage Publications, 1976.

Lyndon Johnson Confronts the World: American Foreign Policy, 1963-1968. New York: Cambridge University Press, 1994.

MacKenzie, Donald. *Inventing Accuracy: An Historical Sociology of Nuclear Missile Guidance*. Cambridge, Mass: MIT Press, 1990.

———. *Knowing Machines: Essays on Technical Change Technology*. Cambridge, MA: MIT Press, 1996.

———. "The Soviet Union and Strategic Missile Guidance." *International Security* 13, no. 2 (1988): 5-54.

MacKenzie, Donald, and Graham Spinardi. "The Shaping of Nuclear Weapon System Technology: US Fleet Ballistic Missile Guidance and Navigation: I: From Polaris to Poseidon." *Social Studies of Science* 18 (1988): 419-63.

Mahley, Donald. "The New Nuclear Options in Military Strategy." *Military Review* 56 (1979): 3-7.

Malcolmson, Robert. *Beyond Nuclear Thinking*. Montreal, Canada: McGill University Press, 1990.

Manchester, William. *The Glory and the Dream*. Boston: Little, Brown, 1974.

Mandelbaum, Michael. *The Nuclear Question: The United States and Nuclear Weapons, 1946-1976*. Cambridge: Cambridge University Press, 1979.

"Man's Awesome Adventure." *Newsweek* 50 (October 14, 1957): 39-40.

Mark, Hans. "War and Peace in Space." *Journal of International Affairs* 39 (Summer 1985): 1-22.

Markey, Edward J., and Douglas C. Waller. *Nuclear Peril: The Politics of Proliferation*. Cambridge, MA: Ballinger Publishing Company, 1982.

Marshall, Eliot. "Nuclear Winter Debate Heats Up." *Science* 235 (January 16, 1987): 271-3.

"Marshall Islands Stagger from Ravages of US Control." *Baltimore Sun*, October 26, 1997, sec A, pp. 1, 14.

Matthews, Herbert L. "West Still Defers Reply to Russians." *New York Times*, July 17, 1948, sec A, p. 3.

May, Ernest R. *American Cold War Strategy: Interpreting NSC 68*. Boston: St. Martin's Press, 1993.

May, Ernest R., John D. Steinbruner, and Thomas W. Wolfe. *History of the Strategic Arms Competition, 1945-1972*. Washington, DC: Office of the Secretary of Defense Historical Office, 1981.

McBride, James Hubert. *The Test Ban Treaty: Military, Technological, and Political Implications*. Chicago: Henry Regnery Company, 1967.

McCormick, Charles P. *The Power of People*. New York: Harper and Brothers, 1949.

McNamara, Robert. *Blundering into Disaster: Surviving the First Century of the Nuclear Age*. New York: Pantheon Books, 1986.

———. *The Essence of Security: Reflections in Office*. New York: Harper and Row, 1968.

———. "The Military Role of Nuclear Weapons: Perceptions and Misperceptions." *Foreign Affairs* 62, no. 1 (Fall 1983): 59-80.

McPhee, John. *The Curve of Binding Energy*. New York: Ballantine Books, 1973.

McWilliams, Wayne C., and Harry Piotrowski. *The World Since 1945: Politics, War, and Revolution in the Nuclear Age*. Boulder, CO: Lynne Rienner Publications, 1988.

Medvedev, Zhores A. *Andropov*. New York: Penguin Books, 1984.

Meilinger, Philip S. *Hoyt S. Vandenberg: The Life of a General*. Bloomington, IN: Indiana University Press, 1989.

Meyer, Stephen M. *The Dynamics of Nuclear Proliferation*. Chicago: University of Chicago Press, 1984.

Middleton, Drew. "Russians Imperil Berlin Air Supply." *New York Times*, 16 July 1948, sec. A, p. 1.

Midgley, John J., Jr. *Deadly Illusions: Army Policy for the Nuclear Battlefield*. Boulder, CO: Westview Press, 1986.

Miller, George. *Report to Congress on Stockpile Reliability, Weapon Remanufacture, and the Role of Nuclear Testing*. Livermore, CA: Lawrence Livermore National Laboratory, 1987.

Miller, Richard L. *Under the Cloud: The Decades of Nuclear Testing*. New York: Free Press, Macmillan, 1986.

Milliken, Robert. *No Conceivable Injury*. New York: Penguin Books, 1986.

Millis, Walter, Harvey C. Mansfield, and Harold Stein. *Arms and the State: Civil-Military Elements in National Policy*. New York: Twentieth Century Fund, 1958.

Moody, Walter. *Building a Strategic Air Force*. Washington, DC: Air Force History Office, 1996.

Morris, Charles R. *Iron Destinies, Lost Opportunities: The Arms Race Between the USA and the USSR, 1945-1987*. New York: Harper and Row, 1988.

Morrison, David C. "Nuclear Winter." *Defense* 18, no. 25 (June 21, 1986): 1570.

Moss, George Donelson, editor. *A Vietnam Reader*. Englewood Cliffs, NJ: Prentice Hall, 1991.

Moss, Norman. *Men Who Play God: The Story of the H-Bomb and How the World Came to Live With It*. New York: Harper and Row, 1968.

Mossberg, Walter S. "Fighting a Nuclear War." *Wall Street Journal*, August 27, 1980, p. 14.

Moulton, Harland B. *From Superiority to Parity: The United States and the Strategic Arms Race, 1961-1971*. Westport, CT: Greenwood Press, 1973.

New Light on Early Soviet Bomb Secrets. Special Issue. *Physics Today* 49, no. 11 (November 1996).

Newhouse, John. *Cold Dawn: the Story of SALT*. New York: Holt, Rinehart and Winston, 1973.

———. *War and Peace in the Nuclear Age*. New York: Alfred A. Knopf, 1989.

Nichols, K.D. *The Road to Trinity*. New York: Morrow, 1987.

Nitze, Paul H. "Vladivostok and Crisis Stability." *Wall Street Journal*, January 24, 1975, p. 10.

Nitze, Paul H., James E. Dougherty, and Francis X. Kane. *The Fateful Ends and Shades of SALT: Past . . . Present . . . And Yet to Come?* New York: Drane, Russak and Company, 1979.

Nolan, Janne E. *Guardians of the Arsenal: The Politics of Nuclear Strategy*. New York: Basic Books, 1989.

Norris, John, and Will Fowler. *NBC: Nuclear, Biological and Chemical Warfare on the Modern Battlefield*. London: Brassey's (UK) Ltd, 1997.

The Nuclear Controversy: A Foreign Affairs Reader. New York: New American Library, 1985.

"Nuclear Energy–Its Peacetime Use." Interview With James R. Schlesinger, Chairman, Atomic Energy Commission." *US News and World Report* 72 (1972): 46-51.

Nuclear Regulatory Commission Special Inquiry Group. *Three Mile Island: A Report to the Commissioners and to the Public. Volume II, part 3*. Washington, DC, 1980.

"Nuclear Survivability Interviews Dr. Don A. Linger, Director for Test, DNA." *Nuclear Survivability* (August 1990).

"Nuclear Survivability Interviews Major General John C. Scheidt, Director of Operations, DNA." *Nuclear Survivability* (April 1990).

"Nuclear Survivability Interviews Vice Admiral Parker, Director, DNA." *Nuclear Survivability* (July 1989).

"Nuclear Threat in Gulf War." *Washington Quarterly* (Autumn 1996).

"Oak Ridge Scientists Deny Any Subversion." *New York Times*, July 13, 1946, sec. 1, p. 13.

Oberdorfer, Don. *The Turn: From Cold War to the New Era: The United States and the Soviet Union, 1983-1990*. New York: Poseidon Press, 1991.

Office of the Secretary of Defense. *Department of Defense, Key Officials, 1947-1995*. Washington, DC: Historical Office, Office of the Secretary of Defense, 1995.

———. *Strategic Defense Initiative: Progress and Promise*, GPO, Washington, DC, 1989.

O'Keefe, Bernard J. *Nuclear Hostages*. Boston: Houghton Mifflin, 1983.

Oliver, Kendrick. *Kennedy, MacMillan, and the Nuclear Test Ban Debate, 1961-63*. New York: St. Martin's Press, 1997.

Operation Sandstone: The Story of Joint Task Force Seven. Edited by Clarence H. White. Washington, DC: Infantry Journal Press, 1949.

Ord, John A. *Evolution of the Technical Training Group, Sandia Base*, 1996. Provided by author.

Ordway, Frederick I., and Ronald C. Wakeford. *International Missile and Spacecraft Guide*. New York: McGraw-Hill, 1960.

Osgood, Robert. *The Nuclear Dilemma in American Strategic Thought*. Boulder, CO: Westview Press, 1988.

Osgood, Robert E., and others. *America Armed: Essays on United States Military Policy*. Edited by Robert A. Goldwin. Chicago: Rand McNally, 1963.

Panofsky, Wolfgang K.H. *Arms Control and Salt II*. The Jessie and John Danz Lecture Series. Seattle, WA: University of Washington, 1979.

Parrish, Noel Francis. *Behind the Sheltering Bomb: Military Indecision From Alamogordo to Korea*. American Military Experience. New York: Arno Press, 1979.

Patterson, James T. *Grand Expectations: The United States, 1945-1974*. New York: Oxford University Press, 1996.

Patton, Phil. "Indeed They Have Invaded. Look Around." *New York Times*, 15 June 1997, Arts and Leisure section, p. 38.

Pearson, Richard. "Vice Admiral Edward Parker, War Hero, Dies." *Washington Post*, 17 October 1989, sec. B, p. 7.

Peeters, Paul. *Massive Retaliation: The Policy and Its Critics*. Chicago: H. Regnery Co., 1959.

Perkins, Ray Jr. *The ABCs of the Soviet-American Nuclear Arms Race*. Pacific Grove, CA: Brooks/Cole, 1991.

Perle, Richard N. "The Strategic Defense Initiative: Addressing Some Misconceptions." *Journal of International Affairs* 39 (Summer 1985): 23-30.

Pfeffer, Robert. "More NATO Help for System Developers." *Nuclear Survivability* (September 1986).

———. "AEP-9: NATO Simulators Available for Testing Nuclear Survivability." *Nuclear Survivability* (September 1986).

Pincus, Walter. "Military Got Authority to Use Nuclear Arms in 1957." *Washington Post*, 21 March 1998, section A, pp. 1, 8.

Polner, Murray. "The Poisoned Battlefield." *Washington Post*, 17 August 1980, Book World.

Poole, Walter S. *The History of the Joint Chiefs of Staff: The Joint Chiefs of Staff and National Policy: Volume IV: 1950-1952*. Wilmington, DE: Michael Glazier, Inc., 1979.

Porro, Jeffrey, editor. *The Nuclear Age Reader*. New York: Alfred A. Knopf, 1989.

Potter, William C. *Nuclear Power and Non-Proliferation: An Interdisciplinary Perspective*. Cambridge, MA: Oelgeschlager, Gunn and Hain, 1982.

Powaski, Ronald E. *The Cold War: The United States and the Soviet Union, 1917-1991*. New York: Oxford University Press, 1998.

———. *March to Armageddon: The United States and the Nuclear Arms Race, 1939 to the Present*. New York: Oxford University Press, 1987.

Preston, Richard. "Test Ban: Optimism on Project Vela." *Bulletin of the Atomic Scientists* 19 (1963): 33-37.

Pringle, Peter, and William Arkin. *SIOP: The Secret US Plan for Nuclear War*. New York: W.W. Norton, 1983.

Progress in Arms Control?: Readings From Scientific American. San Francisco, CA: W.H. Freeman, 1979.

Pry, Peter Vincent. *The Strategic Nuclear Balance, Volume I: And Why It Matters*. New York: C. Russak, 1990.

Rabe, Stephen G. "Eisenhower Revisionism." *Diplomatic History* 17, no. 1 (Winter 1993): 97-115.

Rafferty, Kevin, Jane Loader, and Pierce Rafferty. *The Atomic Cafe: The Book of the Film*. New York: Peacock Press/Bantam, 1982.

RAND Corporation. *An Assessment of Defense Nuclear Agency Functions: Pathways Toward a New Nuclear Infrastructure for the Nation*. Santa Monica, CA: RAND Corporation, 1994.

Rapids, Rich. "New DoD Survivability Directive Published." *Nuclear Survivability* (December 1988).

Rawls, Wendell, Jr. "Warhead of Missile Is Reported As Safe." *New York Times*, September 22, 1980, sec. A, pp. 1, 16.

Rearden, Steven L. *History of the Office of the Secretary of Defense, Volume I: The Formative Years, 1947-1950*. Washington, DC: Historical Office, Office of the Secretary of Defense, 1984.

"Red Moon Over the US." *Time* 70, no. 16 (October 14, 1957): 27.

Reeves, Richard. *President Kennedy: Profile of Power*. New York: Simon and Schuster, 1993.

Register of Graduates and Former Cadets, 1802-1990. Dwight D. Eisenhower centennial ed. West Point, NY: Association of Graduates, USMA, 1990.

Renehart, Eric J., and Harlan Lawson. "Field Command Becomes Center for DSWA Test Operations". *Science and Technology Digest* (August 1996): 15-7.

Rhodes, Richard. *Dark Sun: The Making of the Hydrogen Bomb*. New York: Simon and Schuster, 1995.

———. *The Making of the Atomic Bomb*. New York: Simon and Schuster, 1986.

Roberts, Chalmers M. *The Nuclear Years: The Arms Race and Arms Control, 1945-70*. New York: Praeger Publishers, 1970.

Roman, Peter J. *Eisenhower and the Missile Gap*. Cornell Studies in Security Affairs. Ithaca, NY: Cornell University Press, 1995.

Rosenberg, David Alan. "American Atomic Strategy and the Hydrogen Bomb Decision." *Journal of American History* 66, no. 1 (June 1979): 62-87.

———. "The Origins of Overkill: Nuclear Weapons and American Strategy, 1945-1960." *International Security* 7, no. 4 (1983): 3-71.

———. "'A Smoking, Radiating Ruin at the End of Two Hours': Documents on American Plans for Nuclear War With the Soviet Union, 1954-1955." *International Security* 6, no. 3 (Winter 1981-1982): 3-39.

———. "US Nuclear Stockpile, 1945 to 1950." *Bulletin of the Atomic Scientists* 38, no. 5 (May 1982): 25-30.

Rosenberg, Howard L. *Atomic Soldiers: American Victims of Nuclear Experiments*. Boston: Beacon Press, 1980.

Rotblat, J. *Pugwash–the First Ten Years: History of the Conferences of Sciences and World Affairs*. New York: Humanities Press, 1968.

Rotblat, Joseph, and Ubiratan D'Ambrosio, editors. *World Peace and the Developing Countries: Annals of Pugwash 1985*. London: MacMillan, 1986.

Rowney, Edward L., and others. *Strategic Force Modernization and Arms Control*. Cambridge: Institute for Foreign Policy Analysis, 1986.

"Russians Put the Squeeze on Berlin." *Life* 24 (1948): 47.

"A 'Safe' A-Bomb Drops: Taut World Gets Jitters." *US News and World Report* 44 (21 March 1958): 55, 57.

"A Safer US With a SALT Treaty?" *US News and World Report* 84 (1978): 55-56.

Saffer, Thomas H., and Orville E. Kelly. *Countdown Zero*. New York: G.P. Putnam's Sons, 1982.

Sagan, Scott D. *The Limits of Safety: Organizations, Accidents, and Nuclear Weapons*. Princeton, NJ: Princeton University Press, 1993.

Salomon, Michael D. *American Strategic Thinking*. Pittsburgh, PA: Center for Arms Control and International Security Studies, University Center for International Studies, University of Pittsburgh, 1977.

Sanders, Daun A. "DNA Weapons of Mass Destruction Game Support." *Science and Technology Digest* (September 1995).

Sands, Matthew. "Monitoring a Test Ban." *Bulletin of the Atomic Scientists* 19 (1963): 12-18.

Scheer, Robert. *With Enough Shovels: Reagan, Bush, and Nuclear War*. New York: Random House, 1982.

Schilling, Warner Roller, and others, editors. *Strategy, Politics, and Defense Budgets*. New York: Columbia University Press, 1962.

Schnabel, James F. *The History of the Joint Chiefs of Staff: The Joint Chiefs of Staff and National Policy: Volume I: 1945-1947.* Wilmington, DE: Michael Glazier, Inc., 1979.

Schnabel, James F., and Robert J. Watson. *The History of the Joint Chiefs of Staff: The Joint Chiefs of Staff and National Policy: Volume III: The Korean War.* Wilmington, DE: Michael Glazer, 1979.

Schwartzman, David. *Games of Chicken: Four Decades of US Nuclear Policy.* New York: Praeger, 1988.

Scoville, Herbert, Jr. *MX: Prescription for Disaster.* Cambridge, MA: MIT Press, 1981.

Shalett, Sidney. "Civilians Assume Atom Rule in US" *New York Times*, January 1, 1947, sec. A, p. 28.

Shepley, James R., and Clay Blair, Jr. *The Hydrogen Bomb: The Men, The Menace, The Mechanism.* New York: David McKay Company, 1954.

Sherry, Michael S. *The Rise of American Air Power: The Creation of Armageddon.* New Haven, CT: Yale University Press, 1987.

Sherwin, Martin J. *A World Destroyed: Hiroshima and the Origins of the Arms Race.* New York: Vintage Books, 1987.

Shields, John M., and William C. Potter, editors. *Dismantling the Cold War: US and NIS Perspectives on the Nunn-Lugar Cooperative Threat Reduction Program.* CSIA Studies in International Security. Cambridge, MA: MIT Press, 1997.

Shlaim, Avi. *The United States and the Berlin Blockade, 1948-1949: A Study in Crisis Decision-Making.* Berkeley, CA: University of California Press, 1983.

"Should US Kill the MX Missile?" *US News and World Report* 88 (1980): 59-60.

Simpson, John. *The Independent Nuclear State: The United States, Britain and the Military Atom.* 2nd ed. Houndmills, Basingstoke, Hampshire, England: Macmillan, 1986.

Smith, Jeff. "Reagan, Star Wars, and American Culture." *Bulletin of the Atomic Scientists* 43, no. 1 (1987): 19-25.

Smith, Merritt Roe, editor. *Military Enterprise and Technological Change: Perspectives on the American Experience.* Cambridge, MA: MIT Press, 1985.

Smith, Michael L. "At Home With the Atom: Nuclear Technology and Ideology in the Cold War." Paper Presented at the Society for the History of Technology Annual Meeting, Uppsala, Sweden, August 19, 1992, Session 32: Display Value of Large Technologies.

Smith, R. Jeffrey. "The Dissenter." *Washington Post Magazine* (December 7, 1997): 18-21, 38-45.

Smoke, Richard. *National Security and the Nuclear Dilemma.* 3rd ed. New York: Random House, 1992.

Snow, Donald M. *The Necessary Peace: Nuclear Weapons and Superpower Relations.* Lexington: Lexington Books, 1987.

Snyder, Glenn H. "The 'New Look' of 1953." *Strategy, Politics, and Defense Budgets.* Edited by Warner R. Schilling, Paul Y. Hammond, and Glenn H. Snyder. New York: Columbia University Press, 1962: 463-65.

Snyder, Jed C., and Samuel F. Wells, editors. *Limiting Nuclear Proliferation.* Washington, DC: Wilson Center, 1985.

Snyder, Pat. "Humble Beginnings for the Inspection Professionals at Buzzard Point." *On Site Insights* (January 1998): 7.

Soviet Nuclear Weapons. New York: Harper and Row, 1989.

"Soviet Satellite Sends US into a Tizzy." *Life* (October 14, 1957).

Spaatz, General Carl. "Where We Went Wrong–Plan for the Future." *Newsweek* 50 (December 30, 1957): 19.

"Special Issue: New Light on Early Soviet Bomb Secrets." *Physics Today* 49, no. 11 (1996).

Spector, Leonard. *Nuclear Ambitions: The Spread of Nuclear Weapons, 1989-1990.* Boulder, CO: Westview Press, 1990.

"The Squeeze on the Corridors." *Newsweek* 32 (26 July 1948): 30, 32.

Stein, Jonathan B. *From H-Bomb to Star Wars: The Politics of Strategic Decision Making.* Lexington: Lexington Books, 1984.

Stein, Peter and Peter Feaver. *Assuring Control of Nuclear Weapons: The Evolution of Permissive Action Links.* CSIA Occasional Paper No. 2. Center for Science and International Affairs, Harvard University. Lanham, MD: University Press of America, 1987.

Steiner, Barry H. *Bernard Brodie and the Foundations of American Nuclear Strategy.* Lawrence, KS: University of Kansas Press, 1991.

Stephens, Tom, and Stuart Kelly. "DNA Updates Computational Aids." *Science and Technology Digest* (September 1995): 29-30.

Steury, Donald P. *Intentions and Capabilities: Estimates on Soviet Strategic Forces, 1950-1983.* Washington, DC: Center for the Study of Intelligence, 1996.

"Strategic Arms Debate." *Editorial Research Reports* 1, no. 21 (June 1979): 403-20.

Strauss, Lewis. *Men and Decisions.* Garden City, NY: Doubleday, 1962.

Sugawara, Sandra. "Bomb Testing Victims Seek Right to Sue US." *Washington Post*, 3 October 1985, sec. A, p. 8.

Suid, Lawrence H. *The Army's Nuclear Power Program: The Evolution of a Support Agency.* Westport, CT: Greenwood Press, 1990.

Sykes, Lynn R., and Jack F. Evernden. "The Verification of a Comprehensive Nuclear Test Ban." *Scientific American* 247, no. 4 (October 1982): 47-55.

Sylves, Richard T. *The Nuclear Oracles: A Political History of the General Advisory Committee of the Atomic Energy Commission, 1947-1977.* Ames, IA: Iowa State University Press, 1987.

Szulc, Tad. *The Bombs of Palomares.* New York: Viking Press, 1967.

Talbott, Strobe. *Deadly Gambits: The Reagan Administration and the Stalemate in Nuclear Arms Control.* New York: Alfred A. Knopf, 1984.

———. *Endgame: The Inside Story of SALT II.* New York: Harper and Row, 1979.

———. *The Master of the Game: Paul Nitze and the Nuclear Peace.* New York: Vintage Books, 1989.

Tammen, Ronald L. *MIRV and the Arms Race: An Interpretation of Defense Strategy.* New York: Praeger, 1973.

Teller, Edward. *Better a Shield Than a Sword: Perspectives on Defense and Technology.* New York: Free Press, 1987.

———. *The Legacy of Hiroshima.* New York: Doubleday, 1962.

Terriff, Terry. *The Nixon Administration and the Making of US Nuclear Strategy.* Ithaca, NY: Cornell University Press, 1995.

Thranert, Oliver. *Soviet Policy on Nuclear Testing, 1985-1991.* Kingston, Ontario, Canada: Centre for International Relations, Queen's University, 1992.

Tirman, John, editor. *Empty Promise: The Growing Case Against Star Wars.* Boston: Beacon Press, 1986.

Titus, A. Costandina. *Bombs in the Backyard: Atomic Testing and American Politics.* Reno, NV: University of Nevada Press, 1986.

Toomay, John C. "The Case for Ballistic Missile Defense." *Daedalus* 114, no. 3 (Summer 1985): 219-37.

APPENDIX A: BIBLIOGRAPHY

Towell, Pat. "The Balance of Arms: Nuclear Hardware Debate Masks SALT Political Issues." *Congressional Quarterly Weekly Report* 37 (1979): 3-10.

Trachtenberg, Marc. "A 'Wasting Asset': American Strategy and the Shifting Nuclear Balance, 1949-1954." *International Security* 13, no. 3 (Winter 1988/89): 5-49.

Trask, Roger R. *The Secretaries of Defense: A Brief History, 1947-1985.* Washington, DC: Office of the Secretary of Defense, 1985.

Trask, Roger R., and Alfred Goldberg. *The Department of Defense, 1947-1997: Organization and Leaders.* Washington, DC: Historical Office, Office of the Secretary of Defense, 1997.

Truman, Margaret. *Harry S. Truman.* New York: William Morrow and Company, 1973.

Trussell, C.P. "Peril to Security Seen in Oak Ridge." *New York Times*, 12 July 1946, sec. 1, p. 5.

Tsipis, Kosta, editor. *Review of US Military Research and Development.* Washington, DC: Pergamon, 1981.

Udall, Stewart L. *The Myths of August: A Personal Exploration of Our Tragic Cold War Affair With the Atom.* New York: Pantheon Books, 1994.

"The Ultimate Clean Bomb." *US News and World Report* 83 (1977): 15.

"The US, Ike, and Sputnik." *Newsweek* 50 (28 October 1957): 31-2, 35.

"Using the Tools of Diplomacy." *Carnegie Quarterly* (Spring Summer 1996): 8-13.

"US Nuclear Weapons Accidents: Danger in Our Midst." *Defense Monitor* 10, no. 5 (1981).

"US-USSR Treaty on Peaceful Nuclear Explosions Signed at Washington and Moscow." *Department of State Bulletin* 74 (28 June 1976): 801-12.

Van Creveld. *Supplying War: Logistics From Wallenstein to Patton.* New York: Cambridge University Press, 1977.

Voss, Earl H. *Nuclear Ambush, The Test Ban Trap.* Chicago: Henry Regnery Company, 1963.

Waggoner, Walter H. "60 B-29s Take Off for British Bases." *New York Times*, July 17, 1948, sec. 1 p. 3.

Wagner, Richard L, Jr. "The Strategic Significance of Nuclear Survivable General Purpose Forces." *Nuclear Survivability* (April 1990).

Wainstein, L., and others. *The Evolution of US Strategic Command, Control, and Warning, 1945-1972.* Arlington, VA: Institute for Defense Analysis, 1975.

Wampler, Robert A. *Nuclear Weapons and the Atlantic Alliance: A Guide to US Sources.* College Park, MD: Center for International Security Studies at Maryland, University of Maryland, 1989.

Warner, Michael, editor. *The CIA Under Harry Truman.* Washington, DC: Center for the Study of Intelligence, Central Intelligence Agency, 1994.

Warshaw, Shirley Ann, editor. *Reexamining the Eisenhower Presidency.* Westport, CT: Greenwood Press, 1993.

Wasserman, Harvey, and Norman Solomon. *Killing Our Own: The Disaster of America's Experience With Atomic Radiation.* New York: Dell Publishing, 1982.

Watson, Robert J. *History of the Office of the Secretary of Defense: Volume IV: Into the Missile Age, 1956-1960.* General Editor Alfred Goldberg. Washington, DC: Office of the Secretary of Defense, 1997.

Weart, Spencer R. *Nuclear Fear: A History of Images.* Cambridge, MA: Harvard University Press, 1988.

Webb, Willard J., and Ronald H. Cole. *The Chairmen of the Joint Chiefs of Staff*. Washington, DC: Historical Division, Joint Chiefs of Staff, 1989.

Wells, Samuel F., Jr. "The Origins of Massive Retaliation." *Political Science Quarterly* 96 (Spring 1981): 31-33.

Wentz, Walter B. *Nuclear Proliferation*. Washington, DC: Public Affairs Press, 1968.

Westervelt, Donald R. "Candor, Compromise, and the Comprehensive Test Ban." *Strategic Review* 5, no. 4 (Fall 1977): 33-44.

Wheeler, Michael O. *Nuclear Weapons and the National Interest: The Early Years*. Washington, DC: National Defense University Press, 1989.

Whitfield, Stephen J. *The Culture of the Cold War*. Baltimore, MD: Johns Hopkins University Press, 1990.

Who's Who in Atoms. Guernsey, British Isles: F. Hodgson, 1977.

Wilford, John Noble. "For Pacific's Atomic Nomads, A Symbolic Ground-Breaking." *New York Times*, 10 April 1988, sec. 1, p. 1.

Williamson, Samuel R., Jr., and Steven L. Rearden. *The Origins of US Nuclear Strategy, 1945-1953*. New York: St. Martin's Press, 1993.

Willrich, Mason, and John B. Rhinelander. *SALT: The Moscow Agreements and Beyond*. New York: Free Press, 1974.

Willrich, Mason, and Theodore B. Taylor. *Nuclear Theft: Risks and Safeguards*. Cambridge, MA: Ballinger Publishing, 1974.

Winkler, Allan M. *Life Under a Cloud: American Anxiety About the Atom*. New York: Oxford University Press, 1993.

Wohlstetter, Albert. "Clocking the Strategic Arms Race." *Wall Street Journal*, 24 September 1974, p. 24.

"The Yanks Are Back." *Newsweek* 32 (26 July 1948): 32.

York, Herbert F. *The Advisors: Oppenheimer, Teller, and the Superbomb*. San Francisco: W.H. Freeman, 1976.

———. *The CTBT and Beyond*. New York: United Nations, 1994.

———. "The Great Test-Ban Debate." *Scientific American* 227, no. 5 (November 1972): 15-23.

———. *The Nuclear Cold War: Phases and Transitions*. 1 videocassette (82 min.) Berkeley, CA: University of California, Berkeley, Office of Media Services, 1989.

York, Herbert, and G. Allen Greb. *The Comprehensive Nuclear Test Ban*. California Seminar on Arms Control and Foreign Policy, 1979.

Ziegler, Charles A. "Waiting for Joe-1: Decisions Leading to the Detection of Russia's First Atomic Bomb Test." *Social Studies of Science* 18 (1988): 197-229.

Ziegler, Charles A., and David Jacobson. *Spying Without Spies: Origins of America's Secret Nuclear Surveillance System*. Westport, CT: Praeger, 1995.

Zimmerman, Carroll L. *Insider at SAC: Operations Analysis Under General LeMay*. Manhattan, KS: Sunflower University Press, 1988.

APPENDIX B

ACRONYM LIST

ABM	Anti-Ballistic Missile
ACDA	Arms Control and Disarmament Agency
ACTD	Advanced Concept Technology Demonstration
AEC	Atomic Energy Commission
AFB	Air Force Base
AFRRI	Armed Forces Radiobiology Research Institute
AFOAT	Air Force Office of Atomic Testing
AFSWP	Armed Forces Special Weapons Project
AFTAC	Air Force Technical Applications Center
ALO	Albuquerque Operations Office
ALCM	Air-Launched Cruise Missile
ANFO	Ammonium nitrate and fuel oil
ANMCC	Alternate National Military Command Center
APFA	Accelerator-Pulsed Fast Assembly
ARES	Advanced Research Electromagnetic Simulator
ARPA	Advanced Research Projects Agency
ASCO	Advanced Systems and Concepts Office
ATSD(AE)	Assistant to the Secretary of Defense (Atomic Energy)
ATSD(NCB)	Assistant to the Secretary of Defense (Nuclear and Chemical and Biological Defense Programs)
BITS	Battlefield Information and Targeting System
BMD	Ballistic Missile Defense
BMDO	Ballistic Missile Defense Office
BMO	Ballistic Missile Office
BRDP	Blue Ribbon Defense Panel
C3 or C^3	Command, Control and Communications
C^3I	Command, Control, Communications and Intelligence
CEP	Circular Error Probable
CFE	Conventional Forces in Europe
CDC	Centers for Disease Control
CIA	Central Intelligence Agency
CINC	Commander in Chief
CINCEUR	Commander in Chief, Europe
CINCPAC	Commander in Chief, Pacific
CNO	Chief of Naval Operations
COEA	Cost and Operational Effectiveness Analysis
COMSAT	Communications Satellite
CTB	Comprehensive Test Ban
CTBT	Comprehensive Test Ban Treaty
CTEIP	Centralized Test and Evaluation Investment Program

CTR	Cooperative Threat Reduction	EMP	Electromagnetic Pulse
CWE	Conventional Weapons Effects	EMPRESS	EMP Radiation Effects Simulator for Ships
DARE	Data Archival and Retrieval Enhancement	EPA	Environmental Protection Agency
DARPA	Defense Advanced Research Projects Agency	ERDA	Engineering Research and Development Administration
DASA	Defense Atomic Support Agency	ERDL	Engineer Research and Development Laboratory
DASIAC	DoD Nuclear Information Analysis Center	ERRIC	Electronics Radiation Response Information Center
DDR&E	Director, Defense Research and Engineering	ETC	Electrothermal Chemical
DDST	Deputy Director, Science and Technology	FC	Field Command
DIA	Defense Intelligence Agency	FEMA	Federal Emergency Management Agency
DIHEST	Direct-Induced High Explosive Simulation Technique	FOFA	Follow-On Forces Attack
		FSU	Former Soviet Union
		FXR	Flash x ray
DNA	Defense Nuclear Agency	GLCM	Ground-Launched Cruise Missile
DNWS	Defense Nuclear Weapons School	HA	High Altitude
DoD	Department of Defense	HASP	High-Altitude Sampling Program
DoDD	Department of Defense Directive	HE	High Explosive
DoDI	Department of Defense Instruction	HEMP	High-Altitude Electromagnetic Pulse
DODDAC	Department of Defense Damage Assessment Center	HEST	High-Explosive Simulation Technique
DOE	Department of Energy	HF	High Frequency
DOI	Department of the Interior	HILAT	High Latitude
DSARC	Defense Systems Acquisition Review Council	HLOS	Horizontal Line-of-Sight
		HML	Hardened Mobile Launcher, Hardened Missile Launcher
DSB	Defense Science Board		
DSCS	Defense Satellite Communications System	HMMWV	High-Mobility Multipurpose Wheeled Vehicle
DSWA	Defense Special Weapons Agency	HPC	High Performance Computing
DTRA	Defense Threat Reduction Agency	HPCC	High Performance Computing and Communications
EM	Electromagnetic	IAC	Information Analysis Center
EM-1	Effects Manual-1		

APPENDIX B: ACRONYM LIST

ICBM	Intercontinental Ballistic Missile
INF	Intermediate Nuclear Forces
IRM	Intermediate-Range Missile
JAIEG	Joint Atomic Information Exchange Group
JAWS	Joint-Munitions Effectiveness Manuals/Air-to-Surface or JMEM/AS Weaponeering System
JCS	Joint Chiefs of Staff
JNACC	Joint Nuclear Accident Coordinating Center
JSTPS	Joint Strategic Target Planning Staff
JTF	Joint Task Force
KT	Kiloton
LANL	Los Alamos National Laboratory
LB/TS	Large Blast/Thermal Simulator
LLNL	Lawrence Livermore National Laboratory
LOS	Line-of-sight
LTBT	Limited Test Ban Treaty
MC	Military Committee
MED	Manhattan Engineering District
MT	Megaton
MIRV	Multiple Independently Targeted Reentry Vehicles
MLC	Military Liaison Committee
MOS	Military Occupational Specialty
MRV	Multiple Reentry Vehicle
NARP	Nuclear Weapon Accident Response Procedure
NASA	National Aeronautics and Space Administration
NATO	North Atlantic Treaty Organization
NCB	Nuclear and Chemical and Biological Defense Programs
NIF	National Ignition Facility
NME	National Military Establishment
NPR	Nuclear Posture Review
NRC	Nuclear Regulatory Commission
NRL	Naval Research Laboratory
NSA	National Security Agency
NSC	National Security Council
NTPR	Nuclear Test Personnel Review
NTR	Nuclear Targeting Review
NTS	National Test Site, Nevada Test Site
NUWAX	Nuclear Weapon Accident Training Exercise
NWE	Nuclear Weapon Effects
NWC	Nuclear Weapons Council
OMB	Office of Management and Budget
OSD	Office of the Secretary of Defense
OSIA	On-Site Inspection Agency
OSRD	Office of Scientific Research and Development
PAL	Permissive Action Link
PCBs	Polychlorinated Biphenyls
PD	Presidential Directive
PEACE	Pacific Enewetak Atoll Cratering Experiments
POD	Pacific Ocean Division
PPG	Pacific Proving Ground
PHETS	Permanent High-Explosive Test Site
ppb	parts per billion
psi	pounds per square inch
QDR	Quadrennial Defense Review
RB	Reentry body
RDT&E	Research, Development, Test & Evaluation
ROTC	Reserve Officer Training Corps

RV	Reentry vehicle
SAC	Strategic Air Command
SACEUR	Supreme Allied Commander Europe
SAGE	Scientific Advisory Group on Effects
SALT	Strategic Arms Limitation Talks or Treaty
SDI	Strategic Defense Initiative
SDIO	Strategic Defense Initiative Office
SGEMP	System-Generated Electromagnetic Pulse
SHAPE	Supreme Headquarters Allied Powers Europe
SIOP	Single Integrated Operation-al Plan
SLBM	Submarine-Launched Ballistic Missile
SPEAR	Space Power Experiments Aboard Rockets
SPO	System Program Office
SRAM	Short-Range Attack Missile
SRM	Short-Range Missile
START	Strategic Arms Reduction Talks or Treaty
STP	Silo Test Program
STRATCOM	United States Strategic Command
SUVAC	Scientific Ultravelocity Accelerator
SWEG	Special Weapons Effects Group
TAPS	Targeting and Planning System, Target Analysis and Planning System
TEMPS	Transportable Electromagnetic Pulse Simulator
TNF	Theater Nuclear Forces
TNFS³	Theater Nuclear Force Survivability, Security and Safety
TNT	Trinitrotoluene
TRAC	Threat Reduction Advisory Committee
TREE	Transient Radiation Effects on Electronics
TRIGA	Training, Research, Isotopes, General Atomic
TTBT	Threshold Test Ban Treaty
TTCP	The Technical Coordinating Panel
TTG	Technical Training Group
TTPI	Trust Territory of the Pacific Islands
UN	United Nations
UGT	Underground Test
UNSCOM	United Nations Special Commission
USA	United States of America, United States Army
USAF	United States Air Force
U.S.	United States
USGS	United States Geological Service
USN	United States Navy
USSR	Union of Soviet Socialist Republics
USEUCOM	United States European Command
VA	Veterans Administration
VLOS	Vertical Line-of-Sight
VNTK	Vulnerability Number/Type/K-Factor
WMD	Weapon of Mass Destruction
WOA	Weapons Orientation-Advanced
WSMR	White Sands Missile Range
WS3	Weapon Security and Survivability System

APPENDIX C

CHRONOLOGY

1789. M.H. Klaproth isolated a small amount of a heavy metal from pitchblende found in Saxony. He named the metal uranium for the planet Uranus, which had been discovered in 1781. For the next 100 years the metal was used primarily as a color fixative in ceramics.

1895. Henri Becquerel discovered that the element uranium has radioactive properties.

1896. Marie and Pierre Curie discovered radium.

1903. Ernest Rutherford predicted that a wave of atomic disintegrations might be started that would "make the world go up in smoke" if a suitable detonator could be found.

1905. Albert Einstein published his *Theory of Relativity*.

1914. World War I begun.

1917. The Russian Revolution launched.

1932. James Chadwick discovered the neutron.

Nov. 8, 1932. Franklin D. Roosevelt elected President of the United States.

1934. Enrico Fermi bombarded uranium with neutrons, producing several radioactive elements.

Sep. 1938. At Munich, France and Britain ceded the Czechoslovakian Sudetenland to Germany sowing the seeds for World War II.

Dec. 22, 1938. Otto Hahn and Fritz Strassmann bombarded uranium with neutrons and, unknowingly, split the atom. Lise Meitner and Otto Frisch, in exile, explained the results. Hahn and Strassmann published an article on their experiment in *Die Naturwissen schaften* in January 1939.

Jan. 22, 1939. The uranium-235 atom was split in the United States at Columbia University by J. D. Dunning and H. Anderson.

Jan. 26, 1939. At the Fifth Conference on Theoretical Physics held at the George Washington University in Washington D.C., Nils Bohr first announced the results of the Hahn-Strassmann experiments that demonstrated that slow neutrons caused the "splitting" of uranium.

Mar. 1939. Anderson, Fermi and Hanstein in the United States, Halban, Juliot and Kowarski in France and Szilard and Zinn in the United States found that two or three neutrons are emitted per fission in uranium confirming the possibility of a self sustained chain reaction. Bohr and Wheeler identified U-235 as the fissionable isotope of uranium.

Apr. 29, 1939. A secret uranium research project was established by the German Ministry of Education; a meeting of nuclear scientists considered the possible applications of uranium fission. All available uranium was acquired for the project and a ban was imposed on the export of uranium from Germany.

Apr. 29, 1939. The possibility of a chain reaction was publicly discussed by Bohr and others at the Washington D.C. meeting of the American Physical Society and reported in the press.

Aug. 2, 1939. Einstein signed Szilard's letter addressed to Roosevelt warning him of German atomic research and its implications.

Sep. 1, 1939. World War II began. Germany invaded Poland and quickly reached Warsaw.

Sep. 3, 1939. Britain and France declared war on Germany. Roosevelt declared U.S. neutrality.

Sep. 26, 1939. German scientists formed the Uranium Society, which concluded that power from the fission of U-238 could create a tremendous explosion.

Oct. 11, 1939. Dr. Alexander Sachs met with President Roosevelt and delivered Einstein's letter, his own introductory note on the implications of the German pursuit of the atomic bomb, with input from Szilard's earlier memo on the current and evolving scientific research on uranium fission. Roosevelt recognized the need for immediate action.

Oct. 21, 1939. Lyman Briggs, Director of the Bureau of Standards, held a meeting of the newly appointed "Uranium Committee" of Army and Navy representatives to investigate the feasibility of building and exploding an atomic bomb.

Dec. 6, 1939. Werner Heisenberg sent his conclusions to the German War Office: the surest way to a reactor for energy production is enrichment of U-235; it was also "...the only method of producing explosives several orders of magnitude more powerful than the strongest explosives yet known."

Apr. 1940. A top secret committee of British scientists, code named MAUD, was established under the Ministry of Aircraft Production to explore the possibilities for building a uranium bomb. For reasons of security, uranium was called "tube alloy" and uranium hexafluoride was known as "working gas."

May 3, 1940. German troops in Norway seized control of the world's only heavy water production facility and increased production to supply the German fission program.

Jun. 15, 1940. Philip Abelson and Edward McMillan demonstrated that neutron bombardment of U-238 produced neptunium, which quickly decayed into plutonium. The British government later protested this publication; after significant fission findings were withheld from publication. At a meeting of the Uranium Committee in Washington, Fermi reported that neutron absorption measurements on high-purity graphite showed it could be an effective moderator. Under new secrecy rules, his findings were not published.

Dec. 1940. Franz Simon submitted a memorandum on isotope separation to the British MAUD Committee, projecting that an isotope separation plant using gaseous barrier diffusion would produce one (1) kilogram per day of highly enriched U-235 at a cost of 5 million pounds.

Mar. 1941. Merle Tuve in Washington reported a refined measurement of the U-235 fast-fission cross section. The Frisch-Peierls critical mass estimate for a bomb was recomputed at 8 kilograms or 4 kilograms with a neutron reflector.

Mar. 3, 1941. Glen Seaborg, at the University of California, isolated the first measurable quantities of a new element he named "plutonium."

Aug. 22, 1941. Fritz Houtermans submitted a report to the German Post Office that included a critical mass formula, but without quantitative estimates, and the suggestion that fissionable plutonium would be generated in a reactor. Houtermans' work gained little attention.

APPENDIX C: CHRONOLOGY

Nov. 27, 1941. Office of Scientific Research and Development (OSRD) Director Vannever Bush reported to President Roosevelt that an engineering group was being formed to accelerate physics research aimed at fissionable material plant design. President Roosevelt approved Bush's decision.

Dec. 7, 1941. Japan launched a surprise attack against the U.S. Fleet at Pearl Harbor, Hawaii; the next day the U.S. declared war on Japan; four days later, Germany declared war on the U.S.

Jun. 4, 1942. A secret meeting is held in Dahlem, Germany, with War Minister Speer and leading nuclear scientists attending. Heisenberg described atomic bombs as possible but not in the near future. Speer approved all the scientists' requests, including a bomb resistant bunker for a large reactor, but the project received the lowest priority that allowed it to proceed.

Aug. 13, 1942. The Army Chief of Engineers issued Order No. 33 setting up the Manhattan Engineer District (MED), an engineering district without territorial limits.

Aug. 20, 1942. Glenn Seaborg's research group at Berkeley chemically extracted pure plutonium (Pu-239) from reactor irradiated uranium, the basis for the plutonium production at Hanford.

Sep. 23, 1942. Col. Leslie R. Groves promoted to Brigadier General and appointed the head of the MED.

Nov. 16, 1942. General Groves and Robert Oppenheimer selected the Los Alamos Ranch School (40 miles from Santa Fe) to be the site for an atomic bomb development laboratory.

Dec. 2, 1942. Enrico Fermi's group, at Stagg Field, University of Chicago, operated a self-sustaining critical reactor at a power of 1/2 watt.

Feb. 1943. The Russians initiate their atomic bomb project under the direction of Igor Kurchatov after learning of the U.S. secret effort.

Mar. 1943. The Japanese physics colloquium in Tokyo decided that an atomic bomb was possible but not attainable by anyone for use in the current war.

Sep. 3, 1943. Italy surrendered unconditionally. The tide of the war begins to change.

Oct. 1943. John von Neumann realized that plutonium could be squeezed by high explosives to such high densities as to turn a sub-critical sphere into a super-critical mass; this premise was quickly adopted as the basis for the implosion bomb at Los Alamos.

Jun. 6, 1944. Operation *Overlord* (D-Day) launched; the Allies land on French beachhead against stiff German resistance.

Sep. 8, 1944. The first V-2 rockets hit London and Antwerp, Belgium.

Dec. 1944. Fermi predicted a lightning-like electromagnetic emission from the upcoming *Trinity* atom bomb test. Experimenters tried to shield their instruments.

Apr. 12, 1945. President Franklin D. Roosevelt died at Warm Springs, Georgia. Harry S. Truman assumed the office.

May 7, 1945. 100 tons of high explosive (TNT), seeded with radioactive fission products from the Hanford slug, was exploded as a trial shot to calibrate instruments and to simulate, at a low level, the radioactive products from the nuclear explosion. This was the first time a large scale, high-explosive detonation was used to simulate a nuclear burst.

May 8, 1945. Victory in Europe (VE) Day. The Germans signed an unconditional surrender to the Allies.

Jun. 1945. The Soviets transferred captured German atomic scientists to the USSR, to reactivate their dormant atomic program.

Jun. 26, 1945. The charter of the United Nations was signed in San Francisco.

Jul. 16, 1945. *Trinity*—the first atomic bomb—an implosion type of weapon, was detonated near Alamogordo, New Mexico, with a yield of 21 kilotons (KT).

Jul. 26, 1945. The U.S. and its allies issued the "Potsdam Declaration," calling for the immediate and unconditional surrender of the Japanese forces. The Japanese refused.

Aug. 6, 1945. A B-29 named Enola Gay dropped the *Little Boy* gun-type atomic bomb that destroyed Hiroshima.

Aug. 8, 1945. Russia declared war on Japan and immediately advanced into Manchuria.

Aug. 9, 1945. A B-29 named Bock's Car dropped the *Fat Man* implosion-type atomic bomb that destroyed Nagasaki.

Sep. 2, 1945. Japan formally surrendered to U.S. General MacArthur on the deck of the battleship *USS Missouri*.

Dec. 10, 1945. The Secretaries of War and the Navy publicly announced the proposed nuclear weapons tests for scientific experiments.

Dec. 25, 1945. The first Soviet nuclear reactor became operational.

Jan. 11, 1946. Joint Task Force One (JTF-1) forms, composed of Army and Navy personnel and civilian scientists, for atomic bomb testing.

Feb. 26, 1946. Stalin delivers "Cold War" speech.

Mar. 5, 1946. Winston Churchill delivers "Iron Curtain" speech in Fulton, Missouri.

Mar. 21, 1946. By order of Headquarters, Army Air Forces, Continental Air Forces became the Strategic Air Command (SAC).

Mar. 28, 1946. Department of State formally releases the Acheson-Lilienthal Report. Fashioned primarily by Oppenheimer, it evolves into the Baruch Plan, America's formal proposal for international control of atomic energy.

Jun. 14, 1946. In the first attempt at nuclear arms control, Bernard M. Baruch, who was the U.S. representative on the United Nations (UN) Atomic Energy Commission, (AEC), presented his plan to the UN for the control of nuclear weapons and the development of nuclear technology for peaceful applications. The essence of the Baruch Plan was the centralization and control of all dangerous nuclear processes, i.e., nuclear fuel enrichment and reprocessing, and manufacture of nuclear explosives.

Jun./Jul., 1946. Operation CROSSROADS conducted at Bikini Atoll. ABLE, an airdrop weapons effects test, on June 30 and BAKER, an underwater effects test, on July 24.

Aug. 1, 1946. Through the McMahon Act, President Truman established the AEC, a five-member civilian board serving full-time and assisted by a military liaison committee and a general advisory committee.

Aug. 19, 1946. 2761st Engineer Battalion (Special) activates at Sandia Base. Colonel Gilbert M. Dorland is designated as Commanding Officer. Its mission is to perform assembly functions on atomic bombs, which previously had been performed solely by civilian personnel. In addition, the Battalion is to organize and train military personnel teams in the assembly of atomic weapons.

APPENDIX C: CHRONOLOGY

Sep. 15, 1946. Officers of the 2761st Engineer Battalion (Special) begin reporting to Sandia Base.

Sep. 16, 1946. Maj. O.M. Brumfiel activates Technical Company B of 2761st Engineer Battalion (Special); Company A provides security.

Sep. 25, 1946. Atomic Energy Conference is held at Fort Belvoir, Virginia. Speakers include General Groves, Rear Admiral Parsons, Colonel Nichols, and Colonel Hasbrouck. This conference was the second part of a three-part orientation; the first part was an orientation program held in the Pentagon for the top War Department planners, whereas the third part was to be the conference attendees to return to their headquarters or schools and present to their staff or faculty the information learned at the conference. Concurrently, Lt. Col. A.J. Frolich, Battalion Executive Officer of the 2761st Engineer Battalion (Special), conducts series of orientation lectures for 25 officers. These lectures were designed to present the overall picture of the atomic bomb and its present status.

Sep.-Dec. 1946. Most of initial officers of 2761st Engineer Battalion (Special) arrive at Sandia.

Oct. 7, 1946. 52 new officers form into Command, Mechanic, Electronic, and Nuclear groups. Nuclear group moves to Los Alamos. Major Frank A. Camm becomes Bomb Supervisor.

Nov. 15, 1946. Los Alamos Staff begins giving series of lectures to 2761st Engineer Battalion

Nov. 16, 1946. Newly appointed commissioners of the AEC visit Sandia Base

Dec. 31, 1946. President Truman signs Executive Order 9816, which transfers all MED properties and facilities, including fissionable materials and atomic weapons, to AEC ownership (i.e., custody of weapons became a legal function of the AEC). Secretary of War Patterson and Chairman Lilienthal of the AEC agree that Sandia Base be exempted from transfer to the AEC, under the terms of the Atomic Energy Act. Design work commences on project "Chickenpox," an Army Air Forces project in which the interior of a C-97 cargo aircraft is adapted for forward assembly operations.

Jan. 1, 1947. AEC takes charge officially of the nation's atomic energy program.

Jan. 17, 1947. Secretary of War Robert Patterson and Secretary of the Navy James Forrestal approve charter for the Military Liaison Committee (MLC), listing the committee's statutory functions and setting its membership at six, three apiece from the Army and Navy. Lt. Gen. Lewis H. Brereton, U.S. Army, is designated Chairman. The charter provides that MLC members should serve as the military members of the AEC of the Joint Research and Development Board.

Jan. 29, 1947. The Armed Forces Special Weapons Project (AFSWP) is established January 1, 1947, retroactively by Secretary of War Robert Patterson and Secretary of the Navy James Forrestal. Headed by Gen. Leslie Groves, AFSWP is to be the successor of the MED program, assuming responsibility for function of the Manhattan Project not assigned to the AEC. This includes training of special personnel required, military participation in the development of atomic weapons of all types, technical training of bomb commanders and *weaponeers*, and developing and effecting joint radiological safety measures in coordination with established agencies. AFSWP had no officially appointed chief from January 1, to February 28, Col. S.V. Hasbrouck was the senior officer of the organization. The directive which activates AFSWP states that it would operate under a Chief who would be selected by mutual action of the Chief of Staff Army and the Chief of Naval Operations. A Deputy Chief from the opposite Service would also be selected.

Jan. 31, 1947. Maj Gen Leslie R. Groves becomes member of MLC.

Feb. 1, 1947. Brig Gen James McCormack, Jr., is appointed Director of the Division of Military Application, a division within the AEC.

Feb. 28, 1947. Maj Gen Groves becomes first Chief AFSWP, serving for one year, until his retirement on February 29, 1948; he is promoted to Lt. General on January 24, 1948.

Mar. 1947. AEC (Santa Fe Office) and AFSWP (Sandia Base) divide security and intelligence responsibilities.

Mar. 25, 1947. JCS sends memo to Chief AFSWP, directing him to organize the Joint Radiological Safety Training Committee (JRSTC), to carry out Joint CROSSROADS Committee recommendations.

Mar. 31, 1947. Rear Admiral W.S. Parsons, U.S. Navy, receives appointment as Deputy Chief AFSWP; previously Parsons had become a Navy member of the MLC to the AEC (November 6, 1946), and was Chairman of the Joint CROSSROADS Committee.

Apr. 1947. The AEC inaugurates regular meetings with the MLC to exchange ideas and discuss problems of mutual interest. The commission had put off discussion of military access to nuclear weapons because of the controversy surrounding the appointment of David E. Lilienthal as AEC chairman. At Sandia Base, B Company supervises training of mechanical assembly groups. The 2761st Engineer Battalion (Special) redesignated the 38th Engineer Battalion (Special).

Apr. 15, 1947. AFSWP headquarters moves from the New War Department Building, 21st Street and Virginia Avenue, Washington, D.C., to the Pentagon.

May 7, 1947. At General Groves' urging, first team of 2761st Engineer Battalion officers begins training as *weaponeers* for combat drops of atomic bombs. Battalion members joined 509th Bombardment Wing at Roswell, New Mexico, for a six-week tour.

May 29, 1947. Panel convenes by MLC including representatives from AEC and NME, "deadlocked over the question of whether or not an investigation by the FBI is a necessary prerequisite for clearance of military personnel." AFSWP's Security Division maintains that AEC clearances based upon FBI investigations would be more efficient, more convincing, and more quickly processed. Concurrently, AFSWP initiates plans for permanent under ground storage and bomb assembly sites.

Jun. 10, 1947. Residual functions of Joint CROSSROADS Committee are transferred to the AFSWP, which establishes the CROSSROADS Division. Responsibilities include directing technical and scientific aspects of the Bikini Atoll.

Jun. 12, 1947. First concrete step taken to effectively organize the Radiological Safety Division (changed to Radiological Defense (RD) Division on February 5, 1948). RD Division activities are divided among RD training, defense material, medical, operational development, and technical (including radiological warfare, which previously had been the responsibility of a separate branch and later merged with the Technical Branch).

Jun. 27, 1947. President Truman approves 1948 weapons testing plan (Operation SANDSTONE).

APPENDIX C: CHRONOLOGY

Jul. 1947. Brig. Gen. R.W. Montague becomes Commanding General, Sandia Base.

Jul. 8, 1947. Memorandum from Chiefs of Staff, U.S. Army and Navy, to Chief AFSWP, outlined in detail the organization, responsibilities, and guiding principles surrounding AFSWP operations. Groves and JCS agree to revised directive that narrows the scope of AFSWP's functions to those of a technical agency concerned primarily with training troops to handle and assemble atomic weapons. Revisions to the AFSWP charter includes the coordination by AFSWP of atomic energy activities, military participation in research and development of atomic weapons within the Armed Forces, and furnishing assistance to planning agencies, Service schools, and governmental agencies regarding atomic weapons. The charter also clarifies AFSWP's responsibility for storage and surveillance of weapons in military custody. AFSWP headquarters divided into six divisions: Personnel and Administration; Operations and Training; Fiscal and Logistics; Radiological Defense; Development; and Security.

Jul. 24, 1947. Public Information Officer of the Security Division, AFSWP, issues a guarded statement describing the activities and responsibilities of the AFSWP, and acknowledging, for the first time, the fact that Sandia Base is an installation of the AFSWP.

Jul. 26, 1947. President Truman signs into law the National Security Act (Public Law 253, 80th Congress), which provides "three military departments for the operation and administration of the Army, the Navy... and the Air Force" as well as "for their authoritative coordination and unified direction under civilian control but not to merge them." This act creates the National Military Establishment (NME), consisting of the Departments of the Army, Navy and Air Force. The act created a new Department of the Air Force and directed that the Army Air Forces be transferred to it as the United States Air Force.

Aug. 13, 1947. MLC meeting. MLC Chairman General Brereton recommends a directive clearly detailing the precise division of responsibilities at Sandia between Carrol Tyler, the AEC's recently appointed manager of Santa Fe Directed Operations (including Los Alamos, Sandia Base, and a half dozen other western sites), and General Robert M. Montague, commanding general of Sandia. Brereton suggests that the military and the Commission issue a joint directive; General Groves argues that the Commission and the Secretary of Defense should ask the President to transfer all weapons and weapon parts to the armed forces. After the meeting, Acting AEC Chairman Sumner Pike states that the commission unanimously opposed transferring weapon custody on the ground the AFSWP lacked the technical competence for handling and maintaining atomic weapons. AFSWP teams being trained to assemble weapons, even under close AEC supervision, still had to return all bombs to AEC custody.

Sep. 4, 1947. MLC Chairman Lt. Gen. Lewis H. Brereton asks for and receives support from Service Secretaries on issue of whether AEC should share weapons custody with military.

Sep. 17, 1947. James Forrestal becomes the first Secretary of Defense.

Sep. 30, 1947. Committee on Atomic Energy (CAE) established; is closely allied to the MLC.

Sep. 1947. 38th Engineer Battalion visits *USS Franklin D. Roosevelt* to study its nuclear weapon assembly facility needs.

Oct. 18, 1947. The "first" Joint Task Force Seven (JTF-7) is established, which will perform Operation SANDSTONE at the Enewetak Proving Grounds in April & May 1948. Designation skipped from "1" to "7" for security reasons.

Oct. 21, 1947. Letters from Secretary of Defense to Chiefs of Staff, U.S. Army, Navy, Air Force, confirmed AFSWP as Joint Armed forces atomic energy organization. Memorandum from Secretary of Defense is almost exact duplicate of January 1, 1947 directive, except that it included the Air Force.

Oct. 29, 1947. Joint Strategic Survey Committee completes eight-month report for Joint Chiefs of Staff on "...long range estimates of total military requirements of fissionable material." Based on the report's recommendations, the JCS informed the chairman of the AEC that the military needs 400 atomic bombs of destructive power comparable to that used on Nagasaki. The JCS timetable, completed in early December 1947, called for all 400 bombs to be ready by January 1, 1953.

Nov. 12, 1947. Brereton writes to Lilienthal recommending that "...all weapons now in stockpile and completed weapons and parts thereof, when ready for stockpiling, be delivered to the Armed Forces at the earliest practicable date." More specifically, Brereton requests that AFSWP assume custody of atomic weapons and responsibility for their storage and surveillance, and sollicits the AEC's "...formal views" on the matter. AEC responds by asking MLC to clarify its position in writing.

Nov. 15, 1947. Using B-29s from the 509th Bombardment Group of the Eighth Air Force and the 1st Air Transit Unit, the 38th Engineering Battalion begins conducting joint field exercises at Sandia and Wendover Air Force Base (Utah) for Operation AJAX.

Dec. 5, 1947. Col. R.C. Wilson, USAF, is appointed as a Deputy Chief AFSWP, in order that the Air Force would be properly represented, with the Army and Navy. After this date, there continues to be two Deputy Chief positions in the AFSWP.

Dec. 16, 1947. MLC argues formally to AEC that custody should be transferred to the Armed Forces for reasons of national security and the need to have a single agency responsible for the nation's atomic arsenal. At the same time, the MLC concedes that the armed services were not currently staffed and trained to properly maintain the atomic stockpile, and proposed a gradual transition period.

Dec. 22, 1947. Secretary of Defense issues memo to Secretaries of Armed Forces, MLC, JCS, and others on "Clearance of Personnel of the National Military Establishment for Access to Atomic Energy Act Restricted Data." NME personnel granted access to restricted data only after obtaining clearance based upon a background investigation of the "same standard" imposed upon AEC employees.

Jan. 1948. Charles F. Brown, of Secretary Forrestal's staff, recommends abolishing both AFSWP and the AEC's division of military applications, their functions to be transferred to a more powerful MLC and to the individual Armed Services.

Feb. 25, 1948. At special meeting of the Committee of Four, Forrestal expresses his intention to accept his staff's recommendation to place the MLC under the Secretary of Defense, and replacing Brereton with a "top-level civilian." Navy Secretary Sullivan opposes any alteration to AFSWP's organizational status, arguing that it should continue as a joint agency in the interests of interservice collaboration. The meeting ends with a consensus for MLC reorganization and strengthening, but to further study AFSWP's future.

Feb. 29, 1948. Groves retires from U.S. Army. Parson serves as Acting Chief until Nichols' appointment in late April.

Mar. 1, 1948. The AEC issues report supporting earlier contention that the military did not have the technical knowledge or training to cope with problems of custody. It proposes a joint AEC-military program to prepare the armed forces for surveillance and inspection duties. Lilienthal did not state whether or not he favored their adoption and implementation.

Mar. 1, 1948. Sandia Joint Research and Development Board is established, composed of three members each from Sandia Laboratory and the military staff of the base.

Mar. 3, 1948. Lilienthal meets with MLC. He states that only the President could decide whether the military should have custody, and suggests that he might consult with Truman to determine what recommendations the President would accept. In reaction to March 3 incidents, Brereton notifies Forrestal, sends him a copy of the AEC report, and requests that he intercede. Before signing off on letter to Truman advocating military's views, Forrestal consults Gen. Spaatz, Air Force Chief of Staff, on the feasibility of immediate transfer. Spaatz concedes that he lacked sufficient information to have full confidence in assuming such responsibility. At same time, Spaatz proposes to other Chiefs of Staff that the Air Force be designated executive agent of AFSWP.

Mar. 9, 1948. A simulated Category III attack on Sandia Base by 250 paratroopers was conducted to measure base security.

Mar. 11, 1948. Forrestal meets with Joint Chiefs in Key West (herein referred to as the Key West Conference). Talks include issues of Service relations.

Mar. 15, 1948. Forrestal meets with President Truman, recounts Key West meeting with Joint Chiefs. Suggests that "Navy not to be denied use of A-bomb" and that the Joint Chiefs were of the opinion that custody of the completed bombs should be turned over to the military.

Mar. 26, 1948. Forrestal approves of a revised MLC charter, effective April 12, 1948, which affirms that AFSWP will continue to operate as a separate organization (rather than abolish it and have the three services assume its functions, as suggested in Forrestal's staff's January report). The revised charter also allows the Secretary of Defense to appoint the MLC chairman. The MLC now had the authority, in behalf of the NME, to exercise the authority conferred by the Atomic Energy Act, including surveying the nation's overall atomic military requirements and recommending allocation of responsibility for the conduct of military atomic energy activities.

Mar. 23, 1948. Air Force Chief of Staff, Gen. Carl Spaatz, asks his JCS colleagues to join him in petitioning Forrestal to transfer to the Air Force control over all of AFSWP's operational functions, excluding training and technical activities. In addition, Spaatz feels it only logical that he be named JCS executive agent for AFSWP, in light of the recent Key West agreement that had granted the Air Force primary responsibility for strategic bombing. The other chiefs deferred action on this proposal until the MLC could study the matter.

Mar. 30, 1948. Forrestal decides to wait on Brereton's suggestion to intercede on behalf of military regarding custody dispute.

Apr. 8, 1948. To head a reconstituted MLC (organized on March 26, 1948), Forrestal replaces Lewis Brereton with Donald F. Carpenter.

Apr./May 1948. Operation SANDSTONE conducted at Enewetak (April 14 though May 14, 1948). AFSWP takes part in tests, and also provides security guards, technical assistance, and a radiological safety task group. AFSWP accounts for roughly 40 percent of the newly formed J-Division, the largest fraction provided by any single agency, Los Alamos included. AFSWP also studies weapons effects; physicist Herbert Scoville, Jr., joins "radsafe" as head of technical measurements unit. AFSWP developed improved instruments to measure weapons blast and shock environments during future nuclear weapon tests.

Apr. 19, 1948. MLC adopts resolution recommending that completed atomic weapons be transferred from AEC to NME.

Apr. 21, 1948. Forrestal issues paper entitled "Functions of the Armed Forces and the Joint Chiefs of Staff," the result of the Key West Conference and subsequent discussions.

Apr. 27, 1948. Command change; Gen. Kenneth Nichols replaces Rear Admiral Parsons, as Chief AFSWP, and is promoted to Major General.

Mar. 1948. General Lucius Clay issues war warnings in response to Soviet troop deployments in East Germany, which stimulates the development of the first strategic plan for U.S. atomic bombing of Soviet cities.

May 1948. A joint AFSWP-Air Force team successfully loaded a MK-III bomb into a B-29 aircraft, using aircraft hoists, shoring materials, and a deep pit.

May 19, 1948. Postwar Joint Emergency War Plan, "Halfmoon", was approved. Its objective was to destroy "the will of the USSR, to resist by a main offensive effort in Western Eurasia, and a strategic defensive in the Far East."

May 24, 1948. MLC Chairman Donald Carpenter, taking over from Brereton, inspects Sandia base and listens to concerns of AFSWP and AEC senior staffers. By the time he leaves the base he becomes convinced that a transfer of authority is necessary and feasible within certain limitations.

Jun. 2, 1948. Carpenter directs Nichols to prepare, for discussion with AEC (and ultimately the President) definite recommendations giving the military authority to withdraw weapons from storage either for training or use in times of national emergency.

Jun. 14, 1948. Carpenter sends memorandum to AEC on "Custody and Surveillance of Completed and Stockpiled Atomic Weapons" that suggests weapons be transferred to NME.

Jun. 16, 1948. AEC meets with MLC. Issues of June 14 memo are raised. AEC says it would be willing to join with Secretary of Defense in bringing up custody question to President, but would not suggest to the President that there is only one possible solution; i.e., transfer of custody to military. Lilienthal explained that AEC did not endorse the recommended transfer.

Jun. 23, 1948. Forrestal and Lilienthal meet for lunch at Pentagon to discuss transfer issue before Forrestal took his case to the President. Although they understand each other's point, they can not agree. In Europe, Soviets declare Berlin blockade.

Jun. 26, 1948. Operation *Vittles* begins, in which C-47 and C-54 transport aircraft shuttle food and coal to Berlin's airports.

Jun. 29, 1948. Nichols' letter to MLC Chairman Carpenter states: "I feel now, as I have always felt, that the assignment of custody of atomic weapons to the military is a matter of urgency and the question should be referred to the President for decision at the earliest practicable date."

Jun. 30, 1948. Forrestal, along with Carpenter, Nichols, Vannevar Bush and Secretary Royall, meets with the full commission in his office. The meeting results in an agreement that the President should decide the issue and that the AEC and the military would prepare separate position papers for his consideration.

Jul. 1948. AFSWP participates in a deception plan with the British to announce forward deployment of atomic weapons two years before this actually occurred.

Jul. 12, 1948. Operation BANJO: 38th Engineer Battalion, A Company, conducts exercises at Walker Air Force Base, Roswell, New Mexico. BANJO, the first operational employment of assembly units since AJAX, involved the assembly of five atomic bombs, by the complete assembly method, at a forward base.

Jul. 13, 1948. MLC sends memorandum to Chief AFSWP asking latter to initiate a program for disseminating atomic energy information within the National Military Establishment (NME); the program is initiated on July 28, 1948.

Jul. 1948. SAC's 509th Bombardment Group, containing the nation's only atomic modified aircraft, goes on 24-hour alert due to the Berlin crisis. AFSWP provides Air Force with three assembly teams. Meanwhile, JCS proves unable to resolve the question of command and control over AFSWP. The Army conditionally supported the Air Force proposal for control while the Navy opposed it categorically. Unable to reach consensus, the JCS refers the matter to Forrestal, with written comments from the Air Force and the Navy. Navy Admiral Louis Denfeld expresses concern that exclusive Air Force control over AFSWP would inhibit and possibly prevent the Navy from acquiring atomic weapons necessary for its assigned mission.

Jul. 18, 1948. *New York Times* article describes Air Secretary Symington's speech to aviation engineers in Los Angeles, in which Symington acerbically declares that air power should be put in balance not with the Army or Navy, but with the Air Force. Behind this remark is the issue of responsibility of strategic warfare and the use of the atomic bomb.

Jul. 19, 1948. After dinner with the three Service Secretaries, Forrestal notes that the disagreement between the Air Force and Navy Air is deep. The Navy is willing to concede the responsibility of strategic warfare to the Air Force but not willing to be denied the use of the atomic bomb on particular targets. Secretary Royall expresses his view to Sullivan and Symington that the Navy should accept not only the "dominant interest" of the Air Force in the atomic bomb but also their practical control of it. Forrestal outlines a plan based on this view, which Symington finds largely unacceptable.

Jul. 21, 1948. Confrontation over custody at White House; Forrestal, the five commissioners, and their advisors meet and debate the issue. Truman indicates he needed time to think about the matter.

Jul. 23, 1948. Truman rules in favor of the AEC on the custody issue, officially informing Forrestal on August 6. In his diary, Forrestal notes that Truman spoke with him after that day's Cabinet meeting. The President said that his negative decision on the custody transfer was influenced by political considerations of the immediate moment, and would take another look at the picture after the upcoming election. The next day Truman makes a public statement regarding civilian authority of the atomic energy.

Jul. 28, 1948. In light of Truman's decision, Forrestal writes letters to the Secretaries of the three Services that plans for the emergency transfer of atomic weapons be reviewed. Forrestal speaks with General Vandenberg about differences between Navy and Air Force on use of the atomic bomb. According to Forrestal, fundamental psychoses included Navy's belief that the Air Force wanted control over all aviation; and Air Forces' belief that the Navy was encroaching upon the strategic air prerogatives of the Air Force. Forrestal himself is solidly behind the Air Force in its claim for predominance in the field of strategic air warfare.

Aug. 1, 1948. Sites Able, Baker, and Charlie form respectively at Sandia Base, Camp Hood & Camp Campbell.

Aug. 3, 1948. Influenced by escalation of Berlin Crisis, MLC Chairman Donald Carpenter writes Forrestal that the MLC is prepared to recommend placing AFSWP under the Air Force temporarily to deal with emergencies pending more thorough study of the situation.

Aug.-Sep. 1948. MLC initiates study on military organization for atomic warfare to help advise the War Council. Pressing concerns include continuation of AFSWP as a joint agency and the control of air-atomic operations.

Aug. 20, 1948. Forrestal meets with Joint Chiefs of Staff at Newport, to wrestle once more with problems unresolved at Key West Conference in March. Forrestal reads report by General Spaatz and Admiral Towers recommending that Navy be equipped to bomb strategic targets within the area of Naval operations, even though the Air Force had primary responsibility for strategic missions; they split on the question of atomic bomb custody: The permanent future organization for control and direction of atomic operations was postponed until the MLC could complete its study on the link between the AEC and the Armed Forces. The immediate Navy-Air Force quarrel is settled by the decision to allow each Service to have exclusive responsibility for planning and programming but since all available resources must be used then there could be no preclusive participation.

Sep. 7, 1948. JCS write memorandum to AFSWP Chief Nichols requesting that he review technical requirements for use of atomic weapons, and to take steps to train sufficient personnel so that NME can assume full custody as soon as possible.

Sep. 10, 1948. MLC votes 4 to 2 to maintain AFSWP as a tripartite agency answerable to the three Service chiefs individually.

Sep. 16, 1948. 502d and 508th Aviation Squadrons activate and join 38th Engineer Battalion as Units E and F on September 28, 1948, and October 25, 1948, respectively.

Sep. 29, 1948. Forrestal meets with Joint Chiefs, who advise him that preparations for a potential military emergency in Berlin were proceeding smoothly. AFSWP representatives were to be sent to England in order to establish air-atomic operations. The Air Force had checked with the AEC and AFSWP on prearranged plans to transfer custody of atomic weapons in case of emergency.

Oct. 1948. Gen. Curtis E. LeMay is appointed head of SAC.

Oct. 1948. Operation WHIPPOORWILL: 38th Engineer Battalion, C Company, conducts extensive field exercises on rad-safety at Wendover AFB. WHIPPOORWILL's purpose was to test forward base assembly conditions and the capabilities of the assembly team for an extended operation.

Oct. 21, 1948. AEC confidently predicts that nuclear production goal for creating 400 bombs can be met by January 1, 1951, two years ahead of schedule.

Oct. 28, 1948. Nichols reports to Chiefs of Staff about orderly turn-over of atomic weapons to National Military Establishment (NME) in an emergency; states that AFSWP and Air Force had conducted joint maneuvers in which the AEC turned over the required AFSWP atomic weapons, and that no difficulties were encountered in these tests. Further, Nichols claims AFSWP capable of assuming responsibility for weapons custody.

Nov. 22, 1948. Operation EASTWIND: AFSWP and Navy hold joint exercise at Norfolk, Virginia, to test bomb assembly facilities aboard a modified aircraft carrier.

Dec. 14, 1948. Operation UNLIMITED: AEC and AFSWP hold joint exercise at Sandia to determine the effectiveness of current custody arrangement. Satisfactorily transferred "dummy" weapons.

Dec. 15, 1948. The AEC and NME start a joint study on future storage requirements for atomic weapons; 38th Engineer Battalion (Special), Companies A, B, C, & D convert to 111th, 122nd, 133rd, and 144th Special Weapons Units. Lt. Col. Dorland activates Headquarters, 8460th Special Weapons Group over four Army, one Navy, and two Air Force special weapons units.

Dec. 25, 1948. Navy XAJ-1 aircraft arrives at Kirtland AFB for wiring and test loading of *Little Boy, Fat Man,* and Mark IV atomic bombs.

Dec. 30, 1948. JCS directs AFSWP to accelerate training of personnel so that it would be able to assume "...full custody and surveillance as soon as possible...".

Jan. 1949. JCS assigns responsibility to AFSWP for collecting, reviewing, and disseminating data on atomic weapons effects; this research results in *The Effects of Atomic Weapons* (1950), prepared jointly with the AEC.

Jan. 1949. AEC receives "Nutmeg Report" from project sponsored by AFSWP. Project Nutmeg was a survey of sites, within the continental United States, proposed for future atomic weapons tests.

Jan. 29, 1949. Nichols recommends to Lilienthal that formal agreement be made in the matter of fitting weapons transfer to the actual war plans. AEC agrees to Nichols' proposals on March 7, 1949.

Mar. 1949. Nichols endeavors to enlist support of Joint Committee on Atomic Energy in custody battle.

Apr. 4, 1949. U.S. signs North Atlantic Treaty, formally committing itself to defense of Western Europe.

May 11, 1949. AEC authorizes joint AEC-AFSWP operation and maintenance of storage sites Able, Baker, and Charlie, with the AEC responsible for all stockpile items in storage, undergoing inspection, or surveillance; and AFSWP in custody of AEC weapons released for training and maneuver purposes, and for "...support of operations in the event of national emergency."

Jun. 1949. Nichols agrees to AEC request that AFSWP assume responsibility for measurement of free air pressures during proposed atomic bomb tests in 1951. The AFSWP Free Air Pressure Group would eventually become known as Test Group.

Jul. 11, 1949. MLC requests that AFSWP assume responsibility for a program for the study of military effects of atomic weapons, in response to so-called "Hill Letter". AFSWP's program was to consist of studies of: underwater, underground, atmospheric, blast, thermal radiation, and ionizing radiation effects. Two days later, Chief AFSWP writes to the three Services for information on this topic.

Aug. 29, 1949. First Soviet test, *Joe-1*, provides push to U.S. development efforts. AFSWP begins briefings on the strategic implications of the hydrogen bomb.

Sep. 26, 1949. Board of Officers is established to study the future requirements for storage of atomic weapons, with AFSWP Chief Nichols as Chairman. This board established a new Joint Working Group on Future Storage.

Oct. 30, 1949. AEC's General Advisory Committee recommends against development of thermonuclear weapons.

Oct. 1949. Representatives from AFSWP, the Air Force, Army Chemical Corps, and the AEC conduct contamination experiments at a site in the Dugway-Wendover, Utah, area.

Nov. 1, 1949. Management and technical direction of Sandia Laboratory, formerly operated under research contract between AEC and Univ. of California, taken over by the newly formed Sandia Corporation, a wholly owned subsidiary of the Western Electric Company. JTF-3 established for Operation GREENHOUSE (1951).

Nov. 4, 1949. In a letter from Nichols to McCormack, Chief AFSWP advises AEC that they have met the planned assembly rate of 100 bombs per day.

Dec. 1949. First three operational storage sites (Able, Baker, Charlie) established by AFSWP working with the AEC. Sites are used by 1st, 8th, and 2nd Air Forces.

Jan. 31, 1950. Truman announces that he had "...directed the Atomic Energy Commission to continue its work on all forms of atomic weapons, including the so-called hydrogen or super-bomb."

Mar. 1950. With no more doubt that the military had trained personnel in sufficient numbers to perform the necessary custodial functions, AEC releases a study that recommends that the commission obtain the President's approval of the "transfer of custody of stockpile of non-nuclear components of atomic bombs to the Department of Defense." These proposals were strongly endorsed by the MLC and JCS. MLC asks AFSWP to undertake a weapons vulnerability test program for the MK-4 bomb, which results in development of new systems. A formal AFSWP Weapons Vulnerability Program later emerged in 1955.

Apr. 14, 1950. Paul Nitze authors "National Security Council 68 (NSC-68)," a National Securities policy memorandum which warns that U.S. military resources will have to be substantially increased in order to deter threat of Soviet surprise attack.

Jun. 25, 1950. Korean War begins.

Jul. 11, 1950. Secretary Johnson, with JCS and Service Secretaries support, appeals to the President to turn over non-nuclear components to military as precaution against wider emergency than Korea. As a result, President Truman directs the AEC on case-by-case basis to transfer custody of bomb capsules (without nuclear explosives) to the Air Force and Navy for overseas location deployment

Jul. 1950. Truman approves AFSWP support to SAC nuclear-capable units at overseas bases.

Aug. 1, 1950. AEC-AFSWP Re-acceptance Inspection program becomes operative: surveillance work jointly supervised by Sandia Corporation and AFSWP. AFSWP inspectors responsible for both military and AEC re-acceptance of surveillance work.

APPENDIX C: CHRONOLOGY

Nov. 1950. Truman approves Operation *Windstorm*, a program run by the Department of Defense to be conducted between mid-September and mid-November 1951.

Dec. 29, 1950. The first edition of *The Effects of Atomic Weapons* (retitled: *The Effects of Nuclear Weapons* in later editions), edited by Dr. Samuel Glasstone, is published.

Jan. 1951. AFSWP is assigned, by the JCS, responsibility for test planning and coordinating Service needs for nuclear test data. Command change; Major General Herbert R. Loper replaces Gen. Nichols.

Jan. 27, 1951. Operation RANGER commenced at Nevada Test Site (NTS), the first on-continent nuclear tests since *Trinity*. The five RANGER tests were designed to gather data to improve weapon design; since no weapons effects tests were conducted no AFSWP test group attended these tests.

Mar. 10, 1951. Truman secretly endorses recommendation (made by special committee of Dean Acheson, Louis Johnson, and Henry Smyth) to order the AEC to prepare for hydrogen bomb production.

Apr. 24, 1951. AFSWP orders nuclear component assembly teams at Sandia to go on alert status, ensuring deployment of bomber weapons within 12 hours of notification.

Apr. 28, 1951. AFSWP Field Command formally established at Sandia Base, Albuquerque, New Mexico. AFSWP General Order No. 4, dated April 28, 1951, was the basis for this change. Field Command included the Weapons Effects Test Group.

May 29, 1951. AFSWP Chief Herbert B. Loper sends revised mission statements to Chiefs of Staff of Army, Navy, and Air Force. Loper cites "...need for review and clarification of the mission" of AFSWP due to change in stockpile numbers, stockpile complexity, increased numbers of atomic weapons assembly organizations, and increased activity by military Services in atomic weapons field.

Apr. 7, 1951. Operation GREENHOUSE (four events) commenced in the Pacific. It included the first test of the boosting principle and confirmed the feasibility of thermonuclear weapons. The bulk of the rad-safe unit comes from the AFSWP.

Jul. 9, 1951. JTF-132 is established for Operation IVY (1952).

Jul. 12, 1951. AFSWP charter revised to include more extensive controls over weapons in custody of the military services and greater technical, logistic, and training services. Also calls for increased levels of military training and development of further procedures for weapons usage. Second charter for AFSWP is less specific as to organization, more specific as to responsibilities. AFSWP is still an inter-departmental agency.

Aug. 1951. AFSWP and AEC agree on coordinated procedure for maintaining standards at operational storage sites.

Oct./Nov. 1951. Operation BUSTER-JANGLE (seven events) conducted at NTS. Exercise *Desert Rock* (November 1, 1951) includes use of 2,800 servicemen seven miles from ground zero to test effect of blast on troops. Operation JANGLE was the first series to test surface and sub-surface cratering effects. AFSWP conducted the planning and budgeting to pull the intricate operation together.

Jan. 1952. AFSWP personnel strength peaked with 11,182 authorizations. This included the personnel required to operate the five National Stockpile Storage Sites.

Jan. 29, 1952. AFSWP unit, Test Command, is established with headquarters at Sandia Base, Albuquerque, New Mexico. The personnel in the special group at Kirtland AFB formed the nucleus of Test Command. Its mission was to act as technical supervisor of military participation and to assist the AEC. In August, this unit is merged with Field Command under the Directorate of Weapons Effects Tests. Responsibilities include operating field groups at future tests of atomic weapons involving nuclear detonations within the continental limits of the United States.

Apr. 22, 1952. Operation TUMBLER-SNAPPER (eight events) conducted at NTS, which included 2,000 soldiers placed four miles from the blast site. The test on June 1 called for troops to enter the blast area immediately after the event to determine if they could engage enemy positions.

Aug. 1, 1952. Establishment of the Directorate of Weapons Effects Tests. As a result of the Directorate, Test Command, AFSWP, was disestablished and its responsibilities were assumed by Field Command, AFSWP. This was effective with issuance of FC/AFSWP General Order No. 50, dated August 1, 1952, and FC General Order No. 10, dated July 18, 1952.

Sep. 1952. Truman administration rejects proposition by State Department's Panel of Consultants on Disarmament, led by Vannevar Bush and J. Robert Oppenheimer, to delay first thermonuclear test.

Oct. 3, 1952. Britain explodes its first atomic bomb at the Monte Bello Islands near Australia.

Oct. 29, 1952. Navy's Rear Admiral W.K. Mendenhall, Jr., responds to AFSWP Chief Loper's October 6 memorandum. States that although Services could be prepared to assume all responsibilities and functions now performed by AFSWP within one year of receipt of directives, the Services should choose to leave such duties to AFSWP. Mendenhall stated that it was "...healthy evolution" for AFSWP to not be dissolved by the services, but rather receive additional responsibilities. He saw AFSWP as an expedient functionary of the armed services. He also stated that, "with the relatively small number of weapons in existence, the very idea of dividing them among the Services even for custodial purposes will inevitably give rise to conflicting claims as to priority, numbers, and Marks [sic]. All this can be avoided by making the AFSWP the custodian, AFSWP being responsible solely to the Joint Chiefs of Staff or to the Secretary of Defense for this purpose"

Oct. 31, 1952. Operation IVY, Shot MIKE: U.S. explodes first full-scale thermonuclear device using cryogenic liquid deuterium at Enewetak.

Nov. 15, 1952. Operation IVY, Shot KING: largest fission device, detonated.

Dec. 1952. Teapot Panel headed by Von Neumann recommends development of thermonuclear tipped guided missiles.

Jan. 1953. Command change; Major General Alvin R. Luedecke replaces General Loper.

Jan. 20, 1953. Eisenhower inaugurated President of the United States.

Feb. 1, 1953. The "second" JTF-7, a redesignation of JTF-132, is established for Operations CASTLE (1954), WIGWAM (1955), REDWING (1956), and HARDTACK (1958).

Mar. 17, 1953. Operation UPSHOT-KNOTHOLE (eleven events) begins at NTS.

Mar. 21, 1953. AEC releases "An Agreement Between the AEC and the DoD for the Development, Production, and Standardization of Atomic Weapons." This agreement delineates the responsibilities to be assumed by the DoD and the AEC respectively regarding proposed atomic weapons programs (development, testing, standardization, and production). The statement notes that "it is fundamental to progress that both agencies pursue aggressively [sic] the study of new and radical concepts for military application of atomic energy." Delineated functions fall into six phases: Weapon Conception, Program Study, Development Engineering, Production Engineering, First Production, and Quantity Production and Stockpile.

Apr. 1953. JCS assigns AFSWP the responsibility for technical direction of weapon effects tests and of weapon effects phases within any task force organization.

May 25, 1953. First use of artillery piece to launch nuclear device (GRABLE, a special 280-mm cannon).

Aug. 12, 1953. Soviet test, *Joe 4*, first thermonuclear explosion.

Oct. 1953. President Eisenhower approves the "New Look" strategy, as outlined in NSC 162/2. This strategy includes expansion of forward deployments of nuclear weapons in Europe, and a declaration of readiness to deploy nuclear weapons for strategic bombardment and tactical defense.

Oct. 16, 1953. As part of its command and control mission, AFSWP ordered by Secretary of Defense to establish a centralized system to account for status and location of nuclear weapons "...at all times."

Jan. 21, 1954. Launch of *USS Nautilus*, first nuclear powered submarine.

Feb. 28, 1954. Operation CASTLE (six events) begins at Bikini Atoll. After BRAVO produced heavy fallout, the JCS asked AFSWP to monitor and predict worldwide fallout during testing. Worldwide pressure increases for a nuclear test ban. Using U-2 aircraft, AFSWP initiates a High Altitude Sampling Program (HASP) to measure radiation effects in the upper atmosphere.

Jun. 1954. Under new proposal, the command of AFSWP becomes a rotating position shared by each of the three military branches.

Jul. 21, 1954. The AFSWP mission directive was revised to include the maintenance of a technical inspection system to assist the Service Chiefs with their own technical inspection systems, performance of periodic technical inspections to assure standardization in the procedure, and the maintenance of continuous liaison with the inspection agencies of the Services.

Aug. 30, 1954. Eisenhower signs the Atomic Energy Act.

Jan. 1955. Eisenhower directed that weapons with yields of over 600 kilotons would continue to remain in AEC custody, even if dispersed to military units. This directive required AEC custodians at many SAC bases and on ships at sea.

Jan. 1955. The Special Weapons Materiel Control Division was established at Field Command, AFSWP, as the sole DoD activity responsible for procurement and distribution of training weapons, major components, test and handling equipment, associated spares and base spares in support of War Reserve Weapons.

Feb. 18, 1955. Operation TEAPOT (14 events) commences at NTS.

Apr. 6, 1955. Test HA (High Altitude) employed a three-kiloton device at 36,000 feet to test air defense options under conditions of delayed radioactive fallout.

May 14, 1955. Operation WIGWAM (one event) underwater test in the Pacific.

Jun. 22, 1955. NATO agreements call for bilateral programs to coordinate nuclear deployment. In 1956, NATO adopts plan MC 14/2 which includes forward deployment of nuclear weapons and their tactical usage.

Nov. 22, 1955. First Soviet test of a two-stage thermonuclear weapon.

May 4, 1956. Operation REDWING (17 events) begins in the Pacific. This series of events included the first extensive thermonuclear effects tests involving blast radiation, biomedical, and thermal effects.

Jul. 26, 1956. SAC announces start of its ICBM program.

Oct. 1956. Designated Atomic Energy Commission Military Representative (DAECMR) concept developed: commanding officers of SAC bases and of Naval combatant and ammunition ships become designated AEC custodians directly responsible to the AEC.

Jan. 1957. The Atomic Weapons Safety Board was established to study the safety aspects of weapons under development.

Mar. 28, 1957. At the United Nations Disarmament Commission Subcommittee in London, the U.S. announces it would consider stopping or limiting testing if verification issues could be settled.

May 28, 1957. Operation PLUMBBOB (29 tests) begins at NTS.

Jun. 1957. Command change; Rear Admiral Edward Parker replaces General Luedecke.

Jun. 14, 1957. Soviets propose immediate cessation of nuclear weapons testing for two to three years, monitoring conducted by an international commission, and establishment of manned control posts in the U.S., Britain, the USSR., and the Pacific. According to Seaborg, Eisenhower, who was favorably disposed toward the Soviet offer, was partly dissuaded when AEC Chairman Lewis Strauss brought scientists Edward Teller, Ernest Lawrence and Mark Mills to the White House. The nuclear scientists stated that the U.S. could develop fallout-free weapons within seven years and that the Soviets could negate any test moratorium by undetectable, clandestine tests.

Aug. 21, 1957. President Eisenhower proposes suspension of nuclear testing for up to two years. Soviets criticize proposal's linkage to a cutoff in production of fissionable materials for weapons.

Oct. 4, 1957. *Sputnik I* launch.

Nov. 7, 1957. Eisenhower creates the White House position of special assistant for science and technology, appointing to it MIT President James R. Killian, Jr. Shortly afterward he established a President's Science Advisory Committee (PSAC). Prior to these appointments the scientific advice (vis-a-vis nuclear arms control matters) received by President Eisenhower and Secretary of State John Foster Dulles emanated primarily from Los Alamos, Livermore, and Defense Department scientists. A large part of the advice was filtered through AEC chairman Strauss, who also served as special assistant to the president for atomic energy. The Killian group introduced new voices (and therefore greater diversity) to the test ban debate, arguing that greater difficulties might ensue in the absence of an agreement.

Mar. 11, 1958. A SAC B-47 bomber inadvertently drops a atomic weapon on a training mission near Florence, South Carolina. There had been a non-nuclear yet high explosive detonation on impact, resulting in a large crater. The survey team detected no radiation hazard at the farm on which the bomb had landed.

Mar. 27, 1958. Nikita Khrushchev becomes Premier of Soviet Union.

Mar. 31, 1958. Soviets announce unilateral moratorium on testing; start of the test ban debate. Due to disagreements, all three nuclear-weapons countries continue to test for another several months. Khrushchev urges Eisenhower and British Prime Minister Harold Macmillan to follow Soviet's decree to prohibit further nuclear testing.

Apr. 8, 1958. Eisenhower's answer to Khrushchev proposes that the Soviet Union join the Western nations in an examination of the technical requirements for nuclear test ban verification. Khrushchev expressed his willingness, despite doubts, to try this course of action.

Apr. 28, 1958. Operation HARDTACK I (35 events) begins with YUCCA, a balloon-launched weapons effects test in the Pacific. Thirty-two tests were conducted at Enewetak and Bikini. In anticipation of a testing ban, AFSWP and the AEC jointly sponsor a series of high-altitude tests, TEAK and ORANGE, at Johnston Island. EMP effects from Test TEAK results in the temporary loss of communications in some locations in the Pacific.

Apr. 28, 1958. The U.K. conducts a three-megaton nuclear weapon test at Christmas Island.

Aug. 1958. Bureau of Medicine and Surgery, United States Navy, proposed to AFSWP that a bio-nuclear facility be established at the National Naval Medical Center.

Aug. 21, 1958. The Conference of Experts, composed of scientists from the U.S., Britain, France, Canada, Czechoslovakia, Romania, and Poland, release report after two- month study in Geneva. The report concludes that a comprehensive test ban in the atmosphere, underground, underwater, and outer space within 50 kilometers can be verified with some 160 monitoring stations worldwide.

Aug. 22, 1958. Eisenhower proposes tripartite negotiations to end nuclear tests. Eisenhower announces that the U.S. would stop testing for one year, beginning October 31, 1958, provided that the Soviet Union did not resume testing. The U.K. does the same.

Aug. 27, 1958. Operation ARGUS (three tests) conducted in the South Atlantic. ARGUS verified the "Chistofilos Effect," in which fission electrons become trapped in the atmosphere's magnetic field, creating radiation belts. These tests also demonstrated the vulnerability of electronic components in radiation belts.

Aug. 30, 1958. Soviet Union agrees to idea of negotiations beginning October 31, but refused to indicate whether it would suspend tests during the conference. U.S. rushes to complete its HARDTACK series before the conference.

Sep. 1958. Soviet Union begins extensive test series of 16 shots.

Sep. 12, 1958. HARDTACK II test series begins at NTS.

Oct. 30, 1958. U.S. ceases atmospheric testing with TITANIA on October 30.

Oct. 30, 1958. Soviet Union refuses unconditionally to suspend testing for one year as proposed by U.S. and U.K., and reserved the right to determine when and, under what conditions, they would continue testing.

Oct. 31, 1958. Test ban talks in Geneva begin formally (Geneva Conference on the Discontinuance of Nuclear Weapons Tests). They result in U.S. and Britain declarations of one-year moratorium; Soviets join in a few days later. However, verification issues prove more difficult than had been anticipated.

Nov. 3, 1958. Soviet Union conducts the final shot of its 1958 series and refrains from testing until September 1, 1961.

Nov. 7, 1958. Eisenhower announces that the Soviets' testing after the October 31 deadline relieved the U.S. of any obligation under its offer to suspend tests. Nevertheless, the U.S. and the U.K. would observe the moratorium "...for the time being."

Dec. 1958. Defense Reorganization Act. AFSWP is placed under control of JCS and is to be renamed Defense Atomic Support Agency (DASA). The act authorizes the Director of Defense Research and Engineering (DDR&E) to allocate majority of effects testing funds to AFSWP. AFSWP and the AEC establish a Joint Nuclear Accident Coordinating Center. Sandia Laboratory began research on permissive actions links (PAL) for war reserve weapons. Research and development began on use-denial hardware.

Jan. 1959. Eisenhower directs the transfer of custody to the DoD of all weapons dispersed to the DoD, including those with yields in excess of 600 kilotons. Thus approximately 82 percent of the stockpile is transferred to DoD custody.

May 6, 1959. AFSWP formerly changes to DASA. In a major organizational shift, the DASA changes from an inter-departmental agency reporting to the JCS to an independent agency of the Department of Defense. DASA remains responsible for reporting on nuclear testing requirements and test ban considerations. Under its new charter, DASA was responsible to the Secretary of Defense through the Joint Chiefs of Staff. DASA's five major areas of responsibility included: 1) Staff assistance to the Office of the Secretary of Defense, through the JCS; 2) Research in weapons effects; 3) Atomic tests; 4) Weapons development; and 5) Assistance to the Services.

Aug. 26, 1959. U.S. announces it will extend its testing moratorium until the end of the year.

Aug. 28, 1959. Soviets announce that it will not resume testing as long as the "Western Powers" do not test.

Oct. 1959. Director of Defense Research and Engineering recommended support of DASA proposal for a biomedical research reactor at National Naval Medical Center.

Nov. 27, 1959. JTF-7 assigned as subordinate command of DASA.

Dec. 29, 1959. Eisenhower announces that after the moratorium expires at the end of the year, "...we consider ourselves free to resume nuclear testing", but that any resumption would be announced in advance. In the meantime, the U.S. would continue weapon research, development, and "laboratory-type" experimentation.

Dec. 30, 1959. First Polaris missile submarine becomes operational, *USS George Washington*. First successful launch of Polaris missile takes place several months later.

Jan. 14, 1960. Khrushchev states to Supreme Soviet that the Soviet Union will continue to observe the test moratorium as long as "...the western powers" do not test...".

Feb. 2, 1960. The Department of Army takes over as fiscal agent for DASA, and also provides the agency with procurement authority.

Feb. 11, 1960. U.S. proposes phased agreement with first step prohibiting tests in the atmosphere, tests underwater, and underground tests registering over 4.75 on the Richter scale.

Feb. 13, 1960. France explodes its first nuclear device in the Sahara Desert.

Mar. 4, 1960. AEC-DoD memorandum of Understanding for the Transfer of Weapons is released.

APPENDIX C: CHRONOLOGY

Mar. 19, 1960. Soviets respond to February U.S. proposal by adding ban on all tests in space, and calling for a 4-5 year moratorium on tests below seismic magnitude 4.75.

May 1, 1960. After a U.S. U-2 reconnaissance aircraft is shot down over Sverdlovsk, Khrushchev cancels the "Big Four" Paris summit.

Aug. 1960. Command change; Major General Harold Donnelly replaces Admiral Parker.

Dec. 2, 1960. Charter for Armed Forces Radiobiology Research Institute (AFRRI) approved by the three Surgeons General (of the Armed Services) and DASA.

Dec. 15, 1960. DASA supports the Joint Strategic Target Planning Staff (JSTPS), established at SAC, by providing computer models for nuclear weapons blast effects; DASA sponsors formation of the Defense Atomic Support Information and Analysis Center (DASIAC) in Santa Barbara, California.

Jan. 16, 1961. Command change; Major General Robert Booth replaces General Donnelly as Chief, DASA.

Jun. 30, 1961. JTF-7 discontinued.

Jul. 15, 1961. Air Force forms first Minuteman I missile wing.

Aug. 1961. East Germany begins construction of the Berlin Wall.

Aug. 30, 1961. Soviets announce resumption of testing, citing French testing and tension created by Berlin Crisis as reasons.

Sep. 1, 1961. Soviets resume testing, thus breaking nuclear test moratorium. When the Soviets test a 58-megaton device on October 30, the largest in history, DASA is asked to model the effects of a 100-megaton weapon used on the Pentagon.

Sep. 5, 1961. Kennedy announces that U.S. would resume testing with a series of underground tests at NTS.

Sep. 15, 1961. Operation NOUGAT (1961-1962) (45 events), begins with Shot ANTLER, was the first completely underground nuclear test series at NTS.

Oct. 24, 1961. JTF-8 activated as subordinate command of DASA. Participates in Operations DOMINIC (1962) and FISHBOWL (1962).

Dec. 1961. Using large mainframe computers, DASA begins providing the Atomic Warfare Status Center in the basement of the Pentagon. Its mission is "...to collect, collate, display and disseminate information" on the status of reserve weapons, allocated and dispersed weapons, weapon expenditures and targets, and other operational data. Additionally, in response to the Soviet testing of a 58 MT device, DASA is tasked to analyze the effects of a 100 MT weapon on the underground Alternate National Military Command Center (ANMCC) at Fort Richie, Maryland, and on proposed Washington, D.C., underground facilities. The Department of Defense Damage Assessment Center (DODDAC) begins operating in the Pentagon and at the ANMCC.

Jan. 1962. DASA's joint research with a British team, in conjunction with the Armed Services Explosives Safety Board, results in high-explosive testing of igloo safety. An ad hoc Committee on Radiation Effects, established under Dr. William G. McMillan, identifies retrofit solutions for Minuteman II systems, and advocates designed-in hardening for future strategic missiles.

Jan. 1962. AFRRI begins research.

Mar. 2, 1962. Kennedy announces his decision to resume atmospheric testing unless the Soviet Union agrees to the Western test ban proposals by late April.

Apr. 25, 1962. Operation DOMINIC (36 events) conducted in the Pacific. STARFISH PRIME shot detonated near Johnston Island and produced EMP effects as far away as Hawaii. The *USS Ethan Allen* fired a Polaris missile in the Pacific as part of the test series.

Jul. 31, 1962. Military command of AFRRI vested in the Commanding Officer, National Naval Medical Center.

Jul. 1962. The last atmospheric tests conducted in the continental United States were fired in Nevada in July 1962.

Aug. 1962. In response to the Donnelly Report, DASA Field Command recommends field testing of all components of a nuclear weapon system. DASA solicits test priorities from the McMillan Panel, a nuclear effects task force for the DDR&E (later this panel would be known as the Scientific Advisory Group on Effects (SAGE). From 1961 to 1965, the McMillan Panel urges survivability tests for weapons systems; between 1964 and 1970, DASA designs and funds many of these tests. Of particular concern is the vulnerability of the Minuteman II guidance system to radiation. The panel also raised concern regarding missile reentry hardness, silo design, and electronic system vulnerability to EMP.

Oct. 14, 1962. Cuban missile crisis begins.

Nov. 4, 1962. TIGHTROPE high-altitude test. President Kennedy announces the completion of atmospheric nuclear weapon testing on Operation DOMINIC at Johnston Island in the Pacific.

Nov. 14, 1962. To facilitate future nuclear weapon test operations between AEC-DoD, Glenn Seaborg, Chairman AEC, and Roswell Gilpatric, Deputy Secretary of Defense, signed the AEC-DoD Nuclear Weapon Effects Research Agreement.

Dec. 11, 1962. The Minuteman ICBM becomes operational.

Jan. 1, 1963. Nassau Agreement on British testing at Nevada; U.S. sells Polaris A-3 missiles to the UK; Operation FISHBOWL series measures implications of magnetic pulses produced during explosions - street lights on the island of Oahu, 800 miles away, were shorted out; National Security Council adopts new safeguards for control of nuclear weapons, including Permissive Action Links and safety and security improvements; Department of Defense Damage Assessment Center (DODDAC) transferred from DASA to National Military Command System Support Center (NMCSSC).

Apr. 23, 1963. AEC and DoD meet to follow-up November 14, 1962 meeting regarding future nuclear weapons test operations.

Apr. 29, 1963. Operating under joint agreement of the previous week, AEC and DoD representatives meet at Sandia Base to review test readiness program.

May 6, 1963. President Kennedy formally authorizes the June 1, 1964 readiness date for a new series of atmospheric tests.

Jun. 10, 1963. Kennedy announces initiation of special test ban discussions and a U.S. moratorium on atmospheric tests, if the USSR reciprocates.

Jun. 1963. Agreement is made on establishing a Heads-of-Government Hot Line. DASA is tasked to review the survivability of hotline technical designs. This hotline connected the White House, via the Pentagon's National Military Command Center, to the Kremlin.

Jul. 2, 1963. Khrushchev announces his acceptance of the idea of a Limited Test Ban Treaty (LTBT) banning nuclear testing in the atmosphere, underwater, and in outer space.

APPENDIX C: CHRONOLOGY 379

Jul. 12, 1963. Operation NIBLICK (1963-1964) (43 events) at NTS. All shots were conducted underground in this and all future series.

Jul. 14, 1963. U.S. delegation, headed by Harriman, departs for Moscow to begin Nuclear Test Ban Treaty negotiations.

Jul. 26, 1963. Kennedy addresses the American people on the Nuclear Test Ban Treaty, initialed in Moscow on July 25 by the delegates. The treaty is subsequently formally signed in Moscow on August 5, 1963 by Rusk, Home (U.K.), and Gromyko, and sent on August 8, 1963 by Kennedy to the U.S. Senate for its "advice and consent" for ratification.

Jul. 1963. Prior to LTBT ratification, DASA plans to have several SLEIGH RIDE events to further define Air Force and Navy strategic reentry vehicle (RV) survivability/vulnerability issues.

Aug. 5, 1963. LTBT is signed by the U.S., U.K. and the USSR., banning tests in the ocean, atmosphere, and outer space.

Sep. 24, 1963. The U.S. Senate consents to ratification of the LTBT by a vote of 80 to 19.

Oct. 10, 1963. The LTBT enters into force, ratified by the U.S., U.K. and the USSR.

Nov. 22, 1963. President Kennedy is assassinated in Dallas, Texas.

Dec. 4, 1963. AEC and DoD meet for the "Third Meeting of the Joint AEC-DoD Nuclear Weapons Effects Coordinating Group".

Jan. 1964. JTF-2 established and assigned to Sandia Base on a host-tenant agreement. (It was dis-established on Dec. 31, 1968).

Jan. 27, 1964. Command change; Lt Gen. Harold C. Donnelly replaces Gen. Booth. His official position is now Director rather than Chief.

Jul. 1964. Event SNOWBALL: Joint U.S./Canada high explosive test in Alberta, Canada, to conduct basic blast, ground shock, electromagnetic, and other measurements.

Jul. 1, 1964. Weapons Test Division, Headquarters, DASA established; despite name, is physically located at Sandia Base. Reorganized and redesignated as Test Command, DASA, effective Aug. 1, 1966. Weapons Effects and Test Group redesignated Weapons Test Division (STWT) DASA, a staff division under direct control of HQ/DASA (Not Field Command). Authority for this action was DASA General Order No. 10, dated July 1, 1964.

Jul. 16, 1964. Operation WHETSTONE begins at NTS.

Jul. 22, 1964. New DASA charter redefines top positions, including the creation of two deputy director posts: a civilian Deputy Director, Science & Technology, for the testing program; and a military Deputy Director, Operations and Administration, who also serves as Chief, Joint Atomic Information Exchange Group (JAIEG). The civilian Deputy Director oversaw radiation, blast and shock, biomedical, and test plans and programs activities. Charter is DoD Directive 5103.31.

Aug. 1964. JCS establishes Joint Task Force 2 at Sandia Base to develop strategies to penetrate Soviet nuclear-armed air-defense systems.

Sep. 1, 1964. Director, DASA, assumed command and administrative control over AFRRI.

Oct. 1964. Event SALMON conducted in a salt dome in Mississippi as part of the nuclear test detection program. DASA Director begins sponsorship of the McMillan Panel, with DDR&E approval.

Oct. 16, 1964. China explodes its first fission device at Lop Nor.

Nov. 3, 1964. Lyndon B. Johnson elected President of the United States.

Nov. 16, 1964. Research on weapons effects summarized in the classified publication *Capabilities of Nuclear Weapons*. Publication later replaced by January 1968 edition and later by new manual, *Effects Manual 1 (EM-1)* in 1972.

Dec. 1964. Event MUDPACK: Studied the influence of layering upon the propagation of ground shock between soft and hard medium. Defense Secretary McNamara described the "mutual assured destruction" (MAD) concept. President Johnson announces cutbacks in production of nuclear material.

Feb. 1965. Beginning with WISHBONE, DASA begins a series of vertical line-of-sight (VLOS) tests that exposed electronic components, circuits, and systems to gamma rays and neutrons.

Feb. 1965. SAILOR HAT Event: A 500-ton, high-explosive test in Hawaii to evaluate effects of airblast loading and underwater shock on surface ships.

Sep. 1965. DISTANT MIST Event: A VLOS test of fluence effects on material and electrical samples. This was the first test of different parts of the energy spectrum.

Jan. 1966. DASA develops nuclear stockpile reporting standards. JCS tasks DASA Field Command with responsibility of accounting for entire nuclear stockpile. In the late 1960s, the JCS authorizes transfer of all war reserve nuclear weapons to Service custody. As a result of this custody change, DASA personnel declines from a peak of almost 11,000 in the 1950s to 1,800 in fiscal year 1975.

Apr. 1966. PIN STRIPE Event. A VLOS test using a mobile tower, which was pulled away from the shaft after detonation to evaluate radiation effects.

Jun. 1966. PILE DRIVER Event. A ground motion phenomenology experiment, which examined survival of underground structures and shock propagation in granite materials. 71 tunnel segments were excavated for the various structures and experiments.

Jun. 1966. DASA sponsors DOUBLE PLAY Event, the first exposure of full-scale reentry systems.

Jul. 11, 1966. In a letter to Cyrus Vance, Dr. Seaborg proposes transferring all finished weapons from AEC to DoD custody.

Jul. 28, 1966. Operation LATCHKEY (38 events) begun at NTS. STERLING shot, at Hattiesburg, MS, a Plowshare experiment, NEW POINT and MIDI MIST events were DoD weapon effects tests.

Aug. 1, 1966. Weapons Test Division, Headquarters, DASA is reorganized and redesignated as Test Command, DASA. Commander of JTF-8 was assigned collateral duty as Commander, Test Command. JCS approves of a plan, drafted by the DASA Deputy Director for Science and Technology (DDST), for a series of underground tests to assure weapons system survivability.

Nov. 1966. AEC and DoD work out various changes regarding weapons custody. DASA Field Command and Albuquerque Operations Office (ALOO) revise agreements then in effect.

Feb. 10, 1967. President Johnson directs AEC to deliver weapons and components to DoD in accordance with January 30, 1947 agreement.

Mar. 10, 1967. Dr. Seaborg signs the new Stockpile Agreement, followed by Secretary Vance on March 20, 1967.

Jun. 17, 1967. China explodes a megaton-range hydrogen bomb.

Jun. 26, 1967. MIDI MIST Event. A HLOS test to evaluate radiation effects on several weapon systems. The test incorporated for the first time sample protection systems (SPS) to protect experiments from debris. It was also the first major test conducted under the JCS-approved test program.

Aug. 31, 1967. DOOR MIST Event. This test also evaluated radiation effects and was the first to use a tunnel and pipe seal (TAPS) for containment and experiment protection in a HLOS test.

Jan. 1, 1968. EMP Simulation Panel formed to explore ways of testing for EMP effects. DASA eventually funds ARES, an EMP simulator lab for the Air Force at Sandia Labs, and EMPRESS designed for the Navy.

Feb. 1968. DORSAL FIN Event. An HLOS test which evaluated radiation effects in several weapon systems.

Jul. 1, 1968. Nuclear Nonproliferation Treaty (NPT) is signed, obligating non-nuclear-weapon states not to manufacture or acquire nuclear weapons.

Aug. 1, 1968. Command change; Vice Admiral Lloyd M. Mustin replaces Gen. Harold Donnelly as Director, DASA.

Aug. 24, 1968. France explodes a megaton range hydrogen bomb.

Sep. 1968. HUDSON SEAL Event. A very successful HLOS test of the survivability of several weapon systems.

Nov. 5, 1968. Richard Nixon elected President of the United States.

Dec. 7, 1968. DoD directive terminates DASA activities at Clarksville, Killean, and Lake Mead military bases. DASA activities transferred to nearby military installations.

Dec. 31, 1968. JTF-2, at Sandia Base, is dis-established. After nuclear-related accidents in Palomares, Spain on January 17, 1966, and in Thule, Greenland, on January 21, 1968, DASA provides database of nuclear accidents to the Office of the Secretary of Defense, which later requests suspension of all routine SAC nuclear armed bomber patrols.

Jun. 1969. Construction of first MIRVed warheads begin for use on the Minuteman III and Poseidon missiles.

Sep. 1969. MINUTE STEAK Event: A VLOS test which evaluated Minuteman III systems as well as other missile systems.

Dec. 10, 1969. DoD directive terminates activities of JTF-8 and transfer control of Johnston Atoll to the Air Force.

Dec. 1969. DIESEL TRAIN Event: An HLOS test of the survivability of weapon systems.

Mar. 26, 1970. 500th announced nuclear test takes place in Nevada.

May 19, 1970. By General Order No. 20, Headquarters DASA, May 19, 1970, the Commander of Field Command, DASA, Major General Francis W. Nye, assumes command of Test Command, DASA. JTF8 to be deactivated.

May 1970. MINT LEAF Event: An HLOS test of the vulnerability of the Army Spartan missile system. Due to the size of the experiment and the number of HLOS tests being conducted, the "T" tunnel complex was begun.

Jun. 1970. Construction of B-1 bomber begins.

Jun. 30, 1970. JTF-8 is deactivated. As a result, Commander, Field Command, DASA, assumes command of Test Command, DASA (change occurred on May 19, 1970).

Jul. 1, 1970. Blue Ribbon Defense Panel recommends that DASA be dis-established.

Jul. 1970. DIAL PACK Event. A joint U.S./Canadian high-explosive test in Alberta, Canada, to determine loading and response of military systems subjected to airblast and ground shock. This test, along with PRAIRIE FLAT, helped the Air Force assess and improve Minuteman II silo survivability.

Sep. 1, 1970. Reorganization of DASA Field Command to include subcommands of: Nuclear Weapons School, Stockpile Management Command, Data Automation Command, and the Nuclear Weapons Development Command. These activities had been Directorates of Headquarters Field Command. The Stockpile Management Command also included the Nuclear Material Directorate.

Dec. 18, 1970. Operation EMERY, test BANEBERRY accidentally vents large radioactive cloud. U.S. test program is shut down for six months and new safety (containment) procedures are initiated.

Feb. 11, 1971. Seabed Arms Control Treaty is signed, prohibiting parties from placing nuclear weapons on seabed or ocean floor beyond a twelve-mile coastal zone.

Mar. 29, 1971. DoD publishes Blue Ribbon Panel report recommending that DASA be dis-established and its functions taken over by Deputy Secretary of Defense for Testing and Operations. In an Executive Memorandum, Deputy Secretary of Defense David Packard directs reorganization of DASA as a result of cutbacks recommended by the Blue Ribbon Panel survey, to be effective July 1, 1971. DASA was to be retained as a defense agency under the new title: Defense Nuclear Agency (DNA). Deputy Secretary of Defense memorandum, subject: "Defense Atomic Support Agency," directed the Nuclear Weapons School be discontinued by June 30, 1972.

Jul. 1, 1971. DASA (DNA) reorganized. The new agency is solely responsible for sponsoring all future effects tests. Other duties include consolidated management of the DoD nuclear weapons stockpile, management of DoD nuclear weapons testing and nuclear weapons effects research programs, and providing staff advice and assistance on nuclear weapons matters to the government. Under authority of DNA General Order No. 1, the following major changes in the DASA organization and mission were directed: 1) Field Command was retained but the Albuquerque complex of Sandia Base and Kirtland AFB was consolidated for support purposes under the Air Force. 2) The DASA-oriented national storage site was transferred to the Air Force. 3) The responsibility for nuclear weapons technical training was transferred to the individual military Services. The JCS were tasked to identify general interest courses to be continued on a Joint Service level and to assign a Service as executive agent for these courses. (The Joint Services Nuclear Weapons School on Kirtland AFB began to teach general interest courses on a Joint Service level). 4) DASA's responsibilities for weapons development were transferred to the Services. DNA's new role in weapons research and development was defined as advisory through participation in Service planning groups. 5) Manning levels at the weapons laboratories were cut due to the reduced role of DNA in weapons research and development. The Air Force was designated host of support functions in the Albuquerque area, and DNA was directed to obtain its support through Inter-Service Support Agreements with the host. This decision required the disestablishment of Sandia and Manzano Bases as DASA units and transfer of most of the functions to Kirtland AFB. The closure and transfer of the National Stockpile Sites to the Services in their respective proximities and the transfer of the Nuclear Weapons School and the Sandia Base Hospital to the Air Force brought about drastic decreases in manpower authorizations during the 1969-1973 period; DNA authorizations dropped from about 6,500 to about 1,200.

Aug. 1971. Command change; Lt. General Carroll Dunn replaces Admiral Lloyd Mustin as Director, DASA.

Aug. 20, 1971. Technical Analysis Group established within DNA to replace the Weapons Development Command. DNA to exercise greater responsibility for recommending DoD-wide security standards and operating procedures for nuclear weapons.

Nov. 24, 1971. DIAGNOL LINE event. A VLOS shaft-test evaluation of Poseidon missile components which included investigation of Internal Electromagnetic Pulse (IEMP) effects.

Jan. 1, 1972. Test Command and Field Command consolidated together into single organization at Sandia. Weapons Effects Test Group redesignated as Test Directorate. Test Command was deactivated.

May 26, 1972. SALT I agreement signed by U.S. and USSR.; negotiations began in November 1969. SALT I became an interim (5 year) agreement that focused on the limitation of strategic arms. It was intended to be a holding action designed to complement the ABM Treaty by limiting competition in strategic offensive arms. It provided time for further negotiations.

May 26, 1972. Anti-Ballistic Missile (ABM) Treaty was signed, permitting each side to have one limited ABM system to protect its capitol and an ICBM launch area. It provided for a U.S.-Soviet Standing Consultative Commission (SCC), designed to promote ABM objectives and treaty implementation.

Jun. 30, 1972. The military Services assume responsibility for nuclear training; the Nuclear Weapons School is transferred to the Air Force.

Jul. 20, 1972. DIAMOND SCULLS Event. The largest LOS pipe system test conducted with a drift of 1,900 feet and a test chamber over 26 feet in diameter. The test objective was to evaluate vulnerability of Minuteman III components.

Nov. 1972. SALT II negotiations commence. Talks focus on developing a long-term treaty limiting all nuclear weapon systems. The principal U.S. objectives were to provide for equal numbers of U.S. and Soviet strategic delivery vehicles, and to impose restraints on technological developments like MIRVs.

Nov. 7, 1972. Richard Nixon is reelected President of the United States.

Apr. 25, 1973. Deputy Secretary of Defense memorandum, "Johnston Atoll," directed the U.S. Air Force to transfer the host-manager responsibility for Johnston Island to DNA, effective July 1, 1973.

Jun. 5, 1973. DIDO QUEEN Event. An HLOS test, which evaluated effects on several weapons systems. This test included the first use of the DNA Auxiliary Closure (DAC), an improved version of the SAC, for better sample protection.

Jul. 1, 1973. DNA is asked to take over administration of Johnston Atoll from the Air Force. The agency designs a massive cover for plutonium contaminated sites. Johnston Atoll is to be maintained by Field Command for use as a base of operations should it become necessary to resume atmospheric testing of nuclear weapons under Safeguard C of the Limited Test Ban Treat of 1963.

Oct. 2, 1973. Beginning of Operation ARBOR (21 events) conducted at NTS. HUSKY ACE (10/12/73) and MING BLADE (6/19/74) events were DoD weapon effects tests.

Oct. 1973. Command change; Lt. General Warren Johnston replaces Gen. Dunn as DNA Director.

Dec. 1973. SACEUR asks DNA to make assessments of methods to provide a stronger, improved forward defense in Europe. In particular, the integrated deterrent roles of theater and strategic nuclear forces were to be examined.

Jul. 3, 1974. Threshold Test Ban Treaty (TTBT) signed, limiting underground tests to less than 150 kilotons.

Aug. 9, 1974. Richard Nixon resigns as President of the United States. Gerald Ford assumes office. Vladvistok accord puts cap on U.S. strategic offensive forces of 2,400 strategic nuclear delivery vehicles and of 1,320 MIRVs.

Oct. 28, 1974. HYBLA FAIR Event: Designed to evaluate a lower yield source and shorter LOS pipe for future weapon effect tests.

Nov. 1974. Brezhnev and Ford meet in Valdivostok and agree on an outline for SALT II. Defense Secretary Schlessinger announces an end to MAD (Mutual Assured Destruction) policy, opting for "limited strategic options," which states that deterrence must operate across the entire spectrum of possible contingencies. The Assistant Secretary of Defense (Installations and Logistics) directed DNA to conduct study of the economic feasibility and operational practicality of establishing DNA as the DoD Integrated Material Manager for AEC controlled consumable items, and to submit a proposed implementation plan. This plan was eventually approved.

Jan. 1975. Policy established that DNA conducted Nuclear Weapons Technical Inspections (NWTIs) can suffice for technical operations of Armed Services Technical Proficiency Inspection. Energy Research and Development Administration (ERDA) and Nuclear Regulatory Commission (NRC) begun in place of AEC.

Jan. 1975. DNA is in the forefront of developing microcomputer applications for nuclear effects. DNA DDST oversees development of nuclear effects algorithms for handheld calculators and for the first generation of personal computers. DNA provides field commanders with the first microcomputer-based planing tools, including the Targeting and Planning System (TAPS).

Jan. 1975. DICE THROW tests begin: A series of high-explosive events conducted at White Sands Missile Range (WSMR) to examine blast, cratering, and fireball effects leading up to a 500-ton equivalent event. Tests end in June 1977.

Apr. 5, 1975. DINING CAR Event: An HLOS test in support of the Trident and Minuteman III missile systems.

Oct. 24, 1975. HUSKY PUP Event: An HLOS event to test survivability of Navy reentry vehicles and material phenomenology. A 60-ton granite monolith was placed underground to study energy coupling.

Nov. 1975. The Joint Chiefs of Staff directed that FCDNA inspect nuclear capable units at a rate of 20 to 25 percent annually. Formal agreements between DNA and both the Air Force and USAEUR established surveillance inspections by Field Command of nuclear capable units. National Emergency Airborne Command Post (NEACP) becomes operational.

Dec. 1975. DNA develops its Silo Test Program (STP) to assess new protective structures for U.S. strategic and theater force deployments, as ballistic missile accuracies improve. Although initially created to assess potential vulnerabilities of Soviet hardened targets, STP provided insights into hardening design for U.S. ICBM silos.

Jan. 1976. Along with studying theater force modernization, DNA participates in various Joint Working Groups that provide a forum with allies to model alternative force employment tactics and exercise new scenarios and force mixes. DNA supports CINCPAC's effort to ensure operability of command, control, and communications (C^3) links in nuclear environments, including high-altitude bursts with EMP effects. In addition, DNA assessed C^3 network survivability after both direct attack and exposure to EMP.

May 12, 1976. MIGHTY EPIC Event: An HLOS test in support of Air Force and Navy reentry vehicles. It was the first of two-for-one test to reuse the same tunnel complex for subsequent tests and reduce costs.

Oct. 1976. DICE THROW Event, a 628-ton domed cylinder of ANFO was detonated at the WSMR to test military equipment. The success of this test proved the utility of the technique and launched a progression of tests.

Nov. 2, 1976. Jimmy Carter elected President of the United States.

Dec. 1976. FCDNA Commander represented the United Sates in signing agreements for the return of Enewetok to its people. Field Command developed and monitored procedures to provide base support for the launch of two THOR missiles from Johnston Atoll. FCDNA participated in conferences at Los Angeles Air Force Station and Vandenburg AFB to develop and implement revised configuration of the Johnston Atoll launch facilities upon completion of the program.

Jan. 1977. Secretary of Defense tasks DNA to conduct an evaluation and technology program on Theater Nuclear Force Security and Survivability (TNFS2).

Apr. 1977. Command change; Vice Admiral Robert Monroe replaces Gen. Warren Johnston as Director, DNA.

Jun. 1977. MISER'S BLUFF tests begin: A series of high-explosive events to investigate ground motion generated by multiple bursts. Five allied governments participated. MISER'S BLUFF I was conducted at WSMR and MISER'S BLUFF II was conducted at Plant Ranch, Arizona. The event ended in August 1978.

Aug. 4, 1977. U.S. Congress creates the Department of Energy (DOE), which was given the responsibility for nuclear weapon development and testing.

Oct. 1977. NATO's Nuclear Planning Group establishes task force on modernization. Emphasis is placed on two-track approach of improving tactical weaponry while pursuing arms control. Eventual deployment of 108 Pershing II missiles in Europe during the 1980s.

Nov. 1977. HYBLA GOLD Event: A specialized HLOS test to investigate airblast propagation in proposed MX missile trench, in support of MX basing. DNA tested extensive grounding and shielding improvements and made them mandatory for future events.

Dec. 28, 1977. Charter changed so that DNA placed under the direction, authority, and control of the Under Secretary of Defense for Research and Engineering. DNA to be supervised by the Joint Chiefs of Staff for military aspects of DNA activities, including composition of the nuclear stockpile; allocation and deployment of nuclear weapons; military participation and support of nuclear testing; frequency of technical standardization inspections; and requirements for technical publications. Operational phase of the radiological cleanup of Enewetak Atoll begins; Field Command is designated as operational manager of the cleanup project.

Sep. 1978. DIABLO HAWK Event: An HLOS test to certify an Air Force reentry system and the Navy C-4 missile body. Also included an extensive structure test and a test in EMP phenomenology. The event utilized the same experiment drift and hardware from the MIGHTY EPIC Event.

Dec. 1978. President Carter orders Department of Health, Education, and Welfare to establish program to study fallout effects from nuclear testing. OSD establishes Nuclear Test Personnel Review program to track long-term health effects of fallout exposure on personnel.

Jan. 1979. Field Command provided data to support the search and recovery of the Soviet satellite with on-board nuclear reactor that fell over Canada. Field Command facilitated transfer of emergency destruction information to the Services so they could write their own manuals on the destruction of nuclear weapons.

Feb. 1979. New procedures developed to insure survivability of government communications in the event of a nuclear attack.

Jun. 18, 1979. U.S. and USSR. sign the SALT II Treaty at the Hofber Palace, Vienna, Austria. SALT II replaced the interim agreement of SALT I; it allowed an aggregate limit on strategic offensive arms, and included detailed definitions of limited systems, provisions to enhance verification, and a ban on circumvention of treaty provisions. Treaty signed but not ratified.

Nov. 29, 1979. Operation TINDERBOX (15 events) began at NTS.

Dec. 1, 1979. NUWAX-79 was conducted at NTS to simulate a nuclear weapon accident and test the response of various agencies. The Air Force was the lead agency for this particular exercise. The DOE co-sponsored the event, the first of many biennial emergency response exercises.

Dec. 28, 1979. The Soviet Union invades Afghanistan. U.S. announces plans to deploy Pershing II and cruise missiles in Europe. DNA and DOE begin collaborating on joint emergency response exercises for weapon accidents recovery and post-recovery remediation.

Jan. 1980. With DIA cooperation, DNA reverse-engineers Soviet ICBM silos, and begins subscale testing. New DNA models aid in Single Integrated Operational Plan (SIOP) adjustments. DNA supports hardening of the Supreme Headquarters, Allied Powers Europe (SHAPE) at Mons, Beigium; conducts protective structures assessments for ground-launched cruise missiles (GLCMs); and holds Pershing survivability field exercises. With its programs designed to cope with immediate and delayed nuclear effects, DNA community demonstrates its support for presidential initiatives aimed at procuring survivable C^3 systems and at assuring continuity of government in wartime.

Feb. 1980. On JCS initiative, DNA establishes a Hard Target Kill research program that includes consideration of earth penetrating weapons. DNA begins focusing on applying its technologies towards civilian benefits. For example, DNA develops the e-SCRUB program, which uses electron beams to remove oxides of sulfur and nitrogen from coal stack gases; this technique permits electric power plants to use high sulphur coal in areas with sensitive air restrictions. DNA adapts its nuclear effects models so that the Federal Emergency Management Agency (FEMA) and other relief organizations can predict natural phenomena damage and target disaster relief operations. Using its nuclear effects ground shock research and tools, DNA advises the construction industry on methods to mitigate earthquake damage to buildings.

Jun. 24, 1980. HURON KING Event: A VLOS test that evaluated the hardening of satellites to nuclear radiation. A large evacuation chamber located at the surface contained a full-size mockup of the satellite.

Aug. 1980. Command change; Lt. General Harry Griffith replaces Admiral Monroe.

Oct. 16, 1980. China conducts world's last atmospheric test at Lop Nor.

Oct. 31, 1980. MINOR'S IRON Event: An HLOS test containing MX related materials and phenomenology experiments. A fiber-optic data transmission system was tested for the first time to improve data recovery.

Nov. 4, 1980. Ronald Reagan elected President of the United States.

Nov. 15, 1981. DISTANT RUNNER Event: A series of aboveground, high-explosive tests at WSMR to determine the suitability of quantity and distance criteria and standards for hardening aircraft shelters, runways, and taxiways in Europe, as part of the Theater Nuclear Survivability, Security, and Safety Program.

Dec. 1981. NUWAX-81 was conducted at NTS with the Army as the lead Service.

Sep. 23, 1982. DIAMOND ACE Event: This test was fired simultaneously with HURON LANDING and was designed to evaluate the low-yield testbed design that DNA was developing.

Nov. 10, 1982. Leonid Brezhnev dies. Yuri Andropov assumes power in the USSR.

Dec. 1982. Following a SAC maintenance accident, which resulted in an explosive fire at a Titan II missile site, OSD reinstates emergency response teams under the coordination of DNA's Joint Nuclear Accident Coordinating Center (JNACC). Field Command's JNACC began 24-hour operation. Field Command supported studies on intrinsic radiation, an antisubmarine warfare standoff weapon, plutonium dispersal analysis, and retirement of the Titan II missile system.

Feb. 1983. DNA sponsors summer studies (also in 1986) on high altitude nuclear effects. In 1983, it sponsors the satellite HILAT, for "high latitude," whose transmissions through a striated barium cloud would be measured.

Mar. 23, 1983. President Reagan announces the U.S. Strategic Defense Initiative (SDI). DNA is tasked by the SDI Office (SDIO) to evaluate lethality of all SDI weapons against their targets. DNA conducts underground tests for SDI candidate subsystems.

Apr. 6, 1983. The Scowcroft Commission, on the Future of Strategic Offensive Missiles, releases its report. DNA provided technical support and briefings to the Commission. During the years preceding this report, DNA provided support in the evaluation of how Peacekeeper ICBMs could be based. After the release of this report, DNA would apply its expertise to silo survivability. It also examined nonideal airblast and its simulation for tests of the Small ICBM's Hardened Mobile Launcher (HML). Many of these activities were accomplished jointly with the Air Force's Ballistic Missile Office (BMO)

Jul. 1983. The Judge Clark Memorandum, from the National Security Council, reaffirmed the Presidential action of 1976 which redefined Safeguard C of the LTBT as "the maintenance of the basic capability to resume nuclear testing in the atmosphere should that be deemed essential to national security." This action reconfirmed FCDNA's mission on Johnston Atoll, and FCDNA's decision to undertake the DIRECT COURSE event in October 1983.

Aug. 1983. Command change; Lt. General Richard Saxer replaces General Griffith.

Sep. 21, 1983. MIDNIGHT ZEPHYR Event: The primary objective of the HLOS test was to evaluate performance of low yield test bed concept. For the first time on a DNA event the data was totally recorded underground.

Oct. 26, 1983. DIRECT COURSE Event: A high-explosive aboveground test at WSMR to evaluate blast effects from a simulated one-kiloton airburst. The event included several NATO nations and France.

Nov. 1983. Soviets walk out of the INF and START talks.

Dec. 9, 1983. Operation FUSILEER (17 events) begins at NTS.

Jan. 1984. In response to a DoD Nuclear Survivability Directive, DNA develops a microelectronics hardening program, and encourages the military Services to implement radiation-hardened microelectronics components in their operating systems. In addition, DNA sponsored development of radiation-tolerant satellite and computer microelectronics.

Feb. 9, 1984. Yuri Andropov dies; Constantine Chernenko assumes power in the USSR.

Feb. 15, 1984. MIDAS MYTH (MILAGRO) Event: An HLOS test evaluating the effects of radiation on several weapons systems. A subsistence crater formed on top of Rainer Mesa, destroying a number of Los Alamos recording trailers and fatally injuring one of the technicians in the trailer park.

Apr. 1984. Secretary of Defense memorandum authorizes DNA to begin research on advanced conventional weapons. Later reinforced by agreement with DOE for joint studies on conventional weapons.

Sep. 1984. DNA finalizes its operations plan for removing plutonium contaminated debris from Johnston Atoll. A long range plan was conceived to mine plutonium from contaminated soil at Johnston Atoll and free needed space.

Oct. 10, 1984. Operation GRENADIER (17 events) conducted at NTS.

Nov. 6, 1984. Ronald Reagan re-elected President of the United States.

Jan. 1985. Logistics Directorate, Services Division, completed a sophisticated computer bond system, the Enewetak Radiological Records System (ERRS), designed to retain all necessary operational and radiological data. The ERRS contains all information relating to each individual's exposure (approximately 8,000 personnel).

Feb. 1985. Twenty-seven freight containers filled with plutonium-contaminated debris (weighing a total of 540 tons) were shipped from Johnston Atoll to the Nevada Test Site. At NTS, the containers were placed in the U3AXBL crater, a designated radioactive waste disposal site for "defense" wastes. No person received a measurable radiation dose from this project, and there was no leakage of contamination from the containers.

Feb.- Jun. 1985. EMP testing conducted at the Advance Research Electromagnetic Pulse Simulator (ARES) at Kirtland AFB, New Mexico. Field Command tested EMP effects on the Ground Launched Cruise Missile Support System.

Mar. 10, 1985. Chernenko dies; Mikhail Gorbachev assumes power in the USSR.

Apr. 6, 1985. MISTY RAIN, a HLOS test, conducted. A DoD weapon effects test, MISTY RAIN's objective was to measure satellite survivability and hardening verification on the MK21 and MK5 reentry vehicle. This test's technology allowed satellite hardening study as well as evaluation of functional response of electronics under high stress.

Jun. 1985. MINOR SCALE test conducted. This high-explosive effects test was designed to test precursor effects of a nuclear blast on a Hardened Missile Launcher, and also to test blast effects on foreign military hardware and foreign structures, plus blast effects on U.S. equipment.

Jul. 29, 1985. Gorbachev halts Soviet underground nuclear testing.

Sep. 1985. EMP testing of EC-135 SAC Flying Command Post aircraft is conducted at the Advance Research Electromagnetic Pulse Simulator at Kirtland AFB.

Oct. 1985. DIAMOND BEACH test conducted. The primary objective of this HLOS pipe test was to evaluate performance of the low-yield test bed concept. This test was a follow-on to the MIDNIGHT ZEPHYR event conducted in September 1983. FCDNA conducts two Stockpile Emergency Verification exercises and a relocation exercise. The number of nuclear safety studies increased by 25 percent, with the W48 program providing the most significant improvement in safety.

Jul. 1986. Command change; Lt. General John Pickitt replaces General Saxer.

Nov. 1986. Peacekeeper missile system becomes operational.

Nov. 14, 1986. National Defense Authorization Act of fiscal year 1987 disestablishes the Military Liaison Committee (MLC) and replaces it with the Nuclear Weapons Council (NWC).

Dec. 1986. DNA's AFRRI deploys a Chernobyl Site Restoration Assistance Team to Chernobyl, Ukraine, in wake of the nuclear power plant accident. DNA later provides assistance to environmental remediation efforts at the closed test site at Semipalatinsk Kazakhstan.

Feb. 1987. Exercise *Premier Task 87*, a JCS-coordinated and DNA-sponsored command post exercise, is held.

Feb. 20, 1987. Soviets resume underground testing.

Mar. 1987. New DNA charter authorizes research into non-nuclear systems where the agency has unique, albeit nuclear-derived, capabilities for the research.

Apr. 1, 1987. DoD JNACC is transferred to Headquarters DNA from Field Command.

May 11, 1987. Field Command's Test Directorate, with its functions at Kirtland AFB and the NTS, becomes a part of the Director for Test, Headquarters, DNA.

Aug. 1987. Command change; Vice Admiral John Parker replaces General Pickitt.

Dec. 1987. *Mighty Derringer*, a multi-agency exercise under the direction of the National Security Council, involving Washington level and field activity interactions, is conducted.

Dec. 8, 1987. Reagan and Gorbachev sign the INF Treaty in Washington, D.C. The treaty requires the destruction and elimination of U.S. and Soviet ground launched ballistic and cruise missiles with ranges between 500 and 5500 kilometers, along with all launchers and associated support equipment. 859 U.S. and 1,752 Soviet missiles were to be eliminated from Europe, including U.S. Pershing and Soviet SS-20 missiles.

May 27, 1988. Senate ratifies INF treaty, voting 93 to 5.

Jun. 1, 1988. INF treaty enters into force. TTBT and PNE protocol signed.

Oct. 1988. Gorbachev is selected as Chairman of the Presidium of the Supreme Soviet of the Soviet Union.

Nov. 8, 1988. George Bush elected President of the United States.

Jan. 1989. Headquarters DNA orders Field Command to coordinate with the Logistics Planning Group in the development of a document outlining the considerations on the maintenance of a basic Safeguard C capability.

Apr. 19, 1989. Tianemen Square demonstrations begun in China.

Sep. 1989. Command change: Maj. General Gerald Watson replaces Admiral Parker.

Nov. 1989. DNA creates a Stockpile Emergency Verification Subsystem (SEV), which rapidly disseminates selected or total nuclear weapon stockpile serial inventories for site emergency verification under peacetime conditions. DNA implements its Nuclear Management Information System (NUMIS), whose software maintains and provides to system users status reports from the national nuclear weapons and major components stockpile for peacetime, emergency, and wartime conditions.

Aug. 2, 1990. Iraq invades Kuwait. A U.S.-led coalition of nations deploys forces to Saudi Arabia and surrounding areas.

Sep. 1990. Drell Report to Congress on the safety of aging nuclear weapons calls for implementation of several procedural changes. DNA works jointly with the Services to assess risk of plutonium dispersal in plausible accident scenarios. DNA's inspections bring discrepancies to Services' command attention. DNA-sponsored chemical weapons disposal facility (JACADS) begins operations at Johnston Atoll.

Dec. 1990. DNA verification technology programs expand to include support of practically every arms control and bilateral agreement to which the U.S. is a party. Recent technological achievements include sensors for Open Skies aircraft and improved seismic sensing capabilities to verify the CTBT. DNA begins applying its expertise in C^3 facility survivability towards safeguarding U.S. and allied facilities from terrorist attack. The Agency has performed over 50 Balanced Survivability Assessments of critical DoD and federal agency facilities; findings are used in determining risk reduction measures. Such analytical support is provided to law enforcement agencies during forensic investigations of terrorist events, such as the Oklahoma City and Khobar Towers bombings.

Jan. 1991. DNA provides targeting and damage assessment information to Gulf War operations. DNA sets up a 24-hour command center to assess the consequences of potential Weapons of Mass Destruction (WMD) warheads on the Scud missiles Iraq launched against Israel and Saudi Arabia; DNA proves the results of these assessments to Central Command.

Mar. 1991. DNA officers participate in post-Gulf War inspections to validate lethality and survivability models based on wartime experience. After the Gulf War, DNA begins undertaking counterproliferation initiatives. Early planning includes review of all U.S. non-proliferation and counterproliferation activities headed by the Deputy Secretary of Defense, John Deutch. The Assistant to the Secretary of Defense (Atomic Energy) ATSD(AE) designates DNA as the lead defense agency for the counterforce elements of the counterproliferation support program.

Jul. 31, 1991. Bush and Gorbachev sign the Strategic Arms Reduction Treaty (START), requiring both nations to reduce their strategic nuclear arsenals by about 25 percent. Both states also moved to reduce conventional weapons and continue a phased withdrawal of forces from Europe.

Dec. 25, 1991. Mikhail Gorbachev resigns his post, signaling the disbanding of the USSR, and the end of the Cold War. Reflecting the end of the Cold War, President Bush announces nuclear posture changes. These changes include: withdrawal of tactical nuclear weapons from Europe; cancellation of the Peacekeeper mobile basing programs, of the Short Range Attack Missile II (SRAM-II) and of the Small ICBM; and stand down from alert of strategic bombers.

Jan. 1992. A Presidential decision lays the groundwork for eventual elimination of all 50 Peacekeeper missiles, reduced MIRV deployments, and the shift of nuclear bombers to conventional missions.

Apr. 1992. Command change; Maj. General Kenneth Hagemann replaces General Watson as Director, DNA.

Sep. 18, 1992. HUNTERS TROPHY - last U.S. weapons effects test.

Oct. 2, 1992. Bush signs the Energy and Water Development Appropriations Act. Its Hatfield II Amendment mandates a nine-month moratorium on all U.S. underground nuclear weapons tests, followed by a limited testing program between July 1, 1993 and January 1, 1997. Testing is to be limited to those tests related to the safety of "nuclear explosive devices" and to the reliability of "nuclear weapons". No underground test may be conducted by the U.S. after September 30, 1996, unless a foreign government conducts a test after this date, at which time the prohibition against U.S. testing will be lifted.

Oct. 23, 1992. DIVIDER - last U.S. nuclear test.

Nov. 3, 1992. William Clinton elected President of the United States.

Dec. 1992. Congress mandates reviews of DNA's roles, missions, and functions. The eventual result was reaffirming DNA's central position in the DoD's commitment to maintaining nuclear competencies. Along with CTR and Nuclear Stockpile Stewardship responsibilities. DNA also gained responsibility for non-nuclear development activities that draw upon the Agency's nuclear heritage. This mission shift becomes institutionalized by the new charter issued in 1995. ATSD(AE) tasks DNA with implementing the Cooperative Threat Reduction (CTR) program; previously, the program was known as the Safe, Secure Dismantlement Program.

Jan. 1993. George Bush and Boris Yeltsin sign the START II Treaty.

Jul. 3, 1993. President Clinton announces that the U.S. will extend the year-long moratorium on nuclear weapon testing by another 15 months, with the hope of making the ban permanent. DNA provides technical help to the Deutch Task Force as part of its support new counter-proliferation initiatives.

Oct. 1993. Armed Forces Radiobiology Research Institute (AFFRI) transferred from DNA.

Oct. 1, 1993. DNA begins operating the Inter-Service Nuclear Weapons School (INWS), later renamed Defense Nuclear Weapons School (DNWS), at Kirtland AFB. Reflecting new challenges in its mission, the school's curriculum now includes courses in counterproliferation and counterterrorism. The SAGE Panel is disbanded after its annual meeting as part of a government-wide effort to reduce the number of federal advisory groups.

Nov. 1993. DNA initiates two efforts to preserve nuclear effects information and expertise: Project Graybeard and the DARE program. The Data Archival and Retrieval Enhancement (DARE) program locates, stores, and retrieves effects data from a vast informational inventory. Project Graybeard identifies, locates, and interprets test data and integrates the information into the DARE database.

Dec. 1993. The Clinton administration conducts a Nuclear Posture Review (NPR) that defines the "enduring stockpile" of nuclear weapons. A DNA point-of-contact coordinates NPR requirements with DNA analyses and other activities. DNA military officers participate in the "dual revalidation" process, by which each Department of Energy weapons laboratory independently and periodically examines all data relevant to a specific weapon type still in the inventory. The results are reviewed by DOE headquarters, and provided to the Nuclear Weapons Council for final action.

Sep. 1994. President Clinton approves a reduced strategic force, comprised of Minuteman ICBMs, Trident submarines armed with D-5 missiles, B-2 and B-52 bombers, and non-nuclear B-1 bombers.

Dec. 5, 1994. The Strategic Arms Reduction Treaty (START I) goes into effect.

Aug. 1995. Major General Gary L. Curtin replaces Major General Kenneth Hagemann as Director, DNA.

Jan. 27, 1996. U.S. Senate approves the START II treaty, which would cut the number of nuclear warheads possessed by U.S. and Russia by 50 percent if both nations ratified it. The treaty would eliminate Russia's big multiple-warhead land-based missiles. America would eliminate its large Peacekeeper (MX) missiles and reduce the number of warheads in its Minuteman missile from three to one.

Jun. 26, 1996. A new charter is issued that reaffirms DNA's traditional roles and institutionalizes the new roles as mandated in the 1992 and 1993 Congressional studies. DNA is retitled the Defense Special Weapons Agency (DSWA), reflecting the Agency's evolving role in the post-Cold War environment.

Jul. 1996. DSWA is executing over 50 CTR projects, from supplying Russia with storage containers for fissile materials to projects in the demilitarized zone dedicated to maintaining viable threat reduction efforts. DSWA sponsors joint science programs with institutions in Russia, Ukraine, and Kazakstan.

Jul. 29, 1996. China conducted its last nuclear weapons test.

Aug. 1996. The centerpiece of DoD's counterproliferation activities is an Advanced Concept Technologies Demonstration (ACTD), which improves capability to neutralize WMD targets with minimal and predictable collateral effects. This ACTD can predict, minimize, and measure post-attack collateral effects. DNA/DSWA is Demonstration Manager of the counterproliferation ACTD.

Sep. 24, 1996. President Clinton, along with top officials of China, France, Russia, Britain and more than fifty other nations signed the Comprehensive Test Ban Treaty at the United Nations. India and Pakistan declined. The signatories must go through the usual ratification procedures before the treaty is fully implemented.

Sep. 25, 1996. Terrorist attack the USAF housing complex, Khobar Towers, in Saudi Arabia.

Jan. 29, 1997. Defense Special Weapons Agency (DSWA) celebrates 50-year anniversary as oldest defense agency, ranging from AFSWP-DSWA.

Sep. 30, 1998. Through DoD Directive 5105.62 and following from the November 1997 DoD Defense Reform Initiative, the Defense Special Weapons Agency, the On-Site Inspection Agency, the Defense Technology Security Administration, along with selected elements of the Office of the Secretary of Defense staff, were merged to form the Defense Threat Reduction Agency (DTRA). On October 1, 1998, Secretary of Defense William S. Cohen formally established DTRA in a ceremony at Dulles International Airport in Northern Virginia, where DTRA was initially headquartered. Secretary Cohen outlined the agency's mission areas as maintaining current nuclear deterrent capability, reducing threats from nuclear, chemical, and biological weapons, and countering WMD threats, in order "... to help catapult America, safe and secure, into a new century."

APPENDIX D

AGENCY CHARTERS

Manhattan Engineering District (MED)

Armed Forces Special Weapons Project (AFSWP)

Defense Atomic Support Agency (DASA)

Defense Nuclear Agency (DNA)

Defense Special Weapons Agency (DSWA)

APPENDIX D: AGENCY CHARTERS

MED

WAR DEPARTMENT

WASHINGTON

April 17, 1944.

MEMORANDUM for Major General L. R. Groves.

Subject: Delegation of Authority under Executive Order #9001.

1. The powers delegated to the War Department by Executive Order #9001, dated 27 December 1941, and redelegated to the Under Secretary of War by the Secretary of War by Memorandum dated 30 December 1941, to enter into contracts and into amendments or modifications of contracts heretofore or hereafter made, and to deviate, where necessary, from War Department Standard Forms of contracts, and to make advance, progress, and other payments thereon, without regard to the provisions of law relating to the making, performance, amendment, or modification of contracts, are hereby further delegated to Major General L. R. Groves in connection with the work assigned to and coming within the jurisdiction of the Manhattan District, U. S. Engineer Office. He may, pursuant to Executive Order #9001 and the Memorandum for the Under Secretary of War, dated 30 December 1941, exercise such powers either personally or through the District Engineer of the Manhattan District, U. S. Engineer Office.

2. The authority herein delegated shall be effective as of 1 September 1942.

RLsP Ptt
Under Secretary of War.

WAR DEPARTMENT
P. O. BOX 2610
WASHINGTON, D. C.

10 June 1944

Subject: Delegation of Authority.

MEMORANDUM TO THE DISTRICT ENGINEER, MANHATTAN DISTRICT.

    1. The powers delegated to the War Department by Executive Order No. 9001, dated 27 December 1941, and redelegated to the Under Secretary of War by the Secretary of War by memorandum dated 30 December 1941, and further redelegated by the Under Secretary of War to the undersigned, to enter into contracts and into amendments or modifications of contracts heretofore or hereafter made, and to deviate, where necessary, from War Department Standard Forms of Contracts, and to make advance, progress, and other payments thereon, without regard to the provisions of law relating to the making, performance, amendment, or modification of contracts, in connection with the work assigned to and coming within the jurisdiction of the Manhattan District, U. S. Engineer Office, are hereby further delegated to the District Engineer, Manhattan District, provided, however, that the following contracts shall be subject to the written approval of the undersigned or of higher authority.

    a. All contracts (other than architect-engineer, management, or similar contracts) involving a price of $5,000,000 or more, and supplemental agreements and change orders which have the effect of increasing the price of contracts (other than architect-engineer, management or similar contracts) by $5,000,000 or more.

    b. Architect-engineer, management, or similar contracts when the construction contracts to which they relate involve a price of $5,000,000 or more, and supplemental agreements and change orders affecting architect-engineer, management or similar contracts when the changes being concurrently made in the construction contracts to which they relate have the effect of increasing the price of the construction contract by $5,000,000 or more.

    2. The authority herein delegated shall be effective as of 1 September 1942.

L. R. GROVES,
Major General, C.E.

DECLASSIFIED BY DSWA (OPSSI).
AUTHORITY EO 12958
DATE 10 JUN 98

AFSWP

APPENDIX D: AGENCY CHARTERS

Memo 850-25-8

MEMORANDUM)   WAR DEPARTMENT
No. 850-25-8   )   Washington 25, D. C., 18 March 1947

ARMED FORCES SPECIAL WEAPONS PROJECT

1. The Armed Forces Special Weapons Project established by joint directive of the Secretaries of War and Navy, effective as of midnight 31 December 1946, will operate directly under the Chief of Staff and the Chief of Naval Operations.

2. The Armed Forces Special Weapons Project is responsible for carrying on the military service functions of the Manhattan Project retained under control of the armed forces.

3. The Chief of the Armed Forces Special Weapons Project will assume responsibility for all military service functions of the Manhattan Project as are retained under the control of the armed forces, including training of special personnel required, military participation in the development of atomic weapons of all types (in coordination with the Atomic Energy Commission), technical training of bomb commanders and weaponeers, and developing and effecting joint radiological safety measures in coordination with established agencies.

4. United States Army personnel on duty with the Armed Forces Special Weapons Project will be administered by the Deputy Chief of Staff as part of the Miscellaneous War Department Group.

5. United States Army units assigned to the Manhattan Engineer District at midnight 31 December 1946 are assigned to the Armed Forces Special Weapons Project as of 31 December 1946.

6. Funds for the Armed Forces Special Weapons Project, other than for pay of military personnel, have been made available by working fund advances to War Department from the Atomic Energy Commission, utilizing funds formerly available to the Manhattan Project. Pay of military personnel will be from appropriate War and Navy Department appropriations.

7. Services and supplies will be furnished the Armed Forces Special Weapons Project on a reimbursable basis and in accordance with existing War Department regulations.

Memo 850-25-8

8. Installations and agencies of the War Department are authorized and directed to render all practicable assistance and service to the Armed Forces Special Weapons Project.

(AG 322 (10 Feb 47))

BY ORDER OF THE SECRETARY OF WAR:

OFFICIAL:
EDWARD F. WITSELL
Major General
The Adjutant General

DWIGHT D. EISENHOWER
Chief of Staff

DISTRIBUTION:
War Department General and Special Staff Divisions
Army Air Forces
Army Ground Forces
Administrative and technical services
All armies, ZI.
Military District of Washington
War Department Group agencies

Copies of this memorandum are furnished only to agencies listed above. See paragraph 6, AR 310-20.

APPENDIX D: AGENCY CHARTERS

(G. O. NO. 14)

GENERAL ORDERS)   WAR DEPARTMENT
NO. 14   )   OFFICE OF THE CHIEF OF ENGINEERS
                              WASHINGTON 25, D. C.
                                   8 August 1947

SUBJECT: Abolishment of the Manhattan District

     1. By authority of the Secretary of War and effective 15 August 1947

         a. The Manhattan, District, with headquarters at Oak Ridge, Tennessee, established by General Orders No. 33, Office of the Chief of Engineers, 13 August 1942, is abolished.

         b. Personnel of the Manhattan District is transferred to the Armed Forces Special Weapons Project for administration and to duty with the Atomic Energy Commission. Property and records are transferred to the Atomic Energy Commission.

     2. The District Engineer, Manhattan District will arrange for the necessary transfer of property and records. The Chief of Engineers will arrange for the reassignment of military personnel.

     BY ORDER OF THE CHIEF OF ENGINEERS:

                                   CHAS. G. HOLLE
                                   Colonel, Corps of Engineers
                                   Executive

DASA

APPENDIX D: AGENCY CHARTERS

THE JOINT CHIEFS OF STAFF
Washington 25, D.C.

SM-70-59
6 May 1959

MEMORANDUM FOR THE CHIEF,
ARMED FORCES SPECIAL WEAPONS PROJECT

Subject: Organization and Functions of the Defense Atomic Support Agency (U)

1. Reference is made to a memorandum by the Joint Chiefs of Staff for the Secretary of Defense, dated 2 January 1959, subject: "Relationship of the Armed Forces Special Weapons Project to the Joint Chiefs of Staff (U)", and to his reply thereto, dated 1 May 1959.

2. As of this date, the Armed Forces Special Weapons Project is redesignated the Defense Atomic Support Agency (DASA).

3. The organization, mission, functions and responsibilities of DASA are as set forth in the Defense Atomic Support Agency charter enclosed herewith. A separate directive concerning DASA support arrangements will be issued by the Secretary of Defense.

Distr:
Chairman, JCS (2)	CSA
DOSOPS	ONO
Secy to CNO (JCS)	CSUSAF
Director/Plans, AF	CMC
MarCorps L/O	CINCAL
Director J/S	CINCLANT
J-1 (2)	CINCARIB
J-3 (2)	CINCONAD
J-4 (2)	USCINCEUR
J-5 (2)	CINCPAC
	CINCNELM
	CINCSAC

(Further implementation of JCS 1854/24)

4. You will note that one of the functions set forth in the charter charges DASA with supervising the conduct of full-scale DOD weapons effects tests. Insofar as overseas testing responsibility is concerned, this function will be held in abeyance until the future status of Joint Task Force Seven has been determined.

For the Joint Chiefs of Staff:

H.L. HILLYARD
Brig. General, USA,
Secretary.

Enclosure

APPENDIX D: AGENCY CHARTERS

ENCLOSURE

DEFENSE ATOMIC SUPPORT AGENCY CHARTER

SECTION I

ORGANIZATION

1. The Defense Atomic Support Agency (DASA) is an agency of the Department of Defense commanded by a Chief thereof designated by the Secretary of Defense upon the recommendation of the Joint Chiefs of Staff.

2. This agency will be composed of appropriate representation from each of the Military Services and the Chief, DASA, will be rotated among the Services.

3. The chain of command runs from the Secretary of Defense through the Joint Chiefs of Staff to the Chief, DASA. Orders, program approval and guidance to the Chief, DASA, will be issued by the Secretary of Defense or by the Joint Chiefs of Staff, by the authority and direction of the Secretary of Defense.

4. Requests for advice and assistance in the performance of their assigned functions may be made to the Chief, DASA, by designated responsible officials of the Office of the Secretary of Defense, of the Military Departments, of the Military Services and the Unified and Specified Commands. In those instances where the assistance requested is not clearly within the existing capabilities of DASA, the requesting agency may be asked to provide for the additional resources required or the request may be referred to the Joint Chiefs of Staff.

SECTION II

MISSION

The mission of the DASA is to assist the Office of the Secretary of Defense and the Joint Chiefs of Staff, the Military

Enclosure

Departments and the Military Services within those Departments and the Unified and Specified Commands by providing technical, logistical and training advice and services in the field of atomic weapons, and to supervise Department of Defense (DOD) atomic weapons test activities.

NOTE: The term "atomic weapons" as used in this document refers to AEC produced or procured components of atomic weapons systems.

SECTION III

BASIC FUNCTIONS

1. To provide staff assistance to the Joint Chiefs of Staff in atomic weapons matters.

2. To provide over-all surveillance, coordination, advice, and assistance on major actions affecting the atomic stockpile and to store and maintain atomic weapons as directed.

3. As requested by the Services, provide atomic weapons technical, logistical, training, and stockpile management services.

4. Within approved policies and programs and in consonance with pertinent DOD-AEC agreements, to act as the central coordinating agency for the Department of Defense with the Atomic Energy Commission (AEC) on matters pertaining to the research, development, production, stockpiling, and tests of atomic weapons as specified herein.

5. To supervise the conduct of full-scale DOD weapons effects tests, assist in operational evaluation tests of atomic weapons systems involving nuclear detonations, and coordinate other DOD programs for the investigation of atomic weapons effects.

6. In the field of atomic weapons, assist the Joint Chiefs of Staff and the principal staff assistants of the Secretary of Defense as required in fulfilling their responsibilities for providing advice and assistance to the Secretary of Defense.

Enclosure

APPENDIX D: AGENCY CHARTERS   413

SECTION IV

RESPONSIBILITIES

1. In providing staff assistance in atomic weapons matters, the DASA will:

    a. Advise and assist the Joint Chiefs of Staff in the preparation of plans for dispersal and distribution of atomic weapons.

    b. Provide and maintain contiguous to the Joint War Room for the Joint Chiefs of Staff an atomic warfare status center (Joint War Room Annex) to collect, collate, display and disseminate information on:

        (1) Status and location of reserve weapons,

        (2) Status and location by command of allocated and dispersed weapons.

        (3) Weapon expenditures and targets.

        (4) Other technical and operational data as required to reflect the current atomic warfare status.

    c. Maintain up-to-date information on the status of production, modification, stockpiling, and retirement programs for atomic weapons, and review AEC schedules to insure conformance with Department of Defense requirements.

    d. Provide such other staff assistance as may be required by the agencies specified in Section II above, to include bringing to the attention of the appropriate agencies those matters under DASA cognizance which are not within established policy or which are of a controversial nature and require resolution.

2. In providing over-all surveillance, coordination, advice and assistance on major actions affecting the atomic stockpile and in storing and maintaining atomic weapons as directed, the DASA will:

                                                           Enclosure

a. Arrange with the AEC and the Services for the orderly dispersal and distribution of atomic weapons and associated repair parts.

b. Inform commanders and Military Services, after coordination with the Joint Staff, of the estimated availability of atomic weapons to fill allocations and of technical limitations which affect the operational use of atomic weapons.

c. Operate a reporting system to provide information on the status of the stockpile.

d. Operate those stockpile sites used primarily to store and maintain reserve weapons (present NSS's) and such additional sites as may be assigned by the Joint Chiefs of Staff.

e. Provide centralized coordination among the Services and with the AEC in planning and scheduling modifications, modernization and quality assurance programs, to insure minimum loss of weapon availability.

f. Perform technical inspections as required.

g. Furnish technical assistance as required.

3. In providing to the Services atomic weapons technical, logistic and training services, the DASA will:

   a. Consolidate the requirements for and affect procurement of AEC produced training weapons, Operational Suitability Test (OST) weapons, test and handling equipment, associated repair parts and other AEC produced material.

   b. Provide up-to-date technical information on atomic weapons related to OST and training weapons, test and handling equipment, associated repair parts, and criteria for standardizing inspection procedures.

   c. Furnish guidance as necessary to reflect AEC requirements for accountability and responsibility for Restricted Data material.

Enclosure

APPENDIX D: AGENCY CHARTERS

    d. Conduct orientation, familiarization, qualification, and other type training as required.

    e. Assist the Services in the conduct of atomic weapons training by:
        (1) Training instructors.
        (2) Providing instructional material.
        (3) Recommending as to course content.

    f. Provide other technical information and advice as requested by the Services in connection with their operation of assigned storage sites, weapons maintenance, transportation, and other basic logistical functions in support of forces assigned to the commanders of Unified and Specified Commands.

    g. Provide stockpile management services as requested by the Services.

4. In acting as the central coordinating agency with the AEC on matters pertaining to the research, development, production, stockpiling, and test of atomic weapons, the DASA will, within approved policies and programs and in consonance with pertinent DOD-AEC agreements:

    a. Provide primarily DOD liaison with, and coordinated guidance to, the AEC in those matters not appropriate for the Military Liaison Committee (MLC). This is not intended to preclude direct Service contact with AEC.

    b. Upon approval of the Director, Defense Research and Engineering, to conduct and report on Phase 2 Feasibility Studies in conjunction with the Services, and to provide the Chairman of the Joint Study Groups.

    c. Prepare, coordinate with the Services, and submit to the MLC for approval the desired military characteristics for AEC developed weapons.

    d. Participate as a principal in Joint Working Groups established to coordinate the development effort on atomic weapons approved by the Director, Defense Research and Engineering, for Phase 3 development.

Enclosure

e. Review proposed AEC designs of atomic weapons in conjunction with the Services to insure compliance with the military characteristics.

f. Coordinate arrangements for dispersals, transfers, exchanges, exercises, and returns of atomic weapons and associated repair parts.

g. Obtain the release and coordinate the transfer of AEC produced training weapons, OST weapons, test and handling equipment, associated repair parts, and other AEC produced material.

5. In supervising the conduct of full-scale DOD weapons effects tests, assisting in operational evaluation tests of atomic weapons systems involving nuclear detonations; and in coordinating other DOD programs for the investigation of atomic weapons effects the DASA will:

   a. Obtain the requirements for information on atomic weapons effects for use in operational planning and to meet research and engineering needs within the DOD.

   b. In coordination with the Services and agencies concerned, prepare integrated full-scale weapons effects test programs and submit them to the Joint Chiefs of Staff, for their review and approval, and forwarding to the Secretary of Defense for approval.

   c. Prepare preliminary plans for the military phases of such tests and budget for those items not normally included in the Services' budgets.

   d. Make recommendations to the Joint Chiefs of Staff, after coordination with the Services or commanders of Unified and Specified Commands, as appropriate, for:

      (1) Composition and command or control of task forces to conduct tests, or to support the AEC in conducting the DOD portion of tests.

Enclosure

(2) The phased reduction of task forces and other test personnel upon completion of tests, as well as the minimum essential personnel required for test planning and maintenance of DOD facilities at test sites during periods when tests are not being conducted.

e. Prepare reports and analyses of the results of tests and disseminate data of interest to appropriate agencies.

f. Provide technical liaison and assistance as requested for these operational evaluation tests of weapon systems involving nuclear detonations that have been approved for conduct by the Services or the commanders of Unified and Specified Commands.

g. As a supplement to full scale testing and in order to assure an integrated effort, coordinate laboratory and theoretical programs for the investigation of the effects of nuclear weapons, and make appropriate recommendations to the Services and to the DDRE. Where appropriate, supplement these programs, to include budgeting as necessary.

h. Arrange for the AEC support of DOD weapons effects test programs in accordance with basic DOD-AEC agreements.

6. In assisting the Joint Chiefs of Staff and the principal staff assistants of the Secretary of Defense in fulfilling their responsibility for advice and assistance to the Secretary of Defense in the field of atomic weapons, the DASA will:

a. Provide within the DOD the central agency for the collection and dissemination of technical information as to the effects, characteristics, reliability, safety and vulnerability of atomic weapons relating to research and development by the AEC; and on atomic weapon accidents and incidents.

b. Provide, within the DOD, the central agency responsible for development of environmental criteria and construction

Enclosure

standards for the storage and maintenance of atomic weapons, utilizing available technical data developed by AEC and other agencies, in order to insure operational reliability, safety and security of weapons.

    c. Provide support as required to the Joint Atomic Information Exchange Group.

    d. Furnish atomic weapons effects information to the Office of Civil and Defense Mobilization and other agencies outside of the DOD as may be authorized by the Secretary of Defense.

    e. Provide such other assistance as may be directed.

7. In addition to the above, the DASA will:

    a. As requested, furnish information and advice to the agencies designated in Section II above on matters pertaining to the security of atomic weapons information, material and installations.

    b. Provide advice and assistance to further the development of passive defense measures against atomic weapons, through such means as:

        (1) Coordination and support of training for defense measures where joint Service programs are desirable.

        (2) Evaluation of weapons effect data and dissemination of results of such evaluations to all commands, and other agencies of the Department of Defense as appropriate.

        (3) Maintain current information as to the status of military research and engineering in the field of radiac instruments, individual and collective protective devices, radiological decontamination procedures, and the medical aspects of atomic warfare. In order to assure an integrated effort, make recommendations to the DDRE and the Services as appropriate.

    c. Furnish guidance on environmental criteria and construction standards for the storage and maintenance of atomic weapons

Enclosure

APPENDIX D: AGENCY CHARTERS

world-wide to provide optimum security and safety consistent with operational demands.

d. Coordinate as the principal DOD representative the activities of the Joint Special Weapons Publication Board for the publication of technical directives covering the assembly, storage, maintenance, and modification of atomic weapons and related test and handling equipment to provide:

   (1) Minimum technical qualifications of personnel.

   (2) Minimum standards of technical safety.

   (3) Physical procedures and technical specifications.

e. Maintain and operate a Joint Nuclear Accident Coordinating Center (JNACC) in conjunction with the AEC to provide assistance for handling radiological incidents.

APPROVED:

/s/ Donald A. Quarles
DATE: 1 May 59

APPENDIX D: AGENCY CHARTERS

DNA

APPENDIX D: AGENCY CHARTERS 423

November 3, 1971
NUMBER 5105.31

ASD(C)

Department of Defense Directive

SUBJECT Defense Nuclear Agency (DNA)

References: (a) DoD Directive 5105.31, "Defense Atomic Support Agency (DASA)," July 22, 1964 (hereby cancelled)
(b) DoD Directive 4145.20, "Environmental Criteria and Design Standards for Atomic Weapons Storage and Maintenance Facilities," November 29, 1961 (hereby cancelled)
(c) DoD Directive 5154.4, "The Department of Defense Explosives Safety Board," October 23, 1971
(d) DoD Directive 5030.2, "Procedure for Handling Joint AEC-DoD Nuclear Weapons Development Projects," October 26, 1962

I. GENERAL

Pursuant to the authority vested in the Secretary of Defense, the Defense Nuclear Agency (DNA) is established as a designated agency of the Department of Defense (DoD) under the direction, authority, and control of the Secretary of Defense.

II. ORGANIZATION

DNA will consist of:

A. A Director, a Deputy Director (Operations and Administration), a Deputy Director (Science and Technology), and a headquarters establishment.

B. Such subordinate units, field activities, and facilities as are established by the Director, DNA, or are herein or hereafter assigned or attached specifically to DNA by the Secretary of Defense.

III. **MISSION AND RESPONSIBILITIES**

A. The mission of DNA is to provide support to the Secretary of Defense, the Military Departments, the Joint Chiefs of Staff, and other DoD Components, as appropriate, in matters concerning nuclear weapons as provided herein and such other aspects of the DoD nuclear program as may be directed by competent authority.

B. The Director, DNA, will be responsible for:

1. Consolidated management of the DoD nuclear weapons stockpile in accordance with the functions assigned herein.

2. Management of DoD nuclear weapons testing and nuclear weapons effects research programs. (This does not affect the basic Service responsibility for all aspects of specific weapons system development).

3. Providing staff advice and assistance on nuclear weapons matters within his cognizance to the Secretary of Defense, the Military Departments, the Joint Chiefs of Staff, other DoD Components, and government agencies, as appropriate and when requested.

IV. **SUPERVISION**

Staff supervision of DNA for the Secretary of Defense will be provided as follows:

A. The Joint Chiefs of Staff, acting through the Director, DNA, will exercise primary staff supervision over

DNA activities, except as prescribed otherwise herein. Specifically, they will:

1. Exercise staff supervision over the military operational aspects of DNA activities, including:
   (a) composition of the nuclear stockpile;
   (b) allocation and deployment of nuclear weapons;
   (c) military participation in and support of nuclear testing; (d) frequency of technical standardization inspections; and (e) requirements for technical publications.

2. Review and provide military advice on the adequacy of the DNA efforts in nuclear weapons testing and nuclear weapons effects research which is related directly to military systems considered in the Joint Strategic Objectives Plan, Joint Force Memorandum, and Nuclear Warhead Development Guidance.

B. The Director, Defense Research and Engineering (DDR&E) will exercise staff supervision through the Director, DNA, keeping the Director, Joint Staff, informed, of DNA activities associated with the DoD nuclear weapons effects research and nuclear weapons test programs.

C. The Assistant to the Secretary of Defense (Atomic Energy) will exercise staff supervision through the Director, DNA, keeping the Director, Joint Staff, informed, of DNA activities associated with: (1) technical nuclear safety; (2) logistics aspects of nuclear weapon stockpile management; (3) the application of nuclear energy in other than the weapons field; (4) the transmission of information to the Joint Committee on Atomic Energy, as required by the Atomic Energy Act of 1954, as amended; and (5) agreements between the DoD and the Atomic Energy Commission (AEC) on appropriate nuclear matters. In his role as Chairman of the Military Liaison Committee (MLC), the ATSD(AE) will exercise staff supervision through the Director, DNA, of DNA activities associated with DNA support of the MLC.

V. **FUNCTIONS**

Under its Director, and in accordance with the assignments of responsibility specified in Paragraph III., above, DNA will perform the following functions:

A. Maintain overall surveillance and provide guidance, coordination, advice, or assistance, as appropriate, for all nuclear weapons in DoD custody, including production, composition, allocation, deployment, movement, storage, maintenance, quality assurance and reliability assessment, reporting procedures, and retirement.

B. Provide advice and assistance, as appropriate, to the Secretary of Defense, Military Departments, Joint Chiefs of Staff, Unified and Specified Commands, and other government agencies on the effectiveness of nuclear weapons; the vulnerability of military forces, installations, and systems against nuclear weapons effects; and radiological defense activities. In this connection, when directed by the DDR&E, DNA will serve as DoD coordinator for work in selected technological areas related to nuclear vulnerability activities conducted by the Military Departments or other DoD Components.

C. Provide nuclear weapon stockpile information to the Joint Chiefs of Staff as required.

D. Provide nuclear warhead logistic information to authorized DoD organizations.

E. Plan, coordinate, and supervise the conduct of DoD nuclear weapons effects research and nuclear weapons testing, to include evaluation of the results of these programs.

F. Develop, coordinate, and maintain the national nuclear test readiness program jointly with the AEC and perform associated technical, operational, and safety planning.

G. Develop, coordinate, and conduct test exercises, overseas nuclear tests, and other nuclear-related operations, as directed. Arrange for mutual AEC-DoD support of AEC, DoD, or joint nuclear weapons tests.

H. Act as the central coordinating agency for the DoD with the AEC on nuclear weapon stockpile management, nuclear weapon testing, and nuclear weapons effects research within approved policies and programs and in consonance with the statutory provisions for the MLC and pertinent DoD-AEC agreements.

I. Conduct technical standardization inspections of units having responsibilities for assembling, maintaining or storing nuclear weapons, their associated components and ancillary equipment. Inspections will be performed on a selective sampling basis of nuclear capable units assigned to every major command in the Department of Defense. The Joint Chiefs of Staff will determine the frequency of such inspections. Inspection schedules will be coordinated with the major or component commands and the Service concerned.

J. Command the Armed Forces Radiobiology Research Institute (AFRRI).

K. Maintain and operate a Joint Nuclear Accident Coordinating Center (JNACC), in conjunction with the AEC.

L. Operate the Joint Atomic Information Exchange Group (JAIEG) in accordance with policy guidance furnished jointly by the ATSD(AE) for the DoD and the Assistant General Manager for Military Application for the AEC.

M. Perform for the DoD: (1) integrated materiel management functions for all AEC special designed and quality controlled nuclear ordnance items and for Service designed and quality controlled nuclear ordnance items where such management is mutually agreed upon between DNA and the appropriate Service, or as directed by the Assistant Secretary of Defense (Installations and Logistics); (2) management of

Continuation of V. M.

that portion of the Federal Cataloging Program pertaining to nuclear ordnance items including the maintenance of the central data bank and the publication of Federal Supply Catalogs and Handbooks for all nuclear ordnance items; (3) as the DoD assignee, the standardization of nuclear ordnance items in coordination with the appropriate Service; (4) management of the AEC-DoD loan account for nuclear materials; and (5) management of a technical logistics data and information program.

N. Perform technical analyses and studies for the Secretary of Defense, the Military Departments, and the Joint Chiefs of Staff of nuclear related problems; prepare and coordinate implementing directives and joint technical publications when requested. DNA will provide analysis and study results to Defense Components, as appropriate, when such results are pertinent to stated requirements.

O. In coordination with the AEC and the Military Departments, disseminate technological information of joint interest relating to nuclear technology, development, and weapons through laboratory liaison, technical reports, and nuclear weapons technical publications. Publications pertaining to specific weapons will be the responsibility of the lead Service for the weapon concerned.

P. Provide technical assistance and support to the Secretary of Defense, the Military Departments, and the Joint Chiefs of Staff in developing nuclear warhead safety requirements and reviewing and processing safety rules for nuclear weapons systems. When appropriate, coordination will be effected with the Department of Defense Explosives Safety Board. (See DoD Directive 5154.4 (reference (c)).

Q. Within guidelines established by the Joint Chiefs of Staff, investigate and recommend DoD security and safety standards and operating procedures.

R. Develop, prepare, and publish, in coordination with the AEC, Military Departments, and the Department of Defense Explosives Safety Board, appropriate guidance, environmental criteria, and design standards for the construction of facilities to be used for the storage and maintenance of nuclear weapons.

S. Perform such other functions as may be assigned by the Secretary of Defense.

VI. <u>AUTHORITY</u>

The Director, DNA, is specifically delegated authority to:

A. Command the Defense Nuclear Agency.

B. Have access to and direct communications with all DoD Components and, after appropriate coordination, with other organizations.

C. Exercise the administrative authorities contained in Enclosure 1 of this Directive.

VII. <u>RELATIONSHIPS</u>

A. In the performance of his function, the Director, DNA, will: (1) coordinate actions as appropriate with other Components of the DoD and those departments and agencies of government having related functions: (2) maintain appropriate liaison for the exchange of information and findings related to his assigned responsibilities; (3) make maximum use of established facilities, procedures, and channels for logistic support, procurement, accounting, disbursing, investigative, and related administrative operations; (4) obtain information from any Component of the DoD which is necessary for the performance of DNA functions; and (5) insure that the Military Departments, Joint Chiefs of Staff, and appropriate OSD staff elements are kept fully informed concerning DNA activities.

B. The Military Departments and other DoD Components will: (1) provide assistance within their respective fields of responsibility to the Director, DNA, in carrying out his assigned responsibilities and functions; (2) coordinate with DNA all programs which include or are related to nuclear weapons effects research or nuclear weapons testing: (this includes specifically keeping the Director, DNA informed of systems response to nuclear weapons effects) (3) keep the Director, DNA, informed as to the substance of their major actions being coordinated with other DoD Components, AEC and its laboratories, and other government agencies which relate to DNA functions; and (4) provide the Director, DNA, with requirements for nuclear weapons effects research and nuclear weapons testing.

VIII. ADMINISTRATION

A. The Director, DNA, will be a lieutenant general or vice admiral appointed by the Secretary of Defense, upon recommendation of the Joint Chiefs of Staff. Normally, the position of Director will rotate among the Services.

B. The Deputy Directors will be appointed by the Secretary of Defense. When military officers, the Deputy Directors will be recommended by the Joint Chiefs of Staff and will normally be selected from Services different from that of the Director. Civilian Deputy Directors will be recommended by the DDR&E.

C. DNA will be authorized such personnel, facilities, funds, and other administrative support as the Secretary of Defense deems necessary.

D. The Military Departments will assign military personnel to DNA in accordance with approved Joint Manpower Program authorizations. Procedures for such assignments will be as agreed upon between the Director, DNA, and the individual Military Departments.

IX. EFFECTIVE DATE AND CANCELLATION

This Directive is effective upon publication. References (a) and (b) are hereby superseded and cancelled. Reference (d) will be revised to reflect changed DNA functions.

[signature]
Deputy Secretary of Defense

Enclosure - 1
    Delegations of Authority

5105.31 (Encl 1)
Nov 3, 71

DELEGATIONS OF AUTHORITY

Pursuant to the authority vested in the Secretary of Defense, the Director, DNA, or, in the absence of the Director, a person acting for him is hereby delegated, subject to the direction, authority, and control of the Secretary of Defense, and in accordance with DoD policies, directives, and instructions, and pertinent OSD regulations, authority as required in the administration and operation of DNA to:

1. Exercise the powers vested in the Secretary of Defense by Section 204 of the National Security Act of 1947, as amended (10 U.S.C. 1580) and Section 12 of the Administrative Expenses Act of 1946, as amended (5 U.S.C. 302), pertaining to the employment, direction and general administration of DNA civilian personnel.

2. Fix rates of pay for wage board employees exempted from the Classification Act by 5 U.S.C. 5102(c)(7) on the basis of rates established under the Coordinated Federal Wage System. DNA, in fixing such rates, shall follow the wage schedules established by DoD Wage Fixing Authority.

3. Establish such advisory committees and employ such part-time advisors as approved by the Secretary of Defense for the performance of DNA functions pursuant to the provisions of 10 U.S.C. 173, 5 U.S.C. 3109(b), and the Agreement between the DoD and the Civil Service Commission on employment of experts and consultants, dated July 22, 1959.

4. Administer oaths of office incident to entrance into the Executive Branch of the Federal Government or any other oath required by law in connection with employment therein, in accordance with the provisions of the Act of June 26, 1943, as amended, 5 U.S.C. 2903(b), and designate in writing, as may be necessary, officers and employees of DNA to perform this function.

5. Establish a DNA Incentive Awards Board and pay cash awards to and incur necessary expenses for the honorary recognition of civilian employees of the Government whose suggestions, inventions, superior accomplishment, or other personal efforts, including special acts or services, benefit or affect DNA or its subordinate activities in accordance with the provisions of the Act of September 1, 1954, as amended, 5 U.S.C. 4503, and Civil Service Regulations.

APPENDIX D: AGENCY CHARTERS 433

6. In accordance with the provisions of the Act of August 26, 1950, as amended (5 U.S.C. 7532); Executive Order 10450, dated April 27, 1953, as amended; and DoD Directive 5210.7, dated September 2, 1966 (as revised):

    a. Designate any position in DNA as a "sensitive" position;

    b. Authorize, in case of an emergency, the appointment of a person to a sensitive position in the Agency for a limited period of time for whom a full field investigation or other appropriate investigation, including the National Security Check, has not been completed; and

    c. Authorize the suspension, but not to terminate the services of an employee in the interest of national security in positions within DNA.

7. Clear DNA personnel and such other individuals as may be appropriate for access to classified Defense material and information in accordance with the provisions of DoD Directive 5210.8, dated February 15, 1962 (as revised), "Policy on Investigation and Clearance of Department of Defense Personnel for Access to Classified Defense Information" and of Executive Order 10501, dated November 5, 1953, as amended.

8. Act as agent for the collection and payment of employment taxes imposed by Chapter 21 of the Internal Revenue Code of 1954, and, as such agent, make all determinations and certifications required or provided for under Section 3122 of the Internal Revenue Code of 1954, 26 U.S.C. 3122, and Section 205(p) (1) and (2) of the Social Security Act, as amended, 42 U.S.C., 405(p) (1) and (2), with respect to DNA employees.

9. Authorize and approve overtime work for DNA civilian officers and employees in accordance with the provisions of Section 550.111 of the Civil Service Regulations.

10. Authorize and approve:

    a. Travel for DNA civilian officers and employees in accordance with Joint Travel Regulations, Volume 2, Department of Defense, Civilian Personnel, dated July 1, 1965, as amended.

b. Temporary duty travel only for military personnel assigned or detailed to DNA in accordance with Joint Travel Regulations, Volume I, for Members of the Uniformed Services, dated November 1969, as amended.

c. Invitational travel to persons serving without compensation whose consultative, advisory, or highly specialized technical services are required in a capacity that is directly related to or in connection with DNA activities, pursuant to the provisions of Section 5 of the Administrative Expenses Act of 1946, as amended (5 U.S.C. 5703).

11. Approve the expenditure of funds available for travel by military personnel assigned or detailed to DNA for expenses incident to attendance at meetings of technical, scientific, professional or other similar organizations in such instances where the approval of the Secretary of Defense or his designee is required by law (37 U.S.C. 412). This authority cannot be redelegated.

12. Develop, establish, and maintain an active and continuing Records Management Program, pursuant to the provisions of Section 506(b) of the Federal Records Act of 1950, 44 U.S.C. 3102.

13. Enter into and administer contracts, directly or through a Military Department, a DoD contract administration services component, or other Government department or agency, as appropriate, for supplies, equipment and services required to accomplish the mission of the DNA. To the extent that any law or executive order specifically limits the exercise of such authority to persons at the Secretarial level of a Military Department, such authority will be exercised by the Assistant Secretary of Defense (Installations and Logistics).

14. Establish and use Imprest Funds for making small purchases of material and services other than personal for DNA when it is determined more advantageous and consistent with the best interests of the Government, in accordance with the provisions of DoD Instruction 7280.1, dated August 24, 1970, and the Joint Regulation of the General Services Administration -- Treasury Department -- General Accounting Office, entitled "For Small Purchases Utilizing Imprest Funds."

15. Authorize the publication of advertisements, notices, or proposals in public periodicals as required for the effective administration and operation of DNA (44 U.S.C. 3702).

16. a. Establish and maintain appropriate Property Accounts for DNA.

b. Appoint Boards of Survey, approve reports of survey, relieve personal liability, and drop accountability for DNA property contained in the authorized Property Accounts that has been lost, damaged, stolen, destroyed, or otherwise rendered unserviceable, in accordance with applicable laws and regulations.

17. Promulgate the necessary security regulations for the protection of property and activities under the jurisdiction of the Director, DNA, pursuant to subsections III.A. and V.B. of DoD Directive 5200.8, dated August 20, 1954.

18. Establish and maintain, for the functions assigned, an appropriate publications system for the promulgation of regulations, instructions, and reference documents, and changes thereto, pursuant to the policies and procedures prescribed in DoD Directive 5025.1, dated March 7, 1961.

19. Enter into support and service agreements with the Military Departments, other DoD agencies, or other Government agencies as required for the effective performance of responsibilities and functions assigned to DNA.

20. Issue appropriate implementing documents and establish internal procedures to assure that the selection and acquisition of ADP resources are conducted within the policies contained in DoD Directive 4105.55, dated January 21, 1971, the Federal Property Management Regulations and Armed Services Procurement Regulations.

The Director, DNA may redelegate these authorities, as appropriate, and in writing, except as otherwise specifically indicated above or as otherwise provided by law or regulation.

This delegation of authority is effective immediately and supersedes the Delegation of Authority made to the Director, DNA in Enclosure 1 to DoD Directive 5105.31 dated July 22, 1964.

DSWA

Department of Defense
DIRECTIVE

June 14, 1995
NUMBER 5105.31

DA&M

SUBJECT: ~~Defense Nuclear Agency (DNA)~~ Defense Special Weapons Agency (DSWA)

References: (a) Title 10, United States Code
(b) DoD Directive 5105.31, "Defense Nuclear Agency," January 24, 1991 (hereby canceled)
(c) DoD Directive 8910.1, Management and Control of Information Requirements," June 11, 1993

A. REISSUANCE AND PURPOSE

Pursuant to the authority vested in the Secretary of Defense by section 113 of reference (a), this .Directive reissues reference (b) to update the responsibilities, relationships, and authorities of the ~~DNA~~ DSWA.

B. APPLICABILITY

This Directive applies to the Office of the Secretary of Defense, the Military Departments, the Chairman of the Joint Chiefs of Staff, the Unified Combatant Commands, the Office of the Inspector General of the Department of Defense, the Defense Agencies, and the DoD Field Activities (hereafter referred to collectively as "the DoD Components").

C. MISSION

1. The ~~DNA~~ DSWA shall provide a center for nuclear expertise and perform essential missions in the areas of nuclear weapons stockpile support, nuclear effects research and operational support, and nuclear threat reduction including arms control verification technology development for the Department of Defense. Additionally, DSWA ~~DNA~~ shall support related defense needs including the research and advanced development of capabilities for military responses to the proliferation of weapons of mass destruction.

2. When required, ~~DNA~~ DSWA shall provide support to the Chairman of the Joint Chiefs of Staff and the Commanders of the Unified Combatant Commands in analyzing planning and action options for nuclear and other designated advanced weapons, to include weapon system lethality and operability, and reconstituting forces.

D. ORGANIZATION AND MANAGEMENT

~~DNA~~ DSWA is established as a Combat Support Agency of the Department of Defense under the authority, direction, and control of the Assistant to the Secretary of Defense for Atomic Energy (ATSD(AE)). DNA shall consist of a Director, Deputy Director, and such subordinate organizational elements as are established by the Director within authorized resources.

E. RESPONSIBILITIES AND FUNCTIONS

The Director, ~~DNA~~ DSWA, shall:

1. Organize, direct, and manage the ~~DNA~~ DSWA and all assigned resources.

2. Ensure the preservation of critical nuclear competencies within the Department of Defense, to include serving as lead DoD agency for national nuclear stockpile stewardship programs.

3. Manage and conduct DoD nuclear weapon effects programs.

4. Conduct analysis and testing to evaluate the lethality of nuclear and designated advanced weapon systems, to include analysis appraisal of enhanced payload options, weapon/target interactions, and battle damage assessment. Provide technical support to the DoD Components for matters involving weapon system lethality and to appropriate intelligence agencies for targeting-related matters.

5. Conduct analysis and testing to assess and enhance the survivability and operability of weapon systems; command, control, communications, and computer systems; installations; and forces when exposed to the effects of nuclear and designated advanced weapons to include:

    a. Developing new concepts for cost-effective life-cycle operability, hardness design methodologies, hardware prototypes, and testable hardware concepts;

    b. Serving as the DoD focal point for research, development, test, and evaluation (RDT&E) involving the development, demonstration, and production of radiation-resistant microelectronics, materials, electro-optics, and for integrated hardening of electronics and electro-optics against the full spectrum of electromagnetic hazards;

    c. Providing technical support to the DoD Components and appropriate intelligence agencies for matters involving military system operability, to include validating and maintaining the balanced hardening of systems and facilities.

6. Conduct RDT&E for verification technologies to support implementation of and compliance with arms control treaties and agreements.

7. Serve as the executive agency for the ATSD(AE) in support of the DoD counterproliferation acquisition strategy, RDT&E, and technical assessments that support the counterproliferation initiative. Accomplish other ATSD(AE)-designated tasks dealing with measures to counter the proliferation of weapons of mass destruction and associated systems and capabilities.

9. ~~8.~~ Support the DoD Components, and other organizations, as appropriate, through technical support, guidance, operational support, studies, and joint programs dealing with nuclear weapon effects, nuclear force operability, operational survivability, and other matters assigned to DNA.

10. ~~9.~~ Maintain the ~~DNA~~ DSWA as the DoD center pertaining to ATSD(AE)-designated advanced weapons and their effects, giving particular emphasis to matters that

E.8. Serve as the technical and field agent on force protection, within its assigned areas of cognizance, for the Chairman, Joint Chiefs of Staff. Such areas may include, but are not limited to, vulnerability assessments, technology development, and training.

APPENDIX D: AGENCY CHARTERS

involve the application of nuclear expertise to the development of advanced conventional munitions and to improved understanding of warhead lethality and hard-target interactions. Ensure that the synergy of these technologies contributes to sustainment of DNA's core nuclear competencies.

11. XXX Develop, maintain, and operate the DoD capability for computational modeling, physical simulation, and testing of nuclear and designated advanced weapon effects, to include maintaining and operating aboveground simulators for testing against manmade and natural space radiation environments and maintaining a DoD capability to resume currently precluded types of underground weapon effects testing and simulation.

12. XXX Execute ATSD(AE) Cooperative Threat Reduction projects and related program support activities.

13. XXX Serve as focal point for the Nuclear Test Personnel Review and for other DoD health effects radiation research projects.

14. XXX Preserve nuclear test and system reliability/operability data and perform appropriate data management.

15. XXX Conduct technology transfer programs.

16. XXX Evaluate system acquisition planning documents and provide technical appraisals in areas over which DNA has cognizance.

17. XXX Maintain the national nuclear weapons stockpile databases. Provide surveillance, guidance, coordination, advice, and assistance as appropriate, concerning all nuclear weapons in DoD custody.

18. XXX Provide technical assistance and support to the DoD Components for developing and publishing standards, requirements, and operational procedures dealing with the reliability, safety, security, use-control, and explosive ordnance disposal of nuclear weapons or devices.

19. XXX Provide emergency response support, including training exercises, and operational planning assistance to the Department of Defense and other organizations as appropriate, for matters involving radiological accidents and incidents. Operate the DoD Joint Nuclear Accident Coordination Center and maintain an advisory team to assist in radiological accident or incident management.

20. XXX Conduct, for the Chairman of the Joint Chiefs of Staff, weapons technical inspections of units having responsibility for assembling, maintaining, or storing nuclear weapon systems, their associated components, and ancillary equipment. Provide DoD quality assurance program oversight for nuclear weapons. Provide logistics management support for nuclear weapons under DoD control.

21. XXX Manage and operate the Defense Interservice Nuclear Weapons School. Serve as the DoD executive agent for sustaining nuclear weapons training expertise.

22. XXX Serve as Chairman of the Board of Governors of the Armed Forces Radiobiology Research Institute.

23. ~~22.~~ Operate the Joint Atomic Information Exchange Group in cooperation with the Department of Energy (DoE).

24. ~~23.~~ Perform other functions as may be directed by ATSD(AE).

F. RELATIONSHIPS

1. The Director, ~~DNA~~ DSWA, shall:

   a. Be responsible to the Chairman of the Joint Chiefs of Staff for operational matters as well as requirements associated with the joint planning process. For these purposes, the Chairman of the Joint Chiefs of Staff is authorized to communicate directly with the Director, ~~DNA~~ DSWA, and may task the Director, ~~DNA~~ DSWA, to the extent ~~authorized by~~ coordinated with the ATSD(AE).

   b. Assist the ATSD(AE) in representing the Department of Defense in its relations with the DoE for all matters relating to the ~~DNA~~ DSWA mission.

   c. Coordinate and exchange information with other DoD organizations that have collateral or related functions.

   d. Use established facilities and services in the Department of Defense and other Federal Agencies, whenever practicable, to avoid duplication and to achieve an appropriate balance of modernization, efficiency, and economy of operations.

2. The Heads of DoD Components shall:

   a. Provide ~~DNA~~ DSWA, as appropriate, with the support necessary for accomplishment of ~~DNA~~ DSWA functions.

   b. Coordinate with the Director, ~~DNA~~ DSWA, on all matters concerning the mission, capabilities, and functions of ~~DNA~~ DSWA.

3. The Chairman of the Joint Chiefs of Staff shall review and assess the adequacy of ~~DNA~~ DSWA efforts in nuclear and other weapon testing and effects research and the support required for the execution of operational plans of the Unified Combatant Commands.

G. AUTHORITIES

The Director, ~~DNA~~ DSWA, is specifically delegated authority to:

1. Communicate directly with the DoD Components and other Executive Departments and Agencies, as necessary, in carrying out assigned responsibilities and functions. Communications to the Commanders of the Unified Combatant Commands shall be transmitted through the Chairman of the Joint Chiefs of Staff.

2. Obtain reports, information, advice, and assistance from other DoD Components, consistent with DoD Directive 8910.1 (reference (c)), as necessary in carrying out assigned responsibilities and functions.

3. Establish facilities necessary to accomplish the DSWA mission in the most efficient and economical manner.

4. Exercise the administrative authorities contained in the enclosure.

H. ADMINISTRATION

1. The Director, and Deputy Director, DSWA, shall be appointed by the Secretary of Defense.

2. The Secretaries of the Military Departments shall assign military personnel to the DNA in accordance with approved Joint Manpower Program authorizations and procedures for assignment to joint duty.

3. The DSWA shall be authorized such personnel, facilities, funds, and other resources as the Secretary of Defense deems necessary.

I. EFFECTIVE DATE

This Directive is effective immediately.

William J. Perry
William J. Perry
Secretary of Defense

Enclosure

Delegations of Authority

APPENDIX E

AGENCY THROUGH THE DECADES CHART

APPENDIX E: Agency Through the Decades Chart

AGENCY ARM PATCHES

1940   **1950**   **1960**

MANHATTAN ENGINEER DISTRICT 1942   ARMED FORCES SPECIAL WEAPONS PROJECT 1947   DEFENSE ATOMIC SUPPORT AGENCY 1959

AGENCY SEALS

PRESIDENTS

Franklin Roosevelt 1933-1945   Harry Truman 1945-1953   Dwight Eisenhower 1953-1961   John Kennedy 1961-1963   Lyndon Johnson 1963-1969

DIRECTORS

Major General Groves 1947-1948   Major General Nichols 1948-1951   Major General Loper 1951-1953   Major General Ludecke 1953-1957   Rear Admiral Parker 1957-1961   Major General Booth 1961-1964   Lt. General Donnelly 1964-1968   Vice Admiral Mustin 1968-1971

TECHNICAL DIRECTORS

1948-1955 Dr. Scoville

1955-1959 Dr. Shelton

1960-1964 *Chief Scientist* Dr. Otting

1964-1966 *Deputy Director Science & Technology* Dr. Taylor

FIELD COMMANDERS

1947-1951 Major General Montague

1951-1955 Major General Stranathan

1955-1957 Vice Admiral O'Beirne

1957-1960 Major General Heath

1960-1963 Lt. General Donnelly

1963-1964 Rear Admiral O'Beirne

1964-1966 Rear Admiral Johnson

APPENDIX E: AGENCY THROUGH THE DECADES CHART

1970   **1980**   **1990**   **2000**

DEFENSE
NUCLEAR AGENCY
1971

DEFENSE SPECIAL
WEAPONS AGENCY
1996

| Richard Nixon | Gerald Ford | James Carter | Ronald Reagan | George Bush | William Clinton |
| 1969-1974 | 1974-1977 | 1977-1981 | 1981-1989 | 1989-1993 | 1993-2001 |

| Lt. General Dunn | Lt. General Johnson | Vice Admiral Monroe | Lt. General Griffith | Lt. General Saxer | Lt. General Pickitt | Vice Admiral Parker | Major General Watson | Major General Hagemann | Major General Curtin |
| 1971-1973 | 1973-1977 | 1977-1980 | 1980-1983 | 1983-1985 | 1985-1987 | 1987-1989 | 1989-1992 | 1992-1995 | 1995-1997 |

1969-1972
*Deputy Director
Science & Technology*

–1968 Dr. Northrop   1972-1974
Director   *Deputy Director*
Technology   *Science & Technology*
Wikner   Dr. Rosengren

1979-1983
*Deputy Director
Science & Technology*
Dr. Conrad

1974-1979
*Deputy Director
Science & Technology*
Mr. Haas

1983-1987
*Deputy Director
Science & Technology*
Dr. Atkins

1987-1989
Deputy Director
Dr. Atkins

1990-1999
Deputy Director
Dr. Ullrich

1979-1981
Brig. General
Mitchell   1981-1983
1977-1979   Brig. General
Major General   Brown
Tate

1990-1992
Rear Admiral
Gaston   1992-1993
1988-1990   Brig. General
Brig. General   Miller
Dickey
1986-1988
Brig. General
Kavanaugh

966-1969
ajor General
Honeycutt   1969-1972
Major General
Nye   1972-1975
Rear Admiral
Swanson

1975-1977
Brig. General
Lacy

1983-1984
Rear Admiral
Aut   1984-1986
Rear Admiral
Kersh

1993-1995
Colonel
Singleton   1995-1997
Colonel
Hafner

APPENDIX F

INDEX

Symbols

2761st Engineer Battalion 49
38th Battalion 50
509th Bombardment Group 49

A

ABLE (Test) 13
Accelerator-Pulsed Fast
    Assembly (APFA) 190
Acheson, Dean G. 19
Acheson-Lilienthal Report 19
Advanced Research Electromagnetic
    Simulator (ARES) 307
Advanced Research Projects
    Agency (ARPA) 136
Advanced Systems and Concepts
    Office (ASCO) 323
Agnew, Harold M., Dr. 313
Air Force Office of Atomic Testing
    (AFOAT) 60
Air Force Technical Applications
    Center (AFTAC) 197
AJAX (Operation) 49
Albuquerque, New Mexico 2
Albuquerque Operations Office 147
Alternate National Military
    Command 157
Ammonium Nitrate and Fuel Oil
    (ANFO) 190
Anti-Ballistic Missile (ABM) 143
ARES (Simulator) 307
ARGUS (Operation) 139

Armed Forces Radiobiology
    Research Institute (AFRRI) 206
Armed Forces Special Weapons
    Project (AFSWP) 2
Arms Control and Disarmament
    Agency (ACDA) 251
Army Air Corps 16
Aspin, Leslie, Secretary 308
Assistant to the Secretary of
    Defense, Atomic Energy
    ATSD(AE) 182
Atkins, Marvin C., Dr. 278
Atomic Energy Act 13
Atomic Energy Commission (AEC) 9
Atwood, Donald J., Deputy
    Secretary 313
AURORA (Test Facility) 239

B

B-1 (Aircraft) 218
B-29 (Aircraft) 13
B-52 (Aircraft) 122
Bacher, Robert F. 26
BAKER (Test) 13
Baldwin, Hanson 146
Ballistic Missile Defense Office
    (BMDO) 280
Ballistic Missile Office (BMO) 264
BANJO (Operation) 62
Baruch, Bernard M. 20
Baruch Plan 19
Battlefield Information and
    Targeting System (BITS) 284

Berlin Airlift 52
Bethe, Hans, Dr. 25
Betts, Cyrus, Major General 136
Bikini Atoll 10
BLACKJACK (Simulator) 265
Blandy, W.H., Vice Admiral 13
Blue Ribbon Defense Panel
    (BRDP) 216
Booth, Robert H., Major General 160
Bradbury, Norris E. 8
Bradley, Omar, General 55
Braun, Wernher von, Dr. 133
BRAVO (Test) 111
Brereton, Lewis H., Lieutenant
    General 13
Brezhnev, Leonid, Soviet Premier 249
Brodie, Bernard, Dr. 1
Broken Arrow 178
Brown, Charles F. 40
Brown, Harold, Secretary 171
Bush, George H., President 281
BUSTER (Operation) 80

C

C-47 (Aircraft) 48
C-54 (Aircraft) 226
C-97 (Aircraft) 34
Caldwell, Glynn G., Dr. 233
Camp Desert Rock, Nevada 41
Camp Lejeune, N. Carolina 87
Camp Mercury, Nevada 87
Camp Murphy, Nevada 30
Camp Pendleton, California 87
Carpenter, Donald F., Secretary 52
Carter, James E., President 249
CASINO, (Test Facility) 240
CASTLE, (Operation) 101
Centers for Disease Control (CDC) 233
Central Intelligence Agency (CIA) 57

Chernenko, Konstantin,
    Soviet Premier 281
Cherry, William R., Dr. 31
CHICKENPOX (Operation) 35
Chief of Naval Operations (CNO) 29
Christmas Island 114
Christofilos, Nicholas C., Dr. 136
Chrome Dome (Operation) 200
Churchill, Winston, Prime Minister 114
Circular Error Probable (CEP) 174
Clarkson, Percy W., Major General 96
Clay, Lucius D., General 47
Clifford, Clark, Secretary 57
Clinton, William J., President 270
Cohen, William S., Secretary 323
Colby, Walter F., Dr. 57
Cold War 48
Columbia University, New York 6
Command, Control, and
    Communications (C3) 302
Commander in Chief (CINC) 252
Commander in Chief, Pacific
    (CINCPAC) 301
Comprehensive Test Ban (CTB) 248
Comprehensive Test Ban Treaty
    (CTBT) 301
Compton, K.T., Dr. 13
Congress, U.S. 6
Conrad, Edward, Dr. 218
Conventional Forces in Europe
    (CFE) 299
Conventional Weapons Effects
    (CWE) 319
Cooper, Paul R., Sergeant 232
Cooperative Threat Reduction
    (CTR) 298
Corman, James R., Master Sergeant 31
Cornwall, John, Dr. 308
Corps of Engineers, U.S. Army 2
Corpus Christi Bay 242

APPENDIX F: INDEX

Cost and Operational Effectiveness
   Analysis (COEA) 224
Cotter, Donald 223
COWBOY (Operation) 62
CROSSROADS (Operation) 10
Curtin, Gary L., Major General 314

D

Daigo Fukurya Maru
   (Japanese Trawler) 112
Daniel, Dan, Congressman 250
Data Archival and Retrieval
   Enhancement (DARE) 318
Davis, Jay, Dr. 323
Davis-Monthan AFB, Arizona 62
DECADE (Test Facility) 304
Defense Advanced Research
   Projects Agency (DARPA) 223
Defense Atomic Support Agency
   (DASA) 149
Defense Intelligence Agency (DIA) ... 176
Defense Nuclear Agency (DNA) 216
Defense Nuclear Weapons School
   (DNWS) 205
Defense Science Board (DSB) 308
Defense Special Weapons Agency
   (DSWA) 314
Defense Systems Acquisition Review
   Council (DSARC) 259
Defense Threat Reduction Agency
   (DTRA) 322
DeLauer, Richard, Under Secretary ... 267
Department of Defense 55
Department of Defense
   Instruction (DoDI) 259
Department of Defense Nuclear
   Information Analysis Center
   (DASIAC) 184
Department of Energy (DOE) 216
Department of the Interior (DOI) 227
Deputy Director Science and
   Technology (DDST) 181

Desert Storm (Operation) 295
Deutch, John, Secretary 267
Dewey, Bradley, Dr. 13
Director, Defense Research and
   Engineering (DDR&E) 179
DISTANT LIGHT Program 266
Division of Military Application 40
DoD Damage Assessment Center
   (DODDAC) 157
DOG (Shot) 80
Doll, Edward B., Dr. 134
DOMINIC (Operation) 161
Donnelly, Harold C., Major
   General 160
Dorland, Gilbert M., Colonel 2
dri-Enewetak 226
dri-Engebi 226
Dukakis, Michael, Governor 287
Dulles, John F., Secretary 98
Dunn, Caroll H., Lieutenant
   General 228

E

Early, Stephen T., Secretary 76
EASTWIND (Operation) 65
Eglin AFB, Florida 70
Eisenhower, Dwight D., General 9
Eisenhower, Dwight D., President 95
Electromagnetic Pulse (EMP) 137
Electronics Radiation Response
   Information Center (ERRIC) 320
Enewetak Atoll 58
Engineer Research and Development
   Laboratory (ERDL 69
Enjebi Island 59
Environmental Protection
   Agency (EPA) 225

F

Farrell, Major General 13
Fat Man (Weapon) 12

Federal Emergency Management Agency (FEMA) 271
Fermi, Enrico, Dr. 25
Ferraro, Geraldine 281
Field Command (FC) 79
Fields, Kenneth E., General 95
FISHBOWL (Operation) 161
Flash X-Ray (FXR) 192
Fletcher, James, Administrator 276
FLINTLOCK (Operation) 191
Follow-On Forces Attack (FOFA) 223
Ford, Gerald R., President 251
Former Soviet Union (FSU) 298
Forrestal, James V., Secretary 13
Fort Belvoir, Virginia 17
Fort Hood, Texas 62
Fort Monmouth, New Jersey 30
Fort Polk, Louisiana 285
FRIGATE BIRD (Test) 161
Froehlich, Alexander J., Colonel 22
Fubini, Eugene, Dr. 180
Fuchs, Klaus, Dr. 73

G

Gagarin, Yuri 159
Gates, Thomas, Secretary 156
Gaulle, Charles de, French President 157
Gavin, James M., General 122
Gilinsky, Victor, Dr. 312
Gill, Henry, Dr. 237
Gilpatric, Roswell, Secretary 180
Glasstone, Samuel, Dr. 72
Goldwater, Barry, Senator 174
Gorbachev, Mikhail, Soviet Premier 281
GRAPPLE (Operation) 114
Graves, Alvin C., Dr. 68
Great Britain, United Kingdom 47

GREENHOUSE (Operation) 76
Griffith, Harry A., Lieutenant General 258
Gromyko, Andrei, Premier 48
Ground-Launched Cruise Missile (GLCM) 224
Groves, Leslie R., Major General 1
Gruenther, Albert M., General 55
Guest, W.S., Rear Admiral 201

H

Haas, Peter 218
Hagemann, Kenneth, Major General 297
Hailsham, Lord, British Representative 164
Hamre, John, Secretary 323
Handy, Thomas T., General 9
Hanford Facility, Washington 2
Hardened Mobile Launcher (HML) ... 264
HARDTACK (Operation) 135
HARDTACK II (Operation) 155
Harrison, R.H., Brigadier General 147
Harry Diamond Laboratory 239
Hartgering, James B., Dr. 86
Hasbrouck, Sherman V., Colonel 17
Hickam AFB, Hawaii 163
High Explosive Assemblies 24
High Performance Computing 318
High-Altitude Electromagnetic Pulse (HEMP) 280
High-Altitude Sampling Program (HASP) 142
Hill, Tom B., Admiral 71
Hillenkoetter, Roscoe H., Director 73
Hiroshima, Japan 1
Hitler, Adolph 19
HMS Plym 114
Hoffman, Fred, Dr. 276
Holloway, David, Dr. 53

Hoover, M., Vice Admiral 13
Horizontal Line of Site (HLOS) 189
Horwitz, Solis, Dr. 180
HURRICANE (Operation) 114
Hutchinson, Howard B., Captain 66

I

Information Analysis Center (IAC) 319
Intercontinental Ballistic
    Missile (ICBM) 131
Intermediate Nuclear Forces (INF) 282
ITEM (Test) 77
IVY (Operation) 89

J

James, Jack, Colonel 103
JANGLE (Operation) 80
Jenkins, Bruce, Judge 237
Johnson, Louis A., Secretary 73
Johnson, Lyndon B., President 172
Johnson, Warren, Lieutenant
    General 224
Johnston Atoll (Island), S. Pacific 139
Joint Atomic Information
    Exchange Group (JAIEG) 147
Joint Chiefs of Staff Evaluation
    Board 13
Joint Chiefs of Staff (JCS) 13
Joint Nuclear Accident
    Coordinating Center (JNACC) ... 184
Joint Strategic Target Planning
    Staff (JSTPS) 157
Joint Task Force (JTF) 13

K

KC-135 (Aircraft) 200
Keesler AFB, Mississippi 70
Kennedy, John F., President 160
Keyes, Roger M., Secretary 103
Khrushchev, Nikita, Soviet Premier 48

Killian, James R., Jr. 113
Kiloton (KT) 84
Kirtland AFB, New Mexico 49
Kirtland Field, New Mexico 7
Kissinger, Henry, Dr. 135
Kitral (Compound) 296
Kosygin, Alexis, Soviet Premier 175

L

La Carlotta 225
LaGuardia, Fiorello 3
Laird, Melvin, Secretary 178
Lampert, James B., Colonel 21
Large Blast-Thermal Simulator
    (LB/TS) 259
Lawrence, Ernest O., Dr. 101
Lawrence Livermore National
    Laboratory (LLNL) 101
LeBaron, Robert 76
LeMay, Curtis E., Lieutenant
    General 48
Lewis, John, Dr. 194
Lilienthal, David E., Dr. 19
Limited Test Ban Treaty (LTBT) 164
Line-of-Sight (LOS) 191
Little Boy (Weapon) 25
Lodge, Henry Cabot, Ambassador 114
Loper, Herbert B., Brigadier
    General 76
Los Alamos National Laboratory
    (LANL) 279
Los Alamos, New Mexico 2
Lovett, Robert A., Secretary 56
Luedecke, Alvin R., Brigadier
    General 86

M

Macmillan, Harold, Prime Minister 161
Malenkov, Goergi M., Soviet
    Premier 107

Manhattan Engineer District (MED) 1
Manhattan Project 1
Marshall Plan 47
Martin, Charley 238
Massachusetts Institute of
 Technology (MIT) 2
May-Johnson Bill 38
McArthur, Douglas, General 79
McCone, John 154
McCormack, James 29
McCormick, Charles 171
McElroy, Neil, Secretary 147
McMahon Bill 16
McMahon, Brien, Senator 16
McMillan, William, Dr. 171
McNamara, Robert S., Secretary 171
Midway-Class (Aircraft Carriers) 34
MIKE (Shot) 95
Military Liaison Committee (MLC) 17
Military Occupational Specialty
 (MOS) 205
Minuteman (Missile) 172
MIXED COMPANY (Operation) 242
Mondale, Walter, Vice President 281
Monroe, Robert, Vice Admiral 218
Montague, Robert F., General 50
Montgomery, Bernard, Field
 Marshall 38
Moore, Ivan M. 31
Multiple Independently-Targeted
 Reentry Vehicles (MIRV) 172
Multiple Reentry Vehicle (MRV) 172
Mustin, Lloyd M., Rear Admiral 144
MX Program 239

N

Nagasaki, Japan 3
National Aeronautics and Space
 Administration (NASA) 190
National Ignition Facility (NIF) 307

National Security Act 37
National Security Agency (NSA) 245
National Security Council (NSC) 75
Naval Research Laboratory (NRL) 132
Naval War College 52
Neumann, John von, Dr. 133
Nevada Test Site (NTS) 78
Nichols, Kenneth D., Brigadier
 General 10
Nimitz, Chester W., Admiral 30
Nixon, Richard M., President 202
Norstad, Lauris, General 63
North Atlantic Treaty Organization
 (NATO) 160
Northrop, John A., Dr. 194
NOUGAT (Operation) 159
Nuclear, Chemical and
 Biological (NCB) 298
Nuclear Posture Review (NPR) 296
Nuclear Regulatory
 Commission (NRC) 216
Nuclear Targeting Review (NTR) 258
Nuclear Test Personnel
 Review (NTPR) 232
Nuclear Weapon Effect (NWE) 238
Nuclear Weapons Council (NWC) 283
Nunn, Sam, Senator 222
NUTMEG (Operation) 63

O

Oak Ridge, Tennessee 2
Office of Management and
 Budget (OMB) 285
Office of Scientific Research and
 Development 6
Office of the Secretary of
 Defense (OSD) 223
Offsite, R.A., Rear Admiral 13
Ogle, William E., Dr. 133
On-Site Inspection Agency
 (OSIA) 285

APPENDIX F: INDEX

Oppenheimer, J. Robert, Dr. 1
Ord, John A., Colonel 22
Oxnard Field (Sandia), New Mexico 2

P

Pacific Enewetak Atoll Cratering Experiments (PEACE) 263
Pacific Ocean Division 228
Pacific Proving Ground (PPG) 111
Packard, David, Secretary 216
Palmer House 62
Palomares, Spain 200
Parker, Edward N., Rear Admiral 125
Parker, John T., Vice Admiral 287
Parsons, William S. (Deke), Admiral 18
Patterson, Robert P., Secretary 9
Patton, George, General 38
Pearl Harbor, Hawaii 11
Perle, Richard, Under Secretary 260
Permanent High Explosives Test Site (PHETS) 304
Permissive Action Link (PAL) 199
Permissive Action Links (PALs) 198
Perry, William, Secretary 301
Petersburg, Virginia 84
Pickitt, John L., Lieutenant General 270
Pike, Sumner T., Secretary 39
PITHON (Test Facility) 265
PLUMBBOB (Operation) 123
Polaris (Missile) 138
Powell, Colin, General 295
Powers, Francis G. 158
Project Candor 109
Project Carryall 151
Project Plowshare 150
Project Willow 155

Q

Quarles, Donald A., Secretary 136
Quesada, Elwood R., General 76

R

Rabi, Isador I., Dr. 75
Rainer Mesa, Nevada 195
RAND Corporation 171
RANGER (Operation) 78
RB-57D (Aircraft) 124
Reagan, Ronald, President 257
Reconstruction Finance Corporation 2
REDWING (Operation) 115
Reentry Vehicle (RV) 172
Reis, Victor, Secretary 308
Reserve Officer Training Corps (ROTC) 22
Rio Grande River, Texas 2
ROLLER COASTER (Operation) 203
Royall, Kenneth C., Secretary 38
Rusk, Dean, Secretary 177

S

Sagan, Carl, Dr. 273
Sandia Base, New Mexico 2
SANDSTONE (Operation) 50
Sapwood (Missile) 131
Saxer, Richard K., Lieutenant General 267
Schweitzer, Albert, Dr. 114
Scientific Advisory Group on Effects (SAGE) 182
Scoville, Herbert, Jr. 99
Scowcroft, Brent, Lieutenant General 263
Seaborg, Glenn T., Dr. 151
Shalikashvili, John, General 304
Shelton, Frank H., Dr. 103

Short Range Attack Missile-II (SRAM-II) 296
Shute, Nevil 134
Silo Test Program (STP) 264
Single Integrated Operability Plan (SIOP) 173
Smith, Harold P., Dr., Secretary 298
SMOKY (Shot) 232
Smyth, Henry 76
Snapp, Roy B., Secretary 98
SNOWBALL (Operation) 190
Sorensen, Theodore 159
Spartan (Missile) 210
Sputnik (Satellite) 131
Stalin, Joseph, Soviet Premier 48
Starbird, Alfred D., Major General 161
Stevens, Ted, Senator 308
Stevenson, Adlai, Senator 122
Stilwell, J.W., General 13
Stimson, Henry L., Secretary 3
Stockpile (Nuclear) 69
Stranathan, Leland S., Brigadier General 102
Strategic Air Command (SAC) 53
Strategic Arms Limitation Treaty (SALT) 249
Strategic Arms Reduction Talks (START) 177
Strategic Defense Initiative (SDI) 258
Strategic Defense Initiative Office (SDIO) 277
Strauss, Lewis L., Admiral 28
Stromberg, LaWayne R., Colonel 233
Submarine-Launched Ballistic Missile (SLBM) 162
Sullivan, John L., Secretary 55
Supreme Allied Commander Europe (SACEUR) 219
Supreme Headquarters Allied Powers Europe (SHAPE) 284

SWORDFISH (Test) 161
Symington, W. Stuart, Secretary 51
System-Generated Electromagnetic Pulse (SGEMP) 266

T

Taiki Maru (Japanese Trawler) 225
Taylor, Theodore, Dr. 184
TEAPOT (Operation) 115
Technical Training Group (TTG) 25
Teller, Edward, Dr. 25
Tennessee Valley Authority (TVA) 19
Theater Nuclear Forces (TNF) 224
Threat Reduction Advisory Committee (TRAC) 323
Threshold Test Ban Treaty (TTBT) 249
Thule, Greenland 201
Transient Radiation Effects on Electronics (TREE) 190
Trapnell, Frederick M., Rear Admiral 102
Trident (Missile) 172
Trinitrotoluene (TNT) 13
Trinity (Test Site) 7
Trinity (Test) 3
Truman, Harry S., President 3
Trust Territory of the Pacific Islands (TTPI) 226
Tsarapkin, Semyon, Soviet Ambassador 155
TUMBLER-SNAPPER (Operation) 86
Tyler, Carroll L. 68
Tyler-Montague Agreement 68

U

Udall, Stewart, Secretary 225
Ulam, Stanislaw M., Dr. 77
Ullrich, George W., Dr. 297

Underground Test (UGT) 155
United Nations (UN) 123
United Nations Special
    Commission (UNSCOM) 299
United States (US) 12
United States Geological
    Service (USGS) 262
University of California at
    Berkeley 7
University of Washington 10
UNLIMITED (Operation) 65
UPSHOT-KNOTHOLE
    (Operation) 100
USS Belle Grove 226
USS Boxer 140
USS Cushing 125
USS Ethan Allen 162
USS Missouri 71
USS Norton Sound 144
USS Parrott 125
USS Petrel 201
USS Tarawa 145

V

Vance, Cyrus, Secretary 181
Vandenberg AFB, California 263
Vandenberg, Arthur H., Senator 16
Vandenberg, Hoyt S., General 16
Vertical Line of Site (VLOS) 189
Veterans' Administration (VA) 232
Vittles (Operation) 48
Vulcanus (Ship) 225

W

Wadsworth, James, Ambassador 155
Walker AFB, New Mexico 62
Wallace, Henry A. 20
Wallace, William, Captain 146

Walske, Carl, Asst. Secretary 199
War Department 3
Watson, Gerald, Major General 295
Waymach, William W. 28
Weapons of Mass
    Destruction (WMD) 295
Weapons Orientation-Advanced
    (WOA) 204
Weapons Security and Survivability
    System (WS3) 260
Webster, William 57
Weinberger, Caspar, Secretary 257
Wendover Field, Utah 49
West Berlin, Germany 48
Wheeler, Earl, General 189
WHIPPOORWILL (Operation) 64
White, John P., Secretary 233
White Sands Missile Range
    (WSMR), New Mexico 175
WIGWAM (Operation) 116
Wikner, Fred, Dr. 171
Wilhoyt, Ellis E., Lieutenant
    Colonel 29
Williams, Franklin H.,
    Ambassador 228
Wilson, Bob, Congressman 250
Wilson, Carroll L., Dr. 26
Wilson, Charles E., Secretary 98
Wilson, Delmar E., General 200
WINDSTORM (Operation) 84

X

X-RAY (Event) 59

Y

Y-12 (Plant) 6
Yeltsin, Boris, Soviet Premier 294
YOKE (Test) 59
York, Herbert F., Dr. 146

Z

Z-Division (Sandia Base) 12
Zacharias, Jerrold R. 12
ZEBRA (Test) 59